Disability, Society, and the Individual

Julie Smart, PhD, CRC, NCC, LPC, ABDA
Department of Special Education and Rehabilitation
Utah State University
Logan, Utah

pro·ed
An International Publisher
8700 Shoal Creek Boulevard
Austin, Texas 78757-6897
800/897-3202 Fax 800/397-7633
www.proedinc.com

© 2001 by PRO-ED, Inc.
8700 Shoal Creek Boulevard
Austin, Texas 78757-6897
800/897-3202   Fax 800/397-7633
www.proedinc.com

Library of Congress Cataloging-in-Publication Data

Smart, Julie.
   Disability, society, and the individual / Julie Smart.
      p. cm.
   Originally published: Gaithersburg, MD : Aspen, 2001.
   Includes bibliographical references and index.
   ISBN 0-944480-28-4
   1. Handicapped—Social Conditions.   2. Discrimination against people with disabilities.
3. Sociology of disability.   I. Title.
HV1568.S63 2003
305.9′0816—dc21

      2003046780

(Previously published by Aspen Publishers
as ISBN 834216019)

Printed in the United States of America

   3   4   5   6   7   8   9   10   09   08   07   06   05

*This book is dedicated to my dear parents,
Helen and Ben Fishler.*

Contents

Acknowledgments

I am particularly grateful to my colleagues and friends, who have supported me and assisted me in writing this book. Their enthusiasm and commitment have helped me a great deal in realizing this goal. Susan Nash and Patricia Huff provided administrative support and, for this, I thank them. To all of my colleagues at Utah State University and the Department of Special Education and Rehabilitation, I am grateful. Both the university and the department have been encouraging and supportive, and I am proud to be a faculty member.

I have used many excerpts from various writers, people with disabilities, and disability scholars, and there probably would be no book without their contributions. I have long respected the work and ideas of these individuals and their contributions certainly strengthen this book.

Working with Aspen Publishers has been both fun and productive.

Finally, I wish to thank my students. Over the years, I have taught a course entitled, "Psychosocial Aspects of Disability" in a master's degree program in rehabilitation counseling, during which students and I have discussed all of the ideas in this book. If I have managed to present many sides of a single issue, much of this is a result of these classroom discussions. In addition, students and graduates send me articles, e-mails, and other materials, knowing that I am deeply interested in issues related to disability. Many of these materials have been used in this book. As I reread what I have written, I am struck by—and feel grateful for—the many contributions of my students.

Julie Smart
Utah State University
March 2000

Abbreviations and Terms

ADA   Americans with Disabilities Act

ADL   Activities of daily living, such as eating, bathing, grooming, doing household maintenance tasks, conducting necessary business, and shopping

ASL   American Sign Language

IL   Independent Living

PWD   Person or people with disabilities

PWOD   Person or people without disabilities

TAB   Temporarily able-bodied

Note: "Deaf" with a capital "D" indicates the Deaf Culture (sometimes referred to as the Deaf community) while "deaf" with a small "d" refers to the disability of deafness. Individuals who are deaf do not consider themselves to have a disability, but instead view themselves as part of another culture that speaks another language. Indeed, the symbol of their oppression—sign language—has evolved into a symbol of unity and community.*

---

*Jankowski, K. A. (1997). *Deaf empowerment: Emergence, struggle, and rhetoric*. Washington, DC: Gallaudet University.

Introduction

The purpose of this book is to look at the disability experience from the perspective of the individual who has the disability, to discuss how disabilities are viewed by society, and to consider the relationship between these two viewpoints. As this book emphasizes, a perfect world is not a world without disabilities, but rather a world in which accommodations for people with disabilities (PWDs) are provided and artificial barriers are removed. It is also a world that does not stigmatize or discriminate against those with disabilities.

In contrast to most textbooks on disability, this book is not organized by various disabilities, with each chapter discussing a specific disability. Rather, broad similarities and differences across a wide range of disabilities are considered. There are many psychosocial issues, responses, and tasks required of PWDs and, therefore, this book addresses these broad issues. Society's view of disability and PWDs is also discussed in terms of a wide spectrum of disabilities, rather than discussing society's view of each disability type.

The book is divided into three parts. The first part defines disability and the various models of viewing disability. The definition of disability is not as clear-cut and straightforward as might be thought and, therefore, before embarking upon a discussion of disability, it seems reasonable to devote some attention to clearly defining what a disability is and what a disability is not. The second part of the book discusses society's responses—most of which have included prejudice and discrimination—toward disability and PWDs. The third part concerns itself with the individual's response to the disability. The sequence of these last two parts may appear, at first glance, to be backward. Yet, inasmuch as many PWDs internalize society's view of PWDs and disability, a person's response is very closely tied to the larger society around him or her. Even more important, it is essential to understand the prejudice and discrimination with which the PWD must contend in order to understand his or her response to the disability.

Do these well-defined sections represent the reality of any one person? Of course not. No textbook can truly communicate someone's experience. Moreover, there are no neat divisions between defining disability, society's response, and the individual's experience of living with a disability. Certainly, all three of these concepts interact with each other and no one truly conceives of his or her life in these three neat paradigms. Nonetheless, the purpose of this book is to introduce readers to these paradigms and to provide an introduction to complex, important, and new (to the reader) ideas. Therefore, some sort of organization and conceptualization, even if artificial, is necessary. Hence, these three neat parts of the book and their sequence are provided in order to facilitate learning. Whenever possible, these interrelationships will be noted.

Suggestions for viewing commercially produced videos are provided at the end of each chapter. While there is no one single disability experience, these videos can provide students with first-person accounts of a wide range of disabilities and idiosyncratic circumstances. Nonetheless, the information contained in these chapters will assist students in understanding some of the broad issues that these videos discuss. That is to say, it is hoped that after reading the specific chapter, which presents many sides of particular issues and clarifying background information, the opinions and viewpoints expressed in the videos will be more helpful and understandable to students. Such a combination of background information and first-person accounts can be a powerful tool in beginning to understand the disability experience.

In the past, disability was thought of as a private or family concern. However, due to the increasing numbers of PWDs and the political and educational advocacy efforts of PWDs, including the passage of the Americans with Disabilities Act (ADA), we are now beginning to understand that disability is a universal concern. Chapters 1 and 2 discuss the various definitions and models of disability and also address the six reasons why there are more disabilities than ever before. Indeed, both the rate of disability and the number of PWDs will continue to increase in the future, and this increase is viewed as progress. In these first two chapters, the rationale of the ADA is presented. The ADA was passed in 1990, leading many in the Disability Rights Movement to term PWDs as the "last and least minority." Certainly, most other minority groups in the United States were accorded their civil rights before 1990. These first two chapters also present the rationale behind the correct terminology for disability and PWDs.

Chapters 3, 4, 5, and 6 explain the prejudice, discrimination, and stigma that PWDs have experienced. Ten sources of prejudice and discrimination are outlined. Each PWD, regardless of his or her privilege, economic resources, or achievements, understands that he or she is a member of a devalued group. PWDs are often faced with the need to negotiate a relationship with a society that, in many cases rejects them. Certainly, the focus of these four chapters is on the effect of prejudice on PWDs, but ways in which people without disabilities (PWODs) pay for their prejudice are also discussed. Prejudice against any group literally costs the larger group. Prejudice is expensive; eliminating prejudice against any group improves the economy. By systematically refusing to allow members of any one group the right to fulfill their potential, the larger group forfeits economic benefits. Further, PWODs pay for their prejudice by forfeiting the creativity and diversity of ideas that PWDs could provide, if allowed. For example, most universities offer women's studies courses and African American courses. In contrast, there are few universities that offer disability studies courses. Finally, PWODs pay for their prejudice against PWDs by losing an opportunity to grow because of fear of acquiring a disability. If PWDs and their experiences were socially validated, PWODs would understand the disability experience and not fear it as much.

The focus changes in Chapters 7, 8, and 9. In these chapters, the individual's response to the disability is considered, especially considering factors of the disability itself and factors in the environment. Types of onset, varied courses, levels of severity, degree of visibility, the presence of chronic pain, and the amount of stigma and prejudice toward the particular disability are all known to have an effect on the individual's response. Disability scholars are beginning to recognize that factors in the environment have an important impact on the individual's response to the disability. Of course, most PWDs think of the disability as a personal attribute, not as a tragic problem. For many PWDs, the disability is not the single most important self-identifier. Further, the only shared identity of PWDs is the prejudice and discrimination they experience. Other than this devalued position in society, it is safe to state that there is no single disability experience.

As a society, we are increasingly recognizing the pervasiveness and significance of the disability experience. It is hoped that this book will lend support to a transformation of the way in which we view ourselves.

Part I

Definitions of Disability

Chapter 1

Defining Disability

▶ Does anyone know what "normal" is?
▶ Darwin's theory of evolution and "survival of the fittest" posited that humankind would eventually be free of disability. Has this happened?
▶ Why is it necessary to define or categorize disabilities?
▶ Why are labels and diagnoses depersonalizing for the individual?
▶ Does everybody have a disability of some sort?
▶ Can environmental factors—such as the labor market or societal prejudice and discrimination—change the definition of disability?
▶ If medicine and medical technology have made such great advances, why are there more disabilities than ever before?

DOES ANYONE KNOW WHAT "NORMAL" IS?

In this section, look for—
> ▶ *the reasons why diagnoses of exclusion are frequently ambiguous*
> ▶ *five factors that affect society's determination of normalcy*

The question that heads this section is an important question because the answer has a great impact on the self-concepts of individuals, on how people treat each other, and on the allocation of public resources for services and benefits. Other questions follow. Is it always positive to be labeled "normal"? Where can we see pictures of "normal" people? Is "abnormal" always a negative label, indicating someone inferior, deviant, or deficient? Is there one fixed, correct pattern of human development?

Oftentimes, normal is defined solely as the absence of deviance, illness, or disability, so that the definition becomes a definition of exclusion. In other words, if deviance, illness, or disability are not present, the person is judged to be normal. No definition of exclusion is very helpful. After all, only eliminations are made, usually of those factors considered to be undesirable; there are no further guidelines or clarifications given. Diagnoses of exclusion, including the determination of normalcy, are frequently given due to the ambiguity and lack of specificity of these types of diagnoses. Consequently, there are more clear-cut, standardized, measur-

3

able, and objective guidelines for the definition of abnormal than there are for the definition of normal.

Conceptualizing normalcy as the ideal, as the standard against which everything is measured, is another invalid assumption. For many, normal means perfect. Assumptions, accurate or not, can remain intact throughout centuries of human history. Those who subscribe to this assumption believe that anything, or anyone, that does not meet all the prescribed criteria, guidelines, and standards is judged to be abnormal. Indeed, Wolfensberger (1972) stated, "Normalcy is often confused with humanity."

Following these types of logic—that normal means only the absence of abnormalcy or that normal is considered to be the standard of evaluation—the determination of normalcy would depend upon the combination of three elements: (1) the characteristic(s) to be judged, (2) the environment in which the characteristic(s) appears, and (3) the individual(s) who are making the judgment. Defining power is the authority to determine who or what is normal. Normalcy is, in many ways, in the eyes of the beholder; indeed, the determination of normalcy and abnormalcy may tell us more about the people making the determinations than about the people being judged. The most clear-cut example of defining power is the example of Nazi Germany and the Holocaust. The Nazis defined the criteria of being "normal" and then killed all those who did not meet these criteria, including German children and adults with disabilities (Friedlander, 1996). Nazi pseudoscientists "confirmed" these criteria with "data."

In the original sense of the word, "normal" carries no value judgment; normal is neither good nor bad. Normal simply means typical, prevalent, customary, routine, commonplace, and to be expected (Davis, 1997). Abnormal, therefore, can also be good or bad. Here is an example of abnormality: "I am abnormal because I am good looking and I have a genius level I.Q." Consider this example: "It is normal for 500 murders to be committed each year in the City of Oz." Accordingly, the determination of normalcy or abnormalcy is not an evaluation, because these concepts have no inherent value, but is rather a simple determination based on how typical an event, a characteristic, or a behavior is. Normalcy, then, is more of a statistical concept, which includes the ideas of "most commonly occurring and most likely to happen."

THE LINK BETWEEN THE ACADEMIC DISCIPLINE OF STATISTICS AND EUGENICS

In this section, look for—
- ▶ *the definition of eugenics*
- ▶ *the link between statistics and eugenics*
- ▶ *the lack of a disability identity for real people on Martha's Vineyard*
- ▶ *how the definition of normalcy is becoming more constricted due to managed care*
- ▶ *cost containment policies*

Quantification, measurement, statistical methodologies, and counting of human characteristics all carry the potential to be distorted into value judgments. Eugenics, the study of hereditary improvements of the human race by controlled selective breeding and, in its extreme form, by the elimination of those with disabilities, was a direct result of statistical analyses of biological traits measured on large samples of people. These analyses then led to theories that created the concept of the "normal distribution" curve and the concept of the "norm." Sir Francis Galton (1869), Karl Pearson (originator of the Pearson Product Moment Correlation statistic), and Sir Ronald Fisher, considered to be the "fathers" of the academic discipline of statistics, were eugenicists or, as they are sometimes called, population geneticists (Leakey in Darwin, 1979). Galton was cousin, friend, and colleague to Charles Darwin. It was Galton who coined the term "eugenics" and authored numerous books, including *Hereditary Genius* (1887) and *Inquiries into Human Faculty and Its Development* (1883). Fisher used statistical analyses in the book he wrote, *The Genetical Theory of Natural Selection*. Pearson, another British statistician, argued that "genetically inferior people were outbreeding superior ones and that the human species was degenerating by dysgenics" (*L.A. Times*, October 23, 1994; cited in Jacoby & Glauberman, 1995, p. 386).

Davis (1997) pointed to this link:

> The rather amazing fact is that almost all early statisticians had one thing in common: they were eugenicists....While this coincidence seems almost too striking to be true, we must remember that there is a real connection between figuring the statistical measures of humans so that deviations from the norm diminish.... Statistics is bound up with eugenics because the central insight of statistics is the idea that a population can be normed (p. 14).

Eugenicists then implemented mathematical, scientific, statistical methodology to define that which was normal and that which was deviant. The debate continues, at least for intellectual and cognitive disabilities. Books such as *The Bell Curve* (Herrnstein & Murray, 1994), *Measured Lies: The Bell Curve Examined* (Kincheloe, Steinberg, & Gresson, 1997), and *The Mismeasure of Man* (Gould, 1981) have all focused on the relationship between scientific, statistical concepts and the definition of "normal" intellectual and cognitive functioning.

Darwin's theory of evolution and natural selection, sometimes referred to as the "survival of the fittest," and the improvement of "mammiferous animal species" (including humans) postulated that eventually there would be no individuals with defects or disabilities. Indeed, Darwin posited that variations considered to be harmful would be eliminated. Herbert Spencer (1884) applied Darwin's theories specifically to humans and was a leader in the Social Darwinism movement. Spencer believed that "under the natural order of things society is constantly excreting its unhealthy, imbecile, slow, vacillating, faithless members" (p. 355). Note the use of the word "excreting." Ironically, the opposite has occurred. Today, a greater proportion of humankind has disabilities than ever before. (These increases in disability rates and their sources will be discussed later in this chapter.) These scholars/writers contributed to the false idea that normalcy is natural and the converse, abnormality, is unnatural. Nevertheless, Darwin wrote with clarity, force, and in a style easily understood by the general public, and his theories had, and continue to have, a tremendous influence on the public consciousness (Hofstadter, 1955). Certainly, "the theory of evolution is considered to be one of the fundamental principles that govern the universe" (White & Gribbin, 1995, p. 3).

Notwithstanding the important and widespread acceptance of Darwin's Theory of Natural Selection, this theory does not apply to humans. (Darwin's theory has been scientifically proven for plants and animals, but not for humans.) Indeed, the major thesis of this book stands in direct opposition to Darwin's Theory of Natural Selection. At the time that Darwin and his disciples were developing this theory, advances in medicine that would preserve and prolong life were impossible to predict. Darwin's theory is based on natural processes operating without the effect of human intervention (Diamond, 1999). But, humankind has always struggled, and in many ways has succeeded, in overcoming the effects of nature. As we shall see later in this chapter, medical advances have indirectly increased the number of individuals with disabilities. More and more people have disabilities and, furthermore, due to longer life spans and sophisticated medical management, individuals who have disabilities are living longer. These higher disability rates may, at first glance, appear to be at odds with the trajectory of progress that science and civilization provide. However, considering that the alternative would be death, higher rates of disability are certainly advances.

Olkin (1999) pointed out that society's efforts to eliminate disability can lead to the idea that *people* who have disabilities should also be eliminated. Olkin listed 13 "Human Rights of Children with Disabilities" and included

> Right 6: To not be made to feel that "people like them" should be prevented. Much of the financial resources, most of the charities, and now prenatal screening, put the emphasis on preventing disabilities. It is psychologically hard for children to know that if their mother could have screened for and found out about the condition the child has, the pregnancy may well have been terminated.... We might well say to these children that it is not them [sic], but the disability that we are trying to prevent, but this is a sham message when we're also trying to encourage incorporation of this disability into a self-concept (p. 101).

The Social Construction of Normalcy and Disability

The increasing proportion of the population with disabilities adds a new dimension to the concept of normalcy. If normalcy is based upon numbers, with those in the numerical majority considered to be "normal" and those in the numerical minority considered to be "abnormal," then as more individuals acquire the identification of having a disability, will the definition of normalcy change? An unusual example of a substantial number of individuals having a disability (albeit not a majority), and not being perceived as having a disability due to their large proportion in the population, is described in Groce's book *Everyone Here Spoke Sign Language: Hereditary Deafness on Martha's Vineyard* (1985). In 1633, an inherited trait that causes deafness was brought to the island, Martha's Vineyard. Geographic isolation and intermarriage resulted in deafness for many individuals; many families had members who were deaf. What is unusual about the story is the lack of a disability identity on the island. On Martha's Vineyard, deafness was a natural part of human existence. Deafness was unremarkable. Moreover, as the title of Groce's book suggests, the use of sign language was not regarded as an accommodation and, indeed, the widespread use of a communication system that everyone could understand probably contributed to the lack of a disability identity. Also, because telecommunications had not yet been introduced, most long-distance communication used the written word. Thus, people who were deaf were not disadvantaged. Many disability advocates have theorized that it is not biological conditions that "make" disabilities, but rather the lack of accommodations (Higgins, 1992; Liachowitz, 1988; Scott, 1969). And the story of Martha's Vineyard certainly lends support to this theory.

Often termed "the universality of disability," the theoretical model of everyone in a community having the same disability helps us to understand the social construction of disability. For example, if no one could walk, the community would be completely accessible for wheelchairs. Even more important, there would be no stigma, prejudice, or stereotypes about people who could not walk. The community would adjust to the inability to walk, with both universal accessibility and the corresponding absence of prejudice and discrimination.

If a spaceship from another planet landed, and the aliens could walk, they would find all the drinking fountains in this community to be too low, because the fountains would be at wheelchair height. Also, the aliens would probably experience a great deal of prejudice, discrimination, and stereotyping because of their deviance (their ability to walk). If, instead of the ability to walk, the universal disability was deafness, there would be the same conditions: (1) universal accommodations and (2) lack of prejudice and discrimination against people who are deaf, which, of course, would be everybody. A third result occurs: the identity of people who are deaf then becomes a cultural and social/linguistic identity and not a disability identity.

In spite of the complexities of defining normalcy/abnormalcy, some widely accepted standards of normalcy must be established, depending on both the characteristic(s) and the environment. How can society operate without some broad guidelines in order to provide services that are most appropriate? Naturally, determination of normalcy/abnormalcy must (occasionally) be made, but it is important to consider the following when making these types of assessments:

- value judgments that may mistakenly interfere
- the environment in which the person functions
- who is making the determination and what their motives are. (Remember, it is "normals" who have defining power. Normals define "nonnormals," not the other way around. So it is not a matter of equal differences. "Normal" people, whoever they might be, have power and "nonnormal" people, whoever they might be, do not have power.)
- the purpose of the assessment
- the diagnostic tools, instruments, and classification system used

All five of these considerations are subject to adaptation and revision. We may like to think that our value systems are fixed and unchanging, but societal values do shift, environments evolve, clinicians change their diagnostic criteria and methods, and policy makers pass in and out of power. What is considered to be normal today might not be normal tomorrow (Brown, 1991; Smart & Smart, 1997).

Especially with intellectual disabilities and mental/emotional disabilities, it is important to understand that both the diagnostic instruments and tools and the classification systems are very much linked to the environment/culture in which they are developed and implemented. Smart and Smart (1997), for example, studied the *Diagnostic and Statistical Manual of Mental Disorders IV* (DSM-IV) published by the American Psychiatric Association (1994). The DSM-IV is the classification system used to diagnose psychoses, personality disorders, mental retardation, and other types of mental illness. Many clinicians must render a diagnosis of some sort from the DSM-IV in order to be paid for services. As described by Smart and Smart, the DSM-IV does not take into account the individual's culture or religious/spiritual background. Indeed, Kirk and Kutchins (1992) detailed a highly critical account of the DSM as a *political* rather than a *scientific* classification system. They labeled the DSM-IV as "lily white" (p. 103), questioning the validity of using DSM diagnoses for people of color. Seem and Hernandez (1997, as cited in Ivey & Ivey, 1998) conducted an analysis of the DSM-IV and determined that more attention should be paid to feminist issues. This is not to advocate that the use of the DSM-IV should be discontinued. These cautions, however, clearly point out the necessity of a critical awareness that every diagnosis based on DSM-IV criteria always occurs in the broad sociocultural context of the North American culture.

Having discussed the most-widely used classification system for mental retardation and mental illness (the DSM-IV), it is important to make a brief statement about the diagnostic tools and instruments used to make these types of diagnoses. Many psychological tests have a "fundamental negative bias" (as cited in McCarthy, 1993) in that only pathology is noted and described. Widely used instruments, such as the Minnesota Multiphasic Personality Inventory (MMPI), tap only negative traits and do not give a picture of the individual's adaptive functioning. Surely, if the tools clinicians use are based on deficit and pathology, disability diagnoses will be given. Further, groups considered to be inferior, such as women, gays, and racial/ethnic minority individuals, will be given diagnoses of pathology more often than individuals who are not considered inferior.

Finally, the reason why the assessment of normalcy is made is important. We like to think that "society" is committed to providing the best services for those with disabilities; however, occasionally the considerations of convenience, cost, and the comfort of those without disabilities receive first priority (Hahn, 1988, 1991). Managed care reforms, cost-containment efforts, and financial risk shifting may work together to more narrowly define both disability and normalcy (Vernellia, 1994). It should also be remembered that there are many situations in which such assessments of normal/abnormal are unnecessary and irrelevant.

It is important to discuss the concept of normalcy/abnormalcy early on because everything that follows—the categorization of disability, the individual's adjustment to disability, or society's reaction to those with disabilities—will directly relate to these ideas.

CATEGORIZING DISABILITIES

In this section, look for—

▶ *reasons why it is necessary to categorize disabilities*
▶ *how diagnoses often affect self-image*
▶ *the short leap from categorization to stereotyping*
▶ *why categorization of disabilities is based on symptom manifestation and not etiology*
▶ *the four broad categories of disabilities*
   1. *physical disabilities*
   2. *intellectual disabilities*
   3. *cognitive disabilities*
   4. *psychiatric disabilities*

Categorization of disabilities is necessary in order to provide benefits and services to those who need them (Albrecht, 1976). Government agencies must design some sort of counting and data collection system in order to estimate the resources necessary to serve the needs of their mandated populations and also to establish policy (Thompson-Hoffman & Storck, 1991). The determination of eligibility for services and benefits, the agencies from which applicants are allowed to receive services, and the settings in which individuals live (institutions or in the community) are closely related to the categorization of the disability (Matson & Barrett, 1993). In the move toward managed care and cost containment (which often includes benefit limitations), the categorization, diagnosis, and definition of disability are important, but complex and detailed, considerations. Simply stated, without a diagnosis, third-party payers will not reimburse, nor will government agencies provide services and benefits (Ivey & Ivey, 1998). Advocacy groups, usually individuals with disabilities, need information in understandable categories in order to represent their legislative and judicial interests. Categorization of disabilities also exerts a powerful effect on the type of prejudice and discrimination directed toward individuals with disabilities (Szymanski & Trueba, 1994). The relationship between disability categorization and societal responses will be discussed in Chapter 3. Finally, and most important, the categorization of the disability impacts the self-identity of the individual with the disability, as will be seen in Chapter 5. Professional vocabulary, including diagnoses, often affect self-images of those who are given these diagnoses. Physicians, psychologists, and other clinicians know that the diagnosis describes a condition a person has and not the person himself or herself. However, diagnosis often results in the self-image of those who receive the diagnosis. Further, one disability scholar (Langer, 1983) found that labels affected the performance of those who received them and, moreover, the clinicians formed their expectations of patients based on the label given. Those individuals who received labels of low competence performed poorly (as expected by their physicians), and those individuals who received labels of high competence performed well. This process is known as a self-fulfilling prophecy (Hannah & Midlarsky, 1987).

Categorization of these diagnoses, while necessary, is also fraught with difficulties, and no classification system truly represents the reality and experience of the individual with the disability. Categorization may lead to false stereotypes, such as the stereotype that all or most individuals with the same disability share important characteristics, experiences, or perceptions. (Example: "Most people who are deaf are shy.") It is a short leap from categorization to stereotyping (McCarthy, 1993; Wright, 1991). Also, in theory, these are classifications and categories of disabilities that people experience and not classifications of people themselves. In practice, however, many individuals with disabilities are consigned to categorization. Indeed to be perceived as a person with a disability is to be immediately, and often incorrectly, categorized. (Example: A rehabilitation counselor who states, "I have four quads on my caseload.") Any categorization scheme tends to emphasize differences *between* categories and emphasizes the similarities *within* categories (Schmelkin, 1988). Further, simply because the focus of most categorization systems is on the disability, the strengths, abilities, assets, and resources of the individual are not considered. Finally, and most important, these categorization schemes of disability do not take into account the self-identities of the individuals with disabilities. Two people who experience the same type and severity of disability have differing circumstances, resources, values, interests, and abilities. Everyone has multiple identities, and for people with disabilities, the disability is only one aspect of their identity. Having explained (1) the necessity for categorization and (2) the effects of categorization, it is important to emphasize that categories are only abstractions and never can fully describe or capture reality.

While there is no one universally accepted categorization of disabilities (Olkin, 1999), the most widely accepted categorization is organized by the symptoms and manifestations of disabilities and not by the cause (etiology) or the source (pathogenesis) of the disability (Bowe, 1981, 1984, 1985, 1993; Bradsher, 1997; Brown, 1991). For example, schizophrenia is considered to be a psychiatric disability, but if disabilities were categorized according to etiology, schizophrenia, and many other mental illnesses, would be considered a physical disability, because it has been proven that many mental illnesses are caused by physical factors. Defining or categorizing disability by the etiology or pathogenesis would be difficult because (1) for many disabilities, the cause is not known; (2) for some disabilities, there are multiple causes, such as mental illness (Kiesler, 1999); and (3) clinicians may change their hypotheses concerning the cause of a specific disability. It should also be noted that while professionals know that diagnoses do not carry any implications about cause, many nonprofessionals—including individuals who are given these diagnoses—are unaware that most diagnoses are based only on symptoms and other clinical features, saying nothing about possible causes. Certainly, the categorization of disabilities by their symptoms, whether they are physical, intellectual, cognitive, or psychiatric, has the longest history in both medicine and the social sciences. Another advantage of this categorization system is the treatment and management plans that result from looking at the course, type, and severity of symptoms. Notwithstanding the present wide acceptance of categorization of disabilities by their symptoms, efforts to refine these classification systems continue. This book will use this categorization system, unless otherwise noted.

Some disabilities are chronic illnesses, such as diabetes and lupus. Nonetheless, health conditions and chronic illnesses are considered to be disabilities. Injuries often result in disabilities. So, while injuries are not discussed in the following sections, it should be remembered that following medical stabilization, many injuries do result in disabilities.

Thus, there are four broad categories of disability: physical, intellectual, cognitive, and psychiatric, all of which are based on symptoms. Individuals with physical disabilities experience physical symptoms, those with intellectual disabilities experience intellectual manifestations, those with cognitive disabilities have cognitive manifestations, and psychiatric symptoms are present in those individuals who have been diagnosed as having a psychiatric disability.

PHYSICAL DISABILITIES

In this section, look for—

▶ *visual impairments*
▶ *hearing impairments*
▶ *dual sensory loss, such as deaf–blindness*
▶ *mobility impairments*
▶ *health disorders*

Physical disabilities include mobility impairments; neurologic impairments such as cerebral palsy and seizure disorders; traumatic brain injuries; musculoskeletal conditions, such as muscular dystrophy and arthritis; sensory loss; and health disorders. Most people would be surprised to learn that arthritis is the most frequently occurring disability in the United States (LaPlante, 1991, 1993, 1996, 1997). In Chapter 3, the societal prejudice, discrimination, and stigma directed toward individuals with disabilities will be discussed, and we will see that, of the four broad categories of disabilities (physical, intellectual, cognitive, and psychiatric), individuals with physical disabilities experience the least amount of prejudice and discrimination. Since government policy makers are subject to the same flawed human perceptions as the general public, we will learn that individuals with intellectual, cognitive, and psychiatric disabilities received government funding for benefits and services long after those with physical disabilities. Moreover, intellectual, cognitive, and psychiatric disabilities were not considered to be disabilities until the twentieth century. The longer history of service provision and allotment of resources to individuals with physical disabilities has resulted in more professional experience and knowledge in dealing with physical disabilities (DeJong & Lifchez, 1983). For the individuals concerning the cause of a specific disability, this longer history of self-identification has resulted in stronger advocacy groups, such as the National Federation for the Blind (NFB), established in 1940 (Berkowitz, 1987).

Physical disabilities lend themselves to objective, quantifiable diagnoses, often with standardized laboratory procedures. In contrast, the diagnosis of intellectual, cognitive, or psychiatric disabilities requires more subjective, impressionistic, clinical judgment. Indeed, some disability advocates regard many psychiatric diagnoses as thinly veiled moral judgments (Szasz, 1961). The most clear-cut illustration of a diagnosis of pathology (not a disability) reflecting society's moral judgment is outlined in Clendinen and Nagourney's (1999) book *Out for Good: The Struggle To Build a Gay Rights Movement in America*. The authors devote a chapter to describing the struggle to remove homosexuality as a diagnosis of pathology from the American Psychiatric Association's *Diagnostic and Statistical Manual of Mental Disorders* (DSM).

Visual Impairments

Visual impairments include total blindness from birth; the gradual loss of vision; muscular disorders, such as strabismus or "crossed eyes"; and loss of acuity across the visual field, such as tunnel vision (Falvo, 1991; Rosenthal & Cole, 1993). People who wear eyeglasses are not considered to have a visual impairment simply because the use of a common and easily obtainable device, such as eyeglasses, restores the individual to full functioning. Indeed, in order to be considered a visual impairment, the condition must be severe enough to limit daily functioning. Degenerative conditions, affecting the retina or optic nerve, include retinitis pigmentosa, retinal detachment, and glaucoma (Carroll, 1961). Visual impairments may also be caused by genetic factors such as malformations or may be acquired due to infections, inflammations, accidents, or tumors (Panek, 1992). However, a large percentage of visual impairments have unknown causes. LaPlante (1991) estimated that approximately 1,500,000 individuals of all ages have visual impairments.

The age distribution of visual impairments is different from that of other disabilities inasmuch as these impairments occur, for the most part, at the beginning of life (before the age of 1) or at the end of life (after the age of 70). Indeed, it is estimated that

60 percent of all visual impairments occur before the age of 1. Two factors that, in the past, led to thousands of cases of blindness in newborn infants have now been virtually eliminated. These two factors are maternal rubella and excess oxygen administered to premature infants, which resulted in retrolental fibroplasia. The rubella vaccine and incubators, introduced in the 1960s, that control the amount of oxygen, have almost eliminated blindness due to these causes. However, many adults born before the 1960s have experienced lifelong blindness due to these two causes.

On the other hand, there is a larger percentage of visual impairments than ever before in the United States due to the larger percentage of elderly people (Silverstone, Lang, Rosenthal, & Faye, 1999). Visual impairments are positively correlated with age and as the population ages, the number of people with visual impairments increases. Advances in medicine and medical technology have greatly decreased the number of newborn infants born with blindness, and yet have also indirectly increased the number of elderly individuals who are blind. Due to the fact that medical advances have lengthened the life span of elderly individuals, they now survive with disabilities, many of which are visual impairments.

Individuals with visual impairments, especially those who have been blind since birth, often have been educated in specialized residential schools (Warren, 1984, 1989). While these residential schools are being replaced with specialized programs in regular schools, there are many adults today who were educated in these segregated schools (Tuttle, 1984). Most people with other types of disabilities, except for hearing impairments and mental retardation, were not educated in schools that required them to live apart from their families. Before the advent of special education programs in the public schools, parents had little choice other than to send their children to boarding schools that were equipped with the educational resources, including teachers, to help their children reach their academic potential. Nonetheless, the emotional cost, for the child sent to school, the parents, and the siblings, was high. In another chapter, we will discuss the effects of segregation on the individual and the costs to society of segregating groups.

Historically, people who are blind have been viewed as receiving preferential treatment (Berkowitz, 1987) inasmuch as there have been more services and benefits accorded to them. Individuals with visual impairments, as a group, have been the beneficiaries of legislation that offered services only to those who are blind. The original Social Security Act allowed only those who were blind to qualify for public assistance (welfare), and today, individuals who are blind automatically qualify for Social Security benefits. The Randolph-Sheppard Act allowed only people who were blind to qualify for Social Security benefits. The Randolph-Sheppard Act allowed only people who were blind to operate vending stands in federal buildings, and the Wagner O'Day Act of 1938 required the federal government to purchase products produced in workshops by people who are blind. No other disability group has had legislation and policy written exclusively for it. There is a box on federal income tax forms where taxpayers can indicate if they are blind. Most states (approximately 32) have separate agencies for individuals who are blind. (People with all other types of disabilities are served by a single agency: Vocational Rehabilitation.)

Hearing Impairments

Everyone has viewed closed-captioned television programs, has watched sign language interpreters at meetings and in the classroom, and a few have had to make accommodations for elderly relatives and friends with hearing loss. Indeed, according to Livneh and Antonak (1997), hearing impairments are the most prevalent type of physical disability in the United States. In some ways, then, individuals with hearing impairments have achieved some measure of visibility and integration within the broader American culture (Moore, 1987). Nonetheless, many individuals with hearing impairments and deafness consider themselves to be part of a different culture—Deaf Culture, claiming individual identity as members of a culture, rather than as individuals with a disability (Bauman & Drake, 1997; Stokoe, Croneberg, & Casterline, 1965; Van Cleve & Crouch, 1989). Individuals in no other disability category consider themselves to be a different culture. Those who advocate for the identification of a Deaf Culture cite the use of a different language, American Sign Language (ASL), and the fact that individuals who are deaf tend to marry other individuals who are deaf. The fact that many of these individuals were educated at residential schools may also contribute to their self-identity as a separate culture. Certainly, their unwillingness to accept "the disabled role" of impairment, deviance, and inferiority plays a large part in the Deaf Culture movement. The impetus for Deaf Culture came from within the group of people who are deaf and was motivated, for the most part, by the need for solidarity and mutual support.

Deaf Culture does not view deafness as pathology or disability. Jankowski, in her book, *Deaf Empowerment* (1997) emphasizes that those in the Deaf Culture have been opposed to cochlear implants, devices that have the capability to restore some hearing. Jankowski told of a hearing mother in Canada who claimed the right to have her deaf child implanted with this device, giving her reason as, "it would make him more like her, a hearing person." A former Ontario legislator, Gary Malkowski, replied, "Then you presumably have no objection to Deaf parents requesting surgery to make their hearing child deaf" (p. 145).

Hearing loss is measured in decibels, but in defining the exact level of loss, two other factors are considered: age of onset and site of the loss. Prelingual deafness occurs before the individual develops speech, usually before the age of two, and postlingual deafness occurs after the age of two. Obviously, the functional limitations of prelingual deafness are greater than those of postlingual deafness since with the latter, the individual usually has the capacity to speak. The site of the loss often determines treatment, such as surgery or the use of hearing aids. Estimates of the prevalence of hearing loss in the United States are as high as 28 million people, or 11 percent of the population.

The cause of more than 25 percent of all hearing loss is unknown. Nonetheless, hearing impairments are often the result of many known conditions, which are divided into two broad categories: congenital and acquired. Congenital, meaning existing at birth, includes hereditary factors, such as those that cause otosclerosis, and prenatal disease, such as rubella. Acquired hearing loss includes postnatal infections, such as scarlet fever, measles, mumps, influenza, typhoid fever, meningitis, and otitis media. As would be expected, the development of antibiotics has greatly decreased the number of individuals with postlingual deafness (Higgins, 1980). Environmental factors, such as physical abuse and exposure to prolonged loud noise, can also cause hearing loss.

The presence of a hearing loss in a child often requires parents to make important decisions early in the child's life (Moore, 1987). The type of education, the means of communication, and the use of technology such as cochlear implants and hearing aids are decisions that will have lifelong effects, and yet these decisions must be made early on when the child is too young to be accorded a great deal of input.

Dual Sensory Loss: Deaf–Blindness

As would be expected, individuals who are both deaf and blind experience severe communication deficits. Another obstacle to the education and rehabilitation of individuals who are deaf–blind is the fact that this type of disability is a low-incidence category. Simply because there are so few people whose disabilities fall within this category, it is difficult to provide services and benefits. A biographer of Helen Keller explained the disability of deaf–blindness: "Today, relatively few deaf–blind people suffer [sic] from Helen Keller's condition—that is, being completely deaf and blind from an early age. The life-threatening childhood infections such as meningitis and scarlet fever have been for the most part eradicated, and the simultaneous onset of blindness and deafness seldom occurs....In general, deafness precedes blindness. Today 50 percent of the deaf–blind population suffer [sic] from Usher syndrome, a genetic condition characterized by hearing loss and by retinitis pigmentosa, an irreversible condition causing...eventual total blindness in middle age" (Hermann, 1998, p. 340).

As with simple deafness or blindness, time of onset has an important impact on the functional limitations of the individual. Obviously, learning to speak is a difficult task for these individuals. Individuals with low-incidence disabilities of any type are often educated in residential schools, far from their homes. Communication is an overriding issue. Helen Keller, probably the most well-known person with dual sensory loss, reported a lifetime of difficulty in distinguishing between her own ideas and the ideas of others since most of what she learned she received literally "secondhand." Information was finger-spelled into her hand (Hermann, 1998).

Mobility Impairments

Mobility impairments interfere with the individual's movement and coordination. Examples of such impairments are spina bifida, cerebral palsy, spinal cord injuries, paraplegia, quadriplegia, muscular dystrophy, and amputations, including congenital limb deficiencies.

Many of these conditions are the result of hereditary conditions; others result before or during birth and others occur because of injury or infection. For example, the single largest cause of amputation in the United States is therapeutic surgical procedures necessitated by complications and secondary infections due to diabetes. Spinal cord injuries, which often result in paraplegia (paralysis of the lower limbs) or quadriplegia (paralysis of all four limbs and the trunk), are caused by automobile accidents, falls, gunshot wounds, and stabs, among others. Over 80 percent of individuals with spinal cord injuries are male. Thus, spinal cord injuries are the only physical disability that is more prevalent among one sex.

Mobility impairments are visible to others, and many individuals with these conditions also experience other disabilities, such as hearing loss, intellectual deficits, and general perceptual difficulties. Some mobility impairments, such as muscular dystrophy, will eventually result in death; but most are stabilized after the acute phase.

Health Disorders

Health disorders, such as diabetes, seizure disorders, hemophilia, sickle cell anemia, AIDS, and cystic fibrosis, are considered to be disabilities because they limit functioning; require treatment, care, and management; and force individuals with these conditions to often be the target of discrimination and prejudice. However, health disorders are different from sensory loss or orthopaedic disabilities in some important aspects. For example, some health disorders are invisible and thus the individual must balance the costs of disclosure against the need for accommodation (Livneh & Antonak, 1997). Some health disorders, such as diabetes, are asymptomatic and the individual may not be aware that he or she has the disorder. Indeed, some health disorders may be somewhat "invisible" to the individual who has the condition inasmuch as when symptoms subside, the individual may no longer continue treatment/management, feeling that he or she no longer has the condition. Lifelong management needs and quality of life issues are important to individuals with health disorders. The terminal course of some health disorders (the individuals will eventually die) renders these disabilities different from other disabilities that are stable. Another difference in course or progression of the disability is the episodic nature of many health disorders. Relapses, seizures, or "flare-ups" are often unpredictable and frequently are exacerbated by stress. So, exactly when the individual wants to be symptom-free, such as for job interviews or in social situations, stress may help to bring on an episode of the health disorder.

INTELLECTUAL DISABILITIES

In this section, look for—

▶ *how mental retardation is more than seven times as prevalent as blindness or deafness and 10 times as prevalent as physical disabilities*
▶ *mild mental retardation*
▶ *moderate mental retardation*
▶ *severe mental retardation*
▶ *profound mental retardation*

Intellectual disabilities include mental retardation, Down syndrome, and autism. As stated previously, these disabilities are grouped together because of their similar symptoms or manifestations, yet the range of these symptoms is broad. Government funding for education and services for individuals with intellectual disabilities was initiated only recently. Special education in neighborhood schools began in the 1970s (Hardman, Drew, Egan, & Wolf, 1993) and adult services were authorized in 1943. Therefore, today there are many adults with these types of disabilities who either remained at home in the care of the family or who were institutionalized. Now, there are both community services and specialized education in regular schools for individuals with these disabilities, allowing the majority to live at home with their families while they receive an education.

Mental Retardation

Mental retardation is defined by the American Association on Mental Retardation (AAMR, 1992) as "significantly subaverage general intellectual functioning resulting in or associated with concurrent impairments in adaptive behavior, and manifesting during the developmental period" (Grossman, 1983, p. 11). Individuals with IQs in the range of 55–70 would be considered to have mild mental retardation, those with IQs in the range of 55–40 would be considered to have moderate retardation, those with IQs in the range of 40–25 would have severe retardation, and IQs in the range of 25 or lower indicate profound mental retardation (American Association on Mental Retardation, 1992; American Psychiatric Association, 1994). Adaptive behavior is defined as those behaviors that are necessary to function, such as social, self-help, communication, and occupational behaviors. As with IQ scores, there is a wide range of adaptive behavior, and these levels of functioning are also labeled "mild," "moderate," and "severe." In order to distinguish mental retardation from disabilities that occur later in life (for example, senile dementia), this diagnosis is determined in the developmental period between birth and age 22 (Drew, Logan, & Hardman, 1992).

It is estimated that approximately 6 million people in the United States (3 percent of the population) can be classified as having mental retardation, with 90 percent of these classified as having mild mental retardation (Joseph P. Kennedy, Jr. Foundation, 1991). Mental retardation is more than 7 times as prevalent as blindness or deafness and 10 times as prevalent as physical disabilities. Causes of mental retardation include maternal infection during pregnancy, most often congenital rubella or fetal alcohol syndrome; birth trauma (most often lack of oxygen); postnatal infections such as encephalitis or metabolic problems that result in the body's inability to process certain substances; and chromosomal abnormalities.

COGNITIVE DISABILITIES

In this section, look for—
  ▶ *traumatic brain injury*
  ▶ *learning disabilities*

Cognitive disabilities impair perception, memory, information processing, reasoning, sensory discrimination (auditory and visual), and attention. Learning disabilities and traumatic brain injury are cognitive disabilities (Cruickshank, 1990; Gaddes, 1985; Hallahan, Kauffman, & Lloyd, 1985). The first indication that a child may have a learning disability usually occurs when parents and/or teachers notice a discrepancy between the child's achievement in school and his or her measured intelligence or potential. The child with a learning disability scores lower on achievement tests than his or her classmates, but also scores lower than would be expected given his or her assessed level of intelligence/potential (i.e., IQ scores). These discrepancies are due to the fact that school achievement tests, such as spelling, arithmetic, and handwriting require skill and facility in the cognitive areas of perception, visual discrimination, auditory discrimination, and information processing (Houck, 1984).

Once considered to be a disability that an individual "outgrew" or, at a minimum, to be a disability only in academic settings, learning disabilities are now known to be lifelong impairments (Johnston, 1987). It is difficult for adults to totally avoid tasks that require reading, writing, or math skills and, furthermore, the individual "knows" that he or she is intelligent, but is unable to explain his or her difficulties in academic areas (even to himself or herself). Oftentimes, spouses of adults with learning disabilities undertake the financial responsibilities for the family and all other family tasks that require writing and math. Nonetheless, adults with learning disabilities are frequently underemployed, meaning they work in jobs that do not utilize their full potential.

Hypotheses of the causation generally fall into two categories: neurological causes or genetic causes. Damage to the central nervous system, usually occurring at birth, such as anoxia or abnormal fetal position, or infections, are thought to be associated with learning disabilities. Genetic abnormalities are also thought to be linked to learning disabilities. Traumatic brain injuries can be caused by accidents, strokes, or infections. Traumatic brain injuries are the leading cause of death and disability among children and adolescents; these injuries occur most frequently to individuals aged 15 to 24. Eighty percent of those who sustain traumatic brain injuries are male.

PSYCHIATRIC DISABILITIES

In this section, look for—

▶ *mental illness*
▶ *autism*
▶ *chemical and substance abuse*
▶ *the relationship between the advent of psychotropic medications and the deinstitutionalization movement*
▶ *how the success of psychotropic medication "humanized" mental illness*

Psychiatric disabilities, the disability category which was the last to receive government funding for services and benefits, includes mental illness, autism, and chemical and substance abuse. The disabilities in this category are often viewed by the general public as self-imposed and being caused, or at least exaggerated, by the individual's lack of character or willpower.

Indeed, more than any other disability group, the families of individuals with psychiatric disabilities are often blamed for the disability. The combination of societal stigma and a short history of government funding for services renders the category of psychiatric disabilities vulnerable to reduction in social services and discontinuity of care.

Mental illness includes schizophrenia, delusional disorders, bipolar affective disorders, major depression, and anxiety/panic disorders (American Psychiatric Association, 1994). The treatment of mental illness underwent a dramatic shift with the introduction of psychotropic medications. Before the introduction of these medications, individuals with severe psychoses were institutionalized for decades; many individuals lived in institutions for their entire lives. Medications, while certainly not without problems, triggered the deinstitutionalization movement and allowed these former patients to integrate into the community. Perhaps even more important than community integration, the success of psychotropic medication has "humanized" the disability, helping the general public to understand the role of organic/biological factors in the causation of these mental illnesses (Deegan, 1997).

DOES EVERYONE HAVE A DISABILITY OF SOME SORT?

In this section, look for—

▶ *how disadvantage is not disability*
▶ *examples of "perceived disabilities"*
▶ *the Americans with Disabilities Act (ADA) definition of disability*
▶ *the difference between eligibility programs and entitlement programs*

The answer to the question, "Does everyone have a disability of some sort?," will impact an individual's self-concept, determine funding and benefits for government services, and assist individuals without disabilities to better understand those who do have disabilities. It is often stated that everyone has limitations, challenges, and problems. This is true. However, disadvantage is not disability. The Americans with Disabilities Act (ADA, 1990) clearly defines disability by providing three general guidelines, all of which are necessary: (1) the presence of a physical, cognitive, intellectual, or psychiatric condition, or a combination of conditions; (2) pervasive impairment in social and occupational functioning; and (3) individuals with these impairments are the target of prejudice, discrimination, stigma, and reduced opportunities. So, it can be seen that disability is a combination of the condition, limitations in functioning, and societal prejudice and discrimination.

Are prejudice and discrimination always inherent in the definition of disability? Societal negative response to individuals with disabilities will be discussed in detail in Chapter 3. However, the example of facial disfigurement will illustrate this relationship. There are no functional limitations in many individuals with facial disfigurements, but, not surprisingly, these disabilities are among the most limiting simply because of the reaction of others to the individual with the disfigurement. So, in spite of the fact that the individual has no functional limitations, he or she is often not employed and lives a life of isolation and reduced opportunity. "Perceived" disabilities, such as obesity and stuttering, usually do not involve functional limitations, but individuals who experience these conditions are subject to reduced opportunity, prejudice, and discrimination. The ADA provides protection to people who are *"regarded* as having a disability." Other well-documented examples of visible physical conditions leading to reduced opportunities are lack of height for boys and men and obesity for girls and women. Looking at the newspaper article that described a longitudinal study in Great Britain (1994) (see Exhibit 1–1), it can be seen that, over the lifetime, short men and fat women earned less money. Therefore, individuals with both of these physical traits, the majority of whom experience no functional limitations, fight long-standing prejudice and discrimination. Many of these individuals, as high school students, probably did not get dates for the prom and then continued to be devalued through their lifetimes. This study quantifies the devaluation in terms of lifetime salaries. For the individuals whose daily lives were summarized, categorized, and interpreted in this study, the low salaries and the lack of occupational success and opportunities are probably less hurtful than the social discrimination and alienation they have been forced to endure. There is an interesting aspect to the prejudice and discrimination directed toward height and weight in that the prejudice seems to be very gender-specific. Lack of height among women is not generally considered a negative (short women are described by the positive term "petite") and obesity in men is more accepted by

Exhibit 1–1

Girls' weight, boys' height affect earning power

CHICAGO (AP)—Obese teenage girls and short teenage boys make less money when they become young adults than others their age, a study of thousands of British youths found.

The study doesn't indicate whether the culprit is discrimination or some internal factor such as low self-esteem, but it suggests appearance can have a big effect on teens' transition from school to work, the research said in the July issue of the *Archives of Pediatrics and Adolescent Medicine.*

Dr. James D. Sargent, lead author of the study, said obesity needs to be prevented by teaching children to eat properly. But he said he is also concerned that women are starving themselves or purging to achieve the ideal of thinness prized in British and U.S. society.

Previous studies, including a recent survey of more than 10,000 Americans ages 16 to 24, found that overweight people, especially women, are far less likely to get married or make a comfortable living when they get older.

Dr. William H. Dietz, who led that study, said that the new work "provides once again pretty compelling evidence that obesity is a major social handicap as well as physical handicap."

He said it matters little whether discrimination or factors such as low self-esteem were behind the findings, because both result from societal attitudes.

The new study looked at 12,537 people in England, Scotland, and Wales, where all children born between March 3 and 9, 1958, were enrolled in a national child development study and have been tracked ever since.

The study found that girls in the heaviest 10 percent of their age group at age 16 earned 7.4 percent less than their non-obese peers by the time they reached 23; and those in the heaviest 1 percent earned 11.4 percent less at age 23.

For boys, obesity did not appear to affect earnings, but height did. For every four inches less height at age 16, boys earned 2 percent less at age 23, the researchers found.

the general public than obesity in women. Men who are overweight are described by such positive terms as "stocky" or "husky."

Another clear-cut example of a disability with few, if any, functional limitations is provided by Shapiro (1993) in his book *No Pity*. Shapiro told the story of Paul Steven Miller, a top graduate of Harvard Law School and a dwarf. Miller was told by a law firm in Philadelphia that, although the firm was impressed with his credentials, they would not hire Mr. Miller because clients, upon meeting Mr. Miller, would, in the words of the interviewer, "think we're running some sort of circus freak show" (p. 28).

Someone who uses eyeglasses does have a vision loss, thus meeting the criterion of the first guideline, but is not considered to have a disability because the use of a simple, easily available obtainable technology (eyeglasses) allows the individual to function without impairment. Based on the same argument that an easily available intervention can restore an individual to full functioning (in this case, medication), the U.S. Supreme Court ruled that a mechanic with high blood pressure did not have a disability and, therefore, was not protected under the ADA (*Murphy v. United Parcel Service,* 141 F.3d 1185, 97–1992). Furthermore, most people who wear eyeglasses have not experienced a great deal of prejudice and discrimination. Nor is a severe case of flu comparable to the experience of a disability. While the flu can limit an individual's activities and is an unpleasant and painful episode, it is not a long-term condition. Furthermore, people who have or have had the flu are not the target of prejudice and discrimination, and finally, a bout with the flu has little effect on a person's self-identity. Extreme fear of speaking in public is certainly a limitation, but is not considered to be a disability because, in addition to the difficulty in documenting a physical condition, people with stage fright experience little functional impairment, because they can simply avoid the need to speak in public. Disadvantage is not a disability. In an empirical study published in *Rehabilitation Psychology* in 1996 (Zea, Belgrave, Townsend, Jarama, & Banks, 1996), the authors stated: "Some of the (Latino) participants referred to their disability as 'lack of English'" (p. 235). It appears that 13 subjects or 26 percent of the Latino sample listed lack of English as their disability. Certainly not being able to speak English in the United States is a disadvantage, but it is not a disability. These individuals, who did not have a disability, were compared to others with "physical (disabilities), emotional (disabilities), substance abuse, and cognitive (disabilities)" (p. 230). In spite of the fact that multivariate analyses were used, one quarter of one sample did not have a disability.

Most public agencies that are mandated to serve people with disabilities provide benefits, funds, and services only after eligibility has been determined. Therefore, the individual must apply for services, provide evidence of the disability, which sometimes includes submitting to extended evaluation procedures, and then be determined "eligible for services" or "not eligible." The three guidelines established by the ADA comprise the eligibility criteria for most of these agencies. Rather than an entitlement program, in which individuals who are part of a mandated population are automatically accepted for services, services for people with disabilities are usually eligibility programs and applicants must prove their eligibility. Public education is an entitlement program but most disability agencies are eligibility programs.

THERE ARE MORE DISABILITIES THAN EVER BEFORE

In this section, look for—
   ▶ *the differing definitions of disability used by government agencies*
   ▶ *the six reasons why there are more disabilities than ever before:*
   1. advances in neonatal medicine
   2. advances in emergency medicine and trauma care
   3. aging of the population
   4. PWDs living longer
   5. liberalization and expansion of the definition of disability
   6. more accurate counting

Disability is a natural and ordinary part of life and, certainly, there is a larger proportion of the population with disabilities today than before. It seems likely that this number will continue to grow. An important point to remember is that these rising rates of disability are advances (both for the individual and society) because, in most cases, the alternative to the acquisition of a disability would be the individual's death. Modern medicine has increased the number of individuals with disabilities, increased their life spans, and raised their quality of life. People who would have died now survive with a disability. It is estimated that the number of people with disabilities exceeds 45 million (Americans with Disabilities Act, 1990; Equal Employment Opportunity Commission, 1991; Ficke, 1992; Hahn, 1991, 1993; LaPlante, 1991, 1997). One factor that makes it difficult to determine accurate disability counts is the difference in the definition of disability (LaPlante, 1997; Pfeiffer, 1993; Zola, 1993).

There is no uniform definition of disability because government agencies define disability differently (Zola, 1993). Further clouding the picture is the fact that some health demographers do not define disability as completely as do rehabilitation demographers. For example, while rehabilitation demographers define alcohol abuse and learning disorders as disabilities, health demographers do not. Finally, rehabilitation demographers are also concerned about health conditions such as obesity, diabetes, and hypertension, which, if not defined as disabilities, are disposing factors that lead to disability.

Some federal programs such as Social Security Disability Income (SSDI) and Supplemental Security Income (SSI) define disability in terms of activity limitations either in "major life activities" or "work limitations." This functional limitation definition of a disability, especially with regard to work limitations, is economically motivated. Children under the age of 16 and individuals above the age of 65 are not typically included in these surveys because they are thought to be "excused" from work. Medical organizations and the diagnostic manuals they produce, such as the *International Classifications of Impairments, Disabilities, and Handicaps* (Thompson-Hoffman & Storck, 1991; World Health Organization, 1980), define disabilities in terms of pathology, losses, impairments, defects, and abnormalities in physical, psychological, or anatomical structure or function.

It is probably safe to assume that the narrow definitions and the lack of consistency among agencies and different demographic methods result in underestimations and underreportings of the prevalence of disability. Nonetheless, it is widely understood that the higher rates of disability are due to the following six factors (Jones, Sanford, & Bell, 1997; Kaye, LaPlante, Carlson, & Wenger, 1997; Pope & Tarlov, 1991).

Advances in Neonatal Medicine

There are more congenital disabilities (disabilities present at birth) than ever before due to the capabilities of neonatal medicine to sustain life. Neonatal medicine is a specialty that concerns itself with newborn infants. Infants who, in the past, would have died now undergo treatment in the uterus before they are born and receive better monitoring and care during the birth process and advanced treatment during the first few months of life. As a result, there are more babies born, and more babies who live, with cerebral palsy, spina bifida, and mental retardation. For example, premature and low-birth-weight babies experience high rates of neurological conditions. In the past, premature infants who weighed less than 3.3 pounds rarely survived. Today, it is commonplace for infants as small as 1.5 pounds to survive. The rising number of births to teenage mothers also contributes to greater incidence of congenital disabilities because teenage mothers have higher rates of premature and/or low-birth-weight babies (Himmelstein, Woolhandler, & Wolfe, 1992). Medical advances and technology, such as fertility enhancement, have brought about multiple births. This increased prevalence of multiple births has also augmented the number of congenital disabilities. For example, there is a fourfold increase in the probability of an infant having cerebral palsy if the infant is part of a multiple birth. The strides of neonatology have resulted in higher rates of cerebral palsy, mental retardation, and spina bifida.

Advances in Emergency Medicine and Trauma Care

The Vietnam War was a great impetus to the development of emergency medicine and trauma care and the larger medical community incorporated these military methods of evacuating people with injuries and providing trauma care while en route to the hospital. Due to these advances, victims of accidents or trauma experience high survival rates because they are evacuated from the scene quickly, treated, and stabilized while being transported to the hospital. Fewer individuals die before they reach the hospital. In 1980, for example, less than 10 percent of individuals with traumatic brain injury or spinal cord injuries survived. Today, the survival rate for individuals with these disabilities is over 90 percent.

Individuals with spinal cord injuries experience permanent paralysis and other health problems such as decubitus ulcers or pressure sores (bed sores) and respiratory and bladder complications. Antibiotics that treat, and cure, these secondary infections allow individuals with spinal cord injuries (and amputations) to experience long life spans (Crewe, 1993). After World War I, there were 400 American men with battle injuries that paralyzed them from the waist down. Ninety percent of these men died before they reached home, most as a consequence of secondary infections. After World War II, and the discovery of antibiotics, there were 2,000 veterans with paraplegia and 85 percent were alive 20 years later (Shapiro, 1993). Indeed, most individuals today with paraplegia or quadriplegia consider themselves to be healthy, controlling infections and other complications with the use of antibiotics. It should be noted that individuals with paraplegia or quadriplegia do not live as long as individuals without these conditions; nonetheless, these individuals usually live for a long period after the onset of their disability.

Aging of the Population

Medicine and medical technology have lengthened the life span of Americans. For example, since the 1970s, stroke *mortality rates* have decreased significantly, but the *incidence* of stroke has not decreased. Obviously, more individuals survive strokes, many with disabilities.

Arthritis is very common among older individuals, but arthritis, although very disabling, is rarely fatal. Seventy-five percent of all therapeutic amputations performed in the United States today are performed on people over the age of 65. Most of these amputations are the result of complications of diabetes. Diabetes, a condition often associated with old age, is the leading cause of blindness in the United States. Mobility impairments and sensory loss are prevalent among elderly people. As Americans live longer, they will continue to experience higher disability rates (Higgins, 1992; Zola, 1989). Indeed, by the year 2040, when the younger baby boomers are 85 years old, the number of Americans with disabilities will be triple what it is today. Also, those individuals with congenital disabilities or disabilities acquired early in life are also experiencing longer life spans (Wilkins & Cott, 1993).

People with Disabilities Live Longer

Not only are there more people with disabilities, but also, people with disabilities live longer with the disabilities than before (Becker & Kaufman, 1988; Benedict & Ganikos, 1981; Brody & Ruff, 1986; Mitchell & Kemp, 1996). Trieschmann (1987) noted:

> Aging is synonymous with living....The issue of aging with a disability is a new problem for western societies, one that has caught our health care system by surprise. Currently, individuals who have lived with spinal injury, polio, and other disabilities for 30, 40, and 50 years are arriving in physicians' offices with a variety of complaints that the physicians have not been taught to handle (p. 1).

The overall increase in the life span contributes to the longer lives of people with disabilities; but even more important are the scientific, technological, and medical advances in the management and treatment of chronic disabilities. To cite a single example, 50 years ago, many parents of infants with disabilities were told by physicians that their babies would not survive to adulthood. Fifty years ago, this was an accurate prognosis. Now, the situation is very different, and most infants with congenital or early onset disabilities survive to adulthood. Living longer with a disability has implications for the individual, the family, and the larger society.

Stubbins (1988) asserted that medical science has not only increased the number of people with disabilities, but has, moreover, changed the experience and personal significance of disability: "Medical advances have transformed the central meaning of disability from physical survival to the search for meaning when one is socially isolated, unemployed, or underemployed, and lacking essential environmental accommodations" (p. 24).

Liberalization and Expansion of the Definition of Disability

The expansion or liberalization of the definition of disability has resulted in higher numbers of disabilities. This is termed a "statistical" cause because the number of people with these types of disabilities did not increase; rather, the way in which their disability was defined or diagnosed changed. Nonetheless, changes in definition result in greater numbers of people to be served and more people who consider themselves to have a disability.

Disability used to be thought of as only physical disability by both the general public and government policy makers. Even today, there are many who think of disability solely in terms of physical disabilities. Nonetheless, such impairments as mental illness, learning disabilities, and alcohol dependence and substance abuse are defined as disabilities, and individuals who experience these conditions are eligible for services and accommodations. It should be noted that there are a few experts who do not consider conditions such as alcoholism to be diseases or disabilities (Fingarette, 1988; Peele, 1989). Last to be legally recognized as disabilities, psychiatric and cognitive disabilities are also the first to be eliminated in government agency guidelines. For example, the Social Security Administration recently ruled that individuals with alcohol or chemical dependency were no longer eligible for benefits.

In addition to the liberalization of the definition of disability, it is safe to state that there has also been an expansion in the definition of disability. Examples such as AIDS, post-polio syndrome, and chronic fatigue syndrome illustrate that the number and types of disabilities are expanding. The *Diagnostic and Statistical Manual of Mental Disorders IV* (DSM-IV, 1994), published by the American Psychiatric Association, contains 120 more diagnoses than its predecessor, the *Diagnostic and Statistical Manual of Mental Disorders III-Revised* (DSM-III-R). While most of these 120 new diagnoses are simply refinements or subcategories of long-established diagnoses, several diagnoses are new. Indeed, the editors stress the evolving nature of the DSM. Some clinicians (Turner & Hersen, 1997), interestingly, have noted that many of these new diagnoses fail to make a clear distinction between the disorder and normal functioning. (It should be noted that not all psychiatric disorders are considered to be disabilities.) Other diagnostic guidebooks, such as the *International Classification of Diseases* (ICD, World Health Organization, 1980), also continue to add diagnoses.

More Accurate Counting

As both the general public and government policy makers become more clear on the definitions of disability, the numbers of all individuals *reported* to have disabilities continue to climb. Essentially, more accurate counting is another "statistical" cause for the higher disability rates since the number of people with disabilities did not increase, only the number of people who are counted or reported as having a disability. Further, disability and health demographers (people who count and categorize the number of health conditions and disabilities) consider the reported number of disabilities to be an underestimation, simply because there are many individuals who do not wish to identify themselves as having a disability. Another illustration of more individuals reporting disabilities concerns the inverse relationship between the economy and disability rates (Yelin, 1992). During economic slumps and depressions, more individuals claim disabilities; most of these individuals are unemployed and need to claim their disability in order to receive financial benefits. In times of prosperity, the number of disability claims decreases. Therefore, the number of people with disabilities did not increase, but rather the number of people *reporting* disabilities.

Table 1–1 is a graphic representation of defining (and counting) disability in terms of work limitations. Looking across the first row, it can be seen that a much higher percentage of working-age Americans have "any work disability" than those who have a "severe work disability." (10.1 percent report "any work disability" and 6.2 percent report "severe work disability.") There appears to be little difference between males and females in either disability category. There are five age categories and, in both categories of disabilities, the percentage goes up as age goes up. (Statisticians state, "There is a positive relationship between prevalence of disability and age.")

The biggest single percentage increase is found in the severe disability category from the ages of 45 to 54 and 55 to 64 years old. The 45- to 54-year-old group reports 8.1 percent and the 55- to 64-year-old group reports almost twice the percentage (15.1 percent). Note also that Blacks reported almost double the disability rate (in both disability categories) as did whites.

Figure 1–1 shows the increase, from 1970 to 1994, in the percentage of the U.S. population with a disability. Disability is defined as "activity limitation." Each increment on the chart represents one percentage point. It can be seen that in 1984,

Table 1–1 Prevalence of Work Disability among Persons Aged 16–64, by Gender, Age, Race, and Ethnicity, by Severity of Work Disability, 1995

	Total (millions)	Any Work Disability		Severe Work Disability	
		Number (millions)	Percentage of total	Number (millions)	Percentage of total
All persons aged 16–64	167.7	16.9	10.1	10.4	6.2
Males	82.8	8.5	10.2	5.1	6.2
Females	84.9	8.4	9.9	5.3	6.2
Ages 16–24	32.5	1.4	4.2	0.8	2.6
Ages 25–34	41.4	2.7	6.4	1.5	3.7
Ages 35–44	42.3	4.0	9.4	2.4	5.7
Ages 45–54	30.7	4.1	13.3	2.5	8.1
Ages 55–64	20.8	4.8	22.9	3.1	15.1
Whites	139.1	13.0	9.4	7.5	5.4
Blacks	20.8	3.2	15.4	2.5	11.8
Other races	7.8	0.7	8.5	0.4	5.6
Hispanic origin	17.1	1.6	9.6	1.2	7.1

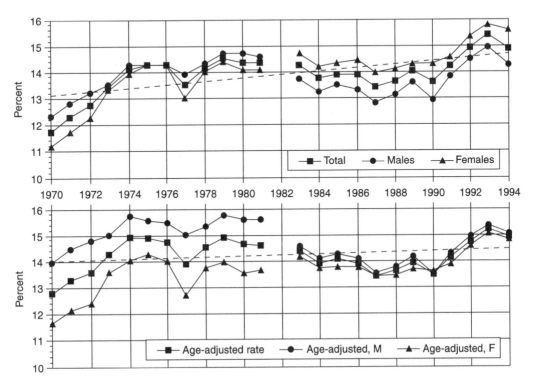

Figure 1–1 Proportion of U.S. Population with Activity Limitation, 1970–1994.

approximately 14.5 percent reported an "activity limitation," while in 1994, this percentage had increased to 15–16 percent. This increase in percentage may not appear, at first glance, to be significant, but the increase in percentage represents tens of thousands of individuals.

Medical Advances and Societal Advances

There is a widespread belief that if medical and scientific communities had the capability to prevent all congenital disabilities, there would be no babies born with disabilities. For example, a producer's description of a videotape about children with disabilities concludes with this sentence: "The program also addresses the growing likelihood that prenatal testing and advances in gene technology may make the current generation of those with physical challenges [sic] the last (generation)." Of course, medical researchers and other scientists should work to prevent disability, but this does not imply that all parents would choose to terminate a pregnancy rather than to give birth to a baby with a disability. Perhaps even more important is society's conceptualization of the "problem."

Such a quick and facile acceptance of the desirability of ending all congenital disabilities demonstrates the widely perceived source of the "problem." The problem is erroneously thought to be the person with the disability. It is more accurate to think of the environment as the problem. For example, the decision-making process of prospective parents who learn that their baby will be born with a disability would be very different if the following conditions were present: (1) all PWDs were accorded full equality and participation in society, including social and intimate relationships; (2) all PWDs had access to the adaptive technology they need and want; (3) all PWDs were provided with the medical resources to manage and control their disabilities; and (4) all PWDs were provided ethical and capable personal care attendants, if needed. Reviewing this list, it is possible to see that none of these conditions relates to the *presence* of disability itself. None of these four conditions proposes to *prevent* or *cure* disability. These conditions propose change—but not in the individual with the disability or his or her parents, but in the broader environment.

In-Class Video

- View the 17-minute video *Understanding Hearing Loss* by Films for the Humanities and Sciences (P.O. Box 2053, Princeton, NJ 08543–2053, 1–800–257–5126, *http://www.films.com*). The producers describe this video: "This program explains sound, hearing, hearing loss, and the relationship between listening to speech and the different kinds of hearing loss. It includes realistic simulations of what speech sounds like with different kinds of hearing loss and useful hints on improving communication."

Learning Activities

1. Read the book *A Nearly Normal Life* by Charlie L. Mee (1999, New York: Little-Brown). Focus on Mee's definition of normal and the "desirability of normal" and his own "deviance from normality." What does the author mean by "The need to expand our concept of normalcy"? Why does he think this is necessary?

2. Read the book *Three Quarters, Two Dimes, and a Nickel* by Steve Fiffer (1999, New York: Free Press). Write a short paper explaining why the title of the book is not *One Dollar*.

3. Read Zola's paper on the various definitions of disability and how each of these definitions reflects the needs and values of the definers. "The Politics of Disability" in *Disability Studies Quarterly, 12,* 1992. Read Hahn's (1993) paper "The Political Implications of Disability Definitions and Data." Write a summary paper.

4. Listen to *On a Roll: Talk Radio on Life and Disability* with host Greg Smith. *On a Roll* airs on 36 radio stations across the country, as well as the Internet live every Sunday at 9:05 P.M. eastern time. The program also has Internet Only streaming audio segments on the Web at http://www.onarollradio.com. *On a Roll* is sponsored by Microsoft (http://www.microsoft.com/enable), the Action Storm Series Power Chairs (http://www.invacare.com), EasyStand (http://www.easystand.com), and Neverland Adventures (619–696–6068).

5. Read the special issue *Disability Policy Studies* (1993, 4) that discusses the differing definitions of disability. Write a paper describing these differing definitions, the source and rationale of each definition, and the legal, clinical, and personal implications of each definition.

6. Give the definition of disability found in the following legislation: SSDI-SSI, ADA. Write a short paper outlining the similarities and differences among the definitions, and the implications these conflicting definitions have for individuals with disabilities.

7. Taking the example of the space aliens on page 7, write a short paper describing the prejudice, discrimination, and stereotyping the aliens would encounter.

8. Go to the library and access the 2nd edition of Radius CD-ROMs. These 19 CD-ROM data sets are the largest single source on disability. Students can analyze disability in terms of demographic, health, employment, and other social variables. Find this CD-ROM: "1998 National Organization of Disability Survey of Americans with Disabilities" and write a paper on some aspect of disability and its relation to demographic variables such as sex, age, geographic area, income, level of education, or ethnicity/race. Note: These data include 438 variables and 1,000 case studies. Radius 1999 Edition is available at most university libraries. Their Web site is *http://www.socio.com* and their e-mail address is socio@socio.com.

Writing Experience

Using any of the seven "bullet" questions listed at the beginning of this chapter, write a paper that responds to one of these questions.

References

Albrecht, G. L. (Ed.). (1976). *The sociology of physical disability and rehabilitation*. Pittsburgh, PA: University of Pittsburgh Press.

American Association on Mental Retardation. (1992). *Mental retardation: Definition, classification, and systems of supports (Special 9th ed.)*. Washington, DC: Author.

American Psychiatric Association. (1994). *Diagnostic and statistical manual of mental disorders* (4th ed.). Washington, DC: Author.

Americans with Disabilities Act of 1990, 42 U.S.C. § 12101 *et seq.* Available: http://www.usdoj.gov/crt/ada/adahoma1.htm.

Bauman, H. D. L., & Drake, J. (1997). Silence is not without voice: Including deaf culture within the multicultural curricula. In L. J. Davis (Ed.). *Disability studies reader* (pp. 307–314). New York: Routledge.

Becker, G., & Kaufman, S. (1988). Old age, rehabilitation, and research: A review of the issues. *The Gerontologist, 28,* 459–468.

Benedict, R., & Ganikos, M. (1981). Coming to terms with ageism in rehabilitation. *Journal of Rehabilitation, 47*(4), 10–18.

Berkowitz, E.D. (1987). *Disabled policy: America's programs for the handicapped.* London, England: Cambridge University.

Bowe, F. (1981). *Demography and disability: A chartbook for rehabilitation.* Hot Springs, AR: University of Arkansas, Arkansas Rehabilitation Services, Arkansas Rehabilitation Research and Training Center.

Bowe, F. (1984). *U.S. Census and disabled adults.* Hot Springs, AR: University of Arkansas, Arkansas Rehabilitation Services, Arkansas Rehabilitation Research and Training Center.

Bowe, F. (1985). *Black adults with disabilities.* Washington, DC: U.S. Census Bureau.

Bowe, F. (1993). Statistics, politics, and employment of people with disabilities. *Journal of Disability Policy Studies, 4,* 83–91.

Bradsher, J. E. (1997). Disability among racial and ethnic groups, #10 [On-line]. *Disability Statistics Abstract.* San Francisco: University of California at San Francisco. Available: http://www.dsc.ucsf.edu.

Brody, S., & Ruff, G. (Eds.). (1986). *Aging and rehabilitation: Advances in the state of the art.* New York: Springer.

Brown, S. C. (1991). Conceptualizing and defining disability. In S. Thompson-Hoffman & I. F. Storck (Eds.), *Disability in the United States: A portrait from national data* (pp. 1–14). New York: Springer.

Carroll, T. J. (1961). *Blindness: What it is, what it does, and how to live with it.* Boston: Little, Brown.

Clendinen, D., & Nagourney, A. (1999). *Out for good: The struggle to build a gay rights movement in America.* New York: Simon & Schuster.

Crewe, N. M. (1993). Aging and severe physical disability: Patterns of change and implications for change. In M. Nagler (Ed.), *Perspectives on disability* (2nd ed., pp. 355–361). Palo Alto, CA: Health Markets Research.

Cruickshank, W. M. (1990). Definition: A major issue in the field of learning disabilities. In M. Nagler (Ed.), *Perspectives on disability* (pp. 389–406). Palo Alto, CA: Health Markets Research.

Darwin, D. (1979). *The illustrated origin of species by Charles Darwin abridged and introduced by Richard E. Leakey.* New York: Hill and Wang.

Davis, L. J. (1997). Constructing normalcy: The bell curve, the novel, and the invention of the disabled body in the nineteenth century. In L. J. Davis (Ed.), *Disability studies reader* (pp. 307–314). New York: Routledge.

Deegan, P. E. (1997). Recovery: The lived experience of rehabilitation. In L. Spaniol, C. Gagne, & M. Koehler (Eds.), *Psychological and social aspects of psychiatric disability* (pp. 92–98). Boston: Boston University, Center for Psychiatric Rehabilitation.

DeJong, G., & Lifchez, R. (1983). Physical disability and public policy. *Scientific American, 248*(6), 40–49.

Diamond, J. (1999). *Guns, germs, and steel: The fate of human societies.* New York: W. W. Norton.

Drew, C. J., Logan, D.R., & Hardman, M. L. (1992). *Mental retardation: Life cycle approach* (5th ed.). Columbus, OH: Merrill.

Equal Employment Opportunity Commission Office of Program Publications. (1991). *National database: Americans with Disabilities Act receipts 100194–093095.* Washington, DC: Author.

Falvo, D. R. (1991). *Medical and psychosocial aspects of chronic illness and disability.* Gaithersburg, MD: Aspen.

Ficke, R. C. (1992). *Digest of data of persons with disabilities: 1992.* Washington, DC: National Institute on Disability and Rehabilitation Research.

Fingarette, H. (1988). *Heavy drinking.* Berkeley, CA: University of California.

Fisher, R. A. (1958). *The genetical theory of natural selection* (2nd ed.). New York: Dover.

Friedlander, H. (1996). *The origins of Nazi genocide: From euthanasia to the final solution.* Chapel Hill, NC: University of North Carolina.

Gaddes, W. H. (1985). *Learning disabilities and brain function: A neuropsychological approach* (2nd ed.). New York: Springer-Verlag.

Galton, F. (1869). *Hereditary genius.* London: Macmillan.

Galton, F. (1883). *Inquiries into human faculty and its development.* New York: Dutton.

Galton, F. (1887). *Hereditary genius: An inquiry into its lows and consequences.* New York: Appleton.

Gould, S. (1981). *The mismeasure of man.* New York: W. W. Norton.

Groce, N. (1985). *Everybody here spoke sign language: Hereditary deafness on Martha's Vineyard.* Cambridge, MA: Harvard University.

Grossman, H. J. (Ed.). (1983). *Manual on terminology and classification in mental retardation.* Washington, DC: American Association on Mental Deficiency.

Hahn, H. (1988). The politics of physical differences: Disability and discrimination. *Journal of Social Issues, 44,* 39–47.

Hahn, H. (1991). Foreword. In R. P. Marinelli & A. E. Dell Orto (Eds.), *The psychological and social impact of physical disability* (3rd ed., pp. ix–x). New York: Springer.

Hahn, H. (1993). The political implications of disability definitions and data. *Journal of Disability Policy Studies, 4,* 41–52.

Hallahan, D. P., Kauffman, J. M., & Lloyd, J. W. (1985). *Introduction to learning disabilities* (2nd ed.). Englewood Cliffs, NJ: Prentice Hall.

Hannah, M.E., & Midlarsky, E. (1987). Differential impact of labels and behavioral descriptions on attitudes toward people with disabilities. *Rehabilitation Psychology, 32,* 227–238.

Hardman, M. L., Drew, C. J., Egan, M. W., & Wolf, B. (1993). *Human exceptionality: Society, school, and family* (4th ed.). Boston: Allyn & Bacon.

Hermann, D. (1998). *Helen Keller: A life.* New York: Alfred A. Knopf.

Herrnstein, R., & Murray, C. (1994). *The bell curve: Intelligence and class structure in American life.* New York: Free Press.

Higgins, P. C. (1980). *Outsiders in a hearing world: A sociology of deafness.* Newbury Park, CA: Sage.

Higgins, P. C. (1992). *Making disability: Exploring the social transformation of human variation.* Springfield, IL: Charles C Thomas.

Himmelstein, D. U., Woolhandler, S., & Wolfe, S. M. (1992). The vanishing health care safety net: New data on uninsured Americans. *International Journal of Health Services, 22,* 381–396.

Hofstadter, R. (1955). *Social Darwinism in American thought* (rev. ed.). Boston: Beacon.

Houck, C. K. (1984). *Learning disabilities: Understanding concepts, characteristics, and issues.* Englewood Cliffs, NJ: Prentice Hall.

Ivey, A. E., & Ivey, M. B. (1998). Reframing the DSM-IV: Positive strategies from developmental counseling and therapy. *Journal of Counseling and Development, 76,* 334–350.

Jacoby, R., & Glauberman, N. (Eds.). (1995). *The bell curve debate: History, documents, options.* New York: Random House.

Jankowski, K. A. (1997). *Deaf empowerment: Emergence, struggle and rhetoric.* Washington, DC: Gallaudet University.

Johnston, R. B. (1987). *Learning disabilities, medicine, and myth: A guide to understanding the child and the physician.* Boston: Little, Brown.

Jones, M., Sanford, J., & Bell, R. B. (1997). Disability demographics. How are they changing? *Team Rehab Report, 38,* 36–44.

Joseph P. Kennedy, Jr. Foundation. (1991). *Facts about mental retardation.* Washington, DC: Author.

Kaye, H.S., LaPlante, M.P., Carlson, D., & Wenger, B.L. (1997). Trends in disability rates in the United States, 1970–1994, #17{On-line}. *Disability Statistics Abstract.* San Francisco: University of California at San Francisco. Available: http://www.dsc.uscsf.edu

Kiesler, D. J. (1999). *Beyond the disease model of mental disorders.* Westport, CT: Praeger.

Kincheloe, J. L., Steinberg, S. R., & Gresson, A. D., III (Eds.). (1997). *Measured lies: The bell curve examined.* New York: St. Martin's.

Kirk, S. A., & Kutchins, H. (1992). *The selling of the DSM: The rhetoric of science in psychiatry*. New York: Aldine Degruyter.

Langer, E. J. (1983). *The psychology of control*. Beverly Hills, CA: Sage.

LaPlante, M P. (1991). The demographics of disability. In J. West (Ed.), *The Americans with Disabilities Act: From policy to practice* (pp. 55–80). New York: Milbank Memorial Fund.

LaPlante, M. P. (1993). State estimates of disability in America. *Disability Statistics Abstracts No. 3*. Washington, DC: National Institute on Disability and Rehabilitation Research.

LaPlante, M. P. (1996). Health conditions and impairments causing disability. *Disability Statistics Abstracts No. 16*. Washington, DC: National Institute on Disability and Rehabilitation Research.

LaPlante, M. P. (1997). How many Americans have a disability: #5 {On-line}. *Disability Statistics Abstract*. San Francisco: University of California at San Francisco. Available: http://www.dsc.ucsf.edu.

Liachowitz, C. H. (1988). *Disability as a social construct: Legislative roots*. Philadelphia: University of Pennsylvania.

Livneh, H., & Antonak, R. F. (1997). *Psychosocial adaptation to chronic illness and disability*. Gaithersburg, MD: Aspen.

Matson, J. L., & Barrett, R. P. (Eds.). (1993). *Psychopathology in the mentally retarded* (2nd ed.). Boston: Allyn & Bacon.

McCarthy, H. (1993). Learning with Beatrice A. Wright: A breath of fresh air that uncovers the unique virtues and human flaws in us all. *Rehabilitation Education, 10*, 149–166.

Mitchell, J. M., & Kemp, B. J. (1996). The Older Adult Disability Scale: Development and validation. *Rehabilitation Psychology, 41*, 187–203.

Moore, D. F. (1987). *Educating the deaf: Psychology, principles, and practices* (3rd ed.). Boston: Houghton Mifflin.

Olkin, R. (1999). *What psychotherapists should know about disability*. New York: Guilford.

Panek, W. C. (1992). Visual disabilities. In M. G. Brodwin, F. Tellez, & S. K. Brodwin (Eds.), *Medical, psychosocial, and vocational aspects of disability* (pp. 217–230). Athens, GA: Elliott & Fitzpatrick.

Peele, S. (1989). *The diseasing of America*. Boston: Houghton Mifflin.

Pfeiffer, D. (1993). The problem of disability definition. *Journal of Disability Policy Studies, 4*, 77–82.

Pope, A. M., & Tarlov, A. R. (Eds.). (1991). *Disability in America: Toward a national agenda for prevention*. Washington, DC: National Academy Press.

Rosenthal, B. P., & Cole, R. G. (1993). Visual impairments. In M. G. Eisenberg, R. L. Gluekauf, & H. H. Zaretsky (Eds.), *Medical aspects of disability* (pp. 38–67). Springfield, IL: Charles C Thomas.

Schmelkin, L. P. (1988). Multidimensional perspectives in the perception of disabilities. In H. E. Yuker (Ed.), *Attitudes toward persons with disabilities* (pp. 127–137). New York: Springer.

Scott, R. A. (1969). *The making of blind men: A study of adult socialization*. New York: Sage.

Shapiro, J. P. (1993). *No pity. People with disabilities forging a new civil rights movement*. New York: Random House.

Silverstone, B., Lang, M. A., Rosenthal, B. P., & Faye, E.E. (Eds.). (1999). *The Lighthouse handbook on vision impairment and vision rehabilitation*. New York: Oxford University Press.

Smart, D. W., & Smart, J. F. (1997). DSM-IV and culturally sensitive diagnosis: Some observations for counselors. *Journal of Counseling and Development, 75*, 392–398.

Spencer, H. (1884). *Social statics: Or the conditions essential to human happiness*. New York: Appleton.

Stokoe, W. C., Croneberg, C., & Casterline, D. (1965). *Dictionary of American Sign Language* (2nd ed.). Washington, DC: Gallaudet College.

Stubbins, J. (1988). The politics of disability. In H. E. Yuker (Ed.), *Attitudes toward persons with disabilities* (pp. 22–23). New York: Springer.

Szasz, T. S. (1961). *The myth of mental illness*. New York: Harper.

Szymanski, E. M., & Trueba, H. T. (1994). Castification of people with disabilities: Potential disempowering aspects of classification in disability services. *Journal of Rehabilitation, 60* (3), 12–20.

Thompson-Hoffman, S., & Storck, I. F. (Eds.). (1991). *Disability in the United States: A portrait from national data*. New York: Springer.

Trieschmann, R. B. (1987). *Aging with a disability*. New York: Demos.

Turner, S. M., & Hersen, M. (Eds.). (1997). *Adult psychopathology and diagnosis* (3rd ed.). New York: Wiley.

Tuttle, D. (1984). *Self-esteem and adjusting to blindness*. Springfield, IL: Charles C Thomas.

Van Cleve, J. V., & Crouch, B. A. (1989). *A place of their own*. Washington, DC: Gallaudet University.

Vernellia, R. R. (1994). Impact of managed care organizations on ethnic Americans and underserved populations. *Journal of Health Care for the Poor and the Underserved, 5*, 224–237.

Warren, D. H. (1984). *Blindness and early childhood development*. New York: American Foundation for the Blind.

Warren, D. H. (1989). Implications of visual impairments for child development. In M. C. Wang, M. C. Reynolds, & H. J. Walberg (Eds.), *Handbook of special education: Research and practice. Vol. 3. Low-incidence conditions* (pp. 155–172). Oxford, England: Pergamon.

White, M., & Gribbin, J. (1995). *Darwin: A life in science*. New York: Simon and Schuster.

Wilkins, S., & Cott, C. (1993). Aging, chronic illness, and disability. In M. Nagler (Ed.), *Perspectives on disability* (2nd ed., pp. 363–377). Palo Alto, CA: Health Markets Research.

Wolfensberger, W. (1972). *The principle of normalization in human services*. Toronto: National Institute on Mental Retardation.

World Health Organization. (1980). *International classification of impairments, disabilities and handicaps: A manual of classification relating to the consequences of disease*. Geneva, Switzerland: Author.

Wright, B. A. (1991). Labeling: The need for person–environment individuation. In C. R. Snyder & D. R. Forsyth (Eds.), *Handbook of social and clinical psychology: The health perspective* (pp. 469–487). New York: Pergamon.

Yelin, E. H. (1992). *Disability and the displaced worker*. New Brunswick, NJ: Rutgers University.

Zea, M. C., Belgrave, F. Z., Townsend, T. G., Jarama, S. L., & Banks, S. R. (1996). The influence of social support and active coping on depression among African Americans and Latinos with disabilities. *Rehabilitation Psychology, 41*, 225–242.

Zola, I. K. (1989). Toward a necessary universalizing of a disability policy. *Milbank Quarterly, 67*, 401–428.

Zola, I. K. (1993). Disability statistics, what we count and what it tells us. *Journal of Disability Policy Studies, 4*, 9–39.

Chapter 2

Models of Disability: The Medical Model, the Environmental Model, and the Functional Model

▶ How does the medical model of disability differ from the environmental and functional models?

▶ Can disabilities be socially and culturally constructed or are disabilities only biological phenomena?

▶ What are the advantages and disadvantages of diagnoses?

▶ What is the difference between a hidden and a visible disability?

▶ What is the difference between a congenital disability and a disability acquired late in life?

▶ Why can't we use the words "cripple," "victim," or "handicapped"? Regardless of which words are used, isn't the meaning the same?

WHAT ARE MODELS OF DISABILITY?

In this section, look for—

> ▶ *why models of disability are important*
> ▶ *how models define our world and influence our attitudes and actions*
> ▶ *the three models of disability:*
>   1. *the medical model*
>   2. *the environmental model*
>   3. *the functional model*

One way in which to conceptualize disability concerns the different models for disability that can be implemented. A model is a set of guiding assumptions, concepts, and propositions about the nature of phenomena or human experience. Models have often been defined as human-made tools for understanding and human-made guidelines for action. As would be expected, treatment and intervention strategies are guided by the type of disability model used. There are three basic models of conceptualizing disability: (1) the medical model, (2) the environmental model, and (3) the functional model. Different models of disability have different uses, and each model has its advantages and disadvantages. On the other hand, all models are, to some extent, incomplete and subject to error, simply because models are *human-made representations* of experiences and phenomena.

33

Nonetheless, these models are important both to individuals with disabilities and to those without disabilities. It is essential to be clear and explicit—especially to ourselves—about the models we use. Occasionally, we should question and examine models to which we subscribe and we should question our ways of explaining the world. Indeed, models define our world and influence our attitudes and actions. Each of the following models formed the basis for the development of different types of government-sponsored services (Bickenbach, 1993; Moore & Feist-Price, 1999; Stone, 1984).

Medical Model of Disability

The medical model is the most familiar and best understood conception of disease and disability, probably because this model has the longest history. This model employs objective, clear-cut, standardized measures and, as the name suggests, uses experts, such as physicians, to provide defining characteristics, causes, prognoses, and methods of treatment (Fowler & Wadsworth, 1991). There are two dimensions of this model, normal and pathological, with the diagnosis of normal often defined as simply the absence of any pathology. As would be expected, the medical model focuses on the anatomy and physiology of the individual and employs standardized procedures to make diagnoses. These standardized procedures allow different medical experts to arrive at the same diagnosis. Due to the high levels of skill and knowledge necessary to render both diagnoses and treatment, the medical model of disability relies on the use of experts, usually physicians. While the contributions of the profession of medicine cannot be overstated, there are deficiencies in the medical model.

Medicine is a profession with a long history; indeed, this profession is thousands of years old. However, it is only within the last 100 years that physicians have faced the challenge of helping patients to manage and treat conditions over the life span. For centuries, medical treatment had two outcomes: a total cure or the death of the person. Of course, there were exceptions to this, such as mental illness or sensory loss. Nonetheless, for many conditions, such as diabetes, there wasn't any management or treatment available and individuals with diabetes died. People with amputations did not survive long after the procedure because, before the advent of antibiotics, infections, which are secondary to amputations, killed these people. People today live with many conditions, both physical and emotional, which are neither acute nor curable, but which could result in death or further disablement if the conditions are not managed and controlled.

The lingering effects of this two-outcome paradigm of the medical model are experienced by people with disabilities today. For example, many individuals with disabilities are very healthy and do not require referral to medical specialists when they have commonplace illnesses that are not relevant to their disabilities or even when they need routine physical exams or dental examinations. Yet, many physicians refer individuals with disabilities to seek treatment from specialists. Indeed, many individuals with disabilities must undergo hospitalization needlessly in order to have simple dental work performed.

The focus of the medical model on pathology and on the biology and physiology of the patient has, for the most part, ignored the individual's role functioning and his or her environmental demands. Disability concerns are divorced from social factors in the medical model. Indeed, the medical model conceived the "problem" as existing entirely within the individual and focused all efforts on "fixing" the individual, rarely acknowledging the social construction of and societal reaction to disability (Phillips, 1990; Sinacore-Guinn, 1995; Szasz, 1961, 1976). The individual with a disability, however severe the disability, is a complete person with family, work, and community requirements, all of which impact the diagnosis of the disability. To cite a single example, in order to determine level of benefits, physicians will often render a numerical rating of a disability, such as 25 percent or 35 percent, not taking into account such factors as the amount of stigma toward the disability, the individual's family support, or the individual's coping resources. Two clear-cut examples of disabilities that are very limiting, not due to any functional or organic limitations, are the disabilities of Paul Steven Miller, found in Chapter 1, and the disabilities of individuals with facial disfigurements. The medical model, with its emphasis solely on the individual, is not broad enough to describe these individuals' experiences or generate plans to change their situations. Surely, two people with the same diagnosis, at the same numerical rating, will have different prognoses. The solution, of course, is multidisciplinary case management in which disability professionals, with their complementary knowledge, skills, and perspectives, provide a complete range of services, including medical, educational, and vocational.

The perspective of the medical model often objectified people with disabilities (PWDs) because these individuals were viewed as a body part, a specific organ, or a type of disability. The PWD becomes a "quad," or a "schizophrenic," or a "diabetic." Clearly, some of this objectification and impersonal treatment of the PWD assists physicians in maintaining an objectivity and emotional distance/detachment. It appears that, rather than easing the discomfort of the patient, physicians have chosen to respond to their own discomfort. The medical model, in its most extreme form, holds that if physicians view patients as whole people and as collaborators in the diagnosis and treatment of their conditions, the effectiveness of physicians will be compromised. As technology and laboratory diagnostic procedures proliferate, less emphasis will be placed on history-taking and learning about the patient from the patient. Thus, in the name of medical pragmatism, the individual and his or her environment are ignored (Cameron, 1982).

The medical model is often perceived to be that of experts delivering services to passive recipients who are expected to be compliant and to whom little information and few treatment options are provided. This "expert-in-control" is referred to as the "omniscience of the experts" (DeLoach & Greer, 1981). Paternalism probably began in the medical model. A practicing attorney with a severe congenital disability stated, "Doctors never bothered asking me what my life could become" (Mikata, 1995). Disability advocates report stories of experts and physicians who did not listen to individuals with disabilities and their family members, other experts who viewed the individuals' disabilities as tragic flaws, and experts who did not have the experience of living with disabilities 24 hours a day, 7 days a week. While these patterns are changing, many individuals with disabilities have felt themselves to have been devalued and treated as inferior by medical professionals, and were allowed very little control over their treatment. Today, some adults with disabilities feel resentment toward their parents, believing that the parents unquestioningly submitted them to all the treatments, procedures, hospitalizations, and institutionalizations "prescribed" by doctors. However, at that time, parents had few options.

A pediatrician, Perri Klass, has described a possible result of the medical model:

If we are at war, then who is the enemy? Rightly the enemy is the disease, and even if that is not your favorite metaphor, it is a rather common way to think of medicine: we are combating these deadly processes for the bodies of our patients. They become battlefields, lying there passively in bed while the evil armies of pathology and the resplendent forces of modern medicine fight it out. Still, there are some very good doctors who seem to think that way, who take disease as a personal enemy and battle it with fury and dedication. The real problem arises because all too often the patient comes to personify the disease and somehow the patient becomes the enemy (Klass, cited in Couser, 1997, pp. 26–27).

One of the greatest leaders in the Disability Rights Movement was Ed Roberts. However, physicians had seen little value in his life when he was a teenager and contracted polio. Furthermore, Roberts internalized those views. He was respirator-dependent. Along with others, Roberts later founded the Independent Living Movement and the World Institute on Disability. He fought to graduate from high school and to be admitted to the University of California at Berkeley, and he organized the "Rolling Quads" to fight for the right to live outside the campus hospital. Roberts was appointed by Governor Jerry Brown to be director of the California State Department of Rehabilitation. He died in 1995.

Shapiro (1993) described the effect of the medical model of disability on Roberts:

Roberts saw himself as a "helpless cripple" overwhelmed by depression, powerlessness, and self-hatred. He asked his parents if he would ever go to college, marry, or hold a job. The answer, based on what doctors, nurses, and counselors had said, was always no. It would have been more humane, a doctor had told his mother, if the high fever of polio had killed him quickly (p. 42).

Due to its long history, most of which was involved with the treatment of physical conditions, the medical model does not lend itself well to intellectual, cognitive, or psychiatric disabilities (Helms, 1992). Only recently have intellectual, cognitive, and psychiatric disabilities been recognized as disabilities. Furthermore, these disabilities are conditions that are, for the most part, managed and treated over the life span of the individual. The medical model, with its emphasis on finding, treating, and curing a problem that exists solely within the individual (without taking the environment into consideration), does not describe cognitive, intellectual, or psychiatric disabilities very well. Interestingly, most writings by and directed to physicians refer to the medical model as the disease model.

Environmental Model of Disability

The environmental model posits that the individual's environment—both social and physical—can cause, define, or exaggerate disability. It is easy to see the relationship between disability and the physical environment. "Disability is viewed as...a product of a disabling, unresponsive, or insensitive environment" (Hursh, 1995, p. 322). Essentially, environments can limit physical access and opportunities for work, education, and social participation (Tannebaum, 1986). If a person with paraplegia does not have a wheelchair, then the impact of the paraplegia is greater.

Barriers in the physical environment can hinder the individual with a disability, and certainly the Americans with Disabilities Act (ADA) is helping to make the environment accessible for all citizens.

It is a little more difficult to understand the relationship between disability and the social and cultural environment. For example, in Manchurian China, infant girls from upper-class homes had their feet bound tightly until the bones were broken and twisted and, as a result, these girls and women were unable to walk. Furthermore, to most people today who look at photographs of these Manchurian girls and women, the feet of the girls and women appear to be deformed. But, the Manchurian people considered the feet of these women to be beautiful and, moreover, judged the inability to walk or stand to be a sign of prestige and status, because these girls and women came from rich homes and, therefore, were not required to work. This is an unusual example, but it does illustrate that disability is not only a biological construction, but also is the result of social and cultural definitions.

Another example of a disability that is often environmentally defined is a learning disability. Learning disabilities, the result of neurological malfunction, probably were not noticeable in preliterate societies. In modern times, individuals with learning disabilities are often called "six-hour retardates" by others and by themselves because their learning disabilities seem environmentally specific during the six hours they are in school. Another example of environmental factors defining disability, rather than anything related to the disability itself, is described by Sobsey (1994). Sobsey recounted that many men with disabilities left institutions during World War I and World War II to fight in the United States military. One institution in Connecticut, Southbury Training School, released 13 men who then enlisted to fight in World War II. Four of these 13 men were wounded in combat and 7 were promoted to higher ranks. When the wars ended, most of these soldiers were returned to institutions.

Today, there are many environmental changes that have transformed the definition of disability. For example, the introduction of psychotropic medications, which allow many individuals with mental illnesses to control their symptoms, has dramatically changed the ways in which both society and the individual view mental illness. Of course, these medications do not work for everyone, and there are many side effects, but nonetheless, these medications have brought about many changes. We can see that this is an environmental change and not a change in mental illness. Other environmental changes that have affected the definition of disability include supported employment and supported living. Used primarily for individuals with mental retardation and individuals with mental illness, these types of community jobs and apartment living are supervised and assisted by professional service providers. Individuals who, in the past, would not have been thought to be capable of working or living outside an institution now do both. Once again, these types of professional services are environmental changes and are not changes in the disabilities. Finally, the accordance of civil rights to PWDs by the Americans with Disabilities Act is another straightforward example of environmental shifts that has transformed the meaning of disability.

Prejudice, discrimination, and stigma are not an inherent part of a disability, but rather are part of the environment (Balcazar, Bradford, & Fawcett, 1988). These attitudes needlessly handicap PWDs. More relevant today as examples are individuals with mental illness who manage their illnesses with medications and, yet, because of societal prejudice, discrimination, and stigma, are handicapped unnecessarily.

Society has created many barriers, both physical and attitudinal, for people with disabilities. For example, in the United States today the attributes of health, strength, youth, fitness, and beauty are highly valued (Buss, 1998), and the emphasis on these attributes increases the impact of disability. In the chapter on society's response to disability, the societal/cultural construction of disability will be discussed more thoroughly.

Functional Model of Disability

The functional model of disability theorizes that the functions of the individual influence the definition of disability. Individuals who enjoy physical activities would probably be more affected by a mobility impairment than those who do not care for such activities. Also, individuals whose work does not require physical strength, movement, or stamina would be less affected by mobility disability. The example most often used to illustrate the functional model of disability is that of the professional pianist who has one finger amputated. The loss of one finger would probably not be considered a disability for most people, and yet, because of the impairment in occupational functioning for the concert pianist, the amputation would be a life-changing disability. Individuals who are visual learners and lose their vision probably experience a greater sense of loss than auditory learners who lose their sight. The relationship between functioning and disability can be very specific to the individual. For example, Stephen Hawking, professor of physics at Cambridge University and world-famous theoretical physicist, considers his disability, amyotrophic lateral sclerosis (ALS), which greatly limits mobility and impairs speech, to be an advantage because it allows him more time to think. Two people can have the same type and degree of disability, but because of their functions and environments, have a very different disability experience.

Which functions should be included in the functional model (Boorse, 1986)? The examples of Stephen Hawking and the concert pianist consider work and wage-earning functions. Should nonessential functions such as leisure and sports be included in the functional model of disability? Most functional models, at present, include only work activities and activities of daily living (ADLs), which assist PWDs in getting to jobs. Due to this exclusive focus on work and ADLs, many individuals in the Disability Rights Movement regard the functional model of disability as an economic model. According to these advocates, the functional model is primarily concerned with the earning capacity of the PWD.

The functional model of disability, of course, is closely related to the availability of adaptive technology and the capability of such technology to assist in role functioning (Spechler, 1996). A professor in a wheelchair can perform his or her occupational functions; an individual who is blind who uses a computer with a speech synthesizer, a brailler, and other assistive technology can perform successfully in many vocational roles. Weisgerber (1991) told of a man named Manny Guitierrez, with Down syndrome, who works with archaeologists from the University of Arizona. Mr. Guitierrez tags all the artifacts unearthed on the digs. Weisgerber summarized: "His work does not entail intellectual tasks but rather the ability to label archaeological artifacts, a task at which he excels" (p. 179).

Three scholars/researchers who study the sources of attitudes toward people with disabilities (Langer, Bashner, & Chanowitz, 1985) found that children can understand disability from a functional model. After speaking to a group of children about disabilities and discussing the various jobs at which PWDs are successful, the researchers showed the children two pictures of male newscasters; one newscaster was in a wheelchair and the other newscaster did not have a visible disability. The children rated both newscasters as equally qualified to perform the job. The children could see that the mobility impairment would not handicap the newscaster on the job.

In addition to role functions of individuals, there are also role functions of society in general, which also impact the definition of disability. The shift of the economy of the United States from an economy that depended on physical labor such as farming, mining, and manufacturing to an economy based on service and information processing has influenced the definition of disability. In an economy based on physical labor, many individuals with cognitive disabilities, such as learning disabilities or mild mental retardation, were successful workers. In contrast, in that economy, an individual (especially a man) with a physical disability would have been severely limited. In today's economy, a cognitive disability is much more limiting than a physical disability because service jobs and technological/information-processing jobs require high levels of cognitive functioning. Today, an individual with a physical disability, who has the use of assistive technology, has many employment options.

Before the advent of industrialized, urban society, disability was both defined and treated differently. In small, rural communities in which members of families worked side by side, day after day, and everyone in the small community knew everyone else, PWDs had their basic needs met and were accorded a place in their community. As described by a noted disability scholar: "In small scale societies, nondisabled citizens knew disabled citizens. People many of us take to be 'bizarre' or 'disturbed' in today's urban areas would often have become familiar, accepted (if not well understood) neighbors of rural communities" (Higgins, 1992, p. 191).

For everyone in these small communities, with or without disabilities, home and family were the basis of everyday life. Everyone was perceived as a unique individual, with both a history and place in the community before the standardization and anonymity of large cities. It was the environment that influenced the status and perception of PWDs and not anything inherent in the disabilities. Another disability scholar described the place of the PWD in these small communities:

> [In preindustrial communities] rigid separation had not yet been made between home and work and where travel was difficult for anyone, citizens with disabilities may not have been exposed to some of the egregious inequities that have subsequently become apparent in highly impersonal autonomous cultures....Deviant or atypical personal characteristics that may have become familiar in a small community seemed bizarre or disturbing in an urban milieu (Hahn, 1997, pp. 177–178).

Scheer and Groce (1988) summarized the negative effect: "Americans have lost familiarity with disabled [*sic*] people so common in small-scale societies" (p. 33). It is interesting that Scheer and Groce view this loss to be greater for PWODs than for PWDs.

Ryan and Thomas (1980) explained the way in which industrialization altered the definition of mental retardation: "The speed of factory work, the enforced discipline, the timekeeping and production norms—all of these were a highly unfavourable change from the slower, more self-determined and flexible methods of work into which many handicapped [*sic*] people had been integrated" (p. 101).

Thirty years ago, Farber and his colleagues (Farber, 1968; Farber & Lewis, 1976; Heiney, 1976) incorporated the functional model of disability into their label for people with disabilities: "surplus populations." People with disabilities, according to these disability scholars, are thought of as surplus populations by the general public because they are not considered to be necessary for institutional efficiency and progress.

Changes in social role functioning also alter the definition of disability. For example, elderly people today live far more active lives than their counterparts did 100 years ago, many today working until age 75, and many more engaging in active community work and physical activity in their retirement years. Today, an older person who experiences a disability, such as blindness or a mobility impairment, probably considers the disability to be limiting rather than simply an expected outcome of aging. As can be seen from these examples, large-scale changes in functioning alter the definition of disability.

Assistive technology also changes the functional definition of disability because these devices allow PWDs to perform many functions and activities. Mobility devices include power wheelchairs, sonic guides, vision enhancement devices, and Functional Electronic Stimulation (FES). In FES, successive bursts of low-level , controlled electricity stimulate paralyzed muscles to contract according to patterns programmed into a computer. This allows the return of coordinated movement to paralyzed muscles, such as those needed for walking. It is used with persons whose muscles have not been damaged and with persons, such as those with spinal cord injuries, whose movements have been blocked by the inability of messages from the brain to get through the spinal cord and to the muscles (Scherer, 1993, p. 18).

There are also augmentative and alternative communication devices that help the individual to "speak"; environmental control devices that allow the individual to lock doors, operate the thermostat, and operate other household appliances; and sensory devices that read for people who are blind.

Scherer (1993) explained the rapid increase in the use of assistive technology. "Each passing year has seen the numbers of assistive technologies in use increase exponentially....As recently as the early 1960s, most equipment available to individuals with disabilities was only of a mechanical nature. Wheelchairs were literally chairs on wheels. Artificial limbs were plastic or, earlier, metal and wooden replacements for lost arms or legs" (p. 19).

Comparison of the Three Models

Each of these models contributes to the understanding of the disability experience and, further, provides guidelines for action. In the medical model, treatment methods are concerned with changing the individual; in the functional model, intervention methods are aimed at adapting the functions of the individual; and in the environmental model, professionals seek to change both the physical and social environments of the individual. In only one of the three models, the medical model, is the "problem" viewed as entirely within the individual. Nonetheless, biology and organic functioning are important. No one would advocate that individuals who are blind should be bus drivers. The clear point, however, is that biology is not as important as it was previously thought to be.

No one today subscribes to a single disability model, although it is safe to state that for centuries there was only one model, the medical model. There is a purpose for each model, and comparison and combination of models can result in greater accuracy and detail in understanding the disability experience. It is important to understand how these models of disability relate to each other. For instance, the most clear-cut example of differing models of disability concerns deafness. For some, deafness is viewed from the medical model as a biological loss/dysfunction that requires some sort of treatment to the individual. In contrast, the Deaf Culture views deafness from the environmental model and regards individuals who are deaf as members of a different culture who use a different language.

In 1980, the World Health Organization (WHO) published a "manual of classification relating to the consequences of disease" entitled *International Classification of Impairments, Disabilities, and Handicaps (ICIDH)*. Careful distinctions were drawn among the terms "impairment," "disability," and "handicap," and the manual is divided into those three sections. In addition, the words "disease," "disorder," and "pathology" were also defined, somewhat synonymously. Diseases, disorders, and pathology can lead to impairment; on the other hand, they often do not. For example, a case of influenza or pneumonia usually does not result in impairment.

According to the *ICIDH*, an impairment is "any loss or abnormality of the psychological, physiological, or anatomic structure or function....Impairment is more inclusive than 'disorder' " (WHO, 1980, p. 47). An impairment "is characterized by losses or abnormalities that may be temporary or permanent, and it includes the existence or occurrence of an anomaly, defect, or loss in a limb, organ, tissue, or other structure of the body, or defect in a functional system or mechanism of the body, including the systems of mental functioning" (p. 27).

The *ICIDH* defined disability as "any restriction or lack of ability to perform an activity in the manner or within the range considered to be normal for a human being....Disabilities may arise as a direct consequence of impairment or as a response by the individual [to the] impairment" (WHO, 1980, p. 143). The *ICIDH* lists diagnostic codes for "Behavior Disabilities," "Personal Care Disabilities," and "Locomotor Disabilities" (pp. 144–145). In addition, the word "handicap" is defined as "a disadvantage for a given individual, resulting from an impairment that limits or prevents the fulfillment of a role that is normal (depending on age, sex, social, and cultural factors) for that individual" (p. 180). Examples of handicaps include social integration handicap, orientation handicap, and economic self-sufficiency handicap. Livneh and Antonak (1997) further explained: "Handicaps are measured against norms and policies of a particular environment, society, or culture. They are generally irreversible conditions of prolonged duration because of well-entrenched social belief and value systems" (p. 6).

The *ICIDH* clearly states that impairments do not always lead to disabilities or handicaps. Also, disabilities do not always lead to handicaps. The logic and intent underlying the definitions of "impairment," "disability," and "handicap" are important. Nonetheless, these three terms and their corresponding definitions are neither widely used nor well known. It seems more straightforward and easily understandable to think in terms of the three models of disability—the medical model, the functional model, and the environmental model. As we have read in this chapter, not all disabilities (the *ICIDH*'s "impairments") result in functional losses (the

ICIDH's "disabilities") and not all disabilities result in environmental restrictions (the *ICIDH*'s "handicaps").

MODELS OF DISABILITY, AMERICAN LEGISLATION, AND AGENCIES THAT SERVE PERSONS WITH DISABILITIES

In this section, look for—
- ▶ *how social security programs are based on the medical model of disability*
- ▶ *how the ADA follows the functional and environmental models of disability*

The sequence of American disability legislation closely parallels the history of models of disability. Social security programs, in place since 1935, are based on the medical model because the presence of a disability must be established and the benefits provided are intended to pay living and disability-related expenses, not to assist individuals in finding employment. The Social Security Administration (SSA) funds two programs for Americans with disabilities. The first is the Supplemental Insurance Income (SII) and the second is Social Security Disability Income (SSDI). In contrast, the state/federal system of vocational rehabilitation (VR) is based on the functional model of disability because, in order to be declared eligible for services, it must be established that the disability impairs the ability of the individual to obtain employment. The workers' compensation system is also based on the functional model because the eligibility is granted when the individual proves that he or she can no longer perform the job. The Americans with Disabilities Act (ADA) appears to have been derived from two models: the functional model and the environmental model. The courts are defining disability, under the ADA, according to the functional model. For example, an individual who could control his high blood pressure with medication was judged not to have a disability because his functioning was intact (*Murphy v. United Parcel Service*, 1992). The ADA derives much of its basis from the environmental model of disability because the statute clearly delineates the prejudice and discrimination that has needlessly handicapped Americans with disabilities.

Thus, the history of American disability legislation closely parallels the sequence of the models of disability. The first model of disability was the medical model; therefore, the first disability legislation was based on the medical model. The second model of disability was the functional model and the next "generation" of disability legislation was based on this model. The newest model of disability is the environmental model, and the Americans with Disabilities Act is based on the environmental model. Indeed, in the next chapter, we shall read Section 2 (Findings and Purposes) of the ADA that outlines the handicaps found in the American environment. When more than one model provides the basis for laws, politics, and service agencies, the onus for change rests with both the individual with the disability and the environment.

This parallel between models of disability and American disability legislation makes sense because American legislation, of any kind, is simply institutionalized public opinion. The medical model of disability (and the resulting legislation and service agencies) theorized that the individual is responsible for solving his or her disability "problem" and, if it could not be "solved," then government should provide financial benefits ("income maintenance"). The functional model, and the resulting legislation and service agencies, advocated looking at the functional requirements of work and considering ways in which the functions could be changed. The environmental model, and the ADA, mandate that environments, both physical and social, must change.

DICHOTOMY OR CONTINUUM?

> *In this section, look for—*
> ▶ *how dichotomies are impermeable and exclusionary—disability or no disability*
> ▶ *the cut-off point on the continuum (disability or no disability), which often changes positions*

Another conceptualization of disability, which takes into account all three models, views the disability experience as either a dichotomy or a continuum. The dichotomy is simple: There is the presence of a disability or the absence of a disability. All individuals must identify with one of the two categories and no one can identify with both categories. A true dichotomy does not allow the categories of "both" or "neither"; the boundaries of the two categories are impermeable and exclusionary.

In contrast, a continuum view of disability has two polar opposites: the presence of a disability or the absence of a disability (Figure 2–1). The closer the individual identifies with either of these polar opposites, the more clear-cut the disability status. Near the end of the continuum designated as "presence of a disability" would be individuals with severe and multiple disabilities, while near the end of the continuum designated as "absence of a disability" would be individuals who have no disability. Somewhere along the continuum, there must be a cut-off point that separates individuals with disabilities from individuals who do not have disabilities. Mild disabilities, which would fall in the middle of the continuum, are more difficult to quantify.

Such a cutoff point requires accurate and sophisticated measuring instruments. Examples of disabilities whose diagnoses rely on accurate diagnostic tools are blindness and deafness. Indeed, diagnostic accuracy and diagnostic reliability are two hallmarks of blindness and deafness. Examples of disabilities for which diagnoses are not the result of precise, reliable diagnostic tools might include mental illness or learning disabilities. Since the diagnosis of these disabilities relies more on clinical judgment, impressionistic data, and psychological measures, there is less diagnostic precision. Certainly, the cutoff points for both blindness and learning disabilities must be considered a range of points rather than a single point. But the range or variability in the cutoff point required for blindness would be smaller than the range of scores required for learning disabilities. Simply stated, the precision in the cutoff point of this disability dichotomy would be directly related to the precision in the diagnostic tools and procedures. Furthermore, some disability experts consider cutoff points for all types of disabilities to be arbitrary. For example, in Chapter 1, we learned that mental retardation is diagnosed as mild, moderate, severe, or

No disability   Presence of a disability

Figure 2–1 The Continuum View of Disability (in Contrast to Discrete Categories)

profound. It is easy to see that the cutoff point between the low end of mild mental retardation and the high end of moderate retardation (to use a single example) might be difficult to establish.

The continuum view of disability allows the cutoff point to change positions— both for society as a whole and for individuals. Therefore, cutoff points are temporary and subject to change. For example, the American Diabetes Association has lowered the diagnostic threshold for diabetes in an effort to diagnose more cases in the early stages and thus avoid many of the secondary complications. The new threshold is 126 milligrams of sugar per deciliter of blood after an eight-hour fast. The previous diagnostic threshold was 140. Legislation, public opinion, the labor market, changes in medicine, and the development of assistive technology adjust the position of the cutoff points. Changes that affect large numbers of people include changes in policy and legislation that redefine what is considered to be a disability. For example, in 1998, the Social Security Administration ruled that alcohol and substance abuse were no longer defined as disabilities and individuals with these conditions were no longer eligible for benefits. Changes that affect an individual might include the development and acquisition of some assistive technology that allows the individual to work.

Cross-Categorical Definitions of Disability: Clinical, Legal, Cultural, and Personal

There are four general categorical definitions of disability: clinical, legal, cultural, and personal. Most of the time, these four definitions of disability are in agreement, although occasionally these cross-categorical definitions may differ. Clinical definitions of disability are usually those found in medical and psychiatric diagnostic manuals, and clinical diagnoses do not always qualify as legal definitions. For example, the *Diagnostic and Statistical Manual of Mental Disorders IV*, published by the American Psychiatric Association, includes many psychiatric disorders that are not legally defined as disabilities. For example, individuals who are clinically diagnosed as having a substance abuse disorder are not protected under the ADA if they are actively using illegal drugs. Nor would gambling addiction be considered a disability when applying for benefits and services, although the American Psychiatric Association considers gambling addiction to be a disorder. Further complicating the picture is the fact that the clinical professions define disability differently, and various government agencies, laws, and policies also often define disability based on different criteria.

Earlier, we read of a single example of a cultural definition of a disability, actually a nondefinition of disability. The example of the bound feet of Manchurian baby girls is an example of cultural definitions of disability that contradict the biological/impaired functioning constructions of disability. More on cultural definitions of disability will be presented in the chapter on the individual and disability.

As expected, the single most important definition of disability is the individual's definition of his or her disability. This personal definition may differ from the clinical, legal, and cultural definitions. For example, a person with diabetes may not view him- or herself as a person with a disability although the individual monitors his or her blood sugar and takes daily injections of insulin. Failure to monitor and control the diabetes would result in death. And yet, due to the fact that there are few functional limitations and that diabetes is a hidden disability, many individuals with diabetes do not consider themselves to have a disability. However, legally and clinically, diabetes is defined as a disability. The Deaf Culture provides the most clear-cut example of the way in which personal definitions of disability can conflict with clinical and legal definitions. Individuals in the Deaf Culture do not consider themselves to have a disability. Certainly the personal definition of disability merits a thorough discussion, and this will be presented in the chapter on the individual and disability.

To summarize, the most widely accepted definition of disability includes three elements: (1) the presence of a physical, intellectual, cognitive, or psychiatric condition; (2) this condition impairs functioning; and (3) the individual is subject to prejudice, discrimination, and reduced opportunity because of the condition.

ADDITIONAL CATEGORIES OF DISABILITIES

In this section, look for—
- ▶ *categorization of disabilities according to severity*
- ▶ *reasons why individuals with severe disabilities often require case management services*
- ▶ *information on congenital and acquired disabilities*
- ▶ *information on hidden and visible disabilities*

Disabilities are also categorized according to their degree. Basically, there are three levels: mild, moderate, and severe. Severe disabilities, sometimes referred to as profound disabilities, are those that impair the individual in several areas of functioning (Matson & Barrett, 1993). For some individuals, a severe disability is a single disability, such as profound mental retardation, because mental retardation impairs functioning in almost every environmental setting. For others, a severe disability is actually multiple disabilities, such as dual sensory loss. Profound cerebral palsy is considered to be a severe disability because this condition can affect the individual's speech, motor abilities, and intellectual functioning. For each type of disability, there are criteria and standards for determining the degree of disability and for assigning the designations of mild, moderate, or severe. For example, mild hearing losses are defined as loss of hearing in the better ear of 25–40 decibels, moderate hearing losses (or being hard of hearing) are defined as loss of hearing in the 40- to 60-decibel range, and severe hearing losses are losses of 60–80 decibels. Severe mental retardation is defined as three standard deviations below normal. Thus, each type of disability has specific diagnostic criteria for determining the degree of impairment.

Individuals with severe disabilities require services from caregivers from many different professions: for example, medical, special education, physical therapy, speech pathology, and vocational rehabilitation. Therefore, case management is important for individuals with disabilities. Case management is the coordination of services of many different professionals in order to provide comprehensive and continuous care for a single individual. In contrast, many individuals with mild disabilities usually do not need case management. For example, a person with a mild case of diabetes would only need services from a physician.

Severe disabilities, as explained when we discussed the concept of disabilities existing along a continuum, are more evident than mild or moderate disabilities. Thus, severe disabilities are more easily and quickly diagnosed (and therefore treated) than are mild disabilities. On the other hand, almost all severe disabilities are also visible disabilities, and the individual is therefore subjected to more prejudice and discrimination. Furthermore, in a time of "rationing" of benefits and services provided to people with disabilities, those whose disabilities meet the criteria for "severe" may or may not receive services. Essentially, when there are not enough resources to serve everyone with a disability, there are two basic choices: (1) Serve *many* people with mild disabilities, or (2) for the same amount of money, serve a *few* people with severe disabilities. Certainly, these two options are a simplification; nonetheless, government agencies are often forced to use waiting lists or to give priority for services to people with certain types or degrees of disabilities. Upon first glance, serving many people with mild disabilities appears economically sound; however, serving only a few people who have severe disabilities may be, in the long run, more economically practical because these people are those who would not be able to integrate into the broader society without these benefits and services.

Finally, in the past, those with severe disabilities were more likely to have been institutionalized. Case management was not considered to be necessary because the people with severe disabilities were literally under a single roof. In the chapter on the individual and disability, a more complete discussion of the effects of institutionalization—on the individual and on society—will be discussed.

Congenital or Acquired

Congenital disabilities are those that are present at birth or shortly thereafter. Acquired disabilities are those that occur some time later. For some disabilities, such as blindness or deafness, there are critical differences in the age of onset. Further, it is safe to say that for all disabilities, the age of onset is important in the adjustment process and in the way in which society views and treats the individual with the disability. The same type and degree of disability, blindness, for example, present at birth, would be a different experience than blindness acquired in old age. For some disabilities, time of onset cannot be determined because the onset is insidious. Therefore, for these types of disabilities, it is the time of diagnosis, rather than time of onset, that is considered.

Hidden or Visible

Some disabilities are visible to others, while other disabilities are hidden or invisible. People with mobility impairments have visible disabilities, while people with learning disabilities have hidden disabilities. This visibility of the disability takes many forms: aspects of the disability itself, such as congenital limb deficiencies; the use of assistive devices such as white canes, hearing aids, and wheelchairs; unusual behaviors that result from the disability, such as responding verbally to hallucinations; or aspects of the treatment/management of the disability, such as side effects from medications or the need to attend therapy meetings. As would be expected, the experience of a hidden disability is different than the experience of a visible disability because society responds to individuals with hidden disabilities differently than it does to individuals with visible disabilities. People with hidden disabilities have the option of disclosure; being able to choose when, or if ever, to disclose. On the other hand, they are not automatically offered accommodations. It should be remembered that hidden disabilities can be severely limiting and present severe impairments for the individual. In the chapter on the individual and disability, we shall learn of the hypervisibility, overobservation, and loss of privacy that individuals with visible disabilities experience.

THE AMERICANS WITH DISABILITIES ACT: EQUAL OPPORTUNITY UNDER THE LAW

In this section, look for—

  ▶ *the five titles of the ADA:*
    1. Title I: Employment
    2. Title II: Transportation
    3. Title III: Public Accommodations and Services
    4. Title IV: Telecommunications
    5. Title V: Miscellaneous

The ADA, which was signed into law by President George Bush in 1990, is considered to be the civil rights law for people with disabilities. There are three components of the ADA: (1) the statute itself; (2) regulations, policy guidance, and technical assistance manuals; and (3) court decisions or what is called "case law." Indeed, the provisions of the ADA are considered to be an application of civil rights principles. "Reasonable accommodations" in policies, practices, and procedures must be put in place in order to end discrimination against people with disabilities. Guidelines must be decided on a case-by-case basis. The ADA has five main sections or titles, each addressing a particular issue and each with different enforcing bodies. In addition to the enforcement of federal bodies, individuals can file lawsuits. A brief summary of each of the five titles of the ADA follows.

Title I: Employment

All employment aspects, including hiring, pay, benefits, job training, promotion, tenure, and termination, are covered in this title. It is important to understand that current users of illegal drugs are not protected by the ADA. No employer with 15 or more employees can discriminate against an individual with a disability who is qualified and capable of performing the essential functions of the job. Further, employers must provide "reasonable accommodations" such as adaptations in employment testing procedures, assistive technology, job restructuring, provision of written materials in alternative formats such as Braille, provision of sign language interpreters, time off for visits to therapists, and architectural access for their employees with disabilities. Employment-testing accommodations include extra time for taking the test, someone to read the test, sign language interpreters, oral tests, large print, allowing the use of a magnifying glass, assisting in marking the answer sheet, and Braille presentations. The rationale behind the provision of these accommodations is to allow the test-taker to demonstrate his or her skill and knowledge level while still maintaining the validity of the test. (Of course, for some jobs, such as air traffic controller, speed of response is an integral part of the job, and therefore accommodations on preemployment tests such as extended time cannot be given.) These reasonable accommodations must be provided unless employers can prove the accommodation(s) presents an "undue hardship." Applicants or employees who pose a direct threat to the health and safety of other individuals may be refused a job or may be fired. Employers cannot make blanket inquiries about the presence of disabilities, such as health "checklists" on application forms, nor are they allowed to ask, verbally or in writing, if the applicant has a disability. Also, employers are allowed to require preemployment medical examinations only after a conditional offer of employment has been made. Of course, individuals whose disabilities are readily visible, such as those who use a sign language interpreter or individuals who use wheelchairs, would not have the option of disclosing the presence of a disability. Employers must pay employees with disabilities at the same rate as comparable employees without disabilities. This equal pay provision extends to benefits, including health insurance. (Health insurance is very important to people with disabilities.) The ADA also prohibits employers from assigning employees who have disabilities to the "back room." In other words, employers are not allowed to segregate an employee because of his or her disability. The Equal Employment Opportunity Commission enforces this title. Private clubs, organizations and churches, and Native American tribes are exempt from this title.

Title II: Transportation

Public entities, such as airplanes, buses, and trains, must provide vehicles that are accessible to people with disabilities. These accessible vehicles must be of a comparable level and comparable response time as vehicles used for people without disabilities. Therefore, accessible public transportation must provide the same schedules and routes that are available to everyone. The Architectural and Transportation Barriers Compliance Board, with members appointed by the President, devises standards for compliance, and the Department of Transportation enforces this title.

Title III: Public Accommodations and Services

Individuals with disabilities cannot be denied full and equal enjoyment of public accommodations solely on the basis of their disability. Public accommodations are hotels, motels, restaurants, theaters, art galleries, libraries, shopping malls, banks, professional offices, recreational facilities, parks, and zoos. For example, movies such as *Titanic, Mask of Zorro*, and *Star Wars: The Phantom Menace* have been audio-described for people who are blind and closed-captioned for people who are deaf, allowing many PWDs to "go to the movies" if the theater is physically accessible. These public facilities may be exempted from compliance if they can demonstrate that the adaptations are not "readily achievable." Private organizations and religious organizations are exempt. The Attorney General enforces this title.

Title IV: Telecommunications

Individuals with speech and hearing disabilities have the right to rapid, efficient, nationwide telephone and telecommunications systems (Equal Access to Software and Information, 1999). Therefore, all telephone companies must provide public telephones that are accessible to people with speech and/or hearing impairments 24 hours a day, 7 days a week, to and from the United States, at no extra cost to the user. These devices include TDDs for deaf people. Federally funded public service announcements must include closed captions.

Frank Bowe (1993) described accessibility to television: "The Television Decoder Circuitry Act of 1990 (P.L. 100–431) requires that all 13" or larger television sets sold or manufactured in the United States after July 1993 include built-in chips enabling the set to receive and display captions or subtitles. The chips themselves cost under $10 to manufacture and are included as part of the purchase price of the set. Broadcasters, advertisers, and others pay the cost of producing the captions themselves" (p. xii).

This title is enforced by the Federal Telecommunications Commission. Electronic databases, Web sites, and electronic mail (e-mail) must be available in alternative formats for individuals who are blind or who have learning disabilities.

Title V: Miscellaneous

Guidelines for historical sites and wilderness to become accessible to individuals with disabilities are included. Accessible wilderness areas, including hunting and fishing locations, were mandated under Section 502 of the Rehabilitation Act of 1973 (Sullivan, 1998). The government is responsible to ensure that Americans with disabilities are able to engage in outdoor activities in the national parks and all other federal lands. The ADA strengthened and reinforced this mandate.

What the ADA Does Not Cover

Clearly noted is the fact that individuals who use illegal drugs and those who have received diagnoses of sexual behavior disorders, kleptomania, pyromania, substance abuse disorders, or compulsive gambling are not covered by the ADA. Individuals, of course, must present documented evidence of a disability, and employers can ask for a second opinion. Further, the individual must be qualified to do the job in order to receive job accommodations under Title I. Employers are not required to lower performance or production standards. Meltsner (1998) stated,

> [employers] do not have to tolerate theft, chronic lateness, insubordination, lewdness, violence, or other clearly inappropriate behavior. The disabled person [*sic*] can be disciplined. It is not discrimination to criticize or to fire for cause. Companies are not required to accommodate low education levels, lack of credentials, or other limitations unrelated to the person's disability....Nor do [employers] have to make a particular accommodation just because it's requested. Some requests...are truly unreasonable (pp. 46–47).

Private houses are exempt from the provisions of the ADA and transit authorities have 30 years to make existing stock accessible to PWDs.

The Intent/Rationale of the Americans with Disabilities Act

The ADA clearly states the rationale of this statute: "Individuals with disabilities are a discrete and insular minority who have been faced with restrictions and limitations, subjected to a history of purposeful unequal treatment and relegated to a position of political powerlessness in our society." Clearly, a bill much like the Civil Rights Act of 1964 was needed to extend legal protection against discrimination to citizens with disabilities. People with disabilities often jokingly refer to the intent of the ADA as "boldly going where everybody else goes." Before the passage of the ADA, it was legal to discriminate against a qualified job applicant solely on the basis of disability. Employers could, and did, candidly inform applicants with disabilities that they did not obtain a job simply because of the presence of a disability and individuals who acquired a disability while they were employed, which did not render them unqualified or incapable of performing the functions of a job, were often terminated. These individuals had no legal recourse.

Furthermore, it makes economic sense to facilitate the employment of capable, qualified people who want to work. Job accommodations that allow people with disabilities to work have been found to be affordable, especially when the reduced costs of public assistance (welfare payments) and the payment of taxes are taken into consideration (Spechler, 1996). Indeed, many consider the passage of the ADA to be based on the economic benefits argument rather than on the argument of according rights to a group of Americans.

President George Bush understood this dollars-and-cents approach when he stated, "When you add together state, local, and private funds it costs almost $1200 billion annually to support Americans with disabilities, in effect to keep them dependent" (cited in Imrie, 1996, p. 64).

Senator Edward Kennedy also emphasized the economic benefits of the ADA, commenting, "Some will argue that it costs too much to implement this bill. But I reply, it costs too much to go on without it. Four percent of the American gross domestic product is spent on keeping disabled [sic] people dependent" (cited in Imrie, 1996, p. 64).

THE ADA DEFINITION OF DISABILITY

In this section, look for—
▶ *the ADA definition of disability*
▶ *the ADA definition of "undue hardship"*
▶ *the ADA definition of "qualified" individual*

The ADA defines mental impairment as "any emotional or psychological disorder, such as mental retardation, organic brain syndrome, emotional or mental illness, or specific learning disabilities" (29 CFR Part 1630. 1[h2]). In order to be considered an "individual with a disability," the person must document a physical or mental impairment and "substantial limitation" in one or more major life activities. It can be seen that the ADA defines disability from both the medical model and the functional model. Reasonable accommodations mandated by the ADA include job restructuring (working part-time, flex time, modified work schedules, telecommunicating, etc.), provision of assistive technology such as computers, and removal of architectural barriers. Indeed, many of the court cases testing the ADA focus on defining disability.

The ADA, as with most laws, must demonstrate general applicability and, at the same time, it should also be specific enough to apply to individual circumstances. The regulations and technical assistance manuals provide flexibility and further explanations of how to interpret the statute. Nonetheless, one of the most difficult issues in the implementation of Title I of the ADA is whether the employer is required to make accommodations. As you will recall, Title I states that if the provision of these accommodations causes "undue hardship," the employer is not required to offer these adaptations. The definition of accommodation, with certain disabilities such as learning disabilities and mental illness, is often hard to establish. Physical disabilities, especially those that are clearly visible, present little difficulty in documentation or in determining the necessary accommodations (O'Keeffe, 1994). Wider doorways for wheelchair users or voice-activated computers for workers who are blind are accommodations that are easily understood. In contrast, the determination and provision of accommodations for workers with cognitive and psychiatric disabilities are often more complex and much less understood.

The ADA Does Not Require Preferential Treatment for People with Disabilities

The ADA is a federal law, although it is not totally universal in its application because private organizations, religious organizations, and Native American tribes are not required to comply. Much of the general public mistakenly believes that the ADA designates Americans with disabilities as eligible for preferential treatment such as lowering or waiving requirements. The ADA clearly states that the individual must be qualified or, stated another way, the individual must be able to perform the essential functions of the job (with or without accommodations) and is not exempted from any legitimate requirement or qualification. In the next chapter, on societal response to disability, a discussion of the differences between ensuring equal opportunity and extending preferential treatment will be presented. The ADA ensures equal opportunity for qualified individuals, based on their American citizenship, and does not require or encourage preferential treatment for people with disabilities.

Before the ADA, Some Employers Could Legally Discriminate Against Qualified Applicants/Employees Solely on the Basis of Disability

The ADA states, "Individuals with disabilities are a discrete and insular minority who have been faced with restrictions and limitations, subjected to a history of *purposeful unequal treatment* [emphasis added] and relegated to a position of political powerlessness in our society." Before the passage of the ADA, there were a few laws that protected the civil rights of individuals with disabilities, and these few laws were enforced on a very limited basis. The story of Paul Steven Miller in Chapter 1, the Harvard Law School graduate who was told by the Philadelphia law firm that he would not be hired because of his disability, illustrates the legality of such actions. Naturally, the law firm was aware that it was totally legal to candidly tell Mr. Miller the reason why he would not be hired. The law firm's actions may have been unethical or immoral, but they were legal at that time.

Before the passage of the ADA, if parents wanted to take their children for a family fun night to the new Disney movie at the neighborhood theater, they would have to leave one child at home—the child who uses a wheelchair. Before the passage of the ADA, some individuals with disabilities could use accessible public buses. However, most often there were so few of these types of buses that they ran on very limited schedules. An accessible bus that travels each route only once a week would now be illegal because of the ADA. So, it can be seen that it is not only the provision of the accessible bus, but also the fact that these buses have comparable schedules and routes to the nonaccessible buses that fulfills the requirement of equal public transportation for people with disabilities.

Weinberg (1988) reported on her study that asked people with physical disabilities, "If there were a surgery available that was guaranteed to completely cure disability with no risk, would you be willing to undergo the surgery?" (p. 144). Twenty-two individuals participated in intensive interviews that varied in duration from 2 to 16 hours. As can be seen from the date, Weinberg's study took place before the passage of the ADA, and the interviewees clearly outlined the difficulties that lack of accommodations and accessibility played in their lives. It is not the disability that the fantasy surgery would "cure," but it is lack of accommodations that make life difficult for many of these individuals. For example, Weinberg reported, "Another respondent, Lois, whose job involves the supervision of teachers, said that her inability to observe classrooms on the second floor of her school building is an obstacle in her effectively carrying out her present position as well as a hindrance to her chances for promotion" (p. 144). Lois did not need surgery; she needed an elevator. It is not her disability that is obstructing a job promotion; it is the lack of an elevator. Furthermore, the surgery is not possible—it is only a hypothetical example, but the installation of the elevator is a very workable and practical solution. Finally, when Lois is not promoted, people without disabilities will probably attribute this failure to Lois' lack of motivation and lack of desire for achievement, never stopping to consider that the absence of essential environmental accommodations prevented her job promotion (and her higher salary).

In another example, Sharon L., a medical social worker in Ogden, Utah, received her bachelor's and master's degrees before passage of the ADA. The difficulties she experienced in obtaining her education would not be legal today. Sharon uses a wheelchair, and the university in her hometown is very hilly and also very snowy during the winter, making the campus very difficult to navigate. Indeed, she simply stayed at home during winter quarter every year. (This is an illustration of reduced opportunities for people with disabilities.) Naturally, her inability to go to school during winter quarter delayed her graduation. In addition, because there were no elevators, when Sharon had a class on the second or third floor of a building, she would roll up to the staircase and wait for any fellow students who appeared to be "strong and kind-looking men" and ask one to carry her up the stairs and the other to carry her chair. (This is an illustration of why individuals with disabilities want their rights and not charity.) Sharon had to rely on the kindness of others and submit to the humiliation of being carried in the arms of a stranger of the opposite sex. Nonetheless, she graduated twice—once with an undergraduate degree and again with a graduate degree. Now, because of the passage of the ADA, students with disabilities do not face these obstacles.

Before the ADA, There Was Only Limited Legal Protection and Limited Enforcement

Until the passage of the ADA, restrictions for discrimination against people with disabilities in the workplace applied to only a few workplaces; some states had laws, and Section 504 of the Federal Rehabilitation Act of 1973 prohibited employers who received federal contracts from discriminating on the basis of disability (Perlman & Kirk, 1991). Sections 503 and 504 of the Rehabilitation Act of 1973 offered some protection against discrimination in employment, and Section 502 mandated architectural access. However, the Rehabilitation Act of 1973 applied only to federal employers or employers who received federal contracts. The Civil Rights Law of 1964 applied only to individuals of racial/ethnic minorities and to women; people with disabilities were not included in this civil rights legislation.

The Supreme Court had only one opportunity to rule on the provision of accommodations (under the Rehabilitation Act of 1973). In *Southeastern Community College v. Davis* (1979), the Court held that the college was not required to admit an applicant with a hearing loss to the nursing program nor to provide accommodations for her training. The fact that only one case concerning the enforcement of the Rehabilitation Act of 1973 was brought to the Supreme Court demonstrates that this act had little relevance for most Americans with disabilities.

Before the ADA, there was no federal mandate that required telecommunications, public places of entertainment, or transportation facilities to be available to people with disabilities. This type of widespread and blatant discrimination was legal until 1990. It would be unthinkable, and justifiably so, if any racial, ethnic, political, cultural, gender, sexual preference, or religious group in the United States experienced such discrimination. Americans with disabilities received their civil rights in 1990.

Resistance to the Americans with Disabilities Act

Why would there be resistance to the ADA? First, there is the mistaken belief that the ADA is reverse discrimination in that people with disabilities are now being given privileges and opportunities and also being afforded exemptions from valid employment and educational qualifications. Accommodations for disabilities are sometimes erroneously confused with special privileges. Indeed, the cost of most job accommodations has been found to be in the $100 to $500 range.

Definitions of such concepts as "disability" and "undue hardship" have been debated in court cases. You will remember that accommodations are not required if it can be proven that the provision of these accommodations causes undue hardship. There have been cases of people who do not have disabilities (as defined by the ADA) and, in spite of this, have sought protection and accommodations under the ADA. Certainly, these types of cases are abuses of the ADA and may make it more difficult for those with legitimate disabilities to assert their rights. For example, many high school students are now claiming learning disabilities and asking the Scholastic Aptitude Test (SAT) administrators to allow them extra time in which to take this college entrance examination. Never before have such large numbers of high school seniors claimed a learning disability and asked for accommodation in testing. Certainly, the majority of these claimants do not have learning disabilities nor are they eligible for the accommodations. The Supreme Court ruled that an individual who wore eyeglasses did not have a disability, and therefore was not protected under the ADA. If the court had ruled in this individual's favor, then over two thirds of all American adults, those who wear eyeglasses, would be considered to have a disability "including the seven out of nine justices who heard this case while wearing glasses" (Becker, 1999, p. 9). Nonetheless, such abuses make it more difficult for those who truly do have learning disabilities to receive the appropriate accommodations. Read the newspaper article in Exhibit 2–1 about athletes who claimed false disabilities in order to receive permits to park in "handicapped parking."

Becker, a Nobel Prize winner and a professor at the University of Chicago, wrote an editorial in *Business Week* entitled "Are We Hurting or Helping the Disabled [*sic*]?" Considering the ADA only as employment legislation, Becker (1999) questioned the passage of the ADA, stating, "The ADA passed without evidence of systematic discrimination against the disabled [*sic*] workers in any way comparable to the discrimination against blacks that gave rise to the civil-rights legislation of the 1960s" (p. 9).

Becker pointed out a weakness in the ADA: "Congress allowed the definition of disability in the act to be vague. I predicted in this magazine that the vagueness of the ADA and the litigious nature of the judicial system would encourage lawyers and workers to widen the concept of disability to absurd extremes" (p. 9).

According to Becker, "the truly disabled [*sic*] may be the principal victims....To prevent costly lawsuits, many companies apparently avoid hiring job applicants whom they believe would prove litigious under the ADA" (p. 9). Many disability advocates would agree with many of Becker's arguments. The ADA has spawned a great deal of litigation, and the overall employment rate of people with disabilities has probably decreased, for the reason that Becker advanced. However, most disability advocates consider that despite these flaws, the ADA is a landmark piece of legislation that has transformed the lives of many Americans.

Exhibit 2–1

Athletes Face Charges over Handicapped Parking Scam

LOS ANGELES (AP)—The fourteen men listed a smorgasbord of complaints—knee and back injuries, asthma, Bell's palsy—to justify requests for handicapped parking permits, authorities said.

In truth, they were arguably among the most able-bodied men on the UCLA campus: members of the football team.

The men, current and former Bruin players, won the permits by claiming fake injuries, investigators said Friday. They were charged Thursday with misdemeanors of illegally possessing the blue handicapped parking placards.

Each count carries a maximum six months in jail and $1,000 fine. One person who allegedly obtained two placards was charged with four counts.

The players' applications to the state Department of Motor Vehicles claimed knee injuries, back injuries, back surgery, torn ligaments, Bell's palsy, and asthma.

All of the claims were bogus, said Mike Qualls, spokesman for the city attorney's office.

Another source of resistance toward the ADA may simply stem from a dislike for governmental interference in such a broad array of public institutions. Some have complained that by allowing access to Americans who have disabilities, liability insurance premiums will increase or employers will not be able to fire incompetent workers who have disabilities; others complain of the inconvenience, and still others insist that the presence of people with disabilities in public life will make others feel ill at ease, uncomfortable, distressed, and embarrassed. Some employers have been fearful that if they hire someone with a disability, coworkers, supervisors, and customers will all be "freaked."

RESULTS OF THE ADA

In this section, look for—

▶ *why the ADA has spurred advances in assistive technology*
▶ *why the ADA has contributed to a collective identity for PWDs*
▶ *how the ADA has increased the employment rate of PWDs*

As would be expected, the ADA has, in the last nine years, facilitated the access of people with disabilities into many aspects of public life. In addition, the ADA has spurred many advances in telecommunications, assistive technology, and job restructuring. Many of these advances have also benefited people without disabilities. For example, closed-captioned television, originally developed for viewers who are deaf, has also been helpful for elderly individuals or people who are learning English, and much of the assistive technology developed for people who are blind is used as memory aids for forgetful people who are not blind. Ramps into buildings that facilitate access for people who use wheelchairs also facilitate access for anyone or anything on wheels, such as infants in strollers, carts, and wheeled suitcases. The first use of the transistor tube, which led to the computer revolution, was in a hearing aid.

The ADA has also contributed to a collective identity of people with disabilities. While this group identity did not begin with the ADA, the ADA has fostered the growth, pride, and awareness of their rights and responsibilities under the law. For example, in the state of Utah, a man named Robert Irons undertook a project to contact people with disabilities and assist them in becoming registered to vote. Mr. Irons helped 900 people to register and then organized telephone committees to ensure that each of these 900 people had transportation to the polls on voting days. Mr. Irons simply informed individuals with disabilities about their large numbers and their ability to vote on legislation that would be favorable to them. It is safe to state that the ADA has increased group solidarity of Americans with disabilities.

Has the ADA increased the rate of employment for people with disabilities? The Harris Survey commissioned by the National Organization on Disability in 1994 showed that people with disabilities were not experiencing higher employment rates. In contrast, in 1996, the U.S. Census Bureau Survey of Income Programs and Participation found a 27 percent decrease in employment of people with severe disabilities. Once again, the conflicting results of these studies can be explained by the differing definitions of "disability" and "work." Some scholars believe that employment of PWDs has increased in small- and medium-sized companies (who employ fewer than 15 workers) because these companies are not afraid of litigation since small- and medium-sized companies are exempt from compliance with the

ADA. Nonetheless, it is safe to state that the passage of the ADA has not facilitated the employment of as many individuals as anticipated.

TALKING ABOUT DISABILITY

In this section, look for—

▶ *how language can be demeaning, distancing, and polarizing*
▶ *how language can determine job opportunities, educational opportunities, and social participation for PWDs*
▶ *how language can communicate deficit*

Using language that conveys respect for people with disabilities is, at times, cumbersome and awkward, and for most of us, there is new terminology to be learned. Language is powerful, and the use of words clearly communicates attitudes toward people. For example, there are many unacceptable words for individuals of various racial, cultural, and ethnic groups. If a parent were to hear his or her child use one of these words, the parent would automatically correct the child, explaining why the word the child used is offensive and what the correct word is.

Language is a mirror that reflects society's views toward certain groups, and the words that are used very accurately reveal social and cultural history. There are many words that are offensive, demeaning, out of date, and lead to inaccurate stereotypes. Much of the language used to describe the disability experience comes from the Bible, illustrating the long history of underlying attitudes toward people with disabilities. Indeed, in reviewing the history of any group of people that has been the target of prejudice, discrimination, and reduced opportunity, we find that the language used by the broader society to speak about these people has these characteristics: (1) the words used to describe these people are both offensive and demeaning; (2) the identifying words that are used to set these people apart from the broader society make very clear that these people do not "belong" with everybody else (this is called "distancing" or "polarization"); (3) usually the language is not a self-identification—people don't use these terms to describe themselves; (4) the language usually "lumps" all the people perceived to be in the group together regardless of individual differences; (5) the labels used to describe people with disabilities describe, often inaccurately, only one aspect of an individual's identity (this is called "reductionism"); and (6) society is very reluctant to change individual language use, using the defense of ease of use or of freedom of speech. Many expressions, used unthinkingly by people without disabilities, are offensive and demeaning to people with disabilities. For example, "blind rage" and "blind jealousy," meaning emotions that are intense, irrational, and uncontrollable, are negative (and inaccurate) uses of the word "blind." Certainly legislation cannot control language, but educating the public about the correct way to discuss disability and the underlying rationale behind this language is a first step in integrating people with disabilities into society.

In the case of people with disabilities, the language used can determine job opportunities, educational opportunities, and social participation (Hahn, 1993). Before behavior and attitudes can be changed, language must be changed. In the chapters on society and disability, it will become clear that people with disabilities have experienced pervasive, systematic, institutionalized prejudice and discrimination and, naturally, the language used by society very clearly reflected these attitudes (Rossides, 1990). Language forces people into pejorative categories.

The language used to describe disabilities and the people who experience disabilities communicates deficit and inferiority. The prefixes "dis" and "dys" mean difficult, impaired, or absent. Words such as disorder, disability, disease, dyslexia, dystrophy, and dysfunction reflect these meanings. The prefixes "im" and "in" mean absence or lack; therefore, the word invalid means without value or validity, impairment means without strength or quality (or spoiled), and infirm means without strength. The prefix "para" (used in the Paralympics) means subsidiary. (Note: Paralympics are competitions for athletes with physical disabilities and the Special Olympics are competitions for people with intellectual disabilities.) It is not surprising that most PWODs think of disabilities as deficits and inferiority, because language shapes our attitudes. In Chapters 5, 7, and 8, we will see that many PWDs do not think of their disabilities as losses or as the absence of something. Moreover, many PWDs consider their disabilities to be assets and an integral part of their self-identities. For example, Dr. Irving King Jordan, the president of Gallaudet College, who is deaf, made this statement: "If there are 1,000 aspects of being deaf, 998 are good and 2 are bad." By quantifying the experience of deafness, Dr. Jordan is making the point that his disability has been an asset and not a deficit.

There are some basic guidelines. The first, and most well known, is the "people-first" approach. It is the Americans with Disabilities Act and not the Disabled Americans Act because this federal legislation is based on people's American citizenship and not their disability. They are Americans first. Also, it is correct to say "individual with a disability," not "a disabled individual." It is correct to say "a person who is blind," not "a blind person." It is "an athlete with a disability" or, even better, simply "an athlete." In spite of this, the term "disabled athletes" is often used. This may appear to be more cumbersome, but it serves the purpose of emphasizing that the individual is a person first and the disability is secondary. In the past, it was legal in many places to institutionalize, sterilize, and even kill people with disabilities because they were not considered to be fully human. Therefore, the importance of "people-first" language can be seen. However, individuals who are deaf, especially those in the Deaf Culture, prefer to be referred to as "a Deaf person." You will see that the word "Deaf" is capitalized. This insistence on putting the word "Deaf" before the word "person" is based on the Deaf's identity as a culture, as a group not unified by a disability, but rather, unified by shared experiences and a common language. Incidentally, the use of the expression "the Deaf" is acceptable. However, it is not correct to use these types of expressions with other disability groups.

There are a few people who do not like the person-first language because they feel that the disability is an important part of their identity. Sobsey (1994) reported: "One physically disabled person told [me] that she is not a *woman with a disability*, she is a *disabled woman*. She feels strongly that her life-long disability is as essential a part of her as her gender or heritage, and she feels that the person-first rule fails to recognize this critical aspect of her identity. People should have the right to reject any labels that they do not like and forcing an unwanted label on anyone is abusive" (p. 320).

Olkin (1999) succinctly remarked, "When we talk about using 'person-first' language...this is what we mean. It's not semantics. It's a way of looking at us and seeing *us*, not the disability" (p. 89).

"Person-first" language is not new; in fact, Beatrice Wright, in her classic book *Physical Disability: A Psychological Approach*, published in 1960, advised against using "shortcuts" in speaking about people with disabilities. Wright explained: "Then, a physically disabled person is also a physically *abled* person. There are things that he [*sic*] *can* do as well as things that he *cannot* do. We may conclude that the designation "a physically disabled person" is a shortcut to the more involved but psychologically sounder expression, "a person with a physical disability." Such a reformulation is far reaching....The shortcut distorts and undermines" (pp. 7–9).

Although Wright was speaking only of physical disabilities, for the last 40 years she has advocated the use of language that separates the disability from the total person.

The second basic guideline is often referred to as "the person is not the condition." So, there are no "diabetics," "schizophrenics," or "quadriplegics," but rather "individuals with disabilities, schizophrenia, or quadriplegia." Once again, this type of language communicates that the individual is not the condition or the disability. No one would speak of a group of people diagnosed with cancer as "the cancerous," but we often hear and read the phrase "the mentally ill" or "the deaf," or "the blind." Sometimes, people with disabilities are identified by their use of assistive technology. A server in a restaurant said, "I have three wheelchairs and two white canes." (Wheelchairs don't eat, they don't pay restaurant bills, and they don't leave tips.) Also, since most people with disabilities are not sick, it is inappropriate to refer to them as "patients." For example, Bickenbach (1993) made the observation that "many people with disabilities make no more use of medical services than anyone else" (p. 83). One publisher of a book for psychologists and psychiatrists recently (1999) advertised a book on adjustment to chronic disease with a photograph of a man in a wheelchair reaching out to a nurse. Most people in wheelchairs do not have a chronic disease, but the media, including a publisher for professionals, presents the idea in a very subtle way that disability (in this case, the wheelchair) and sickness (the title and subject of the book) are synonymous.

The disability should not be mentioned if it is not relevant, and it is surprising how often the disability simply is not pertinent. The following example is not appropriate: "Dr. Smith, who uses a wheelchair, gave a brilliant lecture." Certainly, it is important to mention the use of a wheelchair when planning accommodations such as a lowered podium from which to deliver the lecture or ramps up to the podium. Nonetheless, in the sentence used above, the use of the wheelchair should not be mentioned. When the media includes the disability when it is not relevant, they are giving the incorrect impression that the disability is the focus of the individual's life or that everyone should view the person as his or her disability. Indeed, most of the time, it is probably more accurate to use "people" rather than "people with disabilities." No one likes to be referred to, or thought of, as only one aspect of his or her nature. No single label can capture the meaning of an entire person's personality and character.

Sensational and emotional words should be avoided because these types of words are demeaning. The word "survivor" is preferred over "victim," and it is more correct to say that an individual "experiences" a certain disability rather than he or she "suffers from" the disability (Lynch & Thomas, 1994). A humorous bumper sticker on a car reads "I don't suffer from insanity. I enjoy every minute of it." Clearly, the message of the bumper sticker is twofold: (1) avoid the use of emotional terms such as "suffer," and (2) no one, except for the individual with disability, can describe the experience. It is better to use the expression "congenital disability" rather than "birth defect." A person uses a wheelchair and is not "confined to" a wheelchair. Words such as "cripple," "lame," "dumb" (meaning someone who does not speak), "afflicted," "stricken," "maimed," "invalid," "infirm," "misshapen," or "withered" communicate a condescending attitude. Instead of the word "fit," "seizure" is considered to be more accurate.

The word "handicap" should be avoided simply because of its history. Many believe that the word derived from the act of begging because beggars had their "cap in their hand." In the past, many individuals with disabilities, in the absence of any other opportunity, begged for a living. Certainly today, when it is stated that anyone has "his or her cap in hand," the unstated message is that the person is perceived as humble or inferior. Therefore, it is best to use the word "disability."

Some disability advocates do use the word "handicap" to describe obstacles and impediments in the environment, but never in reference to a condition an individual experiences (Nagi, 1991). The following sentence is an illustration: "The lack of health insurance benefits was a handicap to Ms. Lupino's accepting the position."

"Special" and "exceptional" are words that many people with disabilities dislike because these words invoke a history of segregation. There are many stories of parents being told that their child was going to be placed in a "special" classroom or a "special program." The words "special" and "exceptional" also have a euphemistic quality. "Special" and "exceptional" are labels that people with disabilities instantly recognize as meaning segregated and inferior. They are not innocuous terms because they imply difference and thus are polarizing. Individuals in "exceptional" or "special" programs "are then stigmatized as those who cannot 'get by' under programs designed to meet basic needs" (Bickenbach, 1993, p. 201).

An article once appeared in the *Disability Rag*, a publication written by and for PWDs, entitled "Getting Rid of Special" (Woodward, 1991). The author was clearly opposed to the use of the word "special" to describe PWDs or the services PWDs receive. On the other hand, the author understood that, even among PWDs themselves, there is disagreement about the word's use. The author quoted a National Spinal Cord Injury Association advertisement that showed a sign for "disabled parking." The advertisement read, "We're asking for a special place in your hearts, not just in your parking lots" (p. 41).

Euphemisms are insulting because their use implies that the reality of the disability is negative and unfortunate. Much of the language used to speak about the disability experience has been condescending, trivializing, or euphemistic. Expressions such as "physically challenged" or "mentally different" are both condescending and euphemistic, suggesting that disabilities cannot be discussed in an open and candid manner. The use of these expressions also trivializes the disability experience, suggesting that disabilities are only minor inconveniences. Richard Harris, director of the Office of Disabled Student Development at Ball State University in Indiana, reported that a "point of view article in the May 1991 *Paraplegia News* entitled "Cripplespeak" poked some fun at the newest "acceptable term," that is "people of differing abilities." The coiner of this term won $50,000. Additionally, the article expressed mild amusement at Michigan's politically correct term for an individual with a disability: handicapper (Harris, 1992, p. 210).

People, in their attempts to be positive and complimentary, often inadvertently use insulting qualifying statements such as "Even though she uses a wheelchair, she is beautiful—or intelligent, or funny, or generous, or hardworking, or honest" or "I don't think of you as having a disability." While these types of statements are not intended to be hurtful and condescending, they are both because they clearly communicate the speaker's bias against people with disabilities. The speaker is acknowledging an exception but, at the same time, holding on to the biases and prejudices held against the larger group: people with disabilities.

Finally, it should be noted that these guidelines are used in American English and not necessarily used in British English or other languages. For example, one disability scholar (Charlton, 1998) noted

> The struggle to change language describing disability is particularly interesting in Spanish. The most common expression in Latin America is *minasvalidas*, which translates as "less valid." The term *discapitados* (less capable) is also very common. Pejorative terminology about disabilities abounds in Spanish and, in fact, there is not one politically correct term describing disability in the dictionary. We in the disability rights movement created our own terms, *personas con deshabilidades*, or persons with disabilities. The word *deshabilidades* is not in the dictionary. When people point this out, believing that this means we cannot use the word, we proudly tell them we will not accept the language of the oppressors just because some book perpetuates the stereotypes and myths that we are fighting to break down (p. 67).

Another example of the use of language to describe PWDs has been provided by Ong (1993): "The Chinese term for disabled is 'canfei,' meaning crippled and useless. It depicts the Chinese view of disability" (p. 9).

LABELS THAT ATTEMPT TO DESCRIBE ALL THOSE DIFFERENT FROM THE MAJORITY

In this section, look for—

▶ *what are "catch-all" categories*
▶ *why "crips can call themselves anything they want"*

In an effort to organize and simplify, administrators implement labels to describe people that often become "catch-all" categories. Catch-all categories have often included "exceptional," "multicultural," and "special." People included in these categories often are people with disabilities, people who are intellectually gifted, people of differing cultural/racial/linguistic/ethnic groups, and people of differing sexual orientations (Artiles & Trent, 1994; Pugach & Seidl, 1996). Looking at these various types of people, it becomes clear that they have little in common, with the exception of two factors. First, they all have been targets of prejudice and discrimination, and second, administrators and policy makers often view these different types of people as a single group simply because the "regular" places and services are not viewed as appropriate for any of these people. It is as if everything, and everybody, that defies easy labeling and categorization is put together into a single undifferentiated category. In essence, these catch-all categories are diagnoses of exclusion. These are diagnoses of exclusion in which most of the exclusions are positive and those characteristics or needs that remain are placed in catch-all categories. While it may only be thoughtlessness or an attempt to limit the number of categories, the use of catch-all terms communicates that "these people" are different from the majority, stating, "We don't know who you are, we only know who you are *not*—mainstream." Ironically, "these people" may also be different from others in the same catch-all category—perhaps more different from them than from the majority.

Experts in racial/ethnic/linguistic issues deplore linking racial/ethnic groups with disability groups. Pugach and Seidl (1996) stated this objection: "Unless special educators are willing to view current interpretations of the disability–diversity relationship as problematic in the first place, the richness of cultural diversity will always be transformed into a deficit" (p. 5). These highly educated university professors are stating that disability is a deficit, but cultural diversity is richness. Furthermore, it appears that these special education professors' only concern with including disability groups with racial and cultural groups is the prejudice by association that racial and cultural groups will experience by being somehow related to disability groups, rather than considering that these two groups (both of which are "rich" and neither of which is a "deficit") do not belong together simply because their needs are very different. For example, in public education, what is the commonality, in terms of learning, of a child who does not speak English and a child who uses a wheelchair?

In contrast to all of the above, people who have disabilities can speak about their disabilities, often referring to themselves as "crips" or using other seemingly derogatory terms. Such in-group language reflects their (1) anger at their treatment by people without disabilities, (2) need to choose their own identifiers, and (3) identity of belonging to a group as a sign of solidarity with other people with disabilities. As with all "in-group language," it is not appropriate for individuals without disabilities to use these terms.

Many agencies, legislation, and acronyms of organizations use incorrect language because they were created and named before the use of correct language. Therefore, there is the Equal Education for All Handicapped Children Act of 1975 and the ARC, which stands for Association of Retarded Citizens. The correct usage today would be Individuals with Disabilities Education Act of 1990 and the Association for Individuals with Mental Retardation. (ARC still uses the acronym but has changed the name of the organization.)

In the chapters on society and disability, we will see more clearly the direct relationship between demeaning language and prejudice and discrimination. Certainly, after reviewing the history of treatment of people with disabilities, the correct language will not seem awkward, cumbersome, or difficult to use.

In-Class Videos

All of the following videos (except for *Ways to Move*) show different types of disabilities. After viewing each of these videos, discuss the following in class. If your class is large, divide into groups.

1. In which of the four categories (physical, intellectual, cognitive, or psychiatric) would this disability be placed?
2. Use the functional model to describe this disability.
3. Use the environmental model to describe this disability.
4. Is this disability a hidden disability or a visible disability?
5. What types of accommodations (mandated by the ADA) would be necessary for an individual with this type of disability?

- View the 60-minute video *Ways to Move* by Films for the Humanities and Sciences (P.O. Box 2053, Princeton, NJ 08543–2053, 1–800–257–5126, *http://www.films.com*). The producers describe the video in this way: "This program contains three stories that explore the debate between what has been called the medical model of disability, in which disability is a challenge to be cured, and the independence model, in which the challenge is to make society more accessible. Viewers meet individuals who shatter stereotypes about disability."
- View the 26-minute video *Muscular Dystrophy* by Films for the Humanities and Sciences. The producer states, "This program from *The Doctor Is In* looks at how individuals with muscular dystrophy deal with the disease: a young boy gets physical therapy at an Easter Seals Center, bracing helps a six-year-old girl with spinal muscular atrophy, and a young mother with myasthenia gravis gets help from surgery and medication. The program also covers the search for a cure and the available treatments."
- View the 21-minute video *Diagnosing and Treating Cystic Fibrosis* by Films for the Humanities and Sciences. According to the producers, this video is "divided into four segments and examines the presentation, diagnostic testing, treatment, and biochemistry of CF. Computer graphics and endoscopic imagery enhance this informative program."
- View the 19-minute video *Advancements in Traumatic Brain Injury* by Films for the Humanities and Sciences. The producers describe this video: "Dr. George Zitnay, president of the Brain Injury Association, and other experts discuss the various types of brain injuries within the context of new diagnostic methods and treatments. Innovative rehabilitation techniques are illustrated on actual brain injury sufferers [*sic*]. Several people with brain injuries reveal how the injuries have impacted their lives and the lives of their families."
- View the 19-minute video *The Injured Brain: Closed Head Traumas* by Films for the Humanities and Sciences. The producers state that the video "explains the types and symptoms of closed head injuries—anything from temporary loss of consciousness to coma—though some patients show almost no symptoms." It shows the tests used to determine the nature and extent of the injury, treatment, the problems of recovery, and the role of rehabilitation.
- View the 30-minute video *Mentally Handicapped and Epileptic: They Don't Make a Fuss* by Films for the Humanities and Sciences. The producers state: "This program deals with the combination of mental handicap and epilepsy, showing extensive footage of actual seizures, discussing the special psychosocial implications of this combination of problems, and dealing with first aid, risktaking, and prognosis." The conclusion is that, despite intractable seizures and limited horizons, even severe mental handicaps and severe epilepsy need not preclude a happy and fulfilling life.
- View the 56-minute video *Breaking the Silence Barrier: Inside the World of Cognitive Disabilities*. The producers describe this video as reporting "on the creative technologies and multimedia software programs that are being used to help people with autism, traumatic brain injuries, and learning and speech disabilities. Temple Grandin, an autistic woman with a Ph.D. in animal science, explains how deep pressure therapy helped her. Renowned neurologist Oliver Sacks shares his views on autism. Also profiled is Bob Williams, who is the first person with a significant speech disability to hold a major federal office."

- View the 35-minute video *Mental Disabilities: Organic Disorders* by Films for the Humanities and Sciences. The producers state, "This program demonstrates clinical organic disorders, their characteristics, and differential diagnoses. The disorders discussed include those relating to psychoactive substance use, schizophrenia and delusional disorders; and mood, neurotic stress-related, and somatoform disorders. Each disorder is explained and identified by its characteristics. Included are Alzheimer's, Pick's disease, Huntington's disease, Parkinson's disease, Creutzfeldt-Jakob disease, and HIV dementia. Also included are organic personality disorders, frontal lobe syndrome, primary cerebral disease, systemic disease, endocrine disorders, exogenous toxic substance, and temporal lobe epilepsy."

- View the 46-minute video *Schizophrenia and Delusional Disorders* by Films for the Humanities and Sciences. The producers describe the video in this way: "Schizophrenia, acute and transient psychoses, persistent delusional disorders, and schizoaffective disorders are examined. Their principal abnormalities are divided into the following psychiatric phenomena: disordered thinking, delusions, hallucinations, and abnormal behavior. Specific symptoms of each disorder are discussed."

- View the 24-minute video *Fetal Alcohol Syndrome: Life Sentence* by Films for the Humanities and Sciences. The producers describe the video in this way: "Fetal alcohol syndrome is the result of permanent organic injury to the brain of the fetus, caused by maternal drinking during pregnancy. That injury leads to learning disabilities, poor judgment, antisocial behavior, and worse, if a recent study is correct. This program discusses FAS within the context of that study, which suggests that 20 to 25 percent of all prison inmates may suffer from the condition. The program examines how early identification and treatment of children with FAS can help prevent extreme antisocial behavior in adulthood."

- View the 49-minute video *Empowering People with Disabilities through Technology* by Films for the Humanities and Sciences. The producers describe this video: "In this program, three people determined to be doers, not viewers, demonstrate the adaptive technology that is improving the quality of their lives. For Larry, an adult quadriplegic, mouth-activated remote controls allow him to do high-end computer drafting and even sail a boat. For Carol, born with an underdeveloped visual cortex, an enhanced computer enables her to attend college. And for Matthew, a child born with cerebral palsy, an orthotic walking device has him up and around while helping him condition his bones and muscles. Other innovations include Braille PCs (personal computers), talking book scanners, and a remarkable hands-free office."

- View the 60-minute video *Redesigning the Human Machine* by Films for the Humanities and Sciences. The producers state, "This program explores the use of technological advances. Virtual reality is being used as a learning tool for children with disabilities, as an assistive technology for Parkinson's disease patients, and as a form of empowerment for the disabled. The program also examines the potential use of robotics to assist people with limited mobility. Cochlear implants are also explained."

- View the 60-minute video *Ready to Live* by Films for the Humanities and Sciences. The producers describe this video as looking "at ways adaptive technologies help people with disabilities find independence. Included are profiles of a world-class runner who uses an advanced prosthetic leg, a former Bosnian soldier whose life was transformed by a pair of artificial hands, one of the founders of the 'Independent Living Movement,' and a woman who inspired a revolution in wheelchair design and construction."

- View the 30-minute video *Open to the Public: Complying with the Americans with Disabilities Act* from Aquarius Productions. The producers describe this video as providing "an overview of the Americans with Disabilities Act as it applies to state and local governments. The ADA doesn't provide recommendations for solving common problems, but this film could provide enough information for governments to solve some common problems without turning to high-priced consultants."

- View the 30-minute video *Right at Home: The Fair Housing Act Explained* from Aquarius Productions. The producers describe this video as showing "simple solutions for complying with the Fair Housing Act amendments. Emphasizes low-cost, practical solutions and working with people with disabilities to find the best applicable solution. Ideal for people with disabilities, university courses, and disability awareness organizations."

Learning Activities

1. Give a class presentation on one type of disability, such as blindness, schizophrenia, or mental retardation. Describe this disability from each of these models: the medical model, the environmental model, and the functional model.

2. View the video *My Body Is Not Who I Am* by Lisa Shaffer of the Albany Medical School and Aquarius Productions. Write a short paper listing how the individuals in this video view the medical model of disability. For example, why does one of the interviewees make this statement: "I was angry with my parents for jumping to the beck and call of the doctors. When you're a child and have 'corrective surgeries,' you go through life thinking you're defective"?

3. View the two videos *Open to the Public: Complying with the Americans with Disabilities Act* and *Right at Home*, both by Aquarius Productions. Then, document given places in your community that are not architecturally accessible.

4. After obtaining an ADA technical manual, which will give precise measurements and specifications for accessibility, visit various places in your community, such as entertainment facilities, sports facilities, workplaces, schools, and churches, and other places of worship and write a short paper describing their accessibility.

5. Write a paper or report to class on ADA litigation using these Web sites. After briefly describing each case, either defend the court's ruling or explain why you consider the ruling to be contrary to the intent of the ADA.
   - Americans with Disabilities Act: http://www.usdoj.gov/crt/ada/adahom1. htm
   - President's Committee on Employment of People with Disabilities: http:// www50.pcepd.gov/pcepd/welcome.html
   - President's Task Force on Employment of Adults with Disabilities: http:// www2.dol.gov/dol_sec/public/programs/ptfead/main.htm

6. Look up different types of assistive technology available by using ABLEDATA (ABLEDATA, Silver Spring Centre, 8455 Colesville Road, Suite 935, Silver Spring, MD 20910–3319, telephone 800–277–0216). ABLEDATA is a CD-ROM database and is usually available for public use at most independent living centers. Manufacturers and vendors of assistive technology (both commercial and noncommercial) put information about their products on this CD-ROM database. Users may access information by typing a category of disability or by typing in the function of the assistive technology. Information about the functions, costs, maintenance requirements, and other related equipment is provided.

7. Obtain the following sources:
   – Equal Opportunity Commission, Office of Program Operations. (1993a). *National database: Americans with Disabilities Act receipts 072692–072593.* Washington, DC: Author.
   – Equal Opportunity Commission, Office of Program Operations. (1993b). *National database: Americans with Disabilities Act receipts 100192–093093.* Washington, DC: Author.
   – Equal Opportunity Commission, Office of Program Operations. (1994). *National database: Americans with Disabilities Act receipts 100193–093094.* Washington, DC: Author.
   – Equal Opportunity Commission, Office of Program Operations. (1995). *National database: Americans with Disabilities Act receipts 100194–093095.* Washington, DC: Author.

8. Determine the total number of ADA complaints filed with the Equal Employment Opportunity Commission (EEOC). Are there trends? Of the 35 types of disabilities, which two categories have the highest frequency and percentage of complaints? List the 12 categories of discriminatory behavior.

Writing Experience

Write a paper that responds to one of the six "bullet" questions listed at the beginning of this chapter.

References

Artiles, A. J., & Trent, S.C. (1994). Overrepresentation of minority students in special education: A continuing debate. *Journal of Special Education, 27,* 410–437.

Balcazar, Y., Bradford, B., & Fawcett, S. (1988). Common concerns of disabled Americans: Issues and options. In M. Nagler (Ed.). *Perspectives on disability* (pp. 3–12). Palo Alto, CA: Health Markets Research.

Becker, G. S. (1999, August 2). Are we hurting or helping the disabled? *Business Week* 3635, p. 9.

Bickenbach, J. E. (1993). *Physical disability and social policy.* Toronto: University of Toronto.

Boorse, C. (1986). Concepts of health. In D. Van De Veer & T. Regan (Eds.). *Health care ethics: An introduction* (pp. 359–393). Philadelphia: Temple University.

Bowe, F. (1993). Preface. In M. J. Scherer, *Living in the state of stuck: How technology impacts the lives of people with disabilities* (pp. xi-xvi). Cambridge, MA: Brookline.

Buss, D. M. (1998). *Evolutionary psychology.* Boston: Allyn & Bacon.

Cameron, J. (1982). *For all that has been: Time to live and time to die.* New York: Macmillan.

Charlton, J. I. (1998). *Nothing about us without us: Disability oppression and empowerment*. Berkeley, CA: University of California.

Couser, G. T. (1997). *Recovering bodies: Illness, disability, and life writing*. Madison, WI: University of Wisconsin.

DeLoach, C., & Greer, B. G. (1981). *Adjustment to severe physical disability: A metamorphosis*. New York: McGraw-Hill.

Equal Access to Software and Information. (1999). Web site Available: http://www.rit.edu/~easi. Accessed July 24, 2000.

Farber, B. (1968). *Mental retardation: Its social context and social consequences*. Boston: Houghton Mifflin.

Farber, B., & Lewis, M. (1976). Compensatory education and social justice. *Peabody Journal of Education, 49*, 85–96.

Fowler, C. A., & Wadsworth, J. S. (1991). Individualism and equity: Critical values in North American culture and the impact on disability. *Journal of Applied Rehabilitation Counseling, 22*, 19–23.

Hahn, H. (1993). The political implications of disability definitions and data. *Journal of Disability Policy Studies, 4*, 41–52.

Hahn, H. (1997). Advertising the acceptably employable image: Disability and capitalism. In L. J. Davis (Ed.). *The disability studies reader* (pp. 172–186). New York: Routledge.

Harris, R. W. (1992). Musings from 20 years of hard-earned experience. *Rehabilitation Education, 6*, 207–211.

Heiney, R. W. (1976). Renaissance or retreat for special educators: Issues to explore before 1984. *Journal of Special Education, 10*, 415–425.

Helms, J. E. (1992). Why is there no study of cultural equivalence in standardized cognitive ability testing? *American Psychologist, 47*, 1083–1101.

Higgins, P. C. (1992). *Making disability: Exploring the social transformation of human variation*. Springfield, IL: Charles C Thomas.

Hursh, N. C. (1995). Essential competencies in industrial rehabilitation and disability management practice: A skills-based training model. In D. E. Shrey & M. Lacerte (Eds.). *Principles and practices of disability management in industry* (pp. 303–354). Winter Park, FL: GR Press.

Imrie, R. (1996). *Disability and the city: International perspectives*. New York: St. Martin's Press.

Individuals with Disabilities Education Act of 1990, 20 U.S.C. § 1400 *et seq.*

Langer, E. J., Bashner, R. S., & Chanowitz, B. (1985). Decreasing prejudice by increasing discrimination. *Journal of Personality and Social Psychology, 49*, 113–120.

Livneh, H., & Antonak, R. F. (1997). *Psychosocial adaptation to chronic illness and disability*. Gaithersburg, MD: Aspen Publishers, Inc.

Lynch, R. T., & Thomas, K. R. (1994). People with disabilities as victims: changing an ill-advised paradigm. *Journal of Rehabilitation, 69*(1), 8–11.

Matson, J. L., & Barrett, R. P. (Eds.). (1993). *Psychopathology in the mentally retarded* (2nd ed.). Boston: Allyn & Bacon.

Meltsner, S. (1998). Psychiatric disabilities: What's real, what's protected. *Business Health, 16*(6), 46–47.

Mikata, S. (1995, November). Presentation given at the annual meeting of the Utah Rehabilitation Association, Salt Lake City.

Moore, C. L., & Feist-Price, S. (1999). Societal attitudes and the civil rights of persons with disabilities. *Journal of Applied Rehabilitation Counseling, 30*, 19–24.

Murphy v. United Parcel Service, 97–1992. 526 U.S. 1036.

Nagi, S. Z. (1991). Disability concepts revisited: Implications for prevention. In Institute of Medicine (Ed.). *Disability in America: Toward a national agenda for prevention* (pp. 309–327). Washington, DC: National Academy Press.

O'Keeffe, J. (1994). Disability, discrimination, and the Americans with Disabilities Act. In S. M. Bruyere & J. O'Keeffe (Eds.). *Implications of the Americans with Disabilities Act for psychology* (pp. 1–14). Washington, DC: American Psychological Association [co-published with Springer Publishing, New York].

Olkin, R. (1999). *What psychotherapists should know about disability*. New York: Guilford.

Ong, W. A. (1993). *Asian American cultural dimensions in rehabilitation counseling*. San Diego, CA: San Diego State University, Rehabilitation Cultural Diversity Initiative (RCDI).

Perlman, L. B., & Kirk, F. S. (1991). Key disability and rehabilitation legislation. *Journal of Applied Rehabilitation Counseling, 22*(3), 21–27.

Phillips, M. J. (1990). Damaged goods: Oral narratives of the experience of disability in American culture. *Social Science Medicine, 30,* 849–857.

Pugach, M. C., & Seidl, B. L. (1996). Deconstructing the diversity connection. *Contemporary Education, 68,* 5–8.

Rehabilitation Act of 1973, 87 Stat. 355, 29 U.S.C. § 701 *et seq.*

Rossides, D. W. (1990). *Social stratification: The American class system in comparative perspective* (2nd ed.). Englewood Cliffs, NJ: Prentice-Hall.

Ryan, J., & Thomas, F. (1980). *The politics of mental handicap.* Harmondsworth, UK: Penguin.

Scheer, J., & Groce, N. (1988). Impairment as human constraint: Cross cultural and historical perspectives on variation. *Journal of Social Issues, 44,* 23–37.

Scherer, M. J. (1993). *Living in the state of stuck: How technology impacts the lives of people with disabilities.* Cambridge, MA: Brookline.

Shapiro, J. P. (1993). *No pity: People with disabilities forging a civil rights movement.* New York: Times Books.

Sinacore-Guinn, A. L. (1995). The diagnostic window: Culture and gender-sensitive diagnosis and training. *Counselor Education and Supervision, 35,* 18–31.

Sobsey, D. (1994). *Violence and abuse in the lives of people: The end of silent acceptance.* Baltimore: Brookes.

Southeastern Community College v. Frances B. Davis, 442 U.S. 379 (1979).

Spechler, J. W. (1996). *Reasonable accommodation: Profitable compliance with the Americans with Disabilities Act.* Delray Beach, FL: St. Lucie Press.

Stone, D. A. (1984). *The disabled state.* Philadelphia: Temple University.

Sullivan, D. M. (1998). Hunting and fishing: Ways of life in rural America. In T. S. Smith (Ed.). *Rural rehabilitation: A modern perspective* (pp. 292–312). Arnaudville, LA: Bow River.

Szasz, T. S. (1961). *The myth of mental illness.* New York: Harper.

Szasz, T. S. (1976). *Heresies.* New York: Anchor.

Tannebaum, S. J. (1986). *Engineering disability: Public policy and compensatory technology.* Philadelphia: Temple University.

Weinberg, N. (1988). Another perspective: Attitudes of people with disabilities. In H. E. Yuker (Ed.). *Attitudes toward persons with disabilities* (pp. 141–153). New York: Springer.

Weisgerber, R. A. (1991). *Quality of life for persons with disabilities: Skill development and transitions across life stages.* Gaithersburg, MD: Aspen.

Wright, B. (1960). *Physical disability: A psychological approach.* New York: Harper & Row.

Woodward, J. (1991). Getting rid of special. *The Disability Rag,* November/December, 35–41.

World Health Organization. (1980). *International classification of impairments, disabilities, and handicaps: A manual of classification relating to the consequences of disease.* Geneva, Switzerland: World Health Organization.

Part II

Society and Disability

Chapter 3

Sources of Prejudice and Discrimination, Part 1

▶ Does physical, intellectual, mental, or emotional disability always lead to social inferiority?

▶ Is disability entirely a social construction? Or does biology matter?

▶ Can legislation (such as the ADA) completely eradicate prejudice, discrimination, and segregation?

▶ Since the ADA, has the overall position in society of people with disabilities advanced, stayed the same, or fallen behind?

▶ Why are eugenics movements economically motivated?

SOCIETAL PREJUDICES OFTEN BECOME SELF-IDENTIFIERS

In this section, look for—

▶ *why there is no clear demarcation between society's perception of disability and the individual's perception of his or her disability*

In reality, there is no clear demarcation between society's perception of disability and the individual's adjustment to his or her disability because the individual internalizes a great deal of society's judgments and reactions to the disability (Albrecht, 1976; Gove, 1976; Ince, 1980; Phillips, 1992; Schur, 1971, 1979). For anyone, with or without a disability, society contributes to the individual's sense of self (Allport, 1954, 1958). Perceptions of disability labels, expectations of people with disabilities, and ascribed meanings of the experience of disability are all shaped by the broader culture (Albrecht, 1992). Of course, the degree to which society shapes the identity of the person with the disability depends on several factors (which are discussed in the next chapter). Not all individuals are equally affected by society's judgments. Remember in the preceding chapter from the video *My Body Is Not Who I Am*, the man who states that when he was a child the label used to describe his surgeries, "corrective surgeries," made him think that there was something wrong with him? This is an example of a disability label profoundly affecting an individual's self-concept. In another video, *Tell Them I'm a Mermaid*, a woman states, "[Before I acquired a disability], I used to think I had to feel sorry for disabled [*sic*] people. That they were weirdos and creeps." Another example of the interrelationship between society's judgments and the individual's self-concept is found through the book *The Making of Blind Men: A Study of Adult Socialization* (1969) by Robert Scott. Early in the book, Scott summarized his relationship: "The disability of blindness is a learned social role. The various attitudes and patterns of behavior that characterize people who are blind are not inherent in their condition but rather are acquired through ordinary processes of social learning....Blind men are made, and by the same processes of socialization that have made us all" (p. 14). In spite of this interrelationship between society and the individual in ascribing meaning to the disability experience, this chapter will focus on society and the next chapter will discuss the individual and his or her reaction to a disability.

By Any Standard, People with Disabilities Have Experienced More Prejudice and Discrimination Than Any Other Group in History

Disability has been present in all societies in the world throughout history. In spite of the long history and the universality of disability, almost without exception, people with disabilities have been discriminated against; with that discrimination ranging from minor embarrassment and inconvenience to relegation to a life of limited experience and reduced social opportunity and civil rights (Biklen, 1986: Biklen & Bailey, 1981; Bogdan, 1988; Bogdan & Biklen, 1977; Bogdan & Knoll, 1995; Bowe, 1978, 1990). While there have been a few exceptions of humane treatment, or even veneration, most societies have stigmatized their members with disabilities (Eisenberg, 1982). No other racial, cultural, ethnic, linguistic, religious, political, national, sexual orientation, or gender group has experienced this degree of pervasive and generalized prejudice and discrimination, which included killing babies with disabilities, forced sterilization of PWDs, institutionalization, and mass murder. For example, individuals of racial and ethnic groups are not targets of discrimination in their homeland nor are members of certain religious groups discriminated against in every setting. Certainly history reveals many more attempts to systematically eliminate PWDs than efforts to eliminate racial/ethnic/cultural/religious groups. In contrast, PWDs have been segregated, sterilized, or killed in almost every culture throughout history.

PREJUDICE AGAINST PEOPLE WITH DISABILITIES TODAY IN THE UNITED STATES

In this section, look for—

▶ *the definition of prejudice*
▶ *the ADA's summarization of the prejudice against PWDs in the United States*

Prejudice, according to Allport (1986), is "an avertive or hostile attitude toward a person who belongs to a group simply because he belongs to that group, and is therefore presumed to have the objectionable qualities ascribed to in that group" (p. 7). Allport defined discrimination as

...detrimental distinctions of an active source...exclud[ing] all members of the group in question from certain types of employment, from residential housing, political rights, educational or recreational opportunities, churches, hospitals, or from some other social privileges. Segregation is an institutionalized form of discrimination, enforced legally or by common custom (pp. 14–15).

Condensing Allport's definitions, we can simplify by stating that prejudice is attitudes and beliefs and discrimination is behavior. Therefore, it is easier to disguise prejudice, but discrimination is overt (visible) and can be witnessed by others. Prejudice is hard to challenge and confront, but it is possible to counter blatant discrimination.

It should be noted that there was legislation and public policy that addressed the needs of PWDs before the passage of the ADA. However, these focused on the *service* needs of PWDs, such as education and rehabilitation, rather than focusing on their *civil rights*. The ADA's main thrust is to guarantee the civil rights of PWDs (Moore & Feist-Price, 1999).

The following is the Findings section of the ADA (1990). It is presented in its entirety here for the following reasons: (1) reading the Findings section is one of the best ways to understand the rationale and intent of the law, and (2) this section of the ADA is perhaps the most concise and precise summarization of the history of prejudice and discrimination toward PWDs in the United States.

The Congress finds that

(1) some 43,000,000 Americans have one or more physical or mental disabilities, and this number is increasing as the population as a whole is growing older;

(2) historically, society has tended to isolate and segregate individuals with disabilities, and, despite some improvements, such forms of discrimination against individuals with disabilities continue to be a serious and pervasive social problem;

(3) discrimination against individuals with disabilities persists in such critical areas as employment, housing, public accommodations, education, transportation, communication, recreation, institutionalization, health services, voting, and access to public services;

(4) unlike individuals who have experienced discrimination on the basis of race, color, sex, national origin, religion, or age, individuals who have experienced discrimination on the basis of disability have often had no legal recourse to redress such discrimination;

(5) individuals with disabilities continually encounter various forms of discrimination, including outright intentional exclusion; the discriminatory effects of architectural, transportation, and communication barriers; overprotective rules and policies; failure to make modifications to existing facilities and practices; exclusionary qualification standards and criteria; segregation, and relegation to lesser services, programs, activities, benefits, jobs, or other opportunities;

(6) census data, national polls, and other studies have documented that people with disabilities, as a group, occupy an inferior status in our society and are severely disadvantaged socially, vocationally, economically, and educationally;

(7) individuals with disabilities are a discrete and insular minority who have been faced with restrictions and limitations, subjected to a history of purposeful unequal treatment, and relegated to a position of political powerlessness in our society, based on characteristics that are beyond the con-

trol of such individuals and resulting from stereotypical assumptions not truly indicative of the individual ability of such individuals to participate in and contribute to society;

(8) the nation's proper goals regarding individuals with disabilities are to ensure equality of opportunity, full participation, independent living, and economic self-sufficiency for such individuals; and

(9) the continuing existence of unfair and unnecessary discrimination and prejudice denies people with disabilities the opportunity to compete on an equal basis and to pursue those opportunities for which our free society is justifiably famous, and costs the United States billions of dollars in unnecessary expenses resulting from dependency and nonproductivity.

THE OUTCOMES OF THE ADA

In this section, look for—
- ▶ *the reasons why many experts believe that the economic position of PWDs continues to fall behind that of PWODs*
- ▶ *the difference between de facto and de jure segregation*

The reforms of recent years do not appear to have produced much change in the overall position in society for Americans with disabilities. Americans with disabilities have, of course, made advances; but Americans without disabilities have achieved many *more* gains. Thus the gap between Americans without disabilities and Americans with disabilities has continued to grow (Hahn, 1987). For example, Rossides (1990) reported, "federal aid may have provided better education for all, but without changing relative differences" (p. 352). Rossides was speaking only about one social benefit, that of mass public education, but his statement illustrates this growing gap in spite of government efforts.

At first glance, it may seem incongruous that federal laws (such as the Americans with Disabilities Act, 1990, and the Equal Education Act) and government programs are resulting in advances for people with disabilities and yet their relative position in society continues to go down (Silvers, 1996). Simply stated, PWDs are obtaining more jobs, but PWODs are obtaining even more and better jobs. PWDs and other disenfranchised groups are adversely affected by changes in the labor market, technological advances, inflation, the global economy, and economic depressions (National Disability Statistics and Policy Forum, 1995). Of course PWODs are also affected by these negative conditions but they are not affected as greatly. Gains for PWDs must be judged relative to gains for PWODs (Hahn, 1987). Of course, there is presently low employment and a corresponding need for workers. This type of labor market will naturally assist PWDs. However, this type of labor market also assists PWODs *more.*

Government legislation has effectively eliminated *de jure* segregation of people with disabilities but *de facto* segregation continues. No government can legislate public attitudes and beliefs (Bryan, 1996). It should also be remembered that in addition to the passage of legislation, the issues of funding and of enforcement often decide the impact of the legislation. In other words, if there are no funds allocated to enforce the law, there will be few actual benefits. Further, if the government does not actively enforce the law, the status quo continues. Nonetheless, legislation, such as the ADA and government and private efforts of self-empowerment, are increasing equal opportunity and social justice for PWDs. Later in this chapter, we will discuss disability rights groups and their successes in securing their civil rights.

Without such legislation, government can implicitly legitimize the failure and disadvantaged status of people with disabilities (Charlton, 1998). In other words, the ADA clearly states that PWDs in the United States have experienced pervasive discrimination and, therefore, much (but not all) of their low employment and other disadvantaged and unequal status can be attributed to society. Before the ADA, most Americans considered the disadvantaged status of PWDs to be the result of their own failings and shortcomings (Wright, 1988), which naturally led to the conclusion that the solution for the situation is the responsibility of PWDs. The ADA explicitly and clearly states that the disadvantaged status of PWDs is not solely the result of their organic impairments and functional limitations (Moore & Feist-Price, 1999; Perlman & Kirk, 1991; Shapiro, 1993; Tucker & Goldstein, 1991).

Sources of Prejudice and Discrimination Against People with Disabilities

Here is a brief list of all 10 sources of prejudice discussed in Chapters 3 and 4:

1. The economic threat
2. The safety threat
3. The ambiguity that PWODs ascribe to PWDs
4. The salience or perceived defining nature of the disabilities
5. The spread or overgeneralization of the effects of the disability
6. The idea of moral accountability for the cause of the disability
7. The idea of moral accountability for the management of the disability
8. The inferred emotional consequences of the disability
9. The emphasis on beauty, fitness, and youth
10. The fear of acquiring a disability among PWODs

Many of the sources of prejudice against PWDs are the same sources of prejudice directed toward individuals of certain racial/ethnic/cultural/linguistic groups, or any other minority group. PWDs, however, experience prejudice and discrimination from additional sources. This appears to be a reasonable assertion since, as previously noted, it is known that throughout history, PWDs have experienced more prejudice and discrimination than any other single group.

Sources of prejudice against people with disabilities include (1) the economic threat; (2) the safety threat; (3) the ambiguity that PWODs ascribe to PWDs; (4) the salience of the disability or the perceived defining nature of the disability; (5) the concept of spread or overgeneralization; (6) the idea of moral accountability for the cause of the disability; (7) the idea of moral accountability for the management of the disability; (8) the inferred emotional consequences of disability; (9) the emphasis on beauty, fitness, and youth; and (10) the fear of acquiring a disability among PWODs, sometimes referred to as "existential angst." Interestingly, there is not "equal prejudice" toward all PWDs because some types of disabilities, such as mental illness, are the target of a greater degree of prejudice (Abroms & Hodera, 1979; Antonak, 1980; Obermann, 1965). The first five sources of prejudice listed above are also sources of prejudice directed at other minority groups. Using racial groups as an example, it is well known that racial minority individuals are often perceived by the majority as an economic threat and a safety threat, and ambiguous, and racial identifying characteristics are often thought to be the sole determinant of the individual's attitudes, character, and behavior. However, racial/ethnic minority individuals do not experience prejudice from the five sources listed last. Racial/ethnic minority individuals are not thought to be "responsible" for their ethnic membership; there is not the inferred emotional consequences to being a member of certain racial/ethnic groups, and people of the majority (those in power) do not express fear or anxiety that someday they might become part of a racial/ethnic/cultural group.

With the possible exception of fear of acquiring a disability (or existential angst), all of the sources of prejudice against PWDs are irrational. We shall now discuss each of these 10 sources of prejudice in greater detail. There is a great deal of overlap among all ten.

THE ECONOMIC THREAT

In this section, look for—
- ▶ *the three factors that are considered when determining the economic costs of disabilities*
- ▶ *the economic motivation of the eugenics movement*
- ▶ *the dollar costs of job accommodations that allow PWDs to work*
- ▶ *the effect of financial disincentives on the employment of PWDs*
- ▶ *how PWDs have been an industrial reserve army*

Throughout history, PWDs have been perceived as "burdens" or "drains" on the resources of the community (Berkowitz, 1987). Thinking in terms of three factors, (1) the loss of tax dollars from PWDs who do not work; (2) tax dollars spent on government programs for PWDs, such as special education, vocational rehabilitation, Social Security Disability Insurance (SSDI), and public assistance (welfare); and (3) the increased insurance premiums for all policy holders due to the high costs of disability, it can be seen that disability is expensive and everyone, willingly or unwillingly, bears the cost (Albrecht, 1976: Anderson & Glesnes-Anderson, 1987; Anthony & Young, 1984; Bayles, 1987; Brown, 1987; Ferrans, 1987).

In a climate of "scarcity of resources," waiting lists, rationing of services, and cost containment, the statement "A tax dollar spent on you is a tax dollar NOT spent on me" appears to be rational. Read two letters written to Ann Landers (Exhibits 3–1 and 3–2).

A writer, "Roanoke," had previously written complaining that PWDs "lie around sucking up taxpayers' money" and the two letters reprinted here are responses to Roanoke. In the first letter, S. H. J. from Oakland begins his/her letter by describing the resentful attitudes he or she held toward "freeloaders" and "lazy" people and then goes on to describe his or her own history of independence, and hard work, including 90-hour workweeks. S. H. J. briefly describes some of the effects of his or her disability such as crying in the supermarket and not being able to stand in a line at the pharmacy. By telling us that he or she cannot do these simple, routine tasks, S. H. J. is proving to us that he or she is truly incapable of holding a job. S. H. J. ends the letter by saying, "There are many honorable, hard-working people who used to earn their own way but can no longer do so because they are mentally ill."

Exhibit 3–1

Dear Ann: I want to respond to "Roanoke," who said people on disability would rather sit back and suck up the taxpayers' money than work. A few years ago, I was singing that same ignorant tune. I had worked hard since I was 14 years old and had no respect for anyone on welfare. I put myself through college and graduate school and always had jobs that paid well. I thought, "If I can do it, why can't they?" I remember using words such as "lazy" and "freeloaders."

I am now disabled by what they used to call a "nervous breakdown." Those 90-hour work weeks eventually caught up with me. I have learned, to my sorrow, that in spite of all the therapy and medication, I will have to struggle with my emotional fragility the rest of my days. I would give anything to lead a normal life again, but I know this is impossible.

I am unable to fill out a form or stand in line in a pharmacy or a bank without fearing that I will suddenly go to pieces. Yesterday I had a crying spell in the supermarket because I couldn't find the bouillon cubes. Any little frustration can set me off.

There are many honorable, hard-working people who used to earn their own way but can no longer do so because they are now mentally ill. Most of us manage to make it back into the workplace, but many do not, and we must rely on the generosity of the American taxpayer. Please ask your readers not to condemn the entire system because of a few perceived abuses. We really do hate being dependent, but we have no choice.

—S.H.J., Oakland, Calif.

Dear Oakland: I'm sure you have the heartfelt gratitude of all the people for whom you spoke today. Your eloquent plea for compassion touched millions of readers. Thank you for a letter that will make a difference.

The second writer from Greensboro, North Carolina, describes his or her disability and then makes the main point, "I don't feel that I am a burden to the taxpayers. I earn my disability check because I worked for 36 years and paid into Social Security for my retirement." Note that Greensboro explains (or defends) receiving SSDI funds by telling (1) the severity of the disability (he or she almost died) and the fact that he or she continues to experience pain and other symptoms, (2) he or she paid into the SSDI fund for 36 years, and (3) he or she "contributes to society" by doing volunteer work (with people "more needy," i.e., children and non-English speaking immigrants).

Quantifying the Value of a Human Being

What is the value of an individual? Courts of law often calculate the earning power of the individual in order to arrive at a figure of economic value (Anthony & Young, 1984). The legal system realizes, of course, that economic value is only a single aspect of the individual, but in the absence of any other quantifiable measure, the courts utilize the measure of lifetime earnings. The value of humans is immeasurable; but, nonetheless, we often assume that economic value is a valid and complete measurement.

Putting a dollar value on a person with a disability presents more ethical difficulties. A disability scholar stated, "Utility, even more so than charity, cheapens people with disabilities. Charity exceeds utility in its concern for those with dis-

Exhibit 3-2

Dear Ann: I agree with the reader from Oakland who defended people on welfare after "Roanoke" criticized them so harshly. I am not lying around "sucking up taxpayers' money" as Roanoke would have you believe.

I am on disability because of a head injury. I taught school for 36 years and was told not to go back to full-time teaching because the stress would be too much. I also became an epileptic because of my head injury.

When my family went to the hospital at the time of the accident, they were told I would either die or become a vegetable. I was in a coma for weeks. It took me nine months to learn to walk and write again. I saw double for months.

As long as I stay on my medication and avoid stress, life is beautiful. I don't feel that I am a burden to the taxpayers. I earn my disability check because I worked for 36 years and paid into Social Security for my retirement.

I do volunteer work at the public schools and am helping children learn to read. I also work with adults who come from other countries and want to learn English.

I still have some pain and my neurologist says the Fourth of July is still going on in my head, but I am not complaining. I consider myself one of the lucky ones. I hope Roanoke sees this.

—Greensboro, N.C.

---

abilities, no matter how pitying that concern may be. Utility merely "uses" disabled people [*sic*]. If they (and the policy addressed toward them) cannot produce a "profit" (i.e., if benefits do not exceed costs), then they have little or no value" (Higgins, 1992, p. 199).

Therefore, societies care for their babies and children because babies and children grow up to become economically valuable and societies care for their elderly because, in the past, these elderly individuals have been economically valuable. Neither group, children nor the elderly, can care for themselves and, because of this, they are vulnerable. But, how does society justify caring for people with severe disabilities who are also vulnerable, but who never have and never will economically contribute (Beck, 1999; DeJong & Lifchez, 1983; Eisenberg, Griggins, & Duval, 1982)? If, indeed, the only value a person has is his or her economic value (or potential), then questions of the value of people with severe and multiple disabilities arise.

Furthermore, people with severe and multiple disabilities not only do not work and produce resources, but they also consume resources. Collectivistic societies through history, who believed that the group is more important than individual members, often viewed PWDs as burdens. It was a short leap to segregate PWDs, provide them with a low quality of life and care in order to save money, to forcibly sterilize them, and in extreme cases, to abandon them to die, or to kill them outright. Most eugenic movements have had economic motivations (Gallagher, 1990). One scholar (Pelka, 1997) stated, "Eugenicists opposed social programs for people who were poor and disabled [*sic*], believing such programs aided the unworthy in the struggle for survival" (p. 115). Friedlander (1995), in his book *The Origins of Nazi Genocide: From Euthanasia to the Final Solution,* quoted a German legal scholar, Karl Binder, who spoke of institutionalized Germans with disabilities and the care they received as "the greatest care of beings who are not only worthless but even manifest negative value" (p. 15).

Reading the "publisher's blurb" from Friedlander's book, several points underscore our discussion of the relationship between economics and eugenics. First, note that the first step to murder (not euthanasia) was to reduce the amount of money spent on the care of PWDs. The administrators of institutions were complaining about overcrowding or of having too many residents. One of their first steps was to reduce the amount of food given to the residents. Second, note how the use of language facilitates mass murder. By referring to Germans with disabilities as "life unworthy of life" it became easier to "eliminate these people." Note how unconcerned the Nazi officials were about the method of death. "Just beat them to death" was good enough. Ironically, euthanasia is generally thought of as a merciful, painless, dignified, and peaceful death (Battin, 1986). Although the Nazis called the murder of Germans with disabilities "euthanasia," it was indeed murder and the motivation was economic savings for the Nazi regime, not concern for the individual (see Exhibit 3–3). Finally, notice how the killing of adults (after the killing of children had been in progress) was carefully timed to coincide with Germany's invasion of Poland (September 1939) to take advantage of the fact that the German public would be distracted. Physicians, who subscribed to the Hippocratic Oath that states, "First, do no harm," starved, beat, and gassed their patients.

Hugh Gallagher, in his book *By Trust Betrayed: Patients, Physicians, and the License to Kill in the Third Reich* (1990), quoted a deposition given by a psychologist,

Exhibit 3–3

An excerpt from *The Origins of Nazi Genocide*

The move to rid Germany of institutionalized handicapped adults might have been expected. As we have seen, the funds spent for the upkeep of institutionalized patients had already been reduced drastically, and it had become customary to refer to them as "life unworthy of life." Hitler, who had told Gerhard Wagner in 1935 that he would institute compulsory euthanasia once war came, had not been alone in this desire. At a 1938 meeting of government officials responsible for the administration of mental institutions, for example, one speaker concluded that "a solution for the field of mental health would simply require that one eliminates those people." Fritz Bernotat, the Nazi radical who administered state hospitals in Hessen-Nassau, was later more explicit when he told a meeting of institutional directors who were complaining about overcrowding: "If you have too many patients in your institution, just beat them to death, and then you will have space."

In the summer of 1939 Hitler initiated the policy of killing handicapped adults. This killing operation would involve far larger numbers of victims than the relatively limited operation against children. Hitler turned first to the government agency normally responsible for public health. The Fuhrer sent for Leonardo Conti, who would soon succeed the deceased Wagner as Reich physician leader. Unlike Wagner, who had held only a Nazi party office, Conti also occupied the newly created position of state secretary for health in the RMdI [Reich Ministry of Interior].

Ludwig Lehner, at the Nuremberg trials. A physician, Dr. Pfannmuller, was killing children with disabilities by starving them. Part of Lehner's deposition stated: "I remember the gist of the following remarks of Pfannmuller:

> These creatures (he meant the children) naturally present for me as a Na-
> tional Socialist only the burden for the healthy body of our *Volk*. We do
> not kill (he could have used a euphemistic expression for this word kill)
> with poison, injections, etc.: then the foreign press and certain gentlemen
> in Switzerland [the International Red Cross] would only have new inflam-
> matory material. No, our method is much simpler and more natural, as you
> see." With these words, he pulled, with the help of a ...nurse, a child from
> its little bed. While exhibiting the child like a dead rabbit, he asserted with
> a knowing expression and cynical grin, "For this one it will take two or
> three more days" (p. 127).

A recently published book, *Hitler's Pope: The Secret History of Pius XII* (Cornwell, 1999), sought to access and understand the Catholic Pope's reaction to the Nazi Holocaust. The author concluded that the Pontiff was aware of the mass killings but refused to speak out publicly, citing a desire to protect the neutrality of the Vatican and the Catholic church. Long before the mass extermination of Jewish people, the Romany (gypsies), and political prisoners, the Nazis exterminated Germans with disabilities, many of whom were Catholics and living in Catholic institutions under the care of nuns. When the murder of these Germans with disabilities began, German Catholic clergy implored Pope Pius XII to intervene. The Pope refused and remained silent. Many German clergy did speak out vehemently against the killing of Germans who had disabilities; the most well known of these was Count von Galen, the Bishop of Munster. Many Holocaust scholars posit that Hitler and the Nazis began mass extermination of certain groups of people and waited for world and church leaders to react, and when these leaders did not protest, the Nazis moved on to exterminate another group of people. (Of course, the Nazis carried out their killings in secret, but there is documented evidence that world leaders knew about the killings.) Disability scholars recognize the significance of the Nazis' first choice of victims: Germans with disabilities. Of all the groups of people extermi-nated by the Nazis, people with disabilities were the most stigmatized. Both disabil-ity scholars and Holocaust scholars have questioned if the Holocaust would have taken place if world leaders had protested the killing of Germans with disabilities.

Dr. Hans Sewering, who has been documented as taking part in the killing of Germans with disabilities, was elected president of the World Medical Association in 1992. However, he was forced to resign when protesters objected to his history of mass murder (Sobsey, 1994).

Nazi Germany and mass murder of people with disabilities may seem far re-moved from present-day circumstances and attitudes. Nonetheless, Olkin (1999) demonstrated the power of what she terms "the burden literature" (p. 47) by listing many articles about PWDs from scholarly, academic, and research-oriented journals that use the word "burden" in their titles. Olkin explained that all of these articles have publication dates of 1990 or later. "Then it is not just the disability that is a burden but the person with a disability" (p. 47). Research and scholarly writing mirror the culture in which they originate and scholars/researchers/writers perpetuate (albeit in a very sophisticated manner) the prejudices and misconceptions of the general society. By beginning with the (false) premise that PWDs are burdens to PWODs, these writers then arrive at (false) conclusions.

Disability Losses

It is impossible to quantify the worth of a person. In contrast, it is a relatively simple and straightforward process to calculate the economic impact of disability in the United States. Weisgerber (1991) reported adding the total "aggregate economic losses" and the total "value of resources that are allocated to interventions for persons with disabilities" will result in a number, called national "disability losses." Weisgerber stated,

> Chirikos (1989) estimated that at a national level the annual economic losses (due to disability) for persons with moderate disabilities are $54.1 billion and for persons with severe disabilities, $122.6 billion. In contrasting employability versus dependency, it is estimated that the losses for persons with disability of working age (15 to 64) are about $111.5 billion, for those outside those ages (0 to 14 and 65 and over), the estimated loss is $65.2 billion (p.189).

Weisgerber concluded: "These losses amounted to 6.9% of the gross national product in 1980," or "alternatively, as Chirikos pointed out, the losses can be characterized as a 'tax of about $800 levied on each and every American'" (p.190). Bickenbach (1993) has termed these tax dollars "coerced charity." When the dollar figure of the cost of ADA litigation is added, disability losses will increase.

In spite of these high unemployment rates, most people with disabilities report that they want to work, according to Louis Harris polls (1986, 1994) commissioned by the International Center for the Disabled (ICD). Allowing PWDs to work in the open economy would offset these "disability losses." (The emotional and social benefits of working for PWDs would perhaps be far greater than the economic benefits.) One of the rationales of the passage of the ADA was to allow people with disabilities the opportunity to work. The cost of job accommodations for people with disabilities has been found to be very low. The U.S. General Accounting Office (USGAO, 1990) reported that the average cost of making 34 business facilities accessible was less than one cent per square foot (USGAO, 1990)! In 1982, the GAO reported that the cost of 51 percent of the accommodations cost nothing; 30 percent cost less than $200, and another 30 percent cost less than $500. Those accommodations that were most expensive were audiovisual aids. When comparing the cost of workplace accommodations that allow PWDs to work to the cost of aggregate disability economic losses, which annually costs billions of dollars, it becomes apparent that workplace accommodations make sound economic sense. Bowe (1980) found that architectural accessibility was less expensive than carpet cleaning, stating, "A National League of Cities study found that it costs less than one half of one percent of the total cost of constructing a new building to make it completely accessible and usable by disabled people [*sic*].

We will discuss in greater detail the reasons why the unemployment and underemployment rates of PWDs are so high. Nonetheless, for the sake of brevity, it can be summarized that these high unemployment rates are the result of prejudice and discrimination on the one hand and the financial disincentives that are built into many government programs on the other hand. Financial disincentives occur when individuals are faced with the loss of benefits, including their health insurance, if they accept a job. For a PWD, accepting most jobs would be economic stupidity because of the low salaries paid, especially if the individual has to pay a personal care attendant or has to manage the disability with expensive medication (Berkowitz, 1987; Berry, 1995; Chubon, 1994; DeJong & Batavia, 1990; McCarthy, 1982). Of course, the government is working to dismantle this system of these financial disincentives.

Another way in which the "costs" of disability are perceived to be borne by those who do not have disabilities can be seen in the attitude of many parents whose children do not have disabilities. Turner and Louis (1996) observed "children with disabilities in the classroom were seen as taking away from the educational experience of others" (p. 136). Turner and Louis quote from *Beyond Normal*, written by a mother and educator who chose to remain anonymous. She wrote: "I believe that children with disabilities do not take away from the other children. They do not diminish the community" (p. 136). Certainly, this mother is aware of the public perception that children with disabilities compromise the quality of education for the children without disabilities. Nonetheless, it has been found that whenever PWDs are integrated, the quality of both services and products rises.

PWDs have often been viewed as an "industrial reserve army" (Hahn, 1997, p. 173), in both a figurative and a literal sense, for the American economy. Many men left institutions during World War I and World War II to fight in the U.S. military. Sobsey (1994) told of 13 men from an institution in Connecticut who, in spite of being labeled as having mental retardation, enlisted to fight in World War II. Four of these men were promoted to higher ranks and seven were wounded in action. In spite of their war records, most of these men returned to the institution after the war.

Sobsey (1994) concluded, "Wars and labor shortages have repeatedly redefined who has mental retardation" (p. 132), thus lending support to viewing disability as a continuum, rather than as two discrete categories of disability or no disability. Conditions in the broader environment, such as labor shortages and wars (rather than anything to do with the disability), can change the cut-off point on the continuum. Hahn (1997) reported, "In World War II, physical exams and other conditions of employment were waived by many corporations to open up jobs for disabled [*sic*] persons, and other members of the industrial reserve, who compiled favorable records of productivity and work performance. During the war, the unemployment rate among disabled [*sic*] adults temporarily declined, only to rise again when these job requirements were reinstated to permit the hiring of returning veterans" (p. 173).

Hahn illustrated that when the American economy needs more workers, then PWDs are hired and perform well. Obviously, neither the disabilities nor the PWDs have changed; their sudden employability is due to fluctuations in the labor markets. Therefore, much, if not most, of the unemployment and underemployment of PWDs is the result of lack of opportunity and discrimination, rather than any functional limitations imposed by the disability. The important issue of functional limitations, or better stated, *imputed* functional limitations, is subject to questions when, during periods of great labor needs, PWDs are able to perform all sorts of jobs.

THE SAFETY THREAT

In this section, look for—

▶ *the two causes for perceiving PWDs as dangerous:*
1. *safety*
2. *contagion*

People with disabilities are perceived to be a threat to the physical safety of PWODs in two ways: (1) violence, destructiveness, aggression, and antisocial behavior (Hyler, 1988; Hyler, Gabbard, & Schneider, 1991), and (2) contagion and contamination. Society's perception of a threat posed by PWDs has, throughout the centuries, led to institutionalization for PWDs. Nonetheless, documented facts have shown that it is PWDs who have much more violence, hostility, and aggression directed toward them from PWODs. And yet, deeply ingrained misconceptions persist, including that PWODs have cause to be afraid of PWDs. For millennia, people with disabilities have been institutionalized and subsequently subjected to neglect, abuse, and death (Craine, Henson, Colliver, & McLeland, 1988; Ulicny, White, Bradford, & Matthews, 1990; Waxman, 1991). Ironically, the stated rationale for institutionalization was for the safety of the person with the disability (i.e., "He or she might hurt someone or he or she might hurt himself/herself"). Tragically, once institutionalized, it was the PWD who was hurt by the "caregivers." Much of the rationale for sterilization of female residents of institutions was based on the (resigned) expectation that they would be raped, and sterilization was the only way to avoid unwanted pregnancies (Sobsey, 1994). Violence including assault, robbery, murder, and rape toward PWDs in the community (rather than in an institution) is also much more common than violence toward PWODs (Cole, 1984, 1991; Sobsey & Mansell, 1993). Reasons for these higher rates of violence are that PWDs are more physically vulnerable; they are often unable to get help; and they interact on a daily basis with a wide range of caregivers, many of whom have not been screened for previous arrest records.

Nonetheless, we should briefly discuss the reasons why PWDs would be perceived as a safety threat. Individuals with intellectual and/or mental disabilities are often thought to be dangerous, as can be seen in the following example. A young man working in a sandwich shop had a diagnosis of schizophrenia. His coworkers, aware of the diagnosis, were frightened every time this young man picked up a knife to chop lettuce. This expectation of violent behavior is a misconception because symptoms of many mental disabilities include social withdrawal and, furthermore, many individuals with mental disabilities take daily medication that sedates and calms them. Indeed, it has been proven that people with these types of disabilities are actually less violent than the general population (Schmitt, 1999). Remarkably, patients and staff at the Utah State Hospital exploited the public's fear of people with mental illness. For many years, they sponsored a Halloween "spook alley" and "haunted house" during the month of October. This was a very successful fundraiser for the hospital.

Why, then, this persistent misconception? A great deal has to do with the media and the portrayal of the "psychotic" killer in movies, television, and books (Bower, 1980; Byrd & Elliott, 1988; Hyler, 1988; Hyler, Gabbard, & Schneider, 1991;

Kriegel, 1987; Longmore, 1985a, 1985b; Safran, 1998; Zola, 1985, 1992). Of course, there have been psychotic killers, but such incidences are relatively rare. Irving Zola, a person with a disability (he contracted polio when he was young) and a disability advocate and scholar, loved to read murder mysteries. Zola made a comprehensive study of over 1,000 murder mysteries, sampling 150, and titled his study, "Any Distinguishing Features? The Portrayal of Disability in the Crime-Mystery Genre (1992)." Zola concluded that "villainy has long been associated with abnormality—whether physical, psychological, or mental—and is documented in nonfiction as well as fiction. Thus, from the earliest crime-fiction writing as well as in illustrations and silent films, one could easily recognize the villain by his or her features. She or he was inevitably unkempt, ugly, slobbering, sneering, and often scarred" (p. 236).

Zola observed that it was highly significant that, until recently, the single most watched program in the history of American television was an episode of *The Fugitive*. Zola commented: "Here the wrongly accused hero finally caught the heretofore unseen killer of his wife, the...man with one arm" (p. 236). All the years of chasing a murderer, of whom only one characteristic was known—he had one arm—finally ended. Simply because disability issues were part of his consciousness, Zola was able to point out how pervasively the media links disability with violent and criminal behavior.

Today, when we think of fear of contagion, we probably think of AIDS. However, overwhelming evidence has shown that fears of contagion from AIDS were unfounded. In the 1940s, during the polio epidemics, mothers were afraid to kiss their children who had contracted the polio virus and nurses and doctors wore masks (PBS, 1999—*Paralyzing Fear: The Story of Polio in America*). One author, a polio survivor, explained the fear, before the availability of vaccines, that polio engendered. "Polio's suddenness and unpredictability—the unknowability of where it came from, when, and where it might strike, and how severely—gave it the mystique and fearsomeness almost of the bubonic plague as it swept through the country" (Mee, 1999, p. 50). Currently, while a few disabilities are contagious, most are not and, as stated previously, most people with disabilities are in very good health. Nonetheless, PWODs often feel that they must "maintain a safe distance."

Another way in which to view the perceived threat of contagion, or the idea that one individual can "give" a disability to someone else, is clearly demonstrated by Mackelprang and Salsgiver (1999).

> People with disabilities were to be prevented from marrying or having children for fear of propagating their imperfections. As the 19th century progressed, the number of institutions to deal with the threat and nuisance of persons with disabilities increased dramatically, people with disabilities were increasingly isolated, sometimes under subhuman conditions (p. 39).

Those who believe in such practices as preventing PWDs from marrying or having children and in the rationale for these practices, which is fear that PWDs will propagate their imperfections, are not worried that the general public will acquire the disability or imperfection but that, nonetheless, the disability will be passed on to others (Harrison, 1987; Higgins, 1992; Van De Veer & Regan, 1987). Fine and Asch (1988a) reported that, until recently, many states had laws that banned individuals with epilepsy or individuals with psychiatric disabilities from marrying.

THE AMBIGUITY OF DISABILITY

In this section, look for—
- ▶ *the tendency to ascribe negative aspects or greater limitations to the disability*
- ▶ *the definition and effects of interaction strain*

Stereotyping, making generalizations and categorizations, and sorting people by medical diagnoses all help to simplify and give meaning to a vast array of information. Generating expectations, making sensible judgments or decisions, and feeling in control are all difficult when the environment is novel or ill-defined or lacks meaning. Furthermore, the more ambiguous the situation, the more the individual is required to "guess" about the meaning of the situation and what his or her responses should be. This type of "guessing" in order to make sense of a situation is called personal inference. Personal inference is based on personal factors (including value systems, past experiences, and education) and therefore it reveals more about the observer than the observed. For example, the Rorschach inkblot test is not designed to gather information about the inkblots, but rather to learn about the observer. In much the same way, the perceptions that PWODs have of PWDs often reveal more about PWODs.

Learned responses and attitudes, which in the past were very adaptive, may not be appropriate in ambiguous circumstances. Indeed, using learned responses in a novel and ambiguous environment, which were adaptive in other situations, may actually be very harmful. Frequently, people make inappropriate responses and occasionally they are not aware that their responses have been inappropriate. Finally, an ambiguous environment is automatically assumed to be negative or hostile, even when it is not. This is often called "fear of the unknown." In short, we don't feel in control when our environment, and the people in it, are ambiguous.

This tendency to attribute negative aspects or greater limitations to PWDs simply because they appear ambiguous is found, occasionally, at the professional level. For example, individuals with communication limitations, such as individuals who are deaf or people with cerebral palsy, have been given diagnoses which underestimate their intellectual capabilities merely because these individuals are not able to communicate articulately and fluently, and this ambiguity makes an accurate diagnosis difficult. Nonetheless, the direction of error in these diagnoses is most often downward, ascribing *more* limitation to the individual's functioning.

The opposite of ambiguity is clarity, meaning, and an abundance of previous experience with this type of environment. People feel comfortable, competent, and in control in these types of situations. In fact, people actively seek out these types of environments and experiences. They are able to make fine discriminations and distinctions; the world is not just black or white or comprised of only a few types of people. Well-defined environments are automatically assumed to be pleasant and safe. Individuals in clear-cut situations are able to make sensible decisions and evaluations; they know that their responses are adaptive, and they are able to interpret feedback about themselves. In well-defined environments, there may be decision points or danger points, but people are aware of these and have both the experience and the expertise to successfully negotiate these. And, simply because people have a tendency to seek out well-defined situations, PWODs often seek out other PWODs and avoid PWDs.

The word *ambiguous* comes from the Latin word *ambos* which means *both* and the dictionary definition of the word is "having contrary values or qualities, of doubtful classification." A related word, *ambivalent* has the Latin *ambos* and the second part of the word means *equivalent*. So ambivalent literally means *both equivalent*. Disability, for many, appears to be ambiguous, and the response is often one of ambivalence. The ambiguity leads to tension, discomfort, and ambivalence, all of which are unpleasant, and the PWOD often seeks to reduce or eliminate the ambiguity. There are two equal, but contrary, reactions to the PWD. On the one hand, the observer feels intense aversion and hostility, but on the other hand, he or she also feels strong sympathy and compassion (Antonak, 1985; Bettancourt & Dorr, 1998; Bogdan & Taylor, 1976, 1982; Ferguson, Ferguson, & Taylor, 1991; Gellman, 1959; Goffman, 1963). Often, the tension of this ambivalence leads to what is called *response amplification*, or overreacting. Such response amplification can be exaggerated kindness and solicitude or a quick escape (aversion) from the PWD, the source of the ambivalence and tension. While the need or desire to reduce tension is somewhat understandable, PWDs are aware that people often overreact to their disability (Hastorf, Wildfogel, & Cassman, 1979; Kleck, 1968).

The discomfort, tension, and ambiguity often lead to what has been termed *interaction strain* (Fichten, 1986; Fichten, Robillard, Tagalakis, & Amsel, 1991; Gouvier, Coon, Todd, & Fuller, 1994; Siller, 1976). Interaction strain has been measured in research studies and is most often found to include such factors as (1) shorter duration of contact/conversation—the PWOD wants to leave as quickly as possible; (2) less eye contact and physical contact; and (3) avoidance of personal topics during conversation and a greater focus on impersonal, trivial, polite "small talk" (Antonak, 1988; Belgrave, 1984; Belgrave & Mills, 1981; Gouvier, Steiner, Jackson, Schlater, & Rain, 1991; Grand, Bernier, & Strohmer, 1982; Hannah & Midlarsky, 1987; Livneh, 1982, 1983, 1991; Strohmer, Grand, & Purcell, 1984). Some sophisticated research studies have monitored autonomic responses of PWODs interacting with PWDs, such as pupil dilation, heart rate, blood pressure, galvanic skin (perspiration), and voice pattern (Vander Kolk, 1976a, 1976b). These studies showed that certain types of disabilities elicit more discomfort than other types of disabilities.

Obviously, many PWODs do not feel comfortable, competent, and in control when interacting with PWDs (Safilios-Rothschild, 1970). PWODs may make all sorts of "mistakes" in their interactions with PWDs and may not even be aware of some of their mistakes. The environment is so ambiguous and stressful that PWODs have no way to evaluate their own behavior and the effect their behavior has on others. Also, PWODs often interpret the hard-to-understand behavior of PWDs as negative. If the individual in the wheelchair falls asleep during a meeting, PWODs may interpret the behavior as rudeness and boredom when the behavior is actually a side effect of medication. Indeed, many adaptive coping responses of PWDs are misperceived by PWODs. It is not an enjoyable experience to feel uncomfortable and incompetent, and for many PWODs, the solution is to avoid the experience altogether. Also, the PWD recognizes that he or she (or his or her disability) makes others uncomfortable and that others avoid him or her. Thus, the interaction strain can become circular.

The preferential treatment given by public agencies to those individuals who were blind (discussed in Chapter 1) is thought to be due to the lack of ambiguity ascribed to blindness. In other words, PWODs think they understand blindness. Deshen (1992) stated, "Blindness has an essential distinctiveness and lack of ambiguity relative to other conditions....There is an immediate visible link between the condition and its behavioral manifestations, such as an impaired mobility and lack of ability to read print" (p. 4). Mirzoeff (1997) explained the relative lack of ambiguity of blindness when compared to deafness: "Medico-psychology thus considered the loss of sight to be far less grievous a blow than deafness. This sense that the blind are more "human" than the deaf has persisted to the present and accounts for the greater sympathy and funding that is available for the blind" (p. 390).

Note that Mirzoeff sees a relationship between perceived degree of loss and perceived degree of humanity. In other words, the smaller the perceived loss (disability), the more humanity ascribed to the individual. Ironically, the fact is that "sign language can remedy the 'communication disorder' of deafness in a way that nothing seems to repair the perceptual deficit of blindness" (Couser, 1997, p. 240).

Of course, part of the interaction strain is probably due to the PWODs' awareness that disability is a natural part of life and that he or she could acquire a disability. Nevertheless, most PWDs are acutely aware of this interaction strain and have developed strategies to reduce this. Some PWDs, however, feel that the discomfort of PWODs is the "problem" of the PWODs and feel no need to take steps to make others feel comfortable in their presence. PWDs whose disability can be concealed often choose to avoid this interaction strain by hiding the disability. For example, people with hearing impairments often choose to not wear their hearing aid in public, making a conscious decision to sacrifice the ability to hear for the appearance of being a hearing person (Blood, 1997). Many individuals who are missing a hand choose not to wear the hook in public, but wear a prosthetic hand instead. The hook, infinitely more functional, is used at home in private, but these individuals know that they can avoid a great deal of interaction strain if the cosmetic hand, which really is practically useless in terms of functioning, is worn in public. In reality, probably no one ever thinks that the prosthetic hand is a real hand, but a prosthetic hand does not elicit the intense reaction that a hook does. The following letter illustrates this interaction strain from the perspective of the PWD:

> Soon after I learnt that my failing sight would ultimately lead to blindness, I passed on the information by letter to two old and true friends. In each case I had by letter a warm and sympathetic response, but in each case, when next I came in personal contact with these friends, I sensed at once a nervous reaction, a doubt as to what changes they would find in me and what was the right way to behave....It was a useful experience, teaching me right at the beginning that besides learning to take blindness in my stride, I had to persuade my friends to take it in theirs (Mitchell, 1964, cited in Tuttle, 1984, p. 76).

The fact that the strain was felt by "two old and true friends" rather than strangers underscores the discomfort that disability elicits. Obviously, Mr. Mitchell was aware that his blindness would cause his friends discomfort, and he sought to reduce this discomfort by writing a letter before meeting his friends for the first time as a person with blindness. Like most PWDs, Mr. Mitchell was aware that others would view him as inferior and somehow changed in character and personality. Mr. Mitchell assumed from their "warm and sympathetic" letters that his friends were not uncomfortable with his blindness. Note that Mr. Mitchell suddenly learns that he has a double task—to deal with the blindness and to deal with his friends' reactions to the blindness. Rather than looking to friends for support and assistance in this time of change, Mr. Mitchell must carefully consider and negotiate his friends' reactions. This is a valuable experience because it clearly illustrates how the salience of disability overrides years of "old and true" friendship.

THE SALIENCE OF THE PERCEIVED DEFINING NATURE OF THE DISABILITY

In this section, look for—
- ▶ *the definition of salience and its effects on PWDs*
- ▶ *why the PWD is often viewed as only the disability*

Salience of the disability simply means that the disability is the most important, or the only, aspect of the individual. Nothing else about the individual is acknowledged or noticed, including race, gender, or sexual orientation (Antonak, 1985; Chubon, 1994; Coleman, 1997; Covey, 1998; Davis, 1997; Eisenberg, 1982; Fine & Asch, 1988b; Henderson & Bryan, 1997; Roessler & Bolton, 1978). Moreover, others assume that the disability is the central identity and self-definition of the person with the disability. The word salience means "most noticeable" and, in the case of disability, salience also often means "different from the rest of us." Ascribing such salience and importance to the disability serves to heighten and exaggerate any differences between those with disabilities and those without disabilities (Goffman, 1963; Gordon, Minnes, & Holden, 1990; Schmelkin, 1988). The individual's other characteristics, such as age, sex, educational level, and personality qualities, are neither acknowledged nor understood. The individual becomes his or her disability (Horne, 1988). Two feminist disability scholars, Fine and Asch (1988b), summarized:

> To date almost all research on disabled men and women seems simply to assume the irrelevance of gender, race, ethnicity, sexual orientation, or social status. Having a disability presumably eclipses these dimensions of social experience. Even sensitive students of disability...have focused on disability as a unitary concept and have taken it to be the "master" status but apparently the exclusive status for disabled people (p. 3).

Olkin (1999) described how the salience of her adaptive device, in the view of others, completely overshadows any of her other personal characteristics. When meeting an individual for the first time in her scooter and then meeting the same individual for a second time when she is using crutches, the individual does not remember meeting her. She stated, "I got encoded in their memory as a scooter, and they would sure remember a scooter, if they saw it again. But they don't remember *me*. One year my son's teacher, having met me on my scooter, kept trying to clarify at our second meeting (I was on foot) exactly what my relationship to my son was. I finally understood her confusion, and said, "I'm his mother.""

Others see the disability as the motivator for every thought and action that the PWD has or does. The disability, according to these individuals must be the central identity of the PWD, and therefore PWODs mistakenly believe that the disability is foremost in the individual's comparison of him- or herself to others and also in choosing friends and associates. Counselors often consider the disability to be the "presenting problem" when meeting a PWD for the first time. This is an example of a professional service provider viewing the disability as the salient characteristic of the individual. Many PWDs report that they have to go to great lengths to convince counselors that the disability has nothing to do with the problem or issue they wish to discuss. Similarly, whenever a PWD is in a bad mood, becomes angry, or displays any negative behavior, everyone assumes that such behavior is a result of the disability.

Judith Heumann, the assistant secretary of the Office of Special Education and Rehabilitative Services, who uses a wheelchair, recounted the experience of attending a National Organization for Women (NOW) meeting. The focus of the meeting was to plan strategies to help women gain their rights (Thomson, 1997). Dr. Heumann summarized the impression others had gained of her: "When I come into a room full of feminists, all they see is a wheelchair" (p. 286). Rather than viewing Dr. Heumann as a woman committed to equal rights for girls and women, the NOW members saw her *only* as a person in a wheelchair. The disability was far more prominent than either her gender or her long history of accomplishment and government work. Further, an organization whose main focus is on the rights of individuals and equal access to opportunity could see no further than a wheelchair. The salience of the disability makes all social comparisons dependent on the disability. Rather than comparing individuals based on their value systems, their experiences, or their preferences, the salience of disability reduces all comparisons to the disability.

Attitude scales (Yuker, 1988) include statements such as "It is impossible for a disabled person to lead a normal life." The test-taker responds "true" or "false." Agreement with items like this one demonstrates the salience of the disability. Obviously, automatically assuming that anyone with any type of disability has an "abnormal" life shows that the test-taker assumes (1) the disability is the most important (or only) aspect of the individual, and (2) the disability is a negative and a deficit.

The media, for centuries, have powerfully reinforced the false concept of the salience of the disability. In literature, newspapers, television, and movies, the individual with a disability is shown as (1) having no life other than the disability; (2) existing in a negative light, as evil, weak, or simply pathetic; and (3) usually not being a member of a family. When the media does not portray PWDs as having families, jobs, community affiliations, and all the other types of relationships and achievements, the audience is left to conclude that the only important salient characteristic of the individual is his or her disability. Furthermore, as disability scholars who study the media and their portrayal of PWDs have discovered, most depictions of PWDs are negative (Byrd, 1979; Byrd et al., 1977; Byrd & Elliott, 1985, 1988; Byrd et al., 1986; Gartner & Joe, 1987; Longmore, 1985a, 1985b). In reality, after medical stabilization, the disability is only one aspect of the individual and sometimes a relatively minor part of the individual's self-concept. Most PWDs report that PWODs ascribe far more importance and salience to their disability than they themselves do, and furthermore, most PWODs ascribe more limitations to the disability than actually exist.

SPREAD OR OVERGENERALIZATION

In this section, look for—
▶ *the definition of spread and how spread impacts PWDs*
▶ *how most PWDs view their disability as a single aspect of their identity*
▶ *how FDR knew how to control the effects of spread*

Beatrice Wright, a pioneer in the psychology of disability, coined the term *spread* to describe the overgeneralization (by observers) of the effects of the disability. Another disability scholar (Livneh, 1982) called this the *negative halo effect*. Both describe the widespread discounting and underrating of *all* of the abilities of the individual with the disability. In simplest forms, it is shouting at the person who is blind because it is thought that he or she cannot hear. Such behavior seems laughable, but generalizing the effects of disability is commonplace and usually more insidious. Most PWDs think of their disability as an attribute, not as a problem. Moreover, the disability is only a single aspect of their identity. In contrast, many PWODs consider the disability to be the central, defining characteristic of the PWD. For example, a Washington, DC, lawyer and Congressional lobbyist stated, "People don't think you're smart if you limp." A woman of small stature (a dwarf) commented, "Most people associate my maturity with my size." It can be seen that all of these examples overgeneralize the effects of the disability (and no one is disputing that the disability does indeed have limitations) to totally unrelated aspects of the individuals. In addition, all of these overgeneralizations tend to be negative.

There are a few exceptions when the overgeneralizations are positive and flattering; this is called the "Tiny Tim" syndrome. Tiny Tim, the boy with a disability in Charles Dickens' *A Christmas Carol*, was very sweet, appreciative, and wished everybody well. Dickens used the character of Tiny Tim to show by contrast how mean and miserly Scrooge was. Not only was Tiny Tim poor, but he had a disability. Scrooge, on the other hand, was wealthy and able-bodied, and he was the villain. Nowadays, the "Tiny Tim" syndrome is a derisive term to describe the idea that a disability automatically results in a sweet and saintly personality. Often, we hear that PWDs are compassionate or wise or insightful or are heros or saints. These are examples of the Tiny Tim syndrome.

M. J. Bienvenu (1989) related a joke that communicates the tendency of PWODs to overgeneralize the effects of disability. "A Deaf person is having a difficult time vacuuming the carpet. He goes over the same spot of dirt repeatedly, to no avail. In a fit of frustration, he turns around and notices that the machine is unplugged." Bienvenu then explained why the joke is both uninformed and insulting: "This is a perfect example of humor that is not part of the Deaf culture. Of course, this would never happen in the first place, because a Deaf person would naturally feel the inactive motor and immediately respond appropriately....The fact that the author does not address deaf people's keenly developed sense of sight and touch is rather significant" (p. 19). This joke also illustrates that false and negative stereotypes are readily apparent to PWDs. This joke was published in a book entitled *Hazards of Deafness* (Holcomb, 1977), certainly not a flattering (or accurate) title. Once again, PWODs think they understand the experience of disability (when they do not); PWODs misinterpret the disability experience in negative and insulting ways, and these types of misinterpretation can lead to false stereotypes, for example, the stereotype that Deaf people are easily frustrated. Deaf people do read this joke and laugh. However, it is not for the reason that the author intended.

Far more pervasive, insidious, and damaging is the "twisted body, twisted soul" concept of spread. This widely held view holds that the disability has somehow negatively affected the individual's personality or character. The twisted body, twisted soul concept holds that the individual, because of the disability, is permanently bitter, angry, deviant, and hostile. A variation of this idea states that the PWD is angry and bitter, not directly because of the disability, but because he or she has failed to "accept" the disability, thus "pathologizing" the PWD. Of course, it is others who are making the judgment of the person's character and then ascribing the causes of sources of these character failings.

Esso Leete (1991) has experienced schizophrenia for over 20 years. She summarized the experience of being stigmatized by making a list:

> You understand stigma firsthand when:
> - Your college refuses to readmit you after discharge from the hospital because you now have a history of mental illness.
> - You are denied a driver's license because you are naive enough to answer the questionnaire truthfully.
> - A general hospital emergency room physician brusquely explains, after reading in your chart the diagnosis of "residual schizophrenia" that your fever, nausea, and vomiting are "in your head."
> - Your friends decide they need to develop other relationships on learning of your past troubles and treatment.
> - Stigma is an ugly word, with ugly consequences. (p. 19)

It should be noted that some of this treatment would now be illegal under the ADA.

A well-known example of an individual who had a disability and understood the results of others overgeneralizing his disability was President Franklin Roosevelt. Roosevelt contracted polio at age 39 and never walked again. Before and after the onset of his disability, he pursued a political career. However, after he contracted polio, he and his family went to great lengths (and they had the financial resources) to hide the disability. The American media, mostly print, cooperated by not photographing Roosevelt in his wheelchair or being carried in someone's arms. All of Roosevelt's assistive devices, architectural accommodations, such as ramps into government buildings, and the personal assistance rendered by his sons or members of the Secret Service were systematically hidden from the public view. Roosevelt and his political advisors thought that the American public and international leaders would not accord respect and trust to Roosevelt if they were reminded of his disability too often (Gallagher, 1985). And yet, Roosevelt guided the United States through the Great Depression and World War II, becoming one of the most influential individuals of the 20th century. He was also a great advocate for PWDs, especially for those who had survived polio. Roosevelt's image on the dime is often thought to be due to his work in easing the economic depression, something akin to "Brother, can you spare a dime?" In fact, Roosevelt's image on the dime is an allusion to his work in founding the March of Dimes, a fund raiser for polio research and services for people with polio.

Today, there are those in the Disability Rights Movement who consider Roosevelt to have been a "closet crip," someone who hid his disability for his own convenience and advancement. Another view of Roosevelt and his disability is described in the *Time* magazine article, describing the erection of a monument in Washington, DC, to honor Roosevelt (Exhibit 3–4). Originally, the builders planned to eliminate Roosevelt's wheelchair from the sculpture, but many groups of PWDs protested strongly. The protesters argued that the disability was an inherent part of Roosevelt and, furthermore, it is no longer necessary to prove that the disability of polio was not, or is not, an obstacle to being president. Indeed, many political analysts, not disability analysts (Evans, 1998), consider Roosevelt's disability to have contributed to his national and world leadership achievements because polio forced Roosevelt, for the first time in his life, to interact with, and attempt to understand, the struggles of the "common man."

Contrast the way in which another famous individual, often in the media, has chosen to deal with his disability. Itzak Perlman, the world-famous violinist, has the same disability as did FDR; both had contracted polio and neither could walk unassisted. Perlman has pointedly insisted that his television appearances show him walking on to the stage on his crutches. Of course, Perlman has the option to hide or minimize his disability simply by appearing in a seated position playing the violin. Olkin (1999) described a result of this: "Itzak Perlman…said that when he began playing violin professionally all the stories about him described him as a man who had polio and also played the violin. It was only after he became one of the four premier violinists in the world did the stories switch to describing him as a premier violinist who also happened to have had polio" (pp. 88–89).

Roosevelt felt he could not afford to remind the American people of his disability, while Perlman has chosen to show his self-identity: a violinist who has had polio. This is not to say that one of these individuals is right and the other wrong. These two examples do demonstrate (1) the processes and rationales underlying the choice to disclose or not to disclose; certainly both Roosevelt and Perlman knew/know that their orthopaedic disabilities had no functional impairments for the chosen occupations, and yet each knew that the public would react to the disability and, furthermore, each needed the public to fulfill his occupational aspirations. Roosevelt needed people to vote for him and Perlman needs people to attend his concerts and buy his CDs; (2) the relationship that both Roosevelt and Perlman had, or have, with their public is most often not a personal relationship. A teacher or a physician with a disability meets the individuals with whom he or she works and can, therefore, respond to concerns about the disability on a one-to-one basis; Roosevelt never met or talked to each of the American people on an individual basis, and Perlman meets and speaks with very few of the people who attend his concerts or buy his CDs; (3) the differing results and others' judgments of Perlman and Roosevelt choosing to disclose their disability or to hide their disability; for example, many in the Disability Rights Movement resent the fact that Roosevelt went to such lengths to hide his disability or, more correctly stated, the effects of his disability; and (4) the capability of both these men to hide their disability simply because they are both gifted and famous; certainly the inability to walk and the use of crutches or a wheelchair is considered a visible disability. However, the juxtaposition of fame and media has enlarged the definition of "hidden" disability for those few who are gifted and famous. Furthermore, since most people do not have the choice, they are not criticized for choosing not to disclose.

Exhibit 3–4

A Monumental Mistake:
The FDR Memorial misses the essence of the man

They came humbly and quietly last week in wheelchairs and with leader dogs and a sign-language interpreter, hopeful paraplegic old men, and vigorous middle-age people except for their weakened limbs and dimmed eyes, and glowing youngsters with silence in their ears.

They were a coterie representing 50 million disabled Americans who were invited by the U.S. Park Service to preview the sprawling monument for Franklin Roosevelt to be dedicated May 2. The monument spreads out grandly on 7.5 acres along Washington's Tidal Basin, great blocks of ocher South Dakota granite carved with the soaring phrases of FDR's that brought this nation through economic collapse and war.

But in the $48 million monument there is no depiction of Roosevelt in the wheelchair he used for 24 years, nothing in the gardens and along the pathways to show his disability at a glance for those who remember and for children who never knew the personal struggle that shaped him.

The small vanguard of disabled people left the site saddened, believing to a person that the monument seemed lifeless, lacking the heroic vibrancy of FDR with his radiant smile, head back, steering himself into that destiny he saw beyond all adversity. "The essence of the man is missing," said wheelchair user Mike Deland, chairman of the National Organization on Disability.

And a handful of Gallaudet College students in sign language declared it incomplete history as they had learned it and said they would join a demonstration planned for the dedication day.

Mick Countee sensed the emptiness because after he broke his neck in a diving accident, while he was a Harvard student, his mother told him, "Son, if Franklin Roosevelt could be President, you can finish your education." Countee, a black, not only finished, but also went on to get a law degree from Georgetown and an MBA from Harvard. "Not a day went by," he said last week, "that I did not think of Roosevelt and Roy Campanella." Campanella was the Brooklyn Dodger catcher who was paralyzed in a car accident but never despaired in public.

Jim Dickson, the man organizing the demonstration, stood nearly sightless along the huge monument walls and imagined how a statue of Roosevelt in a wheelchair at the entrance would bring the stone to life. When Dickson was seventeen he was told by his doctor that he had juvenile macular degeneration and would soon be blind. As he walked with his parents out of the doctor's office, his mother told him, "If Franklin Roosevelt, who had polio and was in a wheelchair, could be President, then you can do what you want." He never forgot.

This cry for understanding from the disabled community is being heard. At least 16 Roosevelt family members now seek a design alteration. A demonstration at a New York foundry casting some of the sculptures halted a press conference. Another protest is planned around the office of monument designer Lawrence Halprin in San Francisco.

Former Presidents Bush, Ford, and Carter have urged an additional sculpture to show Roosevelt in a wheelchair, and Bush has sent off a "Dear Bill" note to Clinton in hopes he can encourage a peace before Clinton gives the dedication address. Meanwhile every historian of consequence who has considered the issue has concluded that the monument is a tragic misreading of the spirit of FDR and a grave misstatement of history for the generations to come.

A letter from Ann Landers titled "Angry in Montana," in which a woman in a wheelchair said she did not want to talk to the child in the grocery store about her disability or answer the child's questions, clearly shows Ann Landers' quickness to overgeneralize the effects of the disability. In reply, Landers tells the writer with a disability that she has not accepted her disability and the wheelchair. Never does Landers consider that it is the child, and his or her mother, who are rude, insensitive, and intrusive. This is an example of being a "forced representative." Perhaps the woman in the wheelchair does not have a lot of privacy. For example, maybe a personal care attendant must perform many functions for the woman. Therefore, privacy is precious and important to the woman. Perhaps the woman was in a hurry and did not have time to present a one-woman disability awareness seminar. Perhaps the woman was in a bad mood after having had a hard day. Everyone, including a PWD, is entitled to have bad moods. Perhaps the woman simply did not like children. Landers does not consider for a moment that there is any other explanation for the woman refusing to speak to the child other than her disability. The authors of the following letters written to protest Landers' reply to this woman clearly resent Landers' "twisted body, twisted soul" implication (Exhibit 3–5).

Exhibit 3–5

Ann Gets an Earful on Disability Response

Dear Ann: You goofed. Your reply to "Angry in Montana" about people with physical disabilities and the curiosity of "innocent" children was totally off the mark. "Montana" is right. It is NOT OK for children to ask questions about a physical disability. Just because it comes from a child's "natural curiosity" does not make it all right.

It is natural for a child to want to do away with a new baby who is getting entirely too much attention, but we won't allow it. We also will not allow jumping on the bed in muddy sneakers or taking Daddy's watch apart. When my grandson displayed a bit of "natural curiosity" and attempted to disengage the brake on my car, you'd better believe I lost no time letting him know it was NOT OK. There is no reason to indulge a child's inquisitiveness just because it is "natural."

Your out-of-the-blue statements that Angry in Montana has not come to terms with his disability and the suggestion that he "lighten up" were insensitive and condescending.

—Disappointed in You

Dear D.I.Y.: I appreciate your comment. Keep reading for others.

Lansing, Mich.: I have been confined to a wheelchair since 1957. When I first went to a restaurant back then, a child of about 4 years old came over and asked why I was in that "funny chair." Before I could respond, his mother snatched him away. The child looked startled and probably got the impression that whatever I had must be contagious. I realize the mother didn't want her child to be rude, but her response only made things worse. Times have changed for the better, thank the good Lord. And thanks, too, for those recently installed ramps that now make almost all buildings wheelchair accessible.

The letters are the rebuttals Ann Landers received, commenting on her response to "Angry in Montana." The first letter criticizes Landers, but the second writer, from Lansing, Michigan, states that, as a wheelchair user, she was disappointed when the mother of the curious child "snatches" him away. Perhaps Lansing misperceived the situation and the mother was simply teaching her son rules of courtesy and spoke to her son about "the funny chair" in a more private setting.

In-Class Videos

- View the 19-minute video *disAbility Awareness* (1999) by Insight Media.
- View the 45-minute video *Understanding the Disabled: Dances with the Minotaur* by Insight Media. This video "examines issues of stereotyping and inaccessibility, confronts day-to-day issues" of those with disabilities, and "raises provocative questions about equality" (Insight Media, 2162 Broadway, New York, NY 10024–0621, 800–233–9910). Which of the three types of justice presented in this chapter is or are advocated in this video?
- View the 56-minute video *A New Sense of Place* released by Films for the Humanities and Sciences. The producers describe this video as profiling "individuals who have found a way to 'ramp' their way into the world. Among them is Grammy Award winner Evelyn Glennie, one of the world's leading solo percussionists, and deaf since the age of 12; and NBC News correspondent John Hockenberry, partially paralyzed since the age of 19, who travels the world to report the news. Also featured in the program is a legally blind woman who is not only a district attorney but an accomplished athlete as well."
- View the 56-minute video *Without Barriers or Borders* by Films for the Humanities and Sciences. The producers state: "This program explores the burgeoning global movement for independent living. Among the efforts featured in this program are a group of disabled high school students from Russia, who learn confidence, teamwork, and communication skills through whitewater rafting; Japanese activists who are working to persuade their society to provide access to transportation and buildings; and a Cambodian clinic where over half the workers have disabilities."

Learning Activity

Find examples in the media (films, literature, television, advertising) that communicate prejudice and stereotypes of PWDs. Share these with the class.

Writing Experience

Write a paper that responds to one of the five "bullet" questions listed at the beginning of this chapter.

References

Abroms, K. I., & Hodera, T. L. (1979). Acceptance hierarchy of handicaps: Validation of Kirk's statement "Special education often begins where medicine stops." *Journal of Learning Disabilities, 12,* 15–20.

Albrecht, G. L. (1976). Socialization and the disability process. In G. Albrecht (Ed.). *The sociology of physical disability and rehabilitation* (pp. 3–38). Pittsburgh, PA: University of Pittsburgh.

Albrecht, G. L. (1992). The social meaning of impairment and interpretation of disability. In G. L. Albrecht (Ed.). *The disability business in America* (pp. 67–90). Newbury Park, CA: Sage.

Allport, G. W. (1954). *The nature of prejudice*. Reading, MA: Addison-Wesley.

Allport, G. W. (1958). *The nature of prejudice* (2nd ed.). Garden City, NY: Doubleday Anchor.

Allport, G. W. (1986). *The nature of prejudice* (25th anniversary ed.). Reading, MA: Addison-Wesley.

Americans with Disabilities Act of 1990, 42 U.S.C. § 12101 *et seq.*

Anderson, G. R., & Glesnes-Anderson, V. A. (Eds.). (1987). *Health care ethics: A guide for decision makers*. Rockville, MD: Aspen.

Anthony, R. N., & Young, D. W. (1984). *Management control in nonprofit organizations* (3rd ed.). Homewood, IL: Richard D. Irwin.

Antonak, R. F. (1980). A hierarchy of attitudes toward exceptionality. *Journal of Special Education, 14,* 231–241.

Antonak, R. F. (1985). Societal factors in disablement. *Rehabilitation Counseling Bulletin, 28,* 188–201.

Antonak, R. F. (1988). Methods to measure attitudes toward people who are disabled. In H. E. Yuker (Ed.). *Attitudes toward persons with disabilities* (pp. 109–126). New York: Springer.

Battin, M. P. (1986). Euthanasia. In D. Van De Veer & T. Regan (Eds.). *Health care ethics: An introduction* (pp. 58–97). Philadelphia: Temple University.

Bayles, M. D. (1987). The value of life. In D. Van De Veer & T. Regan (Eds.). *Health care ethics: An introduction* (pp. 265–289). Philadelphia: Temple University.

Beck, M. (1999). *Expecting Adam: A true story of birth, rebirth, and everyday magic*. New York: Times Books/ Random House.

Belgrave, F. Z. (1984). The effectiveness of strategies for increasing social interaction with a physically disabled person. *Journal of Applied Social Psychology, 141,* 147–161.

Belgrave, F. Z., & Mills, J. (1981). Effect upon desire for social interaction with a physically disabled person of mentioning the disability in different contexts. *Journal of Applied Social Psychology, 11,* 44–57.

Berkowitz, E. D. (1987). *Disability policy: America's programs for the handicapped*. Cambridge: Cambridge University.

Berry, J. O. (1995). Employing people with disabilities: Impact on attitude and situation. *Rehabilitation Psychology, 40,* 211–222.

Bettancourt, B. A., & Dorr, N. (1998). Cooperative interaction and intergroup bias: Effects of numerical representation and cross-cut role assignment. *Personality and Social Psychology Bulletin, 24,* 1276–1304.

Bickenbach, J. E. (1993). *Physical disability and social policy*. Toronto, Ont.: University of Toronto.

Bienvenu, M. J. (1989). Reflections of deaf culture in deaf humor. In C. J. Erting, R. C. Johnson, D. L. Smith, & B. D. Snider (Eds.). *The deaf way: Perspectives from the International Conference on Deaf Culture* (pp. 16–23). Washington, DC: Gallaudet University Press.

Biklen, D. (1986). Framed: Journalism's treatment of disability. *Social Policy, 16*(3), 45–51.

Biklen, D., & Bailey, L. (Eds.). (1981). *"Rudely stamp'd": Imaginal disability and prejudice*. Washington, DC: University Press of America.

Blood, I. M. (1997). The hearing aid effect: Challenges for counseling. *Journal of Rehabilitation, 63,* 59–63.

Bogdan, R. (1988). *Freak show: Presenting human oddities for amusement and profit*. Chicago: University of Chicago.

Bogdan, R., & Biklen, D. (1977). Handicapism. *Social Policy, March/April,* 14–19.

Bogdan, R., & Knoll, J. (1995). The sociology of disability. In E. L. Meyen & T. M. Skrtic (Eds.). *Special education and student disability* (pp. 677–711). Denver, CO: Love.

Bogdan, R., & Taylor, S. J. (1976). The judged, not the judges: An insider's view of mental retardation. *American Psychologist, 31,* 47–52.

Bogdan, R., & Taylor, S. J. (1982). *Inside out: The social meaning of mental retardation*. Toronto: University of Toronto.

Bowe, F. (1978). *Handicapping America: Barriers to disabled people*. New York: Harper & Row.

Bowe, F. (1980). *Rehabilitating America: Toward independence for disabled and elderly people.* New York: Harper & Row.

Bowe, F. (1990). Employment and people with disabilities: Challenges for the nineties. *OSERS News in Print, 3,* 2–6.

Bower, E. M. (Ed.). (1980). *The handicapped in literature: A psychosocial perspective.* Denver, CO: Love.

Brown, E. R. (1987). DRGs and the rationing of hospital care. In G. R. Anderson & V. A. Glesnes-Anderson (Eds.). *Health care ethics: A guide for decision makers* (pp. 69–90). Rockville, MD: Aspen.

Bryan, W. V. (1996). *In search of freedom: How people with disabilities have been disenfranchised from the mainstream of American society.* Springfield, IL: Charles C Thomas.

Byrd, E. K. (1979). Magazine articles and disability. *American Rehabilitation, 4,* 18–20.

Byrd, E. K., Byrd, P. D., & Allen, C. (1977). Television programming and disability: A descriptive study. *Journal of Applied Rehabilitation Counseling, 8,* 28–32.

Byrd, E. K., & Elliott, T. R. (1985). Feature films and disability: A descriptive study. *Rehabilitation Psychology, 30,* 47–51.

Byrd, E. K., & Elliott, T. R. (1988). Media and disability: A discussion of the research. In H. E. Yuker (Ed.), *Attitudes toward persons with disabilities* (pp. 82–95). New York: Springer.

Byrd, E. K., Williamson, W., & Byrd, P. D. (1986). Literary characters who are disabled. *Rehabilitation Counseling Bulletin, 30,* 57–61.

Charlton, J. I. (1998). *Nothing about us without us: Disability oppression and empowerment.* Berkeley, CA: University of California.

Chirikos, T. N. (1989). Aggregate economic losses from disability in the United States: A preliminary assay. *The Milbank Quarterly, 67,* 59–61.

Chubon, R. A. (1994). *Social and psychological foundations of rehabilitation.* Springfield, IL: Charles C Thomas.

Cole, S. S. (1984). Facing the challenge of sexual abuse in persons with disabilities. *Sexuality and Disability, 7,* 71–88.

Cole, S. S. (Ed.). (1991). Sexual exploitation of people with disabilities [Special issue]. *Sexuality and Disability, 9* (3).

Coleman, L. M. (1997). Stigma: An enigma demystified. In L. J. Davis (Ed.). *The disability studies reader* (pp. 216–231). New York: Routledge.

Cornwell, J. (1999). *Hitler's pope: The secret history of Pius XII.* New York: Viking Penguin.

Couser, G. T. (1997). *Recovering bodies: Illness, disability, and life writing.* Madison, WI: University of Wisconsin.

Covey, H. C. (1998). *Social perceptions of people with disabilities in history.* Springfield, IL: Charles C Thomas.

Craine, L. S., Henson, C. E., Colliver, J. A., & McLeland, D. G. (1988). Prevalence of a history of sexual abuse among female psychiatric patients in a state hospital system. *Hospital and Community Psychiatry, 39,* 300–304.

Davis, L. J. (Ed.). (1997). *The disability studies reader.* New York: Routledge.

DeJong, G., & Batavia, A. I. (1990). The Americans with Disabilities Act and the current state of U.S. disability policy. *Journal of Disability Policy Studies, 1,* 65–75.

DeJong, G., & Lifchez, R. (1983). Physical disability and public policy. *Scientific American, 248,* 40–49.

Deshen, S. A. (1992). *Blind people: The private and public life of sightless Israelis.* Albany, NY: State University of New York.

Eisenberg, M. G. (1982). Disability as stigma. In M. G. Eisenberg, C. Griggins, & R. J. Duval (Eds.). *Disabled people as second-class citizens* (pp. 1–11). New York: Springer.

Eisenberg, M. G., Griggins, C., & Duval, R. J. (Eds.). (1982). *Disabled people as second-class citizens.* New York: Springer.

Evans, H. (1998). *The American century.* New York: Alfred A. Knopf.

Ferguson, P. M., Ferguson, D. L., & Taylor, S. J. (Eds.). (1991). *Interpreting disability: A qualitative reader.* New York: Columbia University.

Ferrans, C. W. (1987). Quality of life as a criterion for allocation of life-sustaining treatment: The case of hemodialysis. In G. R. Anderson & V. A. Glesnes-Anderson (Eds.). *Health care ethics: A guide for decision makers* (pp. 109–124). Rockville, MD: Aspen.

Fichten, C. S. (1986). Self, other, and situation-referent automatic thoughts: Interaction between people who have a physical disability and those who do not. *Cognitive Therapy and Research, 10*, 571–587.

Fichten, C. S., Robillard, K., Tagalakis, V., & Amsel, R. (1991). Causal interaction between college students with various disabilities and their nondisabled peers: The internal dialogue. *Rehabilitation Psychology, 36*, 3–20.

Fine, M., & Asch, A. (1988a). Disability beyond stigma: Social interaction, discrimination, and activism. *Journal of Social Issues, 44*, 3–21.

Fine, M., & Asch, A. (Eds.). (1988b). *Women with disabilities*. Philadelphia: Temple University.

Friedlander, H. (1995). *The origins of Nazi genocide: From euthanasia to the final solution*. Chapel Hill, NC: University of North Carolina.

Gallagher, H. G. (1985). *FDR's splendid deception*. New York: Dodd and Mead.

Gallagher, H. G. (1990). *By trust betrayed: Patients, physicians, and the license to kill in the Third Reich*. New York: Henry Holt.

Gartner, A., & Joe, T. (Eds.). (1987). *Images of the disabled, disabling images*. New York: Praeger.

Gellman, W. (1959). Roots of prejudice against the handicapped. *Journal of Rehabilitation, 40*, 115–123.

Goffman, E. (1963). *Stigma: Notes on the management of spoiled identity*. Englewood Cliffs, NJ: Prentice Hall.

Gordon, E. D., Minnes, P. M., & Holden, R. R. (1990). The structure of attitudes toward persons with a disability, when specific disability and context are considered. *Rehabilitation Psychology, 35*, 79–90.

Gouvier, W. D., Coon, R. C., Todd, M. E., & Fuller, K. H. (1994). Verbal interactions with individuals presenting with and without physical disability. *Rehabilitation Psychology, 39*, 263–268.

Gouvier, W. D., Steiner, D. D., Jackson, W. T., Schlater, D., & Rain, J. S. (1991). Employment discrimination against handicapped job candidates: An analog study of the effects of neurological causation, visibility of handicap, and public contact. *Rehabilitation Psychology, 36*, 121–129.

Gove, W. R. (1976). Social reaction theory and disability. In G. L. Albrecht (Ed.). *The sociology of physical disability and rehabilitation* (pp. 57–71). Pittsburgh, PA: University of Pittsburgh.

Grand, S. A., Bernier, J. E., & Strohmer, D. C. (1982). Attitudes toward disabled persons as a function of social context and specific disability. *Rehabilitation Psychology, 27*.

Hahn, H. (1987). Civil rights for disabled Americans: The foundation of a political agenda. In A. Garther & T. Joe (Eds.). *Images of the disabled, disabled images* (pp. 181–203). New York: Praeger.

Hahn, H. (1997). Advertising the acceptable employment image: Disability and capitalism. In L. J. Davis (Ed.), *The disability reader* (pp. 172–186). New York: Routledge.

Hannah, M. E., & Midlarsky, E. (1987). Differential impact of labels and behavioral descriptions on attitudes toward people with disabilities. *Rehabilitation Psychology, 32*, 227–238.

Harris, L. (1986). *The ICD survey II: Employing disabled Americans*. New York: Louis Harris.

Harris, L. (1994). *The ICD survey III: Employing disabled Americans*. New York: Louis Harris.

Harrison, J. (1987). *Severe physical disability: Responses to the challenges of care*. London: Cassell.

Hastorf, A. H., Wildfogel, J., & Cassman, T. (1979). Acknowledgment of handicap as a tactic in social interaction. *Journal of Personality and Social Psychology, 37*, 1790–1797.

Henderson, G., & Bryan, W. V. (1997). *Psychosocial aspects of disability* (2nd ed.). Springfield, IL: Charles C Thomas.

Higgins, P. C. (1992). *Making disability: Exploring the social transformation of human variation*. Springfield, IL: Charles C. Thomas.

Holcomb, R. (1977). *Hazards of deafness*. Northridge, CA: Joyce Media.

Horne, M. D. (1988). Modifying peer attitudes toward the handicapped: Procedures and research issues. In H. E. Yuker (Ed.). *Attitudes toward persons with disabilities* (pp. 203–222). New York: Springer.

Hyler, S. E. (1988). DSM-III at the cinema: Madness in the movies. *Comprehensive Psychiatry, 29*, 195–206.

Hyler, S. E., Gabbard, G. O., & Schneider, I. (1991). Homicidal maniacs and narcissistic parasites: Stigmatization of mentally ill persons in the movies. *Hospital and Community Psychiatry, 42*, 1044–1048.

Ince, L. P. (Ed.). (1980). *Behavioral psychology in rehabilitation medicine: Clinical applications*. Baltimore: Williams & Wilkins.

Kleck, R. (1968). Physical stigma and nonverbal cues emitted in face-to-face interaction. *Human Relations, 21*, 19–28.

Kriegel, L. (1987). The cripple in literature. In A. Gartner & T. Joe (Eds.). *Images of the disabled, disabling images* (pp. 31–46). New York: Praeger.

Leete, E. (1991). The stigmatized patient. In P. J. Fink & A. Tasman (Eds.). *Stigma and mental illness* (pp. 17–25). Washington, DC: American Psychiatric Association Press.

Livneh, H. (1982). On the origins of negative attitudes toward people with disabilities. *Rehabilitation Literature, 43,* 338–347.

Livneh, H. (1983). Application of smallest space analysis to the study of attitudes toward disabled persons. *Professional Psychology: Research and Practice, 14,* 406–413.

Livneh, H. (1991). On the origins of negative attitudes toward people with disabilities. In R. P. Marinelli & A. E. Dell Orto. *The psychological and social impact of disability* (3rd ed., pp. 181–196). New York: Springer.

Longmore, P. K. (1985a). A note on the language and social identity of disabled people. *American Behavioral Scientist, 28,* 419–423.

Longmore, P. K. (1985b). Screening stereotypes. *Social Policy, 16,* 31–37.

Mackelprang, R., & Salsgiver, R. (1999). *Disability: A diversity model approach in human service practice.* Pacific Grove, CA; Brooks/Cole.

McCarthy, H. (1982). Partnership as a method of enhancing attitudes and behaviors toward employment of disabled individuals. *Rehabilitation Counseling Bulletin, 26,* 119–132.

Mee, C. L. (1999). *A nearly normal life.* Boston: Little, Brown.

Mirzoeff, N. (1997). Blindness and art. In L. J. Davis (Ed.), *The disability studies reader* (pp. 382–398). New York: Routledge.

Moore, C. L., & Feist-Price, S. (1999). Societal attitudes and the civil rights of persons with disabilities. *Journal of Applied Rehabilitation Counseling, 30,* 19–24.

National Disability Statistics and Policy Forum. (1995). *Working with disability: Employment statistics and policy.* Washington, DC: U.S. Government Printing Office. (ERIC Document Reproduction Service No. 1.21153:2)

Obermann, C. E. (1965). *A history of vocational rehabilitation in America.* Minneapolis, MN: T. S. Dennison.

Olkin, R. (1999). *What psychotherapists should know about disability.* New York: Guilford.

PBS. (1999). *Paralyzing fear: The story of polio in America* (A3317). www.pbs.org/shop.

Pelka, F. (1997). *The ABC-CLIO companion to the disability rights movement.* Santa Barbara, CA: ABC-CLIO.

Perlman, L. B., & Kirk, F. S. (1991). Key disability and rehabilitation legislation. *Journal of Applied Rehabilitation Counseling, 22,* 21–27.

Phillips, M. J. (1992). "Try harder": The experience of disability and the dilemma of normalization. In P. M. Ferguson, D. L. Ferguson, & S. J. Taylor (Eds.). *Interpreting disability: A qualitative reader* (pp. 213–227). New York: Columbia University.

Roessler, R., & Bolton, B. (1978). *Psychosocial adjustment to disability.* Baltimore: University Park Press.

Rossides, D. W. (1990). *Social stratification: The American class system in comparative perspective* (2nd ed.). Englewood Cliffs, NJ: Prentice Hall.

Safilios-Rothschild, C. (1970). *The sociology and social psychology of disability and rehabilitation.* New York: Random House.

Safran, S. P. (1998). The first century of disability portrayal in film: An analysis of the literature. *Journal of Special Education, 31,* 467–479.

Schmelkin, L. P. (1988). Multidimensional perspectives in the perception of disabilities. In H. E. Yuker (Ed.), *Attitudes toward persons with disabilities* (pp. 127–137). New York: Springer.

Schmitt, S. M. (1999, October). Criminalizing the mentally ill. *Counseling Today, 1,* 26–27.

Schur, E. M. (1971). *Labeling deviant behavior: Its sociological implications.* New York: Harper and Row.

Schur, E. M. (1979). *Interpreting deviance.* New York: Harper and Row.

Scott, R. A. (1969). *The making of blind men: A study of adult socialization.* New York: Sage.

Shapiro, J. P. (1993). *No pity: People with disabilities forging a new civil rights movement.* New York: Times Book.

Siller, J. (1976). Attitudes toward disability. In H. Rusalem & D. Malikin (Eds.). *Contemporary vocational rehabilitation* (pp. 67–79). New York: New York University.

Silvers, A. (1996). (In)equality, (ab)normality, and the Americans with Disabilities Act. *Journal of Medicine and Philosophy, 21*, 209–224.

Sobsey, D. (1994). *Violence and abuse in the lives of people with disabilities: The end of silent acceptance.* Baltimore: Brookes.

Sobsey, D., & Mansell, S. (1993). The prevention of sexual abuse of people with developmental disabilities. In M. Nagler (Ed.), *Perspectives on disability* (2nd ed., pp. 283–292). Palo Alto, CA: Health Markets Research.

Strohmer, D. C., Grand, S. A., & Purcell, M. J. (1984). Attitudes toward persons with a disability: An examination of demographic factors, social context, and specific disability. *Rehabilitation Psychology, 29*, 131–145.

Thomson, R. G. (1997). Feminist theory, the body, and the disabled figure. In L. J. Davis (Ed.). *The disability studies reader* (pp. 279–292). New York: Routledge.

Tucker, B. P., & Goldstein, B. A. (1991). *Legal rights of persons with disabilities: An analysis of federal law.* (ERIC Document Reproduction Service No. ED 332–453.) Horsham, PA: PRP Publications.

Turner, C. S. V., & Louis, K. S. (1996). Society's response to differences: A sociological perspective. *Remedial and Special Education, 17*, 134–141.

Tuttle, D. W. (1984). *Self-esteem and adjusting with blindness: The process of responding to life's demands.* Springfield, IL: Charles C Thomas.

Ulicny, G. R., White, G. W., Bradford, B., & Matthews, R. M. (1990). Consumer exploitation attendants: How often does it happen and can anything be done about it? *Rehabilitation Counseling Bulletin, 33*, 240–246.

U.S. General Accounting Office. (1990). *Persons with disabilities: Reports on costs of accommodations* (Human Resources Division Report GAO/HRD 90–44BR). Gaithersburg, MD: Author.

Vander Kolk, C. J. (1976a). Physiological measures as a means of accessing reactions to the disabled. *New Outlook for the Blind, 70*, 101–103.

Vander Kolk, C. J. (1976b). Physiological and self-reported reactions to the disabled and deviant. *Rehabilitation Psychology, 23*, 77–83.

Van De Veer, D., & Regan, T. (Eds.). (1987). *Health care ethics: An introduction.* Philadelphia: Temple University.

Waxman, B. F. (1991). Hatred: The unacknowledged dimension in violence against disabled people. *Sexuality and Disability, 9*, 185–199.

Weisgerber, R. A. (1991). *Quality of life for persons with disabilities: Skill development and transitions across life stages.* Gaithersburg, MD: Aspen Publishers, Inc.

Wright, B. A. (1988). Attitudes and the fundamental negative bias: Conditions and corrections. In H. E. Yuker (Ed.). *Attitudes toward persons with disabilities* (pp. 3–21). New York: Springer.

Yuker, H. E. (Ed.). (1988). *Attitudes toward persons with disabilities.* New York: Springer.

Zola, I. K. (1985). Depictions of disability-metaphor, message, and media: A research and political agenda. *The Social Science Journal, 22*, 5–17.

Zola, I. K. (1991). Communication barriers between "the able-bodied" and "the handicapped." In R. P. Marinelli & A. E. Dell Orto (Eds.). *The psychological and social impact of disability* (pp. 157–164). New York: Springer.

Zola, I. K. (1992). "Any distinguishing features?" The portrayal of disability in the crime-mystery genre. In P. M. Ferguson, D. L. Ferguson, & S. J. Taylor (Eds.). *Interpreting disability: A qualitative reader* (pp. 233–250). New York: Columbia University.

Chapter 4

Sources of Prejudice and Discrimination, Part 2

▶ What does the statement "Disability is a normative experience" mean?
▶ How are disability costs calculated?
▶ How did the Nazi regime justify the murder of Germans with disabilities?
▶ How can allowing PWDs their civil rights and full social integration result in a reduction of PWODs' fear of disablement?
▶ What are four societal responses to disability?
▶ Why do PWDs view charities and telethons as another form of victimization?
▶ What is justice?

MORAL ACCOUNTABILITY FOR THE CAUSE OF DISABILITY

In this section, look for—

▶ *the hierarchy of stigma based on the perceived cause of the disability*
▶ *the relationship between primitive retributivism and the stigma directed toward PWDs*
▶ *how the preventive medicine movement may contribute to blaming the PWD for his or her disability*
▶ *the ethical issue of individuals who cause their own disabilities*

The perceived cause of the disability can influence the degree of stigma directed toward the individual (Augé & Herzlich, 1995; Bordieri & Drehmer, 1988; Couser, 1997; Kravetz, Katz, & Albez, 1994; Safilios-Rothschild, 1982; Shurka & Katz, 1976; Thorn, Hershenson, & Romney, 1994). Generally, disabilities acquired in "noble" and honorable endeavors such as combat injuries or industrial accidents are the least stigmatizing. Defending the nation and working are considered to be both noble and honorable. Higgins (1992) described the way in which American government "assist(s) most generously those who become disabled in the defense of the country, disabled veterans....Disabled veterans have the strongest claim on our disability dollars" (p. 213). Other disability policy analysts (Berkowitz, 1987; Tanenbaum, 1986; Yelin, 1989) have demonstrated that veterans receive more disability benefits than civilians with the same disabilities. Berkowitz (1987) stated that veterans are "entitled to more generous benefits and their programs are older and better established than civilian programs" (p. 169). It should be noted that in 1962, Congress broadened the veterans programs to include those who served in peacetime. Moreover, the *lack* of stigma ascribed to the onset of the disability (and not the disability itself) often translates into more money and other benefits.

Those with congenital disabilities are stigmatized to a greater degree and those with acquired disabilities are often perceived by others to be personally and morally responsible for the onset of the disability, to have somehow "caused" the disability or, at minimum, to have not taken steps to prevent the disability. And, in those cases in which the individual actually does possess a self-inflicted disability (such as a spinal cord injury incurred while riding a motorcycle without wearing a helmet and after drinking alcohol), the stigma is very great. Much of the stigma directed toward individuals with mental illness is a result of society ascribing the responsibility for the illness to the individual's lifestyle choices or lack of character and self-control (Bordieri & Drehmer, 1988; Marantz, 1990; Murphy, 1998; Sontag, 1978; Thorn et al., 1994; Weiner, Perry, & Magnusson, 1988; Wikler, 1987; Zola, 1983). Contrast society's perception of individuals with schizophrenia with the perception of individuals with diabetes. In the case of schizophrenia, the individual is held responsible for the illness, but in the case of diabetes, the individual is not held responsible and therefore is not stigmatized to the same degree. (In many cases, failure to comply with medical regimens such as taking medications may be due, in part, to the individual's unconscious internalization of society's judgment that he or she should be able to control and manage the illness with simple willpower and strength of character.) Walster (1966) suggested that the human tendency to blame the individual for his or her disability is an attempt to protect ourselves from existential angst or acknowledging the randomness of disability. If we can believe the individual *caused* his or her disability, then we can comfort ourselves by saying, "We'll never cause ourselves a disability."

Read the letter from "Smoking Mad" (Exhibit 4–1). Notice that Ann Landers agrees with the writer.

Attitudes about the perceived cause or blame for the disability (and not only the disability itself) result in reduced opportunities for PWDs. Researchers (Bordieri & Drehmer, 1988; Thorn et al., 1994; Weiner et al., 1988) proved that individuals who were judged to be responsible for their disability were offered not as many job interviews or as many actual jobs or offers of assistance as did those individuals who were not held accountable for their disability. These well-designed experiments proved that perceived cause of disability is a factor in the degree of prejudice and discrimination the PWD experiences (Figure 4–1).

PWODs have always been more interested in the cause of an individual's disability than the impact of the disability in the individual's life. This is seen in children's first question to strangers with disabilities: "How did you get this way?" Adults usually do not verbalize the question of "How did you get this way?", but they, like children, are more interested in the cause and/or onset of the disability rather than in the management of the disability.

Moral accountability for the onset of the disability often translates into responsibility or blame. Certainly, when reading the history of the treatment of PWDs, it is clear that many, if not most, societies considered disabilities to be caused by some sort of sin or wrongdoing by the person with the disability or his or her parents or ancestors. Blaming the individual for his or her disability is an erroneous belief that has persisted for centuries in all types of societies. In this day and age of science,

Exhibit 4–1

> **Dear Ann Landers:** Some months ago, I was diagnosed with a disease that my doctor said would be aggravated by cigarettes, even though the disease itself was not caused by smoking. For me, this was a no-brainer—give up smoking.
>
> Several of my co-workers smoke, but not at work, because it is not allowed in our building. One of these co-workers recently had surgery to replace veins in his legs. He was advised by his surgeon to quit smoking, but continues to puff away. Another co-worker had a quadruple bypass, but continues to smoke a pack-and-a-half a day. A third co-worker developed a cancerous growth on his tongue, but continues to smoke like a chimney.
>
> These people share my group insurance, and frankly, I am mad as hell. As my premiums go up, I am tempted to tell the bookkeeper to attach my increases to the bills of the smokers. It is not fair that we should all be penalized by people too selfish to get their own insurance, who instead insist on raising our premiums by continuing with their destructive behavior.
>
> I know there is probably no solution other than for insurance companies to drop the policies of people who continue to smoke against medical advice, but I really needed to vent my anger in a public way.
>
> —Smoking Mad in Minnesota
>
> **Dear Mad in Minn.:** You came to the right place. I am pleased to give you space in which to vent your anger. We now know that smoking is more than just a filthy habit, it is an addiction. I have only one close friend who smokes, and she has the decency to excuse herself when she feels the need to light up. Need I say, I appreciate it.

connecting disability with sin or ill fortune seems absurd. Today, for many disabilities, both the etiology (cause) and the pathogenesis (source) are known. Moreover, many disabilities are known to be hereditary or, at minimum, to be more common among first-degree relatives and, therefore, it would be foolish to blame the individual for his or her disability. For example, many mental illnesses are hereditary, and often several individuals within the same family have the same mental illness. In spite of this, the desire to establish responsibility for the disability appears to be strong.

The natural result of holding *someone* responsible for the disability is to hold that same person totally responsible for the treatment and care of the disability. The rationale is, whoever created the situation should also deal with it. Therefore, the individual and his or her family should manage the disability and not subject others (who are totally blameless) to requests for assistance, accommodations, resources, or rights. Whether the source of the disability is ascribed to ill fortune, the anger of the gods, or bad luck, the disability is thought to be an individual responsibility.

Bickenbach (1993) wrote a very powerful description of two strongly held ideas about disability: (1) the individual (or his or her parents or ancestors) is responsible for the disability, and (2) because the individual with a disability is evil, it is "our duty" to isolate that individual. He added "In a nutshell, primitive retributivism is the view that people who are manifestly defective are living out a just punishment for sins, vices, or other moral faults, known or unknown, that have been inflicted

Noble and honorable endeavors
(e.g., wars, industrial injuries)

Congenital

Acquired

Acquired disabilities in which the individual is
perceived to have "contributed" to the onset
(e.g., use of alcohol, drugs, failed suicide attempts)

Least stigma

Most stigma

Figure 4–1 Stigma Associated with Type of Onset

by some powerful and moral force. At most, in this view, these manifest sinners are entitled to our pity; but it is our duty to dissociate ourselves from them" (p. 189).

Bickenbach's short summary also shows how beliefs about etiology often lead to treatment strategies. Note that we are speaking about *beliefs* about etiology and not about *known* etiology. In Biblical times, outward signs such as blindness or a mobility impairment were thought to be signs of inward evil (Bickenbach, 1993). Today, in some cultures, the idea that disabilities are somehow "God-ordained" still persists and attempts to treat the disability or reduce its effects are resisted because it is believed that if God ordains the disability, God would not approve of any human attempt to alleviate it.

Also note that this primitive retributivism also limits the responsibilities of society and any resulting guilt for not allowing PWDs their civil rights and for isolating them. Bickenbach's (1993) clear-cut statement helps us to see how convenient and guilt-absolving it is to blame the individual for his or her disability. PWDs whose disabilities are visible are often approached by strangers with this question: "What did you do to yourself?"

Today, we can see the same dynamic of searching for the cause, and the blame, for the disability. Mothers who have babies with congenital disabilities are often asked about their pregnancies and what they did and what they did not do. Most mothers of babies without disabilities are not asked about their pregnancies. Autism in children was thought to be caused by remote and cold parents, usually the mother. Nowadays, autism is known to be a genetic biological disorder (Films for the Humanities and Sciences, 1999). Individuals with psychiatric disabilities, such as mental illness, are often perceived to be weak, lacking in self-control and character, and to have been unable to do something that would have prevented the onset of mental illness. In contrast, no one with diabetes is accused of being weak and lacking in self-control. And yet, in both diabetes and mental illness, there is an organ of the body that is malfunctioning.

A noted disability scholar stated, "Indeed, while obesity is not generally considered to be a disability, it is a condition which is highly stigmatized since the notion exists that obese people must be, to some extent, weak and irresponsible people" (Safilios-Rothschild, 1982, p. 43). Today, people who are obese still experience a great deal of prejudice and stigma, in spite of the fact that research has shown (since

1982 when Safilios-Rothschild made the above statement) that body shape and size are primarily a result of hereditary and genetic factors. Yet, simply because people *believe* that individuals are responsible for their condition, they stigmatize them.

Susan Sontag (1978) clearly outlined how society tends to transform illness into moral character in her two books that deal with cancer, tuberculosis, and AIDS. Sontag wrote: "Psychological theories of illness are a powerful means of placing the blame upon the ill. Patients who are instructed that they have, unwittingly, caused their disease are also being made to feel that they have deserved it" (pp. 55–56).

Accountability for the cause of the disability is influenced by social, cultural, and political factors. In individualistic, capitalistic societies, such as the United States, lack of disability is viewed "as a form of individual emancipation" (Cockerham, 1998, p. 95). Lack of disability is also viewed as a form of efficiency, relieving society of the responsibility and expense of rehabilitation. Read the letter (Miller, 1988) on page 266. The mother who gave birth to a baby with a congenital disability felt that she had "failed . . . society." Cockerham explained the relationship between differing political systems and accountability for both the cause and treatment of disability:

> Marxist scholars like Howard Waitzkin and Vicente Navarro claim that an emphasis on individual responsibility for leading a healthy life excuses the larger society from direct accountability in health matters. Waitzkin (1991) maintains that capitalism puts the burden of being healthy squarely on the individual, rather than seeking collective solutions to health problems. The emphasis in capitalist societies on healthy lifestyles is seen as an effort to displace the responsibility for health from the social system and its health sector down to individuals (p. 99).

The preventive medicine movement may actually contribute to the societal response of holding individuals responsible for their illnesses and disabilities (Marantz, 1990). Since it can be empirically shown that preventive measures can *reduce* the incidence of illness and disability, there are many individuals who would then (erroneously) conclude that these preventive measures can *eliminate* all illness and disability (Wang, 1993). For example, frequent routine medical examinations can (and do) detect asymptomatic (without symptoms) chronic health conditions and disabilities or the predisposing factors of disabilities. If left undiagnosed and untreated, these disabilities and chronic health conditions are exacerbated and often result in secondary conditions, further complications, and pervasive functional impairments. Conditions such as diabetes and high blood pressure do not manifest any symptoms, and the individual has no way of knowing that he or she has the condition other than undergoing medical examination. Diabetes, if left untreated, can lead to blindness and lower limb amputation. High blood pressure is an antecedent to strokes. Therefore, submitting to routine medical examinations is both sensible and cost-effective. Should society hold individuals who refuse to undergo medical exams responsible for their disabilities?

Similarly, the emergence of such concepts as "emotional resilience" can also lead to the erroneous conclusion that individuals with mental illness or other psychiatric disabilities could have prevented their disability. Psychologists (Hayes, Barlow, & Nelson-Gray, 1999) outlined the role of prevention in avoiding the onset of psychiatric disabilities: "[Prevention programs] are designed to create competencies and coping skills that are prophylactic" (p. 76). In spite of the fact that proponents of preventive medicine and emotional resilience acknowledge the significant role of prevention, they also understand that most individuals are not to blame for their disabilities and illnesses (Marantz, 1990).

What about those cases in which the individual is truly responsible for the onset of the disability? In rehabilitation counseling, the term "thrills and chills" is used to describe individuals who have a desire or need for danger, intense experiences, novelty, and stimulation. Often, these are the people who enjoy outdoor physical activities and engage in such sports as hang gliding, sky diving, mountain climbing, and other dangerous and exhilarating activities. In the first chapter, we learned about traumatic brain injury (TBI), and learned that, overwhelmingly, the greatest proportion of people with TBI are males between the ages of 19 and 24. TBI, more than any other type of disability, has an onset associated with the use of alcohol and the time of day of the onset is most often between midnight and 5:00 A.M. Individuals with TBI are often described as "thrills and chills" types. Another example of a disability whose onset is well known is fetal alcohol syndrome (FAS). FAS has resulted in many babies being born with learning disabilities, hearing losses, and many other congenital deficits. Women are now being advised to totally abstain from alcohol throughout the course of their pregnancies.

What about thrills and chills people who knowingly disregard safety procedures? What about pregnant women who choose to drink alcohol? What about people who refuse to wear helmets or seatbelts? Are these not lifestyle choices and therefore personal, private, and privileged? What about the use of alcohol during dangerous activities? These are extreme and clear-cut examples, and certainly most people have agreed that these types of choices should be actively discouraged or even declared illegal simply because (1) the evidence clearly points to a cause-and-effect relationship between these choices and injury and death, and (2) the individual who chooses to be "irresponsible" may also harm others in addition to himself or herself. So, the notion of "risk" and "error" are straightforward in the above cases.

Nonetheless, two other significant circumstances in which risk and error are clearly present merit attention. First, almost everybody engages in some types of behaviors, or, more accurately, does not engage in other behaviors, that put them at risk for a disability, injury, or illness. And, because we choose to do or not to do certain things, we raise insurance premiums, consume scarce medical resources, and drive up the costs of disability (Ann Landers, October 6, 1999). Indeed, the costs of most disabilities are paid out of the public purse (insurance or taxes). Everybody, or almost everybody, believes in wisdom, moderation, health maintenance, and prevention of risk (Fox, 1997; Sherrill, 1997). In spite of this, we still smoke, overeat, and refuse to exercise or floss our teeth. The question is this: At what point are individuals allowed to make choices that have a high probability of ending in disability, injury, or illness? Are individuals expected to change their entire personality and lifestyle simply to avoid illness, injury, or disability?

The second situation that involves the principle of responsibility for the onset of disability is the result of medical technology. Should prospective parents who know that their unborn child will have a disability choose to continue the pregnancy and deliver the baby? The availability of technology has expanded the definition of moral accountability for disability. What if the question were "Should prospective parents who know that their unborn child will have *severe* and *multiple* disabilities choose to continue the pregnancy and deliver the baby?" (Hubbard, 1997). Who decides what "severe" and "multiple" are? Will the parents bear all the costs of caring for the baby or will insurance and government dollars be used (*Scholar Under Fire*, 1999)?

Another framework in which to conceptualize disability considers the cause for the disability and the responsibility for dealing with the disability in four forms:

- The individual is responsible for the onset of the disability and the individual is also responsible for dealing with the disability
- The individual is responsible for the onset of the disability; however, the individual is not responsible for dealing with the disability
- The individual is neither responsible for the onset of the disability nor for dealing with the disability
- The individual is not responsible for the onset of the disability, but the individual is responsible for dealing with the disability

It can readily be seen that the second statement reflects the medical model of disability in that the individual is held responsible for somehow causing the disability (or, at minimum, not preventing the disability), but the "cure" or amelioration of disability is best left to trained medical professionals. Obviously, most PWDs consider the last statement to most closely identify their conceptualization of responsibility for the cause of and the response to the disability.

These are difficult, and perhaps unanswerable, questions. Nonetheless, it can be stated that there is a human tendency to want to establish fault, blame, accountability, or responsibility for the onset of the disability. Even with our scientific knowledge and technical expertise, we fall prey to the same questions with which people thousands of years ago grappled. Perhaps we confuse "how" with "why." We don't always know "how" but we often do. Science and medicine can answer many questions of "how." Science does not answer questions of "why." The "why" of disability is a question that religion/spirituality/philosophy attempts to answer.

MORAL ACCOUNTABILITY FOR THE MANAGEMENT OF THE DISABILITY

In this section, look for—

- ▶ *the explanation of the statement "Disability is a normative experience"*
- ▶ *the results when PWDs do not "follow the rules"*
- ▶ *the rules of having a disability*
- ▶ *who is a Tiny Tim, according to the Disability Rights Movement?*

Disability is a normative experience (Augé & Herzlich, 1995). This means that there are rules and expectations of PWDs; certain behaviors and attitudes are obligatory and rule breakers experience severe consequences (Bishop, 1980; Crewe, 1980; Druss, 1995; Leinhardt & Pallay, 1982). Indeed, PWDs who choose not to comply experience the consequences of greater prejudice and discrimination and, in extreme cases, are abandoned medically and socially. On the other hand, those who learn the rules, live the rules, and believe in the rules are rewarded (Lehr & Brinckerhoff, 1996). As with most rules, it is the people in power who make the rules and, in this case, often it is people without disabilities who make the rules about managing the disability. Zola (1991) made the observation that PWDs who are "successful mainstream adapters" (p. 160) are most often accepted by PWODs as spokespersons for all PWDs. Zola stated, "Moreover, almost every 'successful' handicapped [*sic*] person, as well as every 'success' I have met (including myself), usually regards, as a key element, the self-conception: 'I never think of myself as handicapped [*sic*]'" (p. 160).

Indeed, many in the Disability Rights Movement use the derisive term "Tiny Tim" to describe a PWD "who is eager to please the nondisabled people in his or her life, or mainstream society in general, by ignoring slights to his or her rights and dignity and acting the part of the cheerful 'handicapped' person" (Pelka, 1977, p. 305). Evident in this statement are (1) an understanding that to have a disability is a normative role—the words "acting the part" are used, (2) the rules are made by those in power (PWODs) and not by those who have the knowledge and experience of the disability (PWDs), and (3) one of the most important rules is to be cheerful and another rule is to ignore prejudice and discrimination. The term "Tiny Tim" is derived from Charles Dickens' character who is sweet and cheerful. Obviously, to be seen as a Tiny Tim by PWDs is to be seen as someone who, in order to make life easier to him- or herself, does not advance the cause of PWDs.

Society has set the standards of evaluation of dealing with disability without much knowledge or experience about the disability. It is easy to see how lack of capability or loss of function or side effects of medication can be erroneously viewed by others as breaking the rules of managing disability.

What are the rules? PWDs are to face their disability with as much courage and optimism as possible. Self-mastery, emotional robustness, and resilience are all required (Fowler & Wadsworth, 1991). The individual should demonstrate the motivation and desire to recover or, at minimum, to regain as many capabilities as possible. Active and independent management of the disability are expected rather than giving the impression of a passive victim. Individuals who adhere to medical regimens, who appear to "adapt" well to the situation, who request only those necessary accommodations and assistance are subjected to less stigma than those individuals who appear to not manage their disability well.

Even children with disabilities know and understand the "rules." Mee (1999), in his memoir that tells of contracting polio in the 1950s, stated, "Every boy and girl at Sherman Hospital knew this was what was expected, this was the story and the character that needed to be enacted. These were not lessons that had to be learned over a long life; they were so deeply, pervasively embedded in the culture that they were instantly available to any kid in a hospital bed" (p. 88).

PWDs are also expected to make others comfortable with their disabilities. The unwritten rules mandate that the person with a disability initiate the subject of his or her disability, disclose the etiology and any limitations, and finally, and most important, communicate to others that he or she is comfortable with the disability. All of the information must be delivered at the beginning of each new interaction and must be delivered in a fun, upbeat, and semi-indirect manner (Belgrave, 1984; Belgrave & Mills, 1981).

Yet, the PWD is compelled to maintain a balance between active management of the disability, including a highly developed knowledge about the disability, and passive submission to professional treatment plans and decisions. Thus, the rules for managing disability are somewhat contradictory. Most of the time, society expects PWDs to appear in control of both the disability and the emotional reaction to the disability (which, of course, includes the emotional reactions of PWODs to their disabilities). Occasionally, however, society expects and demands that PWDs relinquish their control, their status, and their roles in order to become compliant patients. At these times, the PWD's highly developed knowledge of the disability and accommodations is often viewed by professionals as irrelevant and unnecessary. Part of the responsibility (and skill) of the PWD includes the ability to determine when and where to show assertive independence and when and where to show passive compliance.

One of the most difficult disability ethical issues concerns individuals with mental illness who refuse to take medications to control the symptoms. Should "society" force these individuals to adhere to a medical regimen? If these individuals do not take their medications, they may hurt others, hurt themselves, lose their jobs, alienate their families, or become homeless. Obviously, the scientific and medical advances of psychotropic drugs have led to new ethical issues. On the other hand, perhaps these new antipsychotic medications do not present a new ethical issue because before their advent, individuals with mental illness were physically restrained. Indeed, psychotropic drugs are often referred to as "chemical straitjackets." Nonetheless, "forced medication" and other types of coerced treatment do raise the issue of "society's" right to force an individual to manage his or her disability.

THE INFERRED EMOTIONAL CONSEQUENCE OF THE DISABILITY, OR DIFFICULT DOES NOT MEAN TRAGIC

In this section, look for—
- ▶ *distressed identification*
- ▶ *"the requirements of mourning"*
- ▶ *the three factors of which PWODs are often unaware:*
  1. *the disability is a familiar part of the individual's self-concept*
  2. *the individual has learned how to deal with the disability*
  3. *the individual feels that there are valuable aspects of the disability*

Often termed *distressed identification*, inferred emotional responses usually refer to the fact that most PWODs automatically assume that an individual's disability must be the worst thing that ever happened to the person, an unending, devastating personal tragedy (Thompson, 1982). Certainly, many disabilities are difficult to manage, and the world is not designed for PWDs, but nonetheless, difficult does not automatically translate to bad or tragic. Another way in which distressed identification is expressed is the belief that the PWD must be of no worth to him- or herself or anyone else. Early pioneers in the study and measurement of attitudes toward PWDs, Dembo, Leviton, and Wright (1956) asserted that PWODs expect PWDs to suffer because their suffering proves that their "losses" are valuable. Wright (1960) termed this need that PWDs have a "requirement for mourning" (p. 64). Livneh (1991) explained the reason why PWODs need/want PWDs to suffer: "The nondisabled [*sic*] individual has a need to safeguard his or her values, by wanting the disabled [*sic*] to suffer, and show the appropriate grieving, so as to protect one's own values of the importance of a functioning body. Any attempt on the disabled person's part to deny or reject the 'suffering role' is met with negative attitude" (p. 184).

According to these scholars, when the PWD does not appear to suffer, then PWODs devalue the PWD because he or she has violated one of the rules of having a disability: the person should suffer.

In research studies, PWDs have been asked, using several different types of questions, if the possibility of a "cure" for their disability existed, would they accept it? Most do not automatically say "yes." Some say "no," and others put conditions on their "yes" response. For example, many of the participants responded "yes" if the fantasy cure would not take too long or be too involved. Most people would be surprised to learn that the expectant parents who are deaf want their baby to be deaf. Rather than viewing deafness as a tragic flaw, they see deafness as part of their identity, and most parents want children who are like themselves. Many people who are deaf refuse cochlear implants which would restore some hearing (Lane, 1993).

True–false questions on scales used to measure attitudes of PWODs toward PWDs measure the test-taker's degree of distressed identification of the disability experience. The following are examples of these types of questions: "Most disabled people do not feel that they are as good as other people"; "Most disabled people feel sorry for themselves"; "Disabled people are often grouchy"; "It must be pretty degrading to a blind person to depend so much on others"; "A blind person can never really be happy"; "Disabled people are more easily upset than other people"; and "Most disabled persons worry a great deal." These questions reveal the inferred emotional consequences of inferiority, grouchiness, feelings of degradation, unhappiness, and worry, none of which are positive and pleasant emotions.

In the video *My Body Is Not Who I Am*, the woman with a leg amputation recounts her experience with a physician who, for years, prescribed the tranquilizer Valium for her. All the woman had to do was to telephone the physician's office and the Valium prescription would be renewed, in spite of the fact that the doctor did not see or talk to the woman for years. In the video, the woman explains her view of why the physician gave her tranquilizers. According to her, he simply thought of her disability as so overwhelmingly tragic that the only way in which she could deal with it was to be chemically tranquilized. (It is also of interest to note that it is the woman who decided to terminate the use of Valium and not the physician.)

Individuals who are not blind often conceptualize total blindness as continual darkness and blackness. Congenital, total blindness is relatively rare, but, nonetheless, total blindness is not darkness. In much the same way, individuals who are not deaf conceptualize total deafness as complete silence. Not only is the experience of the disability misinterpreted (usually in an exaggerated, negative way), but also the individual's reaction to the disability is misunderstood. Rarely do people consider three important aspects of the disability experience: (1) the disability is a familiar part of the person's self-concept, (2) the individual has learned how to deal with the disability and often feels a sense of mastery and accomplishment, and (3) the individual often feels that he or she has gained invaluable insights and growth because of the disability experience (Wright, 1988).

Dr. Geerat Vermeij, an evolutionary biologist and professor at the University of California at Davis, has been blind since early childhood. He wrote a book entitled *Privileged Hands* (1997), and in the chapter entitled "A Glow of Yellow" he describes the experience of blindness. Moreover, he discusses how sighted people view blindness:

> Yet opinion polls almost unanimously portray blindness as the most feared of human conditions. Sight is *perceived* as the means by which we gain the bulk of our information about one another and about our surroundings. Accordingly, educators have built curricula almost entirely on a foundation of visual learning. For this reason, blind people are widely regarded as being incapable of learning or interacting fully with others. Skeptics de-

spair that blind people cannot see facial expressions, cannot witness a baby's first tentative steps, cannot respond to a smile, cannot see how others behave. Without such quintessentially visual experiences, the argument goes, the blind are denied a basic dimension of what it means to be human. Naively, [they] fear or loathe blindness (p. 16).

The individual who infers that another's disability is an unending tragedy communicates this attitude clearly. In the video *My Body Is Not Who I Am*, the young man in the wheelchair who fell while rock climbing expresses resentment toward his father, who sat at his hospital bedside and said, "If only this had happened to me." The son feels resentment years after he has left the hospital, probably because the father was saying, "This was the worst thing that could have happened to you." Ed Roberts, founder of the Rolling Quads and the former director of the State of California Office of Rehabilitation, had a doctor who said it was too bad the high fever of the polio did not kill him. Other PWDs have reported that friends and family offered to assist them in committing suicide. Doctors have advised parents of newborns with severe and multiple disabilities to either withhold treatment or allow the baby to die. These are extreme examples of inferring negative consequences (to the point of being unbearable) to the disability. Other examples include the enabling of alcohol and substance abuse because others, including professional caregivers, consider the disability to be so devastating that the PWD "deserves something" to help him or her cope.

Another woman, in an attempt to inform PWODs, stated, "Putting on my artificial leg is no more distressing to me than you putting on your socks" (DeLoach & Greer, 1981). Naturally, it takes more effort and time to put on a prosthesis than socks, but the woman was trying to communicate that it is not an emotionally sad task. In much the same way, a father who, as a boy, contracted polio and wore leg braces from that time on was not viewed by his children as either tragic or an object of pity. Indeed, when this father died, the mortician asked the six adult children if they wanted the leg braces on their father. The children replied "yes," saying that to bury their father without his leg braces would be like burying their mother without her glasses. The braces were a part of their father and, furthermore, were not viewed as a symbol of sadness. In fact, the children reported that the braces were a reminder of happy times. Their father sat on the bed, morning and evening, to put the braces on and off, and each of the six children received a turn sitting on the bed talking one-on-one with their dad.

In Safran's (1998) comprehensive review of the portrayal of disability in film, he concluded that the movie-going public, from the advent of film making, has considered disabilities to be dramatic and out of the ordinary. Such fascination with disabilities, and a little fear, has sold a lot of theater tickets, making disabilities both profitable dramatic and commercial devices.

It is true that (1) most disabilities are difficult (including the prejudice and lack of accommodations) and (2) PWDs are more aware of assistive devices and coping mechanisms used by other PWDs simply because they themselves use them. This is a lot like someone who wears contact lenses is aware of others who wear contact lenses. Those who wear artificial limbs are usually aware of others who wear prostheses; those who wear hearing aids are more aware of others who use hearing aids, and so on. However, the use of these assistive devices/prostheses is not inherently sad and demeaning to PWDs. Of course, people who use these devices are often aware of the emotional reaction of others, and if they have the capability to conceal the use of these devices, the users usually will do so.

Helen Keller presents an example of someone who did use prosthetic devices, but others rarely knew. Helen Keller was a beautiful woman who cared about her appearance and carefully arranged her wardrobe, make-up, and hair. As a result of an infection during her infancy, Helen Keller was deaf and blind. Reporters who interviewed and photographed her throughout her long life often commented on her beautiful blue eyes. Not one reporter questioned if they were glass eyes. Both her eyes had been surgically removed because one of them "bulged" or protruded and Helen Keller wanted to be attractive. Up until the surgery, she allowed photographers to take pictures of her from only one side so as to hide the unattractive eye. But Helen Keller opted for artificial eyes when she began her lecture tours. Obviously, this was a cosmetic, rather than therapeutic, surgery since the removal of her eyes did not make any difference, for either good or bad, in her vision. It was a source of amusement to Helen Keller (and probably everybody who had some knowledge and understanding of blindness) that the media commented on her beautiful blue eyes, and no one ever entertained the idea that the beautiful eyes might be artificial, glass eyes.

SOCIETY'S EMPHASIS ON HEALTH, FITNESS, AND BEAUTY

In this section, look for—

▶ *the advantages of beauty*
▶ *the elements of beauty: health, sexuality, symmetry, and physical fitness*

We worship beauty. Beauty, health, and independence are all judged to be valued and attainable with the prerequisite effort. Goffman (1963), in his classic book *Stigma, Notes on the Management of Spoiled Identity*, included athletic ability in describing a "normal" male. As would be expected, the man's age, marital status, race, ethnicity, sexual orientation, religious affiliation, educational attainment, and employment status are described. Moreover, the last part of the description talks about the male's physical appearance and his athletic record.

> In an important sense, there is only one complete unblushing male in America: a young, married, white, urban, northern heterosexual Protestant father of college education, fully employed, of good complexion, weight, and height, and a recent record in sports. Any male who fails to qualify in any of these ways is likely to view himself—during moments at least—as unworthy, incomplete, and inferior (p. 128).

It is true that individuals who are attractive and independent and appear healthy reap the rewards that society can provide. While both unattractive men and women are disadvantaged because of their lack of beauty, it is well known that it is unattractive women who experience the greatest disadvantage. It is well accepted that attractive people earn more over their lifetimes, receive more social benefits, and experience less rejection and isolation than those who are not good looking.

It is debatable, however, if beauty and attractiveness result from individual effort. And, to promulgate this idea is triply insulting to those who are not attractive because the message is (1) you're ugly, and (2) it's your fault, and, due to the fact that "a woman's beauty is seen as a reflection of a male partner's social status" (Asch & Fine, 1997, p. 244), a married woman who is judged to be unattractive is devalued in three ways: (1) you're ugly, (2) it's your fault, and (3) your husband/mate must be a loser to have settled for you. Furthermore, a woman with a disability is rarely considered to be a "trophy wife."

Most advantaged groups of people are unaware of their privileges, their automatic acceptance, and the advantages that their status brings, and beautiful people are no exception. Beautiful people probably assume that they will have a lifetime partner, perhaps have children, and have an extended family. From birth, beautiful people enjoy many advantages that unattractive people do not.

Mothers give more attention and care to (and are less likely to neglect or abuse) their beautiful babies. Beautiful people do not experience as much punishment and discipline throughout their lives as do unattractive people. Indeed, police, judges, and juries are more lenient toward attractive adults of both sexes. As children, beautiful people were the teacher's pet and the parents' favorite child, and other children realized that beautiful children had the automatic approval and protection of adults. Beautiful people know that job interviews will be fairly easy to obtain, and when they get a job, they will be paid higher starting salaries, and they will be promoted faster. They will not be assigned to the "back room"; they will deal with the customers/clients/patrons. Beautiful people understand that they will not be requested to present as many credentials and achievements to prospective employers simply because beautiful people are automatically considered by others to be intelligent and confident. Beautiful people probably prefer to present themselves in person rather than sending a letter or resume or speaking to someone over the telephone. Others are anxious to do favors for beautiful people.

Research at Harvard found that people "brake for beauty." Experiments in which a beautiful woman and a plain woman had flat tires and were standing by the side of the road waiting for help found that far more people stopped for the beautiful woman (Etcoff, 1999).

Beautiful people know that people enjoy talking to them, prolonging the conversation, laughing, joking, and occasionally touching them. Even young babies prefer beautiful people! Beautiful people understand that others like to be associated with them—as colleagues, as friends, as family members, as classmates. For a beautiful person, belonging to a group is effortless and automatic. If the individual is attractive, others will seek him or her out and make sure that the beautiful person is included. Life is not that difficult when you're beautiful.

Beautiful people know that there are many people who are not attractive and beautiful, and they are also vaguely aware that unattractive people do not receive all the social and occupational rewards that they do. On the other hand, unattractive people know that beauty is skin deep, but they also know that skin deep is all that is necessary to ensure a life full of privileges.

Beauty is important (Schur, 1983). In fact, it continues to become more important. Unattractive people appear to be falling further behind.

> The importance of attractiveness has increased dramatically in the United States in this century....For nearly every decade since 1930, physical appearance has increased in importance for men and women about equally, corresponding with the rise in television, fashion, magazines, advertising,

and other media depictions of attractive models. For example, the importance attached to good looks in a marriage partner on a scale of 0 to 3
increased between 1939 and 1996 from 1.50 to 2.11 for men and 0.94 to
1.67 for women....The sex difference so far remains invariant, however.
The gap between men and women is no more nor less than it was in the
late 1930s (Buss, 1999, p. 145).

The impression that beauty is an unattainable ideal is substantiated by research
(Langlois & Roggman, 1990). Researchers found that subjects judged computer-generated faces to be more attractive than photographs of real people who were beautiful. Computer-generated faces are completely symmetrical, having eliminated all
irregularities; however, these computer-generated images are not pictures of actual
people. Indeed, even the most beautiful people cannot "compete" with computer-
generated composites, proving that individuals with less symmetrical features are
considered less attractive. The media certainly has the power to make everybody
disappointed with his or her body and appearance.

An Associated Press article, dated October 1999, was entitled "Egg Salesman
Defends Web Venture" (Wilson, 1999). The article told of a former photographer
for *Playboy* magazine, Ron Harris, who plans to purchase ovarian eggs from models
and then sell these eggs to prospective parents. The article states Harris' motives:
"The egg auction is an opportunity for parents to give their children a head start in
a society that worships beauty" (p. 1). Harris stated, "I've been around beautiful
women my whole life and I think they have power most of us will never understand" (p. 1). Harris' Web site began accepting bids on Monday morning, and by
noon the site had received 5 million hits. The highest bid for an ovarian egg was
$42,000. Each model decides how long she will allow the bidding to continue and
what price she will accept. Harris' commission is 20 percent of the sale price. The
Web site states, "This site simply mirrors our current society, in that beauty always
goes to the highest bidder" (p. 10).

To summarize: (1) Beautiful people do receive more privileges and advantages
based solely on their appearance; (2) beauty, because of the media, is becoming
even more important than ever before; (3) in some ways, beauty is an unattainable
ideal because people are never completely symmetrical; and (4) there is the widespread notion that beauty is the result of individual effort. It is interesting to note
that the media are expanding the definition of beauty to include older people. The
media have the power to define beauty and also have consciously decided to respond
to the aging of the American population. However, the beautiful older women and
men shown in the media are not typical-looking older men and women, just as the
beautiful younger women and men are not typical-looking younger people.

Unattractive people, especially women, are often assumed to be isolated, unful-
filled, and even tortured (Imrie, 1996). Other characteristics, more extreme, ascribed to unattractive people are monstrosity and deviance. In summary, unattractive people, with or without disabilities, are often viewed as inferior.

What is beauty? We have seen that one component of beauty is symmetry.
Other elements of beauty are health, sexuality, and physical fitness. Many people
with disabilities are not viewed as being symmetrical, healthy, sexy, or physically fit
(Bogdan & Taylor, 1987; Fiedler, 1978; Macgregor, 1951). Further, we have seen that
many quality-of-life issues are a direct function of a person's attractiveness. Indeed,
many prospective employers have told qualified job candidates with disabilities

that they cannot hire them because their appearance would be distressing to customers, coworkers, or supervisors. Viewing the video *Facial Disfigurement*, it can be seen that none of these individuals experiences functional limitations but each is greatly limited by others' reactions to his or her appearance.

FEAR OF ACQUIRING A DISABILITY OR EXISTENTIAL ANGST, OR "THERE BUT FOR THE GRACE OF GOD GO I"

> *In this section, look for—*
> ▶ *the definition of "existential angst"*
> ▶ *why disability challenges our concepts of a fair world and mastery and control over our bodies*
> ▶ *the definition of TAB*
> ▶ *two ways to reduce existential angst*

The onset of a disability challenges our sense of control and *seems* contrary to the natural order. And yet we *know* that disabilities are an inherent, ordinary part of the natural order. We like to believe that we totally control both our destinies and our bodies. We also like to believe that we can overcome anything. None of this is true. Nonetheless, these are deeply held beliefs. We can control many aspects of our bodies and lives, and we can overcome many circumstances. However, no one has total control.

"Disability is a symbol of vulnerability, fallibility, weakness, dependence, and failure to master our bodies" (Bickenbach, 1993, p. 82). PWDs carry this negative and distress-inducing symbol with them, the disability. In the video *Don't Go to Your Room*, one of the participants states, "We confront the other person with what he/she would like to deny or ignore." For many PWODs, seeing someone with a disability reminds them that "I could become *like that.*"

Disability seems to be random, without purpose, and occurs with "unbearable unpredictability" (Augé & Herzlich, 1995, p. 166). The onset of a disability seems to transgress some nonexistent laws of justice and fairness and appears to demonstrate human inequality since not everyone has a disability. Lack of justice, human equality, and predictability are unpleasant to contemplate. And yet, everyone is vulnerable to acquiring a disability. It is difficult for those without disabilities to assign meaning to the disability when it occurs unexpectedly, brings with it a host of secondary losses, reduces the individual's sense of control and independence, and may bring a lifetime of pain. For some, the concept of disability is synonymous with mutilation, deformity, and disfigurement. The onset of a disability may also bring many financial and social costs. Although not inherent in the disability itself, the onset of a disability automatically assigns an individual to the category of "disabled," which usually means a sudden reduction in status and identity. And, the important questions can never really be answered with certainty: "Why him or her?"; "Why here?"; or "Why now?" Medical diagnoses and etiologies are of some help, but the answers to the truly important question of "why" cannot be found in medicine or science.

Fear of acquiring a disability is sometimes referred to as the "existential angst of disability." Angst is the German word for fear, and existentialism is a school of philosophy that holds that human life is fraught with peril, to which everyone is subject. The human condition, according to existential philosophers, is full of un-expected and unwanted circumstances that have the potential to threaten our well-being. Disability is one of these unexpected circumstances, although existentialists usually worry more about death. For an existentialist, every moment as a person without a disability may be the person's last moment without a disability.

Alex Valdez, on the PBS video *Look Who's Laughing*, is a comedian who is blind. Valdez summarizes the audience's first reaction to him: "They don't know what to do with a blind guy on stage. They don't know whether to laugh or cry. They're too preoccupied with how they're feeling." Valdez's last statement concisely describes the existential angst of the audience. Rather than concentrate on the comedian on stage who is telling funny jokes, the audience members are dealing with their indi-vidual reactions to blindness.

Much of the fear, anxiety, and painful reminders of the possibility of acquiring a disability can be easily dealt with by simply avoiding contact with PWDs. When a PWOD meets a PWD, the PWOD often questions his or her own identity as a person totally in control of life. Rather than deal with unpleasant feelings brought on by seeing a PWD, others can simply stay away or, if necessary, institutionalize PWDs so as not to be subjected to their presence. Of course, PWDs are aware of the effect of their disability and they use "in-group" words to describe PWODs, such as TABs (temporarily able-bodied), normies, or ABs (able-bodied). Certainly, the term TABs points to the possibility/eventuality of most individuals acquiring a disability and also plays on the TABs' fear of acquiring disabilities.

We have been discussing the concept of existential angst as an individual re-sponse. However, "collective neurosis" refers to the anxiety and fear of disability experienced by large groups, especially those in power. Collective neurosis often results in segregation and isolation for PWDs.

Fear of acquiring a disability, or existential angst, is a powerful negative emo-tion. Ironically, two methods to reduce (not eliminate) existential angst would be (1) accord PWDs their civil rights and necessary accommodations, and (2) allow PWDs full social integration. In other words, the solution to existential angst is to see disability for what it truly is—a societal concern rather than an individual con-cern. If we choose to view disability as an individual condition, which humans have done for most of history, then we "construct" disability as a terrible reality. If, on the other hand, we choose to view disability as a societal concern, we construct disability as a part of life, which we can negotiate *as a group*. If PWDs were accorded their rights, provided reasonable accommodations, and allowed full equal-status social relationships, the prospect of acquiring a disability would probably not be so anxiety-provoking for PWODs.

Individuals Who Acquire Disabilities Later in Life Have Internalized Many of the Negative Stereotypes of Disabilities

Dr. Fredrick Schroeder, Commissioner of the Rehabilitation Services Administra-tion, became blind at age 16. Dr. Schroeder (1997) commented on his own negative stereotypes of blindness: "I assumed that my life as a blind person would be very lim-ited, isolated, and dependent. I had limited expectations of myself. With blindness did not come any insights into blindness. I attributed to myself all the stereotypes that society holds of blind people. I needed someone to stretch my expectations. I needed someone with a perspective wider than my own. I needed hope."

Holding false and unrealistic beliefs about disabilities limits any individual's view of the world, but if the person should acquire a disability, then he or she literally becomes the object of his or her own prejudice and narrow views. Dr. Schroeder's experiences are valuable because he has insight into the needless self-limitations that his own pervasive, unrealistic, and narrow beliefs inflicted upon himself. He reports, "As I was lying in my hospital bed, I thought, 'I can still talk, so I guess I will be a radio disc jockey or a psychologist.'" Obviously, at that point in his life, Dr. Schroeder had very limited views of what people who are blind can do. (Not that there is anything wrong with being a disc jockey or a psychologist. However, as a 16-year-old boy, Dr. Schroeder needed to consider a wide range of occupational options, which he obviously did, since he did not become a psychologist or a disc jockey.)

The tenacity with which he held his limiting and stereotypical views can be seen in another experience Dr. Schroeder related:

> My rehabilitation counselor was Bob Nessler and he was blind. I remember Bob asked me if I wanted a cup of coffee. I said "yes." He got his white cane and we crossed Van Ness Boulevard (in San Francisco) and went into a coffee shop. (I knew that there was coffee in the rehab office.) I was shocked. I had had mobility and orientation training, but I thought blind people only went where they absolutely had to go. Bob Nessler changed my life and he helped me to see that as a blind person I would live a normal life. He did it without making a speech, making me read a book, but the way in which he lived his life. He took me to a coffee shop for a cup of coffee.

Even after completing his orientation and mobility training (O & M), Dr. Schroeder still retained his narrow and limiting views of the way in which people who are blind should live. But since Dr. Schroeder was blind, these prejudices and stereotypes were now *self*-limiting and *self*-imposed.

Hierarchy of Stigma

There is a "hierarchy of stigma" associated with the four main categories of disabilities (Antonak, 1980; Charlton, 1998; Furnham & Pendred, 1983; Harasymiw, Horne, & Lewis, 1976; Henderson & Bryan, 1997; Horne & Ricciardo, 1988; Jones et al., 1984; Jones, 1974; Olshansky, 1965; Tringo, 1970). In ascending order, this is the hierarchy of stigma. Individuals with physical disabilities have the least amount of stigma directed toward them, individuals with cognitive disabilities have more stigma, individuals with intellectual disabilities experience even more stigma, and, finally, those with psychiatric disabilities experience the greatest amount of stigma (Figure 4–2).

This hierarchy of stigma has implications for individuals with disabilities and also has societal implications. The general history of services and benefits to people with disabilities follows the hierarchy of stigma. Those with physical disabilities received services and benefits first, those with cognitive and intellectual disabilities received services next, and those with psychiatric disabilities received services last. Lawmakers and policy makers are subject to society's judgments and evaluations, and it is understandable that the history of disability services closely parallels the hierarchy of stigma toward disability.

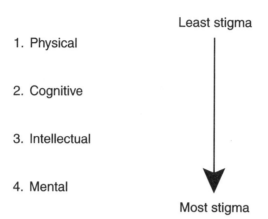

Figure 4–2 The Hierarchy of Stigma of Disability Categories

Those with physical disabilities experience the least degree of stigma and preju-dice, probably because these types of disabilities are the easiest to understand. The cause, the onset, the course, and the limitations are easier for most people to com-prehend. Simply stated, physical disabilities do not have the degree of ambiguity that other types of disabilities do. Indeed, many people consider physical disabili-ties to be the only type of disability. The following quotation explains the greater acceptance of people with blindness than for people with other types of disabilities.

> Possibly it is because the unimpaired can easily imagine and sympathize with their plight; unlike mental illness, for example, the state of blindness involves little stigma. Possibly it is because blindness has existed since the beginning of history, so that the blind have had more time to secure a place for themselves as legitimate objects of aid from the state. The very fact that their impairment is less disabling than others gives the blind ad-vantages in political organization (Berkowitz, 1987, p. 168).

Due to a longer history and greater acceptance by society, people with physical disabilities have been able to receive more professional services and benefits and also have had a longer history and experience of political advocacy for themselves. Just about everyone can identify with a person with a physical disability (Goodyear, 1983; Gordon, Minnes, & Holden, 1990). The prospect of acquiring a physical dis-ability or having a loved one with a physical disability seems (and actually is) pos-sible. In contrast, the prospect of acquiring an intellectual, cognitive, or psychiatric disability is rarely considered by PWODs. The media also follow the hierarchy of stigma in that advertising media most often show people with physical disabilities, most often people in wheelchairs. Rarely would people with other types of disabili-ties, for example, someone with Down syndrome, be shown.

Cognitive disabilities, which include learning disabilities and some types of traumatic brain injuries, are subjected to more stigma and prejudice than are physi-cal disabilities. These types of disabilities appear ambiguous to others because the cause, the course, and the limitations are not clear-cut and well quantified. Even clinicians differ in their diagnoses and treatment plans for individuals with cognitive disabilities. In some environments, cognitive disabilities might be considered "hidden" or "invisible" disabilities because the individual can choose to conceal the disability in those settings where cognitive skills are not required. Choosing not to disclose the cognitive disability may result in others attributing negative motives to the individual. For example, if others are not aware that the individual has a learning disability, they may think the person is lazy, unmotivated, or oppositional, when the reality is that the person does not understand or cannot remember or is unable to filter out extraneous stimuli in order to concentrate.

Individuals with intellectual disabilities, which include mental retardation, autism, and developmental disabilities, experience more stigma and prejudice than those with physical or cognitive disabilities, probably because the limitations of these types of disabilities are so great and affect many areas of the individual's life. And, as we learned in Chapter 1, today's labor market and economy are moving toward service jobs and jobs in technology. For individuals with intellectual disabilities, the changing labor market is redefining their disability. People with intellectual disabilities often appear to be ambiguous and unpredictable or somewhat frightening to the general public. Their disability and its limitations often arouse feelings of discomfort, especially because others feel they do not know how to interact with people with intellectual disabilities. In addition, "appropriate support systems with mental....disabilities are the most complex and necessarily professionalized and technical" (Charlton, 1998, p. 97). Not only are mental disabilities difficult to understand, but, as Charlton observed, the treatment of individuals with these types of disabilities is also difficult to understand.

Throughout history, individuals with intellectual disabilities were often not thought of as being completely "human." Intellectual functioning was considered to be the defining feature of humans, and if a person lacked this capacity, then he or she was often considered to be subhuman.

The types of disability against which the greatest amount of prejudice and discrimination is shown are psychiatric disabilities. Psychiatric disabilities are usually thought to include mental illness, alcohol abuse, and substance abuse. The two letters to Ann Landers in Chapter 3 are from people who have psychiatric disabilities. The writers describe the prejudice and discrimination they feel from others. The fact that these letters were not written by people with physical disabilities or people with cognitive disabilities or people with intellectual disabilities shows us that these types of disabilities have been accepted by the general public as legitimate disabilities. In contrast, individuals with psychiatric disabilities are not fully accepted as having a disability. Often, these individuals are somehow "blamed" for having the disability, as not being "strong enough" to have avoided the onset of the disability. In the video *Depression and Manic Depression* by Aquarius Productions, one of the participants makes this comment: "There is no shame in recognizing that the brain gets sick." This statement very clearly summarizes that there is "shame" in having a psychiatric disability and that the shame is undeserved. No one would say, "There is no shame in recognizing that the heart (pancreas, eyes, ears, or any other organ) gets sick" because there is not the degree of stigma directed toward physical disabilities as there is toward psychiatric disabilities.

Most people have little understanding of psychiatric disabilities. Psychiatric disabilities appear to be both ambiguous and dangerous; people with these types of disabilities have been portrayed for centuries by the media as violent and hostile.

Also, perception, in contrast to actuality, plays a large part in the amount of stigma toward people with disabilities. For example, many cognitive disabilities are often *perceived* to be psychiatric disabilities and, of course, then the stigma directed toward psychiatric disabilities is misdirected toward individuals who have cognitive disabilities.

This hierarchy of stigma is a useful model. However, reality is often more complicated than this simple model, and no one model can ever totally represent what a person experiences. For example, many individuals have more than one disability, and it is safe to state the degree of stigma directed toward these individuals probably is a result of the disability that is most visible or has the greatest number of limitations. Individuals who belong to more than one "minority" group, such as an older African American lesbian with a disability, will experience prejudice, stigma, and discrimination from many sources, and she may not be able to determine the exact source of this evaluation and treatment. Is it racism? Is it ageism? Is it homophobia? Is it sexism? Is it handicapism? Is it all of them? Three of them? Two of them?

Perceived social class is also an important factor. Individuals who are thought to be of higher social classes and who have a disability are perceived more positively than those people with disabilities who are thought to be of a lower social class. Parents of children in wheelchairs often decorate the wheelchair very colorfully in order to attract the other children to their child. In much the same way, adults with disabilities know that they will have a greater chance of being accepted if they can present themselves as well educated and of a high social status. Those PWDs who have some sort of ability that is highly valued by society will experience greater acceptance than someone else who does not have a socially valued role or capability but has the same disability. For example, a lawyer, in *Time* magazine, spoke about her experience with depression and also about the kinship she felt with the homeless people on the street, many of whom the lawyer thought had mental illness. The lawyer appeared in a national news magazine precisely because she was a graduate of an Ivy League law school, was employed in a high-paying job, and had also experienced institutionalization, medication regimens, and other treatment plans. With whom did the lawyer identify most—the other lawyers or the homeless people on the street? She identified with the homeless people because, according to her perception, they were living the 24-hour-a-day experience of mental illness that she was. She was a lawyer for only 8–10 hours a day.

The old joke that a rich person is considered to be eccentric but a poor person who exhibits the same behaviors is considered to be mentally ill reflects the influence that perceived social class exerts on the degree of prejudice and discrimination directed toward the individual. Some of the logic behind the old joke might also refer to the functional definition of disability. Rich people do not have to get up in the morning and go to work and, therefore, their mental illness may seem more benign. Rich people not only have fewer functional demands, but they also have more resources with which to hide their mental illness which, at minimum, would prolong the prediagnosis period. Rich people also have the resources to shield themselves from stress, a known exacerbator of mental illness.

The posters of famous and gifted people with disabilities demonstrate the role the perceived social class of the PWD plays in the degree of stigma or prejudice directed toward him or her. Posters of Beethoven and Einstein, with the question, "Did you know he had a disability?" are designed to help people reevaluate their attitudes toward PWDs. As would be expected, the impact of these posters has been difficult to determine, but many PWDs are offended by these posters because they seem to imply that in order for a PWD to be accepted, he or she must accomplish some superhuman, heroic task, akin to what Beethoven and Einstein did. Certainly, the poster makers needed to use PWDs who were readily identifiable. Celebrities with disabilities today also may present an unrealistic picture of the experience of most PWDs. Nonetheless, most PWDs do not accomplish world-famous acts (nor do most PWODs), and they feel resentful that these posters present only those PWDs who are rich, famous, and extremely gifted. Often, PWDs use the derisive term "supercrips" or "overcomers" to describe the famous individuals with disabilities.

"Society" also includes other people with disabilities. People with disabilities often are not accepting of *other* people with disabilities. Coleman (1997) explained: "Moreover, even among stigmatized people, relative comparisons are made, and people are reassured by the fact that there is someone else who is worse off" (p. 218). For example, in the video *Don't Go to Your Room*, a woman in a wheelchair remarks, "Walking is not all it's cracked up to be. A lot of walking people are depressed or alcoholic." Some PWDs may feel that they are exceptions to the rule, and they therefore can feel prejudice and discrimination toward other PWDs and yet not consider that this is incongruent. These PWDs consider themselves to have worked harder or have somehow done something extraordinary that separates them from other PWDs.

THREE SOCIETAL RESPONSES TO DISABILITY

In this section, look for—
- ► *charity*
- ► *preferential treatment*
- ► *compensation*

Charity

Charity and fund-raising exaggerate and sensationalize disability in order to solicit money. Exaggeration and sensationalism of the disability can lead to segregation and isolation for PWDs. Many PWDs feel that any money raised is not worth the costs to their self-concept.

Joshua Malinga (Disabled Peoples International/Disabled Peoples South Africa) stated,

> Charities play a negative social role. They seek to control us. Charities are not interested in empowerment and integration. They support segregation. In fact, once we have integration and equalization of opportunity, these charities will begin to die. Their institutional interests lie with segregation, ours with integration (Charlton, 1998, p. 92).

Charity, or benevolence or goodwill, is demeaning and insulting to the recipient and is simply another type of victimization. Certainly the benefactor functions from a position of superiority and, furthermore, charity is dependent upon the goodwill of the benefactor (Alder, Wright, & Ulicny, 1991). Stated another way, benevolence is dependent upon the generosity and kindness of the benefactor. The benefactor may or may not decide to give. Furthermore, the benefactor is free to ration the charity, both the amount and the timing of the charity. For example, when money is acquired through charitable fund-raising, it is never possible to accurately predict the amount of money that will be available. People may or may not decide to give. On an individual level, if a personal care attendant does not want to feed his employer, the employer (person with the disability) cannot do much about it. Parents of children who require special education have often had to resort to all sorts of fund-raising, such as bake sales. Parents whose children do not have disabilities are not required to bake brownies in order to ensure that their children receive appropriate public education. These children have the automatic right to education. Furthermore, if parents whose children do not have disabilities had to raise funds to pay for their children's public education, they would probably discontinue asking for charity and start advocating for their rights from the government. Often the public considers education for children with disabilities to be a conditional gift, or charity, rather than an automatic right.

Since the provision of charity is under the control of the benefactor, often the benefactor thinks that he or she knows what the recipient needs and wants. Rather than viewing people with disabilities as experts in their own needs, charitable people provide what they think people with disabilities need (even when their ideas are totally wrong).

The most straightforward example of this is an article that appeared in the September 2, 1990, issue of *Parade* magazine, written by Jerry Lewis, who does not have muscular dystrophy. Lewis wrote, "I know the courage it takes to get on the court with other cripples and play wheelchair basketball." Lewis pretended to write from the point of view of a person with a disability. "I'd like to play basketball like normal, healthy, vital and energetic people....When I sit back and think more rationally, I realize my life is half, so I must learn to do things halfway. I just have to learn to try to be good at being half a person" (Pelka, 1997, p. 301).

And, if the person is to receive help, he or she must submit to the benefactor's definition of him or her, almost to the point of "playing the part." Essentially, the benefactor has inordinate power over the charity receiver. An adult survivor of polio stated, "Those telethons featuring a semimaniacal Jerry Lewis are responded to by men and women who think they are *charitable*. Those well-meaning Shriners interviewed at halftime during the East-West football games they sponsor—let me remind you of the game's motto: "Strong legs run so that weak legs can walk"—do not believe that they have tampered with our reality" (Kriegel, 1982, p. 82).

Children who grew up believing that they needed charity were often "programmed" with learned helplessness. The message of charity, especially to a child, is "someone has to *give* this to you because you are not capable of *earning* it." Indeed, many adults in the disability rights movements feel resentment about the harmful effects of having been recipients of charity as children. They feel that they have paid a very high price for every dollar received.

Charity is polarizing—it is very clear who is the giver and who is the receiver. Generous people give to poor, pitiful, downtrodden, and unfortunate people. We have seen that, due to the rising rates of disability, many Americans are, and will be, in the ranks of persons with disabilities. Defenders of charity will state, "no one, with or without a disability, is completely independent and everyone needs help at one time or another." This is true, but people with disabilities are continuously in the position of accepting charity. Also, PWODs are more often the recipients of invisible and anonymous charity that maintains their dignity and privacy and does not require expressions of gratitude. Poster children, telethons, and neighborhood fund drives are considered by many in the Disability Rights Movement to be modern-day freak shows.

Individuals with disabilities have been protesting telethons since the 1970s. In 1976 and 1979, a disability rights group, Disabled in Action, picketed the United Cerebral Palsy Association, calling their telethons "demeaning and paternalistic shows which celebrate and encourage pity" (Pelka, 1997, p. 302). One of the most well-known charities for PWDs is Jerry Lewis' Labor Day marathon television program for raising funds for muscular dystrophy. Since 1991, a group calling themselves Jerry's Orphans has picketed local television stations that carry the program. Incidentally, Jerry's Orphans was founded by two former Muscular Dystrophy Association poster children, Mike Ervin and Cris Matthews.

Charity to people with disabilities has had a pervasive and insidious effect on our society. It is impossible to establish equal social status relationships, in the workplace or in social situations, when one group is always the benefactor and the other group is always the beneficiary. Morris (1991) stated, "Charities need to present disability in such a way as to encourage people to part with their money. The portrayal of a strong disabled [*sic*] person going about his/her life, and enjoying it, is not going to bring in any money" (p. 108). If the media portray people with disabilities as objects of charity, these individuals will have difficulty in establishing intimate, familial relationships with people who do not have disabilities. Scott-Parker (1989, as cited in Morris, 1991) viewed charities as objectifying PWDs. She stated, "As a study of advertising and disabled put it, charities tend to commission [advertising campaigns] as though they owned their particular 'model' of disabled person, in much the same way that Ford owns Fiesta cars. The charity is assumed to have a similar expert authority, enhanced by unimpeachable motives, and can therefore present its product to the market in any way it sees fit" (Morris, 1991, p. 109).

Charities are businesses. A few charities are big businesses, and many professional, salaried people "live off" charity in that their jobs, their salaries, and their professional identities are dependent upon (1) the existence of pitiful, unfortunate people, and (2) the generosity of others. Albrecht, in his book *The Disability Business* (1992) presented a chart (p. 171) that lists nine large American charities, their 1986 dollar figure, and percentage of these four categories: (1) their total intake, (2) the cost of overhead, (3) the cost of fund-raising activities, and (4) the total payout. Those organizations listed on this chart that seek to assist PWDs are March of Dimes, the American Cancer Society, the American Lung Society, the National Easter Seal Society, and Disabled American Veterans. Albrecht's graphic representation of these charitable organizations shows that overhead costs, which include the salaries of professional workers, vary. For example, the organization World Hunger Year spent 30 percent of its funds on overhead and paid out only 43 percent to its recipients. In contrast, the American Cancer Society used only 7 percent for overhead and paid out 87 percent to its recipients. Albrecht included the column of "fund-raising costs" in order to distinguish between those administrative costs, which include salaries, from those costs that are necessary in order to raise the funds.

Charity given to one group and not to other groups can create factions within the disability community. Factionalizing the disability community can undermine efforts of advocating for civil rights and raising public awareness. The most clear-cut example of this is televised telethons that raise huge amounts of money for a single type of disability. One writer has termed this "brand awareness" in terms of types of disabilities (Campbell, 1990, cited in Morris, 1991, p. 110). Anne Finger (1993) observed, "but each individual charity must compete with other charities for the 'charitable dollar.' Thus, charity advertising aims at simultaneously creating an image of 'its' disease or impairment and of that particular charity as the custodian/savior/earthly representation of all those with that dreaded impairment" (p. 29). Further, benefactors probably do not fully value the objects of their charity. There are no expectations of the recipients other than to be appropriately grateful. Liachowitz (1988) summarized: "Thus, the many handicapped [sic] people whose physical disorder is permanent remain in a position of indebtedness—a position that probably accounts for at least some portion of their socially conferred devaluation" (p. 11).

Also, the clear message of much charitable fund-raising is that the disability must be eradicated. Rarely is any consideration given to improving the quality of life for those who have the disability. The argument can also be made that it is the benefactor who "needs" the charity more than the beneficiary. Finally, recipients of charity must be grateful for whatever they can get. (Often benefactors are irritated if the recipients are not appropriately and sufficiently grateful.) This simply reinforces the power relationship between those with disabilities and those without disabilities. Giving charity comes from a position of superiority and gratitude comes from a position of inferiority. Charity can "objectify" the recipients. Society "needs" objects of charity. The objectifying of people with disabilities is clearly seen in the poster children. (There are never "poster adults" because adults have the ability to fight the objectification. And the public's sympathy would not be as aroused as it is for sweet, innocent, lovable children. Although, according to Shapiro (1993), some adults resent having been poster children.) Everybody feels good when they give to "Jerry's kids." Charity allows the benefactor to defend his or her privileges to him- or herself and to the public (Allport, 1986). However, upon closer scrutiny, people with disabilities want the rights and responsibilities of citizens, not charity. It is no coincidence that Labor Day (the same day that the Jerry Lewis muscular dystrophy telethon is held) was chosen for the "Onarollathon." The "Onarollathon," sponsored by Disability Talk Radio, raised funds for the Literacy Volunteers of America, an organization that helps adults learn to read. Radio host Greg Smith, who has muscular dystrophy, stated, "I know in my heart that our community, people with disabilities, care about important social issues, beyond those that directly impact us. We are a part of a powerful civil rights movement that can create positive change, which is why we are joining forces to help advance another great cause. On this particular weekend when people with disabilities are depicted as hopeless objects of pity, we want to deliver the message that we are important builders of this society."

Preferential Treatment

Like charity, preferential treatment is demeaning and insulting to the individual it is designed to help. Like charity, preferential treatment is also often thought to be a positive response. Preferential treatment for people with disabilities can include such things as hiring preferences, promotion preferences, lowering standards, granting admission to schools solely on the basis of disability, and applying differing standards.

The Americans with Disabilities Act (ADA) does not mandate preferential treatment for people with disabilities. It does not require the hiring, promotion, or admission of unqualified people. Nor does the ADA mandate quotas in jobs or schools. The ADA does mandate accommodations and provision of opportunities to compete for qualified people with disabilities.

Preferential treatment and charity are thought, perhaps at an unconscious level, to be an appropriate compensation, or redress, for the well-documented history of prejudice and discrimination experienced by people with disabilities. Past discrimination can never be fully redressed or compensated. Most people with disabilities do not want, or need, preferential treatment, and furthermore, the *public perception* of preferential treatment may further undermine the position of people with disabilities. If the public thinks that people receive "freebies" and "perks" simply because they are members of a designated group, resentment and factional rivalry will result. The perception of preferential treatment often results in cries of reverse discrimination. Further, there are those who would say, "I am not personally responsible for the prejudice and discrimination experienced by people with disabilities, so why should I have to make amends?"

Preferential treatment communicates, in a not very subtle way, that people with disabilities really are not capable of competing with others who do not have disabilities. The individual is being told that he or she truly is inferior and does not have the ability to be successful on his or her own merit. Preferential treatment for people with disabilities is a fairly common occurrence and, in the long run, usually does not have positive results for the individual. Eventually, standards are upheld, honest feedback is given, and the individual must, at a later date, be judged according to widely accepted standards. For example, someone who is admitted to medical school because he or she is a member of a certain group (disability, gender, or racial/ ethnic group) must graduate from medical school. Simply thinking in terms of the individual, it does this individual little good, and perhaps much harm, to have standards lowered in order that he or she be allowed to enter medical school, only to be "flunked out" later.

Preferential treatment of a person with a disability often results in excusing the individual from widely held standards or expectations. Such indulgence and exemption from standards are seen in ideas such as "Children with disabilities should not be disciplined" or, at minimum, "Parents of children with disabilities should be less strict than other parents." Even as adults, PWDs may be sheltered or protected from life's demands, such as working or managing the disability. In the next chapter, we will discuss the high rates of substance abuse among PWDs, and we will learn that one of the factors is the enabling behavior of PWODs who, out of pity or something else, assist PWDs in obtaining drugs or knowingly choose to ignore the PWD's substance abuse. Such enabling is another form of preferential treatment based on the premise that PWDs should not be held to standards. Preferential treatment of PWDs does not lead to positive results either for the PWDs or for society as a whole.

Compensation and Benefits

Compensation to PWDs includes pensions, insurance benefits, such as workers' compensation and Social Security Disability Insurance (SSDI), and private insurance benefits. Implicit in the assumption of compensation is the idea that no further expectations are required of the individual and, because he or she has documented or proven that he or she has a disability, the individual will receive a monthly check. Also, the idea that the individual has somehow earned the right to benefits is also part of the rationale behind compensating PWDs. Supplemental Security Income (SSI) program, created in 1972, is another form of compensation to PWDs, but it is not based on the premise that the individual has worked and thus "paid into the system." Instead, SSI is a sort of "safety net" for people who have failed to qualify for SSDI because they have not worked. SSI also has a "needs test" that requires the applicant to prove financial need. However, SSDI, workers' compensation insurance, private insurance funds, and military veterans' benefits for disability all consider that the individual has "contributed" to the system and therefore is eligible for benefits. Most compensation schemes do not include individuals with congenital disabilities simply because it is thought that these people never had the opportunity to contribute. (Of course, these congenital disabilities must be sufficiently severe and/or multiple that the individual is unable to work.)

The public purse pays individuals who have acquired disabilities through participating in socially valued activities such as work and war and for whom there is no possibility of returning to work. Often, "in-kind" benefits, such as Medicare and Medicaid, or subsidized housing are included in the benefits. For some PWDs, affordable medical care and medications and vouchers "documenting" a disability may be complicated, but after the disability has been proven, the compensator (government, military, or private insurance company) pays the PWD. Society now feels that it has fulfilled its responsibility to PWDs. And, the PWD knows that he or she has contributed to some sort of "scheme," which has provided the benefits and therefore does not consider the benefits to be charity. Some have conceptualized the relationship between compensator and compensatee as "We'll send you a check if you keep out of our sight" and "I get a check every month simply because I have a label (disability)." There is some truth to this.

First, compensation schemes often have built-in financial disincentives that often make it difficult for the individual to return to work even if accommodations for the disability are provided. Simply stated, the PWD, if he or she were to become employed, would lose the financial benefits. Therefore, there is no economic advantage to accepting minimum wage jobs, especially for individuals who have high costs associated with the management of the disability and/or individuals who have many dependents. Thus, the PWD is caught in a double bind: He or she cannot "afford" to work and, furthermore, he or she is stereotyped as lazy and unmotivated. Policy makers are working to dismantle this system of disincentives, developing strategies that will allow PWDs to work and still guarantee their benefits, especially their medical benefits. The government has the difficult task of providing for those who truly need assistance and, at the same time, not sabotaging a work-based society.

Second, there are those people who do "milk the system." This means that these individuals are capable of working, but they prefer to receive benefits. The most extreme examples of these types of people are seen on television newsmagazine programs where private detectives with video cameras "catch" people with severe back injuries, which supposedly prevent them from working, performing all sorts of recreational activities, such as skiing, painting the house, or hang gliding. Naturally, the public is outraged that there are people who would take advantage of the system. (Television viewers choose to watch these types of programs that may present a one-sided and distorted view of disability issues.) However, most experts consider individuals who fake disabilities (malingerers) to be relatively rare.

Another shortcoming of compensation systems is the difficulty in the determination or diagnosis of a disability. Some applicants are skilled in seeking out those physicians who have a reputation for defining disability very broadly, and insurance companies and government agencies seek to offset this strategy by requesting second opinions from physicians who have reputations for rarely giving disability diagnoses. The determination of disability process can become both complicated and adversarial.

The system of public disability insurance has developed in a patchwork manner due to (1) most public insurance programs, with the exception of programs for federal employees, are administered by the states, and there is wide variation in both the definition of disability and in the amounts of compensation from state to state, and (2) the desire to care for those who truly need assistance often conflicts with the need to keep as many individuals in the labor market as possible.

Interestingly, Liachowitz (1988) recounted that during the American Revolutionary War of 1776, both soldiers and sailors who were judged to be "invalids" were required to stay on active duty if they were "found to be capable of doing guard or garrison duty...or doing any other duty on board the navy or any department thereof, shall be liable to be so employed" (p. 25). Also, "invalid" sailors and soldiers were required to teach various subjects to young soldiers and sailors. Early in American history, military veterans with disabilities were encouraged (or required) to return to work because the military had broadly defined work to include noncombat jobs and because the military recognized the value of these "invalid" sailors and soldiers. Ironically, the word "invalid" means without value! Implicit in this requirement was the assumption that these veterans were capable of making valuable contributions.

CIVIL RIGHTS FOR PWDs

In this section, look for—

▶ *the antecedents of the Disability Rights Movement*
▶ *a discussion that civil rights for Americans are not based on monetary considerations*

The three responses to PWDs of (1) charity, (2) preferential treatment, and (3) compensation are all based on the inherent inferiority of the individual. That is to say, in order for an individual to receive charity, preferential treatment, or compensation, he or she must first be declared inferior, subordinate, and needy. Of course, most would be quick to add that the inferiority of the individual is due to a process of nature (the onset of the disability) for which the individual is not personally responsible. In spite of this, inferiority is the basis of the entitlement.

Furthermore, each of these three responses is viewed as a corrective, virtuous, and benevolent action of the larger society. Rarely do proponents of these types of programs consider that self-empowerment, self-determination, and dignity are not possible for PWDs in these types of systems. In addition, much of the discussion of any response toward Americans with disabilities very quickly arrives at the money question. Costs of workplace and transportation accommodations, costs of care and treatment, and all the other costs can be, and are, calculated. In contrast, the national discussion preceding the passage of the Civil Rights Act of 1964 rarely, if ever, mentioned money or costs. For example, the Civil Rights Act assisted in the deseg-regation of public schools (building upon *Brown v. Board of Education*). Such desegregation must have been expensive, and yet there was little, if any, discussion of putting a dollar figure on the right of American children, regardless of their skin color, to integrated education.

Civil rights for Americans are not accorded on the basis of monetary cost, although the ADA does take into consideration the costs to employers of accommodations. Civil rights for PWDs, as outlined in the ADA, are accorded on the basis of American citizenship. Ensuring, by the power of the law, that all important benefits and opportunities of citizenship are extended to PWDs shifts the responsibility for disability issues from the individual to the American nation. The "problem" of disability, as the ADA states clearly and at length, is society's prejudicial attitudes and actions. Therefore, the solution for the "disability problem" is the responsibility of the American nation, and the first step is the passage of national legislation. Parallel with the rationale behind the Civil Rights Act of 1964, the intent of the ADA is to eradicate prejudice, discrimination, segregation, and reduced opportunities for PWDs.

Civil rights for anyone are individually empowering since these rights are an automatic entitlement and legally protected. The individual does not have to depend on the goodwill of others in order to receive benefits. The ADA, or any other legislation, cannot redress past injustices. However, the ADA states that the status quo (in 1990) was not going to continue, meaning a certain group of American citizens had been intentionally excluded from employment, education, housing, transportation, public buildings, and telecommunications. Further, the responsibility for this disenfranchisement was the collective responsibility of the American people, both for allowing it and for stopping it. Centuries of discrimination and prejudice cannot be redressed, but discrimination and prejudice against PWDs can be stopped.

WHAT IS JUSTICE?

In this section, look for—

> ► *why standardization is important if everyone is to receive the same treatment*
> ► *why the standard of evaluation has been white, middle-class males without disabilities*
> ► *the argument that accommodations cannot be provided for PWDs because everyone else does not receive these accommodations*
> ► *the definition of a meritocracy*
> ► *the relationship between Social Darwinism and meritocracies*
> ► *why a "disability-blind" society is not necessarily good*
> ► *how a society determines which needs are legitimate and which needs are not*
> ► *the concept of "equal outcome"*

Basically, there are three types of justice: (1) Everybody receives equal treatment, (2) everybody receives what he or she has earned, and (3) everybody receives what he or she needs.

Everybody Receives Equal Treatment

This philosophy of justice is based on accurate standards and guidelines that are upheld for everyone. The word *equal* is used in this case to mean "the same." Standardization is very important if everyone is to receive equal treatment. For a long time, the standard of evaluation in the United States, according to many authors, was the white, middle-class male without disabilities. Naturally, not everyone who applied for entrance to schools or for jobs or anything else met all these criteria. In fact, it is debatable whether the numerical majority was ever comprised of individuals who met all these criteria. Despite this, the rationale was not that everyone or even the majority of people were white, middle-class males without disabilities, but that everyone should *compete* with this group. Therefore, testing and evaluation procedures were validated on norm groups comprised of individuals who met the criteria (white, middle-class males without disabilities). Application, admission, promotion, tenure, and termination policies were developed with this standard of evaluation group in mind. Administrative policies could be very clear, straightforward, and without exception. Another advantage was the applicability of the standards and rules to *everyone*. All of these examples are termed "institutional" policies and, until very recently, these institutional policies were not often questioned or challenged. The idea of equal treatment for everybody appeared to be justice.

This type of justice chooses equal opportunity, but also understands that there will not be equal outcomes. For example, everybody is free to apply to Harvard, but not all applicants are accepted.

When teachers or employers argue that they cannot provide certain accommodations for PWDs because they "cannot provide the same thing for everybody else," they are invoking the "everybody receives equal treatment" view of justice. Of course, not all students need (or want) their textbooks in Braille. But, if we follow the "everyone receives equal, meaning same, treatment" logic, then the student who is blind cannot have Braille textbooks because the other students do not have Braille textbooks.

Everybody Receives What He or She Has Earned

In this view of justice, everything is earned, including both rewards and penalties. This type of society is called a "meritocracy." There are some people who are clearly superior because of intelligence, motivation, skills, or other personal characteristics, and they should be able to enjoy more freedom, more justice, and more rights. Conversely, there are some people who are inferior because they lack the requisite personal characteristics to earn their rewards. Further, regardless of the situation in which either of these two types of people (superior or inferior) are placed, the inferior will fail and the superior will rise to the top.

Much of the rationale for this view of justice is derived from Darwinism and Social Darwinism, both of which were based on "survival of the fittest." Social Darwinism was also based on "success of the fittest." Any attempts at "distributive justice" (reallocation of rights and resources) will fail because, as stated before, some people are inferior and some people are superior. If we give the inferior people rights or welfare assistance, they would not know what to do with them and they would end up squandering both. Thus, the inequities in the system are deserved. The superior people do not have to feel guilty about their privileges or feel sorry about the plight of the inferior people. The inferior people should not be jealous of the rights and privileges of the superior people because they could have the same rights and privileges if they would only exert the effort. Social inequities are totally irrelevant to government policy.

Under this type of justice, PWDs are thought to have acquired their disabilities through just plain bad luck; but it is *their* bad luck. Disabilities are seen as deviance and inferiority because this type of justice assumes that the world is a predictable and moral place. If superior people consider their superiority to be justly earned, then they also consider others' inferiority to be justly deserved. Sanctimonious pity is enough for PWDs, and in some societies, such as Nazi Germany, PWDs, because of their (perceived) total lack of merit, were efficiently murdered.

Naturally, when outlined in such a straightforward way, this type of justice makes us uncomfortable, violating our values of compassion and equal opportunity for all. Further, a meritocracy depends on accurate definition and measurement of merit. The most astute authorities cannot agree on what "merit" is. "Inferiority" must also be defined and, in the case of PWDs, much (if not all) of the inferiority is the result of society's handicapping, prejudice, and discrimination.

Everybody Gets What He or She Needs

This view of justice takes individual differences into consideration and also believes that by allowing individuals rights and opportunities, the group as a whole benefits. Of the three types of justice discussed here, the ADA is based on the premise that justice is ensuring that everybody has what he or she needs. The long list of court litigation of ADA issues demonstrates that this type of justice can be complicated and difficult to enact. How does a society determine which needs are legitimate and which needs are not?

Such a view of justice may appear contrary to those who argue that the United States should be "disability-blind" (or "color-blind" or "gender-blind"). Inherent in this view is the idea that there are some groups that have stronger claims for resources, including PWDs. This can result in many groups making claims for resources and accommodations. Where do we stop? But, if we accept that there are biological and functional realities to the experience of disability, then accommodations are both necessary and legitimate. Further, as we have learned in this chapter, if society gives PWDs their civil rights and necessary accommodations, society will benefit economically. In addition, and perhaps more important, are the benefits of having a diverse society.

This view of justice is linked with the "equal outcome" concept, meaning that, if everyone were to receive what he or she needs from infancy, all types of people would succeed in gaining the rewards of society. Everyone would be earning the same reward, at the same standards, but with differing accommodations. All types of people would graduate from Harvard, become movie stars, and become President of the United States.

In-Class Videos

- View the video *Face First* by Mike Grundmann of Fanlight Productions. In this video, several individuals discuss societal reaction to their disability. Discuss the common issues with which each of these individuals must deal. Include a discussion of the relationships between facial disfigurement and the lack of functional limitations. Which of the sources of stigma apply in this type of disability?
- View the 28-minute video *Images in Media*, available from Films for the Humanities and Sciences, P.O. Box 2053, Princeton, NJ 08543–2053 (www.films.com). "The pictures in our heads that define who we are and help us neatly categorize others are increasingly shaped by the newspaper, magazine, film, and TV images that bombard our senses....This program is a behind-the-scenes look at the media's image-makers from the first photographers to today's Madison Avenue wizards, and asks some disturbing questions about the self-selected few who hold a distorted mirror up to our society." Discuss how the media's idea of beauty might be viewed by PWDs.
- View the 51-minute video *Children of Gaia: Living with Physical Challenges* by Films for the Humanities and Sciences. "Powerful personal narratives, plus a history of human deformity traced from ancient times through World War II, create a comprehensive and balanced picture of those whose lives have been altered by undeveloped limbs, facial disfigurement, or dwarfism" (producer's description). Discuss the sources of prejudice and discrimination shown in this video.
- View the 19-minute video *Fetal Alcohol Syndrome and Other Drug Use During Pregnancy* by Films for the Humanities and Sciences. The producers describe this video: "This program profiles an eight-year-old boy born with FAS (fetal alcohol syndrome), showing how alcohol enters the bloodstream of the fetus. It describes the common features of children with FAS and their learning disabilities. The program also illustrates in detail how cocaine affects the fetus."

Learning Activities

1. Read *Expecting Adam: A True Story of Birth, Rebirth, and Everyday Magic* (1999) by Martha Beck. This is a memoir of a woman and her husband who learn that the child they are expecting has Down syndrome. Much of the book relates how the Harvard community—both students and faculty—regarded the opportunity to earn an Ivy League graduate degree (which Beck gives up) to be more important than the birth of a baby with Down syndrome.
2. Write a paper that explains this statement: If PWDs are accorded (1) civil rights, (2) full social integration, (3) all necessary treatment and assistive technology, and (4) capable and ethical personal care attendants (if needed), PWODs would lose many of their own fears of acquiring a disability.
3. Read *Our Guys* (1998) by Bernard Lefkowitz. This book tells the true story of the 1989 Glen Ridge (New Jersey) rape case in which a group of teenage athletes lured a girl who was mentally retarded into a basement and gang

raped her with a broomstick and baseball bat. Write a short paper on the different levels of status and prestige ascribed to the male athletes and to the girl. Discuss your perceptions of the boys' justification of their crime and the town's reaction to the crime. Why is the title of the book *Our Guys*? Why isn't the title *Our Girl*?

4. Read the bestseller *The Broken Cord* (1993) by Michael Dorris. Dorris, a Native American anthropologist, adopted a son with fetal alcohol syndrome (FAS). Before becoming the father of a child with a congenital disability, Dorris was opposed to forced sterilization and advocated for reproductive rights for everyone. Indeed, Dorris' professional work had, up to this point, centered on the genocide of Native American people. However, coping with the FAS of his son, Dorris was tempted to advocate the very practices that he had so vehemently opposed, such as forced sterilization for pregnant women who refuse to stop drinking. Write a paper outlining the changes in Dorris' thinking.

Writing Experience

Write a paper that responds to one of the seven "bullet" questions listed at the beginning of this chapter.

References

Albrecht, G. L. (1992). *The disability business: Rehabilitation in America.* Newbury Park, CA: Sage.

Alder, A. B., Wright, B. A., & Ulicny, G. R. (1991). Fundraising portrayals of people with disabilities: Donations and attitudes. *Rehabilitation Psychology, 36,* 231–240.

Allport, G. W. (1986). *The nature of prejudice* (25th anniversary ed.). Reading, MA: Addison-Wesley.

Antonak, R. F. (1980). A hierarchy of attitudes toward exceptionality. *Journal of Special Education, 14,* 231–241.

Asch, A., & Fine, M. (1997). Nurturance, sexuality, and women with disabilities: The example of women and literature. In L. J. Davis (Ed.). *The disability studies reader* (pp. 241–259). New York: Routledge.

Augé, M., & Herzlich, C. (Eds.). (1995). *The meaning of illness: Anthropology, history, and sociology.* Luxembourg: Harwood Academic Publishers.

Belgrave, F. Z. (1984). The effectiveness of strategies for increasing social interaction with a physically disabled person. *Journal of Applied Social Psychology, 14,* 147–161.

Belgrave, F. Z., & Mills, J. (1981). Effect upon desire for social interaction with a physically disabled person of mentioning the disability in different contexts. *Journal of Applied Social Psychology, 40,* 211–222.

Berkowitz, E. D. (1987). *Disability policy: America's programs for the handicapped.* Cambridge, England: Cambridge University.

Bickenbach, J. E. (1993). *Physical disability and social policy.* Toronto: University of Toronto.

Bishop, D. S. (Ed.). (1980). *Behavioral problems and the disabled: Assessment and management.* Baltimore: Williams & Wilkins.

Bogdan, R., & Taylor, S. (1987). Toward a sociology of acceptance: The other side of the study of deviance. *Social Policy, Fall,* 34–39.

Bordieri, J. E., & Drehmer, D. E. (1988). Causal attribution and hiring recommendations for disabled job applicants. *Rehabilitation Psychology, 33,* 239–247.

Bowe, F. (1990). Employment and people with disabilities: Challenges for the nineties. *OSERS News in Print, 3,* 2–6.

Buss, D. M. (1999). *Evolutionary psychology: The new science of the mind.* Boston: Allyn & Bacon.

Charlton, J. I. (1998). *Nothing about us without us: Disability oppression and empowerment.* Berkeley, CA: University of California.

Cockerham, W. C. (1998). *Medical sociology* (7th ed.). Upper Saddle River, NJ: Prentice Hall.

Coleman, L. M. (1997). Stigma: An enigma demystified. In L. J. Davis (Ed.). *The disability studies reader* (pp. 216–231). New York: Routledge.

Couser, G. T. (1997). *Recovering bodies: Illness, disability, and life writing.* Madison, WI: University of Wisconsin.

Crewe, N. M. (1980). The difficult patient. In D. S. Bishop (Ed.). *Behavior problems and the disabled: Assessment and management* (pp. 98–119). Baltimore: Williams & Wilkins.

DeLoach, C., & Greer, B. G. (1981). *Adjustment to severe disability: A metamorphosis.* New York: McGraw-Hill.

Dembo, T., Leviton, G. L., & Wright, B. A. (1956). Adjustment to misfortune: A problem of social-psychological rehabilitation. *Artificial Limbs, 3,* 4–62.

Druss, R. G. (1995). *The psychology of illness: In sickness and in health.* Washington, DC: American Psychiatric Press.

Etcoff, N. (1999). *Survival of the prettiest: The science of beauty.* Cambridge, MA: Harvard University Press.

Fiedler, L. (1978). *Freaks: Myths and images of the secret self.* New York: Simon & Schuster.

Films for the Humanities and Sciences. (1999). *Autism: The child who couldn't play* [Film]. (Available from Films for the Humanities and Sciences, P.O. Box 2053, Princeton, NJ 08543–2053, 800–257–5126; www.films.com)

Finger, A. (1993). Toward a theory of radical disability photography. *Disability Rag, November,* 29–31.

Fowler, C. A., & Wadsworth, J. S. (1991). Individualism and equality: Critical values in North American culture and the impact on disability. *Journal of Applied Rehabilitation Counseling, 22,* 19–23.

Fox, K. R. (Ed.). (1997). *The physical self: From motivation to well-being.* Champaign, IL: Human Kinetics.

Furnham, A., & Pendred, J. (1983). Attitudes toward the mentally and physically disabled. *British Journal of Medical Psychology, 56,* 179–187.

Goffman, E. (1963). *Stigma: Notes on the management of spoiled identity.* Englewood Cliffs, NJ: Prentice Hall.

Goodyear, R. K. (1983). Patterns of counselors' attitudes toward disability groups. *Rehabilitation Counseling Bulletin, 26,* 181–184.

Gordon, E. D., Minnes, P. M., & Holden, R. R. (1990). The structure of attitudes towards persons with a disability when specific disability and context are concerned. *Rehabilitation Psychology, 35,* 79–90.

Harasymiw, S. J., Horne, M. D., & Lewis, S. C. (1976). A longitudinal study of disability group acceptance. *Rehabilitation Literature, 37,* 98–102.

Hayes, S. C., Barlow, D. H., & Nelson-Gray, R. G. (1999). *The scientist-practitioner: Research and accountability in the age of managed care* (2nd ed.). Needham Heights, MA: Allyn & Bacon.

Henderson, G., & Bryan, W. V. (1997). *Psychosocial aspects of disability* (2nd ed.). Springfield, IL: Charles C Thomas.

Higgins, P. C. (1992). *Making disability: Exploring the social transformation of human variation.* Springfield, IL: Charles C Thomas.

Horne, M. D., & Ricciardo, J. L. (1988). Hierarchy of response to handicaps. *Psychological Reports, 62,* 83–86.

Hubbard, R. (1997). Abortion and disability: Who should and who should not inhabit the world? In L. J. Davis (Ed.). *The disability studies reader* (pp. 187–200). New York: Routledge.

Imrie, R. (1996). *Disability and the city: International perspectives.* New York: St. Martin's Press.

Jones, E. E., Farina, A., Hastorf, A. H., Markus, H., Miller, D. T., & Scott, R. A. (1984). *Social stigma: The psychology of marked relationships.* New York: W. H. Freeman.

Jones. R. L. (1974). The hierarchical structure of attitudes toward the exceptional. *Exceptional Children, 40,* 430–435.

Kravetz, S., Katz, S., & Albez, D. (1994). Attitudes toward Israeli war veterans with disabilities: Combat versus noncombat military service and responsibility for the disability. *Rehabilitation Counseling Bulletin, 37,* 371–379.

Kriegel, L. (1982). Claiming the self: The cripple as American male. In M. G. Eisenberg, C. Griggins, & R. J. Duval (Eds.). *Disabled people as second-class citizens* (pp. 52–63). New York: Springer.

Landers, A. (1999, October 6). Smokes raise insurance for all. *The Herald Journal*, p. 15.

Lane, H. (1993). Cochlear implants: Their cultural and historical meaning. In J. V. Van Cleve (Ed.). *Deaf history unveiled: Interpretations from the new scholarship* (pp. 272–291). Washington, DC: Gallaudet University Press.

Langlois, J. H., & Roggman, L. A. (1990). Attractive faces are only average. *Psychological Science, 1,* 115–121.

Lehr, D. H., & Brinckerhoff, J. (1996). Bases of practice for young children with disabilities who challenge the system. In D. H.Lehr & F. Brown (Eds.). *People with disabilities who challenge the system* (pp. 3–22). Baltimore: Brookes.

Leinhardt, G., & Pallay, A. (1982). Restrictive educational settings: Exile or haven. *Review of Educational Research, 52,* 557–558.

Liachowitz, C. H. (1988). *Disability as a social construct: Legislative roots.* Philadelphia: University of Pennsylvania.

Livneh, H. (1991). On the origins of negative attitudes toward people with disabilities. In R. P. Marinelli & A. E. Dell Orto (Eds.). *The psychological and social impact of disability* (3rd ed., pp. 181–196). New York: Springer.

Macgregor, F. C. (1951). Some psycho-social problems associated with facial deformities. *American Social Review, 16,* 629–638.

Marantz, P. R. (1990). Blaming the victim: The negative consequences of preventive medicine. *American Journal of Public Health, 80,* 1185–1187.

Mee, C. L. (1999). *A nearly normal life.* Boston: Little, Brown.

Miller, J. (1988). Personal statement: Mechanisms for coping with the disability of a child—A mother's perspective. In P.W. Power, A.E. Dell Orto, & M.B. Gibbons (Eds.). *Family interventions throughout chronic illness and disability* (pp. 136–147). New York: Springer.

Morris, J. (1991). *Pride against prejudice: Transforming attitudes to disability.* Philadelphia: New Society.

Murphy, M. A. (1998). Rejection, stigma, and hope. *Psychiatric Rehabilitation Journal, 22,* 185–188.

Olshansky, S. (1965). Stigma: Its meaning and its problems for vocational rehabilitation agencies. *Rehabilitation Literature, 26,* 71–72.

Pelka, F. (1997). *The ABC-CLIO companion to the disability rights movement.* Santa Barbara, CA: ABC-CLIO.

Safilios-Rothschild, C. (1982). Social and psychological parameters of friendship and intimacy for disabled people. In M. G. Eisenberg, C. Griggins, & R. J. Duval (Eds.). *Disabled people as second-class citizens* (pp. 40–51). New York: Springer.

Safran, S. P. (1998). The first century of disability portrayal in film: An analysis of the literature. *Journal of Special Education, 31,* 467–479.

Scholar under fire for views on infanticide. (1999, October 2). *The Herald Journal*, pp. 2, 4.

Schroeder, F. (1997, March). Presentation given at the Annual Training Conference of the National Council on Rehabilitation Education/Rehabilitation Services Administration and Council of State Administrators of Vocational Rehabilitation, Washington, DC.

Schur, E. M. (1983). *Labeling women deviant: Gender, stigma, and social control.* Philadelphia: Temple University.

Shapiro, J. P. (1993). *No pity: People with disabilities forging a new civil rights movement.* New York: Times Book.

Sherrill, C. (1997). Disability, identity, and involvement in sport and exercise. In K. R. Fox (Ed.). *The physical self: From motivation to well-being* (pp. 257–286). Champaign, IL: Human Kinetics.

Shurka, E., & Katz, J. (1976). Evaluations of persons with disability: The influence of disability context and personal responsibility for the disability. *Rehabilitation Psychology, 23,* 65–71.

Sontag, S. (1978). *Illness as metaphor.* New York: Farrar, Strauss, & Giroux.

Tanenbaum, S. J. (1986). *Engineering disability: Public policy and compensatory technology.* Philadelphia: Temple University.

Thompson, T. (1982). Gaze toward the avoidance of the handicapped: A field experiment. *Journal of Nonverbal Behavior, 6,* 188–196.

Thorn, K. R., Hershenson, D. B., & Romney, A. K. (1994). Causal attribution factors in conceptions of disability. *Rehabilitation Counseling Bulletin, 37*, 315–331.

Tringo, J. L. (1970). The hierarchy of preference toward disability groups. *Journal of Special Education, 4*, 295–306.

Vermeji, G. (1997). *Privileged hands: A scientific life*. New York: Freeman.

Waitzkin, W. C. (1991). *The politics of medical encounters: How patients and doctors deal with social problems*. New Haven, CT: Yale University.

Walster, E. (1966). Assignment of responsibility for an accident. *Journal of Personality and Social Psychology, 3*, 73–79.

Wang, C. (1993). Culture, meaning, and disability: Injury prevention campaigns and the production of stigma. In M. Nagler (Ed.). *Perspectives on disability* (2nd ed., pp. 77–90). Palo Alto, CA: Health Markets Research.

Weiner, B., Perry, R. P., & Magnusson, J. (1988). An attributional analysis of reactions to stigmas. *Journal of Personality and Social Psychology, 55*, 738–748.

Wikler, D. (1987). Personal responsibility for illness. In D. Van De Veer & T. Regan (Eds.). *Health care ethics: An introduction* (pp. 326–358). Philadelphia: Temple University.

Wilson, J. (1999, October 20). Egg salesman defends web venture. *The Herald Journal*, pp. 1, 10.

Wright, B. A. (1960). *Physical disability: A psychological approach*. New York: Harper & Row.

Wright, B. A. (1988). Attitudes and the fundamental negative bias: Conditions and corrections. In H. E. Yuker (Ed.). *Attitudes toward persons with disabilities* (pp. 3–21). New York: Springer.

Yelin, E. (1989). Disabled concern: The social context of the work-disability problem. *The Milbank Quarterly, 67*, 114–165.

Zola, I. K. (1983). *Socio-medical inquiries: Recollections, reflections, and reconsiderations*. Philadelphia: Temple University.

Zola, I. K. (1991). Communication barriers between "the able-bodied" and "the handicapped." In R. P. Marinelli & A. E. Dell Orto (Eds.). *The psychological and social impact of disability* (pp. 157–164). New York: Springer.

Suggested Readings

Antonak, R. F., & Livneh, H. (1988). *The measurement of attitudes toward people with disabilities*. Springfield, IL: Charles C Thomas.

Bordieri, J. E. (1993). Self-blame attributions for disability and perceived client involvement in the vocational rehabilitation process. *Journal of Applied Rehabilitation Counseling, 24*(2), 3–7.

Dorris, M. (1989). *The broken cord*. New York: Harper.

Eisenberg, M. G. (1982). Disability as stigma. In M. G. Eisenberg, C. Griggins, & R. J. Duval (Eds.). *Disabled people as second-class citizens* (pp. 1–11). New York: Springer.

Eisenberg, M. G., Griggins, C., & Duval, R. J. (Eds.). (1982). *Disabled people as second-class citizens*. New York: Springer.

Harris, L. (1987). *The ICD survey II: Employing disabled Americans*. New York: Louis Harris.

Harris, L. (1994). *The ICD survey III: Employing disabled Americans*. New York: Louis Harris.

Harrison, J. (1987). *Severe physical disability: Responses to the challenges of care*. London: Cassell.

Watson, J. D. (1984). Talking about the best kept secret: Sexual abuse and children with disabilities. *Exceptional Parent, 14*(6), 15–20.

Whitney, C. R. (1993, January 19). Disabled Germans fear they'll be the next target. *The New York Times*, p. A3.

Chapter 5

The Effects of Prejudice and Discrimination

▶ Are disabilities perceived as difference or are disabilities perceived as deviance?
▶ Are PWDs "differently challenged"?
▶ Does society teach PWDs to think of themselves as inferior?
▶ Why have PWDs experienced more prejudice and discrimination than any other group in history?
▶ What is the difference between institutional handicapism and social handicapism?
▶ Can well-intentioned people be handicapping?
▶ What does this sentence mean? "The world is designed to further the purposes of PWODs."
▶ Do factors inherent in the disability itself lead to prejudice and discrimination?
▶ Why has the contact theory not worked in reducing prejudice and discrimination?
▶ Why are simulation exercises ineffective?
▶ How do PWODs (and society) pay for their prejudice and discrimination against PWDs?

ARE DISABILITIES VIEWED AS DIFFERENCE OR AS DEVIANCE?

In this section, look for—
    ▶ *how difference and diversity are considered to be positive*
    ▶ *how deviance is considered to be negative*
    ▶ *how, in reality, difference, diversity, and deviance do not have an inherent value component*
    ▶ *how society creates deviance*

Many differences among people are considered to be desirable, enriching, valuable, and strengthening to the larger group. We often use the positive word "diversity" to describe these valued differences. These types of differences and diversities usually do not have a hierarchical component. In other words, individuals who are diverse or have differences are considered to be equal to everyone else. Inherent in this notion of equality is the lack of a standard of evaluation or a widely accepted concept of a "norm." In Chapter 1, we discussed the concept of normalcy as a standard of evaluation and concluded that normality was both defined and measured/evaluated/assessed by the group in power.

If there is any hierarchical component applied to people who are different or diverse, these people are most often considered to be superior. Indeed, much of the media today plays upon our fascination with people whom we consider to not be like ourselves. For example, we like to see and hear about film stars and political figures, mostly because they are different from us. Society considers their differences to be desirable, enriching, and strengthening to the larger group. Such diversity and difference are considered to be positive, and while a relatively small portion of the larger society will ever attain such diversity or difference, we still admire and respect these few people who are different. These differences and diversity often translate into power and authority, which is conferred by society, and most people usually like to align themselves with power and authority.

Deviance, on the other hand, is considered to be socially undesirable, weakening to the larger group, and people who are labeled deviant are automatically considered to be inferior. People usually do not aspire to become labeled "deviant"; indeed, most individuals work very hard to avoid this label. People who exhibit differences that are labeled "deviant" are not considered to be assets to the larger group. Indeed, often "deviants" are thought of as "drains" or "burdens" to the group or, at minimum, not having much to contribute. Society tends to avoid, isolate, reject, and segregate people who are labeled as deviants. Also, "deviants" are often feared and invoke hostile reactions.

Of course, the accurate definition of deviance is simply differing from a norm. Chapter 1 presented two important ideas: (1) technically, the concepts of deviance, difference, and norms do not have an inherent value component—all of these concepts are neutral; they can be either good or bad, and (2) defining groups in power develop norms. When these two concepts are taken into consideration, it can be seen that deviance can also mean valuable, extraordinary, superior, and desirable. In addition, simply because societal norms have been in place for literally centuries, it is often easy to leap to the conclusion that these norms are both immutable (unchanging) and completely valid and appropriate. When we pause to think about societal norms, without which judgments of differences and deviance would be impossible, we can see that norms and standards do evolve and change, and often these standards and norms are arbitrary because they are based on the fears, anxieties, and false assumptions of the defining group (Schur, 1971, 1979, 1983).

Deviance, therefore, is not within the individual but rather, deviance is a judgment of the dominant, defining segment of society (Gellman, 1959; Goffman, 1963, 1997). Without social comparison, there can be no judgment of deviance. Or stated in another way: Both deviance and normalcy are defined in relation to each other; thus, sociologists term deviance-labeling an interactionist theory. One sociologist (Becker, 1963) clearly explained:

> Social groups create deviance by making the rules whose infraction constitutes defiance, and by applying these rules to particular people and labeling them as outsiders. From this point of view, deviance is not a quality of the person...but rather a consequence of the application by others of rules and sanctions to an "offender." The deviant is one to whom that label has been successfully applied (p. 9).

Most, if not all, deviance is forced upon the individual. Certainly the individual does not choose to carry this label nor to be subjected to the resulting prejudice and discrimination. Often his or her family and marriage partner are labeled "deviant by association" even when these family members do not exhibit the "deviant" characteristics. Indeed, most individuals considered by others to be deviant do not think of themselves in this way. Furthermore, occasionally, individuals who are stigmatized in this way are not aware of their forced status of being viewed as deviant.

Any attribute can be labeled deviant. Age, racial/ethnic group, nationality, income level, religion, political affiliation, sexual orientation, and gender are all examples of attributes that have been, and to some extent still are, labeled as deviant (Goffman, 1963). However, with all of these examples of types of attributes, the deviancy and stigmatization ascribed to individuals who fit these categories have not been as widespread and pervasive as the deviancy and stigmatization ascribed to PWDs. Reviewing the list of often-stigmatized attributes, we can see that there are environments in which they can escape these negative judgments. For example, individuals of certain races or nationalities are not stigmatized in their native country or in their homes with family members who, most likely, share the same racial/ethnic/cultural identity. For PWDs, there are few such environments.

ARE PWDs "DIFFERENTLY CHALLENGED"?

In this section, look for—

- ▶ *why the expression "differently challenged" is trivializing and demeaning to PWDs*
- ▶ *the relationship between stigmatization and deviancy*
- ▶ *why the medical model of disability has contributed to defining PWDs as deviant*

In the past, have PWDs been labeled as different or deviant? Are PWDs considered to be different or deviant today? Disability scholars have shown that PWDs were, and continue to be, labeled as deviant. Most PWDs consider it incorrect to use the expression "differently challenged" for individuals with disabilities. Difference, as we have seen, is a positive term, and many PWDs do not consider their treatment by PWODs to be positive. The use of the word "differently" denies and trivializes the history (and the current experience) of PWDs being labeled deviant and inferior.

Cheryl Wade (1997) wrote a poem entitled *I Am Not One of The*. The first line is "I am not one of the physically challenged" and another line is "I am not one of the differently abled." Wade organized the stanzas of the poem around each of the trivializing and ill-informed labels that PWODs ascribe to the disability experience. Indeed, the title of the poem clearly shows the poem's purpose and the author's insistence that she be allowed to define and describe herself and her disability experience.

Friedson (1965) stated that a disability "is an imputation of difference from others; more particularly an imputation of *undesirable* difference. By definition, then, a person who is said to be handicapped [*sic*] is so defined because he [*sic*] deviates from what he himself or others believe to be normal or appropriate" (p. 72).

Higgins (1992), in his book *Making Disability: Exploring the Social Transformation of Human Variation,* described the relationship between disability labels/identities and societal norms: "Differences reside in the different persons rather than in relation to norms embedded in prevailing institutions. It is also presumed that the status quo is natural and good" (p. 230). Lerita Coleman (1997) used the term "stigmatization" to describe society's tendency to ascribe deviancy to PWDs: "To further clarify the definition of stigma, one must differentiate between "undesired differentness" that is likely to lead to feeling of stigmatization and actual forms of stigmatization. *It appears that stigmatization occurs only when the social control component is imposed, or when the undesired differentness leads to some restriction in physical and social mobility and access to opportunities that allow an individual to develop his or her potential* [italics added]" (p. 227).

Lennard Davis (1997) used the word "undesirable" instead of "deviance." In the following excerpt from his book *The Disability Studies Reader,* Davis described the tendency to "lump" all people considered to be deviant, or undesirable, into one category: "The problem for people with disabilities was that eugenicists tended to group together all allegedly 'undesirable' traits. So, for example, criminals, the poor, and people with disabilities might be mentioned in the same breath. A leading figure defined the "unfit" as follows: "the habitual criminal, the professional tramp, the tuberculous, the insane, the mentally defective, the alcoholic, the diseased from birth or from excess" (p. 17).

The only factor that people with disabilities have in common with the other types of individuals listed is the deviance and inferiority ascribed to them by the larger society. Davis (1997) judged the results of "lumping" PWDs with these other types of people: "The loose association between what we would now call disability and criminal activity...sexual license, and so on established a legacy that the people with disabilities are still having trouble living down....The conflation of disability with depravity expressed itself in the formulation of 'defective class'" (p. 18).

Deviance also implies shame and blame, holding the "deviant" individual responsible both for his or her own devaluation and for many of society's problems. PWDs historically have been viewed as scapegoats. "People with disabilities have represented a convenient group to blame for a number of problems" (Covey, 1998, p. 12). Thus, the medical model of disability has contributed to the tendency to label PWDs as deviants simply because this model considers the "problem" to be totally within the individual. Rather than acknowledging society's judgments and evaluations as the "problem," the medical model holds that the disability (and the individual who experiences the disability) is the "problem." Therefore, society is not required to change; it is the individual with the disability who has to be "fixed" in order to "fit in." Of course, for most individuals with disabilities, the disability is both permanent and visible, thus making it impossible for the individual to "fit in." Rob Imrie (1996) explained how assumptions of the medical model have resulted in both stigmatization and deviance labeling and architectural inaccessibility for PWDs: "And because the physical or built environment remains a given in the medical theorization of disability, there has been a tendency for disabled people [*sic*] to be stigmatized, or the association of disability with stigma wholly reinforces the notion of disability as an individually derived problem" (p. 39). Therefore, because the medical model views the PWD as the problem, it was thought that there is no need for the physical environment to change.

Occasionally, PWDs are not aware of their "deviant" status. Children with disabilities who have grown up in a loving and accepting home know they have a disability and that they are different from other children, but it is not until they begin activities outside the home, such as school, that these children understand the meaning their disability has for others. At home, the disability was difference but it was not stigma, inferiority, shame, or deviance (Eisenberg, Griggins, & Duval, 1982). The first day of school for these children often is unpleasantly surprising when they realize that others think of their disability as inferiority and as shameful. Adults who acquire a disability later in life often are unpleasantly surprised (or shocked) when they discover that they are viewed as objects of pity and inferiority (Eisenberg, 1982). Before the onset of the disability, they were individuals of status who enjoyed the respect of others. After the onset, the PWD is treated as an inferior, child-like person who is to be avoided.

DO DISABILITIES ALWAYS LEAD TO SOCIAL INFERIORITY?

> *In this section, look for—*
>
> ▶ *examples from history and the present-day media that confer second-class citizenship on PWDs*

People considered to be inferior do not have freedom, dignity, or security (Henderson & Bryan, 1997). Inferior people are often labeled as "second-class citizens" (Eisenberg et al., 1982), meaning that legal, institutionalized practices contribute to their lack of opportunity and segregation. Disability scholars have documented the inferior status of PWDs (Hillyer, 1993, Murphy, 1998). Liachowitz (1988) succinctly stated, "the laws that deal with handicapped [*sic*] people reflect . . . the views that biological deficiency confers social deficiency and that handicapped people deserve . . . a place outside the mainstream of society" (p. 1).

The following are a few examples of prejudice and discrimination.

- A 1997 Associated Press article entitled "Handicapped [*sic*] Used as Guinea Pigs" revealed that Sweden forcibly sterilized 60,000 people with disabilities between the years 1935 and 1976, and hundreds of institutionalized Swedes who were mentally retarded were fed daily diets of candy in order to provide scientists the opportunity to prove the cause and effect relationship between eating sugar and tooth decay.
- A Louis Harris poll, conducted in 1987, found that the unemployment of people with disabilities is the highest of any demographic group in the United States. Furthermore, a Harris poll in 1994 (four years after the passage of the ADA) found no improvement in the rate of employment among people with disabilities compared to 1987. Two-thirds of individuals with disabilities are unemployed, and of those who do work, only 11 percent of people with disabilities have full-time jobs. This high rate of unemployment and *underemployment* persists in spite of the fact that most individuals with disabilities report that they want to work (Hahn, 1997; Trupin, Sebesta, Yelin, & LaPlante, 1997).
- It is often questioned if fetuses with disabilities should be allowed to live. Hubbard (1997) stated, "No one these days openly suggests that certain kinds of people should be killed; they just should not be born" (p. 198).
- The "why bother?" concept is based on the assumption that the individual's disabilities are so severe and multiple "that treatment would make no difference or that the extra expenditures would not be worthwhile or cost-effective" (Lehr & Brinckerhoff, 1996, p. 10). These authors cite examples where "Parents have been told, directly or indirectly, 'What difference would it make if Barry could see better with glasses? He can't understand what he sees

anyway.' 'Why bother continuing to work on oral motor development? The tube feeding is going fine'" (pp. 10–11). Extreme examples of the "why bother?" syndrome are the "Baby-Doe" cases in which infants with severe disabilities were denied life-saving medical treatment because of physicians' predictions about their lack of quality of life. In contrast, infants without disabilities, or with less-severe disabilities, were automatically provided with these life-saving treatments (Anderson, 1987).

- People with disabilities are far more often the targets of crime, physical abuse, and sexual abuse (Cole, 1984, 1993; Craine, Henson, Colliver, & McLeland, 1988; Sobsey & Doe, 1991; Ulicny, White, Bradford, & Matthews, 1990; Waxman, 1991). For example, Sobsey (1994) reported that studies from many countries, such as the United States, the United Kingdom, and Australia "suggest that child abuse, beatings, and rape are common occurrences in the lives of many, probably most, people with developmental disabilities" (cited in Pelka, 1997, p. 260). "[The damaged merchandise myth] provides the offender with a rationalization not only for the choice of victim but also may alleviate any guilt or inhibition about exploiting the disabled [sic] person" (Sobsey & Mansell, 1993, pp. 289–290).

- "It is estimated that only about 20 percent of private practicing dentists are willing to accept patients with minimal disabilities. This failure of the dental profession to treat PWDs persists in spite of the fact that both the prevalence and severity of dental disease are significantly increased in the disabled [sic] population. In many instances, the disability itself either contributes directly to oral disease or greatly exaggerates an existing condition. . . . Accordingly, frequently the treatment regimen indicated for the management of these cases also may be a causative factor in dental disease. Perhaps the most notorious of treatments directly causing oral disease is the resultant gingival hyperplasia seen following the administration of the anticonvulsant dilantin or the antihypertensive nifedpine. . . . The drug is capable of producing an overgrowth of gingival soft tissue to the extent that the crowns of all teeth will be nearly submerged by the overgrowth. Obviously, the condition presents a formidable obstacle to chewing and speaking, not to mention the negative aesthetic aspects. Similarly, many sedatives and psychotropic medications, besides containing sugars in a liquid medium that contribute to tooth decay, also have effects that dramatically reduce the flow of saliva. This lack of salivary flow, or xerostomia, reduces the natural tooth-cleansing effect of saliva. . . . The American Dental Association does not require dental schools to teach students how to manage and provide dental treatment for the disabled [sic] patient (Bennett, 1998, pp. 20–21).

- According to Buss (1999), children with congenital disabilities such as spina bifida, fibrocystic disease, cleft palate, or Down syndrome are "abandoned" (p. 206) more often than children born without disabilities. Buss defined abandonment as institutionalization and adoption. Children with congenital disabilities who are not abandoned "are abused at considerably higher rates" (p. 206). Buss offered an hypothesis to explain this abuse and neglect. Titled the "healthy baby syndrome," this hypothesis states "that the health status of the child affects the degree of positive maternal behavior" (p. 206).

- PWDs are bombarded with negative images of themselves, of which most people without disabilities are unaware. Captain Hook, the Hunchback of

Notre Dame, and Mr. Magoo are demeaning and offensive (Bower, 1980; Byrd & Elliott, 1988; Gartner & Joe, 1987; Kriegel, 1982; Longmore, 1985; Safran, 1998; Zola, 1992). Those without disabilities probably are totally unaware of such media or the lifelong effects these can have on the self-concepts of people with disabilities. Of course, those without disabilities might argue, "Don't be so hypersensitive. It's just a children's cartoon." These same individuals, however, would not want their own racial/ethnic group or religious group portrayed with such triviality and condescension.

- Until recently, it was legal to forcibly sterilize individuals with certain kinds of disabilities. Indeed, in 1931, there were 30 states in the United States that had compulsory-sterilization laws. Individuals who were labeled "insane," "feeble-minded," "epileptic," and "other diseased and degenerate persons" were subjected to sterilization. Many states still have eugenic-sterilization laws today (Hubbard, 1997).

- The Deaf Culture labels society's refusal to accommodate people who are deaf to be "communication abuse" or "communication violence." This communication violence includes refusing to provide education for children in a language they can understand, such as ASL, the inability of many people to communicate with their nonsigning family members, and lack of TTYs (teletypewriters) at public phone booths. One of the most extreme examples of communication violence is the lack of TTYs for 911 emergency phone lines, which has resulted in the deaths of many individuals who are deaf (Jankowski, 1997).

- Many individuals with disabilities have not been allowed to participate in the religious life of their community or to practice their faith due to attitudinal and physical barriers. Rachel Hurst (1998), European Regional Chairperson of Disability, stated, "Religions too have disempowered disabled people [*sic*]...denying them access to the priesthood....The leper is always at the gate of the church—never inside" (p.15). Dr. Judith Heumann, the Assistant Secretary for the Office of Special Education and Rehabilitative Services, spoke about the inaccessibility of Jewish synagogues.

When the environment is made accessible, people have to start going out and becoming more independent, doing things they never did before. A simple example of this occurred in a synagogue that I attended when I lived in Berkeley. The bema, an area where people go to do readings and worship, was not accessible. One day, I told the rabbi, "The bema is not accessible." Two weeks later it was accessible. The rabbi said, "OK, now it's accessible and you have to come up and do some of the things that other people do." I thought, "Oh my god, I've never been trained!" I didn't even know how to participate because I hadn't learned the things that a person needs to learn in order to participate" (Heumann, 1999, p. 53).

The National Organization on Disability (NOD) has begun a program entitled "Accessible Congregations Campaign." In order to join the campaign, an accessible congregation must commit to the following three principles:
1. In our congregation, people with disabilities are valued as individuals, having been created in the image of God;
2. Our congregation is endeavoring to remove barriers or architecture, communications, and attitudes that exclude people with disabilities from full and active participation;

> 3. People, with and without disabilities, are encouraged to practice their faith and use their gifts in worship, service, study, and leadership.

- Before the passage of the Air Carrier Act of 1986, people in wheelchairs were prohibited from flying or they were required to bring an attendant—and to pay for the attendant's fare. In addition, before the ADA, most airports did not have wheelchair-accessible restrooms.
- Holzbauer and Berven (1996) reported these experiences: "In Cologne, Germany, Frank Weber, a wheelchair user, entered a department store to buy a concert ticket. Three neo-Nazis, wearing swastikas, leather jackets, and boots surrounded and began insulting him, saying: 'They must have forgotten you in Dachau.' (This refers to the practice of 60 years earlier of imprisoning people with disabilities along with Jews, Communists, and Gypsies in concentration camps)....Another German, Gunther Schirmer, had lost his leg in a car accident in 1979. He had learned to ride a tricycle. One afternoon...his wife saw boys harassing her husband, spitting on him and saying repeatedly, 'You live off our taxes. You'd have been gassed under Hitler.'...Shortly after this incident, Gunther Schirmer committed suicide. He wrote to his wife that people with disabilities do not have a chance in this world and that he would now personally 'destroy the cripple'" (p. 480). The title of an article (Whitney, 1993) that appeared in *The New York Times* illustrates that for many Germans (those with disabilities and their family members), the Holocaust is not forgotten. The title is "Disabled Germans Fear They'll Be the Next Target."
- From Fries (1997): "It is hereby prohibited for any person who is diseased, maimed, mutilated, or deformed in any way so as to be an unsightly and disgusting object to expose himself to public view" (1911 City of Chicago Ordinance). According to Imrie (1996), these types of ordinances are still on the books in Columbus, Ohio, and Omaha, Nebraska.

People who are considered to be inferior, which often includes PWDs, are avoided, segregated, and marginalized. "Able-bodied" is considered to be better than "disabled." Independence is better than dependence; integration is better than segregation. Active is better than passive. Making contributions is better than receiving charity. Respect is better than pity.

Of course, there are exceptions to these broad generalities. The age, sex, perceived social class, and other characteristics of the individual with the disability contribute to the status ascribed to him or her. We will discuss these later.

HANDICAPISM

In this section, look for—
- ▶ *the definition of handicapism*
- ▶ *the definition of institutional handicapism*
- ▶ *the definition of social handicapism*

Handicapism has been defined as the assumptions and practices that promote the unequal treatment of people because of apparent or assumed physical, mental, or behavioral differences. The clearest and most complete definition of *institutional handicapism* can be found in the Findings section of the ADA (presented in Chapter 2). Handicapism occurs in both the social and physical environment, although handicapism is more visible in the physical environment. For example, the availability of elevators and ramps is easy to see because they are part of the physical environment. Equal status relationships between PWDs and PWODs are part of the social environment and are more difficult to discern. It is, therefore, easier to counter handicapism in the physical environment than handicapism in the social environment. Both the term "handicapism" and the *public awareness* of handicapism are relatively recent developments. In contrast, handicapism itself has persisted in most societies of the world for centuries.

Some of the impetus for the Disability Rights Movement and other organized efforts to combat handicapism derived from the parallel movements of civil rights and women's rights. As racial and ethnic minorities and women began to organize and empower themselves to advocate for their rights as American citizens, PWDs began to develop a group identity and sought to learn from the Civil Rights and Women's Rights Movements and to also build on their successes. Naturally, a first step in such an undertaking is to increase public awareness of the disenfranchisement of PWDs in all facets of life. This chapter will focus on social handicapism, which is the automatic devaluing and marginalization of PWDs in relationships.

In the not-too-distant past, the majority considered the assumed inferiority of racial and ethnic minority individuals and women to be biological. This spurious, but widely held, assumption was supported by so-called science and research. Bickenbach (1993), making reference to Gould's (1981) book, *The Mismeasure of Man,* stated, "Theories of human races based on dubious techniques of craniometry and phrenology, and theories of criminal morphology, such as Cesare Lombroso's infamous theory of the 'criminal type' are some of Gould's examples of how science can come to the aid of racism, sexism, and other prejudices" (p. 190).

If inferiority is biological, then society is not obligated to confer rights upon inferior groups of people, nor is society to be blamed for its unequal treatment of these biologically inferior people. Further, these biologically inferior people cannot, and should not, fight or resist the unequal treatment. It is now well understood and acknowledged that the inferior status (and not the innate, inherent inferiority) of racial groups and women was solely the result of prejudice and discrimination of the broader culture. There is nothing inherently, or biologically, inferior about racial minorities or women.

PWDs, in very much the same way, have also been the objects of widely held views of biological inferiority (Anthony, 1984). The resulting legal disenfranchisement and marginalization of PWDs were also much like the experience of racial and ethnic groups and women. Since the inferiority was thought to be biological, then societies were not obligated to accord rights, privileges, and obligations to PWDs and, furthermore, PWDs should not protest this treatment. The American government, at all levels, supported the assumption of the biological inferiority of PWDs. And, as we have stated, PWDs often internalize the prevailing attitudes of the larger society around them, including society's attitudes toward PWDs. Therefore, many PWDs assumed themselves to be biologically inferior.

PWODs, in the past, have had the power to define who had a disability, define what types of services PWDs needed, and also control the environment, both physical and social. The power to categorize, label, and define is legally conferred by governments and, in the case of PWDs, the people who understood the experience best and knew their needs were not allowed a voice in the labels and categories conferred upon them. Majority and minority status were once theoretically based on numbers, meaning that the majority was the numerical majority. In practice, however, majority and minority status were based on power and not on numbers. A clear-cut example of this is American slavery. Certainly, on a single plantation, there were more slaves than slaveholders. But, majority status was based on power, and the single slaveholder was considered to be the majority. Bickenbach (1993), a Canadian disability scholar, discussed the relationship between the power of the majority to categorize and label the physical realities of disabilities. "Of course, in the case of persons with disabilities it would have to be agreed that disabilities are not entirely arbitrary social or political constructions by those who have the power to label and categorize people. If this were true, then people in power could simply "re-label" or "re-categorize" people. Disabilities do have physical and mental realities. Disabilities are biological facts" (p. 177).

Certainly, there are physical and biological realities to disability. The ADA acknowledges the biological facts of disability when it mandates accommodations. However, as we have seen, these biological realities are not inferiority and, furthermore, accommodations would greatly reduce (if not eliminate) the effects of the biomedical aspects of disability. Indeed, we have discussed such disabilities as facial disfigurements, dwarfism, and even obesity, which have no, or almost no, functional limitations, and we have also observed the prejudice, discrimination, and isolation that society confers upon individuals with these types of disabilities. Of course, there are disabilities that do have functional limitations, which does not mean inferiority. However, most of these limitations could be eliminated with accommodations. (No one would advocate hiring bus drivers who are blind.) Reread the examples of Sharon L. and the woman in Weinberg's research study in Chapter 2. Each of these examples clearly illustrates that it was not the functional limitations (or biological reality) of their disability that handicapped them. Rather, the lack of accommodations was the true handicap. PWDs know that asking for accommodations often results in stigma, categorization, and prejudice.

The false idea of the biological inferiority of PWDs persists. In contrast, the widespread acceptance of the idea of the biological inferiority of racial and ethnic groups and women has ended. In the case of disability, the concept of biological inferiority will be difficult to dispel. When PWODs focus on the disability and its limitations rather than on the person and his or her abilities, it is often an attempt to ascribe biological inferiority to the individual. Society has ascribed inferiority and difference where there is neither.

THE HANDICAPISM OF WELL-INTENTIONED PEOPLE

In this section, look for—

▶ *ways in which well-intentioned people can be handicapping to PWDs*

Well-intentioned people, who view themselves as neither prejudiced nor discriminatory, often promote handicapism. Most of the time, these people are not aware of their handicapism. Nonetheless, it is handicapism, and handicapism results in the disenfranchisement and marginalization of PWDs. The results of their handicapism conflict with their good intentions. Most of these individuals would be quick to assist someone with a disability and also profess to believe in the equality of PWDs; they are well-intentioned people. However, by focusing solely on the disability and its limitations and not viewing the PWD as a unique individual who has strengths, abilities, and skills that far outnumber the limitations of the disabilities, they are engaging in handicapism. Such a narrow focus often is an unconscious attempt to determine and ascribe biological inferiority to the PWD. Proponents of the contact theory and simulation exercises are well-intentioned people who practice handicapism.

The World Is Designed To Further the Purposes of PWODs

The Deaf Culture has a slogan: "It's our world, too." This slogan expresses the right of all PWDs to full social, economic, educational, vocational, and political integration. It may appear to be obvious, but we can ask, "Why do PWDs feel it necessary to remind PWODs that 'it's our world, too'?" Certainly, it is obvious that the world is inconvenient and physically inaccessible for many PWDs, not due to the disability itself, but due to the absence of accommodations. The lack of ramps and elevators, sign language interpreters, and a vast array of other accommodations renders the world an inconvenient place for PWDs.

The medical model of disability regards the PWD as responsible for "adapting" to the environment and does not consider PWODs to have any obligation to modify or change. The medical model probably played a large part in the indifference of the public to provide accommodations. When PWDs claim the world as also belonging to them, they are asserting their right to accommodations. The Deaf Culture provides an easily understood example. Since most hearing people have hands, they have the capability to learn sign language and, indeed, it would be easier for hearing people to learn sign language than for most congenital people who are deaf to learn to speak or to read lips. This example illustrates the need for PWODs to make accommodations rather than simply expecting PWDs to adapt to an indifferent social and physical environment.

Even more important than physical accessibility is the fact that disability public policy, educational services (including goals and curricula), and rehabilitation services, in the past, were designed and executed by PWODs. As a subordinate group, PWDs have been controlled by PWODs. Without any experience of disability or knowledge of the needs/use of accommodations, PWODs have asserted the right to determine the resources and services PWDs received. As PWDs have become more empowered, they have begun to claim the right to determine their own needs, policies, and goals.

For example, Patricia Deegan, in her work describing her recovery from mental illness (1991), described how rehabilitation programs designed by PWODs often impede and handicap the PWD. Deegan stated, "Too often, rehabilitation programs are structured in such a way as to work against this process of recovery. These programs tend to have rigid guidelines for acceptance. They tend to have linear program designs in which a person must enter at point 'A' and move through a series of consecutive steps to arrive at point 'B.' Failure at any point along the way will require that participants return to entry level" (p. 51).

A long list of programs and accommodations to assist PWDs, developed by PWODs, which in reality does not assist and often keeps PWDs marginalized could be presented. Indeed, in almost every first-person narrative, the individual with the disability tells of "professionals" who have, with the best of intentions, withheld accommodations or provided what they considered to be accommodations, but actually made the PWD's functioning more difficult. Both the goals and the accommodations needed to reach them should be decided by the individuals who understand the disability experience. Therefore, the disability rights movement is claiming its right to develop the programs and accommodations for PWDs.

THE CONTACT THEORY

In this section, look for—

▶ *why (initially) the contact theory failed*
▶ *the four conditions necessary for contact to reduce prejudice*

The contact theory was first developed during the 1950s and 1960s as a method to integrate racial and ethnic minorities on a fully equal basis and to facilitate a racially pluralistic society (Allport, 1954, 1958, 1986; Amir, 1969). In the beginning, it was thought that contact of any kind between the majority and minority individuals was sufficient to decrease prejudice, stigma, and discrimination. Contact was defined as direct, one-on-one interaction. Simply stated, it was theorized that contact would lead to attitude change, and attitude change would foster behavioral changes (Yuker, 1965, 1988a, 1988b; Yuker & Block, 1986; Yuker & Hurley, 1987). Contact of any kind was thought to be a solution to the centuries of isolation and segregation which had led to misinformation, stereotypes, and prejudice.

A few years later, the contact theory was expanded to include people with disabilities (Yuker, Block, & Young, 1970). Clearly, both racial/ethnic minorities and PWDs had experienced centuries of institutionalized segregation. Thus, it was thought that by allowing and encouraging PWODs to interact with PWDs, the prejudice and discrimination demonstrated toward PWDs would decrease (Donaldson, 1980; Elliott, Frank, Corcoran, Beardon, & Byrd, 1990; Evans, 1976; Fichten, Robillard, Judd, & Amsel, 1989). When discussing racial/ethnic/cultural/linguistic minority individuals, their right to move within the larger communities is termed "integration," while in discussing PWDs, this right is often termed "mainstreaming," "full social integration," or "inclusion." Nonetheless, the rationale and the methods of the contact theory were basically the same for both types of groups.

Surprisingly, for both types of groups, the initial research suggested that the contact between members of majority groups and members of minority groups did not decrease prejudice and discrimination, but rather *increased* it (Yuker, 1988). For example, when children with disabilities were mainstreamed into regular classrooms with children who did not have disabilities, the amount of playtime at home in the neighborhood between children with disabilities and children without disabilities actually decreased (Woods & Carrow, 1959). It seemed that the contact theory actually *reinforced* prejudice and discrimination. Indeed, many of these interactions were unpleasant, tense, and frustrating and were ended as quickly as possible (Anthony, 1972).

The researchers then sought to define "contact" in a more rigorous way. Cook (1978) summed up the literature on the research dealing with racial/ethnic minorities by stating, "Attitude change favorable to a disliked group will result from equal social status contact with stereotype-disconfirming persons from that group, provided that the contact is cooperative and of such a nature as to reveal the individual characteristics of the person contacted, and that it takes place in a situation characterized by social norms favoring equality and egalitarian association among the participating groups" (pp. 97–98).

Another sociologist (Duckitt, 1992) stated, "The conclusion that only certain kinds of contact actually reduce prejudice has been clearly confirmed. In fact, it has become increasingly apparent that contact does not reduce prejudice nearly as easily as had been hoped" (p. 144). Therefore, it was determined that the following conditions must be present in order for contact situations to decrease prejudice and have positive outcomes:

1. Equal social status relationships are necessary, which is not the situation when the PWD is clearly perceived to be inferior (Dembo, Leviton, & Wright, 1975). This explains, in part, why professionals who serve PWDs and, therefore, experience a great deal of contact, often hold negative stereotypes of PWDs (Bell, 1962; Berkowitz, 1984; Blood & Blood, 1982; Brodwin & Gardner, 1978; Chubon, 1982; Fuchs, Fuchs, Dailey, & Power, 1985; Gaier, Linkowski, & Jaques, 1968; Garske & Thomas, 1990; Horne, 1988; Janicki, 1970; Krauft, Rubin, Cook, & Bozarth, 1976; Larrivee & Cook, 1979; Palmerton & Frumkin, 1969). Indeed, Yuker (1994) stated, "Virtually all helpers perceive themselves as superior to people who need help" (p. 16). Disability scholars have suggested that it is very powerful (in reducing prejudice) if the PWD has a superior status than the PWOD in the contact (Anthony, 1972; Olkin, 1999).

2. The contact occurs under "natural" and voluntary conditions (Sigelman, Spanhel, & Lorenzen, 1979). This probably explains why the schoolchildren without disabilities did not play at home with their classmates who had disabilities (Woods & Carrow, 1959). Indeed, "incidental, involuntary, tension-laden contact is likely to increase prejudice" (Simpson & Yinger, 1985, p. 396).

3. The contact should facilitate viewing the PWD as an individual, rather than as a member of a group, thus disallowing negative stereotypes of PWDs (Jaques, Linkowski, & Seika, 1970; Langer, Bashner, & Chanowitz, 1985; Thomas, Foreman, & Remenyi, 1985; Yuker, 1988). This explains why superficial and casual interactions do not lead to a reduction in prejudice. In these superficial types of interaction, negative stereotypes are actually reinforced (Langer, Fiske, Taylor, & Chanowitz, 1976; McArthur, 1982).

4. Both individuals have the same goal. Such mutual goals are prejudice-reducing, especially if the goal cannot be achieved without the active cooperation of both individuals (Deutsch, 1949).

Reading this list of conditions, we can see that none of these can be legislated by law or mandated by policy. As with any minority group, PWDs can be allowed in schools and jobs and, at the same time, be isolated and segregated. Such laws as the ADA are, of course, necessary and positive influences, but they are simply a *starting point*. True integration is built upon the four conditions listed above. Further, if the contact situations do not include these four conditions, the contact will not reduce prejudice and may, in fact, serve to *strengthen and reinforce* prejudice, the individual mistakenly thinking that he or she now has more "sophisticated" knowledge about PWDs. In the following section, we will discuss each of these four conditions in more detail.

EQUAL SOCIAL STATUS CONTACT

In this section, look for—

▶ *the two components necessary for equal social status relationships: similarities and equal resources*
▶ *why true similarities are not readily apparent*
▶ *when two individuals do not bring equal resources to the relationship, the relationship is considered to be stressful and unbalanced*

Contact, sometimes referred to as "exposure" or "interaction," includes marriage, family relationships, friendships, work colleagues, teacher/student relationships, schoolmates, and professional helping relationships such as doctor/patient relationships. Not all of these types of relationships are equal social status; for example, teacher/student relationships and professional helping relationships usually place the PWD in an inferior position (as a student or patient). The contact theory defines contact as more than simple propinquity (Comer & Piliavin, 1972). Contact between PWDs and PWODs must include equal social status for both individuals if the contact is to lead to a reduction in prejudice and formation of more realistic attitudes. Indeed, Yuker (1983) presented an excellent review and interpretation of 274 studies that investigated the effect of the contact theory. Yuker made a strong point that in most of these studies the variable of contact was very loosely and ambiguously defined. For example, some studies simply asked the PWODs if they had contact with a PWD; in other studies, the "contact" was watching a video of a PWD. Yuker concluded, "We should no longer waste time studying and discussing the effects of experience or contact in general. The precise nature and duration of the contact and the nature of the interpersonal relationships involved must be specified before conclusions can be drawn" (p. 100). Moreover, Yuker and his associates found that when research studies included equal social status, common goals, and were of a voluntary nature, these studies were more likely to find a significant reduction in prejudice on the part of PWODs. On the other hand, studies attempted to measure the effect of "contact" in which the contact was observational tours of residential institutions for individuals with mental retardation or people with mental illness. Indeed, many college courses use these types of "tours" as part of course curricula and these tours/observations are a class requirement (Baker, Baker, & McDaniel, 1975). As would be expected, there was no reduction in prejudice among the tourists and, in some cases, there was an increase in prejudice. Rabkin (1972) explained this increase in prejudice: "Tours of institutions, like tours of zoos, may arouse feelings of pity or revulsion, but almost never stimulate a sense of respect and empathy regarding the inmates; it is only when roles are transformed and patients are given "normal" role assignments that they seem like you or me" (p. 163).

How do two people form equal social status relationships? Experts report that two conditions must be present: (1) similarities and (2) equal resources. Briefly stated, relationships are formed when people have something in common and both individuals bring equal resources such as power, prestige, material resources, and emotional resources, including consideration for and understanding of others. Of course, in the beginning stages of any relationship, the similarities are only *perceived* similarities and the resources are only *perceived* to be equal. As the relationship progresses and builds, the individuals find that true similarities are shared values, goals, and experiences and, therefore, true similarities are not quickly apparent. In any relationship with equal social status, physical appearance and first impressions are important in the initial stages. However, as the relationship builds, personality, character, values, and goals become more important than superficial, readily visible characteristics (Safilios-Rothschild, 1970). Physical appearance becomes less important; nonetheless, the difficulty is in maintaining the relationship beyond the point where these visible characteristics are important, long enough to allow more relevant characteristics to be demonstrated. Whether a job interview or a first date, we all understand that physical appearance has great significance, and we also know that getting past this initial stage will allow us to demonstrate relevant characteristics. Furthermore, these types of contact create a great deal of interaction strain. In much the same way, the PWD knows that the disability causes discomfort to the PWOD and therefore he or she must work harder to advance the relationship beyond the first impression stage (Kleck, 1966; Kleck, Ono, & Hastorf, 1966).

The second condition upon which long-standing relationships are built is that of *equal* resources of each partner, keeping in mind that equal resources do not necessarily mean the *same* resources. Relationships in which one partner has more resources are often termed "asymmetrical" or "unbalanced." Asymmetrical relationships are considered to be stressful; the partner with the greater resources is resentful that he or she brings more to the relationship, and the partner with fewer resources becomes resentful that he or she is always in an inferior position and may fear abandonment. Resources are both visible and invisible. For example, money and prestige are easy to see, while emotional resources can only be discovered as the relationship progresses. Some resources, such as power, are both visible and invisible.

Similarities and equal resources are necessary components for any long-standing social relationship, in which the partners consider themselves to be equal. Equal social status relationships between a PWD and a PWOD are no exception, although these components are more complicated when one partner has a disability. It is not the disability itself that makes these types of equal social status relationships more complex; rather, it is the perceptions and attitudes of others toward the disability. For example, when one marriage partner has a disability, the partner without a disability is often thought to be a "saint" or a "loser." These derisive and insulting judgments reflect the widely held attitude that PWDs have few resources (including social status) and that PWDs cannot contribute anything, but must always be the recipients of their partners' care and compassion. If the PWOD is thought to be a "loser," then the relationship is a balanced relationship (because it is automatically assumed that the PWD is also a "loser"). On the other hand, if the PWOD is thought to be a "saint," then the relationship is not balanced.

Remarkably, the idea that a PWD and a PWOD can have an equal social status relationship of any type—friendship, work colleague, romantic, marriage—wherein both bring resources to the relationship and thus both benefit is rarely considered. Further, the concept of shared similarities of the two individuals is often overlooked because, as we learned in Chapter 4, others mistakenly believe that the disability is the most salient (defining) characteristic of the PWD. This erroneous assumption leads to the equally erroneous conclusion that PWODs and PWDs cannot share common values, goals, and experiences because one partner has a disability. In the video *My Body Is Not Who I Am*, a man in a wheelchair tells us that he is often asked if he has a girlfriend, and when he answers "yes," he is then asked if his girlfriend has a disability. While rude and intrusive, these questions also illustrate the widely held belief that equal social status relationships between PWODs and PWDs are not possible because the PWD is perceived to be (1) dissimilar to PWODs and (2) not bringing equal resources to the relationship.

The Contact Must Be Natural and Voluntary

Having a marriage partner, family member, or a child with a disability is usually not voluntary. (In the case of the marriage partner, it would be voluntary if the individual had the disability before the marriage.) Nonetheless, in order for the contact theory to reduce prejudice in nonfamilial associations, the relationship between the PWD and the PWOD must be perceived as both natural and voluntary. Assigning PWODs to PWDs for tutoring, mentoring, and "best buddies" is neither voluntary nor natural. Both PWODs and PWDs clearly understand that the "relationship" is "coerced" and time limited. The motivation to move beyond the initial stages of the relationship is reduced because both individuals understand that, under typical conditions, they would not associate with each other. These types of contact have the potential to succeed if the relationship evolves beyond the involuntary (assigned) stage.

Many schools have "best buddies" programs in which a student without a disability is assigned to a student with mental retardation. The student without the disability assists his or her "best buddy" with schoolwork and negotiating the school day and engages in social activities with him or her. Due to the disability of mental retardation, the PWD may not understand that the PWOD is simply fulfilling some type of requirement and once this is accomplished, the PWOD will no longer be a "best buddy."

The Contact Should Facilitate Viewing the PWD as an Individual

Once the relationship has progressed beyond the initial stages, the disability should no longer be the focus. This is not to say that the disability is denied or ignored, only that the disability is no longer the defining or most important aspect of the relationship. Other specific, more-relevant characteristics form the basis of the contact. The contact must facilitate the PWOD in viewing the PWD as more than a stereotype, label, or diagnosis (Parenti, Beaufils, & Paicheler, 1987). As the salience of the disability is reduced, the interaction strain felt by the PWOD is also reduced (Amsel & Fichten, 1988; Fichten, Robillard, Judd, & Amsel, 1989; Genskow & Maglione, 1965; Makas, 1993). Yuker (1965) summarized the results of viewing the PWD as an individual. (Note that the labels used to describe various types of individuals are 35 years old and are considered offensive and insulting today.) "If you have known a person over a period of time, you cannot help but think of him as an individual. You think of him as John or Dave, not as a cripple, a Negro, a Catholic, or a Jew. You may not like him, but if you don't like him you don't like him as an individual. Or, if you do like him, you like him as an individual. But the attitude is based on him as a person, not as a member of a particular group" (p. 16).

In this type of contact, the PWD is recategorized as an individual, not as "one of *those* people." Stereotyping and distancing, as we have learned in other chapters, serve (1) to communicate that these types of people are not like us, and (2) to view individuals as their categories. With contact, complex, long-held stereotypes are broken down when the PWOD learns that (1) "this PWD is more like me than I had thought," and (2) "this PWD doesn't act (or think) like I thought PWDs do."

Two Canadian disability scholars, Robert Bogdan and Steven Taylor (1992), conducted interviews with family members of people who had severe and multiple disabilities. Compiling 15 years of qualitative research, they found that those families who had warm and accepting relationships with their member with a disability (or more than one disability) viewed the PWD as a unique individual; indeed, the families described the PWD in positive terms, such as "she has sparkling eyes," "she has beautiful hair," and "he has a great smile." Bogdan and Taylor found that these accepting families often had nicknames for the PWD that were positive, conferred dignity, and described something unique about the individual. These families dressed and groomed the PWDs in age-appropriate, gender-appropriate, stylish clothes. Older men often had beards; the women had makeup and attractive hair-dos. Bogdan and Taylor stated, "By paying attention to clothing style and color and appearance (hair style, nails, makeup, cleanliness, beards for men), they helped construct an identity....Thus, the person is given...an identity as an individual" (p. 104). Further, these families spoke at length about the PWD's likes and dislikes in food, recreation, and music. While Bogdan and Taylor's research focused only on family relationships and was limited to people who had severe and multiple disabilities, clearly one of the components of acceptance was ascribing individuality to the PWD.

The Contact Should Involve Cooperative Goals

The contact must include the contributions of the PWD, and these contributions must be viewed as valued and necessary for success. Some textbooks describe this as "reciprocating" in that both the PWD and the PWOD need the contribution and assistance of the other.

In summary, we can see that previous PWODs' contact or experience with PWDs may or may not reduce prejudice and foster realistic attitudes. Therefore, it is not only the amount or quantity of previous experience with PWDs, it is the quality of the experience that makes the difference. Therefore, both quantity and quality are important. A one-day seminar on disability awareness, viewing a video, or reading a book (such as this one) are only *starting points*. However, each of these methods is an excellent place to begin, but it must be followed up with one-on-one relationships with PWDs that incorporate the four components discussed above.

PERCEPTIONS OF THE DISABILITY THAT MAY BE ASSOCIATED WITH PREJUDICE

> *In this section, look for—*
>
> ▶ *the effects of the following factors:*
> 1. *the degree of visibility of the disability*
> 2. *visibility/aesthetic qualities of the disability*
> 3. *communication difficulties*
> 4. *perceived cause of the disability*
> 5. *perceived threat of the disability*
> 6. *course of the disability*

A disability scholar, Liora Pedhazur Schmelkin (1988) listed the six factors (in the box above) as "six critical dimensions of stigma" (p. 129). Naturally, both the experience of a disability and the reactions of others to an individual with a disability are complex and interrelated. Nonetheless, in order to impose structure and gain a preliminary understanding of the stigma directed toward PWDs, disability scholars have devised categorization schemes, such as the one listed above. Whatever categorization scheme is used, everyone agrees that stigma is multidimensional and any scheme must be considered only a starting point to understanding stigma. Second, the factors listed above are only *perceptions* of PWODs and are not accurate judgments of either the disability itself or the individual with the disability. Third, the degree of stigma directed toward the PWD will affect the PWD's response to his or her disability. Sociologists and psychologists know that the judgments of others profoundly influence an individual's self-concept. In the case of PWDs, if there is a great deal of prejudice and discrimination against a certain type (or level of severity) of disability, it is likely that the individual with this type of disability will incorporate some of these negative judgments into his or her self-identity (Garske & Thomas, 1990; Siller, 1984; Wright, 1983, 1988).

THE DEGREE OF VISIBILITY OF THE DISABILITY

> *In this section, look for—*
>
> ▶ *the fact that lack of visibility does not mean absence of impairment*
> ▶ *how PWODs often attribute negative characteristics to PWDs with hidden disabilities*
> ▶ *how PWDs will often choose to hide the disability, even at the cost of necessary accommodations*
> ▶ *when PWDs must weigh the cost/benefit ratio of disclosure*

Read the following letter sent to Ann Landers (Exhibit 5–1).

Hidden disabilities can include many health conditions, many psychiatric disabilities, hearing impairments, and a vast range of other types of disabilities. Many times, it is not the disability itself that is visible, but rather the accommodations the disability requires, such as hearing aids, wheelchairs, and note-takers in a college classroom for student(s) with learning disabilities, that are apparent to others. There

Exhibit 5–1

> **Dear Ann Landers:** I am handicapped, but one would never know it by looking at me. I have had two back operations and four knee surgeries. If I do any walking or standing, even for a few minutes, I get very tired and must sit and rest.
>
> Recently, I parked in the handicapped spot at the supermarket. I have a handicapped tag hanging on my rearview mirror. Before I could get out of the car, a "gentleman" walked up and said, "You certainly don't look handicapped to me. You should not be parking in that space." I looked at him and said, "And you, sir, look intelligent, but I guess looks can be deceiving."
>
> If more people realized that some handicapped folks have physical disabilities that are not visible, life would be easier for all of us.
>
> —Yes I Am in Palm Harbor, Fla.

is no correlation between the degree of visibility and degree of impairment. Clearly, the Ann Landers letter illustrates that simply because a disability is not visible, it does not mean that there are not severe functional limitations.

Indeed, reactions to hidden disabilities reveal the lack of awareness of many PWODs to disabilities in general. It is not possible to discern if an individual has a disability from his or her appearance. Further, many PWODs attribute negative motives to (1) the functional limitations of the disability, or (2) the accommodations that the individual uses. We learned in Chapter 2 that ambiguity, of any kind, is often interpreted as negative (or hostile). Here are two examples. A young woman student in our department has a heart condition (she breathes from oxygen tanks at home each day from 5:00 P.M. to 8:00 A.M.). Naturally, this student must use the elevators. While waiting for an elevator or riding the elevator, strangers often approach her and say, "Are we feeling a little lazy today?" Interestingly, at some point, this student's disability will become visible when she will be required to breathe oxygen 24 hours a day. The other example concerns the wife of a political candidate who has a progressive neuromuscular disability that affects her coordination and motor abilities. These types of conditions are often exacerbated by stress and fatigue, and episodes of heightened symptoms are impossible to predict. Therefore, when the individual is stressed and tired, symptoms may appear precisely when he or she needs and wants to make a good impression. At a fund-raising cocktail party, the woman held her husband's arm because she was experiencing the heightened symptoms of loss of motor control. The next day, a newspaper article asked, "Do we want a governor who has a wife who gets falling-down drunk?" Adding to the irony was the fact that the wife had not had any alcohol because she understood the serious effects alcohol has for these kinds of disabilities.

But what about people who do not have a disability but fake one? Certainly, there are incentives to fake disabilities, such as to gain financial benefits or drugs or to gain exemption from criminal prosecution, work, or military duty. This is termed "malingering," and one of the criteria of this diagnosis is that the individual must be aware that he or she is trying to deceive others (in contrast to unconscious denial of the disability in which the individual is not aware that he or she is attempting to deceive anyone). In a previous chapter, we read about college athletes who claimed nonexistent disabilities in order to receive "handicapped" parking tags. There are people who fake disabilities. At a large high school in Salt Lake City, 70 percent of the students taking the Scholastic Aptitude Test claimed a learning disability, requesting more time in which to complete the test. It would be rather remarkable if there were such a large number of individuals with documented, diagnosed learning disabilities in one school.

The letter to Ann Landers also illustrates that many individuals mistakenly think of legitimate accommodations for a disability as preferential treatment, and "handicapped" parking spaces are a particularly "hot button." (In the disability community, there are jokes about "handicapped parking stickers" being big sellers at garage sales.) Both people with visible disabilities and people with hidden disabilities are aware that others often resent the accommodations provided for the disability. As we have learned in previous chapters, under the ADA, when PWDs utilize accommodations, they are simply exercising their rights as American citizens.

Obviously, for individuals whose disability (or the accommodations or adaptive technology) is clearly visible, there is no decision about the costs of disclosure. In contrast, when an individual has a disability that can be hidden, he or she must weigh the costs and benefits of disclosure.

Choosing not to disclose a hidden disability is often termed "passing." Individuals with hidden disabilities can *decide when or to whom* to disclose. The option of choosing the point of disclosure allows the individual to display the relevant characteristics, such as work skills and work habits, before telling others about his or her disability. Often, individuals with hidden disabilities choose to never reveal their disability. As you remember, the ADA does not mandate accommodations for the disability unless the individual discloses his or her disability. Therefore, one of the benefits of disclosure is the provision of accommodations.

Foremost among the benefits of choosing not to disclose a hidden disability is the ability to shed the "disabled image" and "disabled role." The disabled image has led to prejudice, discrimination, and stigma, and it is understandable when individuals refuse this devalued role.

Often, the individual who attempts to "pass" sacrifices functioning. Examples of this include individuals who decide not to wear their hearing aids in public (others may think they are rude and conceited, but in reality, they cannot hear), those wearing a prosthetic hand in public that is not very functional because they understand that the very useful hook is distressing to others, and those individuals wishing to keep their disability hidden by not taking medications or injections in the view of others. Listed below are some of the costs/benefits of disclosure (Exhibit 5–2).

Reading the list of "costs" or disadvantages of not disclosing a disability, we can see that sometimes the truth (revealing the disability) is better than allowing others to "think the worst." For example, a gap of time (months or years) on a résumé due to a hospitalization may raise more questions than simply telling the job interviewer the truth. In the example of the political candidate's wife, the truth about the disability was certainly better than the implications drawn by newspaper reporters. Also, the individual is aware that there is more societal stigma directed toward some disabilities than others. For example, an individual with a hidden disability of diabetes (a disability toward which society holds very little prejudice) may be more willing to disclose the disability than an individual with a psychiatric disability (a disability toward which society holds a great deal of prejudice). In addition, those who choose to hide their disability are often considered "disloyal" by others with

Exhibit 5–2

Benefits of Disclosure

1. Accommodations are provided;
2. The truth is often better than negative assumptions.

Costs of Disclosure

1. No accommodations are given;
2. Negative characteristics are attributed to the individual with the disability;
3. Others with the same disability who have disclosed consider the person who "passes" as disloyal;
4. It is stressful to hide something that is part of one's self-identity;
5. The individual has lost an opportunity to advocate and educate others about the disability;
6. There might be more problems if the disability is discovered by others.
7. The individual sacrifices the solidarity, support, and understanding of associating with other PWDs.

---

the same disability. For example, many in the Disability Rights Movement label Franklin Roosevelt a "closet crip" because he hid and minimized his disability. Another cost is the stress of hiding both the disability and the accommodations/treatment of the disability. An individual may need time off from work during the day to attend Alcoholics Anonymous meetings and his coworkers may think that he or she is goofing off. Another example is that of an individual with a psychiatric disability who has chosen not to disclose the disability and then must listen to friends' jokes about "fruitcakes," "whackos," and "psychos" and remain silent.

Cynthia Rich (as cited in Morris' 1991 book *Pride Against Prejudice: Transforming Attitudes to Disability*) described two distinct types of "passing." The first type is that of a "consciously political tactic for carefully limited purposes" and, for her, this type of passing does not have serious, pervasive, and long-term consequences for the individual. The second type of passing, in which the individual loses his or her own identity, has serious results.

> Passing—except as a consciously political tactic for carefully limited purposes—is one of the most serious threats to selfhood. We attempt, of course, to avoid the oppressor's hateful distortion to our identity and the real menace to our survival of his [*sic*] hatred. But, meanwhile, our identity is never acted out, can lose its substance, its meaning, even for ourselves (p. 36).

It should be pointed out that others who have the same disability (or who have a great deal of experience with that type of disability) often are able to detect the disability, while most PWODs are not. Simply due to the fact that these individuals are aware of the symptoms, limitations, treatments, and compensations of that particular disability, they can recognize the disability in others. For example, people who wear contact lenses are usually aware of others who wear contact lenses, when most people would not know. Individuals who have learning disabilities can often "pick up" on the adaptive techniques of others with learning disabilities simply because they know what to look for. People who wear prostheses are aware of others who wear similar prostheses. Others have no "expectation" or "awareness" of prostheses.

In today's age of technology and telecommunications, the concept of hidden disabilities has been changed. John Hockenberry, the news journalist in a wheelchair, worked in Los Angeles and did not tell his bosses in New York City that he had a disability. This is a single example that illustrates the changing definition of a hidden disability. Certainly, the people in Los Angeles saw the wheelchair, but Hockenberry decided that he wanted his bosses to see the quality of his work before disclosing his disability. (Hockenberry also "paid" for his refusal to disclose. He had no accessible bathroom at work.)

Looking at the Ann Landers letter, we can see that the writer chose to disclose the disability in the first paragraph, stressing both the disability and the functional limitations. (Perhaps this would not be considered true disclosure because it is an anonymous letter.) Nonetheless, it is thought-provoking to consider what Ann Landers' response and the reader response would have been if the writer had chosen not to disclose the type of disability and the resulting limitations, but simply stated, "I am handicapped, but one would never know it by looking at me."

OTHER FACTORS THAT INFLUENCE THE PERCEPTION OF PWDs

> *In this section, look for—*
>   ▶ *perceived cause of the disability*
>   ▶ *perceived social class and educational level of the PWD*
>   ▶ *the specific situation*
>   ▶ *functional limitations of the disability*

Certainly in discussing the perception of and response to PWDs, there are many factors—some are situational factors (Dunn, 1996); some are related to the PWD, such as his or her perceived social class, social prestige, and educational level (clinicians are less likely to give certain diagnoses, such as antisocial personality disorder, to individuals they believe to be of higher social status); some are related to the perceptions that others have of the disability; and finally, some factors are related to the disability itself (Gordon, Minnes, & Holden, 1990; Gouvier, Coon, Todd, & Fuller, 1994; Grand, Bernier, & Strohmer, 1982; Greenwood & Johnson, 1987; Harosymia, Home, & Lewis, 1976; Heinemann, Pellander, Vogelbusch, & Wojtek, 1981). Reading the list of factors in the box, we see the word "perceived" precedes the first two listed. The perceptions of others can be inaccurate but, nonetheless, they consider these perceptions to be reality. In Chapter 4, we learned that the stigma attached to the types of onset of the disability or disabilities acquired in war or industrial accidents are considered to be "noble" disabilities and therefore have the least amount of stigma, individuals with congenital disabilities experience more prejudice, and disabilities that are thought to be self-inflicted have the greatest stigma. A student in our department was born with a displaced hip and has had several surgeries. Today, she walks with a limp. When she was a little girl, a rumor circulated around her church that her father had physically beaten her when she was a baby, causing the displaced hip. Not very long ago, many disabilities, such as autism and affective disorders, were thought (by many professionals and by the general public) to be caused by "refrigerator parents." Refrigerator parents were described as cold, distant, and rejecting. Thus, we can see perceptions are not always accurate, and they influence the way in which the PWD (and in this case, her family) is viewed.

The functional limitations of the disability usually do not create many barriers between the PWD and others. However, such limitations as difficulty in communication, which people who are deaf or who have speech disorders experience, have the potential to create tension and frustration for both the PWD and the PWOD. These communication limitations can be overcome with the use of adaptive technology, or interpreters, and patience and a willingness to talk with the PWD. It is safe to state that most PWODs exaggerate the extent and impact of the functional limitations of most disabilities.

"DISABLED HEROES" OR "SUPER CRIPS"

In this section, look for—
- ▶ *the definition of a "disabled hero"*
- ▶ *three reasons why disabled heroes create more prejudice and discrimination against PWDs*
  1. *Most PWODs do not understand the functional limitations of various disabilities and therefore have no basis upon which to judge "heroism"*
  2. *Disabled heroes have extraordinary resources available to them, which most people, with or without disabilities, do not have*
  3. *The disabled hero perpetuates the myth that PWDs should "try harder"*
- ▶ *why those in the Disability Rights Movement label disabled heroes as super crips*

Perceived social class, educational level, income, and occupational level do matter. Most of us do not like to admit that we are influenced by an individual's grooming, style of clothing, manners, and speaking ability. Nonetheless, individuals who are believed to be well educated, well mannered, and of high social status are accorded more respect. This holds true for PWDs (although it should be remembered that as a group, PWDs are far more likely to live in poverty, have inferior educations, and be unemployed or underemployed). PWDs, like anyone else, realize that they will be more readily accepted if they appear in a position of authority and status.

All of us have seen the posters of "disabled heroes," in which individuals who have accomplished extraordinary achievements in science, the arts, athletics, or politics are pictured. Some examples include the physicist Stephen Hawking, American President Franklin Roosevelt, Helen Keller, the composer Beethoven, and Albert Einstein. Their accomplishments are remarkable for anyone, with or without a disability. These posters are intended to reduce the prejudice and discrimination against PWDs, but in reality they perpetuate more prejudice and discrimination simply because they give a false impression of a "typical" PWD and communicate, in a not very subtle way, that anyone can overcome a disability. It is easy to understand why many PWDs resent these disabled heroes.

Further, most PWODs are unaware of the functional limitations of disabilities and, therefore, are not in a position to evaluate the accomplishments of PWDs. For example, Wendell (1997) made the observation that athletes with amputations or spinal cord injuries do not have as many functional limitations as people with arthritis. Arthritis is a very debilitating, painful, pervasive disability that affects many joints in the body. Yet, it is safe to state that most PWODs would consider a spinal cord injury or an amputation (or congenital limb deficiency) as more limiting than arthritis. However, it would be most unusual to see an athlete with severe arthritis.

These individuals who are considered to be disabled heroes have had remarkable resources available to them, including money, education, family support, innate talents, and intelligence and, indeed, they are probably more famous for their accomplishments than they were/are for having a disability. For example, Helen Keller, who was deaf and blind, came from a prominent Southern family, was physically beautiful, and had personal friends such as Alexander Graham Bell, Mark Twain, Eleanor Roosevelt, and Albert Einstein. She graduated from Radcliffe College and lived on the financial support of admiring millionaires. But, by far, her greatest asset, not available to most people who are deaf and blind, was a companion/teacher who stayed with her for over 49 years, Anne Sullivan (Hermann, 1998). (It is interesting to note that her family often could not afford to pay Sullivan, but she remained with Helen Keller until her own death.) Interestingly, Helen Keller's parents wrote to the Perkins Institute for the Blind after hearing about the successful education of a young woman, Laura Bridgman, who was deaf and blind. One of Laura Bridgman's teachers at the Perkins Institute was Anne Sullivan, and the Kellers were able to engage Anne Sullivan as the teacher/live-in companion for their daughter, Helen. Laura Bridgman lived most of her life at the Perkins Institute and died there; today there are few people who know who she was, and yet Helen Keller would not have been a famous celebrity and writer if it had not been for Laura Bridgman. (However, Charles Dickens met Laura Bridgman and modeled his fictional character "Little Nell" after her.)

Often the time of the onset of the disability has an impact on the accomplishments of the individual. For example, Christopher Reeve was able to develop his celebrity status before the onset of the disability, and Stephen Hawking received his education before the onset of amyotrophic lateral sclerosis (ALS). (The disability of ALS would not have prevented him from receiving a PhD, but most universities would not have had the accommodations necessary for Hawking, and, therefore, Hawking probably would not have been admitted.) Beethoven became deaf later in life, after he was a famous composer. The lives of these individuals would have been very different if their disabilities had been congenital or acquired early in life.

Finally, in the case of learning disabilities, it is difficult to know if these celebrities truly had a disability. Individuals of great achievement, such as Einstein; Edison; the Danish writer of fairy tales, Hans Christian Andersen; the British prime minister, Winston Churchill; and the Italian artist, Leonardo da Vinci have been reported to have had a learning disability. However, most experts in learning disabilities do not think that any of these individuals had a learning disability. Of course, all of these individuals lived in a time when learning disabilities were not known and not diagnosed. Many of these assumptions are based on these individuals' handwriting, examples of misspelled words, and reports that they had problems in school. Huston (1987) summarized:

> Frequently, in books and articles on dyslexia, writers report a number of notable adults reputed to have had dyslexia. Repetition of these names has become almost a litany. These names are usually just listed in a series in books with rarely any explanation or evidence given why the person is considered to have been dyslexic. The few times any evidence is given it is scanty—often irrelevant or questionable....Often there are more simple explanations for the difficulties these persons are said to have had (pp. 151–152).

THE DRAWBACKS TO HAVING DISABLED HEROES

In this section, look for—

▶ *the two harmful prejudices perpetuated by super crips*
  1. *The public wrongly believes that it is very rare for PWDs to succeed*
  2. *By focusing on individual achievements, the accomplishments of advocacy groups are ignored*

Many PWDs use the derisive term "super crip" to label these disabled heroes. Indeed, many in the Disability Rights Movement regard super crips as perpetuating two harmful ideas/prejudices. First, by focusing only on the individual, the efforts and successes of the Disability Rights Movement, the passage of legislation such as the ADA, and the realities of the physical and attitudinal barriers that PWDs confront are ignored. The concept of a super crip concentrates on a remarkable individual and conveniently overlooks the accomplishments of disability advocates who facilitated the creation of the super crip. Once again, by focusing on *individuals*, society can reassure itself that the difficulties that PWDs encounter can be solved by individual effort. Second, posters and other advertisements of disabled heroes subtly plant the idea in the mind of the general public that *all* people with the same type of disability should be able to accomplish at the level of the super crip. However, for the "typical" PWD (whoever that might be) who does not have all the resources of the super crip, this is impossible. In spite of these realities, in the minds of the public, the super crip now becomes the standard by which *all* PWDs are judged. Covington (1997, as cited in Pelka, 1997) summarized:

> Super crip is usually a character struck down in the prime of life who fights to overcome insurmountable odds to succeed as a meaningful member of society. Through strength of will, perseverance, and hard work, the disabled individual achieves a *normal* life. . . . Too often, the news media treats an individual with disabilities who has attained success in his [sic] field or profession as though they [sic] were one-of-a-kind. While this one-of-a-kind aspect might make for a better story angle, it perpetuates in the mind of the general public how rare it is for the citizen with disabilities to succeed (p. 292).

If the public thinks it knows *by name* the few PWDs who have succeeded, then it is also logical, though wrong, to think that most PWDs are failures. Irving Zola, the sociologist, college professor, and disability scholar, was a survivor of polio. He died in 1994 at the age of 59. Zola (1991) described the message and effects of "super crips."

> It is the...message that I have recently begun to abhor. It states that if a Franklin Delano Roosevelt or Wilma Rudolph could OVERCOME their handicap [sic], so could and should all the disabled [sic]. And if we fail, it's *our* problem, *our* personality, *our* weakness. And this further masks what chronic illness is all about. For our lives or even our adaptations do not center around one single activity or physical achievement but around many individual and complex ones. Our daily living is not filled with dramatic accomplishments but with mundane ones. And most of all, our physical difficulties are not temporary ones to be overcome once-and-for-all but ones we must face again and again for the rest of our lives. That's what chronic means! (p. 161)

Exhibit 5–3

Charles Krauthammer

RESTORATION, REALITY AND CHRISTOPHER REEVE

"Paralyzed people fooled by a Super Bowl ad showing Christopher Reeve walking have been calling an advocacy group to find out how he was cured." —Associated Press, Feb. 1, 2000

I have long been reluctant to criticize Christopher Reeve. It is not easy attacking someone who suffered such a devastating injury and has carried on with spirit. Nor am I particularly keen to violate the Brotherhood of the Extremely Unlucky. (I injured my spinal cord when I was 22 and have been in a wheelchair ever since.)

But his Super Bowl ad was just too much. Why did he do it? To raise consciousness, he says. Convinced that a cure is imminent, he wants to share the good news with the largest possible audience. For 28 years I've been hearing that a cure is just a few years away. Being a doctor, I have discounted such nonsense. Most of the spinal-cord injured, however, are not doctors.

These are the facts. Yes, there is research into spinal-cord regeneration and, occasionally, there are some positive results in animal models. But the research is preliminary, at best suggestive. There remain enormous scientific obstacles even beyond the extremely problematic question of getting the neurons to regrow. Yes, this research will bear fruit one day. Unhappily, it is overwhelmingly likely that this day lies many years in the future.

Second, when that time does come, the principal beneficiaries will be the newly injured. People long injured—who've developed scar tissue at the site of the break and whose distal spinal cord (the part below the injury) often turns to mush as the old neurons die—will be the last people to be helped by this research, if they'll be helped at all. The "cure" will probably end up like the polio vaccine: preventing paralysis, not abolishing it.

Third, even in the unlikely event there is a cure for those presently paralyzed, it will at best be partial. The idea so dramatized in the Super Bowl commercial—that someone with a completely severed cord will actually walk—is very farfetched. Walking is a hugely complex motor and feedback activity. Look at how long it takes babies, who have totally intact nervous systems to learn it. Look at how, despite decades of research to develop robots that walk, they remain primitive, often comical. Perhaps the long-injured will enjoy some partial return, some movement in the hands or chest or even legs. That would be a considerable boon. But it is far from the fantasy Reeve promotes; walking, i.e., restoration to preinjury status.

Reeve believes restoration is just around the corner. Fine. I have no quarrel with a man who wants to believe that. If he needs that to get through his day, who am I to disabuse him of his fantasies?

But Reeve insists on parading his fantasies in public with the express purpose of converting others to them. In his public pronouncements and now in his disgracefully misleading Super Bowl ad, he is evangelizing the imminent redemption. He goes so far as to criticize those who believe otherwise.

"The biggest problem, actually," he told *Good Morning America* the day after the commercial aired, "is people who've been in a chair for a very long time, because in order to survive psychologically they've had to accept 'O.K.., I'm going to spend my life in a chair.'"

In Reeve's view, reality is a psychological crutch. His propaganda to that effect undermines those—particularly the young and newly injured—who are struggling to face reality, master it, and make a life for themselves from their wheelchairs.

Odder still is Reeve's belief that people in wheelchairs don't dream enough about getting out of them. (Hence the $2 million ad.) On the contrary. The problem is that some—again, the newly devastated young especially—dream about it too much.

When I was injured, I had a roommate in my four-bed ward who was making no effort to continue his education or plan for a new career. One day he told me why: "I'm going to wait seven years for a cure. Then I'm going to kill myself."

The false optimism Reeve is peddling is not just psychologically harmful, cruelly raising hopes. The harm is practical too. The newly paralyzed young might end up emulating Reeve, spending hours on end preparing their bodies to be ready to walk the day the miracle cure comes, much like the millenarians who abandon their homes and sell their worldly goods to await the Rapture on a mountaintop. These kids should instead be spending those hours reading, studying, and preparing themselves for the opportunities in the new world that high technology has for the first time in history made possible for the disabled.

They can have jobs and lives and careers. But they'll need to work very hard at it. And they'll need to start with precisely the psychological acceptance of reality that Reeve is so determined to undermine.

If I am wrong, the worst that can happen is that when the miracle comes, the nonbelievers will find themselves overtrained and overtoughened. But if Reeve is wrong, what will his dreamers be left with?

Christopher Reeve's appearance on an advertisement shown during the Super Bowl 2000 illustrates why many PWDs feel that super crips do not speak for most PWDs, and further, Reeve and other super crips may actually promote more stereotyping of PWDs. The advertisement was for Nuveen, a "wealth management" corporation (an investment company), that manages $71 billion in assets and trades on the New York Stock Exchange (Hersey, 2000). In 1999, Nuveen had a record sales of $14.1 billion. The advertisement was not for any disability organization. In the advertisement Reeve, through the use of special effects, appears to be walking, wearing a tuxedo, presenting some type of award for the "great strides" in AIDS, cancer, and spinal cord injury research. Christopher Reeve said that he did the commercial to raise public consciousness.

The disability community was outraged. First, Nuveen paid millions of dollars to air this commercial during the most expensive television time slot, the Super Bowl (January 23, 2000). Second, Nuveen blatantly used disability issues to promote its investment company, implying that a few rich people (like their customers) would fund research and eventually eliminate many kinds of disability (including spinal cord injuries). Laura Hersey, a writer with a disability stated, "Nuveen was not advertising a product or service during this Super Bowl; it was selling an idea: That the very rich are good, powerful people who think deeply and through their thoughtful action, help society.... Nuveen's new ad latches onto and amplifies the idea of clobbering the problem of disability, by leveraging the accumulated funds of the upper classes. 'Invest well' means to pay now to eliminate physical differences which, otherwise, will haunt society later with complex, expensive legal and architectural demands." Ironically, most PWDs have monthly incomes that are far less than PWODs; therefore, Nuveen probably does not have many PWDs as customers.

Charles Krauthammer, a physician who acquired a spinal cord injury 28 years ago, wrote an editorial for *Time* magazine (February 14, 2000, p. 100) (see Exhibit 5–3). Krauthammer labels the Christopher Reeve Super Bowl advertisement as "disgracefully misleading" and "cruel": "The false optimism Reeve is peddling is not just psychologically harmful, cruelly raising hopes. The harm is practical too. The newly paralyzed young might end up emulating Reeve, spending hours on end preparing their bodies to be ready to walk the day the miracle cure comes, much like the millenarians who abandon their homes and sell their worldly goods to await Rapture on a mountaintop" (p. 100). As a physician, Krauthammer understood, "The idea so dramatized in the Super Bowl commercial—that someone with a completely severed spinal cord will walk—is very farfetched...the principal beneficiaries will be the newly injured. People who are long injured—those who have developed scar tissue at the site of the break and whose distal spinal cord (the part below the injury) often turns to mush as the old neurons die—will be the last people to be helped by this research" (p. 100).

Reeve is what Hersey terms a "baby crip." She said, "Four years post-injury, he still doesn't know what hit him, nor what lies ahead." Although Hersey does not use the term, "super crip," she does mention Reeve's resources in dealing with his disability, which most PWDs do not have: "He still thinks that being disabled means you need two RNs attending you around the clock" and Reeve is "insulated by his wealth and celebrity." Reeve is insulting to other PWDs, giving television interviews in which he is critical of others with spinal cord injuries who are content to live their lives in a wheelchair. Further, he avoids associating with disability groups.

People with disabilities resent the assumption that he speaks for all PWDs. Hersey explained, "Reeve's message doesn't reflect how most disabled people live their lives. For most of us, things like work, personal relationships, having fun, and basic survival occupy far more of our attention and energy than any eventual cure. We come to terms with life as it is—complete with the disability and all its hazards, revelations, inconveniences, and adaptations. Many, though not all, come to value the crip life as a bold deviation from the boring norm....For me, being disabled is part of life. I'm baffled when someone wants to talk cure with me. It's not something I seriously contemplate; I feel no connection. When someone insists on a cure as a prerequisite for my happiness, I am angry. What's wrong with being who I am?"

AESTHETIC QUALITIES OF THE DISABILITY

> *In this section, look for—*
>
> ▶ *the increased stigma directed toward individuals whose disability is perceived as "disfiguring"*
> ▶ *often there are no functional limitations to a disfigurement*
> ▶ *in the past, there were only two alternatives for those with disfigurements*
> ▶ *most PWDs whose disabilities are disfiguring have even less privacy than most other PWDs*

It is clear that there is a great deal of stigma directed toward individuals whose disabilities are considered to be "maiming," "deforming," or "disfiguring." It is less clear, however, why there is increased prejudice. Disability scholars hypothesize that the anxiety and existential questioning that these types of disabilities evoke in others is at the root of this stigma. Upon viewing someone with a disfiguring disability, often we are reminded that disability, and disfigurements, can happen to anyone. Another source of stigma may be the overgeneralization and "spread" that is accorded to PWDs. Simply stated, when we see someone who looks very different from our expectations, or who is ugly, deformed, or maimed, we might assume that his or her personality and character are also very different or ugly, deformed, and maimed. Morris (1991) explained, "Our physical characteristics evoke such strong feelings that people often have to express them in some way. At the same time, they feel able to impose their feelings on us because we are not considered to be autonomous human beings" (p. 29). Perhaps another reason for violating the PWD's privacy is that the observer mistakenly thinks that the PWD is responsible for the strong feelings that the observer is feeling when, in reality, the observer is responsible for his or her own feelings and reactions.

Disfigurements illustrate the relationship between the disability itself and the handicapism of society. Most facial disfigurements, for example, have no functional limitations and yet they are considered to be disabilities and, moreover, one of the most handicapping disabilities. The handicaps and limitations have nothing to do with the disfigurement, but rather these handicaps are the result of society's reaction. Individuals with these types of disfiguring disabilities experience even less privacy than do PWDs with other types of disabilities. JoAnne Rome was born without a left arm below the elbow and in the following excerpt, she discussed her lack of privacy.

> I used to believe I owed an explanation to whomever demanded one. I felt fearful, intimidated, ashamed, out of control, and outraged, yet "what happened to your arm?" was not a question that I could choose to answer or not. I was a freak, an outsider, an "other" and the world made it very clear that I owed them an explanation. I was also a little girl who was chased home from school with taunts of "Captain Hook!" ringing in my ears, the object of whispers, stares and laughter (Morris, 1991, p. 28).

We have discussed the various ways in which the reactions of PWODs to an individual with a disability may become part of the PWD's self-concept. Persons with a disfiguring disability understand that they are not the disfigurement and may be forced to isolate themselves from others in order to maintain this self-identity. One woman called her facial scars "my mask," therefore, making it not part of her self-identity, and felt she could be herself only at home. Molly McIntosh was burned as a child and has scars on her face and the upper part of her body. She stated,

> I have horrible scars on my face. What I mean by that is that people react to them with horror. Forty years ago, when I was in my twenties, and also when I was a child, I so hated the way that I looked. I tried not to think about it but every time I went out in the street I would be reminded about how I looked because of the way people reacted to me. As I walked down the street and someone was coming towards me, they would look and then drop their eyes or move their heads, as if the horror was too much. But then they could never, ever resist looking again. I used to have bets with myself about the second look. I would promise myself a treat if they didn't look again, but they always did (Morris, 1991, p. 24).

In the past, there were only two ways for individuals with disfiguring disabilities to live. Most simply secluded themselves at home, thereby avoiding a lifetime of being objects of revulsion and rejection. A few chose to display themselves in freak shows and circuses, choosing to use people's horror and fascination as a money-maker (Bogdan, 1988).

IMPRESSION MANAGEMENT

In this section, look for—
- ▶ *disability-specific impression management*
- ▶ *an answer to the question, Should PWDs be concerned with reducing interaction strain? Or, stated differently, whose problem is it that PWODs are uncomfortable around PWDs?*
- ▶ *how even the most socially adept PWDs experience more rejection than most PWODs*

Most everybody, with or without a disability, engages in some type of impression management. We wear appropriate clothing, are well groomed, speak appropriately, and practice good manners. Especially when interacting with people whom we do not know very well and whom we wish to favorably impress, we invest a great deal of time and effort in impression management. First dates and job interviews are classic examples of these types of situations in that we wish to impress an individual(s) who does not know us very well and, furthermore, there is always the possibility that we will be rejected.

PWDs are aware that their disability creates discomfort in others and, therefore, impression management for them becomes even more complicated. In fact, many PWDs employ disability-specific impression-management techniques in an effort to reduce the tension felt by others (Belgrave, 1984; Belgrave & Mills, 1981; Kleck, 1968; Kleck et al., 1968). These techniques do not assist the individual's functioning and may, in fact, actually jeopardize his or her functioning. The sole purpose of these impression-management techniques is to reduce discomfort in others. Such impression-management techniques are criticized by many in the Disability Rights Movement because activists believe that the discomfort felt by PWODs is an issue with which PWODs should deal and it is not the responsibility of PWDs to become "court jesters" or "Tiny Tims." Some impression-management techniques are so costly to PWDs, in terms of time and physical pain, that they decide to abandon these attempts.

In spite of this controversy, many PWDs do actively engage in impression-management techniques to cope with the reactions of others. Some general techniques are the use of humor, the skillful introduction of the topic of the disability, and tactfully correcting PWODs when they make a mistake. Disability-specific techniques include a person who is blind maintaining "eye contact" with those who are speaking and turning on the lights at night. Individuals who are deaf have undergone years of speech training in order to have a more pleasant-sounding voice, and individuals with motor difficulties are subjected to "gait-training" in order to appear more "normal" to others. Other types of impression management include wearing prostheses for their cosmetic value rather than for their functional use. Franklin Roosevelt was a master at impression management. For example, he developed a type of "walk" in which he used a cane and a man walked on each side of him. (Often these men were his sons.) The three men had devised a carefully rehearsed act, at Roosevelt's request, to talk and laugh as they walked, appearing re-laxed. In reality, all three were exerting themselves, carefully shifting Roosevelt's weight with each step, and taking turns lifting him. (Roosevelt was lifting his legs with his body muscles because he had no hip muscles.) It was hard work, but it appeared that Roosevelt was walking on his own. Another example of Roosevelt's impression-management techniques was the navy blue cape that he wore. The public mistakenly thought this cape to be part of his "style," much as his cigarette holder was. In reality, it is easier to wear a cape rather than a coat when using a wheelchair, and therefore the cape was an accommodation to Roosevelt's disability.

SIMULATION EXERCISES

> *In this section, look for—*
>
> ▶ *what simulation exercises are designed to accomplish*
> ▶ *why simulation exercises fail to accomplish these purposes*
>   *1. How can a congenital disability, such as blindness, be simulated?*
>   *2. Is "forced empathy" possible?*
>   *3. Is it possible to simulate a significant aspect of an individual's self-concept?*
> ▶ *Often, simulation exercises increase prejudice and discrimination*

Simulation exercises are designed to give those without disabilities insight into the experience of disability (Baesler, 1995; Fichten, Compton, & Amsel, 1985). Individuals wear blindfolds to simulate blindness, use wheelchairs and other devices to simulate other types of disabilities, and often students in drug/alcohol abuse counseling classes are required to forego one type of food or drink for two or three weeks (often chocolate, coffee, or beer). However, it is now known that these exercises are not only useless but they may actually increase prejudice and discrimination toward PWDs (Kiger, 1992; Olkin, 1999; Pfeiffer, 1989; Wright, 1975).

Allport, in his classic work, *The Nature of Prejudice* (1954; 1958; 1986), discussed the usefulness of role playing techniques in which a member of the dominant group takes on the role of an individual of a minority group. In Allport's examples, the groups are racial/ethnic groups. Allport explained that the white person is "required to act out the roles of other people—of employees, of students, of Negro servants, he [sic] learned through such 'psychodrama' what it feels like to be in another's shoes. He [sic] also gains insight regarding his own motives, his anxieties, his projections" (Allport, 1986, p. 491). Indeed, Allport used the expression "forced empathy" to describe the purpose of these simulations.

Is it possible to simulate a disability? Simulation exercises, regardless of how carefully designed, cannot allow a PWOD to assume the identity of a PWD. As discussed before, most PWDs consider their disability to be a valued part of their self-identity, are proud of their mastery of the disability, and have developed many idiosyncratic responses and accommodations. None of these self-defining characteristics can be simulated. Voluntarily giving up coffee, chocolate, or beer may allow an individual to see how difficult such self-control can be, but the experience cannot begin to parallel the experience of recovery from alcohol and/or drug abuse. Furthermore, how can a PWOD simulate a congenital disability, such as blindness, deafness, or a limb deficiency?

On the other hand, it is possible to glimpse some of the prejudice and discrimination PWDs encounter. If a person is required to use a wheelchair for 24 hours, he or she can understand the frustration of nonaccessible restrooms, water fountains, and doorways. Nonetheless, the simulator knows that the simulation is of short duration (Sawyer & Clark, 1980).

Most important, simulation exercises reinforce and strengthen prejudice against PWDs because simulations often evoke feelings of dependence, hopelessness, and discouragement in the simulator. People who are blind or deaf or who use a wheelchair are skilled in mastering their environment; people who wear a blindfold or earmuffs or use a wheelchair for a simulation exercise, on the other hand, experience 24 hours of frustration, dependence, and hopelessness. Using a wheelchair requires strength and technique, both of which necessitate time to develop. The experience of blindness would be very different if an individual did not know how to read Braille. However, learning Braille is a difficult and time-consuming process. Wandering around the corridors of a university building with a blindfold would probably give the simulator a discouraging and frustrating view of blindness because Braille is used on doors and elevators. (In addition, people who are blind have had orientation and mobility [O & M] training.) Further, the simulator mistakenly thinks that he or she now has "expert knowledge" of the disability experience. However, it is not knowledge of disability that has been acquired, but rather the myth that PWDs feel helpless, dependent, and discouraged all the time.

Lifchez and Wade (1982) described simulation exercises and their unexpected results:

> Workshops where one temporarily "tries on" a disability constitute attempts to give...an entry into the subjective experience of the disability. Trying on a disability offers...a sense of the physical issues involved, but it often backfires, as it can generate so much anxiety....Trying on fails to offer...any sense of the way in which the environment affects, feeds, and is sustained by social and cultural prejudices and expectation (p. 91).

Kiger (1992) undertook a review of 60 studies of simulation exercises and found that none had any positive effect on the attitudes of PWODs toward the disability experience. There are other issues in using simulation exercises; one of these issues concerns the response of PWDs to PWODs attempting to "imitate" them. Olkin (1999), a polio survivor who uses a wheelchair, summarized her feelings about simulation exercises: "I find it rude for people to 'imitate' me as a way of understanding my minority status. It implies that only through direct experience can one come to understand 'minority status,' as if the word of people with disabilities isn't good enough. For no other minority status do we direct students to use imitation as a means of enlightenment" (p. 330).

Experiential learning is valuable and most disability scholars advocate the use of such learning methods to help PWODs understand the experience of disability. Indeed, if done correctly, experiential learning activities can decrease the heightened sensitivity and interaction strain PWODs often feel in the presence of PWDs. Beatrice Wright required her university students to undertake a semester-long advocacy project, such as overseeing the accessibility of a public playground or generating a list of public entertainment facilities which are not accessible to PWDs and then developing a plan to facilitate change. Other projects included listing negative, condescending portrayals of PWDs in the media (McCarthy, 1993). Olkin

(1999) used other types of experiential learning, including having her students use assistive devices, such as TTY telephones, and requiring students to go to the Department of Rehabilitation office and learn how to fill out an application form. (TTY telephones, used by people who are deaf, have a keyboard and a screen. The two "callers" type to each other. TTY stands for teletypewriter.) Both these professors/scholars emphasize that these types of learning activities need to be preceded and followed by the appropriate knowledge and discussion.

The Costs of Handicapism for PWODs and Society

Thus far, we have discussed the costs of prejudice and discrimination against PWDs (handicapism) only in terms of PWDs. Indeed, the costs to PWODs, and society in general, are rarely considered. Nonetheless, whether acknowledged or not, there are consequences and costs to the dominant group—PWODs. There are three ways in which society pays for its prejudice against PWDs: (1) the economic costs; (2) the collective, and individual, fear of acquiring a disability; and (3) the narrow (and inaccurate) view of the world and human experience that PWODs have when they choose to ignore the disability experience. Perhaps there is an additional "cost" of prejudice, that of our moral ambivalence. A society (or individual) is morally ambivalent when the society (or individual) publicly *professes* one set of values and *acts* on another set of values. For example, our society professes that all people are created equal; however, as we have seen, PWDs have systematically been treated as second-class citizens. Handicapism is deeply rooted, legitimized, institutionalized, and individually internalized throughout American society. Moreover, society blames the victims, telling PWDs that their disabilities are the cause of the prejudice and discrimination. Believing this premise, many consider handicapism to be an inevitable and unavoidable outcome. In contrast, if we could understand that our prejudices and discrimination (and the resulting lack of accommodations) were both irrational and unjustified, then institutional changes could be made.

The Economic Costs of Prejudice and Discrimination, or "Do the Math"

Of course, it is impossible to generate an accurate dollar cost of what a society loses in wasted skills, lower production, and fewer customers to buy products. Nonetheless, economic costs are incurred in three ways: (1) the loss of productivity of PWDs, (2) the financial costs to compensate PWDs rather than to employ them, and (3) the loss of a customer base to buy products. The economic costs of keeping PWDs unemployed or underemployed do not begin to consider the social and emotional costs of unemployment to the PWD. Work for anyone, with or without a disability, brings financial security and economic empowerment, but there are other benefits such as social relationships, the opportunity to learn and develop skills, and the chance to make a contribution. These types of benefits are not easily translated into dollar costs, but they may, in many respects, be more important than the financial benefits. Yet, PWDs continue to be denied entrance into the labor market.

Lest anyone think that government financial compensation, such as Social Security, allows PWDs a life of economic comfort and dignity, most Social Security benefits keep the individual below the poverty line. Who pays for the unemployment and underemployment of PWDs? The American taxpayer. The taxpayer pays in two ways: for the loss of productivity of PWDs and for the financial compensation required to keep PWDs unemployed. Sociologists (Simpson & Yinger, 1985) cited another cost: "That discrimination prevents the training and use of workers as their highest possible skill is shown not only in the failure to employ fully the trained carpenter or pilot or teacher if he or she belongs to the "wrong groups," but more particularly in the failure to train many individuals in the first place" (p. 161).

Hahn (1997) stated: "The concept of an 'industrial reserve army' seems to provide an explanation for the depressed economic position of men and women with disabilities. Available estimates indicate that approximately two-thirds of disabled persons in most industrialized nations are unemployed, a level that exceeds the unemployment rate among other deprived and disadvantaged groups" (p. 173).

Weisgerber (1991) reported, "These losses amounted to 6.9 percent of the gross national product in 1980," or "alternatively, as Chirikos pointed out, the losses can be characterized as a 'tax of about $800 levied on each and every American'" (p. 190). Since these are 1980 statistics and the rate of employment of PWDs has not improved, we can conclude that at the present time, each American pays more than $800.

Fear of Acquiring a Disability

If PWODs were to understand the disability experience more accurately, they would fear it less. Disability has been termed "the only open minority group," meaning that anyone, at any time, can become a member of the group by acquiring a disability. Rosemarie Garland Thomson concisely stated, "There is no 'we' and 'they' when it comes to disability" (1997, p. 297). Clearly, such assumptions that PWDs are the "other" or "those" people and the belief that we will never acquire a disability defy logic. Disability is a universal concern. The existential angst, or fear of acquiring disability, is self-inflicted by PWODs' indifference to learning about the disability experience. We learned from Groce's book, *Everybody Here Spoke Sign Language,* that when a child was born deaf on Martha's Vineyard, the birth was not considered tragic nor were the baby's social or vocational opportunities automatically reduced due to the deafness. On Martha's Vineyard, because of the large number (relatively speaking) of residents who were deaf, everyone "spoke" sign language and people who were deaf were not considered to have a disability, to be different, or to be inferior. Deafness, to everyone, seemed natural and nothing to be feared. Hearing people who were "bilingual" might be regarded as an accommodation for people who are deaf, but certainly the bilingualism of everyone on Martha's Vineyard helped hearing people not to fear deafness. Wendell (1997) stated, "If disabled people and their knowledge were fully integrated into society, everybody's relation to his or her own body would be liberated" (p. 260). Dorothy Hermann (1998), after writing the biography of Helen Keller, wrote that she had learned that disability is "not inevitably accompanied by deformity, suffering, and limitations" and that disability was "not inevitably sacrifice and loss of freedom. Disability is not to be feared" (p. xxxiii). Accommodations for PWDs also assist PWODs. For example, the Americans with Disabilities Act requires standardizing admission requirements for schools and job functions for employment. Such standardization and widening of the pool of qualified applicants help both PWDs and PWODs. Employers and educational programs will now have a larger and more qualified pool from which to hire/admit, and all applicants, with or without a disability, will have clear, written job qualifications and admission standards.

A Narrow and Inaccurate World View

PWODs have designed a society based on the false assumption that there are few PWDs when, in fact, disability is both common and natural. Believing this assumption, PWODs rob themselves of the richness and diversity that PWDs could contribute, if PWODs would allow them. A society is richer when it appreciates, understands, and respects a wide range of experiences, values, points of view, and self-identities. On the other hand, when society reduces (consciously or subconsciously) its level of tolerance for difference of any kind, its framework for viewing the world is both narrow and inaccurate. However, in times of change, boundaries between groups are less clear-cut. The rising movement of PWDs (and their families) to claim their civil rights and the higher rates of disability incidences have begun, and will continue, to blur the demarcations between PWODs and PWDs.

Franklin Roosevelt, one of the world's greatest leaders, who guided the United States through the worst financial crisis in history, the Great Depression, and oversaw the creation and deployment of the largest military and industrial force to win World War II, had a disability. Everyone knew that Roosevelt was a survivor of polio and could not walk, but they cooperated in minimizing and hiding the effects of the disability. Historians and biographers, in the past, judged Roosevelt to have made his world-changing accomplishments *in spite* of his disability. Now, Geoffrey Ward, in his book *A First Class Temperament: The Emergence of Franklin Roosevelt* (1989), advances the thesis that Roosevelt's disability experience *contributed* to his accomplishments. Ward stated that the experience of surviving polio "humanized" Roosevelt, changing him from "a superficial opportunist, self-centered lightweight who sacrificed old friends in the interest of personal advancement" (p. 74). Ward continued, "To win that battle (polio)...would demand of him qualities not conspicuously displayed so far as his largely charmed life: patience, application, recognition of his own limitations, a willingness to fail in front of others and try again" (p. 75). Ward's biography of Roosevelt makes it clear that it is not possible to understand Roosevelt or his achievements without understanding his experience with polio.

In-Class Videos

- View the video *How Difficult Can This Be?*, produced by The Fat City Workshop, Public Broadcasting Company. This is an example of a simulation exercise. Concentrate on the defense mechanisms these individuals use.
- View the video *Without Pity: A Film about Disabilities*. This documentary, narrated by Christopher Reeve, introduces the audience to several people of different ages, professions, and disabilities. In this video, Reeve makes this comment: "Disabled [*sic*] people are tired of being invisible and are declaring their right to an equal chance at life." Available from Films for the Humanities and Sciences.
- View the 60-minute video *Ways To Move*. The producers describe this video: "[It] contains three stories which explore the debate between what has been called the medical model of disability (in which the disability is a challenge to be cured) and the independence model (in which the challenge is to make society more accessible). Viewers meet individuals who shatter stereotypes about disability: dancers who use wheelchairs as part of their choreography, researchers

on the quest for a cure for paralysis, and a candidate running for Congress who happens to be disabled." Available from Program Development Resource.

- View the video *My Country*. This video tells the stories of three people with disabilities and their hard-won success for equal rights under the law. Available from Aquarius Health Care Videos, 5 Powderhouse Lane, P.O. Box 1159, Sherbon, MA 01770; telephone, 508–651–2963; fax, 508–650-4216; e-mail, aqvideo@tiac.net (www.aquariusproductions.com).

- View the 50-minute video *The Ragin' Cajun: Oliver Sacks Investigates Usher Syndrome* by Films for the Humanities and Sciences. The producers describe this video: "The deaf–blind community in Seattle is extraordinarily vibrant, with a strong sense of pride and independence. That is why Danny Delcambre moved there. Deaf from birth, and steadily losing his sight, Danny suffers [*sic*] from Usher syndrome. The region in Louisiana he left behind has the highest concentration of Usher syndrome in the world. This program takes a sensitive look at this degenerative condition as neurologist/author Oliver Sacks and Danny explore the nature of Deaf Culture and the marvelous richness of American Sign Language, which includes a sophisticated touch-based variation called tactile signing. A BBC (British Broadcasting Company) production."

- View the 40-minute video *Signs of Life* by Films for the Humanities and Sciences. The producers describe this video: "People with hearing impairments have been a misunderstood minority for too long. This program blows away the stereotypes and should be required viewing for everyone, including the Deaf and hard-of-hearing."

- View the 30-minute video *The Right Future: Beyond Institutionalization* by Films for the Humanities and Sciences. The producers describe this video: "For people with developmental disabilities, misunderstanding, fear, and financial constraints historically have created barriers to successful community living. This documentary is a compelling profile of the Right Future project, a model program that integrates people with developmental disabilities into a supportive and welcoming community."

- View the 25-minute video *Ethics, Residents' Rights, and Dignity* by Insight Media, 2162 Broadway, New York, NY 10024–0621, 1–800–233–9910, *www.insight-media.com*. The producers describe this video: "Legal issues and advances in technology make it imperative to consider ethics and residents' rights. This video explores the difference between law and ethics, details the rights of every resident, and helps viewers to determine standards of personal conduct for the workplace." Note: This video discusses issues of elderly people in residential care. However, there are many ethical issues that apply to PWDs in residential care.

- View the award-winning video *Fred's Story*. This 27-minute video is described by the producers: "A charming older gentleman tells about the 40 years he spent inside Mansfield Training School, a Connecticut institution closed in 1990. Fred Calabrese tells of the unpleasant realities of decades of institutional life, then a move to his own apartment. Fred is a disturbingly honest but overwhelmingly charming speaker on his own behalf." Mr. Calabrese states, "He said he'd get me out when the time comes. Well, the time never came and I was there for 40 years." Available from Program Development Resource, P.O. Box 2038, Syracuse, NY 13220, 1–800-543-2119, fax 315–452–0710. This video comes with four discussion guides.

- View the 26-minute video *Waddie Welcome*. The producers describe this video: "The many fascinating stories, the heartbreak, and the triumphs experienced by Waddie Welcome are presented by his circle of friends. They listened to his pleas, learned to communicate in his language, and used person-centered planning to enable Mr. Welcome to live with a family after a 10-year stay in a nursing home. This video signifies an effort to sustain justice and challenges us to redesign the responsiveness of community delivery systems." Available from Program Development Resource.
- View two 30-minute videos, *This Is YOUR Right*. The producers describe these videos: "Imagine a news magazine type television program like *60 Minutes* or *20/20*. Then imagine the anchors, segments, field reporters, and commercials. Now imagine instead that the news magazine type show is called *Human Rights TB*, the anchors and field reporters all have concrete strategies for promoting and strengthening self-advocacy. Learn the rich history of self-advocates, disability rights advocates, and the civil rights struggles. Viewers will have a stronger sense of empowerment and understand the importance of self-advocacy." Available from Program Development Resource.
- View the 60-minute video *Ready To Live*. Producers describe this video: "This program looks at ways adaptive technologies help people with disabilities to find independence. Included is a profile of the late Ed Roberts, a national disability rights activist, once called a 'helpless cripple,' who became one of the founders of the 'Independent Living Movement.' Other profiles include a world-class runner who used an advanced prosthetic leg, a former Bosnian soldier whose life was transformed by a pair of artificial hands, a woman who inspired a revolution in wheelchair design and construction." Available from Program Development Resource.
- View the 29-minute video *Self-Advocacy: Freedom, Equality, and Justice for All*. The producers state: *"Freedom, Equality, and Justice for All is a remarkable package of specific disabilities, and tonight's entire show will be devoted to people with disabilities and be called This is YOUR Right.* If you can imagine all of this, you'll have a pretty good idea of what this humorous production is all about. The production includes funny commercials about fictitious products and services that are intended to lampoon situations that people with disabilities encounter in everyday life." An Irene M. Ward and Associates Production, available from Program Development Resource.
- View the 22-minute video *A Little History Worth Knowing: Disability Down Through the Ages*. The producers describe this video: "From ancient times to telethons, to today's burgeoning disability movement, *A Little History Worth Knowing* traces the often-overlooked history of people with disabilities. With a combination of hard-hitting facts and rare historical footage, the video looks at:
  1. stereotypes in films, TV, and other media
  2. the ongoing struggle for disability rights
  3. the effects of technology on people's ability to work and live independently
  4. historical stereotypes, including the "medical model."
  Although the video doesn't shy away from the abuses of the past (including Hitler's extermination of more than 200,000 people with disabilities), it ends with a hopeful look at the future as changing attitudes and advancing tech-

nology help people with disabilities to enter the global economy." This Irene M. Ward and Associates production is available from Program Development Resource.

- View the 48-minute video *Vital Signs: Crip Culture Talks Back* by David Mitchells and Sharon Snyder. The producers describe this video as an "edgy, raw documentary [that] explores the politics of disability through the performances, debates, and late-night conversations of activists at a recent national conference on Disability and the Arts. Including interviews with well-known disability rights advocates such as Cheryl Marie Wade, Mary Duffy, and Harland Hahn, *Vital Signs* conveys the intensity, variety, and vitality of the disability culture today. Available from Fanlight Productions, 4196 Washington Street, Boston, MA 02131, 800–9374113, www.fanlight.com.

- View the 24-minute video *Voices in a Deaf Theater*. The producers describe this video: "This perceptive documentary follows a mixed cast of deaf and hearing actors as they prepare to stage *The Glass Menagerie*. As they rehearse, each group experiences a difficult but rewarding journey into the culture of the other. This outstanding video offers viewers a window into the Deaf world, with its rich culture and expressive language, as well as an opportunity to witness the way two groups, with a common goal but very different communication tools, can bridge their language barrier." A study guide is included. Available from Fanlight Productions.

Learning Activities

1. Read and discuss two or three issues of *The Ragged Edge: The Disability Experience in America*. Available from The Advocado Press, Box 145, Louisville, KY 40201; e-mail: circulation@ragged-edge-mag.com; Web site: *www.advocadopress.org*. This is the most widely circulated disability rights magazine.

2. Read and discuss two or three issues of *Mouth: Voice of the Disability Nation*. This is a very direct and straightforward publication written by those who have disabilities. Write to 4201 SW 30th Street, Topeka, KS 66614–3023.

3. Obtain the transcript from the NBC Dateline Sept. 9, 1997 program. This program, featuring John Hockenberry, showed prejudice and discrimination against PWDs in applying for jobs, trying to rent an apartment and other situations. Hidden cameras were used to record apartment owners and store managers refusing to rent an apartment or give a job interview to people in wheelchairs. Available from Burrelle's Information Services, Box 7, Livingston, NJ 07039. Ask for transcript Number 560.

Writing Activity

Using one of the 11 "bullets" listed at the beginning of this chapter, write a response paper.

References

Allport, G. W. (1954). *The nature of prejudice.* Reading, MA: Addison-Wesley.

Allport, G W. (1958). *The nature of prejudice* (2nd ed.). Garden City, NY: Doubleday Anchor.

Allport, G. W. (1986). *The nature of prejudice* (25th anniversary ed.). Reading, MA: Addison Wesley.

Amir, Y. (1969). Contact hypothesis in ethnic relations. *Psychological Bulletin, 71,* 319–342.

Amsel, R., & Fichten, C. S. (1988). Effects of contact on thoughts about interaction with students who have a physical disability. *Journal of Rehabilitation, 54,* 61–65.

Anderson, G. R. (1987). Paternalism. In G. R. Anderson & V. A. Glesnes-Anderson (Eds.). Health care ethics: A guide for decision makers (pp. 177–191). Rockville, MD: Aspen.

Anthony, W. (1972). Societal rehabilitation: Changing society's attitudes toward the physically and mentally disabled. *Rehabilitation Psychology, 19,* 117–126.

Anthony, W. (1984). Social rehabilitation: Changing society's attitudes toward the physically and mentally disabled. In R. Marinelli & A. Dell Orto (Eds.). *The psychology and social impact of physical disability* (2nd ed., pp. 193–203). New York: Springer.

Baesler, E. J. (1995). Persuasive effects of an involving disability role play. *Journal of Applied Rehabilitation Counseling, 26*(2), 29–35.

Baker, F. M., Baker R. J., & McDaniel, R. S. (1975). Demoralizing practices in rehabilitation facilities. *Rehabilitation Literature, 36,* 112–115.

Becker, H. S. (Ed.). (1963). *Outsiders: Studies in the sociology of deviance.* New York: Free Press.

Belgrave, F. Z. (1984). The effectiveness of strategies for increasing social interaction with a physically disabled person. *Journal of Applied Social Psychology, 14,* 147–161.

Belgrave, F. Z., & Mills, J. (1981). Effect upon desire for social interaction with a physically disabled person of mentioning the disability in different contexts. *Journal of Applied Social Psychology, 11,* 44–57.

Bell, A. H. (1962). Attitudes of selected rehabilitation workers and other hospital employees toward the physically disabled. *Psychological Reports, 10,* 183–186.

Bennett, C.R. (1998). Dentistry and the disabled. *Rehab Team, January,* 20–24.

Berkowitz, E. D. (1984). Professionals as providers: Some thoughts on disability and ideology. *Rehabilitation Psychology, 29,* 211–216.

Bickenbach, J. E. (1993). *Physical disability and social policy.* Toronto: University of Toronto.

Blood, I. M., & Blood, G. W. (1982). Classroom teachers' impressions of normal-hearing and hearing-impaired children. *Perceptual and Motor Skills, 54,* 877–878.

Bogdan, R. (1988). *Freak show: Presenting human oddities for amusement and profit.* Chicago: University of Chicago Press.

Bogdan, R., & Taylor, S. J. (1992). The social construction of humanness: Relationships with severely disabled people. In P. M. Ferguson, D. L. Ferguson, & S. J. Taylor (Eds.). *Interpreting disability: A qualitative reader* (pp. 275–294). New York: Teachers College, Columbia University.

Bower, E. M. (Ed.). (1980). *The handicapped in literature: A psychosocial perspective.* Denver, CO: Love.

Brodwin, M. G., & Gardner, G. (1978). Teacher attitudes toward the physically disabled. *Journal of Teaching and Learning, 3*(3), 40–45.

Buss, D. M. (1999). *Evolutionary psychology: The new science of the mind.* Boston: Allyn & Bacon.

Byrd, E. K., & Elliott, T. R. (1988). Media and disability: A discussion of the research. In H. E. Yuker (Ed.). *Attitudes toward persons with disabilities* (pp. 82–95). New York: Springer.

Chubon, R. A. (1982). An analysis of research dealing with the attitudes of professionals toward disability. *Journal of Rehabilitation, 48,* 25–30.

Cole, S. S. (1984). Facing the challenge of sexual abuse of persons with disabilities. *Sexuality and Disability, 7,* 71–88.

Cole, S. S. (1993). Facing the challenges of sexual abuse in persons with disabilities. In M. Nagler (Ed.). *Perspectives on disability* (2nd ed.) (pp. 273–282). Palo Alto, CA: Health Markets Research.

Coleman, L. M. (1997). Stigma: An enigma demystified. In L. J. Davis (Ed.). *The disability studies reader* (pp. 216–231). New York: Routledge.

Comer, R. J., & Piliavin, J. A. (1972). The effects of physical deviance upon face-to-face interaction: The other side. *Journal of Personality and Social Psychology, 23,* 33–39.

Cook, S. W. (1978). Interpersonal and attitudinal outcomes in cooperating interracial groups. *Journal of Research in Developmental Education, 12,* 97–113.

Covey, H. C. (1998). *Social perceptions of people with disabilities in history.* Springfield, IL: Charles C Thomas.

Covington, G. (1997). Super crip. In F. Pelka (Ed.), *The disability rights movement* (p. 92). Santa Barbara, CA: ABC-CLIO.

Craine, L. S., Henson, C. E., Colliver, J. A., & McLelan, D. G. (1988). Prevalence of a history of sexual abuse among female psychiatric patients in a state hospital system. *Hospital and Community Psychiatry, 39,* 300–304.

Davis, L. J. (Ed.). (1997). *The disability studies reader.* New York: Routledge.

Deegan, P. E. (1991). Recovery: The lived experience of rehabilitation. In R. P. Marinelli & A. E. Dell Orto (Eds.). *The psychological and social impact of disability* (3rd ed., pp. 47–54). New York: Springer.

Dembo, T., Leviton, G. L., & Wright, B. A. (1975). Adjustment to misfortune: A problem of social-psychological rehabilitation. *Rehabilitation Psychology, 2,* 1–100.

Deutsch, M. (1949). A theory of cooperation and competition. *Human Relations, 2,* 129–152.

Donaldson, J. (1980). Changing attitudes toward handicapped persons: A review and analysis of the research. *Exceptional Children, 46,* 504–514.

Duckitt, J. (1992). *The social psychology of prejudice.* New York: Praeger.

Dunn, M. (1996). Subscale development of the Rehabilitation Situations Inventory. *Rehabilitation Psychology, 41,* 255–264.

Eisenberg, M. G. (1982). Disability as stigma. In M. G. Eisenberg, C. Griggins, & R. J. Duval (Eds.). *Disabled people as second-class citizens* (pp. 1–11). New York: Springer.

Eisenberg, M. G., Griggins, C., & Duval, R. J. (Eds.). (1982). *Disabled people as second-class citizens.* New York: Springer.

Elliott, T. R., Frank, R. G., Corcoran, J., Beardon, L., & Byrd, E. K. (1990). Previous personal experience and reactions to depression and physical disability. *Rehabilitation Psychology, 35,* 111–119.

Evans, J. H. (1976). Changing attitudes toward disabled persons: An experimental study. *Rehabilitation Counseling Bulletin, 19,* 572–579.

Fichten, C.S., Compton, V., & Amsel, R. (1985). Imagined empathy and attributions concerning activity preferences of physically disabled college students. *Rehabilitation Psychology, 30,* 235–239.

Fichten, C. S., Robillard, K., Judd, D., & Amsel, R. (1989). College students with disabilities: Myths and realities. *Rehabilitation Psychology, 34,* 243–257.

Friedson, E. (1965). Disability as social deviance. In M. Sussman (Ed.). *Sociology and rehabilitation* (pp. 71–99). Washington, DC: American Sociology Association and the US Vocational Education Administration.

Fries, K. (Ed.). (1997). *Staring back: The disability experience from the inside out.* New York: Plume.

Fuchs, D., Fuchs, L. S., Dailey, A. M., & Power, M. H. (1985). The effects of examiners' personal familiarity and professional experience on handicapped children's test performance. *Journal of Educational Research, 78,* 141–146.

Gaier, E. L., Linkowski, D. C., & Jaques, M. E. (1968). Contact as a variable in the perception of disability. *The Journal of Social Psychology, 74,* 117–126.

Garske, G. G., & Thomas, K. R. (1990). The relationship of self-esteem and contact to attitudes of students in rehabilitation counseling toward persons with disabilities. *Rehabilitation Counseling Bulletin, 34,* 67–71.

Gartner, A., & Joe, T. (Eds.). (1987). *Images of the disabled, disabling images.* New York: Praeger.

Gellman, W. (1959). Roots of prejudice against the handicapped. *Journal of Rehabilitation, 40,* 115–123.

Genskow, J. K., & Maglione, F. D. (1965). Familiarity, dogmatism, and reported student attitudes toward the disabled. *The Journal of Social Psychology, 67,* 329–341.

Goffman, E. (1963). *Stigma: Notes on the management of spoiled identity.* Englewood Cliffs, NJ: Prentice-Hall.

Goffman, E. (1997). Selections from stigma. In L. J. Davis (Ed.). *The disability studies reader* (pp. 203–215). New York: Routledge.

Gordon, E. D., Minnes, P.M., & Holden, R. R. (1990). The structure of attitudes toward persons with a disability, when specific disability and context are considered. *Rehabilitation Psychology, 35,* 79–90.

Gould, S. (1981). *The mismeasure of man.* New York: Norton.

Gouvier, W. D., Coon, R. C., Todd, M. E., & Fuller, K. H. (1994). Verbal interactions with individuals presenting with and without physical disability. *Rehabilitation Psychology, 39,* 263–268.

Grand, S. A., Bernier, J. E., & Strohmer, D. C. (1982). Attitudes toward disabled persons as a function of social context and specific disability. *Rehabilitation Psychology, 27,* 165–174.

Greenwood, R., & Johnson, V. A. (1987). Employer perspectives on workers with disabilities. *Journal of Rehabilitation, 53*(3), 37–54.

Hahn, H. (1997). Advertising the acceptably employable image: Disability and capitalism. In L. J. Davis (Ed.). *The disability studies reader* (pp. 172–186), New York: Routledge.

Harosymia, S. J., Home, M. D., & Lewis, C. A. (1976). A longitudinal study of disability group acceptance. *Rehabilitation Literature, 37,* 98–102.

Heinemann, W., Pellander, F., Vogelbusch, A., & Wojtek, B. (1981). Meeting a deviant person: Subjective norms and affective reactions. *European Journal of Social Psychology, 11,* 1–25.

Henderson, G., & Bryan, W. V. (1997). *Psychosocial aspects of disability* (2nd ed.). Springfield, IL: Charles C Thomas.

Hermann, D. (1998). *Helen Keller: A life.* New York: Knopf.

Hersey, L. (2000). *Commentary on the Super Bowl Ad: Quad Man Walking.* Available from Compuserve.com.

Heumann, J. (1999). Personal narrative. In R. Mackelprang & R. Salsgiver (Eds.). *Disability: A diversity model in human service practice* (pp. 51–54). Pacific Grove, CA: Brooks/Cole.

Higgins, P. C. (1992). *Making disability: Exploring the social transformation of human variation.* Springfield, IL: Charles C Thomas.

Hillyer, B. (1993). *Feminism and disability.* Norman, OK: University of Oklahoma.

Holzbauer, J., & Berven, N. (1996). Disability harassment: A new term for a longstanding problem. *Journal of Counseling and Development, 74,* 478–483.

Horne, M. D. (1988). Modifying peer attitudes toward the handicapped: Procedures and research issues. In H. E. Yuker (Ed.). *Attitudes toward persons with disabilities* (pp. 203–222). New York: Springer.

Hubbard, R. (1997). Abortion and disability: Who should live and inhabit the world? In L. J. Davis (Ed.). *The disability studies reader* (pp. 187–200). New York: Routledge.

Hurst, R. (1998). Forget pity or charity: Disability is a rights issue. *Disability International, 5*(3), 14–16.

Huston, A. M. (1987). *Common sense about dyslexia.* New York: Madison.

Imrie, R. (1996). *Disability in the city: International perspectives.* New York: St. Martin's Press.

Janicki, M. P. (1970). Attitudes of health professionals toward disabilities. *Perceptual and Motor Skills, 30,* 77–78.

Jankowski, K. A. (1997). *Deaf empowerment: emergence, struggle, and rhetoric.* Washington, DC: Gallaudet University.

Jaques, M. E., Linkowski, D. C., & Seika, F. L. (1970). Cultural attitudes toward disability: Denmark, Greece, and the United States. *International Journal of Social Psychiatry, 16,* 54–62.

Kiger, G. (1992). Disability simulations: Logical, methodological, and ethical issues. *Disability, Handicap, & Society, 7,* 71–78.

Kleck, R. (1966). Emotional arousal in interactions with stigmatized persons. *Psychological Reports, 19,* 1226.

Kleck, R. (1968). Physical stigma and nonverbal cues emitted in face-to-face interaction. *Human Relations, 21,* 19–28.

Kleck, R., Buck, P. L., Goller, W. L., London, R. S., Pfeiffer, J. R., & Vukcevic, D. P. (1968). Effect of stigmatizing conditions on the use of personal space. *Psychological Reports, 23,* 111–118.

Kleck, R., Ono, H., & Hastorf, A. H. (1966). The effects of physical deviance upon face-to-face interaction. *Human Relations, 19,* 425–436.

Krauft, C. C., Rubin, S. D., Cook, D. W., & Bozarth, J. D. (1976). Counselor attitudes towards disabled persons and client program completion: A pilot study. *Journal of Applied Rehabilitation Counseling, 7,* 72–77.

Krauthammer, C. (2000, February 14). Restoration, reality and Christopher Reeve. *Time, 155*(6), 100.

Kriegel, L. (1982). Claiming the self: The cripple as American male. In M. G. Eisenberg, C. Griggins, & R. J. Duval (Eds.). *Disabled people as second class citizens* (pp. 52–63). New York: Springer.

Langer, E. J., Bashner, R. S., & Chanowitz, B. (1985). Decreasing prejudice by increasing discrimination. *Journal of Personality and Social Psychology, 49,* 113–120.

Langer, E. J., Fiske, S., Taylor, S. E., & Chanowitz, B. (1976). Stigma, staring, and discomfort: A novel-stimulus hypothesis. *Journal of Experimental and Social Psychology, 12,* 451–463.

Larrivee, B., & Cook, L. (1979). Mainstreaming: A study of the variables affecting teacher attitude. *Journal of Special Education, 13,* 315–324.

Lehr, D. H., & Brinckerhoff, J. (1996). Bases of practice for young children with disabilities who challenge the system. In D. H. Lehr & F. Brown (Eds.). *People with disabilities who challenge the system* (pp. 3–21). Baltimore: Brookes.

Liachowitz, C. H. (1988). *Disability as a social construct: Legislative roots.* Philadelphia: University of Pennsylvania.

Lifchez, R., & Wade, C. (1982). What every architect should know. In M. G. Eisenberg, C. Griggins, & R. J. Duval (Eds.). *Disabled people as second class citizens* (pp. 88–102). New York: Springer.

Longmore, P. (1985). Screening stereotypes: Images of disabled people in television and motion pictures. *Social Policy, 16,* 31–38.

Louis Harris and Associates, Inc. (1986). *The ICD survey of disabled Americans: Bringing disabled Americans into the mainstream.* New York: Author.

Louis Harris and Associates, Inc. (1994). *N.O.D. L. Harris survey of disabled Americans.* Washington, DC: National Organization of Disability.

Makas, E. (1993). Getting in touch: The relationship between contact with and attitudes toward people with disabilities. In M. Nagler (Ed.). *Perspectives on disability* (2nd ed., pp. 121–136). Palo Alto, CA: Health Markets Research

McCarthy, H. (1993). Learning with Beatrice A. Wright: A breath of fresh air that uncovers the unique virtues and human flaws in us all. *Rehabilitation Education, 7,* 149–166.

Morris, J. (1991). *Pride against prejudice: Transforming attitudes to disability.* Philadelphia: New Society.

Murphy, M. A. (1998). Rejection, stigma, and hope. *Psychiatric Rehabilitation Journal, 22,* 185–189.

Olkin, R. (1999). *What psychotherapists should know about disability.* New York: Guilford.

Palmerton, K. E., & Frumkin, R. M. (1969). Contact with disabled persons and intensity of counselors' attitudes. *Perceptual and Motor Skills, 28,* 434.

Parenti, J. F., Beaufils, B., & Paicheler, H. (1987). Stereotyping and intergroup perceptions of disabled and nondisabled children: A new perspective. *The Exceptional Child, 34,* 93–106.

Pelka, F. (Ed.). (1997). *The ABC-CLIO companion to the disability rights movement.* Santa Barbara, CA: ABC-CLIO.

Pfeiffer, D. (1989). Disability simulation using a wheelchair simulation. *Journal of Post Secondary Education and Disability, 7,* 53–60.

Rabkin, J. G. (1972). Opinions about mental illness: A review of the literature. *Psychological Bulletin, 77,* 153–171.

Safilios-Rothschild, C. (1970). *The sociology and social psychology of disability and rehabilitation.* New York: Random House.

Safran, S. P. (1998). The first century of disability portrayal in film: An analysis of the literature. *Journal of Special Education, 31,* 467–479.

Sawyer, H. W., & Clark, W.D. (1980). Disability simulation as a strategy for attitude change. *Journal of Applied Rehabilitation Counseling, 11,* 132–135.

Schmelkin, L. P. (1988). Multidimensional perspectives in the perception of disabilities. In H. E. Yuker (Ed.). *Attitudes toward persons with disabilities* (pp. 127–137). New York: Springer.

Schur, E. M. (1971). *Labeling deviant behavior: Its sociological implications.* New York: Harper and Row.

Schur, E. M. (1979). *Interpreting deviance.* New York: Harper and Row.

Schur, E. M. (1983). *Labeling women deviant: Gender, stigma, and social control.* Philadelphia: Temple University.

Sigelman, C. K., Spanhel, C. L., & Lorenzen, C. D. (1979). Community reaction to deinstitutionalization. *Journal of Rehabilitation, 45,* 52–54, 60.

Siller, J. (1984). The role of personality in attitude toward those with physical disabilities. In C. J. Golden (Ed.). *Current topics in rehabilitation psychology* (pp. 201–227). Orlando, FL: Grune & Stratton.

Simpson, G. E., & Yinger, J. M. (1985). *Racial and cultural minorities: An analysis of prejudice and discrimination* (5th ed.). New York: Plenum.

Sobsey, D. (1994). *Violence and abuse in the lives of people with disabilities: The end of silent acceptance.* Baltimore: Brookes.

Sobsey, D., & Doe, T. (1991). Patterns of sexual abuse and assault. *Sexuality and Disability, 9,* 243–260.

Sobsey, D., & Mansell, S. (1993). The prevention of sexual abuse of people with developmental disabilities. In M. Nagler (Ed.), *Perspectives on disability* (2nd ed., pp. 283–292). Palo Alto, CA: Health Markets Research.

Thomas, S. A., Foreman, P. E., & Remenyi, A. G. (1985). The effects of previous contact with physical disability upon Australian children's attitudes toward people with physical disabilities. *International Journal of Rehabilitation Research, 8,* 69–70.

Thomson, R. G. (1997). Integrating disability studies into the existing curriculum: The example of "Women and Literature" at Howard University. In L. J. Davis (Ed.). *The disability studies reader* (pp. 295–306). New York: Routledge.

Trupin, L., Sebesta, D. S., Yelin, E., & LaPlante, M. P. (1997). Trends in labor force participation. Disability Status Report No. 10. San Francisco, CA: University of California, Institute for Health and Aging.

Ulicny, G. R., White, G. W., Bradford, B., & Matthews, R. M. (1990). Consumer exploitation by attendants: How often does it happen and can anything be done about it? *Rehabilitation Counseling Bulletin, 33,* 240–246.

Wade, C. M. (1997). *Poems.* In L. J. Davis (Ed.). *The disability studies reader* (pp. 408–409). New York: Routledge.

Ward, G. C. (1989). *A first class temperament: The emergence of Franklin Roosevelt.* New York: Harper and Row.

Weisgerber, R. A. (1991). *Quality of life for persons with disabilities.* Gaithersburg, MD: Aspen Publishers, Inc.

Wendell, S. (1997). Toward a feminist theory of disability. In L. J. Davis (Ed.). *The disability studies reader* (pp. 260–278). New York: Routledge.

Whitney, C. R. (1993, January 19). Disabled Germans fear they'll be the next target. *The New York Times,* p. A3.

Woods, F. J., & Carrow, M. A. (1959). Choice rejection status of speech defective children. *Exceptional Children, 25,* 279–283.

Wright, B. A. (1975). Sensitizing outsiders to the position of the insider. *Rehabilitation Psychology, 22,* 129–135.

Wright, B. A. (1983). *Physical disability: A psychosocial approach* (2nd ed.). New York: Harper and Row.

Wright, B. A. (1988), Attitudes and fundamental negative bias: Conditions and corrections. In H.E. Yuker (Ed.). *Attitudes toward persons with disabilities* (pp. 3–21). New York: Springer.

Yuker, H. E. (1965). Attitudes as determinants of behavior. *Journal of Rehabilitation, 31,* 15–16.

Yuker, H. E. (1983). The lack of a stable order of preference for disabilities: A response to Richardson and Ronald. *Rehabilitation Psychology, 28,* 93–103.

Yuker, H. E. (1988). The effects of contact on attitudes toward disabled person: Some empirical generalizations. In H. E. Yuker (Ed.). *Attitudes toward persons with disabilities* (pp. 262–274). New York: Springer.

Yuker, H. E. (1994). Variables that influence attitudes toward persons with disabilities: Conclusions from the data. *Journal of Social Behavior and Personality, 9,* 3–22.

Yuker, H E., & Block, J. R. (1986). Research with the Attitude Toward Disabled Persons Scales: 1960–1985. Hempstead, NJ: Hofstra University Center for the Study of Attitudes Toward Persons with Disabilities.

Yuker, H. E., Block, J. R., & Young, J. H. (1970). *The measurement of attitudes toward disabled persons.* Albertson, NY: Human Resources Center.

Yuker, H. E., & Hurley, M. K. (1987). Contact with and attitudes toward persons with disabilities: The measure of intergroup contact. *Rehabilitation Psychology, 32,* 145–154.

Zola, I. K. (1991). Communication barriers between "the able-bodied" and "the handicapped." In R. P. Marinelli & A. E. Dell Orto (Eds.). *The psychological and social impact of disability* (3rd ed., pp. 157–180). New York: Springer.

Zola, I. K. (1992). "Any distinguishing features?" The portrayal of disability in the crime-mystery genre. In P. M. Ferguson, D. L. Ferguson, & S. J. Taylor (Eds.). *Interpreting disability: A qualitative reader* (pp. 233–250). New York: Columbia University.

Suggested Readings

Blood, I. M. (1997). The hearing aid effect. *Journal of Rehabilitation, 63*(4), 59–63.

Fichten, C. S., & Amsel, R. (1986). Trait attributions about college students with a physical disability: Circumplex analyses and methodological issues. *Journal of Applied Social Psychology, 16,* 401–427.

Fichten, C. S., Tagalakis, V., & Amsel, R. (1986). Effects of cognitive modeling, affect, and contact on attitudes, thoughts, and feelings toward college students with physical disabilities. *Journal of the Multihandicapped Person, 2,* 119–137.

Furnham, A., & Pendred, J. (1983). Attitudes toward the mentally and physically disabled. *British Journal of Medical Psychology, 56,* 179–187.

Gallagher, H. G. (1985). *FDR's splendid deception.* New York: Dodd & Mead.

Havranek, J. E. (1991). The social and individual costs of negative attitudes toward people with disabilities. *Journal of Applied Rehabilitation Counseling, 24,* 16–18.

Ladd, G. W., Munson, H. L., & Miller, J. K. (1984). Social integration of deaf adolescents in secondary level mainstreamed programs. *Exceptional Children, 50,* 420–428.

Livneh, H. (1983). Application of smallest space analysis to the study of attitudes toward disabled persons. *Professional Psychology: Research and Practice, 14,* 406–413.

Livneh, H., & Thomas, K. R. (1997). Psychosocial aspects of disability. *Rehabilitation Education, 11,* 173–183.

Millington, M. J., Strohmer, D. C., Reid, C. A., & Spengler, P. M. (1996). A preliminary investigation of the role of differential complexity and response style in measuring attitudes toward persons with disabilities. *Rehabilitation Psychology, 41,* 243–254.

Morgan, S. R. (1987). *Abuse and neglect of handicapped children.* Boston: Little, Brown.

Nosek, M. A., Zhu, Y., & Howland, C. A. (1992). The evolution of independent living programs. *Rehabilitation Counseling Bulletin, 35,* 174–189.

Obermann, C. E. (1965). *A history of vocational rehabilitation in America.* Minneapolis, MN: T. S. Dennison.

O'Connell, B. (1999). *Civil society: The underpinnings of American democracy.* Hanover, NJ: University Press of New England.

Olkin, R., & Howson, L. (1994). Attitudes toward and images of physical disability. *Journal of Social Behavior and Personality, 9,* 81–96.

Rees, L. M., Spreen, O., & Harnadek, M. (1991). Do attitudes toward persons with handicaps really shift over time? Comparison between 1975 and 1978. *Mental Retardation, 29,* 81–86.

Richardson, S. A. (1971). Children's values and friendships: A study of physical disability. *Journal of Health and Social Behavior, 12,* 253–259.

Sagatun, I. J. (1985). The effects of acknowledging a disability and initiating contact on interaction between disabled and nondisabled persons. *The Social Science Journal, 22*(4), 3343.

Satcher, J., & Bookey-Dickey, K. (1992). Attitudes of human-resource management students towards persons with disabilities. *Rehabilitation Counseling Bulletin, 35,* 248–252.

Scheer, J., & Groce, N. (1988). Impairment as human constraint: Cross cultural and historical perspectives on variation. *Journal of Social Issues, 44,* 23–37.

Soder, M. (1990). Prejudice or ambivalence? Attitudes toward people with disabilities. *Disability, Handicap, & Society, 5,* 227–241.

Strauch, J. D. (1970). Social contact as a variable in the expressed attitudes of normal adolescents toward EMR pupils. *Exceptional Children, 36,* 495–500.

Strohmer, D. C., Grand, S. A., & Purcell, M. J. (1984). Attitudes toward persons with a disability: An examination of demographic factors, social context, and specific disability. *Rehabilitation Psychology, 29,* 131–145.

Strohmer, D. C., Leierer, S. J., Cochran, N. A., & Arokiasamy, C. V. (1996). The importance of counselor disability status. *Rehabilitation Counseling Bulletin, 40,* 96–115.

Vander Kolk, C. J. (1976). Physiological and self-reported reactions to the disabled and deviant. *Rehabilitation Psychology, 23,* 77–83.

Watson, F. (1930). *Civilization and the cripple.* London: John Bales, Sons, & Danielson.

Waxman, B. F. (1991). Hatred: The unacknowledged dimension in violence against disabled people. *Sexuality and Disability, 9,* 185–189.

Weinberg, N. (1978). Modifying social stereotypes of the physically disabled. *Rehabilitation Counseling Bulletin, 22,* 114–124.

Weinberg, N. (1978). Preschool children's perception of orthopedic disability. *Rehabilitation Counseling Bulletin, 21,* 183–189.

Chapter 6

Experiencing Prejudice and Discrimination

▶ What are the effects for PWDs of the following behaviors and attitudes?
  • Stereotyping
  • Role entrapment
  • Lowered expectations
  • Lack of privacy
  • Hypervisibility and overobservation
  • Solo status
  • Token status
  • Infantilization, paternalism, and "motherese"
  • Objectification
  • Viewing PWDs as animals
  • Unnecessary dependence
  • Marginality
  • Lack of equal social status relationships
  • Second-class citizenship

INTRODUCTION

> *In this section, look for—*
>
> ▶ *similarities in the prejudice and discrimination experienced by PWDs and by individuals of racial/ethnic minority groups*

Itzak Perlman, the world-famous violinist and a survivor of polio, stated that PWDs experience two problems: (1) the environment that is not physically accessible, and (2) the attitudes of PWODs toward disability and PWDs. As difficult as these problems are, it can be seen that neither problem concerns the disability itself (or the individual with the disability). Indeed, one of the results of the Americans with Disabilities Act (ADA) has been the increased public awareness that many of the problems and obstacles experienced by PWDs are due to their environments (both social and physical).

None of the behaviors and attitudes listed above helps create a socially valued and respected position for PWDs. PWDs are subjected to many types of negative and harmful responses from PWODs, in much the same manner as individuals who are members of racial/ethnic/cultural minority groups. Indeed, many of these behaviors, such as stereotyping, infantilizing, and withholding equal social status, are also experienced by individuals belonging to other types of minority groups. People allow degrading stereotypes for what (and whom) they do not understand and do not like. However, PWDs also encounter added prejudice and discrimination. For example, PWDs have less privacy than PWODs and are often considered to be dependent. These two conditions/characteristics are usually not part of the racial/ethnic minority individual's experience. In discussing the experience of PWDs, it is important to remember (1) while the PWD considers the behaviors and attitudes of PWODs to be prejudicial and negative, often PWODs do not; (2) it is then logical to assume that many PWODs are unaware of their behaviors and the effects (or at least minimize and rationalize their attitudes and behaviors). Many times, we operate on the assumption that if we are not aware of attitudes and behavior, then they cannot be important; (3) these types of behaviors and attitudes are found in all types of people, including professionals who provide services to PWDs, policy makers, and program administrators; and (4) many of these behaviors and attitudes are closely related to each other, although there are important differences among them. For example, the concepts of lack of privacy and hypervisibility are closely related, but there are also important differences between these two concepts.

STEREOTYPING

> *In this section, look for—*
> ▶ *the difference between a category and a stereotype*
> ▶ *how PWDs can internalize society's false stereotypes*
> ▶ *how seemingly positive stereotypes about PWDs are handicapping the results of stereotypes*
> ▶ *the three factors that serve to maintain and reinforce false stereotypes*

To be viewed as a person with a disability is to be both categorized and stereotyped. The person is no longer viewed as an individual. Stereotyping is defined as "an exaggerated belief associated with a category. Its function is to justify (rationalize) our conduct in relation to that category" (Allport, 1986, p. 191). Most stereotypes about PWDs are unsupported by fact. For example, we have seen in Chapter 2 that PWODs have a tendency to sensationalize the disability and to impute emotional reactions to disabilities that PWDs simply do not experience. Some examples of stereotypes that are unsupported by fact include the ideas that blindness is a dark pit and that PWDs do not have "normal" sexual feelings. It would, therefore, appear logical that PWDs would not adopt these stereotypes as self-identifiers. However, especially in the past, some of the stereotypes held by PWODs have been so pervasive and widespread that PWDs (and their families) have internalized these false stereotypes. Reread the story of Gunther Schirmer in Chapter 5. Tragically, Schirmer had taken society's prejudice and discrimination as his self-concept. Speaking of himself, he said he would "destroy the cripple." And he did.

A stereotype is not a category, but rather a belief about a category. Therefore, it is not prejudicial to recognize someone as having a disability. It is prejudicial to assume that this one category (or any other one category) is the sole determinant of the individual's attitudes and behaviors. Categorization of people is sometimes necessary, although not as often as we think. Both the tendency to overcategorize and to stereotype people in categories are the result of our need to simplify a vast array of different types of people and their individual characteristics and identities.

Stereotypes are usually negative and categorize people in subordinate positions. Of course, there is the *possibility* of positive stereotypes. For example, consider this stereotype: PWDs are compassionate and wise because their suffering has given them sensitivity and insight. On the surface, this appears to be a positive statement. However, this stereotype is false, but it is also negative. In much the same way as unintentional handicapism, positive stereotypes may not be malicious in *intent* but their *results* are harmful to PWDs. All types of stereotyping (even those we think are positive) are detrimental for the following reasons: (1) stereotypes do not portray individuals in the category as individuals, (2) stereotypes are polarizing because they make a clear demarcation between those in the category and those not in the category, and (3) stereotypes of any kind lead to behaviors and actions that limit and reduce the opportunities of people in that category. Using our example of a false stereotype of PWDs being compassionate, we can see that many professions that require assertive, competitive, win-or-lose behaviors (such as being a lawyer) would automatically be ruled out for a PWD because PWDs are thought to be too nice and compassionate. In Chapter 3, we learned that our culture, especially the media, reinforces and builds upon our stereotypes. In short, stereotypes are socially supported.

Professionals also fall prey to stereotypes. In his autobiography, Henry Kisor, who became deaf at age 3, discussed standardized testing and diagnostic procedures and concluded that these professional tools are based on false stereotypes. For example, Kisor was offended by the mandatory psychological counseling that people who are deaf are required to undergo before they are allowed to receive speech therapy. Kisor submitted to the psychological counseling and therefore did receive speech training, but decades later, he found it insulting that "deaf experts" automatically assumed that he needed counseling. Kisor termed his practice of mandatory psychological counseling as "official stereotyping" (Kisor, 1990).

Stereotypes are not harmless because job, housing, educational, and social decisions are based on stereotypes (Allport, 1954, 1958). Also, legislation is based on deeply held assumptions that are often stereotypes. (Policy makers and legislators are subjected to the same media as everyone else.) Stereotypes circumscribe opportunities for individuals and handicap society as a whole. Stereotypes are resistant to the truth, probably as a result of these three factors: (1) constant reinforcement by the media; (2) the human need to simplify and organize people; and (3) the prejudice and discrimination that allow those in power to benefit and profit from the subordinate status of stereotyped groups.

More than 20 years ago, an article appeared in a scholarly rehabilitation journal that strongly argued that there is no one personality type associated with a certain disability (Shontz, 1977). For example, there is no "rheumatoid arthritis personality" or "paraplegia and quadriplegia personality." Well written and comprehensive, much of the value of this article lies in its extensive listing of scholarly writings that have stereotyped individuals according to the type of disability they experience. As long ago as 1977, the listing of the stereotypes was amazingly long! For example, the list of personality attributes ascribed to patients with arthritis is long. They have been said to have weak egos, to repress hostility, to be compliant and subservient, to be potentially psychotic, to be depressed, dependent, conscientious, masochistic, emotionally labile, compulsive, introverted, conservative, perfectionistic, moody, nervous, worried, tense, over-concerned about personal appearance, and prone to express psychopathology in physical symptoms (Shontz, 1977, p. 339).

Shontz summarized much of the scholarly writing on various types of disabilities (in addition to rheumatoid arthritis) and concluded that "the recent literature provides no support for the hypothesis that particular disabilities are associated with particular personality characteristics or for the hypothesis that disability is a sufficient cause of maladjustment" (pp. 340–341). The Deaf have had many stereotypical psychological characteristics applied to them. Lane, Hoffmeister, and Bahan (1996) reviewed the scientific literature on the "psychology of the deaf"(there is no such thing as the "psychology of the deaf"), reading more than 350 journal articles and books. Lane et al. then developed a list of these characteristics and divided them into four columns: (1) social, (2) cognitive, (3) behavioral, and (4) emotional. There are 67 adjectives on Lane et al.'s list. Lane et al. summarized:

In general, people who are deaf are characterized as socially isolated, intellectually weak, behaviorally impulsive, and emotionally immature. The list of traits attributed to the Deaf is inconsistent: they are both *aggressive* and *submissive; naive, shrewd, detached, passionate, explosive, shy, stubborn and submissive, suspicious and trusting.* However, the list is consistently negative; nearly all of the traits ascribed, even many in pairs of opposites, are unfavorable. Clearly we must suspect that the "psychology of the deaf" consists of hearing people's stereotypes about others who are deaf (p. 349).

Obviously, none of these stereotypes has been confirmed. Further, these examples demonstrate that stereotyping can occur in very sophisticated and scholarly settings. The perpetuation of these stereotypes was labeled "education," "science," "scholarship," and "research." In the not-too-distant past, university students memorized these disability stereotypes for exams. The better the students learned these stereotypes, the more successful they were in their "education." Physicians and psychologists, who are the products of their professional education, approach their patients with disabilities with these false stereotypes in mind. Furthermore, the continuing education and upgrading of skills required to maintain the licensure and certification of most clinicians is often accomplished through reading the professional/scholarly journals. And, as we have seen, many of the professional journals have simply maintained then reinforced these false stereotypes of individuals with disabilities. The stereotypes held by physicians, psychologists, and other clinicians have negative consequences for their patients with disabilities. For example, individuals who are deaf experience longer lengths of stay in psychiatric hospitals than people who are not deaf, inappropriate placement of people who are deaf in institutions that care for individuals with mental retardation, and psychiatric misdiagnosis. Lane et al. attribute much of this to negative stereotypes of the Deaf. Stereotypes are not harmless.

Reread the description of the "arthritis personality" on the preceding page and ask yourself if you would like to go out on a date with this type of individual (not an individual with arthritis, but someone who has a weak ego, represses hostility, is potentially psychotic, depressed, emotionally labile, moody, nervous, tense, and worried). Of course not, it would be the date from hell. People with arthritis are not like this, but if these stereotypes persist, it will be difficult for people with arthritis (or any other disability) to enjoy equal-social-status relationships.

For the individual who is the target of these stereotypes, it is often easier to accept the stereotypes than to fight them. We have learned that the "disability role" is a normative role, meaning that there are rules and expectations that describe how an individual should act. Obviously, the individual knows that these stereotypes are untrue and, indeed, much of the humor of the Disability Rights Movement makes fun of these stereotypes. Nonetheless, when the PWD acts according to these expectations and stereotypes, he or she is rewarded, and when the PWD violates the expectations of PWODs, often PWODs withhold the rewards and even punish the individual. Therefore, often it is simply easier for PWDs to accept the stereotype than to fight it. For those who have hidden disabilities and therefore have the option of disclosure, they may choose to keep the disability hidden. On the other hand, those with visible disabilities may react to stereotyping by attempting to downplay or minimalize the disability or to conceal the effects of the disability. Many PWDs have consciously developed "presentation strategies" in order to comply with these stereotypes. Certainly before the advent of disability rights groups, an individual with a disability understood that if he or she decided to fight the stereotypes, it would be a difficult (and probably losing) battle since these stereotypes have had a history of centuries of development and have been ascribed to by millions of people. For a single individual contemplating these formidable odds, he or she may decide to focus his or her attention and energy elsewhere and simply comply with the stereotype. Also, it should be remembered that societal stereotypes were often held by family members of the PWD. Therefore, the PWD had few places of refuge where he or she could escape the stereotyping. Recall the letter to Ann Landers from "Angry in Montana" in Chapter 3. Angry in Montana, a woman in a wheelchair, did not want to answer a curious child's question about her disability. Ann Landers replies that "Angry in Montana" was unwilling to speak to the strange child because "Angry in Montana" has not accepted her disability. Ann Landers responded with punishment and blame. There are many PWDs who, unwillingly, answer the questions of strangers simply because it is easier than fighting stereotypes.

Some PWDs internalize these stereotypes and these false assumptions become a part of their self-concept. Simply due to the fact that they have heard these stereotypes so often and from prestigious and authoritative sources, PWDs may accept these stereotypes as truth. Certainly, before the disability rights movement, when PWDs were often isolated with little access to peers, role models, and leaders/authorities who had disabilities, PWDs had little basis upon which to judge these false stereotypes. They simply accepted them as truth, truth about themselves. This situation was especially common for individuals with congenital disabilities or disabilities acquired early in life, due to the fact that all young children unquestioningly accept the attitudes and viewpoints of the adults around them. PWDs who have experienced institutionalization, residential schooling, or prolonged hospitalizations often have no point of comparison because they are isolated from the broader culture and have no way to disprove these stereotypes and, as a result, these PWDs internalize society's stereotype. Society has effectively taught them to feel inferior.

ROLE ENTRAPMENT

In this section, look for—

> ▶ *the definition of role entrapment*
> ▶ *why the individual may choose to accept the role entrapment*
> ▶ *the Bulova Syndrome and the four "Fs"*
> ▶ *how the inferior education given to PWDs may contribute to their occupational role entrapment*

Role entrapment occurs when the group in power, in this case PWODs, defines those roles minority individuals can and cannot assume. Role entrapment can be social or occupational and usually includes only inferior and undesirable roles. Often occupational role entrapment has been termed "occupational stereotyping." Ethnic and racial minority individuals have long been aware of role entrapment; for example, Black men were expected to do certain jobs. Obviously, role entrapment is not self-imposed unless the minority individual comes to internalize the majority's view of himself or herself. Once again, as in categorization and stereotyping, the person is not viewed as an individual and certainly his or her strengths and abilities are never considered. It is a matter of "Your kind of people do or do not do these kinds of things." Here is an often-told riddle that relies on occupational role entrapment to confuse people: A young boy is injured in an automobile accident. The boy's father dies in the accident. He is taken to the hospital. The boy needs emergency surgery. The surgeon says, "I cannot operate on this boy. He is my son." The surgeon was not the boy's father (the father is dead). What relation was the surgeon to the injured boy?" Answers often include stepfather, adopted father, or grandfather. Very few people respond that the surgeon is the boy's mother. This is an example of gender occupational role entrapment, and as more and more women become physicians and surgeons, this riddle will probably no longer be told because without gender stereotyping, the answer is obvious.

As with stereotyping, often the PWD simply accepts the role entrapment rather than fight it. Since it is the group in power that makes the rules, they "reward" those minority people who "know their place," keep their aspirations and achievements at a modest level, and refrain from testing the limits of acceptance (Yuker, 1988). Individuals who attempt to assume roles that are not endorsed by the majority are called "uppity" and told that "they don't know their place." For PWDs, the entrapment may be more powerful (than for racial and ethnic groups) because "society" often feels that they have provided many benefits to PWDs (charity, special services, etc.) and consider these attempts to escape role entrapment to be lack of gratitude. According to this viewpoint, PWDs should accept their inferior quality of life with gratitude and equanimity. Davis (1997) summed up this view: "[PWDs should] accept our [PWODs'] construction of your life or give up your access to equal citizenship" (p. 167).

Social role entrapment occurs when PWDs are told that they should associate with their own kind. In the video *My Body Is Not Who I Am,* the young man in the wheelchair tells of being asked if he has a girlfriend. When he replies "yes," the next question is, "Does she have a disability?" This is an example of social role entrapment. It is automatically assumed that PWDs have romantic/sexual relationships only with other PWDs. Social relationships in which one individual has a disability and the other does not have a disability are often automatically assumed to be asymmetrical. Obviously, the most extreme example of social role entrapment is segregation and institutionalization.

Occupational role entrapment for PWDs has been so widespread as to gain derisive nicknames. The "Bulova Syndrome" refers to the tendency to place men in wheelchairs in watch repair. While the Bulova Watch Company should not be faulted because they were hiring PWDs when very few companies were, the Bulova Syndrome refers to a time when people with a certain disability (usually paraplegia) were often automatically "assigned" a life's occupation. Today, the nickname for role entrapment for PWDs, especially those with mental retardation, is "The Four F's." The Four "F's" are food, filth, flowers, and folding. Food is work in fast food restaurants, filth is janitorial and housekeeping work, flowers refers to work in yard maintenance and landscaping, and folding refers to work in laundry facilities. Men who were deaf were often placed in printing jobs because their disability was viewed as an asset because they could not hear the loud machinery. Women who were deaf and not homemakers were often placed in textile mills, and in the late 1960s, girls in residential schools who were deaf were trained for keypunch work or to be seamstresses; men who were blind often trained for photographic darkroom work (Sinick, 1969). At the Perkins School for the Blind, girls were trained to be typists or dictaphone users and boys were trained to be piano tuners (Holcomb, 1990). It is not an exaggeration to state that, first, most individuals with physical disabilities were placed in lower-level jobs requiring manual skills and, second, much of this role entrapment was due to the false stereotypes that held that individuals with physical disabilities were intellectually incapable of managerial or professional-level jobs. Further, most of these jobs were low paying. For example, men who were deaf were rarely the managers of printing companies; they were allowed only to run the machinery and produce the printing products.

In the past, occupational role entrapment was often termed occupational stereotyping, and there is some indication that the tendency of professionals to relegate an individual to a job on the sole basis of his or her disability is decreasing. It should be noted that Hahn (1997) strongly asserted that relegating PWDs to lower-paid jobs has little to do with the disability itself, but rather, is the result of a capitalist system that needs workers willing to work for low wages in order for employers to maintain high profits. Simply stated, according to Hahn, keeping PWDs in low-level jobs maintains the social order. Occupational role entrapment began early in life for PWDs. The little education that children with disabilities received emphasized manual skills and vocational training. There were no "career days" at schools for children with disabilities nor were there individual career/college planning sessions with the school counselor for these children. The type of disability determined the child's career. Sharon L., the medical social worker we met in Chapter 2, tells that she clearly remembers the day that the school counselor told her that she should become a professional artist. The counselor told Sharon that (1) she was good at art, (2) she would not have to be around people, and (3) no one would recognize her art as "disabled art." Probably the reason why this one day in Sharon's high school career is so indelibly etched in her memory is that she was surprised by the role entrapment that the counselor was attempting to enforce. Also, as we will see in the chapter on the individual's adjustment to disability, "stigma recognition" is often shocking to the PWD. In many situations, PWDs are not aware of the stigma that others hold toward their disability. For example, what did the counselor mean by "disabled art," other than to imply that such art would be inferior to "nondisabled art"? Even individuals like Sharon, who have had their disabilities for many years, are unpleasantly surprised when confronted with prejudice, discrimination, and stigma. Disability scholars have labeled this experience "stigma recognition." As a teenager, Sharon was unaware that some school officials thought she would be forced to choose a profession that would not require interaction with people; after all, she had been attending high school, church, and community activities all her life. The high school counselor, probably out of good intentions, tried to guide Sharon to art. (This is an example of the handicapism of well-intentioned people.) There is nothing wrong with being an artist. The error lies in (1) someone else choosing Sharon's life work, and (2) choosing a profession based on how others *might* react to the disability.

When considering the situation of PWDs, we can indulge in the circular argument: Did the inferior education of children with disabilities lead to occupational role entrapment? Or, did the occupational role entrapment lead to inferior education for children with disabilities? The answer to each question is "yes." An extreme example of the practice of preparing children with disabilities for a life of occupational entrapment is presented in Margret A. Winzer's (1993) work *Education, Urbanization, and the Deaf Community: A Case Study of Toronto, 1870–1900.* Winzer makes two points: (1) "The Ontario institution tried to reproduce the factory conditions as a means of socializing its students and disciplining them to the rigidity and monotony of modern industrial labor" (p. 127), and (2) "these efforts were a mistake...they limited the opportunities for deaf workers and made them easily expendable as technology changed" (p. 127). It does not sound like school was much fun for these children.

David Wright, a South African who is deaf and who now works as a university professor of literature in England, wrote an autobiography. He related his lifelong response to the role entrapment perpetuated in schools for children who are deaf:

> Since then, I have had an aversion to doing anything with my hands. To this day, I cannot draw, or tie up a parcel properly, if it comes to that....But, for a long time, dating from my attendance at this school, if it was a school, I refused on principle to learn, or was deliberately bad at manipulatory skills like carpentry, painting, and so on. Schools of this type, where the teacher was usually untrained—they probably do not exist nowadays—took the line of least resistance and while teaching their deaf pupils a little speech and lip-reading, concentrated on instruction in handicrafts. This seemed to me, even then, to be equating deafness with stupidity; and I resented it. So much so that I took cleverness with the hands to be a badge of deafness, and I would not wear that badge. Instead of being taught to use my head, because I was deaf, I was being fobbed off with handicrafts (Wright, 1994, p. 40).

Another way in which career options may be limited for PWDs is the idea that PWDs should "help their own kind." In the video, *Irving King Jordan,* the President of Gallaudet College, Dr. Jordan, reports that 20 years ago, entering students who were deaf usually had a career goal of teaching the deaf. Now, Jordan notes that students at Gallaudet prepare for all types of careers and professions.

The concept of "helping your own kind" probably arose from the assumption that PWDs could best understand other PWDs (Strohmer, Leierer, Cochran, &

Arokiasamy, 1996). Also, the need to counter the paternalism of PWODs who worked with PWDs probably activated the desire for PWDs to be taught by other PWDs. However, we have learned that PWDs can, and do, hold false prejudicial views about individuals with other types of disabilities. Further, it would be impossible to match each individual with a counselor or teacher who has the same type of disability. This is to say nothing about limiting the career opportunities for PWDs. In addition, the "help your own kind" philosophy is blatantly ascribing disability to be the most salient characteristic of the individual.

LOWERED EXPECTATIONS, OR "LET'S GIVE THOSE POOR DISABLED PEOPLE A BREAK"

In this section, look for—
- ▶ *how lowered expectations can result in fewer opportunities for PWDs*
- ▶ *overprotection and sheltering and their results*
- ▶ *the difference between providing accommodations and lowering standards*
- ▶ *misguided acts of perceived kindness*

Related to both stereotyping and role entrapment of PWDs is the practice of automatically lowering expectations and inappropriate pessimism. Such a relaxing of standards communicates that PWDs should be excused or indulged and, furthermore, PWDs are not considered capable to be judged against high standards. In the video *Tell Them I'm a Mermaid*, one of the women, who is in a wheelchair, states, "All that lack of belief does something to you." Another PWD stated, "When people stop having expectations of you, you know they have given up on you."

The provision of accommodations for the disability is often confused with lowering standards. Brenda Premo, the director of the California Department of Rehabilitation, who is legally blind, described this difference when she stated,

> I really appreciated the teachers in high school who would accommodate me but who had high expectations. They would ask me, "What can I do that would make this better for you?" but they wouldn't let me slide at all academically. There was a math teacher, an old gruff guy. He would accommodate me, but I had to achieve and I had to earn my grade. I always got B's from him but I respected him so much more than some other teachers who always gave me easy A's. The same thing happened in college. I always appreciated the teachers who expected the most out of me and worked my hardest in their classes. I got the most out of them (Mackelprang & Salsgiver, 1999, p. 142).

Behaviors and attitudes that (1) do not allow the PWD to be an equal partner, (2) communicate the message that he or she is not capable, and (3) reduce the range of opportunities open to the individual are harmful. Lowered expectations, which at first glance may appear to be kindness and generosity, harm the individual because he or she does not receive helpful and honest feedback. And, without honest feedback, an individual is kept in an inferior and dependent position. Praising the individual for small achievements (when the individual is capable of much more) is insulting and demeaning for the individual. Robert Scott (1969), in his book *The*

Making of Blind Men: A Study of Adult Socialization, observed one additional result from lowered expectations: The individual begins to believe that the disability (in this case, blindness) is the cause of his or her incompetence: "Clients are rewarded by trivial things and praised for performing tasks in a mediocre fashion. This superficial and overgenerous reward system makes it impossible for most clients to assess their accomplishments accurately. Eventually, since anything they do is praised as outstanding, many of them come to believe that the underlying assumption must be that the blindness makes them incompetent" (p. 85).

PWDs are aware when standards are relaxed for them, which implicitly stated, "You're never expected to be any good." Those who have lowered expectations of PWDs often do not allow PWDs opportunities for achievement. One woman with a disability experienced this when she said, "Even if you can, no one will let you." Often, overprotection and "sheltering" of the PWD are other forms of lowered expectations. Thus, the PWOD falsely assumes that he or she is not reducing the PWD's independence and achievement; the PWOD thinks he or she is protecting the PWD. Lowered expectations of PWODs often result in failure to inform PWDs of available opportunities and the standards and requirements for gaining these opportunities. Often, educational opportunities, job openings, and social occasions are not considered relevant because PWODs are quick to judge such opportunities to be unobtainable and unrealistic for the individual with a disability. Lowered expectations often lead to lack of challenge and achievement for PWDs.

Harris (1992), a coordinator of a university program designed to provide services for students with disabilities, summarized the effects of lowered expectations: "Misguided acts of perceived kindness are a much harder construct to deal with than even overt negative discrimination. One of the reasons for this is generally neither party understands the pernicious effects of this behavior. It may be years before the person with the disability realizes that he/she has been victimized by inadequate preparation and a lack of necessary independence" (p. 208).

Failing to discipline children with disabilities and "mercy graduations" for schoolchildren with disabilities are examples of the lowered expectations of PWODs. Lowering expectations, excusing, indulging, and tolerating poor performance from PWDs are all forms of discrimination.

LACK OF PRIVACY

In this section, look for—

▶ *reasons why PWDs enjoy less privacy than others*
▶ *explanations of why the "dehumanization" of assistive technology is appealing to many PWDs*

Most PWDs enjoy less privacy and anonymity than do PWODs. Goffman (1963), speaking of a stigmatized person, described this lack of privacy: "To be present among normals nakedly exposes him [*sic*] to invasions of privacy" (p. 212). Some of this lack of privacy may be due to the disability itself. Individuals who are deaf and use sign language interpreters and individuals with visual impairments who often require readers/scribes are examples of loss of privacy that are a result of the disability itself. Personal care attendants dress PWDs and assist them in using the bathroom and using suppositories and catheters, and assist with menstrual needs. Furthermore, these types of losses in privacy are unavoidable. Such a continuous, daily loss of privacy, in areas of life that are considered to be the most personal, is difficult for most PWODs to understand. Higgins (1980), in his book *Outsiders in a Hearing World,* interviewed a married couple who use sign language. He explained: "When one deaf couple dines in a restaurant, they imagine that they have drawn a curtain between themselves and the hearing people who stare at them" (and mimic their signing) (p. 128). PWDs who must sustain this loss of privacy often regard privacy and anonymity as precious resources to be carefully defended. Individuals who use sign language must occasionally guard against others "overseeing" (not overhearing) them. For example, Groce (1985) related a story in her book *Everybody Here Spoke Sign Language.* On the island of Martha's Vineyard, because a large number of people were deaf, everybody knew and used sign language. Groce interviewed a woman who remembered young teenage boys (hearing and deaf) gathering at the general store to socialize and tell stories. Many of these stories were sexually oriented, and therefore, whenever anyone (hearing or deaf) entered the store, the boys would have to turn around to hide their signing. They did not want adults to oversee the jokes and stories. (The fact that the woman was aware of the boys' attempts to hide their signing indicates that the adults knew exactly what type of stories and jokes were being told.)

Miller and Morgan (1980) spoke about the need for emotional privacy in the context of marriage. Citing the change in attitudes of caregivers toward PWDs marrying, Miller and Morgan concluded that married PWDs now have to deal with "overenthusiasm" for their marriage. While undeniably the result of good intentions, the intrusion of PWODs into the private, personal spheres of an individual's life is another form of denying PWDs privacy. "Emotional privacy is as important as physical privacy for a couple who are severely disabled [*sic*] and physically dependent, and probably more difficult to ensure" (p. 353).

Hospitalization, institutionalization, and resident schooling of PWDs all greatly decrease the PWD's opportunity for privacy. Living with large groups of people, whom the individual has not chosen to live with, day after day, allows little chance for either private time or private space. Chubon and Moore (1982) studied individuals in a large rehabilitation center for spinal cord injuries. They observed that many people spent large amounts of time in bed with the blankets pulled over their heads. When they interviewed these individuals, they learned these patients were attempting to gain some seclusion and privacy. Chubon and Moore termed this behavior "cocooning."

Often, PWDs interpret and define privacy differently than PWODs (Lane, Hoffmeister, & Bahan, 1996). Beisser (1989), who contracted polio after graduating from medical school, was paralyzed from the neck down and placed in an iron lung. Dr. Beisser related that hospital caregivers asked permission before they touched his head. In contrast, caregivers poked, prodded, handled, and displayed the rest of his body without asking permission or giving prior warning. Beisser realized that everyone was very respectful of his head! Assistive technology, such as voice-activated computers and TTD telephones, offer a measure of privacy to PWDs and thus eliminate the need for a family member or a personal care attendant to perform certain types of functions. Ironically, the very "dehumanization" of technology is very appealing to PWDs. Technology, in contrast to people, always maintains confidentiality, does not get sick, and does not refuse to assist when irritated or in a bad mood, thus allowing the user more independence. Technology can, and does, break down and "crash," but technology is far more reliable than most people. Technology provides both independence and privacy to PWDs.

HYPERVISIBILITY AND OVEROBSERVATION

In this section, look for—

▶ *the definitions of hypervisibility and overobservation*
▶ *the power relationship between the individual who is staring and the individual who is being stared at*
▶ *the effects of hypervisibility*
▶ *having unintended meanings attributed to PWDs' actions*

Individuals with visible disabilities also enjoy less privacy and anonymity and experience more hypervisibility and overobservation. The letters to Ann Landers from individuals in wheelchairs who are the target of curious children are examples of this reduced privacy. Kenneth Fries (1997) compiled a book of essays, poetry, and fiction written by PWDs, entitling the book *Staring Back.* There is a clear message in the fact that all the writers and artists, with their differing life histories and various types of disabilities, shared one experience in common: being stared at. A woman who acquired a spinal cord injury at age 36 stated, "When I was first in a wheelchair, I was terrified that people were going to stare at me" (Mackelprang & Salsgiver, 1999, p. 100). In American Sign Language, the sign for the word "stare" communicates both the intrusiveness and hostility felt by the Deaf. The sign is "the fingertips of both hands almost poking into one's own face" (Walker, 1986, p. 100). A student of mine, a middle-aged, former professor who is blind, was stopped by a young student at the doorway of my classroom. The student said, "I've been watching you walk down the street and seeing how many times you mess up." From a distance, my student's white cane made him hypervisible. Obviously, most people who do not have visible disabilities are not stopped by strangers and asked questions or told they had "messed up." Thomson (1997) perceptively noted the power differential between the person who is staring ("the spectator") and the person who is being stared at ("the spectacle"), stating, "One role is to look, judge, and act while the other role is to be gazed upon, measured, and passive" (p. 300). Read the letter from the mother of an infant with a disability (Exhibit 6–1).

For everyone, there are times when we wish to remain in the background, or totally anonymous. For someone with a visible disability or someone who uses some sort of assistive technology (such as a hearing aid or wheelchair), this is not possible. A woman with a disability explained: "Having a visible disability means always being noticed, standing out, being different *everywhere you go.*" Indeed, she terms her disability "a blinking neon sign" (Olkin, 1999, pp. 80–81). Here is an example when anonymity would be desirable. A professor in a large class of 300 students states that attendance will not be taken and therefore will not affect students' grades. Almost every student can skip class, realizing that the professor has no way of knowing who is attending and who is not. Anonymity is not possible for the one student enrolled in the class who uses a wheelchair, or the one student who uses a sign language interpreter, or the one African American student.

For someone who is subjected to hypervisibility, life can become an unending public performance in which he or she is expected to exhibit positive behaviors and

Exhibit 6–1

Dear Ann Landers: I gave birth to my first child last April. "Crystal" was 12 weeks premature and weighed less than 2 pounds. We were afraid that she would die or have severe handicaps, but we were blessed with good fortune as her only remaining requirement is the extra oxygen she receives through a nasal tube worn 24 hours a day.

Her doctors told us, "Don't let her alter your lifestyle." We took their advice and take Crystal everywhere. She's been to the mall, five restaurants, a small boat harbor, and the county fair.

Because the nasal tube makes her look different, I have received a lot of unsolicited and rude comments. People ask, "What's wrong with her? Was she born that way? What's her problem?" I do not wish to discuss my daughter's medical condition with strangers, and considering the handicaps she might have had, my husband and I feel there's nothing wrong with Crystal at all.

Ann, please alert the boneheads out there that if they see a child who is "different," to coo over the baby the way they would a "normal" child. The parents already know their child looks different, and they love the child anyway. The anguish they have already gone through doesn't need to be rehashed to satisfy a stranger's curiosity. A kind word would make a world of difference.

—Grateful Mom in Buffalo, NY

Dear Buffalo Mom: Thank you for speaking up about an intensely personal matter. You have performed a valuable service by sharing your problem with millions of readers today. Many of them will see themselves and be reminded of your letter when they see a child who is "different."

attitudes. In Chapter 2, we discussed that "disability is a normative experience," meaning that there are rules, usually unwritten but strongly held, about how PWDs should behave. Coupled with these "rules of disability" is the general lack of knowledge about disabilities. Nonetheless, PWDs are aware that they are being scrutinized and often judged. The individual in the wheelchair who falls asleep during an important meeting is thought to be rude simply because it never enters the minds of others that this PWD must take large doses of medication, which make him or her sleepy. With hypervisibility, everything the PWD does takes on added meaning, and this added meaning is often the result of negative inferences. Public performance, with the subsequent judgment of others, is stressful and anxiety-provoking. The individual is not allowed to relax and "just hang out." Some individuals can escape hypervisibility by returning "home" or someplace where there are a lot of other people who look like themselves. These people have a place where they can "blend in." Often, PWDs do not have this haven or sanctuary. Frequently, the PWD feels very alienated and different from even his or her own family. Many PWDs cannot shed their hypervisibility and simply be a person, not for an evening, not for a weekend, not for the Christmas holidays.

Much of the attention directed toward PWDs is well-intentioned and certainly not planned to annoy or inconvenience anyone. Unintended or not, attention that is not wanted or attention that is directed solely toward the disability, rather than the person, is both irritating and inconvenient. Intrusive and insulting questions, which would never be asked of PWODs, are often asked of PWDs. In the video *My Body Is Not Who I Am,* an adult woman with a disability remarks, "It's like I am a child. People can ask me anything they want. I have no boundaries." In that same video, a single young man (in a wheelchair) tells that he is often asked by strangers if he has a girlfriend. He always replies, "Of course I do. Why do you ask?" This question is insulting and intrusive on at least two counts: (1) it is a question that would not be asked of an adult man without a disability because romantic relationships are considered to be private, and (2) it conveys the questioner's stereotypical, prejudicial view of PWDs as sexually neutered (not desiring or capable of intimate relationships) and unattractive to the opposite sex. His response of "why do you ask?" shows some irritation at being asked such a demeaning question. The young man goes on to say that after he answers "yes," some questioners continue to ask, "Does your girlfriend have a disability?"

Read the following letter to Ann Landers (Exhibit 6–2).

There are two circumstances that may account for the different responses of Grateful Mom in Buffalo, New York, and S. R. in Meraux, Louisiana. Grateful Mom was dealing with adults who were strangers, while S. R. was responding to children who may have been friends of her own children, people with whom she had a relationship. It is probably safe to say that the curiosity and fascination of complete strangers has more potential to insult and irritate PWDs than the interest of people with whom they are acquainted. Second, PWDs often report that children are more honest and forthright in their interest than are adults who often display subtle (and

---

Exhibit 6–2

Dear Ann Landers: I was interested in the letter from "Upfront in Vermont," who taught children to ask questions rather than just state people are different. As a person who has had a disability since birth, I was especially pleased that you printed it. Growing up, I was hurt far more by people who gawked and made comments among themselves than by those who asked me questions.

My right arm ends just below the elbow, and when I see children looking at it curiously, or if they ask what happened, I explain that God makes each of us different. Some people have brown hair, some blond; some people are tall, some are short; some people have two hands, some may have only one. But each of us is special in our way. Sometimes, the children touch my arm or want to know how I can drive with one hand. I never take offense to their questions. I simply hope they learn that we can all be and do whatever we want—it's about ability, not disability.

Some parents are embarrassed when their child asks a question, but I believe children should feel free to ask questions so long as they do so politely. How else are they to learn? I was worried that my daughter would be upset by other children's reactions to my arm. Now, at age 6, she answers questions, saying, "That is how God made her and my mom can do anything."

—S. R., Meraux, LA

Dear S.R.: What a wonderfully positive attitude! Some people would see the cup as half empty, but in your case, it is overflowing. Thanks for writing.

sometimes not so subtle) hypocrisy about the disability. Further, children have not yet acquired the stereotypes and myths about disabilities and, therefore, their questions are free of demeaning, preconceived ideas. Susan Wendell (1997) summarized the experience of being an object of curiosity: "Visibly disabled women report that curiosity about medical diagnoses, physical appearance and the sexual and other intimate aspects of disability is more common than willingness to listen and to understand the experience of disability" (p. 267).

Such intrusions of privacy also affect the partners and family members of PWDs. Most people on family outings do not enjoy being approached by strangers and being forced to deal with others' misinformed and negative attitudes toward disability. Lefley (1991) summarized: "Generalization of stigma to families is an additional source of psychological risk" (p. 127).

Often, PWDs do not want to be ignored; however, instead of asking intrusive, personal questions, it is more appropriate to engage in simple "small talk." Sports, weather, current events, and other innocuous subjects are good starting places for developing a relationship or chatting with any individual we do not know. As one PWD summarized, "At least PWDs in circuses and freak shows got paid."

SOLO STATUS

> *In this section, look for—*
> ▶ *the definition of solo status*
> ▶ *what it means to:*
>   *1. be a forced representative*
>   *2. be in an unending public performance*
>   *3. have no role models*

Related to lack of privacy and hypervisibility is solo status. Solo status is when an individual is the only person with a particular visible characteristic and certainly, in many settings, there may be only one PWD. Solo status often constrains PWDs to become "forced representatives." Regardless of whether an individual has the desire or inclination, he or she now becomes the spokesperson for the disability group. At any time or place, the individual is expected to speak for individuals who have the same disability or to present extemporaneous educational and entertaining lectures. Being a solo, for whatever reason—gender (the only woman), race (the only African American), nationality (the only American), profession (the only professor)—adds another duty to the individual's list of jobs. Whenever a committee needs (1) a woman, (2) an African American, (3) an American, or (4) a PWD, there will be no question who will be asked! Goffman (1963) explained: "A new career is likely to be thrust upon him, that of representing his category" (p. 26). At the committee meeting, the members will turn to the solo and ask, "How do women (African Americans, Americans, professors, or PWDs) feel about this issue?" It is automatically assumed that the forced representative will know. If this occurs frequently, it can be burdensome for the PWD (Olkin, 1999). When an individual states, "I am not the poster boy (or girl)" for whatever disability the individual has, he or she is refusing the forced representative role.

In addition to being a forced representative and feeling isolated, the solo may be viewed as his or her category rather than as an individual. The solo is often viewed as "the disabled," "the deaf," and so on. Everything the solo does and says takes on unintended meaning simply because the solo has, in the eyes of others, become the group he or she is thought to represent. Olkin (1999) explained: "One's failings or mistakes also can be misinterpreted as representative of the group. Thus, the person with a visible disability is always an ambassador from the disability community on assignment to the able-bodied (AB) world" (p. 82). Ironically, occasionally solos do not subscribe to the identity that the larger group has given them. Once again, it is not the *actual* identity or characteristics of the individual that determines his or her treatment, but the *perceived* identity.

Often solos do not have access to informal communication networks, such as office gossip; they have no role models or mentors. Informal communication, role models, and colleagues are all sources of professional development and emotional support. Much of the helpful (and interesting) information at school and work is derived from informal sources. In addition, professional development can be facilitated by coworkers and mentors who can "clue the new person in." However, the one individual who is perceived as different, the solo, the PWD, will be accorded all his or her rights under the ADA, but often coworkers do not view the solo as a peer. The solo may sit alone at lunches and on coffee breaks and will not be "in" on the office gossip. The importance of role models for PWDs can be seen in the experience of Dr. Schroeder, whom we met in Chapter 4. Although he had received orientation and mobility training (O & M), Schroeder wrongly assumed that people who were blind went to only those places in the community which were necessary, such as work or school. As you remember, his rehabilitation counselor, who was also blind, asked Schroeder if he would like to go out for a cup of coffee. The two of them then went to a coffee shop, crossing busy streets in downtown San Francisco. This short outing for a cup of coffee was a life-changing experience for Schroeder. His rehabilitation counselor was a role model who helped Schroeder to understand (1) how to make better use of his O & M training, and (2) his life as a person who is blind did not have to be isolated and lacking in social contact. As a young man who had experienced the onset of blindness, Schroeder was given high-quality professional services to assist him in dealing with the disability, but he also needed a role model, an individual who was blind, who could *show* (not *tell*) Schroeder ways in which to expand his world. When an individual is a solo, he or she has no access to role models. The fact that Schroeder remembers this single cup of coffee years later attests to the importance of role models.

Harilyn Rousso, a woman with cerebral palsy, tells of the importance of role models in her book *Disabled, Female, and Proud!* (1993).

> When I was about twenty-two, I had an unexpected, important experience. I worked one summer for a prominent woman economist who happened to have cerebral palsy. I can't tell you my surprise when I met her at the job interview. It was a bit like looking at myself in the mirror. Betty had a powerful effect on me. I was impressed that a woman with cerebral palsy, not a very socially acceptable disability in our culture, could become so successful in her career, particularly in a "man's field," anti-trust economics. I was even more impressed that she was married....It never occurred to

me that I had any alternative, that I could have *both* a career and a romantic life. Betty's lifestyle, her successful marriage to an interesting, dynamic man made me question for the first time the negative assumptions that I had made about my social potential (p. 2).

As can be seen, meeting and working with this economist occurred at an age, 22 years old, when Ms. Rousso could take advantage of an expanded view of both work and romantic options available to her. We can also see that Ms. Rousso identified with her employer because she states, "It was a bit like looking at myself in a mirror."

TOKEN STATUS

In this section, look for—

▶ *the definition of token status*
▶ *why tokens are not acknowledged for their achievements and talents*

Token status refers to being viewed as having received rewards and privileges as a result of membership in a certain category. When we discussed the ADA in Chapter 2, we learned that this law does not mandate hiring for jobs or entrance into schools of anyone with a disability who is not qualified. In spite of this, many PWODs think that PWDs have special privileges or exemptions from qualifications. On a personal level, being perceived as a token is both demeaning and frustrating. On a national level, these misperceptions can impact both legislation and policy. It would make no economic sense to hire someone who is not qualified, although he or she belongs to a minority group or has a disability. Further, the law does not mandate that companies hire or schools admit individuals from any particular group. The law does require that application and hiring processes be open to all.

As would be expected, when an individual is considered to be a token (for membership in any type of group), years of hard work, preparation, study, and sacrifice are disregarded and ignored. The individual is thought to have received his or her position because he or she is a member of some "disadvantaged group." Further, the token's talents, abilities, skills, intelligence, and work habits are also unacknowledged. Thus, the token fully understands that if he or she were not a member of "some disadvantaged group," his or her accomplishments would be recognized and acknowledged as *individual* achievements. Certainly, the token realizes that it is his or her membership in the group that results in being perceived as a token. It is clear that being viewed as a token is the result of the mistaken stereotypes of the token's associates.

In the video *Look Who's Laughing,* a comedian with a disability relates that he was told by another comedian, who did not have a disability, that he was "lucky" to have a disability. Implied in this statement is the idea that the comedian with a disability did not have the qualification to be a comedian, which is to be funny, but that his disability helped him to get comedy jobs. Another comedian states, "You can get only so far on any type of gimmick (speaking of her disability). You need talent."

PATERNALISM

In this section, look for—

▶ *why the practice of paternalism is common when serving PWDs*
▶ *when paternalism is justified*
▶ *when paternalism is not justified*
▶ *what "limited paternalism" and "paternalism by permission" mean*
▶ *the principle of informed choice*
▶ *the principle of self-determination*

Paternalism has been defined as "acting upon one's own idea of what is best for another person without consulting that other person" (Marchewka, cited in Anderson, 1987, p. 177). Sissela Bok (1979) defined paternalism as "to guide and even coerce people in order to protect them and serve their best interests, as a father might his children. He must keep them out of harm's way, by force if necessary" (p. 215). Both these definitions emphasize that the individuals for whom this guidance, protection, and service are provided are, at best, not consulted, and, at worse, coerced. Therefore, an individual's autonomy has been violated. On the other hand, the concept of a father implies someone who (1) has the best interests of the child in mind and would not want to harm his child, and (2) is more knowledgeable and qualified than his child. The "child," or patient, or client is considered to be vulnerable and in need of guidance. It is not difficult to determine that paternalism is a product of the medical model of disability. As you will remember, the medical model relies on the expert knowledge of physicians and other health care providers.

Of course, there are situations in which paternalism is both appropriate and desirable, and therefore society provides the power and resources for paternalism to be enforced. For individuals with severe mental retardation who do not have the ability to understand the nature, extent, and ramifications of important decisions, paternalism is desirable. Indeed, Anderson (1987) stated,

> Some might argue that because of cognitive impairment, the incompetent or severely mentally retarded [*sic*] have no right to the truth as they have no "true liberty." This leads to a logical difficulty: if people have no liberty, it is not possible to abridge that liberty, and therefore it is not paternalistic to choose for them; in fact it is not possible to be paternalistic (pp. 183–184).

Paternalism is justified when it is thought that the individual may make decisions that would cause harm to himself or herself. (Another obvious example is that of children and their parents.) However, many PWDs feel that paternalism has been overused. In the video *Don't Go to Your Room*, one woman with a physical disability states, "I have the right to control my body," and another woman remarks, "We have the right to all aspects of our lives." A third PWD states, "Let me define who I am and what I want to do with my life." Such statements as these reflect a long history of needless paternalism toward PWDs.

The unethical use of paternalism is readily apparent when decisions are made for individuals who have the capability to make their own decisions. A woman who has experienced schizophrenia for 20 years related her experiences with paternalism: "You are given insulin coma therapy and ECT (electroconvulsive therapy) without being consulted or informed because your psychiatrist and your family assume you are too ill to understand" (Leete, 1991, p. 19). Ruth Morris has a degenerating physical disability. She worries that as her condition deteriorates, physicians may make paternalistic decisions about the quality of her life. Further, she knows that physicians have the power to enforce their decisions, regardless of how wrong or patronizing:

> The neurosurgeon told me that he was only interested in quality of life and that in no way would he be looking to prolong my life if he didn't feel the quality would be acceptable. However, neither he nor anyone else has asked me what criteria I would use in judging what was an acceptable quality of life. I am very worried that if I get admitted unconscious or without the power of speech, he will make a decision based on his judgment and his criteria about what is an acceptable quality of life (Morris, 1991, p. 62).

Here is another example of paternalism: "Upon retirement, the head of the Spastic Society of Britain was asked if he could envision the day when a person with spasticity would head that charity. 'That'd be like putting dogs and cats in charge of the Humane Society,' he quipped" (Pelka, 1997, p. 3 – quoted from the November/December 1993 issue of *Mouth: The Voice of Disability Rights*). Incidentally, this short story also illustrates other concepts that we have discussed in this book: (1) the use of improper language ("The Spastic Society"), (2) comparing PWDs to animals, (3) the use of humor to stereotype and devalue PWDs, and (4) the harm that so-called "charities" perpetuate on people whom they claim to help. Not so quickly discernible is the unintentional misuse of paternalism for individuals who are not capable of making decisions (and therefore society deems paternalism to be appropriate), but these important decisions are made based on false stereotypes and/or inaccurate information about the PWD. Certainly, we have seen that highly trained professionals hold many false stereotypes of PWDs. And, in those cases where paternalism is both necessary and desirable, it is important to ensure these judgments and choices, made on the behalf of another person, are based on accurate and complete knowledge of the individual. Many disability rights advocates have argued that an individual's worst behavior, regardless of how infrequently that behavior occurred, determined the individual's placement and treatment plans.

Thus, there are types of abuse of paternalism. The first, and most clear-cut, is enforcing paternalism when the individual can make decisions for him- or herself. The second, and less obvious, is enforcing paternalism when the individual cannot make decisions, but unintentionally basing decisions on inaccurate information and/or false stereotypes. Indeed, unjustified paternalism has resulted in restrictive and humiliating treatment for PWDs.

Why have PWDs been subjected to so much paternalism? First, the normative role of a PWD demands dependency, compliance, and passive acceptance of treatment, benefits, and rehabilitation. Certainly the power is in the hands of the physicians and counselors who, if they chose, could withhold treatment and benefits if a PWD questions or challenges their decisions. Second, the overgeneralization or perceived spread concerning the effects of the disability often contributes to the mistaken idea that a PWD does not have the mental capacity to make decisions in his or her own behalf. Third, the (unnecessary) need to protect and shelter the PWD may lead some service providers to withhold information from the PWD. Fourth, simply due to the nature of the living and treatment environments, many PWDs experience daily, lifelong contact with care providers. These types of settings promote and encourage paternalism, rather than any characteristic or need of the client. Fifth, some service providers may be paternalistic simply for the convenience and ease of the institution/hospital/agency. These service providers often feel that "things just go more smoothly when the client/patient does what he or she is told to do." (This last example may not be true paternalism because paternalism implies beneficence or consideration of the individual's best interests.)

What are the ways in which paternalism is promoted? As mentioned above, withholding of important information about the disability, about treatment options and their consequences, or about alternative placements is a common form of paternalism. Forcing PWDs to undergo treatments, such as cochlear implants for individuals who are deaf, or forced sterilization of people with mental retardation, is another type of paternalism. Paternalism is often directed toward "the hateful client" (Purtilo, 1991, p. 29), especially individuals who are perceived as difficult or demanding. Occasionally, paternalism is deemed to be justified because the resulting decisions will be "better for all concerned." Often, the "all concerned" means family members of the PWD. On the other hand, parents of children with disabilities have often felt they have been manipulated by professionals. Paternalism on the behalf of PWDs is often considered to be appropriate when a PWD wishes to undertake a particular activity and his or her caregiver considers the activity to be unobtainable or impractical. As can be seen, there is a very thin line between paternalism and coercion. Today, there is a heightened sensitivity about the risks of paternalism. As would be expected, several methods to reduce the risk of abusing paternalism have been devised. Concepts such as "limited paternalism" are often implemented with individuals who have the capability to make some decisions but are incapable of making other decisions. Therefore, instead of completely controlling the individual's life, it may be necessary, for example, to make financial decisions for the individual, but he or she can guide and control all other aspects of his or her life. On the other hand, "paternalism by permission" can be justified. When a patient acknowledges that the health professional is in a better position to decide on a course of action, a patient may actually exercise autonomy by appointing the health professional as a decision maker. The patient must explicitly acknowledge that he or she chooses to follow the professional's judgment (Purtilo, 1991, p. 29). Inherent in these two concepts is the idea that a certain degree of paternalism may be necessary, but the need for total control and complete paternalism may be quite rare.

Two other movements, both supported by federal legislation, designed to minimize paternalism are (1) informed choice in which the client is given all available information about the disability, the various treatment plans and options, and their consequences, and (2) self-determination in which the individual has the right to make decisions about his or her treatment, living arrangements, job placement, and social networks. Often, self-determination is called empowerment. Both of these movements acknowledge that the individual is the expert in his or her own needs and desires.

Indeed, PWDs have had to *fight* for their rights while all others are automatically *given* their rights. The right to control their own lives has often been denied (needlessly) to PWDs.

INFANTILIZATION

In this section, look for—
- ► *the definition of infantilization*
- ► *the definition of "motherese"*
- ► *which types of people are subjected to motherese*

PWDs have often been viewed as "eternal children," in need of control, management, and spiritual guidance (Imrie, 1996). Wolfensberger (1981) explained: "Adults [with disabilities] may be cast into the roles of eternal children by being encouraged to play children's games and to follow children's school schedules rather than adult work schedules; by children's decoration and children's clothing; by funding of services for adults coming from departments charged with serving children; and by such names as "day care center" for day programs for adults (p. 205).

Thus, it can be seen that infantilization is practiced both on an individual level and on an institutional level.

Sharon L., a medical social worker with a congenital bone disease that has resulted in her small stature, stated, "It is difficult to cross that border from childhood to adulthood." Sharon has developed "presentation strategies" in order to offset the tendency of others to, as she states, "associate my maturity with my size." For example, when she speaks on the telephone, her voice sounds like the voice of a child; therefore, she "uses big words" so as to "sound" like an adult. Charities have often used "poster kids" and, indeed, some celebrities have demonstrated a tendency not only to infantilize people with a certain type of disability, but also to claim a paternalistic relationship. For example, Jerry Lewis terms individuals with muscular dystrophy (MD) as "Jerry's Kids." It is safe to say that most people with MD do not consider themselves either to be children or to belong to Jerry Lewis.

Another example of infantilization is seen in the remark made by a woman in the video *My Body Is Not Who I Am*. She states, "It's as if I am a child and I have no boundaries." PWDs are often spoken to in a speech pattern that has been labeled "motherese" (Gouvier, Coon, Todd, & Fuller, 1994). Other authors label this type of speech pattern as "child-directed speech" (Warren-Leubecker & Bohannon, 1989). Motherese "involves exaggerated prosodic inflections and other characteristics such as the use of diminutives in naming (e.g., Bobby rather than Bob) and shortened phrase and sentence length,...greater redundancy and higher usage of questions and concrete referents" (Gouvier et al., p. 264). Prosodic means sing-song speech. Gouvier and his colleagues surreptitiously audiotaped conversations of bookstore employees giving directions to customers in wheelchairs and customers who had no visible disability. Employees speaking to customers in wheelchairs used more words, more repetition, and more questions than when these employees were speaking to customers without a visible disability. Incidentally, none of these fake customers had a disability of any kind (they simply used the wheelchair for the purpose of the experiment) and all were university students. Furthermore, each student played both roles; he or she would use the wheelchair one time and then on another day walk into the bookstore. These students reported that when they used the wheelchair, they sensed "a reverse discrimination in which people actually seemed 'nicer' to them than when they approached in the walking condition" (p. 267).

Gouvier and his colleagues concluded, "This study offers clear behavioral validation that people do speak differently to individuals with disabilities, and that some of these differences parallel those observed in the way people speak to their infant children, pets, and other individuals of lower social standing" (p. 266).

We can hear motherese spoken when a nurse asks someone, "How are we feeling today?" or "Did we eat all our dinner?" Terms of endearment such as "honey" or "sweetheart" used when addressing adult strangers are another indication of "motherese." PWDs are often addressed in this insulting and degrading manner. Indeed, adults in institutions were/are often deprived of some small pleasure as a form of punishment. "If you don't do your physical therapy, you won't get dessert" and "If you don't take your medication, you won't be allowed to watch television." These are all examples of motherese.

PWDs are subjected to intrusive touching by strangers. In our society, adults usually do not touch other adults whom they do not know. Other than a handshake, in which both individuals must cooperate, a stranger touching another adult is usually considered to be intrusive. PWDs are patted on the head and hugged, and their assistive devices (such as wheelchairs) are moved. All of these behaviors are viewed as intrusive and infantilizing by PWDs.

Certainly, there is a complex relationship between infantilization, paternalism, dependence, and the medical model of disability. PWDs are often thought to be sexually neutered and to not be capable of working and making contributions to society; both of these characteristics we usually attribute to children. Furthermore, PWDs are expected to comply with the rules made by PWODs, again a characteristic of childhood in that a child is expected to obey his or her "elders and superiors." Indeed, Ludwig and Adams (1968) undertook a study in a large rehabilitation center in order to assess the relationship between patient dependency and subordination and patient rehabilitation success rate. The authors stated, "The role of a patient has been likened to that of children by many....What is held in common, of course, among these...social positions is the lack of independence, the necessity of accepting a subordinate position and submitting to others" (p. 227). Their study, which included 406 PWDs, "hypothesized that persons whose normal role relationships and social position contained elements of dependency or subordination would be more inclined to successfully perform such a role and complete treatment. Persons in dependent age status, females, Negroes, the unemployed...were found more likely to complete recommended services, thus supporting the general hypothesis" (p. 235).

This study was completed over 30 years ago. Nonetheless, the straightforward and clearly stated hypothesis (and the entire purpose of the study) sought to demonstrate that childlike patients were more successful in their rehabilitation. Hypothesizing that PWDs who were women, African Americans, or unemployed would be more submissive clearly shows that these types of individuals, with or without disabilities, also are not accorded full adult status in our society.

VIEWING PWDs AS OBJECTS

In this section, look for—
▶ *the history and purpose of freak shows*
▶ *present-day freak shows*

The long history of freak shows and circuses in which PWDs were put on display for the entertainment of others provides a clear definition of the objectification of PWDs. Nervous curiosity and fascination with people who are not viewed as being human, but rather as objects, continue today. However, our media, such as movies and television, have replaced most of the freak shows and circuses. It was thought that there were moral lessons to be learned by viewing these "freaks" and, indeed, these individuals who were put on display were thought to be symbols of evil, disease, and sin. Pelka (1997) described these "sideshows":

> The Catholic Church, during the Middle Ages in Europe, sponsored traveling exhibitions of disabled people, while families exhibited their disabled members for a fee or sold them to royalty at court. By Victorian times, these forms of "entertainment" had evolved into carnival sideshows or "dime museums," where the public paid to see "armless and legless wonders," "giants," "dwarfs," "seal boys," "living skeletons," and "pinheads." Such exhibits were particularly popular in small-town America (p. 127).

Ironically, many, if not most, of these individuals experienced no functional limitations. It was simply their appearance that made them "freaks."

Circuses and freak shows were often viewed by PWDs as sources of income when there were not many opportunities for employment and integration with the general population (Thompson, 1968). Furthermore, these PWDs who worked in circuses and freak shows felt a sense of acceptance and understanding by living, working, and traveling with other people who knew what it meant to be labeled a "freak." There was a dark and brutal side to these traveling circuses, and many PWDs were abused and exploited simply because the operators of these circuses and freak shows knew very well that there were few places to which the PWD could escape (Bogdan, 1988). Clearly, these PWDs were exploited and objectified for the entertainment of avid audiences with the express purpose of making money for others.

The efforts to raise awareness and funds for the education of PWDs often included prestigious authorities, such as physicians and teachers, "displaying" a PWD and showing the audience what the PWD could do. Basically, these types of demonstrations consisted of a teacher putting a PWD "through his or her paces." Thus, physicians and teachers used PWDs as objects, albeit under the guise of advancing education and medical science. Helen Keller, an honors graduate of Radcliffe College, performed in vaudeville for four years, twice a day, much to Helen's mother's disappointment, who had claimed that her daughter would "go on stage over my dead body" (Hermann, 1998). After the act, the audience was allowed to ask Ms. Keller questions. Ms. Keller said that she enjoyed acting in vaudeville, but it also solved her financial problems. Before her vaudeville days, and after, Ms. Keller had relied on the charity of millionaire philanthropists and income from lecturing. She did view herself as a "spectacle." She wrote of herself and her fellow actors "for the sake of many for whom fate is unkind. . . . I can conceive that in time the spectacle might have grown stale" (Hermann, 1998, p. 223).

Paul Higgins, a disability scholar, forthrightly labels telethons and other charitable fund-raising activities as modern-day freak shows. Higgins (1992) explained: "Fund raisers still exhibit disabled [sic] people for 'profit.' Audiences marvel at the accomplishments of the disabled people who are presented to tug at our heartstrings—and our purse strings" (p. 94).

Today, PWDs feel viewed as objects when they state, "I was *something* to stare at," or "I was interesting to people and that's dehumanizing" *(My Body Is Not Who I Am)*. A woman who was born with spina bifida described an unforgettable experience of objectification. "I was barely human. One time, as a 14-year-old, I was paraded in front of a whole class of doctors so they could see my "abnormal gait." I was wearing only my panties. They would never have done that to a nondisabled girl but it was OK to parade me almost naked. The crazy thing is, it wasn't until years later that I realized they had dehumanized me" (Mackelprang & Salsgiver, 1999, p. 39).

Two ideas are immediately apparent from reading this adult's memory of the treatment she received as a teenager. First, the woman has become aware that the doctors could have had the same quality of training and demonstration while, at the same time, according the girl some measure of respect and dignity (i.e., allowing her to wear more clothing). Second, rather than being overly sensitive and hypervigilant for any evidence of prejudice and discrimination, the 14-year-old willingly complied with the doctors' requests and, amazingly, only comes to an awareness of this disrespectful treatment years later. Mee (1999) reported the same experience:

> Dr. Blount, proud of his work, kept inviting me back to Milwaukee whenever he brought together a group of doctors from around the world, to put me on the stage in the medical theater. I would arrive early, strip, and put on a little loincloth, like a diaper. This, in itself, was a disagreeable experience. I was, in any case, an embarrassable adolescent boy. But to be reduced to an object, as these days, finally everybody knows, is profoundly diminishing. In fact, I was reduced to something even less than an object: I was a specimen (p. 175).

An extreme example of objectification of PWDs is a practice called "dwarf-tossing." Patrons at bars or clubs pay a fee to throw a person, who is a dwarf, onto a padded surface. Dwarf-tossing is a competition with those who throw the person the farthest or the most accurately, winning the "game" (Higgins, 1992, p. 94). The perpetrators of crime against PWDs and sexual abuse of PWDs often defend themselves, stating that they did not view their victims as people. Reading David Hevey's (1997) essay *The Enfreakment of Photography*, we learn that modern-day photography has exploited PWDs. A line from the first paragraph states, "I ask the reader to join me on a journey into oppressive disability imagery" (p. 332). PWDs report that they feel objectified when PWODs, including their own families, "put them on a pedestal." While this might be admiration and may be thought to be a positive experience for the individual with the disability, it is both distancing and objectifying.

VIEWING PWDs AS ANIMALS

In this section, look for—

> ▶ *ways in which society views PWDs as less than human*
> ▶ *the four dimensions of ascribing humanness to PWDs, according to Bogdan and Taylor (1987)*

You will remember that in Chapter 1 when we discussed the concept of normalcy, we read the following statement of Wolfensberger (1972): "Normalcy is often confused with humanity" (p. 205). Implied in this statement is the corresponding idea that disability is not associated with humanity. Davis (1997) stated, "To have a disability is to be an animal" (p. 20). A brief listing of the derisive names applied to PWDs illustrates Wolfensberger's statement: Joseph Merrick, the 19th century Englishman with neurofibromatosis was called the "Elephant Man"; a woman who was born with hands missing some fingers is called "Lobster Claws"; freak shows exhibited "Jo-Jo, the Dog-faced Boy," and "Lionel, the Lion-faced Man"; Samuel D. Parks, a dwarf without legs was billed as "Hopp, the Frog Boy"; a native of New Guinea, Prince Randian, had no arms or legs and was billed as the "Snake Man" and the "Caterpillar Man" (Pelka, 1997); a man with mental retardation is called "Monkey Boy." Mackelprang and Salsgiver (1999) proposed that "disabilities suggest to people humankind's imperfections and dissimilarities to God while illuminating humankind's relationship to the imperfect animal kingdom" (pp. 37–38). Recently, in Utah, a manager of a large grocery store referred to and addressed an employee who bagged groceries (and who was mentally retarded) as "Monkey Boy." When the bagger was out in the parking lot gathering up shopping carts, the manager would use the loudspeaker to call the bagger back into the store, addressing him as "Monkey Boy." The bagger's parents sued the grocery store chain (Mims, 1998).

People who used sign language were called "ape-like." A teacher at the Pennsylvania School for the Deaf observed in 1873 that sign language was "being decried, denounced, and ridiculed...as a set of monkey-like grimaces and antics" (Pettingill, 1873, cited in Baynton, 1997). Furthermore, the ability to speak was often "the constituting force of humanity" (Nelson & Berens, 1997, p. 52), and therefore people who were deaf and did not speak were not considered to be human "in the relentlessly aural world of early modern England...[where] civilization was possible only through *spoken* [italics added] language" (Nelson & Berens, 1997, p. 52). St. Augustine denied church membership to individuals who were deaf, including the right to communion or the other sacraments, based on the assumption that they could not confess their sins.

Commenting on the experiences of Joseph Merrick, Darke (1993) made the observation that English Victorian society dehumanized and objectified PWDs "rather than representing abnormality/disability as human and valid in itself" (p. 340). Darke remarked that PWDs were thought of as "potential exhibits in what was a cross between a zoo and a museum" (p. 339). What are typically viewed in a museum? Objects. What are typically viewed in a zoo? Animals. Goffman (1963), speaking about all types of stigmatized people, stated, "[they] are not quite human" (p. 3).

A famous deaf actor, Bernard Bragg, provided another example of viewing PWDs as less than human, perhaps on a subconscious level. Bragg was approached by a producer of documentaries who wished to make a film on language and asked Bragg to write and star in a segment on sign language. Upon asking about the other segments of the proposed film and learning that the other parts of the film would present communication among whales and chimpanzees, Bragg refused to participate. The film producer was surprised and perplexed, not understanding how insulting such associations are (Bragg, 1989).

It is well known that people who live in institutions are often not thought to be fully human by their caregivers (Livneh, 1980). Criminals often choose PWDs as their targets because they often do not think of PWDs as "people" and therefore these criminals do not experience guilt and remorse for their crimes. Also, the myth that PWDs are insensitive or indifferent to pain increases the likelihood that they will be abused. Sobsey, in his book *Violence and Abuse in the Lives of People with Disabilities: The End of Silent Acceptance* (1994), conceives of the dehumanization of people with disabilities who live in institutions to take three forms. He labels these forms "1) conceptual dehumanization, 2) ecobehavioral dehumanization, and 3) reactive dehumanization" (p. 311). Conceptual dehumanization includes "attitudes, expectations, beliefs, labels and language"; ecobehavioral dehumanization includes segregating people, putting them into uniforms, thus robbing them of their humanity and individuality, humiliating them, and denying them the necessities of life"; reactive dehumanization occurs when "the behaviors and appearance of people who are dehumanized deteriorate to conform to their societal status" (pp. 311–312). Sobsey sees dehumanization of people with disabilities to be a circular process. In other words, the more they are treated as less than human, the more they conform to these expectations. Other examples of not viewing PWDs as fully human include scientists and researchers who have, in the past, used PWDs as research subjects. Of course, it is not unethical to use people as research subjects; however, PWDs have often been used in unethical medical experiments simply because PWODs would have refused to participate (and had the power to enforce that refusal). For instance, in the 1960s in Sweden, individuals with mental retardation were fed high-sugar diets in order to establish a causal link between sugar and tooth decay. The headlines of the news stories that reported these experiments included the words "guinea pigs" and "laboratory rats" to describe the subjects of these studies.

Wolfensberger and Tullman (1982) described ways in which society views children with disabilities as animals:

> If a group of children is [unconsciously] viewed as animals, then they may be segregated in a special class that is given an animal name—often even the name of animals that are seen as expressive of the devalued children's identity. Thus, a class for retarded children may be called "The Turtles." The animal kingdom may serve as an analogue for or source of service measures for that group of people (pp. 134–135).

Two disability scholars, Robert Bogdan and Steven Taylor, wrote *The Social Construction of Humanness: Relationships with Severely Disabled People* (1989), in which they describe 15 years of qualitative research. Bogdan and Taylor interviewed over 100 family members and caregivers of individuals with severe and multiple disabilities. They describe the PWDs in their study in this way: "Some scholars and professionals would argue that [our research subjects] lack the characteristics of a human being....The severely and profoundly retarded people in our study have often been the target of the indictment 'vegetable'" (p. 279). Bogdan and Taylor analyzed the interviews and found four dimensions of humanness: (1) ascribing thinking to PWDs, (2) seeing individuality and personality in the PWD, (3) viewing the PWD as reciprocating and contributing to the family, and (4) defining a social place for the PWD and thinking of the PWD as an integral part of the family. This research presents a monumental shift in the way in which PWODs view individuals with severe and multiple disabilities.

Technology and neonatal medical science have added another dimension to the question of ascribing humanity to PWDs. Such questions of humanity now apply to unborn babies. Now that it is possible, in some cases, to determine the presence of severe and multiple disabilities in unborn children, should these babies be born? (Fletcher, 1979; Frohock, 1986).

Bogdan and Taylor concluded, "We [PWODs] can show that they [PWDs] are human by proving we are capable of showing humanity to them" (p. 29).

UNNECESSARY DEPENDENCE

In this section, look for—
- ▶ *how PWDs define dependence differently*
- ▶ *how PWODs often misinterpret adaptive coping responses of PWDs to be dependence*
- ▶ *how PWODs often promote unnecessary dependence for PWDs*

The idea of independence/dependence is probably defined a little differently by everyone. Stated differently, independence/dependence is very idiosyncratically defined. Nonetheless, we can broadly state that independence means having control over one's life and one's decisions, which includes (1) control of the resources necessary to care for oneself; (2) the choice of affiliation with other people, in families, in friendships, and in colleague groups; and (3) the freedom to make choices for oneself (Chesler & Chesney, 1988). For anyone, with or without a disability, the resources necessary to care for oneself include economic empowerment (which usually means a job); in addition for PWDs, included in the resources necessary to care for oneself may be medical care, certainly complete information about the disability, assistive technology, personal care attendants, and the services of other types of caregivers (Crewe & Zola, 1983; Deegan, 1992). Physical independence is relatively easy to describe and define; emotional independence is more difficult to define. However, Anne Finger (1991) observed that some types of physical dependence are acceptable to PWODs while others are not. She uses the examples of using a car (acceptable to PWODs) and using a wheelchair (unacceptable to PWODs). A second set of examples includes going to a hairstylist for a haircut (acceptable to PWODs) and having an attendant wash your face (not acceptable to PWODs). For instance, what one person describes as emotional independence, another might describe as loneliness and isolation.

Of course, no one, with or without a disability, is completely independent. Everyone depends on someone else to some extent; however, most of us would agree that the greater the degree of independence an individual experiences, the more options he or she enjoys. Indeed, independence is considered to be one of the *sine qua non* of quality of life.

It is safe to state that our "value system distrusts and devalues dependence in other people and vulnerability in general" (Wendell, 1997, p. 261). And, PWDs are often viewed as both dependent and vulnerable.

PWDs often define and interpret dependence/independence differently. While independence is valued and needless dependence is avoided, PWDs do not "glorify independence" (Wright, 1960). Control and consent are important components of independence. Indeed, what is thought to be independence, for many PWDs, is neither possible nor a great need. A professional artist who needs the services of a personal care attendant explained:

My attendant is an extension of my body. It takes a very emotionally strong as well as spiritually strong person to understand that and not resent it. If I don't direct the person, then I'm dependent on that person. Then I'm not autonomous and ultimately it's harder on the attendant. I made it very clear that I'm not making decisions for *them,* only for myself (Panzarino, as cited in Rousso, 1993, p. 111).

Notice the way in which Panzarino redefines the concept of autonomy (or independence). Most people who have had no experience with personal care attendants would assume that being fed, bathed, and dressed by a paid attendant would make an individual feel dependent and helpless. In contrast, when Ms. Panzarino is directing the attendant, she feels "autonomous" and in control. Notice also that she is aware that when she does not remain independent and directive, it makes the attendant's job harder. Ms. Panzarino also explains that it is possible for an individual to become "overly dependent" on an attendant.

Leonard Kriegel, in his book *Falling into Life* (1991), details how learning to fall was a turning point in the recovery of his independence. When he was 11 years old, Kriegel contracted polio and his legs were paralyzed. In order to learn how to walk in his braces, it was necessary to learn how to fall "properly" and to get back on his feet. The physical therapists taught these skills to all the patients, but Kriegel would not allow himself to fall, explaining, "The prospect of letting go was precisely what terrified me. That the other boys in the ward had no trouble falling added to my shame and terror. I knew there was virtually no chance of injury when I fell, but the knowledge simply made me more ashamed of a cowardice that was as monumental as it was unexplainable" (pp. 10–11).

For Kriegel, falling down meant a loss of independence and succumbing to failure. When he does learn to fall, he writes in almost biblical language of how learning to deliberately and autonomously sacrifice his independence by falling is the beginning of learning how to control his body: "I dropped. I did not crash. I dropped. I did not collapse. I dropped. I did not plummet. I felt myself enveloped by a curiously gentle moment in my life. In that sliver of time before I was kissed by the mat, I could sense my shame and fear drain from my soul, and I knew that my sense of my own cowardice would soon follow. In falling, I had given myself a new life, a new start" (p. 8). Kriegel, at age 11, had redefined independence.

In the American culture, independence is both highly valued and narrowly defined. Naturally, PWDs value independence and autonomy and also know that they have a right to independence. They simply redefine these concepts. Also, they manipulate both their personal environment and the disability to achieve independence. However, PWDs cannot manipulate all of the physical environment or the attitudes of PWODs. Obviously, for some PWDs, there are activities that they will not be able to do, regardless of how much they "try harder" (Phillips, 1991). PWODs may unwittingly curtail the independence of PWDs in an attempt to be helpful. For example, encouraging the use of prostheses which serve no functional purpose, but instead are uncomfortable and confining, diminishes the independence of the PWD.

Often PWODs misinterpret assertive and independent behaviors of PWDs. For example, the use of certain assistive devices to conserve energy (an individual using a wheelchair or scooter when he or she is capable of walking but wants to conserve his or her energy for something more important), the side effects of medication (falling asleep in public places), and all sorts of strategies to complete activities of daily living (such as keeping the clean dishes in the refrigerator) are sometimes viewed, erroneously, by PWODs as maladaptive and dependent behaviors. When PWDs ask for accommodations or assistance, for example, they are often seen as being dependent and passive. Does it make sense for a very highly paid corporate attorney to spend two and a half hours in the morning dressing him- or herself, finishing exhausted, or should a personal care attendant be hired? Obviously, the attorney is capable of dressing him- or herself, but how rational is the decision to do as much for oneself as possible in this particular case? At other times, when PWDs resist or refuse assistance, they are seen as rude and ungrateful. Unwanted assistance may be viewed by PWDs as attempts to control them. Certainly, due to the fact that PWODs have so little understanding of the experience of disability, it is difficult for them to judge the degree of independence a PWD has.

Society can, and does, impose unnecessary dependence upon PWDs. Certainly, the medical model of disability has never encouraged PWDs to be active, assertive, or independent (Zola, 1972). Medical and human service bureaucracies are often dehumanizing, expecting passive compliance from patients/clients. The services provided are intended to assist the individual; however, the expectations of passive compliance promote needless dependence and prevent the individual from making his or her own choices and decisions. Residential schooling, institutionalization, and prolonged hospitalizations also contribute to promoting needless dependence. Decision making is a learned skill that individuals learn in small incremental steps. For example, kindergarten children make their daily clothing choices and young adults choose marriage partners and careers. In between kindergarten and young adulthood, there are many choices and decisions, appropriate to the individual's age. For individuals who have lived in institutions and have not been allowed to make decisions of when they will sleep, when they will eat, or what they will eat, typical adult independence can seem overwhelming.

Society institutionalizes dependence for PWDs. By giving children with disabilities inferior education, by making policies and regulations that incorporate financial disincentives that make it difficult for PWDs to go to work, and by refusing to provide accommodations, society has institutionalized unnecessary dependence for PWDs.

The unwillingness to provide accommodations (as mandated by the ADA) can be recognized in thoughtless comments such as "Don't these people lip read?" It can be seen in a sign with a picture of a wheelchair that states "Ring for assistance" or in signs that direct wheelchair users to use the delivery entrance. Another example of reluctance to provide accommodations is reflected in efforts to determine if PWDs will attend specific events. As we have already learned, it is both irrelevant and illegal to provide physical accessibility *only* after it has been determined that PWDs will need them. Certainly, it is clear from these examples that the independence of PWDs has been needlessly limited. Surprisingly, most individuals would consider the above examples to be adequate accommodations for PWDs. Imrie (1996) summarized: "Mobility [is] liberty for the human body" (p. 18). Facilities, both public and private, which are accessible to PWODs and are necessary for day-to-day living, are unavailable to PWDs. This is an example of institutionalizing needless dependence for PWDs.

A court interpreter for the New York State Supreme Court (English/Spanish) who is blind told how difficult it was to ask for accommodations when she was new on the job. (She had threatened a lawsuit in order to be considered for the job and was therefore unwilling to appear demanding.)

Having Braille indicators on the elevators would have made my life easier, but I didn't ask for them because I felt I shouldn't make any special demands. Now, eight years later, I feel a lot more comfortable asking for what I need, but I feel silly demanding changes in the elevator at this point, when I have been using them as they are for so long. I guess asking for help is not yet as easy for me as I would like it to be. But it is an issue that all of us as disabled people need to keep struggling with—to make sure we get what we need (Crespo, 1993, p. 98).

Dependence is also fostered by the false stereotype that PWDs can never contribute. According to this stereotype, all assistance and contribution is one-way—all given to the PWD, with the PWD never being acknowledged as a benefactor or a contributor. Looking back to Chapter 4 and the example of Greg Smith and his Rollathon fund-raiser for Literacy of America, we can see that PWDs, like everyone else, like to contribute to the community and to their families. Smith planned his fund-raiser to coincide with the Labor Day Jerry Lewis telethon in order to make a strong point that PWDs participate in community service.

Marginality

Everyone wants to know where he or she "belongs" in the world. The concept of marginality was originally discussed in relation to members of racial and ethnic minority groups (Stonequist, 1937). The condition of marginality occurs when an individual, because of his or her membership in a devalued group (sometimes referred to as "defining status") is not allowed to participate fully in the life of the community according to his or her interests and abilities. Stonequist posited that because racial and ethnic minority individuals were barred from full participation in the life of society, these individuals are "caught" between two groups—the dominant, powerful majority group and their own minority group. Gist and Dworkin (1972) described a marginal person as "one who lives in two worlds, in both of which he [sic] is more or less a stranger" (p. 10).

The solution to remedying the condition of marginality seems simple—the individual should choose his or her identity in one of the two groups. This is not possible because the power of definition is held by the dominant group. In other words, it does not matter how the individual defines him- or herself because the individual's position is determined by how the dominant group defines him or her. Therefore, the defining characteristic must be visible. The theory of marginality holds that (1) the majority group will not allow the minority individual entrance, stating that the individual has no legitimate claim to this status, and (2) the minority individual does not want to identify with his or her minority group because of the subordinate status. Therefore, the individual belongs to neither group and lacks a strong identification with any one group. Minority group individuals know far more about the majority group than the reverse. In order to survive, minority group members, including PWDs, must know about the majority culture. In contrast, majority group members often have little interest in or need to know about the minority group. Indeed, PWODs, unless they have had a family member with a disability, usually have not been interested in learning about the experiences and perspectives of PWDs.

Some aspects of marginality can be applied to individuals with disabilities while others cannot. Charles Mee, a survivor of polio, wrote of one of his first realizations of his own marginality. He described marginality perfectly: "This world seemed too foreign to me, and at the same time so familiar" (p. 131). Notice how, as a teenager, the only way in which he can describe this realization is to compare his situation with that of a racial minority.

> I spent many hours in the living room, watching Ed Sullivan's *Toast of the Town* and Sid Caesar's *Your Show of Shows* and *Ozzie and Harriet* and *I Love Lucy*.
>
> These shows, and their commercials, made me dizzy with their vision of a world so wholesome, intact, healthy, vigorous, upbeat, smooth-skinned, smiling, sleek, plump; with all the unattainable girls in swimming suits, each one of them incredibly sexy even as they were evidently not thinking about sex or anything other than purity, purity of soap and purity of complexion and purity of thought, the purity of a perfect Ipana toothpaste smile; clean people, good people, winning people, with their milk shakes and hamburgers and French fries, bobby sox and swirling skirts and snug sweaters, their pep and vigor. This world seemed too foreign to me, and at the same time so familiar: actually, in many confusing ways, this vision of the close-knit, happy family, secure in the possession of the basic consumer durables, described my life. But at the same time, in some way I couldn't put my finger on, I knew this was not my world at all. I thought: Oh, I think I know how *Negroes* feel. I thought: These people on television could be from the moon (Mee, 1999, p. 131).

In 1948, a disability scholar (Barker, cited in Goffman, 1997) stated that PWDs "live on a social-psychological frontier constantly facing new situations" (p. 215). Disability scholars use words such as "marginality" and "frontier" to describe the experience and identity of PWDs. An individual who is deaf and blind communicated his sense of marginality when he stated, "I see myself within the world, against the world, but not really part of the world" (Petty, 1979, p. 10).

Certainly, in the case of visible disabilities, the PWD is often denied membership in the dominant culture (Hannaford, 1985). However, the concept of marginality includes the necessity of two cultures, between which the PWD can be caught. Until recently, there was no disability culture with which a PWD could identify. Indeed, much of the literature on the marginality of racial/ethnic minority individuals speaks about the loss of minority cultures due to the fact that individuals have decided to take on the identity of the dominant group or, at minimum, to have their children and grandchildren take on this identity. Again, until very recently, there has been no disability culture to lose or to retain. Nonetheless, many PWDs do feel "caught." For example, the title of Higgins' (1980) book, *Outsiders in a Hearing World*, clearly communicates the alienation of the Deaf. Any kind of marginality, it can be argued, must be based on clear-cut demarcations between majority and minority. It is doubtful if, other than a few types of disabilities, such as deafness, there is such a standardized, widely understood demarcation.

The term "status inconsistency" describes the experience of the marginal person. Status inconsistency refers to the ambivalence, self-hatred, and heightened sensitivity to insult and threat that, supposedly, the marginal person experiences.

Rather than viewing these individuals as bicultural, adaptable, and flexible, social scientists and scholars viewed them as being "pulled in two directions" or having internalized the negative views of the dominant group toward their own group. Thus, the dominant group has effectively "taught" minority individuals to feel inferior. The well-known study (Clark & Clark, 1947) of young African American children (ages 3–7) choosing a white doll instead of an African American doll was used to support the hypothesis that minority individuals prefer to identify with the dominant group.

Simpson and Yinger (1985), two sociologists, stated,

> Other authors emphasize the personal instability that they believe is likely to characterize persons who lack a strong feeling of identification with one group. Minority-group members who feel torn between association with the group in which they are categorically placed by prejudice and their feelings of identification with the dominant society may lack some of the security that comes from stable and acceptable group relationships (p. 124).

Whether the psychopathology, psychological strain, personality disorganization, ambivalence, and lack of identity (none of which is a positive trait) must always be present in the marginal person is somewhat unclear. The "scientific" theory of the marginal person may have added to the prejudice and discrimination against minority individuals.

Sociologists describe individuals who experience status inconsistency as people who have acquired many of the achievements and statuses of the dominant group but, nonetheless, are still identified as being a member of a minority group. Therefore, PWDs with high occupational positions, high incomes, high levels of education, and prestige are aware that, notwithstanding these accomplishments, they are readily perceived as members of a devalued group. Therefore, when these PWDs are among strangers, the strangers have no way (usually) of knowing the *achieved status* (the education, money, prestige) but only see the PWD's *ascribed status* (as a PWD).

In summary, PWDs must negotiate a relationship with a world that ignores, devalues, and rejects them. Further, the PWD may be open to attack from both sides—from PWODs and PWDs. If the PWD tries to "pass" as not having a disability, other PWDs may think of him or her as a "closet crip." If the PWD appears to be overly eager to please PWODs and "grateful for any crumbs" (Pelka, 1997, p. 305), other PWDs may call him or her a "Tiny Tim."

EQUAL SOCIAL STATUS RELATIONSHIPS

In this section, look for—

▶ *the differing levels of social distance*
▶ *how dating, for PWDs, is Mount Everest*

Friendships, family relationships, and loving and sexual relationships are quality-of-life issues. Most people seek out and develop these types of equal social status associations. However, the segregation, isolation, and institutionalization of PWDs has created physical distance between PWDs and PWODs, which in turn has created social distance. Moreover, the stereotyping, role entrapment, lowered expectations, solo status, infantilization, paternalism, objectification, and unnecessary dependence that PWDs experience work together to make equal social status relationships difficult to initiate and maintain.

Social distance is defined by sociologists as "the degree of intimacy which group norms allow between any two individuals" (Poole, 1927, p. 115). Theories of social distance were originally developed to describe relationships between individuals of differing racial, ethnic, cultural, and religious groups. Bogardus (1928) devised a numerical scale which listed six degrees of social distance. These include allowing members of a certain group (6) to visit my country, (5) to gain citizenship in my country, (4) to gain employment in my occupation, (3) to live on my street as neighbors, (2) to join my club as personal friends, and (1) to close kinship by marriage. This order, from least intimate to most intimate, describes the degree of social relationship desired/allowed.

Olkin (1999) has also quantified social distance when speaking of PWDs, stating,

> For people with disabilities, dating is Mount Everest. Disability discrimination is most felt in the romantic realm. Studies of attitudes toward disability repeatedly show that people's attitudes become more and more negative as the relationship with the person with the disability gets closer. Those who indicate that they would be fine with the idea of a neighbor with a disability draw the line at their children dating a person with a disability, and most people indicate that they would not marry a person with a disability (p. 223).

Mount Everest may not be a numerical rating, but it does communicate the difficulty of dating for PWDs. Many PWDs report that going out for an evening of fun with a group of men and women is relatively easy for a PWD. As long as specific couples are not identified (i.e., John is with Mary), PWODs are willing to go out with PWDs. However, it is much more difficult for a PWD to arrange a one-on-one date with a PWOD.

Other measures of social distance include the progressive steps of speaking acquaintance, work colleague, having a member of a family marry this type of individual, and marrying this type of individual oneself. While these measures of social distance may be somewhat outdated (and were originally developed for racial/ethnic minority relationships), there are several ways in which they apply to PWDs. As we have discussed, perceived characteristics of PWDs, such as intelligence, social class, and level of education, influence the judgment of others. Those PWDs who are thought to be of higher social class, with more education, will probably experience less social distance than PWDs who are thought to not possess these characteristics. Therefore, there is an interplay of both the disability status and other types of desired characteristics.

However, it is safe to state that most PWDs experience more difficulty in establishing all types of equal social status relationships (DeLoach, 1994; Fisher & Galler, 1988). The widely held idea that PWDs are not able to contribute and must always be passive recipients contributes to this difficulty. On an impersonal level, we have seen how the idea that PWDs are incapable of making contributions has led to their high underemployment and unemployment rates. In spite of this widely held myth, PWDs have made important contributions as workers during labor shortages and world wars. On a personal level, this false idea has led to the unquestioned assumptions that PWDs must overachieve in order to be considered equal. Often, others, including professionals, automatically assume that a child with a disability is an unwanted burden to his or her parents, never considering that a child with a disability can be a source of joy to the parents.

Intimate, loving relationships are even more difficult (than friendships or workplace colleagues) for PWDs to achieve due to two widespread ideas: (1) PWDs are not interested in or capable of intimate and loving relationships, and (2) an intimate relationship between a PWD and a PWOD must be asymmetrical, or unbalanced, with the PWOD holding the position of power.

Many PWODs think that the onset of a disability means the end of all sexuality for the individual. For those with congenital disabilities, it is often thought that the individual will experience neither sexuality nor intimate, loving relationships. In the video *Tell Them I'm a Mermaid,* one woman stated that when she acquired her disability, a psychologist told her that "romance would mean less, work would mean more, and religion a lot more." We can readily recognize the psychologist's statement as paternalizing, but we can also see how, in a very concise way, the psychologist neatly assigned values to the important parts of this woman's life. Romance is assigned the lowest value. The sexuality of PWDs is often misunderstood (Lesh & Marshall, 1984). At times, PWDs, such as those with mental retardation or mental illness, are viewed as sexually dangerous and threatening; at other times, PWDs are seen as sexually unattractive, and at still other times, PWDs are viewed as uninterested or incapable. None of these views is true, but all these ideas consider PWDs to have some sort of sexual maladjustment (Olkin & Howson, 1994; Rousso, 1981).

Intimate relationships between a PWD and a PWOD are viewed as asymmetrical and stressful because the PWD is often thought to be a burden. Several scholars have written on the perceptions of PWODs who choose to marry a PWD or to engage in any long-term relationship with a PWD. Asch and Fine (1997) reported that others view the PWOD "as a saint or a loser" or someone who was forced into a "default position" (p. 247). Unbalanced relationships of any kind, in which one individual is seen as the contributor and the other as the passive recipient, are stressful for both partners. The contributor (saint) might become resentful and the recipient (burden) may feel insecure, fearing his or her partner will leave. DeLoach and Greer (1981) devoted several pages of their book *Adjustment to Severe Physical Disability: A Metamorphosis* to discussing individuals who are sexually attracted to PWDs.

> The "walking wounded"...those persons who have been so deeply hurt in a previous relationship with a "normal" person that they seek out persons who seem unlikely to injure them again....The "would-be dictators" are persons who are so insecure that they feel the need to dominate another human being. Such persons seek out disabled [*sic*] persons because they feel superior to those with physical limitations....The "unsolicited missionaries" are persons who develop a relationship with disabled persons in order to save them....The "gallant gesturers" are persons who discount the disabled [*sic*] as sexual beings, and thus view any liaison with them as a basis for self-congratulation (pp. 95–96).

These scholars underscore the imbalance that is automatically assumed in relationships between PWDs and PWODs. In each of DeLoach and Greer's examples, the PWOD is using his or her partner to meet his or her own needs.

PWDs have often internalized this view of relationships and have made comments such as, "There is a tendency for PWDs to feel grateful when someone loves them or pays attention to them." Another PWD says, "We are perceived as burdens"

(Nordqvist, 1980). Abby Kovalsky stated, "I joined a dating service a year and a half ago. All I hear from the agency is that anyone who reads my profile and then sees my photo is basically not willing to meet someone with my disability" (Mackelprang & Salsgiver, 1999, p. 17). Equally distancing is the perception (held by PWODs) that PWDs are either "saints" or "heroes." One woman with a disability stated, "I have a lot of people who respect me, but I have no friends."

Naturally, there are difficulties related to the disability itself when initiating and establishing relationships between PWDs and PWODs (Perduta-Fulginiti, 1996). Scheer (1993) quoted a man: "On the romantic side, women have a tendency to move away from me....It's like 'see ya later.' I mean, it's easy to find someone to say, 'Okay, let's go out,' but when it comes to the romantic side of it, they're not quite sure what to do, what to expect. Too, it's hard to approach someone when you're in a wheelchair, as opposed to the way it was before. I mean, what do you say? Can I buy you a drink, and, by the way, would you help me with mine?" (p. 9).

Ironically, research shows that married people enjoy better health, probably due to eating better, having emotional support, and having someone to monitor one's health, including such behaviors as regular exercise, seat belt use, and undergoing routine medical examinations.

SECOND-CLASS CITIZENSHIP (FOR WHICH AMERICANS MUST ASSUME COLLECTIVE RESPONSIBILITY)

As a conclusion to these six chapters, a list of the ways in which PWDs experience second-class citizenship seems to be in order.

- PWODs are the standard of evaluation, beauty, and good. For example, PWDs are rarely part of norm groups used in standardized testing. Thus, PWODs are both the norm and the ideal to which individuals should strive.
- Their sense of "otherness" is perpetuated; their sense of "differentness" is exaggerated.
- PWDs are "pathologized" in order that PWODs can legitimize and rationalize their treatment of them.
- They are pressured to hide or minimize their identity as PWDs.
- They have a long history of segregation, isolation, and marginalization. When PWDs are institutionalized, the institutions are administered for the convenience of PWODs. When the public does not see PWDs, their absence is not noticed.
- They are consistently undervalued and demeaned.
- They are denied their dignity.
- They must fight for their rights while PWODs are automatically given their rights. For example, school entrance for children with disabilities was often conditional, rather than automatic.
- They are given secondary, inferior facilities (schools, housing, transportation, public buildings, telecommunications).
- Other minority groups (such as racial and ethnic groups, women, and gays and lesbians) do not recognize their members with disabilities.
- When they are given accommodations (which is their right under federal law), they are expected to be grateful.

- They are underemployed and unemployed (when most express a desire to work). They are also first to be laid off in times of economic distress.
- PWODs create and reinforce *unnecessary* dependency, including financial disincentives for not working and physically inaccessible facilities.
- They are more likely to be poorer than the general population.
- Their abilities and capabilities are underestimated.
- They are less educated than the general population.
- The physical and psychological experience of PWDs is not acknowledged and shared (Wendell, 1997).
- They are considered to be sexually maladjusted, including neutered, incapable of or uninterested in sex, undersexed, or oversexed.
- The contributions and accomplishments of PWDs are not acknowledged. (Sharon L.'s high school counselor told her that no one would know that Sharon's art was "disabled art." Geerat Vermeij refused to participate in "Handicapped Science" Fairs.)
- Their history is ignored; people, including PWDs, do not have access to this history.
- They are given charity and pity rather than their rights as citizens.
- They are less likely to be married or to be a part of a family.
- Their mobility is obstructed.
- They experience abuse and are targets of crime far more often than the general population.
- They are the targets of harassment and hate crimes.
- They are not assigned positions of authority.
- Others, without much knowledge of the disability experience, make decisions for them and, in some cases, define the disability experience.
- PWDs provide jobs for PWODs and therefore PWDs are a source of income.
- When PWDs advocate for their rights, others become angry.
- They are at high risk for substance abuse.
- They must assume the burden of proof when they experience prejudice and discrimination. Moreover, until recently, the maintenance of this system of inequality was both legally and socially acceptable. Discrimination must be proven on a case-by-case basis.

In-Class Videos

- View the 13-minute, open-captioned video *Disabled Women: Visions and Voices*. The producers describe this video: "Women from around the world passionately share their concerns and success! Their stories demonstrate the diversity and commonality of women's issues." This video comes with a 35-page discussion guide. Available from Program Development Resource, P.O. Box 2038, Syracuse, NY 13220, 1–800–543–2119, fax 315–452–0710.
- View the 56-minute video *Look Who's Laughing*. The producers describe this video as a "funny and compelling documentary about the lives, experiences, and humor of six working comedians who have various types of disabilities. Shot at comedy clubs across the country, *Look Who's Laughing* spotlights some of the most talented and truly funny comics working today. *Look for examples of stereotyping, role entrapment, lowered expectations, lack of privacy, hypervisibility, infantilization, objectification, marginality, and lack of equal social status relationships*. Available from Program Development Resource.

- View the 31-minute video CASA: *The Community Attendant Services Act.* The producers state: "Mike Auberger, Director of Denver-based Atlantis Community and one of the key leaders of American Disabled for Attendant Programs Today (ADAPT), provides insights into ADAPT which has been labeled 'the radical arm of the disability movement,' the CASA bill, and the advocacy movement in the U.S. today." Available from Program Development Resource.
- View the 60-minute video *Redesigning the Human Machine.* Producers describe this video: "This program explores the use of technological advances. Virtual reality is being used as a learning tool for children with disabilities, as assistive technology for Parkinson's disease patients, and as a form of empowerment for people with disabilities. The program also examines the potential use of robotics to assist people with limited mobility and cochlear implants for the hearing impaired." Available from Program Development Resource.
- View the 57-minute video *If I Can't Do It...* by Walter Brock. This is a presentation of the Independent Television Service, with funding provided by the Corporation for Public Broadcasting. It was shown on the PBS series P.O.V. The producers describe this video: "Born with cerebral palsy in an isolated Kentucky cabin, Arthur Campbell spent his first thirty-eight years sheltered by his overprotective parents at home. 'I watched a lot of television,' he says, 'and I never saw a program about anyone whose life is like mine.' Today, he lives independently and is an advocate and activist for disability rights. Witty, stubborn, and often exasperating, Campbell is neither a hero nor a saint, but a complex individual working to fulfill his dreams by seizing control of his own existence and living on his own terms." Available from Fanlight Productions, 4196 Washington Street, Boston, MA 02131, 800–937–4113, wwwfanlightcom.
- View the 16-minute video *Shaking Off Stereotypes.* The producers state: *"Shaking Off Stereotypes* will help people with disabilities and others recognize that we are all unique individuals with something to contribute. It is an entertaining story about a woman wheelchair user who discovers her own self-worth in spite of the everyday stereotypical situations she encounters." Available from Program Development Resource.

Learning Activities

Choose one of the 14 bulleted attitudes and/or behaviors listed at the beginning of this chapter and write a paper that (1) describes the behavior or attitude and (2) explains their effects and results.

Writing Experiences

Using any of the 14 bullet experiences listed at the beginning of this chapter, write a paper describing and giving examples of this experience.

References

Allport, G. W. (1954). *The nature of prejudice.* Reading, MA: Addison-Wesley.

Allport, G. W. (1958). *The nature of prejudice* (2nd ed.). Garden City, NY: Doubleday Anchor.

Allport, G. W. (1986). *The nature of prejudice* (25th anniversary ed.). Reading, MA: Addison-Wesley.

Anderson, G. R. (1987). Paternalism. In G. R. Anderson & V. A. Glesnes-Anderson (Eds.), *Health care ethics: A guide for decision makers* (pp. 177–191). Rockville, MD: Aspen.

Asch, A., & Fine, M. (1997). Nurturance, sexuality, and women with disabilities: The example of women and literature. In L. J. Davis (Ed.), *The disability studies reader* (pp. 241–259). New York: Routledge.

Baynton, D. (1997). A silent exile on this earth: The metaphorical construction of deafness in the nineteenth century. In L. J. Davis (Ed.), *The disability studies reader* (pp. 128–150). New York: Routledge.

Beisser, A. (1989). *Flying without wings: Personal reflections on being disabled.* New York: Doubleday.

Bogardus, E. S. (1928). *Immigration and race attitudes.* Lexington, MA: D. C. Heath.

Bogdan, R. (1988). *Freak show: Presenting human oddities for amusement and profit.* Chicago: University of Chicago.

Bogdan, R., & Taylor, S. J. (1987). Toward a sociology of acceptance: The other side of the study of deviance. *Social Policy, Fall,* 34–39.

Bogdan, R., & Taylor, S. J. (1989). Relationships with severely disabled people: The social construction of humanness. *Social Problems, 36*(1).

Bok, S. (1979). *Lying: Moral choice in public and private life.* New York: Vintage.

Bragg, B. (1989). *Lessons in laughter: The autobiography of a Deaf actor. As signed to Eugene Bergman.* Washington, DC: Gallaudet University.

Chesler, M. A., & Chesney, B. K. (1988). Self-help groups: Empowerment attitudes and behaviors of disabled and chronically ill persons. In H. E. Yuker (Ed.), *Attitudes toward persons with disabilities* (pp. 230–244). New York: Springer.

Chubon, R. A., & Moore, C. T. (1982). The cocoon syndrome: A coping mechanism of spinal cord injured persons. *Rehabilitation Psychology, 27,* 87–96.

Clark, K. B., & Clark, M. P. (1947). Racial identification and preference in Negro children. In T. Newcomb (Ed.). *Readings in Social Psychology.* New York: Henry Holt and Company.

Crespo, A. (1993). Alice Crespo, court interpreter. In H. Rousso (Ed.). *Disabled, female, and proud!* (pp. 95–104). Westport, CT: Bergin & Garvey.

Crewe, N. M., & Zola, I. K. (1983). *Independent living for physically disabled people.* San Francisco: Jossey-Bass.

Darke, E. (1993). The Elephant Man: An analysis from a disabled perspective. *Disability and Society, 9,* 327–343.

Davis, L. J. (Ed.). (1997). *The disability studies reader.* New York: Routledge.

Deegan, P. E. (1992). The independent living movement and people with psychiatric disabilities: Taking back control over our own lives. *Psychosocial Rehabilitation Journal, 15*(3), 3–19.

DeLoach, C. P. (1994). Attitudes toward disability: Impact on sexual development and forging of intimate relationships. *Journal of Applied Rehabilitation Counseling, 25,* 18–25.

DeLoach, C., & Greer, B. G. (1981). *Adjustment to severe physical disability: A metamorphosis.* New York: McGraw-Hill.

Finger, A. (1991). *Past due: A story of disability, pregnancy, and birth.* Seattle, WA: Seal Press.

Fisher, B., & Galler, R. (1988). Friendship and fairness: How disability affects friendship between women. In M. Fine & A. Asch (Eds.). *Women with disabilities: Essays in psychology, culture, and politics* (pp. 172–194). Philadelphia: Temple University.

Fletcher, J. F. (1979). *Humanhood: Essays in biomedical ethics.* Buffalo, NY: Prometheus.

Fries, K. (Ed.). (1997). *Staring back: The disability experience from the inside out.* New York: Plume.

Frohock, F. M. (1986). *Special care: Medical decisions at the beginning of life.* Chicago: University of Chicago Press.

Gist, N. R., & Dworkin, A. G. (1972). *The blending of the races: Marginality and identity in a world perspective.* New York: Wiley Interscience.

Goffman, E. (1963). *Stigma: Notes on the management of spoiled identity.* Englewood Cliffs, NJ: Prentice-Hall.

Goffman, E. (1997). Selection from *Stigma.* In L. J. Davis (Ed.). *The disability studies reader* (pp. 203–215). New York: Routledge.

Gouvier, W. D., Coon, R. C., Todd, M. E., & Fuller, K. H. (1994). Verbal interactions with individuals presenting with and without physical disability. *Rehabilitation Psychology, 39,* 263–268.

Groce, N. E. (1985). *Everybody here spoke sign language: Hereditary deafness on Martha's Vineyard.* Cambridge, MA: Harvard University Press.

Hahn, H. (1997). Advertising the acceptably employable image: Disability and capitalism. In L. J. Davis (Ed.). *The disability studies reader* (pp. 172–186). New York: Routledge.

Hannaford, S. (1985). *Living outside inside: A disabled woman's experience. Towards a social and political perspective.* Berkeley, CA: Canterbury Press.

Harris, R. W. (1992). Musings from 20 years of hard-earned experience. *Rehabilitation Education, 6,* 207–211.

Hermann, D. (1998). *Helen Keller: A life.* New York: Alfred A. Knopf.

Hevey, D. (1997). The enfreakment of photography. In L. J. Davis (Ed.). *The disability studies reader* (pp. 332–347). New York: Routledge.

Higgins, P. C. (1980). *Outsiders in a hearing world: A sociology of deafness.* Newbury Park, CA: Sage.

Higgins, P. C. (1992). *Making disability: Exploring the social transformation of human variation.* Springfield, IL: Charles C Thomas.

Holcomb, L. P. (1990). Disabled women: A new issue in education. In M. Nagler (Ed.). *Perspectives on disability* (pp. 381–388). Palo Alto, CA: Health Markets Research.

Imrie, R. (1996). *Disability and the city: International perspectives.* New York: St. Martin's Press.

Kisor, H. (1990). *What's that pig outdoors? A memoir of deafness.* New York: Hill and Wang.

Kriegel, L. (1991). *Falling into life.* San Francisco: North Point.

Lane, H., Hoffmeister, R., & Bahan, B. (1996). *A journey into the deaf-world.* San Diego, CA: Dawn Sign Press.

Leete, E. (1991). The stigmatized patient. In P. J. Fink & A. Tasman (Eds.). *Stigma and mental illness* (pp. 17–25). Washington, DC: American Psychiatric Association Press.

Lefley, H. P. (1991). The stigmatized family. In P. J. Fink & A. Tasman (Eds.). *Stigma and mental illness* (pp. 127–138). Washington, DC: American Psychiatric Association Press.

Lesh, K., & Marshall, C. (1984). Rehabilitation: Focus on women with disabilities. *Journal of Applied Rehabilitation Counseling, 15,* 18–21.

Livneh, H. (1980). Disability and monstrosity: Further comments. *Rehabilitation Literature, 41,* 280–283.

Ludwig, E. G., & Adams, S. D. (1968). Patient cooperation in a rehabilitation center: Assumption of the client role. *Journal of Health and Social Behavior, 9,* 328–336. Reprinted in J. Stubbins (Ed.). *Social and psychological aspects of disability: A handbook for practitioners* (pp. 225–236). Baltimore: University Park Press.

Mackelprang, R., & Salsgiver, R. (1999). *Disability: A diversity model approach in human service practice.* Pacific Grove, CA: Brooks/Cole.

Mee, C. L. (1999). *A nearly normal life.* Boston: Little, Brown.

Miller, S., & Morgan, M. (1980). Marriage matters: For people with disabilities, too. *Sexuality and Disability, 3,* 203–211.

Mims, B. (1998, January 24). Mentally disabled worker files $10M suit charging Smith's co-workers ridiculed him. *Salt Lake Tribute,* Bl, B5.

Morris, J. (1991). *Pride against prejudice: Transforming attitudes to disability.* Philadelphia: New Society.

Nelson, J. L., & Berens, B. S. (1997). Spoken daggers, deaf ears, and silent mouths: Fantasies of deafness in early modern England. In L. J. David (Ed.). *Disability studies reader* (pp. 52–74). New York: Routledge.

Nordqvist, I. (1980). Sexual counseling for disabled persons. *Sexuality and Disability, 3,* 193–198.

Olkin, R. (1999). *What psychotherapists should know about disability.* New York: Guilford.

Olkin, R., & Howson, L. J. (1994). Attitudes toward and images of physical disability. *Social Behavior and Psychology, 9,* 81–96.

Panzarino, C. (1993). Connie Panzarino: Art therapist. In H. Rousso (Ed.). *Disabled, female, and proud!* (pp. 107–118). Westport, CT: Bergin & Garvey.

Pelka, F. (1997). *The ABC-CLIO companion to the disability rights movement.* Santa Barbara, CA: ABC-CLIO.

Perduta-Fulginiti, P. S. (1996). Impact of bowel and bladder dysfunction on sexuality and self esteem. In D. M. Krotoski, M. A. Nosek, & M. A. Turk (Eds.). *Women with physical disabilities: Achieving and maintaining health and well-being* (pp. 287–298). Baltimore: Brookes.

Petty, D. (1979). What is it like to be deaf-blind? *Consumers Contemporary, 1,* 10–11.

Phillips, M. J. (1991). "Try harder": The experience of disability and the dilemma of normalization. In P. M. Ferguson, D. L. Ferguson, & S. J. Taylor (Eds.). *Interpreting disability: A qualitative reader* (pp. 213–227). New York: Columbia University Teachers College Press.

Poole, W. C., Jr. (1927). Social distance and personal distance. *Journal of Applied Sociology, 11,* 114–120.

Purtilo, R. B. (1991). Ethical issues in teamwork: The context of rehabilitation. In R. P. Marinelli & A. E. Dell Orto (Eds.). *The psychological and social impact of disability* (3rd ed., pp. 18–31). New York: Springer.

Rousso, H. (1981). Disabled people are sexual, too. *The Exceptional Parent, 11,* 21–25.

Rousso, H. (1993). *Disabled, female, and proud!* Westport, CT: Bergin & Garvey.

Scheer, M. J. (1993). *Living in the state of stuck: How technology impacts the lives of people with disabilities.* Cambridge, MA: Brookline.

Scott, R. (1969). *The making of blind men: A study of adult socialization.* New York: Russell Sage Foundation.

Shontz, F. (1977). Physical disability and personality: Theory and recent research. In J. Stubbins (Ed.). *Social and psychological aspects of disability: A handbook for practitioners* (pp. 333–353). Baltimore: University Park Press.

Simpson, G. E., & Yinger, J.M. (1985). *Racial and cultural minorities: An analysis of prejudice and discrimination* (5th ed.). New York: Plenum.

Sinick, D. (1969). Training, job placement, and follow-up. In D. Malikin & H. Rusalem (Eds.). *Vocational rehabilitation of the disabled: An overview* (pp. 129–153). New York: New York University Press.

Sobsey, D. (1994). *Violence and abuse in the lives of people with disabilities: The end of silent acceptance.* Baltimore: Brookes.

Stonequist, E. V. (1937). *The marginal man: A study in personality and culture conflict.* New York: Charles Scribners.

Strohmer, D. C., Leierer, S. J., Cochran, N. A., & Arokiasamy, C. V. (1996). The importance of counselor disability status. *Rehabilitation Counseling Bulletin, 40,* 96–115.

Thomson, R. G. (1997). Integrating disability studies into the existing curriculum: The example of "women and literature" at Howard University. In L. J. Davis (Ed.). *The disability studies reader* (pp. 296–311). New York: Routledge.

Walker, L. A. (1986). *A loss for words: The story of deafness in a family.* New York: Harper.

Warren-Leubecker, A., & Bohannon, J. N. (1989). Pragmatics: Language in social contexts. In J. Berko-Gleason (Ed.). *The development of language* (pp. 327–368). Columbus, OH: Merrill.

Wendell, S. (1997). Toward a feminist theory of disability. In L. J. Davis (Ed.). *The disability studies reader* (pp. 260–278). New York: Routledge.

Winzer, M. A. (1993). Education, urbanization, and the Deaf community: A case study of Toronto, 1870–1900. In J. V. Van Cleve (Ed.). *Deaf history unveiled: Interpretations of the new scholarship* (pp. 127–145). Washington, DC: Gallaudet University.

Wolfensberger, W. (1972). *The principle of normalization in human services.* Toronto, Canada: National Institute on Mental Retardation.

Wolfensberger, W. (1981). The extermination of handicapped people in World War II Germany. *Mental Retardation,* Vol. 1–7.

Wolfensberger, W., & Tullman, S. (1982). A brief outline of the principle of normalization. *Rehabilitation Psychology, 27*(3), 131–145.

Wright, B. A. (1960). *Physical disability: A psychological approach.* New York: Harper & Row.

Wright, B. A. (1983). *Physical disability: A psychosocial approach* (2nd ed.). New York: Harper & Row.

Wright, D. (1994). *Deafness: An autobiography.* New York: Harper Perennial.

Yuker, H. E. (Ed.). (1988). *Attitudes toward persons with disabilities.* New York: Springer.

Zola, I. K. (1972). Medicine as an institution of social control. *Sociological Review, 20,* 487–504.

Part III

The Individual and Disability

Chapter 7

The Individual's Response to Disability

▶ Why would many PWDs choose not to eliminate their disability if they could?

▶ Is there a real difference between the terms "acceptance of disability" and "response to disability"?

▶ How does an individual's ethnic/racial/cultural/linguistic identification influence his or her response to a disability?

▶ When discussing an individual's response to a disability, why is it important to consider the individual's environment?

▶ Of the three types of response to disability, affective, cognitive, and behavioral, which is the most difficult to measure?

▶ Why is the PWD's subjective judgment of his or her disability often more important than the objective medical diagnosis?

▶ What are the four components of Beatrice Wright's "cognitive restructuring" model?

▶ What is the difference between coping strategies and defense mechanisms?

▶ What is a somatization disorder?

▶ What are some possible secondary gains of a disability?

▶ What is psychogenic pain? Why is it necessary to establish a temporal relationship between environmental stimuli and onset of pain?

▶ Why would anyone malinger?

▶ What are possible problems in measuring adjustment to disability?

▶ What are the advantages of the stage theory of adaptation/response?

▶ What are the three types of denial?

▶ Why is denial often considered to be therapeutic?

▶ What are some cautions in implementing the stage theory?

The three major divisions of this book are (1) defining disability, (2) society and disability, and (3) the individual and disability. These convenient, easily understood demarcations are a starting point to learning about the disability. However, these divisions are not actually experienced by anyone, nor do they represent reality. For instance, it is important to learn about the various definitions of disability—what a disability is and what a disability is not. So far we have learned that there are four definitions of disability: clinical, legal, cultural, and personal. This final section of the book will discuss the personal definitions of disability. But, definitions of disability are closely tied to society's perception of disability and, furthermore, the individual's experience with a disability involves both the definition of disability and society's response to his or her disability (Antonak & Livneh, 1991; DeLoach & Greer, 1981; Dembo, Leviton, & Wright, 1956; Wright, 1991). These are complex interrelationships and are idiosyncratic (specific to each individual) (Heinemann & Shontz, 1984; Roessler & Bolton, 1978). No one with a disability thinks of his or her disability in these three divisions; indeed, to the individual there can be no neat, three-division paradigm to the disability experience. Nonetheless, it does make sense to discuss some basic issues in order to gain a preliminary understanding, but with the knowledge that these basic issues are only a starting point and that some aspects of the disability experience apply only to specific individuals. Disability happens to one person at a time.

Perhaps the title of this chapter should be "The Individual's Response to *Acquired* Disability" because an individual with a congenital disability, or a disability acquired during infancy, has incorporated the disability into his or her identity. Individuals with congenital disabilities have no memory of not having the disability. Nonetheless, there are adjustment demands for these individuals, not to a new identity, but to stigma recognition. Very often, children with disabilities do not know until they enter school that their disabilities are perceived as inferiority and deviance. These children understand that (1) they have a disability, and (2) the disability requires management, treatment, and/or accommodations, but they may not have experienced prejudice and discrimination. Therefore, a child with a disability must learn to adjust to and negotiate a prejudiced and discriminating environment.

For these reasons, this section of the book will use many first-person narratives, individuals telling us what they have experienced and learned. Can the disability experience be understood by someone who has not lived it? Probably not, but PWODs can begin to learn about the disability. However, most PWDs have not written about their experiences and, thus, their experiences with disability are unrecorded (Couser, 1997; Frank, 1991, 1995; Hawkins, 1993). Some of these narratives have found publishers because the authors are seen as "super crips," people with extraordinary resources or celebrity. Indeed, most of those who have written about disability experience have been white, upper-class, highly educated individuals (Ballin, 1930; Beisser, 1989; Brookes, 1995; Callahan, 1989; Cohen, 1994; Hull, 1991; Keller, 1990; Kisor, 1990; Kriegel, 1991; Murphy, 1987; Padden & Humphries, 1988; Price, 1994; Schaller, 1991; Sienkiewicz-Mercer & Kaplan, 1989; Spradley & Spradley, 1985; Zola, 1982). Also, on the one hand, first-person accounts carry the weight of someone who has lived the experience, giving us an immediate and direct look at disability (Kleinman, 1988; Mairs, 1997). On the other hand, every disability account must, of necessity, speak about individual circumstances. Nonetheless, there are some universal aspects of the disability experience, and furthermore, we can learn from the idiosyncratic aspects of these narratives (see Appendix 7–A for a listing of published narratives).

VIEW FROM THE OUTSIDE VERSUS LIFE ON THE INSIDE

> *In this section, look for—*
> ► *how PWODs assume that all PWDs would eliminate their disability if they could*
> ► *how most PWDs*
>   *1. consider their disability to be an integral part of their identity*
>   *2. are proud of their mastery of the disability*
>   *3. consider their disability to have positive options*
> ► *how PWODs assume that the onset/acquisition/diagnosis of every disability is distressful to the individual*

Myths Held by PWODs

Outsiders (meaning those who do not have a disability) often think they understand how PWDs feel about their disability. Naturally, such conceptions are based on an outsider's point of view; it is difficult to imagine the life of someone else. Moreover, rarely do PWODs question their own assumptions. (We learned in Part II that most PWODs sensationalize and misunderstand disability, thinking that all disabilities are an unending source of tragedy and grief for the individual.) One misconception, widely and strongly held, is that if the PWD were offered a way to eliminate the disability, he or she would enthusiastically accept it. Rarely do PWODs consider the possibility that the disability is an integral part of the PWD's self-identity or that the PWD might be proud of the mastery and control that he or she has gained over the disability. Many of the first-person accounts of disability reveal that the individual would *not* choose to eliminate the disability (Davis, 1995). The most straightforward example is that of cochlear implants for individuals who are deaf. Cochlear implants are comprised of electrodes that are surgically placed in the inner ear to stimulate the nerve cells along a pathway to the auditory region of the brain. Designed to improve the individual's speech perception and oral communication, the cochlear implant has not been unanimously accepted by the Deaf community. First, it should be stated that not all cochlear implants are successful. But, even more important, the Deaf Culture feels that, as one scholar wrote, "in America, the recognition of the status of the Deaf community, fueled by the civil rights movement, is leading to greater acceptance of people who are deaf. The interest of the child who is deaf and his [*sic*] parents may best be served by accepting that he is Deaf, with an elaborate culture and linguistic heritage that can enrich his parents' life as well as his own. We should heed the advice of the teenager who was deaf who, when reprimanded by her mother for not wearing the processor of her cochlea prosthesis, hurled back bitterly: 'I'm deaf. Let me be deaf'" (Lane, 1992, p. 238).

In learning about how the individual experiences his or her disability, it seems appropriate to begin by making the point that most PWDs consider their disability to be an integral part of their identity—not their sole identity, or even the most important part of the identity, but an important part (Higgins, 1980). It therefore follows that PWDs would not eliminate the disability if they could. Cochlear implants, very much favored by people who are not deaf, including parents of children who are deaf and physicians, are often refused by the Deaf.

Other first-person accounts describe PWDs who think of their disability as part of their identity and have no wish to eliminate it. In Rousso's book *Disabled, Female, and Proud!* (1993), Rousso interviews Barbara Cole-Appel, a woman paralyzed in an automobile accident. Cole-Appel told of a friend who asked her if she would rather win a $30 million lottery or regain the use of her legs. (Neither winning the lottery nor regaining the use of her legs was actually possible.) Cole-Appel responded, "I decided that I would rather have the $30 million because losing the use of my legs has not inhibited me other than walking, as far as I'm concerned. Not being able to walk is something I have learned to live with. It's no longer something that I have to be able to do in order to feel complete" (p. 41).

In the video *Irving King Jordan*, the interviewer asks Dr. Jordan, President of Gallaudet College, twice about the disadvantages of being deaf. Dr. Jordan replied, "If there are 1,000 differences (between hearing and being deaf), 998 are good opportunities and 2 are bad." In the video *Don't Go to Your Room*, a woman states, "I believe that I've had wonderful experiences because of my disability." Another woman states, "I present my disability as a strength."

Disability also involves impairment, sometimes the loss of valued activities, sometimes pain; often makes time demands on the individual; and most often includes the prejudice and discrimination of the larger society. Nonetheless, the onset/acquisition/diagnosis of a disability is not automatically distressing to everyone. Shontz (1991) summarized:

> Though many efforts have been made to correlate disability with overall personality maladjustment, no systematic evidence has yet been published to show that reactions involving psychiatric disturbance occur any more frequently with a truly representative sample of people with disabilities than within the general population. . . . The personality resources of an individual may be strengthened, not weakened, when the stresses that disability imposes are successfully managed (p. 108).

We have seen in Part II that the tendency of PWODs to view all disability as devastating and overwhelming tragedy has resulted in abortion, murder, and institutionalization of PWDs.

ACCEPTANCE OF DISABILITY OR RESPONSE TO DISABILITY

In this section, look for—
▶ *four reasons why "response" to disability is now the preferred term*
1. *It is not the disability itself, but the meaning the individual ascribes to it*
2. *There are many other types of acceptance, not just psychological acceptance*
3. *The word "response" does not pathologize the disability experience*
4. *The individual copes with and responds to a disability throughout his or her life*

Disability scholars have used the terms *adjustment, adaptation,* or *acceptance* of disability to describe the end result of coping with a disability and successfully integrating the disability into the individual's life and identity (Lindemann, 1981; Linkowski & Dunn, 1974; Livneh, 1986a, 1986b; Moos, 1984). In the early stages of scholarship, adjustment to disability was conceptualized as a series of stages through which the individual passed, ending with acceptance of the disability. The current model of coping with a disability uses the term *the individual's* **response to** *disability* (Livneh & Antonak, 1997). The word *response* is more accurate because it communicates more fully that (1) it is not disability itself, but the meaning that the individual ascribes to the disability that will determine the response to the disability; (2) there are many types of responses or adjustments to disability in addition to the psychological adjustment, including occupational and social adjustment or response; (3) the words *adjustment, adaptation,* and *acceptance* pathologize the experience of a disability, meaning a disability is automatically assumed to be an undesirable state (we would not say that a person adjusts to being a woman or a person of color); and (4) the individual copes with disability and makes adjustments throughout his or her lifetime, including those with stable disabilities, and therefore *acceptance* is not a one-time event (Kendall & Buys, 1998; Schlossberg, 1981; Wortman & Silver, 1989). In this chapter, both the expressions "response/reaction" and "adaptation/acceptance/adjustment" will be used, but with the awareness that "response/reaction" is the more accurate term.

In this section, we shall discuss the individual's response to disability in terms of the American culture. At times, references will be made to other cultures because an individual's cultural/linguistic/ethnic identity certainly impacts the way in which the individual views and treats the disability. Further, behavioral manifestations of responding to a disability can only be interpreted with knowledge of the individual's cultural identity. What is considered to be "acceptance of disability" in one culture may not apply in another culture. Moreover, we have learned that disability itself is culturally defined and, further, symptom recognition is also culturally and socially determined. For example, someone with a large family to support and who works at a physically demanding job may not recognize his or her chronic back pain as a disability. Obviously, in this case, the individual's economic situation does not allow him or her to recognize (much less respond to) subjective discomfort. Also, the individual's perception of etiology is shaped by his or her cultural identification. For example, someone from a culture that is deterministic and fatalistic may feel that his or her automobile accident was "meant to happen" and not the result of anything that individual did or did not do. In contrast, an individual who identifies with the American culture may view the same automobile accident as his or her fault and thus engage in self-blame (Bordieri, 1993).

Carolyn Vash (1981) another disability scholar, introduced the concept of "transcendence," which is a step beyond acceptance or adjustment to disability. Transcendence of a disability is a combination of refusing to idealize normality (lack of disability), adopting a spiritual/philosophical orientation to the disability, and "embracing the experience" (p. 135). Inherent in the concept of transcendence are the questions "What can I learn from this disability? and "What positive options are available?" The disability is seen as a catalyst for the individual to grow and develop, with the individual feeling that he or she is a "better" person for having experienced a disability. According to Vash, when an individual has achieved transcendence, he or she views the disability as a tool, an asset, and an opportunity.

Consideration of the Individual's Environment

Shontz (1977) emphasized that reacting to a disability is not only a response to a physical, intellectual, cognitive, or psychiatric impairment, but also includes other factors in the individual's environment. Factors such as economic security, educational level, family support, and availability of treatment influence the disability experience. Therefore, Shontz argued that clinicians and researchers should include environmental resources of the individual, rather than simply focusing on the psychodynamics of the PWD.

The factor that has not been fully addressed in the individual's response to the disability concerns the degree of prejudice, discrimination toward the type and severity of disability, and if the individual is also subject to prejudice or discrimination because of other perceived identities, such as belonging to other cultural/ethnic/racial groups, being a woman, being older, or having a different sexual orientation (Corbett & Bregante, 1993; Fine & Asch, 1988). Certainly, the degree of stigma and prejudice the individual experiences will influence his or her response to the disability. For example, gay people with disabilities have a humorous way to describe their doubly-stigmatized status: "I want to come out of the closet, but the doorway isn't wide enough for my wheelchair."

WHAT IS A "GOOD" RESPONSE TO A DISABILITY?

In this section, look for—

▶ *the three categories of response to disability: behavioral, cognitive, affective*
▶ *which is easiest to define and measure?*

There is a vast range in the definitions of disability, great variability in the severity or degree of disability, and PWDs have many environmental factors and varying types of psychological/emotional coping abilities. Added to this combination of disability variables are the differing levels of stigma directed toward specific disabilities. In Chapter 4, we learned about the hierarchy of stigma toward disabilities and, therefore, the clinical picture of an individual's adjustment to a psychiatric disability would not be complete without recognizing that psychiatric disabilities are the most stigmatizing disabilities in our society. Having stated the great variability of the experience of disability, it is nonetheless possible to list some general attributes, behaviors, and manifestations of a "good" response to disability.

Generally speaking, response to a disability can be divided into three categories: cognitive, behavioral, and affective. Cognitive means thinking or how one chooses to view (or to think about) the disability. A positive or good cognitive response to disability includes redefining reality rather than ignoring it or denying it. Behavioral responses to disability include active mastery of the disability, compliance with treatment regimens, seeking out social support, returning to work, and, for many PWDs, actively fighting against the stigma and prejudice of society. Affective response means how the individual feels about the disability and how he or she manages emotions. Of course, the individual does not view his or her coping responses as neatly divided into these three categories. Behavioral acceptance/response to disability is relatively easy to operationally define and measure. Cognitive and affective responses are more difficult to measure. These types of assessments are made by either interviewing the PWD and/or family members or by paper-and-pencil psychological instruments. Of course, extreme and severe affective/emotional responses such as total denial of the disability, externalized anger and aggression, abuse of alcohol and/or drugs, family conflict and dissolution, and self-blame are readily observable. However, most affective responses are less extreme and, therefore, are less obvious and more difficult to measure and assess.

COGNITIVE RESTRUCTURING

In this section, look for—

▶ *Beatrice Wright's theory of cognitive restructuring*
1. *Enlargement of the scope of values*
2. *Subordination of the physique*
3. *Containment of disability effects*
4. *Transformation from comparative values to asset values*

Beatrice Wright (1960) pioneered the study of the individual's response to physical disability, working with veterans of World War II. Her theory of cognitive restructuring described how the individual with a disability can redefine reality. Wright's cognitive restructuring has four points:

1. Enlargement of the scope of values. The PWD subscribes to values that are not in conflict with the disability. A clear-cut illustration of this is the large number of professors, editors, and writers with physical disabilities who have devoted their lives to intellectual pursuits that are not affected by the physical disability. Psychological theories describe well-adjusted individuals as being able to generate many options and responses to the demands of their environment. This capability is also termed "having more cards to play." Certainly, the PWD who is able to enlarge his or her value system will have more options and choices.
2. Subordination of the physique. The individual does not think of his or her body as a symbol of worth, desirability, or competence. The title of the video *My Body Is Not Who I Am* illustrates subordination of the physique. Later, we shall discuss the importance of body image.
3. Containment of disability effects. The individual does not deny the disability but *contains* or limits the effects, realizing that there are other activities that he or she can do. Rather than thinking that his or her life has no value or meaning, the individual finds meaning in other areas.
4. Transformation from comparative to asset values. Rather than comparing oneself to others who do not have disabilities or thinking only in terms of the limitations and losses of the disabilities, the individual focuses attention on his or her assets.

The literature on the individual's response to disability describes an individual with a positive response as someone who is flexible, demonstrates active mastery, rallies social support, and is capable of tolerating a degree of ambiguity. Upon acquiring a disability, normality (which is the absence of ambiguity because it is familiar to the individual) is gone. For most people, the experience of acquiring a disability, especially a severe disability or multiple disabilities, is a novel situation, one with which he or she has not had any experience. One of the first responses of a PWD is a desire to return to normality, that is to say, the individual's idiosyncratic conception of normality. A positive response does not view normality as the absence or cure of the disability, but rather conceptualizes normality as the reinstatement of the individual's identity, family, social system, home, status, income, professional identity, and sexuality (after the medical stabilization of the disability). Certainly the extent to which the individual is able to regain these aspects of his or her life will determine his or her response to the disability. An individual who is considered to have a positive response is judged to have a realistic view of the disability, aware of the limitations but not exaggerating them (Yoshida, 1993).

As would be expected, it is easier to judge/assess the behavioral manifestations of response to disability than the affective or cognitive responses. Behavioral responses can be observed, measured, and quantified. In contrast, clinicians must rely on the self-report of the PWD in order to get some understanding of affective or cognitive responses. Behavioral responses such as complying with treatment and rehabilitation regimens, increased activity levels, seeking out social support, and returning to work are relatively easy to operationally define and measure. The degree of emotional stress, physical pain, hope, and optimism for the future, on the other hand, are difficult to define and measure. Nonetheless, it is these subjective responses to disability that influence the individual's help-seeking behaviors and response to the disability. These assessments are made by either interviewing the PWD and/or family members or by paper-and-pencil psychological instruments. Well-planned, goal-directed activity and stress reduction are considered necessary for a positive response. Naturally, extreme and severe affective/emotional responses such as denial of the disability, externalized anger or aggression, abuse of alcohol and/or drugs, family conflict and dissolution, and self-blame are readily observable. However, it is safe to say that most affective/emotional responses are less extreme and therefore less obvious.

WHAT IS A POOR RESPONSE TO DISABILITY?

In this section, look for—

▶ *the indicators of a "poor" response to disability*
▶ *the difference between coping skills and defense mechanisms*

An individual may perceive his or her disability as (1) loss of status, (2) loss of social support, (3) loss of functioning, and (4) loss of control, thinking that he or she will be isolated, dependent, and a burden on others. Further, in the American culture, the PWD may well feel that he or she has somehow violated his or her duty to *not* acquire a disability.

Other studies of individuals with various types of disability have described poor response to disability as including unnecessary dependence on others, social isolation due to "shame" about the disability, feelings of helplessness, negative body image and self-esteem, anger and aggression toward others, long-standing feelings of dissatisfaction, high levels of stress, hypersensitivity to criticism, passivity, developmental immaturity, exhibiting an external locus of control, hypermorality, internalized anger and depression, holding unrealistic hopes of a cure, relying on defense mechanisms such as rigidity, holding on to the past, emotional lability (widely fluctuating moods, temperamental, easily upset), resignation (giving up), and humorlessness (Livneh & Antonak, 1997; Marshak & Seligman, 1993). Coupled with these poor responses is the lack of a realistic plan for dealing with the disability.

Coping strategies are different from defense mechanisms. Coping strategies are considered to be goal-directed, positive steps such as rallying social support, obtaining treatment and rehabilitation, redefining life goals, and seeking information. In contrast, defense mechanisms are an effort to avoid anxiety and reality and, most often, the individual is not aware that he or she is using them. Examples of defense mechanisms are regression (preoccupied with the past when the individual did not have the disability or returning to a less mature pattern of behavior), projection (attributing one's own feelings to someone else), displacement (blaming others), withdrawal (socially isolated and unable to form therapeutic alliances with service providers), denial (at certain stages in the adjustment period, denial is considered to be therapeutic), and depersonalization (detached from self). Professional caregivers *reinforce* coping strategies, but *challenge* the use of defense mechanisms.

SECONDARY GAINS, MALINGERING, AND PSYCHOGENIC PAIN DISORDER

In this section, look for—

▶ *reasons why an individual would seek secondary gains*
▶ *the difference between malingering and somatization disorders*
▶ *the importance of a temporal relationship between the onset of pain and environmental stimuli*

Four responses to disability are considered to be counterproductive: (1) maintaining secondary gains, (2) somatization, (3) malingering, and (4) psychogenic pain disorder. Although relatively rare and often confused with adaptive responses and/or the symptoms of the disability itself, there are clear distinctions that characterize these responses. Furthermore, in all four of these responses, physicians must first rule out valid physical, cognitive, or psychiatric disorders.

Secondary gains that may result from a disability include financial compensation; freedom from responsibility (such as working or family obligations); receiving pity, attention, and care from others; free time; and freedom from evaluation. Seeking secondary gains is a self-protection strategy (of which the individual may or may not be aware). The individual who seeks secondary gains maintains his or her dependence, seeking environmental supports when they are not necessary, trying to maintain the sick role as long as possible. As would be expected, it is difficult to make an accurate distinction between adaptive, coping responses to the realities of a disability and secondary gain seeking. Nonetheless, seeking secondary gains is viewed as an avoidance behavior.

In somatization, the individual reports symptoms of long duration that have caused serious impairment in his or her life. However, there is no organic basis for these symptoms or, stated differently, the individual has functional symptoms without organic cause (American Psychiatric Association, 1994). The distinguishing feature of somatoform disorders is the fact that the individual is not consciously aware that he or she has produced the symptoms or is faking the symptoms. Somatization is "a process in which emotional and/or psychosocial stress is expressed in physical symptoms, precedes the development of these disorders and accounts for a large number of patients seeking medical care for symptoms that have no organic cause (Spelic, 1997, p. 30)." As would be expected, there is a great deal of frustration on the part of medical service providers and on the part of the patient. Individuals with somatization disorder utilize medical resources frequently, having had many diagnostic procedures and visited many physicians (sometimes termed "doctor shopping"). Often, patients are perceived as manipulators. On the other side, patients are defensive because they sense the resentment, distrust, and irritation of medical care providers. Patients feel overwhelmed, helpless, and inadequate. Recently, with the emerging awareness of the frequency of childhood sexual abuse, somatization has been hypothesized, at times, to be an adaptive strategy on the part of the child. Illness and pain may have provided the child an escape from sexual abuse, starting a pattern that continues into adulthood. Indeed, many physicians now screen for childhood abuse when they suspect that a patient has somatization disorder. The difficulty of somatization disorder is that often individuals with invisible chronic diseases (especially autoimmune diseases), such as multiple sclerosis, lupus, chronic fatigue syndrome, and Crohn's disease, are thought to be engaging in somatization when, in reality, their pain, fatigue, numbness, and muscle weakness are real. For example, "on average, from the first onset of symptoms to diagnosis of multiple sclerosis, an individual will endure 40 baffling months" (Donoghue & Siegel, 1992). Therefore, in addition to experiencing the symptoms of a real disease without treatment, the individual has also endured the distrust of medical care providers.

Malingering is deliberate. According to the *Diagnostic and Statistical Manual - IV (DSM-IV)* of the American Psychiatric Association (1994), "The essential feature of malingering is the intentional production of false or grossly exaggerated physical or psychological symptoms, motivated by external incentives such as avoiding military duty, avoiding work, obtaining financial compensation, evading criminal prosecution, or obtaining drugs" (p. 683). Like somatization, there are symptoms without organic causes (or the symptoms are "grossly exaggerated"). Unlike somatization, in malingering the individual is not experiencing some underlying emotional conflict and is also aware that he or she is faking. When malingering is suspected, clinicians look for incentives to fake, such as receiving workers' compensation benefits or an insurance settlement. However, often malingering is difficult to detect because the individual is very medically knowledgeable and sophisticated.

Psychogenic pain disorder (the *DSM-IV* has changed the name to "pain disorder associated with psychological factors") is pain that "causes significant clinical distress or impairment in social, occupational, or other important areas of functioning" (*DSM-IV*, 1994, p. 461). The symptoms of pain are not intentionally produced or feigned , but psychological factors are thought to play an important part in the onset, severity, exaggeration, or maintenance of the pain. Therefore, when psychogenic pain disorder is suspected, physicians look for a temporal relationship between the psychological factors and the onset or exaggeration of the pain. Stated another way, the physician attempts to establish if a psychological stimulus precedes the onset of the pain. This is often difficult to establish since the patient often is not aware of the distressing nature of the psychological stimulus. For example, a college student may not think that final exam week is stressful. However, if the physician is able to establish a temporal relationship, that is to say, that if the student's physical pain begins every final exam week, then it is reasonable to suspect that the stress of final examinations is responsible for the onset of the pain.

Although relatively rare and often confused with legitimate symptoms and/or coping strategies, these four responses to disability are counterproductive.

PROBLEMS IN MEASURING AN INDIVIDUAL'S RESPONSE TO A DISABILITY

In this section, look for—

▶ *10 difficulties in measuring response to disability:*
   1. *Most measurements are unidimensional*
   2. *Most measurements do not include the stigma of society*
   3. *There has been little longitudinal research*
   4. *Most measurements have been on people with physical disabilities*
   5. *For some disabilities, it is difficult to distinguish between response to the disability and symptoms of the disability*
   6. *Many of the research instruments are psychological instruments that render diagnoses of exclusion*
   7. *Much of the research is based on self-report*
   8. *Many of the research instruments report little or no reliability or validity studies*
   9. *Some disability scholars argue that response to disability should be measured by disability-specific instruments*
   10. *Most research studies do not take into account the individual's level of premorbid (predisability) functioning*

Research Is Only as Good as the Model Upon Which It Is Based

The research that has sought to understand the individual's adaptation/response to a disability has been grounded in the medical model. As you remember, the medical model posits that the "problem" lies entirely within the individual and, therefore, the responsibility for resolution/adaptation lies with that individual. Psychological instruments that have been used to assess a person's adjustment to a disability have not attempted to assess (1) the availability of resources to the individual, (2) the degree of stigma directed toward the type of disability that the individual experiences, or (3) the functions that are affected by the disability. The medical model deals with the treatment and rehabilitation of PWDs and does not usually consider such interventions as changing the social and physical environment.

Disability scholars (Anson, Stanwyck, & Krause, 1993; Krause, 1998a, 1998b; Krause & Anson, 1997; Krause, Coker, Charlifue, & Whiteneck, 1999) have begun to incorporate measures such as the *Life Situations Questionnaire* (LSQ) and the *Reciprocal Support Scale* (RSS) in their studies of the ways in which individuals respond to disabilities. The LSQ and the RSS ask questions about the individual's finances, career opportunities, living circumstances (whether he or she lives in an institution or whether he or she lives at home), his or her level of education, and the degree of social interaction and emotional support the individual receives. The environmental and functional models of disability are the bases of these types of questionnaires. Instruments such as these are used *in addition* to instruments that assess the individual's emotional response to the disability. As would be expected, by incorporating all three models of disability—medical, functional, and environmental—a more complete and accurate picture of the individual's response to the disability can be obtained.

Research Is Only as Good as the Instruments Used

Up until the publication of Linkowski's (1971, 1987) *The Acceptance of Disability Scale*, acceptance of disability was usually measured using psychological instruments such as the *Minnesota Multiphasic Personality Inventory* (MMPI) or the *California Personality Inventory* (CPI). There are two disadvantages in using these types of instruments. First, many of these instruments were designed to assess personality characteristics indicative of psychological abnormality....Each of the nine scales on which the MMPI is scored consists of items that distinguish between responses of a specified psychiatric patient group and a control group of normal people (Aiken, 1997, p. 317).

These instruments were designed for use in psychiatric hospitals to assess and diagnose pathology and psychological disorder, and when psychopathology is not found, a diagnosis of exclusion is rendered. In other words, the person is "normal" (whatever that means). Such a diagnosis of exclusion does not provide information on the individual's adaptive functioning and psychological growth. The diagnosis simply declares that psychopathology was looked for and none was found. No one would want to brag about high scores on the MMPI!

Second, these psychological inventories are comprised of scales such as Hypochondriasis (the MMPI and the *Basic Personality Inventory*) and Somatoform Disorders (Scale H of the *Millon Clinical Multiaxial Inventory*), which do not adequately describe the disability experience. Many PWDs are healthy, not sick, and, furthermore, concerns with body functioning, which the psychological instrument would score as pathology, would reflect active, adaptive management of the disability. For example, an individual with diabetes probably thinks about his or her body more than someone without diabetes. Other scales, such as the *Edwards Personal Preference Scale*, have Independence scales. Independence, for many PWDs, has been redefined and therefore their scores on these types of scales would not truly reflect their experience and certainly not be indicative of psychopathology. For example, someone who depends on a respirator to breathe carefully devises back-up systems and emergency responses. However, such plans and considerations should be viewed as positive, productive adaptive responses to the disability and not as pathological dependence.

These psychological instruments also depend on self-report and, for this reason, several of these instruments have validity scales that can detect quite accurately when the examinee is not being truthful. Stated simply, there are two basic ways in which a person can answer dishonestly. The first is intentional deception in which the person deliberately attempts to make him- or herself appear better ("faking good") or attempts to make him- or herself appear worse ("faking bad"). The second type of dishonesty is unintentional and termed "response sets." The individual is not aware that he or she is giving distorted answers.

Psychometrists and psychologists agree that the results of psychological instruments are valid only when test-takers understand that "they have nothing to gain by failing to answer thoughtfully and truthfully" (Aiken, 1997, p. 308.) Yet, many service programs for PWDs, such as vocational rehabilitation, are eligibility programs, meaning that the individual must demonstrate the presence of a disability. For this reason, there would be a tendency to "fake bad" in order to establish eligibility for services and benefits. The best-case scenario of the examinee having nothing to gain by failing to answer thoughtfully and truthfully probably rarely exists.

Livneh and Antonak (1997) presented a review of the 10 available instruments that measure psychosocial adaptation to disability. The authors concluded their review by noting "the considerable variability" in the theoretical orientations of the developers of these instruments and the concomitant variation in the operational definitions of psychosocial adaptation to chronic illness and disability.

> For instance, psychosocial adaptation (or maladaptation) has been operationalized as (a) presence of new and distressing physical, behavioral, and psychosomatic complaints (*General Health Questionnaire, Millon Behavioral Health Inventory*, and *Sickness Impact Profile*); (b) the alteration of vocational and avocational productivity (*Psychosocial Adjustment to Illness Scale*); (c) reduction in performance of domestic activities or daily living skills (*Psychosocial Adjustment to Illness Scale* and *Sickness Impact Profile*); (d) coping style (*Millon Behavioral Health Inventory*); (e) degree of disability acceptance (*Acceptance of Disability Scale* and *Acceptance of Loss Scale*); (f) pathological dimensions of personality that influence the course of disability or the efficacy of treatment (*Millon Behavioral Health Inventory*); (g) impact on interpersonal relations, communication, and sexual behavior (*Psychosocial Adjustment to Illness Scale* and *Sickness Impact Profile*); and (h) emotional and psychological distress, as manifested by the reasons of anxiety, shock, guilt, depression, anger, hostility, and denial (*Heinemann and Shontz Q-Sort* and *Reactions to Impairment and Disability Inventory*) (p. 63).

The Few Instruments That Measure Acceptance to Disability Are Designed for *Physical* Disabilities

Paper-and-pencil instruments are derived from theory. Linkowski's (1987) *Acceptance of Disability Scale* (AD) provides an easily understood example in that Linkowski operationalized Wright's theory of cognitive restructuring. However, as we have seen, Wright's theory applies only to *physical* disabilities and does not consider the response of individuals who have intellectual, cognitive, or psychiatric disabilities. (Linkowski reports that he is in the process of changing and adapting the AD scale.) Both Wright and Linkowski are considered to be pioneers, having developed their theory and instrument in the 1960s. Nonetheless, there are few, if any, instruments currently available to assess the response of an individual to an intellectual, cognitive, or psychiatric disability.

Most Often, No Premorbid Empirical Measure of the Individual's Psychological Functioning Exists

Many disability scholars have posited that the single most important variable in responding to the disability is the individual's premorbid psychological functioning. (It should be noted that the thesis of this book holds that environmental variables are also important.) Psychological functioning thought to be related to a positive response to a disability includes such factors as high levels of stress and tension control, excellent problem-solving and decision-making abilities, high levels of assertiveness and goal direction, capability of mobilizing a social-support system, accurate and positive appraisal abilities, high levels of emotional control, high levels of self-esteem, well-developed cognitive flexibility, high levels of self-insight, and a well-developed sense of humor (Linkowski & Dunn, 1974).

However, measurements of the individual's psychological functioning prior to the onset/diagnosis of the disability rarely exist. Therefore, there is no "baseline" to which to refer. Of course, this can be *inferred* by reading the individual's history, asking the individual him- or herself, or by relying on the reports of family members and other significant people in the PWD's life. Nevertheless, such inferences lack empirical precision and quantification.

Another issue in the psychodynamic functioning of the individual before the onset/diagnosis of a disability concerns the confounding of psychological functioning with environmental resources. For example, research has shown that individuals with higher levels of education and income tend to accept disabilities better. Intuitively, this makes sense because the individual has more options at his or her disposal, and these options act as stress moderators (for anyone—with or without a disability). The problem arises when trying to separate the individual's psychological functioning from the resources in his or her environment. The individual's functional demands also impact his or her emotional acceptance or response to the disability. For example, generally speaking, it is acknowledged that older people tend to accept disability better. However, it is not entirely understood *why* this relationship between age and acceptance has been found. Is it because older individuals have had more experience in dealing with life situations and therefore possess more emotional/psychological resources with which to respond? Or is it because older individuals usually have fewer functional demands, such as working or child care? Elderly people are usually "excused" from work or child care. Or, perhaps it is easier for an individual to accept his or her disability if all of his or her agemates have disabilities and/or functional limitations; the elderly individual may have reduced expectations concerning his or her quality of life.

Some Disability Scholars Advocate Disability-Specific Instruments

In contrast to general instruments that measure psychosocial response/adaptation to disability, such as the *Acceptance of Disability Scale*, there are 11 instruments that measure adaptation to eight specific disabilities: hearing impairment, arthritis, spinal cord injuries, visual impairment, cancer, diabetes, traumatic brain injury, and seizure disorders. For example, the *Communication Profile for the Hearing Impaired* measures the communication skills and personal adjustment and asks questions about the environment of individuals with hearing impairments. The *Arthritis Impact Measurement Scale* elicits information on the individual's mobility, social activity, and ability to perform household activities and activities of daily living, and the *Washington Psychosocial Seizure Disorder Inventory* seeks to measure overall psychological and social functioning, but also assessed financial status, management of medications, vocational adjustment, and adjustment to seizures. Certainly, these instruments would have a great deal of face validity for the test-takers. Even more important, these disability-specific instruments assess function and environment in addition to the individual's response. Therefore, all three models of disability—

medical, functional, and environmental—are used to more completely assess the individual's response.

Often, It Is Difficult To Distinguish Between Symptoms of the Disability and the Individual's Response to Disability

It is important, albeit difficult, to separate symptoms of the disability from the individual's response to the disability. For example, depression is a disability triggered, organically based manifestation of several disabilities, including spinal cord injury, multiple sclerosis, and traumatic brain injury. Garland and Zis (1991) suggested that affective disorders in people with multiple sclerosis, such as depression, result from structural lesions (wounds) in the neurological system. Instruments such as the *Beck Depression Inventory* and the *Minnesota Multiphasic Personality Inventory* can determine the presence and degree of depression present in the individual; however, these instruments cannot distinguish between depression that is a direct result of the disability and depression that is a response to the disability. Naugle (1991) addressed the reaction of denial of deficit as a "psychological sequelae" of disability or, in other words, denial as an emotional response to a disability. However, Naugle clearly distinguished denial as an emotional response from another type of denial or "'anosognosa' associated with and directly attributed to a focal cortical lesion" (p. 139). Obviously, the psychologist or psychometrist who is administering and interpreting these instruments should be knowledgeable about disabilities and their symptoms, course, and outcome in addition to adaptation/response theories. If not, the results of these instruments could be misinterpreted.

Most Research on Acceptance to Disability Has Not Been Longitudinal

Overwhelmingly, the majority of research investigating the adaptation/reaction to disability has gathered data at one point in time (Shontz, 1975). There are exceptions to this, such as Krause and colleagues' longitudinal studies (data gathered from the same people at several points in time) with people with spinal cord injuries (Krause, 1997, 1998a, 1998b). Longitudinal studies, using participants with or without disabilities, are expensive and difficult to implement. As would be expected, participants tend to drop out of studies; therefore, in most longitudinal studies, the size of the sample becomes smaller and smaller. Longitudinal studies have the potential to assess growth and development in adaptation, to assess the interaction of the various psychosocial developmental stages with the disability, and measure the impact of legislation such as the Americans with Disabilities Act in the lives of PWDs. Not only has most research on adaptation to disability gathered data only at one point in time, often the timing of the data collection was relatively soon after the onset/diagnosis of the disability. Due to the fact that patients in hospitals or residents of institutions are more accessible to researchers, PWDs were often "recruited" into studies that are purported to measure their adaptation to disability.

Acceptance of Disability Instruments Does Not Always Translate to Other Cultures

In order for any psychological instrument to be translated into another language, there must be cultural equivalence on the psychological concepts measured between the two languages. In other words, translating *The Acceptance of Disability Scale* into another language, such as Spanish, from the English in which Linkowski originally developed it, requires that the construct of acceptance of disability is defined in much the same way in the American cultures as in the Hispanic cultures (Smart, 1993; Smart & Smart, 1991, 1992a, 1992b, 1993a, 1993b, 1994a, 1994b, 1995a, 1995b, 1995c, 1995d, 1995e, 1996). You will remember that earlier in the book we learned that being a PWD is a "normative" role. In other words, there are rules (norms) that govern the "correct" or "socially acceptable" way in which to have a disability. Moreover, this normative role is culturally defined and, therefore, the role of a PWD may be different in an Asian culture than it is in a Hispanic culture.

Using the Hispanic cultures and the Spanish language as an example, it can be seen that the broad concept of acceptance/response to disability is probably viewed and defined differently in Hispanic cultures than it is in North American cultures. Hispanic cultural values, such as familism, well-defined sex roles, and religious beliefs influence how Hispanics with disabilities respond to and accept a disability. However, if a Hispanic individual were to be administered a Spanish translation of the *Acceptance of Disability Scale* (the author did translate this instrument into Spanish), his or her responses might spuriously indicate low acceptance of disability. Such cultural distortions have been found in other psychological instruments, such as the *Minnesota Multiphasic Personality Inventory* (Butcher & Garcia, 1978; Butcher & Pancheri, 1976; Darlington, 1971; Greene, 1987; Velasquez & Callahan, 1991). Simply stated, regardless of how accurate and elegant a foreign language translation may be (the words of the test), the psychological concepts of the instrument must be equivalent in both cultures in order to present an accurate clinical picture.

THE STAGE MODEL OF ADAPTATION TO DISABILITY

In this section, look for—

> ▶ *how not all disabilities have a traumatic, acute onset/diagnosis*
> ▶ *how, for most disabilities, the individual is not able to engage in anticipatory adjustment*
> ▶ *how difficult does not always mean tragic*
> ▶ *how the stage model does not apply to deteriorating conditions*
> ▶ *how it is helpful to have some broad guidelines in predicting the course and outcome of the adjustment/response process*

The stage theory of adaptation/response to disability provides some helpful guidelines in understanding and predicting the course and outcome of the individual's response process. This process is a gradual assimilation of an altered identity and is a process, not a one-time event (Livneh, 1986a, 1986b). Not all disabilities have a sudden, acute, traumatic onset. For example, disabilities such as diabetes and lupus have an insidious onset and therefore it is more accurate to speak of the time of diagnosis rather than the time of onset (Moos, 1984). Moving through these stages requires goal-directed changes in attitude and behavior, but this does not imply that the onset/diagnosis of every disability is thought to be tragic. The stage theory is based on theories of adaptation to loss, especially Kübler-

Ross's theories of acceptance of one's death (Kübler-Ross, 1969). The value of these theories to individuals (and their families) facing loss and death cannot be underestimated. However, there are two differences in the stage theory for death/loss and the stage theory of adaptation to disability. First, in many losses, or with regard to one's impending death, there is a period of anticipatory adjustment that allows the individual to both behaviorally and emotionally prepare for the loss before the loss actually happens. Such an anticipatory period rarely occurs for a PWD. (Exceptions to this would include situations such as individuals who have time to prepare for a therapeutic amputation.) Second, in losses such as divorce or death, the individual experiencing the loss usually does not experience prejudice, stigma, and discrimination from society and, therefore, these stage theories do not consider the added stress of prejudice and discrimination. Indeed, many PWDs report that their greatest difficulty is not in dealing with the disability, but in confronting prejudice and discrimination. However, the stage theory of adaptation/response to disability remains silent on the prejudice and discrimination of society.

The stage theory of adaptation/response to disability probably does not apply to individuals who have gradually deteriorating conditions, especially elderly individuals. For example, persons who experience the onset/diagnosis of a chronic, degenerating disability, such as arthritis or old-age deafness, typically do not experience the initial shock stage, nor would such individuals tend to undergo long-term depression or mourning.

THE STAGES OF RESPONSE IN DISABILITY

In this section, look for—

▶ *shock*
▶ *defensive retreat*
▶ *depression or mourning*
▶ *personal questioning*
▶ *adaptation, change, and integration*

Shock or Initial Impact

Robert Perkins, in his book *Talking to Angels: A Life Spent in High Latitudes* (1996), described the shock of the diagnosis/onset of his mental illness:

> In the spring of 1968, I was nineteen and a freshman at Harvard College. I was soon to leave school, without even passing "GO" or finishing the year, to start a journey. A journey I have yet to complete....To have the wind knocked out of you, hard, at nineteen. To give you the feeling of it, I'd hit you on the side of the head, when you were not expecting it, with a flat board or a piece or rubber tubing. The shock of the thing! (pp. 5, 15)

In this stage, the individual's thinking is often disorganized, and he or she may be feeling overwhelmed and confused. Rereading Perkins' description, we can see the total unexpectedness and the devastating impact. First, he relates the abruptness of the onset as not being able to pass GO. Then he describes the devastating impact in physical terms: being hit on the side of the head. Individuals in this stage of initial shock often feel that more is happening to them than they can understand or absorb. They are unable to think or feel.

It is not only the diagnosis/onset of a disability that precedes this type of shock. For some individuals, it is a point in the treatment or rehabilitation process that has idiosyncratic shocking meaning. For example, one individual with a progressive neurological disease stated, "Going into the wheelchair was awful!" Another individual stated, "Going into the assisted living center was the worst day of my life. I will never forget it."

Defensive Retreat or Denial

As the word "defensive" implies, this stage is often considered to be a therapeutic, adaptive strategy on the part of the PWD. Denial can take three basic forms: (1) denial of the presence of the disability, (2) denial of the implications of the disability, or (3) denial of the permanence of the disability. Denial allows the individual to maintain his or her self-identity (Langer, 1994; Stewart, 1994). An individual who denies the implications of the disability may think "I'm the same as I always was" or may think "I'll soon be walking" or "I don't need to change any of my plans" or "Everything will be like it was before." The individual understands that he or she has the disability, but minimizes and downplays the effects of the disability and often tries to live in his or her "predisability world." (Franklin Roosevelt denied the implications of his disability because he maintained that some day he would be able to walk.) When an individual denies the permanence of the disability, he or she may feel that the disability will disappear or "Soon, I'll be my old self again." Denial of the presence of the disability is quite rare; denial of the implications or the permanence of the disability is more common. Families of PWDs frequently engage in denial when they view the disability as not changing the PWD's life or insist that the PWD will "return to normal." For example, a wife asks physicians, "When will he walk out of here?" (Dunn, 1996) In individuals with amputations, the stage of denial is often complicated and compounded by phantom limb pain.

Defensive retreat or denial can prevent what is called "emotional flooding" and allows the individual to gradually assimilate both the permanence and the full implications of the disability. Individuals in this stage, in an attempt to guard against the trauma, may refuse to accept information, insist that there has been a mistake, and/or may seek out other service providers. Deegan (1991), in *Recovery: The Lived Experience of Rehabilitation*, described denial:

> Needless to say, we didn't believe our doctors and social workers. In fact, we adamantly denied and raged against these bleak prophesies for our lives. We felt it was all just a mistake, a bad dream, a temporary set-back in our lives. We just knew that in a week or two, things would get back to normal again. We felt our teenage world was still there, just waiting for us to return to it. Our denial was an important stage in our recovery. It was a normal reaction to an overwhelming situation. It was our way of surviving those first awful months (p. 48).

Obviously, the individual in denial does not have any motivation (or understanding) to learn to live with the disability. For this reason, denial, or defensive retreat, is considered to be therapeutic if it does not continue too long. Service providers often counter denial with the concept of "dosage of information" (Naugle, 1991). Timing of information is also important. Naugle summarized, "Equally important is the concept of dosage. If the individual is overwhelmed with information, that material is less likely to be accepted. Failure to recognize and accommodate an individual's tolerance level for distressing information may have the effect of interfering with participation in any treatment regimen. Smaller "doses" of information allow the individual to assimilate that information at a more controlled, self-determined rate" (p. 147).

Depression or Mourning

Denial is often considered to be past-oriented, in that the individual is trying to retain his or her former identity. Depression is considered to be future-oriented because the individual now struggles with questions of an uncertain future and an uncertain identity (Austin, 1990; Johnson, 1993; Powers, 1993). Often, the PWD feels "My family would be better off without me." In this stage, the PWD often does not have the energy or motivation to invest in a rehabilitation program. The individual often withdraws from others and has trouble sleeping and eating, and concentrating.

A man with a spinal cord injury described the grieving process, "If someone is stuck in the grieving process...it's like an adjustment to a death. The only thing is, for an injury or disability, it's not as easy to adjust as with a death because with a death, the person's no longer there. With a disability, you have a constant reminder. So, sometimes it takes even longer to grieve and adjust. A lot of people turn to alcohol and drugs, which is a way of going through denial. As long as you're smashed, you can forget about your disability" (Scherer, 1993, p. 115).

It is often typical (or "normal") for the PWD to experience cycles of loss of hope, apathy, and deep depression. Also associated with depression are feelings of guilt and self-blame. As the grief subsides, the individual is able to acknowledge that he or she feels better.

Regression

Closely tied to the stage of depression, regression occurs when the PWD simply gives up or regresses to an earlier, less mature, stage of life. Deegan (1991) described regression in herself and a fellow resident:

> Our denial gave way to despair and anguish. We both gave up. Giving up was the solution for us. It numbed the pain of our despair because we stopped asking "Why? and How will I go on?"....Giving up meant that for 14 years he sat in the day rooms of institutions gazing at soap operas, watching others live their lives. For months I sat in a chair in my family's living room, smoking cigarettes and waiting until it was 8:00 p.m. so that I could go back to bed. At this time, even the simplest of tasks were overwhelming. I remember being asked to come in to the kitchen to help knead some bread dough. I got up, went in to the kitchen and looked at the dough for what seemed to be an eternity. Then I walked back to my chair and wept. The task seemed overwhelming to me (p. 49).

Another type of regression occurs when the individual romanticizes and idealizes "normality" or his or her premorbid identity. A lot like reminiscing about the "good old days," which may or may not have been so good, the individual nostalgically idealizes the memories of him- or herself without a disability. Charles Mee, the writer who contracted polio as a teenager, deeply resented his father's regression. Mee (1999) wrote:

> For the rest of his life after I had polio, my father carried a picture of me in his wallet that he had taken at the halftime of a football game. I was sitting on the grass with my teammates while the coach talked to us. My father had come around to the side of the group, and as I turned to look at him, he took the picture: an adolescent boy in the vigor of youth, a strong jaw and neck, a crewcut, massive shoulders with the football pads....I always took the fact that he carried that picture with him as a sign of disappointment in me, and it filled me with rage....The photograph was still on a table not far from his bed when he died at the age of ninety-four (p. 170).

Personal Questioning and/or Anger

In this stage, the individual may ask, "Why did God allow this to happen to me?" The onset of a disability seems unfair. Anger is often a combination of feelings of helplessness, frustration, fear, and irritability. Other types of personal questioning may take the form of the PWD "replaying" the accident or prediagnosis period, in an attempt to find ways in which the disability could have been avoided. In trying to find the reason or meaning (which are not the same as the cause), the individual may lose trust in the world and in his or her value systems. For some individuals, this type of questioning is both lonely and futile. The responsibility or cause of the disability often becomes self-blame for the individual; for some individuals, holding oneself responsible for the disability is the price they pay for maintaining their belief that the world is not a random and unpredictable place.

If carried on for too long, compulsive, obsessive questioning and search for cause and meaning can delay the treatment and rehabilitation process. Helping the individual to understand the difference between the cause (responsibility) for the disability and the meaning and purpose can be therapeutic. Oftentimes, the individual's religious, spiritual, or philosophical belief systems can be implemented to help the individual clarify his or her beliefs about the purposes of his or her disability. Mee (1999), a survivor of polio, had the following conversation with a Jesuit priest.

> "I've lost my faith. I no longer believe in God."

> "I see," the priest said. And then he made a mistake. Instead of honoring my thoughts and feelings—instead of gently exploring the anger that had taken me to this place I was in—he decided to bully me, to intimidate me back into the church with his superior reasoning (p. 202).

Mee tells what the priest did wrong, which was not honoring his thoughts and feelings, and also states what the priest should have done, which was to gently explore the anger.

A man with a spinal cord injury spoke of "anger that just sits there and grows." He said, "I wish I'd had counseling regularly...on a fairly regular basis. I'm not sure what would've come out of it, but if you see someone enough, eventually you're going to say something. Try to bring things out, some of the anger, and things like that. That was something that was never done, and that anger just sits in there and grows" (Scherer, 1993, p. 160).

Integration and Growth

The individual reaches this stage when he or she (1) understands and accepts the reality and implications of the disability, (2) establishes new values and goals that do not conflict with the disability, and (3) explores and utilizes his or her strengths and abilities. Often, integration and growth necessitate changes in the environment such as assistive technology, changes in role functioning, and assuming responsibility for the management of the disability. Carolyn Vash (1981) has termed this stage "transcendence," in which the individual feels that the disability is an opportunity for growth and learning. This stage is never complete; life continues to make demands and challenges of everyone. However, PWDs, upon reaching this stage, often begin advocacy and support work with other PWDs and their families. Further, they view their advocacy, service, and political activity as a means of bringing meaning and purpose to their own disability experience.

ADVANTAGES OF THE STAGE THEORY

In this section, look for—
- ▶ *how the theory facilitates the selection of the most suitable forms of treatment*
- ▶ *how the theory emphasizes the need for both short-term treatment and long-term support*
- ▶ *how the theory allows the PWD to understand his or her own feelings and reactions*
- ▶ *common variables that can be tailored to the individual PWD*
- ▶ *how the theory helps to validate and normalize the PWD's intense and often contradictory emotions*
- ▶ *how the theory recognizes that adjustment/response is a process and not a one-time event*

Educating the PWD and his or her family about these stages helps to "normalize" and "universalize" the experience of adaptation/response. When the PWD, and his or her family, learn that other individuals experience the same types of feelings, the PWD will not feel as isolated. It is strengthening to an individual to know that others understand his or her experience. The individual feels validated and is able to put his or her feelings into context. Proponents of the stage theory maintain that these types of responses of PWDs (and their families) are neither pathological nor dysfunctional. Occasionally, however, if the responses are prolonged or associated with major impairment, then interventions can be implemented.

The stage theory also assists service providers in understanding the process of response/adaptation and, in so doing, helps service providers to choose the best treatment goals (Livneh, 1986b). Tailoring concrete short-term goals compatible with the stage of adaptation/response can provide a task-oriented approach that does not overwhelm the individual. Conceptualizing the adaptation/response to a disability as a process can also assist service providers in encouraging and supporting the individual to progress to the next stage while not permitting coping mechanisms of one stage to become long-term habits. Caregivers cannot counter maladaptive responses and behaviors unless they understand the demands of each stage. Case management, in which many different professionals provide services to a single individual, is facilitated when there is agreement and understanding concerning the stage in which the PWD is operating. This agreement among members of the treatment team will ensure that all treatment will be coordinated. Furthermore, educating and supporting PWDs and their families can assist in maintaining family equilibrium and help families to avoid making major life changes until they are further along in the process.

Understanding the stages of adaptation/response assists family members in their efforts to support the PWD. For example, family members can be educated about the importance of noncritical acceptance of the PWD's denial. Family members learn that confronting or arguing with the PWD is counterproductive. Another example concerns the individual who is in the anger stage. Often, this anger is expressed toward the most accessible people—family members or care providers. Helping family and caregivers to understand that the anger of the PWD is an attempt to regain balance and control will reduce their stress and help to eliminate compassion fatigue and burnout. Therefore, if caregivers and family members understand the stages of adaptation, it is less likely that the PWD will become socially isolated. The stage theory promotes hope and optimism and provides a starting point for assisting the PWD. Deegan (1991) stated, "Hope is contagious" (p. 53).

Often professional caregivers minimize or purposely avoid certain stages of the adaptation/response process. For example, some professionals are not comfortable with individuals who are experiencing the anger stage (Clanton, Rude, & Taylor, 1992). By understanding the stage theory and developing an awareness of their own responses to certain stages, professional caregivers can develop alternative treatment strategies, such as referring PWDs to other caregivers.

Assisting PWDs to understand the stages of adaptation/responses can allow them to draw upon their strengths and capabilities at each stage (Livneh & Antonak, 1990). Of course, such an understanding is more than an intellectual understanding, but is a deep, therapeutic conceptualization of a long-term process. Often, PWDs join support groups with individuals who have experienced the same disability. Due to the fact that group members may be at different stages in the adaptation/response process, members often learn from the experiences of others. These self-help groups can do much to promote and maintain hope. Further, group members know that others understand their experiences.

CAUTIONS IN IMPLEMENTING THE STAGE THEORY

In this section, look for—

▶ *some stage theories that are specific to the disability, such as therapeutic amputations*
▶ *how, in some disabilities, the stages do not progress in a linear fashion, but in a curvilinear fashion*
▶ *how each stage encompasses a wide variety of behavioral characteristics*
▶ *how the stage theory does not consider the prejudice and discrimination of others and how these affect the adjustment/response process*
▶ *how individuals can recycle through the stages, repeat a stage, or skip a stage*
▶ *how disability is not a single event, but a process*

Recently, there have been some criticisms of the stage theory of adaptation/response to disability, even to the point of terming the stage theory as "social oppression" (Kendall & Buys, 1998, p. 17). The idea that *every* PWD, and his or her family, regardless of the type or severity of disability, experiences a predictable, orderly, sequential, linear, hierarchical progression through these stages has never been suggested by the proponents of the theory. Nor has the wide variability in behavioral characteristics of each stage been disputed. One critique does, however, have merit. Kendall and Buys argued, "Stage models of adjustment also normalize responses such as denial and distress following acquired disability, which may lead rehabilitation workers to expect, or even encourage, such responses" (p. 17). Nonetheless, proponents of the stage model have noted that

> The process of adaptation is not irreversible. Individuals who experience a chronic illness or sustain a permanent disability may regress to an earlier phase or skip one or more phases of psychosocial adaptation. Phases of adaptation comprise nondiscrete and categorically overlapping reactions. These reactions may fluctuate and blend with one another, providing for the experience of more than one reaction at a time. Attempts to specify the duration of each phase, or of the entire adaptation response, are futile at best (Livneh & Antonak, 1997, p. 19).

Therefore, it is difficult to understand the criticism that rehabilitation workers, and other care providers, might encourage certain responses such as denial or distress. The stage theory provides *only* guidelines and acknowledges that PWDs do not proceed through these stages in a one-time-only, sequential, time-dated process. PWDs (whose disability has been medically stabilized) may recycle through these stages as the demands and stresses of developmental tasks and other life transitions arise.

The stage theory does propose a linear process but it also acknowledges that, for some disabilities, the response/adaptation process is a curvilinear process. Many individuals with chronic, degenerating disabilities and chronic illnesses are thought to experience a curvilinear response, with a positive response in the beginning (when the symptoms and pain are not very great), experience a negative response in middle age (when the symptoms and pain increase), and experience a positive response in older age (when the individual has few functional demands).

There are a few specific disabilities for which the stage theory has been specifically adapted. For instance, the stage theory has been applied to individuals with amputations and congenital limb deficiencies. Individuals who undergo a surgical (therapeutic) amputation are thought to experience four phases: (1) realization that the loss of a limb is imminent, (2) early postoperative hospitalization, (3) in-hospital rehabilitation in which the individual receives such treatments as the fitting of a prosthesis, and (4) home rehabilitation in which the individual returns to his or her "normal" life (Bradway, Malone, Racy, Leal, & Poole, 1984).

Certainly, the stage theory advocates viewing the person as someone with resources and capabilities. By acknowledging various stages, PWDs can understand their own feelings better and the feelings of family members. For example, clients (with or without disabilities) tend to terminate counseling/psychotherapy when they feel they are not "getting better." Recognizing and understanding that "you might feel worse before you feel better" may help clients to continue in counseling. Caregivers (both professional and family members) will be less likely to withdraw support if they understand that some of the typical stages a PWD experiences are often unpleasant. Rereading Patricia Deegan's *Recovery*, we can see that her family members never withdrew their support and encouragement, in spite of the fact that she sat on the couch all day. Arnold Beisser, the physician who contracted polio, explained his relationship with his disability as like a marriage, especially when he realized that there was no final and complete stage to accepting his disability.

The argument that the stage theory promotes the idea that a disability is an undesirable state ("pathologizing" disability) has not been validated by research or by anecdotal evidence. Powers (1993) explained:

> The topic of disability-related grief is also associated with sensitivity and controversy when considered in relation to current positive perspectives of disability. Theories that postulate the existence of grief or chronic sorrow in response to a disability are sometimes regarded as promulgating the notion that disability is an inherently tragic event with an enduring negative impact on families. Yet,...it can be through the validation and processing of grief that many family members shift their perspectives of disability from tragedy to challenge and opportunity (p. 120).

An excellent summarization on the need for counseling support (and the dangers of not providing it) is provided by a PWD who said, "People in this condition need mental rehabilitation more than anything else. Because that is 90 percent of physical rehabilitation. [Rehabilitation doesn't] want to face that because it's too expensive. So you adapt. You develop coping mechanisms and some of them, like drinking, are not good ones. If way back then they had given us good coping mechanisms, a lot of problems could have been prevented" (Scherer, 1993, pp. 159–160).

In-Class Learning Activity

- Dr. Donald Linkowski, a professor of rehabilitation at George Washington University, developed the *Acceptance of Disability Scale* (AD) in 1969. Linkowski has given permission to reprint this scale in the book (Appendix 7–B), with two provisos: (1) he is aware that the more accurate term is "response" to disability, and (2) he is in the process of making revisions. Nonetheless, the *Acceptance of Disability Scale* can be a useful learning tool for students (in addition to the original purpose of assessing an individual's acceptance of disability).

  You will remember that Linkowski derived this instrument from Beatrice Wright's theory of cognitive restructuring. Wright's theory has four components:
  1. Enlargement of the scope of values;
  2. Subordination of the physique;
  3. Containment of disability effects;
  4. Transformation from comparative values to asset values (instead of viewing the limitations, viewing the assets the individual has).

  As you read and answer the questions of the AD Scale (see Appendix 7–B), determine which of the four components Linkowski based each question on.

Learning Activities

1. Using one of the 17 "bullets" listed at the beginning of this chapter, write a response paper.
2. Read any of the following first-person accounts of disability. Look for these points:
   - Is the author white, middle-class, and highly educated?
   - What is the disability? Is it a physical, intellectual, cognitive, or psychiatric disability?
   - Is the disability part of the author's identity?
   - Are there any extraordinary environmental resources?
   - Are there examples of Beatrice Wright's cognitive restructuring coping mechanisms?
   - Is there evidence (or lack of evidence) of the stage theory of acceptance/response to disability?

References

Aiken, L. R. (1997). *Psychological testing and assessment* (9th ed.). Needham Heights, MA: Allyn & Bacon.

American Psychiatric Association. (1994). *Diagnostic and statistical manual of mental disorders* (4th ed.). Washington, DC: Author.

Anson, C. A., Stanwyck, D. J., & Krause, J. S. (1993). Social support and health status in spinal cord injury. *International Journal of Paraplegia, 31,* 632–638.

Antonak, R. F., & Livneh, H. (1991). A hierarchy of reactions to disability. *International Journal of Rehabilitation Research, 14,* 13–24.

Austin, J. K. (1990). Assessment of coping mechanisms used by parents and children with chronic illness. *Maternal and Child Nursing, 15,* 98–102.

Ballin, A. (1930). *The deaf mute howls.* Los Angeles: Grafton.

Beisser, A. R. (1989). *Flying without wings: Personal reflections on being disabled.* New York: Doubleday.

Bordieri, J. E. (1993). Self-blame attributions for disability and perceived client involvement in the vocational rehabilitation process. *Journal of Applied Rehabilitation Counseling, 24*(2), 3–6.

Bradway, J. K., Malone, J. M., Racy, J., Leal, J. M., & Poole, J. (1984). Psychological adaptation to amputation: An overview. *Orthotics and Prosthetics, 38,* 46–50.

Brookes, T. (1995). *Catching my breath: An asthmatic explores his illness.* New York: Vintage.

Butcher, J. N., & Garcia, R. E. (1978). Cross-national application of psychological tests. *Personnel and Guidance Journal, 56,* 472–475.

Butcher, J. N., & Pancheri, P. (1976). *A handbook of cross-national MMPI research.* Minneapolis, MN: University of Minnesota.

Callahan, J. (1989). *Don't worry, he won't get far on foot.* New York: Random House.

Clanton, L. D., Rude, S. S., & Taylor, C. (1992). Learned resourcefulness as a moderator of burnout in a sample of rehabilitation providers. *Rehabilitation Psychology, 37,* 131–140.

Cohen, L. H. (1994). *Train go sorry: Inside a Deaf world.* Boston: Houghton Mifflin.

Corbett, J. O., & Bregante, J. L. (1993). Disabled lesbians: Multicultural realities. In M. Nagler (Ed.). *Perspectives on disability* (pp. 261–271). Palo Alto, CA: Health Markets Research.

Couser, G. T. (1997). *Recovering bodies: Illness, disability, and life writing.* Madison, WI: University of Wisconsin.

Darlington, R. B. (1971). Another look at "cultural fairness." *Journal of Educational Measurement, 9,* 71–82.

Davis, L. J. (1995). *Enforcing normalcy: Disability, deafness, and the body.* London: Verso.

Deegan, P. E. (1991). Recovery: The lived experience of rehabilitation. In R. P. Marinelli & A. E. Dell Orto (Eds.). *The psychological and social impact of disability* (3rd ed.) (pp. 47–45). New York: Springer.

DeLoach, C., & Greer, B. G. (1981). *Adjustment to severe physical disability: A metamorphosis.* New York: McGraw-Hill.

Dembo, T., Leviton, G. L., & Wright, B. A. (1956). Adjustment to misfortune—A problem of social psychological rehabilitation. *Artificial Limbs, 3*(2), 4–62.

Donoghue, P. J., & Siegel, M. E. (1992). *Sick and tired of feeling sick and tired: Living with invisible chronic illness.* New York: Norton.

Dunn, M. (1996). Subscale development of the Rehabilitation Situations Inventory. *Rehabilitation Psychology, 41,* 255–264.

Fine, M., & Asch, A. (1988). Introduction: Beyond pedestals. In M. Fine & A. Asch (Eds.). *Women with disabilities: Essays in psychology, culture, and politics* (pp. 1–37). Philadelphia: Temple University.

Frank, A. W. (1991). *At the will of the body: Reflections on illness.* Boston: Houghton Mifflin.

Frank, A. W. (1995). *The wounded storyteller: Body, illness, and ethics.* Chicago: University of Chicago.

Garland, F. J., & Zis, A. P. (1991). Multiple sclerosis and affective disorders. *Canadian Journal of Psychiatry, 36,* 112–117.

Greene, R. L. (1987). Ethnicity and MMPI performance: A review. *Journal of Consulting and Clinical Psychology, 55,* 497–512.

Hawkins, A. H. (1993). *Reconstructing illness: Studies in pathography.* West Lafayette, IN: Purdue University.

Heinemann, A. W., & Shontz, F. C. (1984). Adjustment following disability: Representative case studies. *Rehabilitation Counseling Bulletin, 58,* 3–14.

Higgins, P. C. (1980). *Outsiders in a hearing world: A sociology of Deafness.* Newbury Park, CA: Sage.

Hull, J. M. (1991). *Touching the rock: The experience of blindness.* New York: Pantheon.

Johnson, D. L. (1993). Grieving is the pits. In G. H. S. Singer & L. E. Powers (Eds.). *Families, disability, and empowerment: Active coping skills and strategies for family interventions* (pp. 151–154). Baltimore: Brookes.

Keller, H. (1990). *The story of my life.* New York: Bantam.

Kendall, E., & Buys, N. (1998). An integrated model of psychosocial adjustment following acquired disability. *Journal of Rehabilitation, 64*(3), 16–21.

Kisor, H. (1990). *What's that pig outdoors? A memoir of deafness.* New York: Hill and Wang.

Kleinman, A. (1988). *The illness narratives: Suffering, healing, and the human condition.* New York: Basic Books.

Krause, J. S. (1997). Adjustment after spinal cord injury: A nine-year longitudinal study (1985–1994). *Archives of Physical Medicine and Rehabilitation, 78,* 651–657.

Krause, J. S. (1998a). Changes in adjustment after spinal cord injury: A 20-year longitudinal study. *Rehabilitation Psychology, 43,* 41–55.

Krause, J. S. (1998b). Dimensions of subjective well-being after spinal cord injury: An empirical analysis by gender and race/ethnicity. *Archives of Physical Medicine and Rehabilitation, 79,* 900–909.

Krause, J. S., & Anson, C. A. (1997). Adjustment after spinal cord injury: Relationship to gender and race. *Rehabilitation Psychology, 42,* 31–46.

Krause, J. S., Coker, J., Charlifue, S., & Whiteneck, G. G. (1999). Depression and subjective well being among 97 American Indians with spinal cord injury: A descriptive study. *Rehabilitation Psychology, 44,* 354–372.

Kriegel, L. (1991). *Falling into life.* San Francisco: North Point.

Kübler-Ross, E. (1969). *On death and dying.* New York: Macmillan.

Lane, H. (1992). *The mask of benevolence: Bio-power and the Deaf community.* New York: Knopf.

Langer, K. G. (1994). Depression and denial in psychotherapy of persons with disabilities. *American Journal of Psychotherapy, 48,* 181–194.

Lindemann, J. I. (Ed.). (1981). *Psychological and behavioral aspects of physical disability.* New York: Plenum.

Linkowski, D. C. (1971). A scale to measure acceptance of disability. *Rehabilitation Counseling Bulletin, 14,* 236–244.

Linkowski, D. C. (1987). *The acceptance of disability scale.* Washington, DC: The George Washington University Medical Center, Department of Psychiatry and Behavioral Sciences, The Rehabilitation Research and Training Center (originally published in 1971).

Linkowski, D. C., & Dunn, M. A. (1974). Self-concept and acceptance of disability. *Rehabilitation Counseling Bulletin, 17,* 28–32.

Livneh, H. (1986a). A unified approach to existing models of adaptation to disability—I. A model of adaptation. *Journal of Applied Rehabilitation Counseling, 17*(1), 5–16, 56.

Livneh, H. (1986b). A unified approach to existing models of adaptation to disability—II. Intervention strategies. *Journal of Applied Rehabilitation Counseling, 17*(2), 6–10.

Livneh, H., & Antonak, R. F. (1990). Reactions to disability: An empirical investigation of their nature and structure. *Journal of Applied Rehabilitation Counseling, 21*(4), 13–21.

Livneh, H., & Antonak, R. F. (1997). *Psychosocial adaptation to chronic illness and disability.* Gaithersburg, MD: Aspen.

Mairs, N. (1997). Foreword. In G. T. Couser (Ed.). *Recovering bodies: Illness, disability, and life writing* (pp. ix-xiii). Madison, WI: University of Wisconsin.

Marshak, L.E., & Seligman, M. (1993). *Counseling persons with physical disabilities: Theoretical and clinical perspectives.* Austin, TX: Pro-Ed.

Mee, C. L. (1999). *A nearly normal life: A memoir.* Boston: Little, Brown.

Moos, R. H. (Ed.). (1984). *Coping with physical illness. Volume 2: New perspectives.* New York: Plenum.

Murphy, R. (1987). *The body silent.* New York: Henry Holt.

Naugle, R. I. (1991). Denial in rehabilitation: Its genesis, consequences, and clinical management. In R. P. Marinelli & A. E. Dell Orto (Eds.). *The psychological and social impact of disability* (3rd ed.) (pp. 139–151). New York: Springer.

Padden, C., & Humphries, T. (1988). *Deaf in America: Voices from a culture.* Cambridge, MA: Harvard University Press.

Perkins, R. (1996). *Talking to angels: A life spent in high latitudes.* Boston: Beacon.

Powers, L. E. (1993). Disability and grief: From tragedy to challenge. In G. H. S. Singer & L. E. Powers (Eds.). *Families, disability, and empowerment: Active coping skills and strategies for family interventions* (pp. 119–149). Baltimore: Brookes.

Price, R. (1994). *A whole new life: An illness and a healing.* New York: Atheneum.

Roessler, R., & Bolton, B. (1978). *Psychosocial adjustment to disability.* Baltimore: University Park Press.

Rousso, H. (1993). *Disabled, female, and proud! Stories of ten women with disabilities.* Westport, CT: Bergin & Garvey.

Schaller, S. (1991). *A man without words.* New York: Summit.

Scherer, M. S. (1993). *Living in the state of stuck: How technologies affect the lives of people with disabilities.* Cambridge, MA: Brookline.

Schlossberg, N. K. (1981). A model for analyzing human adaptation to transition. *The Counseling Psychologist, 9,* 2–18.

Shontz, F. C. (1975). *The psychological aspects of physical illness and disability.* New York: Macmillan.

Shontz, F. C. (1977). Physical disability and personality: Theory and research. In R. P. Marinelli & A. E. Dell Orto (Eds.). *The psychological and social impact of physical disability* (pp. 105–129). New York: Springer.

Shontz, F. C. (1991). Six principles relating to disability and psychological adjustment. In R. P. Marinelli & A. E. Dell Orto (Eds.). *The psychological and social impact of disability* (3rd ed.) (pp. 107–110). New York: Springer.

Sienkiewicz-Mercer, R., & Kaplan, S. B. (1989). *I raise my eyes to say yes.* Boston: Houghton Mifflin.

Smart, J. F. (1993). Level of acculturation of Mexican Americans with disabilities and acceptance of disability. *Rehabilitation Counseling Bulletin, 36,* 199–211.

Smart, J. F., & Smart, D. W. (1991). Acceptance of disability and the Mexican American culture. *Rehabilitation Counseling Bulletin, 34,* 356–367.

Smart, J. F., & Smart, D. W. (1992a). Cultural issues in the rehabilitation of Hispanics. *Journal of Rehabilitation, 58,* 29–37.

Smart, J. F., & Smart, D. W. (1992b). Curriculum changes in multicultural rehabilitation. *Rehabilitation Education, 6,* 105–122.

Smart, J. F., & Smart, D. W. (1993a). Acculturation, biculturism, and the rehabilitation of Mexican Americans. *Journal of Applied Rehabilitation Counseling, 24,* 46–51.

Smart, J. F., & Smart, D. W. (1993b). The rehabilitation of Hispanics with disabilities: Sociocultural constraints. *Rehabilitation Education, 7,* 167–184.

Smart, J. F., & Smart, D. W. (1994a). The rehabilitation of Hispanics experiencing acculturative stress: Implications for practice. *The Journal of Rehabilitation, 60*(4), 8–12.

Smart, J. F., & Smart, D. W. (1994b). Rehabilitation of Hispanics: Implications for training and education. *Rehabilitation Education, 8,* 360–369.

Smart, J. F., & Smart, D. W. (1995a). Acculturative stress: The experience of Hispanic immigrants. *The Counseling Psychologist, 23,* 25–42.

Smart, J. F., & Smart, D. W. (1995b). Acculturative stress of Hispanics: Loss and challenge. *Journal of Counseling and Development, 73,* 390–396.

Smart, J. F., & Smart, D. W. (1995c). Response to Leal-Idrogo's "Further thoughts." *Journal of Rehabilitation, 61,* 24–25.

Smart, J. F., & Smart, D. W. (1995d). The use of translators/interpreters in rehabilitation. *Journal of Rehabilitation, 61,* 14–20.

Smart, J. F., & Smart, D. W. (1995e). Vocational evaluation of Hispanic clients with disabilities. *Directions in Rehabilitation Counseling, 6,* 1–12.

Smart, J. F., & Smart, D. W. (1996). The rehabilitation of Hispanics: Topics of interest to educators. *Rehabilitation Education, 10,* 171–184.

Spelic, S. S. (1997). Somatization and hypochondriasis. *Treatment Today, Winter,* 30–34.

Spradley, R., & Spradley, J. (1985). *Deaf like me* (2nd ed.). Washington, DC: Gallaudet University.

Stewart, J. R. (1994). Denial of disabling conditions and specific interventions in the rehabilitation counseling setting. *Journal of Applied Rehabilitation Counseling, 25*(3), 7–15.

Vash, C. L. (1981). *The psychology of disability.* New York: Springer.

Velasquez, R. J., & Callahan, W. J. (1991). Psychological testing of Hispanic Americans in clinical settings: Overview and issues. In K. F. Geisinger (Ed.). *Psychological testing of Hispanics* (pp. 253–256). Washington, DC: American Psychological Association.

Wortman, C. B., & Silver, R. C. (1989). The myths of coping with loss. *Journal of Consulting and Clinical Psychology, 57,* 349–357.

Wright, B. A. (1960). *Physical disability: A psychological approach.* New York: Harper and Row.

Wright, B. A. (1991). Labeling: The need for greater person–environment individuation. In C. R. Snyder & D. R. Forsythe (Eds.). *Handbook of social and clinical psychology* (pp. 469–487). Elmsford, NY: Pergamon.

Yoshida, K. K. (1993). Reshaping of self: A pendular reconstruction of self and identity among adults with traumatic spinal cord injury. *Sociology of Health and Illness, 15,* 217–245.

Zola, I. K. (1982). *Missing pieces: A chronicle of living with a disability.* Philadelphia: Temple University.

First-Person Narratives of People with Disabilities

Ballin, A. (1930). *The deaf mute howls*. Los Angeles: Grafton.

Beisser, A. R. (1989). *Flying without wings: Personal reflections on being disabled*. New York: Doubleday.

Black, K. (1996). *In the shadow of polio*. White Plains, NY: Addison Wesley Longman.

Brookes, T. (1995). *Catching my breath: An asthmatic explores his illness*. New York: Vintage.

Callahan, J. (1989). *Don't worry, he won't get far on foot*. New York: Random House.

Cohen, L. H. (1994). *Train go sorry: Inside a Deaf world*. Boston: Houghton Mifflin.

Fries, K. (Ed.). (1997). *Staring back: The disability experience from the inside out*. New York: Plume.

Gallagher, H. G. (1985). *FDR's splendid deception*. New York: Dodd and Mead.

Hannaford, S. (1985). *Living outside inside: A disabled woman's experience. Towards a social and political perspective*. Berkeley, CA: Canterbury Press.

Hockenberry, J. (1995). *Moving violations: War zones, wheelchairs, and declarations of independence*. New York: Hyperion.

Hull, J. M. (1991). *Touching the rock: The experience of blindness*. New York: Pantheon.

Keller, H. (1903). *The story of my life*. New York: Doubleday.

Kisor, H. (1990). *What's that pig outdoors? A memoir of deafness*. New York: Hill and Wang.

Mee, C. L. (1999). *A nearly normal life*. Boston: Little, Brown.

Merker, H. (1994). *Listening*. New York: Harper Collins.

Murphy, R. (1987). *The body silent*. New York: Henry Holt.

Perkins, R. (1996). *Talking to angels: A life spent in high latitudes*. Boston: Beacon.

Price, R. (1994). *A whole new life: An illness and a healing*. New York: Atheneum.

Rousso, H. (1993). *Disabled, female, and proud!* Westport, CT: Bergin & Garvey.

Schaller, S. (1991). *A man without words*. New York: Summit.

Scott, R. (1969). *The making of blind men: A study of adult socialization*. New York: Russell Sage Foundation.

Sidransky, R. (1990). *In silence: Growing up in a deaf world*. New York: St. Martin's Press.

Sienkiewicz-Mercer, R., & Kaplan, S. B. (1989). *I raise my eyes to say yes*. Boston: Houghton Mifflin.

Vermeij, G. (1997). *Privileged hands: A scientific life*. New York: Freeman.

Wright, D. (1994). *Deafness: An autobiography*. New York: Harper Collins.

Zola, I. K. (1982). *Missing pieces: A chronicle of living with a disability*. Philadelphia: Temple University.

Acceptance of Disability Scale

READ EACH STATEMENT AND PUT AN "X" IN THE SPACE INDICATING HOW MUCH YOU AGREE OR DISAGREE WITH EACH STATEMENT.

1. A physical disability may limit a person in some ways, but this does not mean he or she should give up and do nothing with his or her life.
   ___I disagree very much   ___I agree a little
   ___I disagree pretty much   ___I agree pretty much
   ___I disagree a little   ___I agree very much

2. Because of my disability, I feel miserable much of the time.
   ___I disagree very much   ___I agree a little
   ___I disagree pretty much   ___I agree pretty much
   ___I disagree a little   ___I agree very much

3. More than anything else, I wish I didn't have this disability.
   ___I disagree very much   ___I agree a little
   ___I disagree pretty much   ___I agree pretty much
   ___I disagree a little   ___I agree very much

4. Disability or not, I'm going to make good in life.
   ___I disagree very much   ___I agree a little
   ___I disagree pretty much   ___I agree pretty much
   ___I disagree a little   ___I agree very much

5. Good physical appearance and physical ability are the most important things in life.
   ___I disagree very much   ___I agree a little
   ___I disagree pretty much   ___I agree pretty much
   ___I disagree a little   ___I agree very much

6. My disability prevents me from doing just about everything I really want to do and from becoming the kind of person I want to be.
   ___I disagree very much   ___I agree a little
   ___I disagree pretty much   ___I agree pretty much
   ___I disagree a little   ___I agree very much

Source: Courtesy of Donald C. Linkowski, PhD, CRC.

7. I can see the progress I am making in rehabilitation, and it makes me feel like an adequate person in spite of the limitations of my disability.
   ___I disagree very much   ___I agree a little
   ___I disagree pretty much   ___I agree pretty much
   ___I disagree a little   ___I agree very much

8. It makes me feel very bad to see all the things nondisabled people can do which I cannot.
   ___I disagree very much   ___I agree a little
   ___I disagree pretty much   ___I agree pretty much
   ___I disagree a little   ___I agree very much

9. My disability affects those aspects of life which I care most about.
   ___I disagree very much   ___I agree a little
   ___I disagree pretty much   ___I agree pretty much
   ___I disagree a little   ___I agree very much

10. Though I am disabled, my life is full.
   ___I disagree very much   ___I agree a little
   ___I disagree pretty much   ___I agree pretty much
   ___I disagree a little   ___I agree very much

11. If a person is not entirely physically able, he or she is that much less a person.
   ___I disagree very much   ___I agree a little
   ___I disagree pretty much   ___I agree pretty much
   ___I disagree a little   ___I agree very much

12. A person with a disability is restricted in certain ways, but there is still much he or she is able to do.
   ___I disagree very much   ___I agree a little
   ___I disagree pretty much   ___I agree pretty much
   ___I disagree a little   ___I agree very much

13. There are many more important things in life than physical ability and appearance.
   ___I disagree very much   ___I agree a little
   ___I disagree pretty much   ___I agree pretty much
   ___I disagree a little   ___I agree very much

14. There are times I completely forget that I am physically disabled.
   ___I disagree very much   ___I agree a little
   ___I disagree pretty much   ___I agree pretty much
   ___I disagree a little   ___I agree very much

15. You need a good and whole body to have a good mind.
   ___I disagree very much   ___I agree a little
   ___I disagree pretty much   ___I agree pretty much
   ___I disagree a little   ___I agree very much

16. There are many things a person with my disability is able to do.
    ___I disagree very much   ___I agree a little
    ___I disagree pretty much   ___I agree pretty much
    ___I disagree a little   ___I agree very much

17. Since my disability interferes with just about everything I try to do, it is foremost in my mind practically all the time.
    ___I disagree very much   ___I agree a little
    ___I disagree pretty much   ___I agree pretty much
    ___I disagree a little   ___I agree very much

18. If I didn't have my disability, I think I would be a much better person.
    ___I disagree very much   ___I agree a little
    ___I disagree pretty much   ___I agree pretty much
    ___I disagree a little   ___I agree very much

19. My disability, in itself, affects me more than any other characteristic about me.
    ___I disagree very much   ___I agree a little
    ___I disagree pretty much   ___I agree pretty much
    ___I disagree a little   ___I agree very much

20. The kind of person I am and my accomplishments in life are less important than those of nondisabled persons.
    ___I disagree very much   ___I agree a little
    ___I disagree pretty much   ___I agree pretty much
    ___I disagree a little   ___I agree very much

21. I know what I can't do because of my disability, and I feel that I can live a full and normal life.
    ___I disagree very much   ___I agree a little
    ___I disagree pretty much   ___I agree pretty much
    ___I disagree a little   ___I agree very much

22. Though I can see the progress I am making in rehabilitation, this is not very important since I can never be normal.
    ___I disagree very much   ___I agree a little
    ___I disagree pretty much   ___I agree pretty much
    ___I disagree a little   ___I agree very much

23. In just about everything, my disability is annoying to me so that I can't enjoy anything.
    ___I disagree very much   ___I agree a little
    ___I disagree pretty much   ___I agree pretty much
    ___I disagree a little   ___I agree very much

24. How a person conducts himself or herself in life is much more important than physical appearance and ability.
    ___I disagree very much   ___I agree a little
    ___I disagree pretty much   ___I agree pretty much
    ___I disagree a little   ___I agree very much

25. A person with my disability is unable to enjoy very much in life.
    ___I disagree very much   ___I agree a little
    ___I disagree pretty much   ___I agree pretty much
    ___I disagree a little   ___I agree very much

26. The most important thing in this world is to be physically normal.
    ___I disagree very much   ___I agree a little
    ___I disagree pretty much   ___I agree pretty much
    ___I disagree a little   ___I agree very much

27. A person with a disability finds it especially difficult to expand his or her interests and range of abilities.
    ___I disagree very much   ___I agree a little
    ___I disagree pretty much   ___I agree pretty much
    ___I disagree a little   ___I agree very much

28. I believe that physical wholeness and appearance make a person what he or she is.
    ___I disagree very much   ___I agree a little
    ___I disagree pretty much   ___I agree pretty much
    ___I disagree a little   ___I agree very much

29. A physical disability affects a person's mental ability.
    ___I disagree very much   ___I agree a little
    ___I disagree pretty much   ___I agree pretty much
    ___I disagree a little   ___I agree very much

30. With my condition, I know just what I can and cannot do.
    ___I disagree very much   ___I agree a little
    ___I disagree pretty much   ___I agree pretty much
    ___I disagree a little   ___I agree very much

31. Almost every area of life is closed to me because of my disability.
    ___I disagree very much   ___I agree a little
    ___I disagree pretty much   ___I agree pretty much
    ___I disagree a little   ___I agree very much

32. Because of my disability, I have little to offer other people.
    ___I disagree very much   ___I agree a little
    ___I disagree pretty much   ___I agree pretty much
    ___I disagree a little   ___I agree very much

33. Besides the many physical things I am unable to do, there are many other things I am unable to do.
    ___I disagree very much   ___I agree a little
    ___I disagree pretty much   ___I agree pretty much
    ___I disagree a little   ___I agree very much

34. Personal characteristics such as honesty and a willingness to work hard are much more important than physical appearance and ability.
    ___I disagree very much   ___I agree a little
    ___I disagree pretty much   ___I agree pretty much
    ___I disagree a little   ___I agree very much

35. I get very annoyed with the way some people offer to help me.
___I disagree very much   ___I agree a little
___I disagree pretty much   ___I agree pretty much
___I disagree a little   ___I agree very much

36. With my disability, there isn't a single area of life that is not affected in some major way.
___I disagree very much   ___I agree a little
___I disagree pretty much   ___I agree pretty much
___I disagree a little   ___I agree very much

37. Though I can see that disabled people are able to do well in many ways, still they can never lead normal lives.
___I disagree very much   ___I agree a little
___I disagree pretty much   ___I agree pretty much
___I disagree a little   ___I agree very much

38. A disability, such as mine, is the worst possible thing that can happen to a person.
___I disagree very much   ___I agree a little
___I disagree pretty much   ___I agree pretty much
___I disagree a little   ___I agree very much

39. No matter how hard I try or what I accomplish, I could never be as good a person as one without my disability.
___I disagree very much   ___I agree a little
___I disagree pretty much   ___I agree pretty much
___I disagree a little   ___I agree very much

40. There is practically nothing a person in my condition is able to do and really enjoy it.
___I disagree very much   ___I agree a little
___I disagree pretty much   ___I agree pretty much
___I disagree a little   ___I agree very much

41. Because of my disability, I am unable to enjoy social relationships as much as I could if I were not disabled.
___I disagree very much   ___I agree a little
___I disagree pretty much   ___I agree pretty much
___I disagree a little   ___I agree very much

42. There are more important things in life than those my physical disability prevents me from doing.
___I disagree very much   ___I agree a little
___I disagree pretty much   ___I agree pretty much
___I disagree a little   ___I agree very much

43. I want very much to do things that my disability prevents me from doing.
___I disagree very much   ___I agree a little
___I disagree pretty much   ___I agree pretty much
___I disagree a little   ___I agree very much

44. Because of my disability, other people's lives have more meaning than my own.
    ___I disagree very much   ___I agree a little
    ___I disagree pretty much   ___I agree pretty much
    ___I disagree a little   ___I agree very much

45. Oftentimes, when I think of my disability, it makes me feel so sad and upset that I am unable to think of or do anything else.
    ___I disagree very much   ___I agree a little
    ___I disagree pretty much   ___I agree pretty much
    ___I disagree a little   ___I agree very much

46. A disability changes one's life completely. It causes one to think differently about everything.
    ___I disagree very much   ___I agree a little
    ___I disagree pretty much   ___I agree pretty much
    ___I disagree a little   ___I agree very much

47. I feel that I should be as able as the next person, even in areas where my disability prevents me.
    ___I disagree very much   ___I agree a little
    ___I disagree pretty much   ___I agree pretty much
    ___I disagree a little   ___I agree very much

48. Life is full of so many things that I sometimes forget for brief periods of time that I am disabled.
    ___I disagree very much   ___I agree a little
    ___I disagree pretty much   ___I agree pretty much
    ___I disagree a little   ___I agree very much

49. Because of my disability, I can never do most things that normal people can do.
    ___I disagree very much   ___I agree a little
    ___I disagree pretty much   ___I agree pretty much
    ___I disagree a little   ___I agree very much

50. I feel satisfied with my abilities, and my disability doesn't bother me too much.
    ___I disagree very much   ___I agree a little
    ___I disagree pretty much   ___I agree pretty much
    ___I disagree a little   ___I agree very much

Chapter 8

The Onset and Diagnosis
of the Disability

▶ Why is psychoeducation often therapeutic?
▶ Do you agree that parental response to a baby with a congenital disability is often not validated by society?
▶ What are low incidence disabilities?
▶ What are some of the atypical experiences of children with disabilities?
▶ Do CODAs assume responsibilities beyond their capabilities?
▶ What is prelingual deafness?
▶ Why do many in the Deaf Culture advocate residential schooling for children who are deaf?
▶ Why is the distinction between time of onset and time of diagnosis sometimes important?
▶ For individuals with acquired disabilities, why do their prejudices often become self-identifiers?
▶ Explain this statement: Many disabilities and chronic illnesses of children are low incidence.
▶ Why is the time of onset of schizophrenia so disabling?
▶ Why is the role of women traditionally one of "caring for vulnerable people"?
▶ Why have few rehabilitation services been provided for elderly people with disabilities?
▶ Why is old age itself often considered to be a disability?
▶ Why do elderly people often respond positively to the onset of the disability?
▶ What are the differences between insidious onset disabilities and acute onset disabilities?
▶ What is the impact on the individual of a long prediagnosis period?

FACTORS THAT AFFECT THE IMPACT OF THE ONSET OF DISABILITY

In this section, look for—

▶ *the three broad categories of variables that impact the individual's response/adaptation to disability*
1. *Factors in the disability*
2. *Factors in the environment*
3. *Factors in the individual*

Carolyn Vash (1981), a disability scholar, constructed a model that assists in understanding the factors (or variables) that impact an individual's response to a disability. The broad categories are (1) factors in the disability itself, (2) factors in the environment, and (3) factors in the individual. Factors in the environment include the degree of family support and acceptance (Cook & Ferritor, 1985; Danek, 1988; Danek & Lawrence, 1985; Darling & Baxter, 1996; Eisenberg, Sutkin, & Jansen, 1984; Huberty, 1980; Perlesz, Kinsella, & Crowe, 1999; Power, & Dell Orto, 1980), the availability of self-help and mutual support groups, assistive technology available, the quality of professional services rendered, and the individual's income level. As can be seen, most of these factors in the environment are tangible, measurable elements.

In contrast, factors in the individual are often difficult to measure. These factors include the individual's previous experience with PWDs, the individual's premorbid (before the onset of the disability) coping skills (Affleck, Tennen, Pfeifer, & Fifield, 1987), problem-solving and decision-making abilities, challenge orientation, level of emotional control, cognitive appraisal skills, levels of self-esteem and self-confidence, and, finally, the individual's religious/spiritual/philosophical belief system. Reviewing this list of factors, it can be seen that all of these pose difficulties in measurement and clinical assessment. However, the individual's marital status (PWDs who are married or have a partner usually respond better to a disability), the individual's level of education (PWDs who are highly educated usually respond better to a disability), and the individual's work history and transferability of skills (PWDs who have a long and varied work history usually respond better to a disability) are factors that can be more easily measured and assessed.

This chapter will focus on the onset of the disability itself, including time of onset and type of onset. Below is a listing of all these factors. Each factor will be discussed in some detail in this chapter and in the next chapter. Remember, as we discussed previously, this model is an oversimplification of reality. For example, many PWDs have more than one disability and, furthermore, it is not the disability itself that influences the way in which the individual views the disability; it is the meaning the individual ascribes to the disability. Therefore, each disability is a very idiosyncratic experience and, moreover, there is no one "personality type" associated with a particular disability. Nonetheless, there are some general guidelines in understanding specific types of disabilities. Indeed, knowledge and understanding of specific disabilities and their impact on individuals is one of the main functions of mutual support and self-help groups (Chilman, Nunnally, & Cox, 1988; Goodheart & Lansing, 1997; Kriegsman & Celotta, 1981). In these types of groups, individuals with the same disability (and their families) meet together to discuss all of the factors listed below (Drotar, Crawford, & Bush, 1984). This is what is termed psychoeducation, and psychoeducation alone, just learning about the disability itself from others who have experienced the same disability, is therapeutic (Pearson & Sternberg, 1986; Power & Rogers, 1979). Psychoeducation can do much to eliminate anxiety and ambiguity and create a feeling of universality or the feeling that "someone else is experiencing the same thing I am."

Exhibit 8–1 contains a list of all 10 factors. Two factors will be discussed in this chapter.

Exhibit 8–1

Factors in the disability that influence an individual's response to disability:

1. Time of onset
2. Type of onset
3. Functions impaired
4. Severity of disability
5. Visibility of the disability
6. Degree, if any, of disfigurement
7. Degree of stigma
8. The course of the disability—stable, progressive, episodic
9. Prognosis of the disability
10. Treatment required

TIME OF ONSET

In this section, look for—

▶ *time of onset—congenital or acquired*
▶ *some aspects of congenital disabilities:*
   1. *often involve treatment considerations of the parents and siblings of the PWD*
   2. *the individual has no memory of not having a disability*
   3. *there is no premorbid functioning with which the individual compares himself or herself*
   4. *the parents must make treatment/habilitation choices*
   5. *individuals with congenital disabilities often have atypical childhood experiences*
   6. *society attributes less stigma to congenital disabilities (than to acquired disabilities)*

Basically, the time of onset of a disability is divided into two categories: congenital and acquired. Congenital disabilities are, by definition, those disabilities that exist at or before birth as a result of hereditary or environmental factors. Some disabilities are *only* congenital, such as Down syndrome, muscular dystrophy, cerebral palsy, spina bifida, and achondroplasia (dwarfism) (Batshaw, 1998; Bernbaum & Batshaw, 1998). Other disabilities, such as blindness, deafness, and mental retardation can be either congenital or acquired later in life. You will remember that we learned in Chapter 4 that the type of onset of the disability influences the degree of stigma directed toward the individual. Generally speaking, congenital disabilities elicit less prejudice and stigma than do acquired disabilities. (This lack of stigma may be due to the fact that individuals are usually not held responsible for the cause of a disability with which they are born.) Of course, disabilities acquired for "noble purposes," such as war, are viewed with less stigma than congenital disabilities.

Also, keep in mind that we are discussing "perceived" onset because, in many cases, others do not actually know if the disability is congenital or acquired.

Generally, the earlier the age of onset, the better the response and adjustment (Alfano, Nielsen, & Fink, 1993; Krause, 1992; Krause & Crew, 1991; Schulz & Decker, 1985; Woodrich & Patterson, 1983). While this is not always true, it has been found that, for example, children with congenital limb deficiencies adjust better than children with acquired amputations and children whose diabetes is diagnosed early adapt better than those who are diagnosed with diabetes later in life. This may be due to several factors: (1) the cognitive and affective resiliency and flexibility of children; (2) the fact that there are no premorbid identity or functional losses; (3) children have not internalized society's prejudices and discriminations about disability; and (4) children have not fully developed their body image. Children can be resilient and accepting of disability, able to learn medical self-management technique and other adaptive strategies that are appropriate to their developmental level. For example, using a dialysis machine or hearing aids or putting on a prosthesis, for most children, is not a distressing and emotionally fraught experience. For these children, the adaptive strategies are part of daily living. Also, these children have no nondisability identity. Geri Jewell, a comedienne, explained, "It's not like I wake up every morning and say, 'Oh my goodness, I have cerebral palsy!' I was born like this." Finally, it is safe to say that the older the individual is when he or she acquired the disability, the more he or she has acquired the prejudices, stereotypes, and attitudes of the tragic, limited view of life with a disability. Of course, there are some exceptions to this. For example, individuals who have a family member with a disability would have a more accurate view of life with a disability. In addition, a child with a disability will not confront, on a daily basis, all the prejudices and discrimination against disabilities until he or she enters school.

PARENTS OF CHILDREN WITH CONGENITAL DISABILITIES

In this section, look for—

▶ *how knowledge or perception of the cause of the disability is very important in determining how the family deals with the disability*

When a baby is born with a congenital disability, it is the parents who respond/adjust to the disability (Lindenberg, 1980; Olshansky, 1962; Patterson, 1988; Powers, 1993). Often, the parents grieve over the loss of the baby that they had imagined, the baby without a disability (Collins-Moore, 1984; Featherstone, 1980; Mitsos, 1972). At the same time, parents are grieving for the "loss of one baby," they must care for and provide treatment for the "baby that remains" (Powers, 1993, p. 121). Furthermore, although the onset/diagnosis of the disability occurred at the time of birth (or before), the symptoms, manifestations, or medical crises that occur later may create additional losses for the parents. Often, the unpredictability of the course of the disability, or even the prospect of the baby's death, makes the response/adjusting process difficult and unpredictable for parents and siblings (Frantz, 1981). As we learned in Chapter 1, there are more congenital disabilities than ever before because of the advances in neonatal medicine. Many adults with disabilities report that the doctors, and their parents, did not expect them to live (when they were infants) and, moreover, doctors were not quite sure of the type of medical treatment to provide for them (Knoll, 1992, 1996). In addition, many adolescents who had congenital disabilities or acquired disabilities early in life were not provided with either sex education or career counseling/exploration services because no one thought these children would survive to adulthood. Therefore, both sex education and career counseling were considered to be irrelevant for these teenagers (Ireys & Burr, 1984). However, many did (and do) survive to adulthood.

As we discussed in Chapter 7, there is a stage theory of response/adaptation to disability. The stage theory holds that there are predictable, "normal" stages of responding; however, the stage theory is most often thought of in terms of the individual who is experiencing the disability. In the case of congenital disabilities, nonetheless, the parents and siblings (and perhaps grandparents) progress through these stages (Austin, 1990; Damrosch & Perry, 1989; Sutkin, 1984). Parental response/adaptation to a congenital disability in their baby is often not validated or even "normed" by society. That is to say, others, such as relatives or neighbors, may not understand the grief, anger, or questioning experienced by the parents (Harper, 1999; Singer & Irvin, 1989; Singer, Powers, & Olson, 1996). Reread the letter from "Grateful Mom in Buffalo" in Chapter 6.

Parental guilt plays a role in the adjustment/adaptation response (Downey, Silver, & Wortman, 1990; Heller, Rafman, Zvagulis, & Pless, 1985). You will remember that in Chapter 7, we learned that many PWDs engage in self-blame and guilt for the onset of the disability (Young, 1974). With congenital disabilities, it is the parents who attribute the cause of the disability to something they did or did not do (Nixon, 1993). Often, parents, especially mothers, feel responsible for the disability. One father did not assist his wife in caring for their newborn baby with a disability because he held his wife responsible for the baby's disability (Nixon, 1993). Genetically based disabilities elicit guilt in both the mother and the father. Friends and neighbors may ask what the mother did or did not do during the pregnancy; thus, unintentionally blaming the mother for the disability. Parents also blame themselves when they are not able to "help" the child (Cummings, 1976). The role of a parent is to protect the helpless infant, and when a baby is born with a disability, the parents may feel that they failed to protect the child from harm. Often, parents feel directly or indirectly blamed by medical professionals, either for the cause of their child's disability or for the management of their child's disability (Wasow & Wikler, 1983). We also learned that self-blame is the price some individuals pay for devising an etiology for the disability. Rather than viewing the infant's disability as a random event, parents blame themselves and thus alleviate the stress of an unknown etiology. Parents can blame each other and, in so doing, place stress on the marital relationship with comments such as "This came from your side of the family." Older brothers and sisters often think that they "did" (or did not do) something to cause the disability. The "superparent" ideals of doing everything possible for the child and/or of being 100 percent responsible for the child often lead to parental guilt when these unrealistic and self-imposed expectations cannot be met.

Families who have an infant with a congenital disability must deal with all the typical family demands, and at the same time begin to negotiate a host of disability-related concerns (Singer & Powers, 1993; Turnbull & Turnbull, 1991). Parents must learn about the disability itself and must also learn to deal with a complex medical system. These parents are faced with a staggering amount of technical and medical information (Spaniol, Zipple, & Fitzgerald, 1985). Further, some of the information and treatment recommendations are contradictory. For the first time for many families, they are required to contact and elicit the assistance of governmental agencies (Summers, Behr, & Turnbull, 1989). Simply moving through the medical and legal service systems can be bewildering. The parents are faced with these changes and tasks, while experiencing the shock and grief many experience at the birth of a child with a disability (Head, Head, & Head, 1985; Rolland, 1994). In addition, many of their familiar social supports may have disappeared (Dell Orto, 1988). Friends and relatives often distance themselves from the parents who have a child with a disability; therefore, exactly when the parents need support, stability, and instrumental assistance, they slowly begin to understand that their familial and social networks are no longer there (Santelli, Turnbull, Lerner, & Marquis, 1993). Often, the parents are sleep-deprived and/or have just finished a physically stressful pregnancy. In addition, there may be older siblings that require care and support in their adjustment process (Graliker, Fishler, & Koch, 1962; Keydel, 1988). Often, one of the parents (usually the mother) must quit his or her job in order to provide care to the infant, further straining the family's financial status. Many parents feel overwhelmed (Fewell, 1986; Pearson & Sternberg, 1986).

One mother told of her experience, "There are heavy demands for a highly functional, two-parent family that is financially stable. However, many families that have children with disabilities do not enjoy these advantages. The increasing number of single parents (most often, mothers) and the mobility of the U.S. population make it far more common for the family of a child with a congenital disability to be a single mother without extended family nearby."

Another mother (Miller, 1988) did not feel that she experienced the "typical" stages of adjustment, "I had read many times about the grief surrounding the birth of a child with defects, but the literature had not seemed to apply to me. My life certainly included denial, anger, bargaining, depression, and acceptance. But for me these were not milestones on a timeline, but were aspects of every day, sometimes every hour. Furthermore, there was little grief attached to the "expected baby." The grief was tied up with the whole mental picture I had for myself, my family, and our future. Feeling I had failed myself, Kurt [her husband], Beth [the baby], the family, and even society itself, what I really had lost was my whole sense of self-esteem" (p. 145).

Parents often must make decisions concerning medical care, living arrangements, and the type of education for their child with a disability, all of which have long-range ramifications for both the child and the family (Greenberg, 1980). For many community services, such as schools, children with severe congenital disabilities are "peripheral" to their basic mission (Sailor, Kleinhammer-Tramill, Skrtic, & Oas, 1996, p. 329) or insurance policies may not pay for noninstitutional care or the prevailing professional opinion advocates a certain type of treatment or education. Faced with an array of needs, a complicated structure of services and payment requirements, parents make decisions. And occasionally, as would be expected, these children grow up and later question or resent the decisions made by the parent(s). Remember the man in the video *My Body Is Not Who I Am* who stated, "I resented my parents jumping at the requests of the doctors." This man had undergone many "corrective" surgeries during his childhood. Today, there are elderly parents with middle-aged children who have been in institutions for decades. These parents feel themselves unjustly maligned when they are asked why they allowed their children to "be put into an institution." These parents remind us that when their children were born, there were no special education classes in the neighborhood schools, no home nursing care, no respite care, nor the array of community and home services available today. Moreover, if the disability was/is a low-incidence disability, such as deaf–blindness, there were (and are) still fewer services. For example, if the parents live in a rural area and their child has a severe disability, the physician may have no experience in treating people with this disability. In sum, these parents felt they had no choice.

Couser (1997) stated, "The prevailing norms of the modern American family presume the absence of a disability" (p. 252). For example, most television comedies or dramas that feature families do not show families that have a member with a disability. Television programs portray families with gay parents, biracial families, and single parent families. This makes sense because these types of families are representative of typical American life and viewers can relate to these imaginary TV families. Nonetheless, there are few, if any, families on television who have a member with a disability.

Not all families are Euro-American and middle-class (Brown, 1997). Westbrook and Legge (1993) conducted a study in Australia that provides a glimpse of the difference in familial coping with children with disabilities. Westbrook and Legge sought to learn the perceptions and attitudes of families toward children with disabilities because, as they stated, "The family's perception of the cause and meaning of the disability is communicated to the child and also influences the experiences which are provided for the child and the life roles that he or she is expected to achieve" (p. 176). The researchers studied six communities in Australia, labeling two of the communities "individualistic" and four of the communities "collectivistic." The collectivistic communities were the Arab, Chinese, Greek, and Italian groups, and the individualistic communities were Anglo-Australian and German groups. Westbrook and Legge found

> In all four collectivistic communities, there were significant differences [when compared with the individualistic communities] in believing that it is a greater tragedy to have a son with a disability and that it is desirable to conceal the existence of a child with a disability. However, they considered that such a child places less strain on the parents' marriage than do Anglo-Australians. Giving birth to a disabled [*sic*] child was considered more shameful in the Greek and Chinese communities. In these and the Arabic communities there was a stronger belief that disability in a family reduces relatives' marital chances (p. 183).

> There was significantly less expectation within the Italian, Greek, Arabic, and Chinese communities that children with disabilities would attend school, accompany their families on social outings, or behave like other children (p. 182).

This is a single study, and as the authors themselves concluded, there are few studies that seek to examine cultural differences in family attitudes toward children with disabilities. Nonetheless, the questions they asked merit consideration because questions such as these underscore the importance of considering the family's cultural values before automatically assuming that the family responds to the child with a disability in the same way that Euro-American, middle-class families do.

ATYPICAL CHILDHOOD EXPERIENCES

In this section, look for—

▶ *how atypical childhood experiences of individuals with congenital disabilities may include:*
1. *prolonged hospitalizations*
2. *early socialization into the role of patient*
3. *overprotection*
4. *relaxation of discipline*
5. *a large number of adults with whom to relate*
6. *abuse, neglect, and abandonment*

Individuals with some types of congenital disabilities often have atypical childhood experiences. Repeated hospitalizations, frequent surgeries and other types of medical treatments, and, occasionally, residential schooling are experiences that children with certain types of congenital disabilities (and disabilities acquired early in life) undergo. Thus, the infant or young child is completely socialized into the role of patient. These are not the typical childhood experiences; however, as the child is experiencing many of them, he or she is often not aware that his or her life is unusual. Nonetheless, most adults with congenital disabilities view their childhoods, in retrospect, as unique and different from the experiences of most children. Children without disabilities usually have very little contact with physicians. In contrast, children with disabilities are thoroughly socialized into the world of medical professionals.

One of the most commonly reported experiences of children with congenital disabilities is the overprotection of their mothers. Linda Pelletier, a woman with cerebral palsy, told of two experiences of overprotection. The first is somewhat humorous. "One of the complications of this birth trauma was that I was more susceptible to respiratory infection...[my mother] was afraid to allow me to go outdoors for fear of my getting a chill....One of my most vivid recollections is going to see fireworks on the Fourth of July. I was sitting in a car with the windows rolled up, wearing ski pants, thermal underwear, and a winter coat. I became nauseous and almost fainted before the fireworks were even over" (Pelletier, 1988, p. 55).

In contrast, Ms. Pelletier labels her mother's overprotectiveness as "destructive" in the second description.

> My mother's overprotection was also a destructive element in my development. She assumed complete care of all of my physical needs. This meant that I was lifted in and out of bed, onto the toilet, and in and out of our car. I was bathed, dressed, groomed and fed without my lifting a finger to help myself. I realize now that it would have been extremely difficult for her to sit by passively and watch me struggle to perform these basic activities of daily living. Although my mother meant well by catering to me in this way, it retarded my physical development because I was never given the opportunity to work on doing these essential tasks. Such a relationship caused me to be completely dependent upon my parents (Pelletier, 1988, p. 58).

Often, children with congenital disabilities are not disciplined or standards of behavior are lowered for them. Parents, caregivers, and teachers often tolerate inappropriate behavior, explaining they don't "have the heart" to discipline children with disabilities. Remember, this is related to the concept of sympathy and pity for PWDs or "let's give these poor PWDs a break" that we discussed earlier. Read the following statement in which a young child begins to suspect that he is sick when the discipline is relaxed. "I know I'm very sick...because everyone treats me differently. Before I became ill, my parents never let me get away with bad behavior. Now, I can even hit my little sister without being punished" (Whitt, 1984, p. 77).

Overprotection and relaxation of discipline can result in a lack of mastery, competence, and self-confidence, and can often isolate the child. Those behaviors and attitudes, begun in earliest infancy, often continue until the individual reaches adulthood. Thus, often children with congenital disabilities are needlessly handicapped.

One clearcut exception is the case of children with learning disabilities (LD) and/or attention deficit disorder (usually boys) who are overpunished. Parents, relatives, and teachers attribute their inability to focus, sit still, control impulses, complete tasks on time, and respond to multiple requests at one time, as defiance and willful lack of cooperation. Due to misunderstanding or lack of a diagnosis, these children are subjected to a great deal of punishment and negative feedback. Indeed, many experts on LD attribute the high rate of school dropout for children with LD to be due to their wish to escape the punishment and humiliation of school.

Abuse and Neglect of Children with Congenital Disabilities

Parental depression and/or caregiver stress can lead to abuse or neglect of the infant or child with a congenital disability. Stressors that are thought to lead to abuse and neglect include: "(1) Regular loss of sleep because of caregiving demands, (2) the child's severe medical problems, (3) the child's severe behavior problems, (4) the child's unusual appearance, and (5) adversity in the family combined with caregiving responsibilities" (Singer, 1996, p. 25). Obviously, the more support the parents have in providing care for an infant, the smaller the probability of abuse and neglect occurring. Such support includes linking parents with self-help groups in which they can meet with "veteran" parents who have a child with the same type of disability, providing respite care, in-home health care for complicated medical procedures, financial subsidies, and supportive counseling. Two generations ago, all these types of support were usually provided by extended family members. With the changing demographics of America, such as divorce and geographic mobility, these types of support are now provided by professional caregivers.

A Large Number of Adults with Whom To Relate

Simply due to the fact that the world of medical care is populated by adults, many children with congenital disabilities are in the care of a large number of different adults. Children probably do not form long-term relationships with many, if not most, of these caregivers because (1) there are too many of these caregivers, (2) these relationships are often transient in nature, (3) the caregivers must obey hospital and agency rules, and (4) most caregivers are motivated by pay. A secretary at a residential school for children who are deaf reported, "They have so many people to relate to. They go to bed with one houseparent and wake up with another one, and then numerous adults engage them all day long, they must deal with various administrators and different security officers throughout their lives here...." (Evans & Falk, 1986, p. 100).

There are risks for children who are exposed to a great many adults, including: (1) the lack of ability to develop healthy reciprocal, empathic feelings (attachment bonds) and (2) vulnerability to physical and/or sexual abuse. Rutter (1989) found that young children in institutions/hospitals typically encounter 50–80 caregivers before reaching school age.

Remember the woman in the PBS video "Polio" who told of a night in the hospital when she was a little girl with polio. The little girl was crying because she was homesick and missed her family. The nurse came in and told her if she did not stop crying, she would unplug her respirator. The little girl stopped crying that night; but she wept, as an adult, when she recounted the experience. When an adult is exposed to many different caregivers, he or she usually has the ability to question and challenge the treatment or the lack of treatment. However, children with disabilities are powerless and must submit to adults. Indeed, many adults report that it is only in retrospect that they understand the power that adult caregivers wielded over them when they were children.

The child who lives at home and attends community schools has daily reminders that, because of the disability, he or she is different from other children. Medical treatments, assistive devices, and doctors' appointments serve to remind the child that he or she is different. If the course of the disability is episodic and/or life threatening, medical treatments can be unexpected emergencies that require aggressive treatment. At these points, the child understands that hospitalization/treatment is more important than school attendance.

Children with disabilities are at risk for emotional maladaptation including behavioral problems, low self-esteem, and poor resolution of developmental tasks (Breslau, 1982; Breslau & Marshall, 1985; Heller, et al., 1985). These researchers found that (1) central nervous system involvement in the disability (i.e., mental retardation) was associated with greater psychosocial problems; and (2) the family's coping responses impact the child's response.

HEARING CHILDREN OF PARENTS WHO ARE DEAF

> *In this section, look for—*
>
> ▶ *Children of Deaf Adults (CODAs)*
>   *1. how hearing children of parents who are deaf act as interpreters*
>   *2. the argument that CODAs find themselves "caught" between the Deaf world and the hearing world*
>   *3. how some CODAs feel that they have been "deprived" of a "normal" childhood*

There is another situation in which a disability is present from the individual's birth; however, the disability is not the individual's disability, but rather the disability of his or her parents. Children of deaf adults (CODAs) are children who are born hearing to two parents who are both deaf. Naturally, the CODAs grow up bilingual, learning both sign language and spoken language. CODAs, unlike parents of deaf children, assume that Deafness is "normal," have a way in which to communicate with their parents, and do not feel that their parents should try to enter the hearing world. (In contrast, hearing parents of a child who is deaf assume that deafness is an abnormality and deficit and have no way in which to communicate with their child because not all hearing parents learn sign language, and they want their child to become part of the hearing world.)

One child in the family, usually the oldest daughter, assumes the role of "designated interpreter." Thus, it can be seen that age is an important factor in choosing the designated interpreter, but gender is even more important (it is the oldest *female* child, even when there is an older son). The role of the designated interpreter requires sacrifice and the need to consider the parents' needs, often before his or her own needs. On the other hand, the role of the designated interpreter offers power not usually accorded to children (Couser, 1997). Because CODAs must speak for their parents, they are required to assume adultlike roles in assisting their parents in dealing with the adult hearing world, often when these CODAs are very young children. Many CODAs, in retrospect, view the responsibilities they assumed as children as beyond their capabilities. Paul Preston wrote a book entitled, *Mother Father Deaf: Living Between Sound and Silence* (1994). Preston described the power and responsibility of being a CODA, "Although the negative associations of diminished identity and status were true for several women and men, a few other informants stressed that interpreting provided them with a much greater degree of visibility and control....Rather than being a passive and objective translation, interpreting could be understood as authoritative and dynamic cultural brokering" (p. 102).

Ruth Sidransky spoke of "never quite fitting into either [the Deaf world or the hearing world], never knowing who I was" (p. 95). In her book, *In Silence: Growing Up Hearing in a Deaf World* (1990), Sidransky related her own experience and that of other CODAs. Note her use of such words as "sucked into," "buried," and "invisible."

> There were those of us who were sucked into a silence we carried with us always. There were those of us defiantly proud of our parents yet secretly ashamed of their garish sounds. There were those of us who, as soon as we were able, left home and abandoned our parents to grow old alone in withering silence. There were those of us who ignored our deaf parents, never quite learning to sign well enough to tell them what was in our hearts and minds. There were those of us who deliberately turned our heads when our parents raised their arms and hands to speak to us. And there were those of us who loved our parents with passion. We were the ones who buried the silence within. We abandoned our dreams and took care of our deaf mothers and fathers. They were our children, and we were their parents. We, the children, were invisible (p. 96).

Lou Ann Walker, a CODA, wrote about her embarrassment of her parents' writing. Notice that she is in third grade and correcting her parents' written English. She wrote, "Mom and Dad's sentences sounded as if a foreigner had written them, as if English weren't their native tongue at all—and of course, it wasn't really. Still, I was to find out later their writing was far superior to most done by deaf adults—even deaf college graduates. Back then, a proud and self-conscious third grader correcting her parents' letters, I was filled with a mixture of pleasure and embarrassment—pleasure because I was useful to my parents, embarrassment because they couldn't do what I thought all other parents did with ease" (1986, p. 81).

CODAs protect their parents from the hearing world. Couser (1997) summarized Walker's feelings about protecting her parents. "On the one hand, she takes pride in her competence as a mediator and in her ability to shield her vulnerable parents from thoughtless and sometimes hostile hearing people. She is candid about the quite literal 'gaze' of the hearing world....On the other hand, she makes clear the cost of providing such protection. When she censors, rather than passes on, rude remarks from hearing people, she becomes the receptacle of animosity directed at her parents; she contains both the hostility of the hearing world and the resentment it stirs in her. So, in interpreting for her parents, she absorbs much of the friction between the worlds" (p. 254).

CODAs often feel that they have been deprived of a normal childhood, a childhood in which parents protect children. Ruth Sidransky wrote of how her own needs were denied: "I didn't dare hear myself. It meant breaking an unforgivable taboo; to hear myself could only diminish my capacities to hear others who needed me. My mother said, 'I am helpless.' My father said, 'Take care of us.' I did not ask, 'Who will take care of me?' I was alone, walled in their silence and mine. Incommunicado. Blank" (p. 153).

Sidransky also wrote: "I did not recognize that this...was an abuse of my childhood. No one was to blame for this abuse. It was simply so" (p. 243). Other CODAs feel that they have had an advantaged childhood because they have grown up bilingual and bicultural, and learned to empathize with others (Filer & Filer, 2000). Nonetheless, most CODAs deal with two conflicting sets of identity: (1) deaf and hearing and (2) parent to his or her parents and child to his or her parents. Support groups for CODAs help them to sort these issues out (Preston, 1994). Regardless of how they view their childhood or the way in which they established their identities, CODAs are a unique group of individuals. Indeed, there is "coda-talk," a combination of spoken English and sign language, reflecting the bilingual language heritage of CODAs. The use of coda-talk is controversial, some CODAs feeling that it trivializes sign language. However, those CODAs who do use coda-talk consider it to be (1) in-group communication, (2) identity reinforcement, and (3) self-help.

PRELINGUAL DEAFNESS

In this section look for—
- ▶ *prelingual deafness*
  1. *individual does not have speech abilities*
  2. *individual does not have a memory of sound or language*
- ▶ *differences between a deaf child born to hearing parents and a deaf child born to deaf parents*

Time of onset is an important factor in deafness; however, time of onset is not thought of as either congenital or acquired, but rather as prelingual deafness or postlingual deafness. Prelingual deafness refers to deafness acquired before the development of speech and postlingual deafness refers to deafness acquired after the development of speech. (Of course, prelingual deafness can also be congenital deafness.) An example of an individual with prelingual deafness was Helen Keller. She was not born deaf or blind, but at the age of 19 months she developed what was then called "brain fever." Most physicians today think that the baby Helen Keller either had scarlet fever or meningitis. After her recovery, she was both deaf and blind with few, if any, memories of vision or hearing.

The earlier in life a child acquires deafness, the more likely he or she is to identify with the Deaf Culture. Gershon (1994, cited in Edwards, 1997) used the term "permanent exile" to describe all people who are deaf because they are exiled from the hearing world and used the term "immigrant" to describe individuals who become deaf later in life. These individuals are immigrants to the Deaf Culture because "they never lose their hearing accent." Those who grow up deaf are natives in the Deaf Culture (Edwards, 1997, p. 42).

Individuals with prelingual deafness have no memory of sound, language, or of being able to hear and to speak. Congenital deafness also involves another element that most congenital disabilities do not—whether or not the parents are also deaf. Harlan Lane (1996) describes the reaction of parents who are deaf to the birth of a deaf child: "In general...many members of the DEAF-WORLD would prefer to have a Deaf child to having a hearing child, those whose happiness at the advent of a Deaf child is tinged with sadness (after all, that child will face many extra challenges) commonly overcome their reservations quickly. If you belong to a hearing culture, you may find such Deaf preferences hard to understand" (pp. 24–25).

Lane explains why parents who are deaf often want deaf children:

> The birth of a Deaf baby in a Deaf household signifies that the Deaf heritage of the family will be secure. Deaf families with many Deaf members are commonly proud of their genealogy.
>
> In other words, when a Deaf infant of Deaf parents is diagnosed as Deaf, the joy of the parents reflects the fact that most Deaf parents, like parents generally, look forward to having children who are a reflection of themselves....Deaf parents bring their Deaf baby home to a nurturing environment in which communication is naturally dependent on visual, not aural (hearing) cues. Almost all use the signed language of the DEAF-WORLD to interact with their child. Their home is already functioning as an environment conducive to using vision as the main means of learning and communication....Like the hearing child born to a well-functioning hearing family, the Deaf infant in a Deaf family...is immediately exposed to a world suited to maximizing his or her social, emotional, psychological, cognitive, and linguistic development (pp. 25–26).

Some couples in which both partners are deaf have undergone genetic testing when they are expecting a baby to ascertain the "risk" of having a hearing infant (Mackelprang & Salsgiver, 1999). Deaf parents of a baby who is deaf realize that their baby's physician and other medical care providers view the deafness as a negative and as a condition which must be ameliorated as quickly as possible. Many parents who are deaf appreciate the concern of the physician, but resist the physician's attempts to pathologize the deafness of their baby or to subject the baby to hearing aids and other prostheses. Obviously the physicians often view disability from the medical model and deaf parents of children who are deaf view it from the environmental model.

However, most children who are deaf, whether the time of onset is congenital, prelingual, or postlingual, are children of hearing parents. Indeed, 80 percent of all congenitally deaf babies are born to hearing parents, and further, the diagnosis of deafness usually occurs months or years after birth. Most often, the child is isolated within his or her own family because of the lack of communication. Both the parents and the child are frustrated.

People who are deaf, like most PWDs, have been handicapped by medical and educational professionals who have advocated treatment and education that have not been in their best interests. Nonetheless, the Deaf have been subjected to more professional misjudgment, paternalism, and control than any other disability group. For example, for years, most educators of the Deaf (who usually were not deaf themselves) advocated the oralism method in which children were not allowed to use sign language and instead were required to speak. (Alexander Graham Bell was the most famous advocate of oralism.) Oralism was impossible for many and, for most children who were deaf, oralism provided years of frustration and failure. At the same time, these children were not allowed to learn and use sign language. (In some schools, children were required to go sit on their hands or had their hands tied, so they could not use their hands to sign.) Lip reading was taught, in spite of the fact that lip reading is not very accurate. Training/educating children who were deaf in oralism and lip reading were attempts to reduce discomfort in people without disabilities and force the Deaf to fit into a hearing world, without making any demands upon the hearing world. In so doing, children who were deaf were deprived of a language and a culture. Today, the Deaf Culture actively fights against these types of attempts by hearing physicians and educators to "make deaf people fit in."

CONGENITAL BLINDNESS OR BLINDNESS ACQUIRED IN INFANCY

In this section, look for—

▶ *individuals with congenital blindness:*
1. *have no visual experience with concepts such as color, shape, distance, or proportion*
2. *are not able to learn by observation*

People who are born blind or become blind early in life have no visual experiences with concepts such as colors, distance, depth, or proportion. Falvo (1991) explained:

[Individuals who have congenital blindness] because of their lack of visual experience in their environment, such as the observation of tasks or behavior of others, they must learn by other means concepts that sighted individuals often take for granted. This adaptive learning of tasks then becomes a natural part of their developmental process so that the adjustment to visual limitations is incorporated into their self-perception and daily activities as a normal part of growing up. Individuals who lose their vision later in life have the advantage of being able to draw on visual experiences in the environment as a frame of reference for physical concepts, but they may find it more difficult to accept their blindness than those who have never had vision (p. 255).

RESIDENTIAL SCHOOLS

In this section, look for—

▶ *mainstreaming children in the community school is not always better than placing the child in a residential school*
▶ *children in residential schools, "school is family"*
▶ *negative aspects of residential schools, which include:*
   –quality of education can be poor
   –bureaucracy and regulations can lead to regimentation
   –abuse and molestation can occur
   –can contribute to child's lack of social skills
   –children are not socialized into their parents' world

Some children, especially those who are blind and/or deaf, attend residential schools. Up until the 1960s, residential schooling was the only educational option for children who were deaf and/or blind; indeed, before the 1960s, 80 percent of all children in the United States who were deaf attended residential schools (Lane, Hoffmeister, & Bahan, 1996). Residential schools offered education from preschool through high school and sometimes adult education. Since the 1960s, mainstreaming or inclusion into community schools has been facilitated by (1) providing sign language interpreters, (2) using "itinerant" teachers (teachers who teach at several different schools), and (3) providing self-contained classrooms for children who were deaf. Nonetheless, most children with severe hearing loss attend residential schools. Fifty-nine percent of all "profoundly deaf" and 41 percent of all "severely deaf" children attend residential schools (Karchmer & Trybus, 1977).

Thus, at an early age, children who attend residential schools are separated from their families and, indeed, many of these children are "homesick" for the school when they are at home for the holidays. In essence, school is their family. Residential education offers these children communication skills and socialization (Meadow-Orlans, 1996). Children in these types of schools, because everyone is deaf and/or blind, participate in all school activities, including student body offices, athletics, and debate (opportunities they probably would not be afforded if they were mainstreamed in a community school). Other advantages of residential schooling include the availability of role models—teachers who are deaf, other students, and alumni of the school. Indeed, many individuals with congenital deafness or blindness have reported that their parents had very low educational and vocational expectations of them. It was the role models at residential schools who encouraged these individuals to fulfill their potential. Individuals in the Deaf Culture have campaigned against the closing of residential schools for deaf children. Dr. Geerat Vermeij, the evolutionary biologist/paleontologist/professor at the University of California, Davis, has been blind since infancy. Dr. Vermeij argued for mainstreaming in local schools, but also advocated that the child receive a solid foundation in learning certain skills in a separate classroom before being allowed to attend class with sighted children.

The ideal situation, it seems to me, is for a blind child to attend a local school. At first, full attention should be devoted to learning the essential skills—Braille, independent travel, getting to know one's physical and so-cial surroundings—in a class wholly dedicated to that purpose. Gradually, blind children should be eased into class with their sighted peers, with time being set aside to hone and expand the fundamental skills of blind-ness. Whatever the right solution is for any particular child, the goal of providing the necessary techniques as well as the self-confidence and social adaptations to live and compete successfully in sighted society must re-main clearly fixed at center stage (Vermeij, 1997, p. 36).

Mainstreaming children in the community school is not always better than residential schooling. In a community school, the quality of education and accom-modations for the disability may not be very good and a child may simply "attend" school rather than receive an education. In the case of children who are deaf, sign language interpreters often have poor skills and, even more frequently, are not trained in the subject matter they are interpreting (such as chemistry). In addition, many children need to ride a bus for as long as two hours each way in order to attend a community school, thus consuming a large part of each school day. There-fore, the educational placement of children with deafness or blindness is compli-cated and, further, mainstreaming is not always superior to residential schools. Added to the complexity is the lack of coordination between medical services and educational services. For example, physicians who treat babies who are deaf often are not trained in or aware of available educational programs. Further, parents may receive conflicting advice from medical caregivers and educational professionals.

As would be expected, the quality of residential schools varies. Some of the negative aspects include:

- The quality of education at some schools was/is very poor; indeed, some schools concentrate on vocational education, especially in the manual trades. For example, in the past, the majority of graduates of residential schools for the Deaf did not continue on to college. (This is also a result of lack of accommodations at colleges/universities.)
- The bureaucracy, rules, and regulations often lead to regimentation. One graduate of a residential school, spoke of the "damned bells" (Evans & Falk, 1986). This individual was referring to the fact that every minute of the day was controlled by the bells and a set, unchanging, monotonous schedule was enforced. This organization of every detail of daily life can inhibit children's sense of self-mastery, independence, individuality, creativity, and initiative.
- Any bureaucracy may respond more to the administrators' needs and conve-nience than to the needs of the students. For example, one book I read had a schedule of a residential school for the Deaf. The children were allowed to go home for Thanksgiving the Thursday and Friday *after* Thanksgiving.
- Families assume that they are placing their children in a safe, secure environ-ment when, in reality, abuse of children occurs in residential schools. Indeed, one houseparent stated, "You have to break deaf kids when they're young." This houseparent whipped the children with a large leather belt when they "misbehaved" (Evans & Falk, 1986, p. 100). These beatings were administered for relatively minor infractions. Another type of abuse is discussed in this statement, "A top administrator estimates that one-third of all students were 'abused and molested' children" (Evans & Falk, 1986, p. 99).

- Children may become dependent because all their basic needs of life are met. Indeed, there is a risk of "learned helplessness" or overcompliance when the child is required to yield self-mastery or never learned self-mastery in the first place.
- Children educated in residential schools usually experience less privacy and may have difficulty in adjusting to being alone, and may be unprepared to take risks. Indeed, those in the Disability Rights Movement speak of the "dignity of risk" in which an individual is allowed, and encouraged, to take risks, even with the possibility of failure. The dignity of risk is better than overprotection.
- The assumption that children can "practice" social behaviors in a supportive learning environment is not always true. Wolfensberger & Tullman (1991) argue that residential schools can be "culture-alien" and thus residential education can contribute to a child's lack of social skills and ability to live outside the school. Wolfensberger noted, "The skills, habits, and relationships that are prerequisites for a meaningful life in open society are difficult to acquire in settings that are culture-alien, that lack familiar cues, reduce opportunity, suggest or impose alien or devalued roles, and so on."
- Regardless of how excellent the education, a residential school is not a home. Children educated in residential schools are often not socialized into their parents' world, including such aspects as siblings, extended family, racial/ethnic/cultural identification, and religion.

It should be noted that we are not discussing institutions, such as those institutions that care for individuals with severe mental retardation or individuals with severe mental illness. These types of institutions typically do not offer education as residential schools do.

The Cost of Residential Schools to PWODs

By failing to provide quality accommodations and adequate education in the community schools to children with disabilities, society "pays" for this segregation. First, our tolerance for diversity and difference is, unnecessarily, reduced, and second, society reinforces the existential angst and fear of acquiring a disability. In other words, if, as children, everyone were educated and socialized with children with disabilities, PWODs would understand the experience of disability more realistically and not fear it. Wendell (1997) clearly explained: "The public world is the world of strength, the positive [valued] body, performance and production, the able-bodied and youth. Wellness, illness, rest, recovery, pain, and death and the negative [de-valued] body are private, hidden, and often neglected" (p. 266).

Although Wendell was not speaking of residential schools, she made the point that by not acknowledging and trying to understand the disability experience (by relegating PWDs to a "private, hidden" world), PWODs harm themselves.

ACQUIRED DISABILITIES

In this section, look for—

    ▶ *aspects of acquired disabilities*
    ▶ *the distinction between diagnosis and onset*

> ▶ *how the PWD may have internalized prejudices about disability*
> ▶ *how the individual may have a well-defined social role and status*
> ▶ *how, often, there is a literal overnight change*

When we discussed congenital disabilities, we read that Geri Jewell said, "It's not like I wake up every morning and say, 'Oh my goodness, I have cerebral palsy!' I was born like this." Christopher Reeve, the actor, told in a television interview, that upon awakening every morning, he is surprised to find that he has quadriplegia. Obviously, the individual's disability identity, or lack of disability identity, differs in those with congenital disabilities and those with acquired disabilities.

It is important to make a distinction between onset and diagnosis. In many disabilities, the onset and the diagnosis occur at the same time; however, in some congenital and acquired disabilities the time of the onset and the time of the diagnosis are different (Donoghue & Siegel, 1992; Gordon, Lewis, & Wong, 1994; Maloney, 1985; Strauss, 1981; White & Lubkin, 1998). For example, deafness can be congenital and yet is often not diagnosed until the infant is older and therefore the time of onset (birth) and time of diagnosis are different. (The average age of diagnosing congenital deafness is 15 months.) In the case of some types of acquired disabilities, such as diabetes, macular degeneration, and schizophrenia, the time of onset is unknown (the onset is considered to be "insidious") and it is the time of diagnosis that is referenced. (Although, in these types of disabilities, the genetic predisposition to develop these disabilities is present at birth.) Nonetheless, for many disabilities, such as spinal cord injuries, traumatic brain injuries, and amputations, the time of onset and time of diagnosis are the same. In these types of disabilities, the onset is considered to be "acute."

Acquired Disabilities and Prejudice and Discrimination

An individual who acquires a disability later in life has often internalized prejudices and discrimination about the disability. For an individual who has not had much experience with or knowledge of PWDs, he or she has been subjected to the prejudicial stereotypes and inaccurate views of disability. PWDs are often thought to be victims of tragic circumstances, without any quality of life, with few choices, and socially isolated. Kevin Shirley, who acquired a traumatic brain injury at age 30 remarked, "Before I became disabled, I used to feel sorry for disabled people. I would feel sorry for them and do what I could to avoid them" (Mackelprang & Salsgiver, 1999, p. 205). If an individual has internalized these inaccurate assumptions and prejudices and then acquires a disability himself or herself, these prejudices, stereotypes, and attitudes now become *self-perceptions* (Glueckauf & Quittner, 1984). Reread Dr. Schroeder's comments in Chapter 4. Note the limited career options he thinks he has (as a 16-year-old who has become blind) and his remark, "With blindness, did not come any insight into blindness."

Karen Pendleton, acquired a spinal cord injury at age 36. In the following excerpt she explains how little she knew about disability, even after she sustained her spinal cord injury:

It seems weird now, but it took me a while to become really accepting of others with disabilities. A really good eye-opener for me was a college course I took on the psychological aspects of disability. I took the class thinking I would know everything and get an easy A. But I really learned a lot in the class about other disabilities. Since then, I've learned a lot from other people with disabilities. I'm much more accepting of people with disabilities and of myself with a disability (Mackelprang & Salsgiver, 1999, p. 99).

Lifelong attitudes and beliefs can be difficult to change and, furthermore, most individuals never consider the possibility that one day they might have a disability, or they consider the possibility to be very remote. As we have stated before, disability is the only "open" minority group, meaning that anyone can "join" the minority at any time. Nonetheless, most people deny the possibility that they might acquire (or discover) a disability and, moreover, most people unquestioningly accept the widely held stereotypes of what life must be with a disability. Then, in some cases, overnight, these prejudices become self-perceptions. It is "safer" to hold prejudices and stereotyped attitudes about racial/ethnic/cultural groups, religious groups, sexual orientation groups, or political groups because, in all likelihood, prejudiced individuals will never become a member of one of these groups.

An Acquired Disability Often Requires a Change of Identity

While not all acquired disabilities are considered to have a traumatic onset, such as the result of an accident, injury, or violence, most acquired disabilities are unpredictable and occur without warning. Due to this lack of warning, the individual has not been allowed to engage in anticipatory preparation. Many of life's transition points can be anticipated, including the natural results of aging, widowhood, retirement, the death of one's parents, and sudden loss of a job/career. Instrumental preparations include financial arrangements such as retirement plans and insurance policies. Perhaps even more helpful are the emotional preparations for life's transitions. Many of life's transitions require a change in self-identity and changes in self-identity are stressful. Transitions include a new beginning and a simultaneous ending. In addition, many life transitions are viewed as universal (they happen to everybody sooner or later). However, the onset of a disability is not thought of as happening, especially in the earlier years of life.

An acquired disability may seem like the loss of identity, status, and independence. Individuals who acquire a disability in mid-life often have earned a place of status and prestige in the community and, certainly, are people with well-developed self-concepts. Individuals in mid-life often feel that this will be a period of life to enjoy. Due to this well-established identity, the disability can seem to be an overwhelming loss. Karen Pendleton, who acquired a spinal cord injury at age 36 spoke about her change in identity. Notice how she speaks of herself before the onset of the disability in the third person and how she "buried" the old Karen. The word "buried" communicates the total change in identity—she is implying that the old Karen is dead. "Over time, I figured out that old Karen was no more. It's like I had to bury her and get to know the Karen that was left here. I found that I like the new Karen a lot better than the old one!...Now all I have left is me" (Mackelprang & Salsgiver, 1999, p. 98).

We can see that Ms. Pendleton feels that she has sustained a loss, but she views it as a positive loss.

Family and friends also react to an acquired disability. These associates often change the way in which they view the PWD, feeling that he or she has sustained a loss of identity and belonging. However, the individual knows that he or she is the same person as before the acquisition of the disability; but is also aware of the ways in which others do not relate to him or her (Crewe, 1997). Re-read the letter from Mr. Mitchell in Chapter 3 when he talks about the reactions of his friends to his blindness.

THE DEVELOPMENTAL STAGE OF ACQUISITION

In this section, look for—

> ▶ *developmental stages*
> ▶ *required age-appropriate mastery of tasks*
> ▶ *how development theories are silent on the topic of disability*
> ▶ *how PWDs must negotiate the development tasks of each stage IN ADDITION to managing the disability*

Developmental stages are usually defined as predictable phases which require certain responses from the individual. Basically, a child develops from requiring full support to an adult with full autonomy, with the individual mastering the tasks of each stage before moving on to the next stage. In other words, certain achievements are expected at each stage; indeed, there are "age-appropriate" tasks (or demands) that must be mastered. Each level of growth and development requires readjustment. Further, psychologists theorize that the successful, or unsuccessful, completion of these developmental tasks has a lifelong impact on the individual. Of course, these developmental stages do not proceed exactly on schedule for any individual; nonetheless, developmental stages provide a framework in which to view the phases of life. Before we begin our discussion of these developmental stages and their corresponding tasks, it should be noted that psychologists, such as Erikson (1963) and Havighurst (1951), devised their theories without much attention or awareness of disability issues. Nonetheless, individuals with disabilities must negotiate all the developmental stages that PWODs are required to negotiate. In addition, PWDs must respond to and manage the disability and society's prejudices and discrimination.

Infancy and Preschool Children

In infancy, the most important developmental task is that of establishing trust with the world. According to Erikson (1968), this trust is established primarily through the infant's relationship with the mother, or other primary caregiver. For the infant with a disability, this may be difficult if he or she is hospitalized for long periods and is cared for by a host of different professionals (Bendell, 1984). In this situation, caregivers change with every 8-hour shift and a trusting relationship with the mother is difficult to develop. Even when the infant with a disability is cared for at home, the parents may be depressed, withdrawn, exhausted, and resentful and, therefore, find it difficult to care for and relate to their baby. Of course, this type of parental withdrawal does not always occur.

A preschool child masters his or her environment by (1) learning sex roles (for example, little children know whether they are a boy or a girl), (2) gaining some independence from the mother (feeding and dressing himself or herself), and (3) learning to communicate. Children with cognitive or intellectual disabilities are often unable to master some of these tasks, and children with hearing impairments may not learn to communicate. Children with motor impairments may not learn as much independence. Overprotection by family members may needlessly limit the child's independence. At this age, the preschooler's parents may not allow him or her to explore the environment. Reread the excerpts of Linda Pelletier and her appraisal of the effects of childhood overprotection on her adult life. Many disabilities (and chronic illnesses) of children are relatively rare (also called "low-incidence disabilities"). In spite of the fact that medical advances, such as neonatal medicine, have resulted in more babies surviving with a disability, these types of disabilities are relatively rare. For example, Patterson (1988, p. 72) calculated the "estimated prevalence" of the following disabilities (Table 8–1).

Patterson (1988) explained:

> Unlike adults, where the type of chronic illnesses [disabilities] are few in number but are prevalent, each of the hundreds of different conditions in children is relatively rare....Except for a few common disorders such as mild asthma, the prevalence of any single condition is less than 1 per 100 children. This low incidence rate of many types of disabilities in children means that many families must seek treatment in large metropolitan hospitals. Frequent travel, or perhaps moving the family residence, may be necessary in order to obtain treatment and services for the child with a disability.

School-Age Children

School-age children begin to learn what Erikson terms "industry," meaning that children learn to start and complete schoolwork. For young children, the completion of schoolwork is a major developmental task. School age children also begin to emotionally separate from the family and develop peer relationships. Therefore, a disability that separates a child from peers can have a profound impact on the child's developmental progress. Disabilities that interrupt schooling or are visible (especially disfiguring disabilities) can make it difficult for the child to build

Table 8–1

Condition	Estimated Prevalence in Children Ages Birth to 20 Years in the United States
seizure disorder	3.50
cerebral palsy	2.50
arthritis	2.20
diabetes mellitus	1.80
Down syndrome	1.10
blindness	.60
spina bifida	.40
cystic fibrosis	.20
hemophilia	.15
deafness	.10
muscular dystrophy	.06

peer relationships. There is stigma in attending "special" classes. Also, disabilities, such as cognitive or intellectual disabilities that interfere with the child's self-concept as a competent student, can make school, and any school-related activity, unpleasant and frustrating. Children with undiagnosed learning disabilities are often subjected to a great deal of punishment and criticism.

Adolescence

The tasks of adolescence include: (1) emotionally separating from parents and family; (2) beginning to develop occupational identity; (3) establishing intimate, romantic relationships; (4) establishing an adult identity; and (5) establishing a strong sexual identity. Adolescents with disabilities must forge their new identity as an adult, discovering their identity, their values, and their career choices. In addition, they must integrate the disability into this new adult identity. Often, there are few role models for these teenagers. Friends and peers, and the companionship and feedback they provide, are important to teenagers. Disabilities that are disfiguring, or are visible, often make peer relationships difficult. One teenager with a therapeutic leg amputation (due to cancer) stated, "I know young men, especially, really pay a lot of attention to looks and physical attractiveness. I wonder—will a boy accept me just the way I am? You hear them talking about how a girl's really built, or how she looks in a bathing suit and I hope they understand that they just amputated my leg, they didn't take my heart and soul and personality. I don't know if they'll ever accept me" (Darling, cited in Blumberg, Lewis, & Susman, 1984, p. 141).

As we can see in this statement, the treatment of illness and disabilities can be disfiguring. Weight gain (a frequent side effect of medication), tremors or spasticity, wearing hearing aids, or using a wheelchair can make teenagers self-conscious at a time in their life when they want to be attractive and "fit in." Disabilities with unpredictable episodes of symptom manifestation can undermine the teenager's social confidence. Robert J. Neumann, wrote about the effects of rheumatoid arthritis on his relationship, or lack of relationship, with girls:

> During my high school days, my social life was virtually nonexistent. Because I received physical therapy at home in the afternoon and because my stamina was poor in any event, I only attended school until about 1 p.m. This eliminated any possibility of interacting with peers in extracurricular activities....Meanwhile, I unsuspectingly continued to...dream of the day I would start college and the active love life I had fantasized about for so long. Finally the big day arrived. Armed with a body of knowledge about women derived solely from TV, James Bond movies, and the *Playboy* magazines my younger brother smuggled in, I arrived at a small Midwestern college....It took only a short while before I noticed my actual accomplishments with women were falling far short, not only of my expectations but also of the experiences of my friends...there was no need for me to call on social-sexual skills I had never learned (1988, p. 159).

Seizure disorders and epilepsy are unpredictable in that the individual cannot predict the time, frequency, or level of intensity of the seizures. Livneh and Antonak (1997) summarized, "Psychosocial adaptation to epilepsy appears to have a complex curvilinear relationships with age of the individual, with increased risk of psychosocial maladaptation among adolescents and reduced risk among children and adults. The same conclusion appears to apply to the relationship between psychosocial adaptation and age at onset of epilepsy" (p. 302).

Teenagers typically experience more independence and freedom than younger children because they are capable of performing more functions. For example, learning to drive a car is a very important milestone and a step toward more freedom and independence. The child with epilepsy or mental retardation probably will never be able to drive a car. For a teenager, this is more than a functional loss—it is a loss of independence and "normality." Every other 16-year-old is getting a driver's license. With the passage of the Americans with Disabilities Act teenagers with disabilities are now afforded more than educational and career options. Before the ADA, these teenagers were often automatically excluded from high school career days or from interviews with visiting college and university representatives.

Teenagers, of any age, are concerned about their future. When a teenager acquires a disability, such concerns are intensified: "Will I be able to have a baby?" "Will I be able to go to college?" "What kind of a career will I have?" and "Will anybody want to marry me?" are questions often asked (Bregman & Castles, 1988; Farrell & Hutter, 1984; Hahn, 1993; Houser & Seligman, 1991).

Schizophrenia is considered to be very disabling, in part, because of its time of onset. The symptoms of schizophrenia usually begin during late adolescence or in the early 20s. Therefore, exactly when the individual is confronting lifelong questions of occupational choice, educational issues, and choices in partners, he or she becomes ill. Schizophrenia would not be such a disabling illness if the typical time of onset were, for example, during the elderly years. The treatment of schizophrenia often requires long periods of hospitalizations and medications with many visible side effects, making it difficult for the teenager to "fit in" with his or her peers.

Spinal cord injuries (SCI) often occur during the teenage years. Over 50 percent of individuals with spinal cord injuries acquired them between the ages of 15 and 24 and over 80 percent of persons with SCI are male (Livneh & Antonak, 1997). Most spinal cord injuries are caused by car accidents, falls, and stab and gunshot wounds.

Early Adulthood

The development tasks of young adulthood include establishing a family and beginning a career. Responding to the onset of a disability in early adulthood often includes not only the individual, but also his or her marriage partner. For example, the time of onset for multiple sclerosis usually occurs during the prime working years and, for a woman, during the childbearing years (Mairs, 1996). Therefore, the rehabilitation of individuals with this disability often includes family counseling in order to provide support to the spouse and children. Livneh and Antonak (1997) described the spouses of individuals with multiple sclerosis: "Spouses felt trapped, overwhelmed, and resentful" (p. 319). Disabilities that are acquired during the early years of marriage often require extensive assistance and custodial care of the partner with the disability. This type of custodial care may undermine the sexual relationship and render the partner with the disability sexually unattractive. Medications may interfere with sexual functioning (Schover & Jensen, 1988). Further, a parent–child relationship can evolve when one partner acquires a disability. The partner without the disability becomes a parent to the partner with the disability. Issues of power and control in a marriage are complicated when one partner is a custodial caregiver to the other. ("If you don't agree with me about decorating the living room, I won't bathe or feed you.") Surprisingly, many insurance policies do not cover marriage therapy for individuals with disabilities.

Disabilities, acquired at any age, are financially stressful. For a young couple trying to establish a household, disability expenses can be devastating. Treatment and adaptive technology are expensive and many times, as the individual ages with the disability, these types of costs continue to rise. Medical crises and unexpected technology breakdowns can make budgeting difficult.

Pace of life issues are part of any marriage; one partner may be energetic, hardworking, and enjoy activity and achievement while the other may be relaxed, laid-back, and content to "kick-back." However, in some disabilities, such as multiple sclerosis or rheumatoid arthritis, fatigue and pain are common symptoms. Individuals with these types of disabilities learn to conserve their energy (Rustad, 1984). The spouse without a disability may not totally understand these symptoms or may resent the partner with the disability, feeling that life is not as fun as before. Symptom exacerbation is often unpredictable and therefore scheduling for family activities is difficult. In addition, the partner with the disability often must spend considerable time in treating/managing the disability.

Middle Adulthood

Since most individuals have established strong identities by middle adulthood, adjusting to the new identity as a PWD may pose certain questions. Middle adulthood is a time of peak achievement and career achievement. Indeed, many individuals in this period of life have reached their life goals and have gained some measure of status and prestige. Individuals now look forward to reaping the benefits of careful planning, hard work, and progressive success. In addition, marital happiness often increases in middle adulthood with the departure of the grown-up children from home. At this age, many individuals have resolved, or are in the process of working on, questions on the personal meaning of life. In short, middle adulthood is a time of life when personal satisfaction and feelings of mastery are greatest. Preparation for retirement also begins in this stage of life and individuals begin to anticipate disengagement from the world of work.

The onset of a disability, for a man or a woman, during the middle adulthood years may prove to be interpreted as a loss of identity, status, and economic security. Since the individual in middle adulthood has established a strong, secure identity and a (perceived) place in society, a disability may appear to be an overwhelming shift in identity. Peak earning years may be lost and the years which individuals looked forward to now may appear lost. Disabilities acquired earlier in life, such as arthritis or diabetes, may not have exhibited many symptoms, but with the advent of the aging process in the middle adulthood years, these symptoms frequently exacerbate and functioning now becomes impaired. Perhaps physical disabilities are easier to accept for individuals in this age range, ages 25–65, because they have begun to subordinate the importance of their physical body and their physical appearance. This is a developmental task of all individuals in this stage of life.

Middle adulthood is a time when many individuals are involved in the care of elderly parents with disabilities. Most of this care is provided by women, for both their own parents and the parents of their husband. Singer (1996) stated, "Currently, a woman can expect to spend more years caring for a parent than looking after dependent children" (p. 13). Such caregiving demands on women are difficult because these women most often work outside the home and therefore have multiple role demands (Elliott, Shewchuk, & Richards, 1999; Vash, 1982). Indeed, Singer (1996) labeled the traditional caregiving responsibilities of women as "The role of women as sources of support for vulnerable people" (p. 13). Rather than enjoying the benefits of more time and money to themselves and freedom from responsibility of raising children, women in middle adulthood frequently find themselves providing long-term care for elderly parents.

As Fine and Asch (1988) pointed out, women with disabilities are more likely to be cared for by strangers while men with disabilities are more likely to be cared for by female family members. Certainly, there are demographic explanations for this: (1) some women have never been married; (2) some women are divorced or widowed; and (3) women tend to marry older men. However, caring for family members has been viewed as a female gender role. Ties of obligation and love "represent a defining aspect of femininity. Nurturing and connecting with others...evoke feminine associations. Many informants spoke of needing to be adaptable, invisible, and even subordinate....These characteristics coincide with the generally tentative or inferior status traditionally available to women and, as such, contrast with the more fixed, visible, and dominant roles available to men" (Preston, 1994, p. 101).

Age 65 and Older

Despite the fact that disability onset is positively correlated with age, very few services have traditionally been provided to older PWDs. Until recently, there were few existing programs to meet the needs of elderly PWDs. This is a reflection of the functional model of disability in that paid employment is the only function considered. In other words, rehabilitation has been focused on job placement and vocational skill development, because such services are regarded as "investments" which would be paid back when PWDs go to work, get off public assistance, and start paying taxes. Elderly PWDs are not of working age and therefore are not considered to be able to "make a contribution to society" (Ouellette & Leja, 1988; Rubin & Rubin, 1988). Often, old age itself is seen as a disability. Of course, there is a loss of physical and cognitive functioning associated with aging, and there is also prejudice and discrimination directed toward elderly individuals (Blackburn, 1988; Hersen & Van Hasselt, 1990; Mitchell & Kemp, 1996). Stein and Cutler (1998) remarked on the physical effects of aging: "The normal wear and tear on the body takes its toll on the individual. Eyesight becomes weaker, hearing more difficult, range of movement in joints becomes limited, the muscles are not as strong, and the blood vessels begin to lose elasticity" (p. 204). The increased life span of Americans puts them at greater risk (and longer risk) for acquiring a disability (Wilkins & Cott, 1993). Added to these physical changes are the losses and stresses of isolation from family, decreased income, vulnerability to crime, and a lack of usefulness to a society that stresses youth and physical fitness.

Loss occurs at any age, of course, but as people grow older they experience more losses, more frequently, and these losses have a cumulative effect (Lawton, 1996). Indeed, the loss of energy for general functioning often leads to social isolation; the person simply does not have the energy to socialize (Smith & Kampfe, 1997). Therefore, reduced activity and mobility, and occasionally reduced cognitive ability are viewed as part of old age. Further, the incidence of various stressful conditions often adds up cumulatively, thus reaching their peak as the individual ages (Schienle & Eiler, 1984). The major developmental task for individuals in the elderly stages of life is adaptation to loss. Erikson, and other developmental psychologists, viewed old age (over the age of 65) as a time to avoid ego despair and disengagement from life's activities and relationships. Nonetheless, it should not be assumed that growing old means inevitable loss or that the normative physiological changes of aging *always* result in disabilities (Schienle & Eiler, 1984). In addition to these physical losses, the elderly individual must deal with the agism of a society that values youth, productivity, independence, achievement, and competition. Frequently, the knowledge and experience of elderly people are considered to be obsolete due to the fast pace of technological change. Much like PWDs, elderly people today may be viewed as "burdens" or "drains" due to the fact that they no longer contribute to the economy (Zola, 1988). Another manifestation of society's agism is the fact that hypochondriasis is overdiagnosed in people who are elderly. (This is not to say that there are not elderly hypochondriacs who use their physical complaints to exert control; it is to say that medical professionals overdiagnose hypochondriasis.) It is very logical for people of advanced age to be preoccupied with their bodies. Also, just as PWDs often incorporate society's handicapism into their self-identity, many elderly people accept agism as a self-identifier (Young & Olsen, 1991).

There are two types of elderly people with disabilities: (1) Those who acquired a disability early in life (Trieschmann, 1987), and (2) those who acquire a disability later in life (Verbrugge, 1989). Disabilities acquired in old age may have an acute onset (such as a heart attack or a broken hip) or may have an insidious onset (such as diabetes or Parkinson's disease). Acute onset disabilities often move the individual quickly into old age. Insidious onset disabilities, on the other hand, manifest symptoms which are difficult to distinguish from the natural changes of aging. To further complicate the picture, in some old age onset disabilities, the individual's cognitive abilities and personality fade away (Lubkin & Larsen, 1998).

Individuals who are elderly may have acquired disabilities earlier in their life. The aging process often interacts with the disability to produce complications or more severe decline in functioning. For example, individuals who acquired a spinal cord injury early in life experience greater loss of energy, strength, stamina, mobility, and flexibility at an earlier age than do their age mates without a spinal cord injury. Growing older with a disability is often associated with an earlier decline in functioning. Nonetheless, growing older with a disability requires that the individual negotiate all the tasks of old age and, at the same time, manage the disability. Some disability scholars have theorized that living an adult life with a disability assists the individual in adjusting to the demands of old age.

Elderly people often feel that they have not been accorded any input into design of agencies and programs intended to serve them (Szymanski & Trueba, 1994; Zarit & Zarit, 1984). This also parallels the disability experience in that many programs for PWDs are developed and administered by PWODs. Also, elderly people are frequently reluctant to accept services from government agencies, viewing such services as "charity" or some sort of admission of failure or lack of control. Seeking psychotherapy or counseling may be stigmatizing to these individuals (Chilman, Nunnally, & Cox, 1988). Due to the fact that during their adult lives, very few people received such services and the people receiving psychotherapy were experiencing severe problems, elderly people today often avoid counseling, viewing supportive counseling to be unnecessary.

Despite the previous discussion, PWDs who are elderly are thought to respond to disability more positively than PWDs who are young adults. This positive response is thought to be a function of the following factors: (1) Disability is often seen as "normative" for old age. Everyone else one's own age has some sort of a disability; (2) Elderly people often have fewer functional demands, such as a career or taking care of children; (3) Elderly people have had a lifetime of transition and changes and have developed effective idiosyncratic ways in which to deal with them. Indeed, the onset of a disability may appear relatively minor to someone who has lived a successful and long life.

TYPE OF ONSET

> *In this section, look for—*
>
> ▶ *two broad categories of type of onset:*
> 1. *Insidious*
> 2. *Acute*

Thinking only of *onset* of disability (and not the time of *diagnosis*), we can conceptualize time of onset as falling within two broad categories, insidious onset and acute onset. An acute onset refers to a disability which has a sharp, definite beginning point (sometimes termed "clinical presentation") and an insidious onset refers to a disability which begins in a subtle, stealthy manner. A spinal cord injury would be considered to have an acute onset while diabetes is thought to have an insidious onset. Further, with many insidious onset disabilities, it is the time of diagnosis that is referenced because no one can really accurately pinpoint the actual time of onset. (Although to be truly accurate, with many mental illnesses, the onset can be considered to be both acute and insidious. For example, the onset of schizophrenia is considered to be acute in that the individual has an intensification of symptoms that greatly impairs the individual's functioning and usually requires immediate hospitalization. Therefore, the onset is considered to be an acute emergency, requiring immediate treatment, but it is acknowledged that the onset was also insidious, meaning that symptoms, in reality, did not appear "out of the blue.")

Acute Onset Disabilities

Acute onset disabilities are considered to be medical emergencies; the individual is often required to disengage from his or her normal life activities, such as school, work, and family obligations, and the treatment of the disability becomes top priority (Verbrugge & Jette, 1994). There is a sharp, decisive turning point for the individual, his or her family, and professional service providers. Rapid mobilization of medical, individual, and family resources is required (Chilman, Nunnally, & Cox, 1988; Lesak, 1986). Acute onset disabilities, as would be expected, usually are a shock. Such events as accidents, disease presentation, or the birth of a baby with a congenital disability are unexpected, thus allowing no time for anticipatory and preparatory reaction. In the case of amputations, individuals with cancer or diabetes who were required to undergo a therapeutic amputation and who had only a few days' advance notice responded better to the amputation than did those individuals who experienced traumatic amputations. This makes intuitive sense because time for acceptance, even a few days, helps individuals to respond to the loss of a body part. In contrast, individuals with traumatic amputations experience more problems with acceptance. In one sentence, a man tells of his acute onset spinal cord injury with the accompanying feelings of suddenness, unexpectedness, and the need to deal with a medical diagnosis: "I was 22, a recent college graduate, and all of a sudden, I'm a T8 bilateral paraplegic, whatever the hell that is!" (Crewe, 1997, p. 32) This man, Roy, had gone on a graduation trip to the American West with friends. The driver fell asleep at the wheel and rolled the van. Roy was the only one seriously hurt.

Insidious Onset Disabilities

Insidious onset disabilities include such conditions as multiple sclerosis, diabetes, and rheumatoid arthritis. No one can definitively state the time of onset, not professional care providers nor the individual himself/herself. More support is usually given for acute onset disabilities because friends and family can clearly understand a sharp, sudden (often traumatic) onset. Insidious onset disabilities appear to be more ambiguous than acute onset disabilities. Frequently, individuals with insidious onset disabilities (that have been diagnosed) must seek emergency medical care, undergo hospitalization, and disengage from their major life activities. For example, the diagnosis of depression or diabetes often requires that the individual go to the hospital for immediate treatment. Many people who experience insidious onset disabilities speak about "something not quite being right for a long time," probably speaking of warning signs or prodromal symptoms which, at the time, were not understood or acknowledged (Viney & Westbrook, 1982).

Implications and Cautions

Viewing onset of disability from this simple dichotomy leads to these implications: (1) We are not discussing *course* of the disability; only the beginning. (2) Nor are we discussing the *cause* of the disability, only the onset. (3) We are not talking about the *visibility* of the disability; both acute onset disabilities and insidious onset disabilities can be either hidden or visible. (4) Those with insidious onset disabilities are less likely to seek treatment than those with acute onset disabilities. (5) An unknown time of onset (an insidious onset) can be stressful. (6) A diagnosis leads to family support. (7) For many psychiatric disabilities, knowing the onset of the disability can help in arriving at an accurate diagnosis. Therefore, physicians will ask, "When did you first start having problems?" "What happened next?" Many psychiatric and cognitive disabilities have similar symptoms but different types of onset and therefore it is necessary to establish the type of onset in order to make the right diagnosis. Ziporyn (1992) stated: "Symptoms associated with more than one disease can underlie years of misdiagnosis" (p. 104). Parkinson's disease and a stroke have many of the same symptoms; however, the first is an insidious onset disability and the second is an acute onset disability. Head injuries have an acute onset while dementia has an insidious onset and yet, they share many of the same symptoms. Therefore, physicians will ask, "Have you been in a car accident or bumped your head in the last few weeks?" If the answer is "yes," then further probing for the presence of a head injury is warranted.

THE IMPACT OF A LONG PREDIAGNOSIS PERIOD

In this section, look for—
▶ *the impact of prolonged uncertainty*
▶ *how individuals are given less support and validation*
▶ *how individuals are often labeled with negative diagnoses*
▶ *how people need diagnoses in order to receive services*

Many disabilities with an insidious onset, such as multiple sclerosis, lupus, thyroid disease, Crohn's disease, and a host of autoimmune diseases have a long prediagnosis period. When the diagnosis is finally made, the individual is torn between relief at having a name for the symptoms that he or she has been experiencing and the shock of having a serious disability. There is a simple and straightforward explanation for their symptoms (Ziporyn, 1992). On the other hand, the diagnosis can be a very devastating disability (Donoghue & Siegel, 1992). Nonetheless, the diagnosis ends "a frightening array of possibilities" (Goodheart & Lansing, 1997).

These types of disabilities often present with the following symptoms: muscle weakness, fatigue, pain, sleep disturbances, numbness, and/or vision disturbance, all of which impair the individual's functioning, but are also easily dismissed by physicians. Therefore, the individual undergoes an exhaustive, long diagnostic period while dealing with the symptoms. Even more important, the individual is often diagnosed as having psychological problems, drug abuse, or alcoholism. According to Donoghue and Siegel (1992), on average, from the first onset of symptoms to diagnosis of multiple sclerosis, an individual will endure 40 months of prediagnosis.

Rereading the definitions of secondary gains and hypochondriasis, we can see how easy it is for both professionals and family members to think that the individual is engaging in trying to obtain secondary gains or is being hypochondrical (Davidhizar, 1994). The doctor says, "The tests show nothing. There is nothing wrong with you." Friends and family often stop being supportive (and may, in fact, resent the individual for being such a "wimp") (Friedberg & Jason, 1998). On the other hand, those with less ambiguous disabilities and chronic illness are given support and validation including medical care, time off from work, time to rest, flowers, cards, and the general solicitude of others. Further adding to the stress of the unknown problem are the negative labels given to the person. Physicians may accuse the individual of "doctor shopping," when in reality the individual is trying to seek help for the debilitating symptoms. These individuals may be told to buy a new hat, take a vacation, have the fillings in their teeth replaced, take herbs and vitamins, or see a psychologist. Occasionally, spouses and other family members are aware of the effects of the symptoms on the individual, but their observations are discounted or dismissed by physicians. The cyclic or intermittent nature of some symptoms makes it difficult for others to understand their severity. After all, at times, the individual seems like "himself/herself." On the other hand, because the individual has no medical diagnosis, he or she may overcompensate and overexert himself/herself during times of symptom remission. Indeed, "many energy depleting conditions have no visible manifestations, they are nevertheless incapacitating" (Kohler, Schweikert-Stary, & Lubkin, 1998, p. 129).

Lack of a Diagnosis Does Not Mean Absence of Impairment

It is not uncommon for the individual who has insidious onset disability (which has not been diagnosed) to begin to wonder if he or she is "crazy." The pain, fatigue, and muscle weakness often work together to drastically change the individual's functioning and activities. Accordingly, these individuals devise coping devices such as spending the entire weekend in bed in order to be able to go to work on Monday morning. Kohler, Schweikert-Stary, and Lubkin (1998) included an account of a woman with arthritis who found it difficult to accept her fatigue. She said, "It's hard to justify my fatigue to friends and relatives; my husband often asks, 'Why are you so tired?' It took an article in the *National Arthritis News* to finally help me to convince myself and him that my fatigue was real, physiologically, as well as emotionally" (p. 129).

Often, these individuals become "medical detectives," learning as much as possible about their symptoms and the best way in which to communicate the seriousness of these symptoms to physicians. As would be expected, some of these individuals become depressed (which, in itself can lead to loss of energy). Without a diagnosis, without family support and validation, and with the symptoms and functional loss, these individuals often report their emotional responses to feel like riding a roller coaster. The emotional roller coaster feels like helplessness, lack of control, and unpredictability. Furthermore, others (physicians, family members, and employers) perceive the individual as fully functional and, because of this, do not change their expectations of the individual. Donoghue and Siegel, in their book *Sick and Tired of Feeling Sick and Tired,* referred to a study that examined the psychological impact of multiple sclerosis. To the researchers' surprise, the group of participants who reported the greatest distress and depression were men (with multiple sclerosis) who had few physical impairments. Indeed, these men were more depressed than others with more severe physical and functional impairments. The researchers determined that the ambiguity and stress of the prediagnosis period was associated with their depression. Many of these men reported low feelings of self-worth and the need to constantly defend and explain themselves to skeptical physicians and family members. These stressors, ambiguity and the skepticism of others, in this one study, were more depressing than physical impairments.

Tosca Appel (1988) wrote of her prediagnosis period before she was determined to have multiple sclerosis. Her young age may have contributed to some of the misdiagnoses since the typical age of onset for multiple sclerosis is about age 20. Note: (1) that none of these symptoms were invisible, (2) the number of misdiagnoses, (3) the severity of the first symptom (her parents took her to the emergency room of the hospital) (4) the prolonged period, and (5) the negative labels given to her.

I was 11 years, 9 months old when my first symptom appeared. My first attack of MS took the form of a lack of motor coordination of my right hand. I was unable to hold utensils and my hand was turned inward; my parents in their concern rushed me to the emergency room of the hospital. The intern who saw me at the emergency room told my parents without any exam, that I had a brain tumor.... I was admitted to the hospital, where I stayed for 12 days. Ten days after the initial attack the symptoms abated.... The doctors had put the blame of the attack on a bad case of nerves....My second attack occurred when I was 16 years old and in the

11th grade....One day...my history teacher asked me a question. I stood up to answer and my speech came out all garbled. I was unable to string the words into a sentence. I was even unable to utter words. All that came out were sounds. I clutched my throat to help the words come out easier....I remembered the teacher's look. He looked at me in utter surprise and a little bit helplessly....Again, my parents rushed me to the emergency room where another intern did his initial workup on me....The intern, in his wisdom, thought this behavior was an attention-getter. He thought I was faking the whole thing (pp. 253–254).

In-Class Videos

- View the 26-minute video *Multiple Sclerosis* from *The Doctor Is In* series by Films for the Humanities and Sciences. Focus on (1) the adjustment demands of a progressive disability, and (2) the adjustment demands of a hidden disability.
- View the 24-minute video *A Full Stride: Overcoming the Challenge of Amputation* by Films for the Humanities and Sciences. The producers describe this video in the following: "Focusing on three people, this program shows the many sides of what is often a generic label: disabled or amputee. Old, young, partial loss, complete loss, each story is different. From the time of hospitalization to the triumph of accomplishing small and large tasks, we see the many challenges and the small victories: the psychological pain of losing a limb, the stigma of being 'disabled,' and the vivid 'phantom' pain of a lost limb, but also the process of adjustment to a prosthesis and the freedom and mobility it can bring."
- View the 19-minute video *Rehabilitation: The Road to Recovery*, by Films for the Humanities and Sciences. This program shows both the rehabilitative techniques used with stroke and spinal cord injury patients and the techniques and tools available to patients after rehabilitation has proceeded to the maximum physiologically possible. The program stresses the role played by the patient as well as by rehabilitation specialists in the patient's recovery, contrasting the very expensive technologies at the forefront of rehabilitation techniques with the counterbalancing requirement of the patient's commitment and willpower.
- View the 40-minute video *Misha: Recovery from a Serious Accident*, by Films for the Humanities and Sciences. This is the powerful story of 16-year-old Misha Heselwood and her successful fight to regain her life after being seriously injured. The program begins with Misha's hospitalization with severe brain injuries suffered in a car accident and follows Misha, her family, and the medical staff over a nine-month period, charting her recovery from coma as she relearns how to walk, talk, eat, and eventually regain self-reliance and independence.
- View the 16-minute video *Abilities Taken for Granted: The Disabled*. This video profiles a woman who has not allowed her disability to interfere with her successful career or fast-paced lifestyle. It discusses the arduous path a disabled person faces in American society and addresses some of the laws and legislation that deal with disabilities.

- View the 27-minute video *Epilepsy: The Storm Within*, by Films for the Humanities and Sciences. Epilepsy is the second most common neurological disorder in the United States. This program examines its causes, what happens in the brain during a seizure, and what should and should not be done to help someone having a seizure. The diagnosis and treatment of the condition are discussed by physicians who present up-to-date information to help families, friends, and coworkers recognize the needs and capabilities of epileptics. Sufferers describe what it is like living with the condition.
- View the 28-minute video *Dancing from the Inside Out*. This video profiles three dancers from AXIS, a dance troupe of disabled and nondisabled dancers. Members discuss adapting to disabilities and reveal their rediscovery of physical expression in dance. Spliced into the discussion are scenes from the dancers' daily lives, rehearsals, and a performance. "Exuberant! Lends perspective to the unlimited potential in people of differing abilities" (*Booklist*).
- View the 25-minute video *Mental Illness in the Family*. In this film, Bonnie and members of her family talk about her illness and its impact on all of them. They recall their helplessness and confusion when she became ill, and their emotions and reactions in the years that followed. Topics include keeping the illness a secret; "could I have done something to prevent her illness?"; Bonnie's anger, paranoia, delusions—and guilt; the threat to the marriage; and special problems that affect siblings. Available from Mental Illness Education Project Videos, 22-D Hollywood Avenue, Hoboken, NJ 07423, 201–652–1989, 800–343–5540, fax 201–652–1973, www.miepvideos.org.
- View the 27-minute video *Recovering from Mental Illness*. What does it feel like to have schizophrenia? Bonnie talks about learning to cope with her illness, and she and her family discuss her progress. With Andrea Blodgett, MSW, of McLean Hospital, Belmont, MA. Topics include the devastation of realizing you're ill, being written off, the reality of the voices, not wanting to take medications, the difficulty of deciding how much to expect, and recognizing recovery. Available from Mental Illness Education Project Videos, 22-D Hollywood Avenue, Hoboken, NJ 07423, 201–652–1989, 800–343–5540, fax 201–652–1973, www.miepvideos.org.
- View the 22-minute video *My Sister Is Mentally Ill*. Bonnie's sister Kathy talks candidly about her emotions and the problems she has faced having a sister with schizophrenia. A unique tape on sibling issues that will interest other family members as well as professionals. With Linda Husar, MSW (Includes some scenes from *Mental Illness in the Family*.) Topics include being afraid but not talking about it, guilt, trying to be perfect, and concerns about marriage, having children, estate planning, and the future. The *Bonnie* tapes are available from Mental Illness Education Project Videos, 22-D Hollywood Avenue, Hoboken, NJ 07423, 201–652–1989, 800–343–5540, fax 201–652–1973, www.miepvideos.org.
- View the 25-minute video *Family Challenges: Parenting with a Disability: Exploring Family Relationships When a Parent Has a Disability*. When a parent has a disability, everyone in the family is affected. For children, these experiences may profoundly influence their lives and views of the world. In this sensitive film, you will hear about different roles that all the family members take on at varying times. *Family Challenges* looks at three families coping with different kinds of disabilities. In *Family Challenges*, the viewer has the opportunity to

understand how different families share their stories of accepting and acknowledging the disability. The video explores the relationship with the spouse as well as the insights and perceptions of the children. This film helps the viewer experience firsthand the feelings and emotions of a family that has a parent with a disability. This is an excellent video for those living with a disability and their families as well as professionals in rehabilitation, mental health counselors, hospitals, and psychology and nursing professionals. Winner of the Silver Award, INTERCOM SuperFest '99 Award. Available from Aquarius Health Care Videos, fax 508–650–4216, Web: www.aquarius productions.com.

- View the 47-minute video *Beyond the Barriers*. Follow sport enthusiast and paraplegic Mark Wellman on his extreme adventures. For too many years, paraplegics, amputees, quadriplegics, and the blind have felt trapped by their disabilities. No more! Mark Wellman and other disabled adventurers rock climb the desert towers of Utah, sail in British Columbia, body-board the big waves of Pipeline and Waimea Bay, scuba dive with sea lions in Mexico, and hang glide the California coast. This film delivers the simple message: Don't give up, and never give in. If you can't ever lose, then you can't ever win. Available from Aquarius Health Care Videos, fax 508–650–4216, Web: www.aquariusproductions.com.

- View the 21-minute video *In the Mind of the Beholder*, a film about newly blind adults. This documentary is about newly blind adults making the transition to using their nonvisual senses. In a society in which most people are terrified of losing their vision—and yet know virtually nothing about vision loss—the blind are wrongly viewed as mysterious, pitiful, or courageous. Produced by Karen Brown Davison, this film puts a human face and voice to blindness. By sharing the experience of losing their eyesight and relearning skills they once took for granted, the people in this film demystify blindness and the nonvisual clues they use to navigate the world. "The interviewees talk openly about how they do not allow their vision loss to prevent them from living full lives despite many difficulties and obstacles they face....*In the Mind of the Beholder* shatters the notion that the blind are helpless or to be pitied" (Samantha J. Gust, *MC Journal: The Journal of Academic Media Librarianship*). Available from Aquarius Health Care Videos, fax 508–650–4216, Web: www.aquarius productions.com.

- View the 22-minute video *Families and Health: A Child's Voice*. Children share their thoughts and fears with having a serious illness in their family. A moving documentary about children communicating their concerns over a family health condition—be it their own, a sibling's or parent's. These children talk openly about conditions such as HIV, diabetes, asthma, and cancer and how they affect them at home, the hospital, and school. Available from Aquarius Health Care Videos, fax 508–650–4216, Web: www.aquariusproductions.com.

- View the 28-minute video, *I Am Dekel: Portrait of a Life with Down Syndrome* by Films for the Humanities and Sciences (P.O. Box 2053, Princeton, NJ 08543–2053, 1–800–257–5126, http://www.films.com). The language of this video is Hebrew with English subtitles. The producers describe this video, "Dekel Shekarzi, a 21-year-old who defines himself as an actor, a poet, a dancer, and a romantic in love with love itself, is defined by many others not by who he is, but what he was born with: Down syndrome. This engaging documentary follows Dekel in his everyday life, which is anything but 'everyday.' Film of Dekel on stage and at home, candid interviews with his family members, and reflections from this remarkable individual reveal an intriguing personality."

Learning Activity

As a class, write some possible questions to ask a PWD. Have several class members interview a PWD using these questions. Report the results of these interviews to the class.

Writing Experience

Using one of the 17 "bullets" listed at the beginning of this chapter, write a response paper.

References

Affleck, G., Tennen, H., Pfeifer, C., & Fifield, J. (1987). Appraisals of control and predictability in adapting to a chronic disease. *Journal of Personality and Social Psychology, 53,* 273–279.

Alfano, D. P., Nielsen, P.M., & Fink, M. P. (1993). Long-term psychosocial adjustment following head or spinal cord injury. *Neuropsychiatry, Neuropsychology, and Behavioral Neurology, 6,* 117–125.

Appel, T. (1988). Personal statement: Living in spite of multiple sclerosis. In P. W. Power (Ed.). *Family interventions throughout chronic illness and disability* (pp. 253–257). New York: Springer.

Austin, J. K. (1990). Assessment of coping mechanisms used by parents and children with chronic illness. *Maternal and Child Nursing, 15,* 98–102.

Batshaw, M. L. (Ed.). (1998). *Children with disabilities* (4th ed.). Baltimore: Brookes.

Bendell, R. D. (1984). Psychological problems of infancy. In M. G. Eisenberg, L. C. Sutkin, & M. A. Jansen (Eds.). *Chronic illness and disability through the life span: Effects on self and the family* (pp. 23–38). New York: Springer.

Bernbaum, J. C., & Batshaw, M. L. (1998). Born too soon, born too small. In M. L. Batshaw (Ed.). *Children with disabilities* (4th ed.) (pp. 115–139). Baltimore: Brookes.

Blackburn, J. (1988). Chronic health problems of the elderly. In C. S. Chilman, E. W. Nunnally, & F. M. Cox (Eds.). *Chronic illness and disability: Families in trouble.* (pp. 108–122). Newbury Park, CA: Sage.

Blumberg, B.D., Lewis, M.J., & Susman, E.J. (1984). Adolescence: A Time of Transition. In M.G.Eisenberg, L. C. Sutkin, & M.A. Jansen (Eds.). *Chronic illness and disability through the life span: Effects on self and the family* (pp. 133–163). New York: Springer.

Bregman, S., & Castles, E.E. (1988). Insights and intervention into the sexual needs of the disabled adolescent. In P.W. Power, A.E. Dell Orto, & M.B. Gibbons (Eds.). *Family interventions throughout chronic illness and disability* (pp. 184–200). New York: Springer.

Breslau, N. (1982). Psychiatric disorder in children with physical disabilities. *Journal of the American Academy of Child Psychiatry, 24,* 87–94.

Breslau, N., & Marshall, I. A. (1985). Psychological disturbances in children with physical disabilities: Continuity and change in a 5-year follow-up study. *Journal of Abnormal Child Psychology, 13,* 199–216.

Brown, D. (1997). Implications of cultural values for cross-cultural consultation with families. *Journal of Counseling and Development, 76,* 29–35.

Chilman, C. S., Nunnally, E.W., & Cox, F. M. (Eds.) (1988). *Chronic illness and disability: Families in trouble.* Newbury Park, CA: Sage.

Collins-Moore, M. S. (1984). Birth and diagnosis: A family crisis. In M. G. Eisenberg, L. C. Sutkin, & M. A. Jansen (Eds.). *Chronic illness and disability through the life span: Effects on self and the family* (pp. 39–66). New York: Springer.

Cook, D., & Ferritor, D. (1985). The family: A potential resource in the provision of rehabilitation services. *Journal of Applied Rehabilitation Counseling, 16*(2), 52–53.

Couser, G. T. (1997). *Recovering bodies: Illness, disability, and life writing.* Madison: University of Wisconsin.

Crewe, N. M. (1997). Life stories of people with long-term spinal cord injury. *Rehabilitation Counseling Bulletin, 41,* 26–42.

Cummings, S. (1976). The impact of the child's deficiency on the father: A study of fathers of mentally retarded and of chronically ill children. *American Journal of Orthopsychiatry, 46,* 246–255.

Damrosch, S. P., & Perry, L. A. (1989). Self-reported adjustment, chronic sorrow, and coping of parents of children with Down syndrome. *Nursing Research, 38,* 30.

Danek, M. (1988). Deafness and family impact. In P. W. Power, A. E. Dell Orto, & M. B. Gibbons (Eds.). *Family interventions throughout chronic illness and disability* (pp. 120–135). New York: Springer.

Danek, M. M., & Lawrence, R. E. (1985). Women in rehabilitation: An analysis of state agency services to disabled women. *Journal of Applied Rehabilitation Counseling, 16,* 16–18.

Darling, R. B., & Baxter, C. (1996). *Families in focus: Sociological methods in early intervention.* Austin, TX: Pro-Ed.

Davidhizar, R. (1994). The pursuit of illness for secondary gains. *Health Care Supervisor, 13*(3), 49–58.

Dell Orto, A. E. (1988). Respite care: A vehicle for hope, the buffer against desperation. In P. W. Power, A. E. Dell Orto, & M. B. Gibbons, (Eds.). *Family interventions throughout chronic illness and disability* (pp. 265–284). New York: Springer.

Donoghue, P. J., & Siegel, M. E. (1992). *Sick and tired of feeling sick and tired: Living with invisible chronic illness.* New York: Norton.

Downey, G., Silver, R. C., & Wortman, C. B. (1990). Reconsidering the attribution-adjustment relation following a major negative event: Coping with the loss of a child. *Journal of Personality and Social Psychology, 59,* 925–940.

Drotar, D., Crawford, P., & Bush, M. (1984). The family context of childhood chronic illness: Implications for psychosocial intervention. In M.G. Eisenberg, L.C. Sutkin, and M.A. Jansen (Eds.). *Chronic illness and disability through the life span: Effects on self and the family* (pp. 103–235). New York: Springer.

Edwards, M. L. (1997). Deaf and dumb in ancient Greece. In L. J. Davis (Ed.). *The disabilities studies reader* (pp. 29–51). New York: Routledge.

Eisenberg, M. G., Sutkin, L. C., & Jansen, M. A. (Eds.). (1984). *Chronic illness and disability through the life span: Effects on self and the family.* New York: Springer.

Elliott, T. R., Shewchuk, R.M., & Richards, J.S. (1999). Caregiver social problem-solving abilities and family member adjustment to recent onset physical disability. *Rehabilitation Psychology, 44,* 104–123.

Erikson, E. (1963). *Childhood and Society* (2nd ed.). New York: Norton.

Erikson, E. H. (1968). *Identity and Crisis.* New York: Norton.

Evans, A. D., & Falk, W. W. (1986). *Learning to be deaf.* Berlin: Mouton de Gruyter.

Falvo, D. R. (1991). *Medical and psychosocial aspects of chronic illness and disability.* Gaithersburg, MD: Aspen Publishers, Inc.

Farrell, F. Z., & Hutter, J. J. Jr (1984). The family of the adolescent: A time of challenge. In M.G. Eisenberg, L. C. Sutkin, & M. A. Jansen (Eds.). *Chronic illness and disability through the life span: Effects on self and the family* (pp. 150–163). New York: Springer.

Featherstone, H. (1980). *A difference in the family: Living with a disabled child.* New York: Basic Books.

Fewell, R. (1986). A handicapped child in the family. In R. Fewell & P. Vadasy (Eds.). *Families of handicapped children* (pp. 3–34). Austin, TX: Pro-Ed.

Filer, R.D., & Filer, P. A. (2000). Practice considerations for counselors working with hearing children of deaf parents. *Journal of Counseling and Development, 78,* 38–43.

Fine, M., & Asch, A. (1988). *Women with disabilities: Essays in psychology, cultural, and politics.* Philadelphia: Temple University.

Frantz, T. T. (1981). *When your child has a life-threatening illness.* Bethesda, MD: Association for the Care of Children's Health.

Friedberg, F., & Jason, L. A. (1998). *Understanding chronic fatigue syndrome: An empirical guide to assessment and treatment.* Washington, DC: American Psychological Association.

Glueckauf, R. L., & Quittner, A. L. (1984). Facing physical disability as a young adult: Psychological issues and approaches. In M. G. Eisenberg, L. C. Sutkin, & M. A. Jansen (Eds.). *Chronic illness and disability through the life span: Effects on self and the family* (pp. 167–183). New York: Springer.

Goodheart, C.D., & Lansing, M. H. (1997). *Treating people with chronic disease: A psychological guide.* Washington, DC: American Psychological Association.

Gordon, P. A., Lewis, M. D., & Wong, D. (1994). Multiple sclerosis: Strategies for rehabilitation counselors. *Journal of Rehabilitation, 62,* 34–38.

Graliker, B. V., Fishler, K., & Koch, R. (1962). Teenage reaction to a mentally retarded sibling. *Journal of Mental Deficiency, 66,* 838–843.

Greenberg, M. T. (1980). Hearing families with deaf children: Stress and functioning as related to communication method. *American Annals of the Deaf, 125,* 1063–1071.

Hahn, H. (1993). Can disability be beautiful? In M. Nagler (Ed.). *Perspectives on disability* (2nd ed.) (pp. 213–216). Palo Alto, CA: Health Markets Research.

Harper, D. C. (1999). Social psychology of difference: Stigma, spread, and stereotypes in childhood. *Rehabilitation Psychology, 44,* 131–144.

Havighurst, R. J. (1951). *Developmental tasks and education.* New York: Longman Green.

Head, D. W., Head, B., & Head, J. (1985). Life or death of severely disabled infants: A counseling issue. *Journal of Counseling and Development, 63,* 621–624.

Heller, A., Rafman, S., Zvagulis, I., & Pless, I B. (1985). Birth defects and psychosocial adjustment. *American Journal of Diseases of Children, 139,* 257–263.

Hersen, M., & Van Hasselt, V. B. (Eds.). (1990). *Psychological aspects of developmental and physical disabilities.* Newbury Park, CA: Sage.

Houser, R., & Seligman, R. (1991). Differences in coping strategies used by fathers of adolescents with disabilities and fathers of adolescents without disabilities. *Journal of Applied Rehabilitation Counseling, 22,* 7–10.

Huberty, D. J. (1980). Adapting to illness through family groups. In P. W. Power & A. E. Dell Orto (Eds.). *Role of the family in the rehabilitation of the physically disabled* (pp. 433–443). Austin, TX: Pro-Ed.

Ireys, H. T. & Burr, C. K. (1984). Apart and a part: Family issues for young adults with chronic illness and disability. In M.G. Eisenberg, L. C. Sutkin, & M. A. Jansen (Eds.). *Chronic illness and disability through the life span: Effects on self and the family* (pp. 184–206). New York: Springer.

Karchmer, M.A., & Trybus, R. J. (1977). *Who are deaf children in "mainstream" programs?* Washington, DC: Gallaudet College.

Keydel, C. (1988). The impact of a handicapped child on adolescent siblings: Implications for professional intervention. In P. W. Power, A. E. Dell Orto, & M. B. Gibbons (Eds.). *Family interventions throughout chronic illness and disability* (pp. 201–215). New York: Springer.

Kohler, K., Schweikert-Stary, & Lubkin, I. (1998). Altered mobility. In I. M. Lubkin & P. D. Larsen, *Chronic illness: Impact and interventions* (4th ed.) (pp. 122–148). Sudbury, MA: Jones & Bartlett.

Knoll, J. A. (1992). Being a family: The experience of raising a child with a disability or chronic illness. In V. J. Bradley, J. Knoll, & J. M. Agosta (Eds.). *Emerging issues in family supports* (Monograph Series No. 18, pp. 9–56). Washington, DC: American Association on Mental Retardation.

Knoll, J. A. (1996). Charting unknown territory with families of children with complex medical needs. In G. H. S. Singer, L. E. Powers, & A. L. Olson (Eds.). *Redefining family support: Innovations for public-private partnerships* (pp. 189–223). Baltimore: Brookes.

Krause, J. S. (1992). Adjustments to life after spinal cord injury: a comparison among three participant groups based on employment status. *Rehabilitation Counseling Bulletin, 35,* 218–229.

Krause, J. S., & Crewe, N. M. (1991). Chronologic age, time since injury, and time of measurement: Effect on adjustment after spinal cord injury. *Archives of Physical Medicine and Rehabilitation, 72,* 91–100.

Kriegsman, K. H., & Celotta, B. (1981). A program for group counseling for women with physical disabilities. *Journal of Rehabilitation, 47,* 36–39.

Lane, H. L. (1996). The hearing agenda I: To mitigate a disability. In H. Lane, R. Hoffmeister, and B. Bahan, *A journey into the deaf-world.* (pp. 334–366) San Diego, CA: Dawn Sign Press.

Lane, H., Hoffmeister, R., & Bahan, B. (1996). *A journey into the deaf-world.* San Diego, CA: Dawn Sign Press.

Lawton, M P. (1996). The aging family in a multigenerational perspective. In G. H. S. Singer, L. E. Powers, & A. L. Olson, (Eds.). *Redefining family support: Innovations in public-private partnerships.* (pp. 1335–149). Baltimore: Brookes.

Lesak, M. D. (1986). Psychological implications of traumatic brain damage for the patient's family. *Rehabilitation Psychology, 31,* 241–250.

Lindenberg, R. E. (1980). Work with families in rehabilitation. In P. W. Power & A. E. Dell Orto (Eds.). *Role of the family in the rehabilitation of the physically disabled* (pp. 516–525). Austin, TX: Pro-Ed.

Livneh, H., & Antonak, R. F. (1997). *Psychosocial adaptation to chronic illness and disability.* Gaithersburg, MD: Aspen.

Lubkin, I. M., & Larsen, P. D. (Eds.) (1998). *Chronic Illness: Impact and Interventions.* Sudbury, MA: Jones & Bartlett.

Mackelprang, R., & Salsgiver, R. (1999). *Disability: A diversity model approach in human service practice.* Pacific Grove, CA: Brooks/Cole.

Mairs, N. (1996) *Waist-high in the world: A life among the nondisabled.* Boston: Beacon.

Maloney, F. P. (1985). Rehabilitation and patients with progressive and remitting disorders. In F. P. Maloney (Ed.). *Interdisciplinary rehabilitation of multiple sclerosis and neuromuscular disorders,* (pp. 3–8). Philadelphia: Lippincott.

Meadow-Orlans, K P. (1996). Socialization of deaf children and youth. In P. C. Higgins & J. E. Nash (Eds.). *Understanding deafness socially: continuities in research and theory* (pp. 60–70). Springfield, Il: Charles C Thomas.

Miller, J. (1988). Personal statement: Mechanisms for coping with the disability of a child—A mother's perspective. In P. W. Power, A. E. Dell Orto, & M. B. Gibbons (Eds.). *Family interventions throughout chronic illness and disability* (pp. 136–147). New York: Springer.

Mitchell, J. M., & Kemp, B. J. (1996). The Older Adult Disability Scale: development and validation. *Rehabilitation Psychology, 41,* 187–203.

Mitsos, S. B. (1972). The grieving process of parents with atypical children. *Journal of Rehabilitation, 38*(2), 5–7.

Neumann, R. J. (1988). Personal statement experiencing sexuality as an adolescent with rheumatoid arthritis. In P. W. Power, A. E. Dell Orto, & M. B. Gibbons (Eds.). *Family interventions throughout chronic illness and disability* (pp. 156–163). New York: Springer.

Nixon, C. D. (1993). Reducing self-blame and guilt in parents of children with severe disabilities. In G. H. S. Singer & L. E. Powers (Eds.). *Families, disability, and empowerment: Active coping skills and strategies for family interventions* (pp. 175–201). Baltimore: Brookes.

Olshansky, S. (1962). Chronic sorrow: A response to having a mentally defective child. *Social Casework, 434,* 190–194.

Ouellette, S. E., & Leja, J. A. (1988). Rehabilitation counseling considerations with sensory-impaired persons. In S. E. Rubin & N. M. Rubin (Eds.). *Contemporary challenges to the rehabilitation counseling profession* (pp. 153–182). Baltimore: Brookes.

Patterson, J. M. (1988). Chronic illness in children and the impact upon families. In C. S. Chilman, E. W. Nunnally, & F. M. Cox (Eds.). *Chronic illness and disability* (pp. 69–107). Beverly Hills, CA: Sage.

Pearson, J. E., & Sternberg, A. (1986). A mutual project for families of handicapped children. *Journal of Counseling and Development, 65,* 213–216.

Pelletier, L. (1988). Personal statement: The challenge of cerebral palsy: Familial adaptation and change. In P. W. Power, A. E. Dell Orto, & M. B. Gibbons (Eds.). *Family interventions throughout chronic illness and disability* (pp. 54–59). New York: Springer.

Perlesz, A., Kinsella, G., & Crowe, S. (1999). Impact of traumatic brain injury on the family: A critical review. *Rehabilitation Psychology, 44,* 6–35.

Power, P. W., & Dell Orto, A. E. (1980). Approaches to family interventions. In P. W. Power & A. E. Dell Orto (Eds.). *Role of the family in the rehabilitation of the physically disabled* (pp. 321–330). Austin, TX: Pro-Ed.

Power, P. W., & Rogers, S. (1979). Group counseling for multiple sclerosis patients: A preferred mode of treatment for unique adaptive problems. In R. G. Lasky & A. E. Dell Orto (Eds.). *Group counseling and physical disabilities* (pp. 115–127). North Scituate, MA: Duxbury.

Powers, L. E. (1993). Disability and grief: From tragedy to challenge. In G. H. S. Singer & L. E. Powers (Eds.). *Families, disability, and empowerment: Active coping skills and strategies for family interventions* (pp. 119–149). Baltimore: Brookes.

Preston, P. (1994). *Mother father deaf: Living between sound and silence.* Cambridge, MA: Harvard University.

Rolland, J. S. (1994). *Families, illness, and disability.* New York: Basic Books.

Rubin, S. E., & Rubin, N. M. (Eds.) (1988). *Contemporary challenges to the rehabilitation counseling profession.* Baltimore: Brookes.

Rustad, L. C. (1984). Family adjustment to chronic illness and disability in mid-life. In M.G. Eisenberg, L. C. Sutkin, & M. A. Jansen (Eds.). *Chronic illness and disability through the life span: Effects on self and the family* (pp. 222–242). New York: Springer.

Rutter, M. (1989). Intergenerational continuities and discontinuities in serious parenting difficulties. In D. Crichetti & V. Carlson (Eds.). *Child maltreatment: Theory and research on causes and consequences of child abuse and neglect* (pp. 317–348). Cambridge, England: Cambridge University.

Sailor, W., Kleinhammer-Tramill, J., Skrtic, T., & Oas, B. K. (1996). Family participation in new community schools. In G. H. S. Singer, L. E. Powers, & A. L. Olson (Eds.). *Redefining family support: Innovations in public-private partnerships* (pp. 313–332). Baltimore: Brookes.

Santelli, B., Turnbull, A. P., Lerner, E., & Marquis, J. (1993). Parent to parent programs: A unique form of mutual support for families of persons with disabilities. In G. H. S. Singer & L. E. Powers (Eds.). *Families, disabilities, and empowerment: Active coping skills and strategies for family interventions* (pp. 27–57). Baltimore: Brookes.

Schienle, D. R., & Eiler, J. M. (1984). Clinical intervention with older adults. In M.G. Eisenberg, L. C. Sutkin, & M. A. Jansen (Eds.). *Chronic illness and disability through the life span: Effects on self and the family* (pp. 245–268). New York: Springer.

Schover, L. R., & Jensen, S. B. (1988). *Sexuality and chronic illness: A comprehensive approach.* New York: Guilford.

Schulz, R., & Decker, S. (1985). Long-term adjustment to physical disability: The role of social support, perceived control, and self-blame. *Journal of Personality and Social Psychology, 48,* 1162–1172.

Sidransky, R. (1990). *In silence: growing up hearing in a deaf world.* New York: St. Martin's.

Singer, G. H. S. (1996). Introduction: Trends affecting home and community care for people with chronic conditions in the United States. In G.H.S. Singer, L. E. Powers, & A. L. Olson (Eds.). *Redefining family support: Innovations in public-private partnerships* (pp. 3–38). Baltimore: Brookes.

Singer, G. H. S., & Irvin, L. K. (1989). Family caregiving, stress, and support. In G. H. S. Singer & L. K. Irvin (Eds.). *Support for caregiving families* (pp. 3–25). Baltimore: Brookes.

Singer, G. H. S., & Powers, L. E. (1993). Contributing to resilience in families: An overview. In G. H. S. Singer & L. E. Powers (Eds.). *Families, disabilities, and empowerment: Active coping skills and strategies for family interventions* (pp. 1–25). Baltimore: Brookes.

Singer, G. H. S., Powers, L. E., & Olson, A. L. (Eds.). (1996). *Redefining family support: Innovations in public-private partnerships.* Baltimore: Brookes.

Smith, S. M., & Kampfe, C. M. (1997). Interpersonal relationship implications of hearing loss in persons who are older. *Journal of Rehabilitation, 63,* 15–20.

Spaniol, L., Zipple, A. M., & Fitzgerald, S. (1985). How professionals can share power with families: A practical approach to working with families of the mentally ill. *Psychosocial Rehabilitation Journal, 8,* 77–84.

Stein, F., & Cutler, S. K. (1998). *Psychosocial occupational therapy: A holistic approach.* San Diego, CA: Singular Publishing Group.

Strauss, A. L. (1981). Chronic illness. In P. Conrad & R. Kerns (Eds.). *The sociology of health and illness: Critical perspectives.* New York: St. Martin's.

Summers, J. A., Behr, S. K., & Turnbull, A. P. (1989). Positive adaptation and coping strengths of families who have children with disabilities. In G. H. S. Singer & L. K. Irvin (Eds.). *Support for caregiving families: Enabling positive adaptation to disabilities* (pp. 27–40). Baltimore: Brookes.

Sutkin, L. C. (1984). Introduction. In M. G. Eisenberg, L. C. Sutkin, & M. A. Jansen (Eds.). *Chronic illness and disability through the life span: Effects on self and the family* (pp. 1–19). New York: Springer.

Szymanski, E. M., & Trueba, H. T. (1994). Castification of people with disabilities: Potential disempowering aspects of classification in disability services. *Journal of Rehabilitation, 60*(3), 12–19.

Trieschmann, R. B. (1987). *Aging with a disability.* New York: Demos.

Turnbull, A. P., & Turnbull, H. R. (1991). Understanding families from a systems perspective. In J. M. Williams & T. Kay (Eds.). *Head injury: a family matter* (pp. 37–64). Baltimore: Brookes.

Vash, C. L. (1981). *The psychology of disability.* New York: Springer.

Vash, C. (1982). Women and employment. In L. Perlman (Ed.), *Women in rehabilitation: The sixth Mary E. Switzer memorial seminar monograph* (pp. 15–24). Alexandria, VA: National Rehabilitation Association.

Verbrugge, L. (1989). Gender, aging, and health. In K. Markides (Ed.). *Aging and health: Perspectives on gender, race, ethnicity, and class* (pp. 55–75). Newbury Park, CA: Sage.

Verbrugge, L. M., & Jette, A. M. (1994). The disablement process. *Social Science and Medicine, 38,* 1–14.

Vermeij, G. (1997). *Privileged hands: A scientific life.* New York: Freeman.

Viney, L. L., & Westbrook, M. T. (1982). Psychological reactions to the onset of chronic illness. *Social Science and Medicine, 16,* 899–905.

Walker, L. A. (1986). *A loss for words: The story of deafness in a family.* New York: Harper.

Wasow, M., & Wikler, L. (1983). Reflections on professionals' attitudes toward the severely mentally retarded and the chronically mentally ill: Implications for parents. *Family Therapy, 10,* 299–308.

Wendell, S. (1997). Toward a feminist theory of disability. In L. J. David (Ed.). *The disability studies reader* (pp. 260–278). New York: Routledge.

Westbrook, M. T., & Legge, V. (1993). Health practitioners' perceptions of family attitudes toward children with disabilities: A comparison of six communities in a multicultural society. *Rehabilitation Psychology, 38,* 177–185.

White, N., & Lubkin, L. M. (1998). Illness trajectory. In I. M. Lubkin & P. D. Larsen (Eds.). *Chronic illness: Impact and interventions* (pp. 53–76). Sudbury, MA: Jones & Bartlett.

Whitt, J. K. (1984). Children's adaptation to chronic illness and handicapping conditions. In M. G. Eisenberg, L. C. Sutkin, & M. A. Jansen (Eds.). *Chronic illness and disability through the lifespan: Effects on self and the family* (pp. 69–102). New York: Springer.

Wilkins, S., & Cott, C. (1993). Aging, chronic illness and disability. In M. Nagler (Ed.). *Perspectives on disability.* (2nd ed.) (pp. 363–377). Palo Alto, CA: Health Markets Research.

Wolfensberger, W., & Tullman, S. (1991). A brief outline of the principle of normalization. In M. G. Eisenberg & R. S. Glueckauf (Eds.). *Empirical approaches to the psychosocial aspects of disability* (pp. 202–215). New York: Springer.

Woodrich, F., & Patterson, J. B. (1983). Variables related to acceptance of disability in persons with spinal cord injuries. *Journal of Rehabilitation, 49*(3), 26–30.

Young, R. K. (1974). Chronic sorrow: Parent's response to the birth of a child with a defect. *Maternal-Child Nursing, 3,* 59–76.

Young, R., & Olsen, E. (1991). Introduction. In R. Young and E. Olson (Eds.). *Health, illness, and disability in later life: Practice issues and interventions* (pp. 1–7). Newbury Park, CA: Sage.

Zarit, S. H., & Zarit, J. M. (1984). Psychological approaches to families of the elderly. In M. G. Eisenberg, L. C. Sutkin, & M. A. Jansen (Eds.). *Chronic illness and disability through the life span: Effects on self and the family* (pp. 269–288). New York: Springer.

Ziporyn, T. (1992). *Nameless diseases.* New Brunswick, NJ: Rutgers University.

Zola, I. (1988). Policies and programs concerning aging and disability: Toward a unifying agenda. In S. Sullivan & M. Lewin (Eds.). *The economics and ethics of long-term care and disability* (pp. 90–130). Washington, DC: American Enterprise Institute for Public Policy Research.

Chapter 9

Other Factors of the Disability

▶ Why can the unpredictable course of a disability be more disturbing than the actual symptoms?

▶ Why is symptom recognition culturally determined?

▶ What does this statement mean, "As the course of the disability progresses, social support often disintegrates"?

▶ What does "temporal disruption" mean in relation to a disability?

▶ What are the four phases of the course of a disability?

▶ Is there a relationship between the episodic course of some disabilities and learned helplessness?

▶ What does this statement mean, "With each level of loss, the individual is faced with adjustment/response demands"?

▶ Why is the importance of functional losses idiosyncratically and culturally defined?

▶ Why has the revolution in assistive technology changed the definition of functioning for many people with disabilities (PWDs)?

▶ What are the factors that determine the level of severity of a disability?

▶ Is there a clear-cut relationship between severity of disability and psychopathology?

▶ What is the difference between chronic pain and acute pain?

▶ With invisible disabilities, why is choosing the point of disclosure important?

▶ What does the term "social death" mean?

▶ How is the treatment of disfiguring disabilities different from the treatment of other disabilities?

▶ What does the phrase, "most enabling environment" mean?

▶ Why do you think that originally physicians often felt mutual support groups were a challenge to their authority?

▶ Do professionals who serve PWDs contribute to prejudice and discrimination at times?

▶ What are the four resources that professionals can bring to the therapeutic alliance?

You will remember that there are 10 factors of a disability that influence an individual's response. Factors in the disability that influence an individual's response to disability are:

1. Time of onset
2. Type of onset
3. Course of the disability

4. Functions impaired
5. Severity of the disability
6. Degree of stigma
7. Visibility of the disability
8. Degree (if any) of disfigurement
9. Prognosis
10. Treatment required

Having discussed the onset/diagnosis of the disability and its meaning to the individual in the last chapter, this chapter will begin with a discussion of the course of a disability, the physiological advancement of the disability and the emotional and psychological responses to the progression of the disability.

THE COURSE OF THE DISABILITY

In this section, look for—
- ▶ *three factors in the course of a disability*
  1. direction
  2. pace of movement
  3. degree of predictability
- ▶ *in (chronic) disabilities the focus is on:*
  1. symptom control
  2. prevention of secondary disabilities or complications
  3. maintaining the highest quality of life possible

Often termed the trajectory of the disability, the course of a disability includes three factors: (1) the direction (stays the same, improves, or deteriorates), (2) the pace of movement, and (3) the degree of predictability (White & Lubkin, 1998). The course is the way in which a disability or chronic illness advances and, once again, it is the individual's *perception/response* to these stages that is most important (Woog, 1992). Reviewing Chapter 2 and the medical model of disability, it becomes apparent that the entire concept of the course of a disability is a relatively new approach since, for centuries, the practice of medicine involved only two outcomes—total cure or death. The idea that an individual would manage and treat a disability throughout his or her life span, working for the highest quality of life possible, is a new concept. We have also discussed how many people without disabilities (PWODs), including physicians, do not consider people with disabilities (PWDs), especially those with severe and multiple disabilities, to have any kind of quality of life. The concept of a normative "disability role" was derived from Talcott Parson's 1951 idea of a "sick role" (Mechanic, 1978). Inherent in Parson's sick role was the idea that the individual would eventually recover. Therefore, it is not possible to transfer the entire concept of "sick role" to "disability role," simply because disability is chronic and, in most cases, lifelong (Curtin & Lubkin, 1998). In the disability role, symptom control and prevention of complications and secondary disabilities are very important. Further, while this chapter will be discussing the physiological and emotional responses to the stages or phases of the course of the disability, it should be remembered that the individual's developmental stage of life, family resources, and personal resources also impact the course of the disability (Feldman, 1974; Lubkin & Larsen, 1998). Finally, the course of the disability should not be confused with the stages of adaptation; although both involve movement and direction and they certainly influence each other, the course of the disability is thought to be related more to actual physiological changes and symptom manifestation.

We have also discussed the stress, anxiety, and depression associated with ambiguity (Mishel, 1993). The individual with the disability, his or her family, and caregivers feel more in control with a clear-cut, on schedule, predictable course. The idea of "planning for uncertainty" is difficult to accept. For an individual who cannot explain the cause of his or her disability, nor the course, the uncertainty may be more distressing than the actual symptoms of the disability (Strauss, et al., 1984; Strauss & Glaser, 1975). Humans demand explanations and often, in disability, there are no explanations. Despite an inability to know for sure, individuals (both physicians and PWDs) try to predict the phases of the disability, the rate of the course, and symptom manifestation. Support groups can offer a newly diagnosed individual an opportunity to "rehearse" the later stages of his disability by seeing and talking with "veterans" of the same disability (Power & Rogers, 1979). The course of some disabilities is more variable than the course of others.

Complications and secondary disabilities must also be factored into this complex prediction. A straightforward example of unexpected and, heretofore unknown, complications is post-polio syndrome. Indeed, polio was considered to be a disability with a stable course in that once an individual reached medical stabilization, it was thought that he or she would continue to function at that level. However, 25 percent of polio survivors experience new symptoms of muscular weakness, severe fatigue, muscle and joint pain, and respiratory difficulties (Zola, 1988). Many of those who used braces or crutches must now use a wheelchair; many have been required to take early retirement from their careers. Physicians could not and did not predict post-polio syndrome. Nor are physicians able to agree on the cause. Falvo (1991) told of the impact of post-polio syndrome. "Those who adjusted to and compensated for their disability, attaining active, independent lives, may find the occurrences of new symptoms and the limitations of post-polio syndrome difficult to accept. No specific treatment is available" (p. 196).

Factors such as the visibility of the symptoms influence the way in which the course of the disability is perceived. For example, for some disabilities, symptoms can progress to a very advanced stage and the individual himself/herself may not be aware. High blood pressure and diabetes, conditions which can lead to serious disabilities and even death, often have invisible symptoms (Cott & Wilkins, 1993). Also, symptoms in remission are invisible symptoms and some individuals may feel that they no longer have the disability and may terminate treatment/management. We have also learned that symptom recognition is influenced by the individual's culture and social class (Robinson, 1988). Therefore, the course of an individual's disability is also culturally determined since it is the individual's recognition of symptoms and the meaning that he or she ascribes to the symptoms that regulate the course of the disability. In sum, *the individual's assessment* of symptoms is more important than the *physiological course* of symptoms (Dunn, 1996; Sinacore-Guinn, 1995; Spector, 1991).

Another factor in the course of a disability is the degree of social support offered at each phase. Usually, during the acute stage, friends and family rally to the aid of the PWD. However, as the course of the disability progresses, often this support disintegrates. In a study of individuals with brain injuries (Kozloff, 1987), it was found that with the passage of time after the injury, the size of the social network of the individual decreased. Friends disappeared. Kosciulek and Lustig commented, "As a result, the number of multiple relationships increased (i.e., family members served more functions as nonrelatives dropped out of the picture). The ultimate consequences of such changes was the social isolation of families" (1998, p. 8).

The course of a disability can only be fully known in retrospect (Lubkin & Larsen, 1998). The course can be predicted, and should be, but even the most predictable disabilities can be unpredictable. Disability scholars term this "temporal disruption," meaning that the PWD cannot accurately predict his or her future or the course of the disability. A disability usually disrupts the individual's future. "How long will this last?" "Will I be able to marry?" "Will I be able to have children?" "Will I have to go into a nursing home?" For the individual planning medical treatment, lifestyle changes, and family adaptations, the greater the predictability of the disability's course, the easier the adjustment. Temporal disruption also is associated with the predictability of the length of time of each stage.

THE PHASES OR STAGES OF THE COURSE OF A DISABILITY

In this section, look for—

▶ *the four phases of the course of a disability*
   1. onset/diagnosis phase
   2. acute phase
   3. chronic phase
   4. symptom exacerbation phase (sometimes termed "relapse")

Generally speaking, there are four phases of the course of a disability: (1) the onset and diagnosis, (2) medical stabilization, (3) chronic, and (4) symptom exacerbation, sometimes referred to as the "crisis" phase or relapse. Each of these phases or stages may be long or short in duration (Rolland, 1988). All of these stages involve both a change in self-identity and role adaptation in addition to medical treatment (Muller-Rohland, 1987). During the onset phase, the individual is required to think of himself/herself as a person with a disability; during the medical stabilization phase the individual is required to think of himself/herself as a compliant patient/client. And, as we have discussed before, any change in self-identity is stressful and often viewed as both negative and stressful. During the onset and medical stabilization phases, the PWD learns to negotiate hospital life and begins to deal with the symptoms of the disability, which sometimes includes pain (Kohler, Schweikert-Stary, & Lubkin, 1998). Both of these phases are regarded as acute emergencies, with available resources being marshaled. These resources include medical treatment and family care and support (Huberty, 1980). During the chronic stage, however, the PWD is required to accept his or her permanently changed status and identity. The chronic stage is the day-to-day living with a disability (Corbin & Strauss, 1988; Feldman, 1974; Power, Dell Orto, & Gibbons, 1988; Robinson, 1988).

The Three Types of Courses

In this section, look for—

▶ *the three types of courses*
  1. *stable course*
  2. *progressive course*
  3. *episodic course*

In rehabilitation, it is generally accepted that there are three broad categories of courses: (1) stable, (2) progressive (sometimes termed degenerating), and (3) episodic (sometimes termed recurring or relapsing). A stable course is one in which after medical stabilization, the symptoms are permanent, but they do not vary (assuming good management and treatment) (Trieschmann, 1988). Life is changed, and for most, there are limitations in functioning. Spinal cord injuries, mental retardation, and deafness are considered to be stable disabilities. Disabilities with a progressive or degenerative course exhibit symptoms that worsen over time and require careful monitoring of former symptoms, the exacerbation of old symptoms, and the appearance of new symptoms. Multiple sclerosis and retinitis pigmentosa are types of degenerative disabilities (Gordon, Lewis, & Wong, 1994; Gulick, 1994; McReynolds, Koch, & Rumrill, 1999). Relapsing and episodic disabilities include asthma, seizure disorders, and some types of mental illness. Episodic disabilities, as would be expected, are unpredictable and yet the individual attempts to live a "normal" life. A simple graph that illustrates each of these three types of courses will be provided.

Stable Course Disabilities

It would appear that stable course disabilities would present fewer adjustment demands simply because the individual knows with what he or she is dealing. After diagnosis and medical stabilization, the individual reaches a plateau of functioning and symptom manifestation and is expected to continue at that level indefinitely. However, there are three factors to be considered: (1) It is the individual's perception of the disability that determines his or her response to the disability and, as we have discussed, one of the responses to a disability is denial, more specifically the denial of the stability of the disability ("I'm going to walk out of here") and (2) most disabilities are not stable in that secondary disabilities or complications often appear. Perhaps it should be stated that some disabilities have courses that are *more stable* than others. And (3) for some disabilities, such as traumatic brain injury, the diagnostic period (even after an acute, traumatic onset such as an automobile accident) may take a long period of time, for some up to two years. (See Figure 9–1.)

Spinal cord injuries are considered to be stable course disabilities; however, individuals with these types of injuries experience (1) frequent genitourinary and respiratory infections, (2) sexual dysfunction (especially in males) (Ducharme, Gill, Biener-Bergman, & Fertitta, 1993; Knight, 1989), (3) autonomic hyperreflexia, an abnormal stimulation of the autonomic nervous system which results in headaches, sudden increase in blood pressure, decreased heart rate, sweating, nasal congestion, or blurred vision, (4) spasticity, (5) pain, and (6) decubitus ulcers (pressure

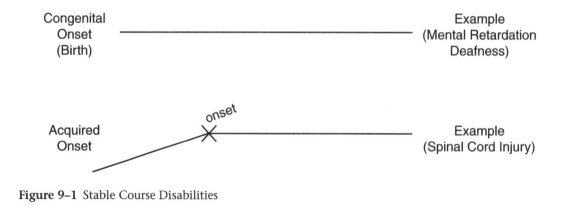

Figure 9–1 Stable Course Disabilities

sores that can become infected) (Livneh & Antonak, 1997, p. 135). Jubala (1990) described the episodic course of these complications of spinal cord injury and the hospitalizations they require.

Jubala explained autonomic dysreflexia: "a syndrome where neural stimulation below the level of injury causes dangerous autonomic processes to occur in the body. These include uncontrolled sweating and a significant increase in blood pressure that can lead to death if not treated. Furthermore, uncontrolled spasms of the paralyzed muscles are not uncommon, and at times can be severe enough to throw people from their wheelchairs. The spinal cord injured [*sic*] are very susceptible to skin pressure sores because of the long periods of sitting or lying without movement. Frequent weight shifts are necessary to prevent such complications...it is not unusual for them to have several hospital admissions over the years because of breakdowns in the biological systems outlined above" (Jubala, 1990, p. 230).

Episodic Course Disabilities

Episodic course disabilities usually have a great deal of unpredictability which acts as a stressor (Gordon, Lewis, & Wong, 1994; Gulick, 1994). Therefore, stress over the prospect of symptom exacerbation may cause symptom exacerbation and symptom exacerbation causes more stress. Obviously, the individual feels a loss of control since he or she cannot predict when an episode will occur. However, many individuals with asthma, some types of mental illness, and other disabilities become very skilled in detecting prodromal symptoms (warning signs), such as fatigue and stress. For some disabilities, individuals can become proficient enough to prevent some of the relapses while with other disabilities the individual can only predict and therefore plan for the relapse. However, there are disabilities for which it is impossible to either predict or prevent symptom exacerbation.

Vocational placement, family life, and social life all become difficult. Repetitive recurrences of symptoms or relapses become burdensome for professional caregivers and family members. Compassion fatigue burnout is quite common (Elliott, et al., 1996; Maslach & Florian, 1988; Power, Dell Orto, & Gibbons, 1988; Shinn, Rosario, Morch, & Chesnut, 1984). The uncontrollable and unpredictable aspects of these disabilities may lead to learned helplessness (Peterson, Maier, &

Seligman, 1993). Kohler, Schweikert-Stary, and Lubkin summarized the emotional response of some PWDs to episodic course disabilities. "Clients have compared times of adjustment to riding a roller coaster; constantly challenged or angered by the uphill struggles, never knowing when another curve will come, and unable to stop the motion. During this period of mixed and conflicting emotions, they have a sense of instability, of bewilderment, and of helplessness" (1998, p. 129).

Individuals with episodic course disabilities often hope for prolonged remissions and stabilization, and fewer and shorter relapses. Each relapse or symptom exacerbation requires an emotional response.

Naturally, PWDs with episodic disabilities (1) follow treatment regimens closely and (2) control their environment at all times with the understanding that symptom exacerbation could occur at any time. For example, individuals with seizure disorders take their anti-seizure medication on time, do not engage in any activity that might trigger a seizure, wear a medical identification bracelet, and do not engage in dangerous activities alone (such as swimming). Naturally, if the PWD is a child, it is the parents who assume these treatment/management regimens. Read the following account of a woman with rheumatoid arthritis and how she deals with its episodic nature: "I have a handicap placard....I feel so bad when I park in that spot, then I finally tell myself—I'm talking [about parking in] handicap spots—that on those days I'm so tired that I wonder how I even got out, it's all right to park in that spot. And on those good days, leave those spots for someone else" (Gordon, Feldman, & Crose, 1998, p. 8).

Finally, both the frequency and intensity of the relapses must be considered. If relapses occur very infrequently and/or are not very visible or impairing, there are not many response demands. In summary, three factors of symptom exacerbation contribute to the individual's response: (1) the predictability, (2) the intensity of the symptoms (is the individual hospitalized?), and (3) the frequency (symptom exacerbations that occur once every 10 years would not impair an individual as much as those that occur every 2 weeks). As would be expected, researchers have found that those who expressed the highest degree of disability ambiguity—including course and treatment—were more likely to respond less positively. (See Figure 9–2.)

Chronic Degenerative Course Disabilities

With each level of loss, the individual is faced with adjustment and response demands and, often, the need to change his or her self-identity. In addition, the "day-to-day" living with a chronic disability must be managed, including the financial costs, costs of time, and costs of seeking out accommodations and adaptations and with uncertainty of the future (Corbin & Strauss, 1988). Indeed, some of the end result of some chronic degenerative course disabilities is the death of the individual (Allen & Sawyer, 1983).

Some degenerative disabilities have a steady rate of progression of symptoms without remission, while others have cyclic periods of symptom stability coupled with periods of degeneration. For most of these types of disability, there is no cure, no prevention, only treatment for symptom relief. Many autoimmune disorders, such as rheumatoid arthritis and lupus, are degenerative course disabilities. Not all degenerative course disabilities result in death. With these specific disabilities, the individual's life span is not shortened; however, 50 percent of those diagnosed with amyotrophic lateral sclerosis die within three years of disease onset. (See Figures 9–3 and 9–4.)

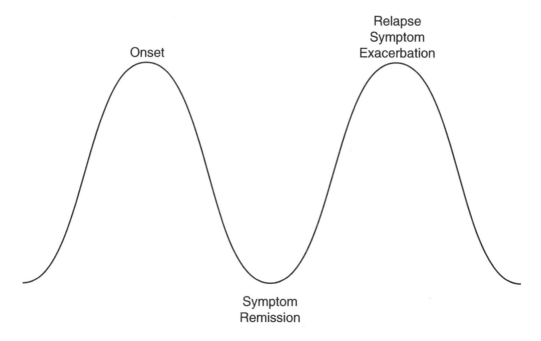

Figure 9–2 Episodic Course Disabilities (i.e., seizure disorder)

Robert Neumann described the progression of his rheumatoid arthritis:

Early in 1960 I went to the Mayo Clinic, where my arthritis was diagnosed at last, and where more appropriate treatment was prescribed. Nonetheless, even this was not able to halt the progression of the disease to my other joints. First, it was my other knee, then my ankles, then my fingers, then my elbows, then my neck, then my hips, then....With a sort of gallows humor, I'd say that I had joined the Joint-of-the-Month Club. But behind this façade, I was terrified at how my body was progressively deteriorating right before my eyes (1988, p. 157).

DEGENERATING EPISODIC DISABILITIES

In this section, look for—
- ▶ *how some disabilities:*
  1. are system-specific
  2. affect many systems of the body
- ▶ *how the degree of cognitive functioning impaired is important*

A disability usually results in loss of function. Some functions, such as respiratory functions, are more important than others. Some disabilities affect many different systems of the body, while other disabilities are system-specific (Livneh & Antonak, 1997). Arthritis affects many different joints and thus affects functioning and mobility to a greater degree than does an amputation. Diabetes, often considered by the general public to not be a very limiting disability, affects all systems of

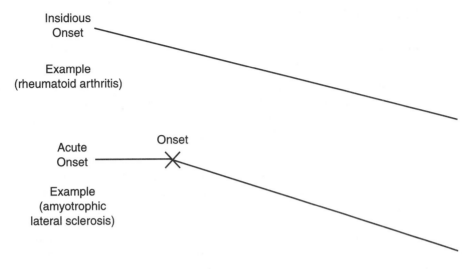

Insidious
Onset

Example
(rheumatoid arthritis)

Acute
Onset

Onset

Example
(amyotrophic
lateral sclerosis)

Figure 9–3 Progressive Course Disabilities

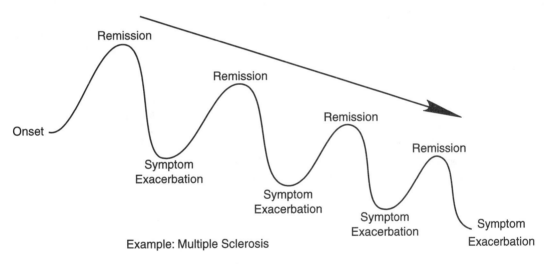

Remission

Remission

Remission

Remission

Onset

Symptom
Exacerbation

Symptom
Exacerbation

Symptom
Exacerbation

Symptom
Exacerbation

Example: Multiple Sclerosis

Figure 9–4 Degenerating Episodic Disabilities

the body and can result in many secondary disabilities and complications. The amputation of an arm is considered to be more disfiguring than the amputation of a leg but less of a loss of function. Ninety percent of all amputations are lower limb amputations (Livneh & Antonak, 1997).

Some disabilities affect functioning in many different areas of the individual's life. Mental retardation, especially severe mental retardation, affects academic, social, and vocational functioning (Hardman, Drew, Egan, & Wolf, 1993). Fatigue, pain, and muscle weakness/numbness, while considered to be invisible to others, can affect functioning in many different areas of the individual's life. Fatigue, which has no direct relationship to physical activity, can render an individual totally immobile.

COMMUNICATION DIFFICULTIES

> *In this section, look for—*
>
> ▶ *the problem of loss of communication*
>   1. *people with communication difficulties are often misdiagnosed as having mental retardation or behavior disorders.*
>   2. *the Deaf Culture asserts that it is not the impairment of deafness that prevents communication but the lack of accommodations.*

Communication is an important function that affects many different areas of an individual's daily life. As we have discussed, there are many ways in which to communicate other than the spoken language, but most people do consider spoken language to be synonymous with communication. A great deal of learning (both formal and informal) uses spoken language. Daily interactions usually require communication, including interacting with family members. Therefore, parents, siblings, and spouses are affected by their family member's inability to communicate. Individuals with hearing impairments, cerebral palsy, speech disorders, and some developmental disabilities experience functional limitations in speaking and hearing. Often the true cause of the individual's lack of ability to communicate is not diagnosed and the individual is erroneously thought to have mental retardation or behavior disorders. Some individuals are able to hear and understand spoken language, but cannot speak, such as those with cerebral palsy, while others can neither hear nor speak, which is the case with individuals who are profoundly deaf.

Those in the Deaf Culture state that it is not the functional limitations of the individual's hearing impairment that renders him or her unable to communicate, but rather the lack of accommodations in the environment (Higgins & Nash, 1987). The Deaf Culture believes that people who are deaf can and do communicate; they simply use another language (Higgins, 1980; 1992). Obviously, individuals who experience limitations in speaking and/or hearing depend on visual channels of communication. Assistive technology, such as communication boards and visual/vibrating warning devices, are helpful.

Individuals who lose their hearing later in life often feel isolated and lonely because they have not learned sign language and they are embarrassed to associate with people who speak. Further, these individuals may feel vulnerable because of their inability to hear sounds that alert them to danger, such as the honking of a car, a fire alarm, etc. Naturally, those who have been deaf for the greater part of their lives have learned to use assistive devices.

Read the following account of two women in a nursing home. Ann (age 42) can walk but her speech is difficult to understand, and, therefore, she uses a communication board. Linda (age 52) uses a wheelchair and speaks very slowly. Notice also the lack of privacy.

> The attendants couldn't speak English and our speech is not so good so there was no communication. Also, we had no privacy. Men, women, anyone would just walk in at any time. They treated us like non-persons and I guess they felt that you can't intrude on a non-person. We were going crazy just trying to be sane. Now I just use it (the communication board) when people don't understand me. Places like the doctor's office where it's

important for people to understand me. It's really a last resort. I know my-self and when I get anxious, I can't talk (cited in Scherer, 1993, p. 96).

THE MEANING OF THE LOSS OF FUNCTIONING

In this section, look for—
- ▶ *the idiosyncratic meaning of functioning*
- ▶ *the degree of "intrusiveness"*
- ▶ *the importance of capitalizing on residual functioning and skills*
- ▶ *the revolution in assistive technology for PWDs*

The importance of certain functions is also idiosyncratically defined. In other words, the individual's value system and lifestyle determine the importance of certain functions (DeLoach & Greer, 1981). For example, some individuals are adventuresome, enjoy outdoor, physical activities, and like taking risks. For such types of individuals, the loss of mobility may be felt as a great loss. On the other hand, the loss of mobility may not seem catastrophic to someone who enjoys intellectual pursuits. Stephen Hawking, the English physicist with amyotrophic lateral sclerosis, remarked that his disability gave him more time to think and thinking is obviously an important function for a physicist. Indeed, many individuals with mobility impairments or sensory impairments have reported, "I escaped into my mind."

It is no coincidence that the leaders in the Disability Rights Movement have been intellectually gifted individuals. Irving Zola, Ed Roberts, Judith Heumann, and Leonard Kriegel were or are survivors of polio and therefore their disability did not diminish their intellectual functioning. Livneh and Antonak (1997) use the term "intrusiveness" to describe the effects of a disability that interferes with an individual's functioning. The loss of valued activities (or "intrusiveness") is idiosyncratically defined because valued activities are defined by the individual.

The example most often used to describe the importance of the idiosyncratic meaning of function is that of a piano player missing a little finger. For most people, the loss of a single finger would not be defined as a disability nor as a loss of function. However, for an individual who had spent his or her life preparing to be a concert pianist, the loss of a single finger would greatly change his or her life. An individual's learning style can affect the unique meaning he or she ascribes to a loss of functioning. For example, auditory learners would experience difficulty in responding to late-onset hearing impairment, just as visual learners would have difficulty in responding to blindness. Personality characteristics, such as privacy and independence needs, also affect the meaning of the loss of certain functions.

Functioning is also culturally and gender defined, meaning that both the loss of function and the role expectations of a PWD are, to some extent, determined by his or her culture and gender (Sasao & Sue, 1993; Sinacore-Guinn, 1995; Spector, 1991). For example, Alice Crespo, the court interpreter who is blind, remarked: "My parents came from Puerto Rico....There, women stay at home and raise babies. If you have a disability, it is assumed that you can't or won't have babies, but you stay home anyhow, being taken care of by your family" (Rousso, 1993, p. 101).

Source: Disabled, Female, and Proud!, Harilyn Rousso. Copyright © 1993 by Bergin & Garvey. Reproduced with permission of Greenwood Publishing Group, Inc., Westport, CT.

For many individuals it is not the onset of the disability which is most life-changing, but the related loss of function which may occur years after the diagnosis/onset of the disability. Many individuals with arthritis, multiple sclerosis, or muscular dystrophy report that the day they began to use a wheelchair was far more lifechanging than the day they received their diagnosis. Other such functional losses include individuals who are required, because of a progressive disability, to move into an assisted living home, or wear hearing aids, or relinquish their driver's license.

Obviously when an individual loses the ability to function in one area, the solution is to use and develop and capitalize on his or her residual skills (Wright, 1960). Generally speaking, therefore, individuals with a broad range of interests and abilities are capable of responding more positively to a disability simply because they have more options. Individuals with unifocal interests, such as athletics and sports, often find responding to a loss of mobility to be difficult. On the other hand, individuals with a great deal of education, varied work skills and experience, and multifocal interests will be able to shift their functioning to the areas of their residual abilities and capabilities.

An example of a valued function that was idiosyncratically defined is presented in Marcia Scherer's book, *Living in the State of Stuck: How Technology Impacts the Lives of People with Disabilities* (1993). Brian sustained a spinal cord injury in a motorcycle accident at age 17. Note the impact of an idiosyncratically defined function, attending a Grateful Dead concert:

> My friends came up to visit as usual and said that [my favorite group] the Grateful Dead were playing here in November. My mind was back, but I had to get my strength. The doctors said I would have to sit 4 to 5 hours straight if I were to go to the concert. Every time I got into the wheelchair, I blacked right out. Each day for only a short time, I would sit in a semi-reclined position determined to reach my goal. After a couple of days I was up to three hours. The day of the show I reached my goals and I was psyched. The concert was the first time I had been out of the hospital. I had reached my destination (p. 22).

Before closing this discussion of loss of functioning, it is important to point out that assistive, or adaptive, technology has greatly decreased the loss of functioning that PWDs experience. Until the invention of computers, the design and use of assistive devices for PWDs changed little for literally hundreds of years. Before computers, these devices were simple mechanical equipment that were most often homemade. These included prosthetic devices, such as artificial arms or legs, orthotic (straightening) devices such as braces, and mechanical wheelchairs (without power) (Weisgerber, 1991). Now, most assistive technology is either computerized or electromechanical (Scherer, 1993). Examples of these newer technologies include: power wheelchairs; Functional Electrical Stimulation (FES) that sends bursts of low level electricity to paralyzed muscles; augmentative and alternative communication systems; environmental control computers that lock doors, turn on the furnace, and turn off the lights; and voice-activated computers that allow individuals who do not have the use of their hands to type. This revolution in assistive technology has changed the meaning of loss of function.

SEVERITY OF THE DISABILITY

In this section, look for—

▶ *how some disabilities have clear-cut levels of severity.*
▶ *how the level of severity of most disabilities is judged on several factors, including*
   1. the number of disabilities the individual experiences
   2. the number of areas of functioning affected
   3. the treatment necessary
   4. the degree of stigma directed at the individual

Some types of disabilities have clear-cut cutoff points between the categories of mild, moderate, and severe. For example, deafness is defined as the loss of hearing 80 decibels or greater; a severe impairment is the loss of hearing within the 60–80 decibel range; a moderate loss (sometimes called "hard of hearing") is defined as loss of hearing in the 40–60 decibel range, and a mild hearing loss is a loss of 25–40 decibels (Hardman, Drew, Egan, & Wolf, 1993). Mental retardation also has categories: an IQ of 55–70 is considered to be mild mental retardation; an IQ of 40–55 is considered to be moderate mental retardation, 25–40 is severe mental retardation and an IQ score below 25 is considered to be profound retardation (American Psychiatric Association, 1994). Vision impairments also have numerical guidelines that designate categories. These types of categories are possible only when there is great diagnostic precision, usually using objective, standardized measuring instruments. Many disabilities do not have this diagnostic precision and, therefore, it is more difficult to determine the medical treatment, educational placement, and living situation for individuals with these types of disabilities.

Disabilities that cannot be measured precisely are usually determined to be severe, moderate, or mild by several different standards. First, the number of disabilities an individual experiences can help to determine level of severity. For example, individuals who are both blind and deaf are considered to have a severe disability. Second, the number of areas of functioning affected can lead to a diagnosis of severity. An individual with quadriplegia would be considered to have a severe disability. Third, the treatment necessary can, in an indirect way, determine the level of severity. For example, an individual whose schizophrenia can be controlled by medication would not be considered to have as severe a disability as someone who must be institutionalized because he or she does not respond to the medication. Finally, the episodic nature of some types of disability often lead to a diagnosis of a severe disability, based on the premise that the individual's functioning is very impaired.

Degree of severity is never based on visibility of the disability; however, degree of severity is sometimes based on the level of prejudice directed toward the individual. Therefore, an individual with a heart condition (a hidden disability) could be considered to have a severe disability because the heart condition limits many different functions (and yet this person appears to not have a disability). Someone with a facial disfigurement, with few or any functional limitations, is also considered to have a severe disability due to the stigma and prejudice that limits the individual's functioning. Many people with facial disfigurements report that they stay at home, always. Those who wear eyeglasses (which restore their vision to full functioning) experience little prejudice and stigma. On the other hand, those who wear hearing aids (which improve their hearing) are subjected to prejudice and discrimination. Finally, it should be remembered that it is the individual's *judgment/assessment/perception* of the disability that is most important. Further, the individual's judgment often differs from that of medical and educational professionals.

QUALITY OF LIFE

> *In this section, look for—*
> ▶ *how quality of life is both subjective and multidimensional*
> ▶ *how minimum requirements usually include*
>   *1. social and economic independence*
>   *2. freedom to function at one's highest level*
>   *3. social support*
>   *4. access to medical and psychological care*
> ▶ *how often it is the lack of accommodations that lowers the individual's quality of life (and not the disability)*

Disabilities can be categorized according to how much quality of life an individual with that type of disability enjoys. However, the concept of quality of life is very subjective and multidimensional (Fabian, 1991; Taylor, Jones, & Burns, 1998). Due to the fact that there are more PWDs than ever before, and these individuals (like everyone else) continue to live longer, the already vague concept of "quality of life" becomes even more cloudy. The chronic, long-term nature of disability coupled with longer life spans has done much to increase the *quantity* of life and *quantity* can be measured. *Quality* of life cannot be measured, but is usually defined in terms of minimum requirements. For PWDs, quality of life is thought to be social and economic independence (within the limits of the disability); the freedom to function at one's highest level; social support, including family life; and the right to medical and psychological care. Others have felt that in order to have quality of life, an individual should be able to ascribe some sort of meaning or spiritual component to his or her life (Kilpatrick & McCullough, 1999; McCarthy, 1995; Vash, 1981; Yalom, 1980). We can see that included in the above definitions are the concepts of having one's basic needs met, economic independence, social support, and self-actualization (Weisgerber, 1991; Whiteneck, 1994).

Often it is the lack of accommodations that diminishes a PWD's quality of life, rather than the disability itself. Accounts of PWDs tell of the day they received their van, their wheelchair or, for one girl with legal blindness, a magnifying glass. The quality of life changed for these people. The prejudice, discrimination, and limited opportunities that PWODs direct toward PWDs also needlessly reduce the quality of life for PWDs. Accounts of PWDs tell of their first day at the neighborhood school, their first time in a movie theater, their first day on the job, their first paycheck, and their first date. Many PWODs cannot remember most of these "firsts," probably because these opportunities were automatically given to them. For many PWDs, these are memorable events and, occasionally, some PWDs thought that they would never be able to experience them. Quality of life for PWDs can be limited by the disability itself, but it is safe to state that quality of life is more likely to be limited needlessly by PWODs. Sexual intimacy, considered to be a component of adult quality of life, may be altered or the PWD's partner may leave, after the onset of the disability (Ducharme, et al., 1993). Partners who do stay in the relationship often report that they are hesitant to resume the sexual relationship.

Many PWDs report an increase in self-esteem, and feelings of mastery and control because they are able to manage their disability. Barbara Waxman (1991) reported that she is "quite skilled at being a disabled person."

> I don't think society understands anything about disability. People look at me and they ask me how do I live my life. I think what they're really saying is *why* do I live my life? They believe that the pain that I experience is derived from my functional limitations. What they don't understand is that the pain and rejection I've experienced have been purely socially based. I'm not depressed about being disabled. I'm quite skilled at being a disabled person. I'm quite proud of my identity as a disabled person. But the pain is social (cited in Morris, p. 62).

In contrast, read the following excerpt:

> I was born, educated, broke my neck, and I'll die and be buried just down the road here about half a mile, so my life hasn't been that much....My life had no value. [The interviewer then asks, "Not even to you?"] No, because I didn't get a chance to do anything with it. It was not mine when I was a kid; it belonged to the parents. By the time I got to be 16, getting ready to go out and do something for myself, you break your neck, and that's it. You can't do anything. I suppose that a person could go to work; I mean, a lot of people do work that are handicapped; they earn money and have families—stuff like that. But once I was hurt, none of that applied to me any longer. I didn't care about it or think about it or nothing. I just kind of hunkered down for the long pull, I guess. You make the best of what you've got. There's nothing going to happen to me in life after that—not to me there wasn't. I knew that (Crewe, 1997, p. 38).

The following are two more PWDs with disabilities speaking of the quality of their lives.

> I look at it like this, I was a 25-year-old hellion with a shaved head before my accident. I think I'm a better person than what I was then. I took life for granted, and boom, I got a big awakening (Boswell, Dawson, & Heininger, 1998, p. 30).

> It's like a gift...over the years, I've evolved into thinking about the greater scheme and believing, that we all exist in our pigeon holes for a reason. And believing that, you can take this [disability] and be a burden with it. You can live with it as a burden or you can live with it as a gift (Boswell, Dawson, & Heininger, 1998, p. 30).

PAIN AND TRAUMA OF THE DISABILITY

> *In this section, look for—*
>
> ▶ *how some disabilities involve or require:*
> 1. *pain*
> 2. *frequent surgeries*
> 3. *loss of income*
> 4. *loss of valued activities*
> 5. *expensive treatment*
> 6. *hospitalization and/or institutionalization*

The treatment/management of a disability can be both time consuming and expensive. Often, sleep disturbances are part of the disability. PWDs often have to alter their lifestyle, relinquishing valued activities. If the PWD has been forced to give up his or her employment, there is a substantial loss of income, coupled with expensive medical and rehabilitation costs. Further, the money and time needed to manage the disability often is the PWD's "disposable" income and time. In other words, the individual must give up social opportunities and fun times in order to find the time and money to deal with the disability.

The treatment and management of some types of disabilities require repeated surgeries (for example, spina bifida), prolonged medical treatment, and frequent hospitalizations. Indeed, for many PWDs, several hospital stays each year is typical. Fatigue and muscle weakness, both of which are invisible to others, limit the functioning of some PWDs. These individuals learn to conserve their energy for what they consider to be important activities. Read the following account of Zachary, a man with a spinal cord injury. Note the repeated surgeries, his limited functioning, and the goals he has set for himself:

> The rods in my back were dissolving through a process of electrolysis. My doctor had no explanation—he said the metal was turning into bubble gum and axle grease. When we redid the rods, I was playing the perfect quad—I wouldn't get a glass of water; I wouldn't put any stress on them at all, and the second set still broke. The third set was actually a double operation, first anterior and then a week later, posterior....The last 5 years has been "staying alive." I haven't really accomplished much that could be written down on paper except for staying alive. On April 11, I've been a quad for as many days as I was able-bodied. Right now I have no goals in my life other than that I want to leave this life consciously (Crewe, 1997, p. 36).

Some disabilities result in the eventual death of the individual. For example, amyotrophic lateral sclerosis is a rapidly progressing motor neuron disease and 50 percent of diagnosed individuals die within three years. On the other hand, retinitis pimentosa, a progressive type of blindness, does result in total blindness, but not in death. Some types of disabilities are thought to have both degenerative and episodic courses, meaning that there are episodes of symptom exacerbation. However, when the symptoms remit, the individual does not return to the level of functioning he or she experienced before the relapse. In other words, the person does "get somewhat better," but with each relapse, the individual returns to a lower level of functioning than before.

It would seem reasonable that severity of disability would be associated with psychopathology (Cook, 1991). In other words, those individuals with very severe disabilities would be maladjusted, depressed, lacking social skills, angry, and/or suicidal. Rehabilitation and disability researchers have sought, for over 30 years, to find a relationship between severity of disability and degree of psychological impairment. Cook (1991) interpreted the research findings: "In his extensive review of the literature, Shontz (1971) concluded that there is little support for the theory that severity of disability causes psychological maladjustment. In his review of research on emotional factors and disability, McDaniel (1976) cautiously concluded that severity of disability was a determinant of psychological adjustment. Based on their review, Roessler and Bolton (1978) also argued for a relationship, albeit complex, between severity of disability and degree of psychological impairment "(Cook, 1991, pp. 85–86). It appears, therefore, that there are few researchers who would state that severity of disability is directly related to degree of psychopathology.

CHRONIC PAIN

In this section, look for—
- ▶ *how there is limited knowledge about pain*
- ▶ *the difference between acute pain and chronic pain*
- ▶ *how medical professionals often have negative stereotypes of individuals with chronic pain*

Pain is a part of many disabilities and, yet, there is limited medical knowledge about "the specific mechanism for transmission and perception of pain" (Lubkin & Jeffrey, 1998, p. 149). Further clouding the diagnostic picture is the fact that pain is invisible, experienced subjectively, and impossible to measure objectively. Physicians ask patients questions about the location of the pain; the intensity of the pain using a numerical scale of 1–10; the onset, duration, variations, and rhythm of the pain; what relieves the pain; what causes or exacerbates the pain; and the effect of the pain on the individual's functioning. In spite of all this specificity, the experience of pain is impossible to describe fully.

Chronic pain, in contrast to acute pain, persists for a period of time, usually three to six months, or occurs at intervals for months or years (Bonica, 1990). Acute pain is a different experience: first, the individual knows that acute pain is temporary, second, acute pain subsides when healing occurs, and third, acute pain can usually be controlled by medications. Acute pain, therefore, is viewed as "having a purpose" and an end. In contrast, chronic pain usually is not related to any malignancy; rather it is associated with musculoskeletal disabilities, such as low back pain. There is no end to chronic pain.

Chronic pain can become the central focus of an individual's life, curtailing work, family life, and social activities. "The individual with chronic pain may undergo a change from being someone with multiple roles (worker, friend, family member, and so forth) to someone who only identifies with the pain" (Lubkin & Jeffrey, 1998, p. 153). Individuals often tire of defending themselves and trying to explain their pain to others. Indeed, they may even begin to question their own perceptions of the pain ("Maybe I *am* crazy"). Rereading the descriptions of malingering and secondary gains, it can be seen that chronic pain is often confused with these maladaptive responses. Chronic pain often leads to sleep disturbances, fatigue, depression, and poor concentration (Latham & Davis, 1994; Linton, 1986). Those who experience chronic pain often lead very restricted, dependent lives. Their lives are controlled by the pain. Family members take on additional responsibilities, trying at the same time to understand and respect the experience of chronic pain. Pain is both a physiological experience and an emotional experience. According to Gallagher (2000), individuals who experience chronic pain are at high risk for depression. Gallagher stated the effect of depression: "Depression may lower both the pain threshold and tolerance" (p. 28). Therefore, it would appear that the relationship between pain and depression can become circular.

Medical professionals often have negative stereotypes of individuals with chronic pain. Thus, there is frustration and anger on the part of the physician and on the part of the patient. The physician cannot understand the pain and the patient feels, justifiably, demeaned and devalued. The idea of pain and the possibility that everyone has of experiencing pain give the individual who does live with chronic pain an unpleasant reminder of an unpleasant possibility. Further, the ambiguity of chronic pain also contributes to the negative stereotypes of individuals who experience it. Pain is a private experience because there is no socially acceptable way to express it. No one wants to hear about someone else's pain and discomfort. Chronic pain often has no clear-cut cause, no end in sight, and, occasionally, no suitable relief (Bowman, 1994; Hadjistavropoulos & Craig, 1994). Everyone involved feels frustrated. Medical professionals often discount patients' reports of pain due to the following factors: (1) "Professionals do not always give credence to pain complaints unless there is some identifiable pathology," (2) "Professionals also often assume that all clients have the same pain perception threshold and therefore perceive the same intensity of pain from the same stimuli," and (3) "Many professionals have become desensitized to the client's pain experience and rate pain as less important than clients do" (Lubkin & Jeffrey, 1998, p. 151).

PSYCHOGENIC PAIN DISORDER

In this section, look for—

▶ *problems in diagnosing psychogenic pain disorder*
  1. often there are undiagnosed organic factors
  2. the diagnosis has no specific treatment
  3. the diagnosis is demeaning to the patient
  4. the diagnosis can lead to unjustified loss of insurance benefits
  5. the diagnosis may conceal an organically based diagnosis

Dr. Gallagher, in a section of his article titled, "Problems in using 'psychogenic pain' and other related diagnoses, " (2000, p. 24) stated,

> The notion that psychological problems cause pain disorder is speculative and based on unsystematic studies beset by methodological problems. One interpretation of the hardiness of these diagnoses is that they meet a need to label pain patients in a way that explicitly (i.e., "psychogenic") or vaguely (i.e., "somatoform") suggests a psychologic causation to justify psychiatric treatment or to absolve an employer, workers' compensation, or a physician from further responsibility in the case (p. 24).

Gallagher lists the problems in diagnosing psychogenic pain disorder, including: (1) in case reviews of patients diagnosed with psychogenic pain disorder, "a high prevalence of previously undiagnosed organic factors" were found; (2) the diagnosis of psychogenic pain disorder has no specific treatment or outcomes; (3) the diagnosis of psychogenic pain disorder "may be perceived as hostile to the patient. Suggesting psychological causation is interpreted by patients to mean that their pain is 'not real,' that they are crazy" (pp. 24–25); (4) such diagnoses can lead to unjustified loss of insurance benefits for the patients; and (5) such diagnoses "are useless clinically, for they suggest no specific treatment and always obfuscate a more refined, biopsychosocial, clinical assessment that does lead specific treatment approaches" (p. 25).

MORE ABOUT PAIN

In this section, look for—

▶ *the widespread fear of pain*
▶ *how often individuals who experience chronic pain are blamed for*
   1. the pain itself
   2. the management of the pain
   3. reminding others of the human possibility of pain

Pain is invisible. Individuals who appear "normal" often experience chronic pain that effectively curtails many of their life functions.

Wendell (1997) explained both the fear of pain and how we might overcome it:

People with painful disabilities can teach us about pain, because they can't avoid it and have had to learn how to face it and live with it. The pernicious myth that it is possible to avoid almost all pain by controlling the body gives the fear of pain greater power than it should have and blames the victims of unavoidable pain. The fear of pain is also expressed or displaced as fear of people in pain, which often isolates those with painful disabilities. All this is unnecessary. People in pain and knowledge of pain could be fully integrated into our culture, to everyone's benefit (p. 270).

THE DEGREE OF STIGMA DIRECTED TOWARD THE DISABILITY

In this section, look for—

▶ *how the PWD has two tasks*
   1. manage the disability
   2. deal with stigma
▶ *stigma recognition*
▶ *stigma management*

An individual with a disability has two tasks: (1) he or she must manage/treat the disability and (2) deal with the degree of stigma that others direct toward the disability. All PWDs, regardless of their type or severity of disability, personal achievements, or socioeconomic status, understand that they are members of a stigmatized and devalued group. However, it is safe to state that there is more stigma toward certain types of disabilities than there is toward other disabilities. We learned earlier that there is a hierarchy of stigma: individuals with physical disabilities experience the least degree of stigma, individuals with intellectual and cognitive disabilities experience more stigma, and individuals with psychiatric disabilities experience the most stigma.

Therefore, individuals with physical disabilities, such as blindness, mobility impairments, and chronic illness, experience less prejudice, less segregation, and are allowed more choices than are individuals with schizophrenia (Fink & Tasman, 1992; Friesen, 1996; Garske & Stewart, 1999). If medical and rehabilitation care providers were to attempt to quantify the degree of impairment of a mobility impairment and the degree of impairment of schizophrenia, such considerations as functions impaired, residual capacities available to the individual, treatment and hospitalizations required, and impact on the individual's vocational functioning would be examined. However, even with a comprehensive review of these important factors, the experience of living with these two types of disabilities is very different. Probably the greatest difference between these two types of disabilities (orthopaedic impairment and schizophrenia) is the prejudice and stigma that is directed toward one, but not toward the other. In Chapters 3, 4, 5, and 6 we discussed the concepts of prejudice, stigma, and discrimination from a societal viewpoint, largely looking at these concepts as a large group in power (society) holding prejudicial and stigmatizing views toward PWDs. In this chapter, the focus is on the individual's experience of stigma.

Stigma recognition and stigma management are two skills that PWDs are required to develop. Stigma recognition is the simple act of acknowledging that someone's judgments, appraisals, and actions are both inaccurate and hurtful. If the PWD is not able to recognize stigma and prejudice, he or she may be affected in the following ways: (1) engage in self-doubt, (2) feel angry, (3) feel depressed, or (4) feel humiliated (Holzbauer & Berven, 1996). Indeed, Holzbauer and Berven quoted an individual who felt the stigma to be justified, saying, "The worst part about it is that I felt it was my fault" (p. 481). Those PWDs who are adept at recognizing stigma may "forgive" the stigmatizer, thinking that he or she "doesn't know any better" or is "having a bad day." Other PWDs may become angry. Most important, however, is that by recognizing stigma as inaccurate, the PWD does not internalize these types of judgments. In other words, the PWD does not believe the insults and they do not become part of his or her self-concept. Naturally, a great deal of stigma recognition is dependent upon the PWD's age (adults are better at stigma recognition than children) and the PWD's social skills and awareness. Stigma recognition becomes an even more difficult issue when the stigma/handicapism is unintentional. Remember the story of Sharon L., who was told by her high school counselor that she could be an artist because (1) she would not have to associate with others; she could work alone and (2) those who purchased her art would never realize that it was "disabled art." Such attitudes are stigmatizing and hurtful, and yet, in this particular case, the professional career guidance was intended to be helpful. How should a PWD respond to such an unintentional stigma?

Stigma management can be handled with skillful humor and/or assertive and direct responses. Of course, the PWD must be especially proficient at correcting misconceptions and refusing to be denied his or her rights. Often, the skillful humor and assertiveness "backfires" and the PWD has more stigma directed toward him. In the video, *Irving King Jordan,* Dr. Jordan, who is president of Gallaudet University, skillfully manages the stigmatizing questions and comments of the interviewer. For example, Dr. Jordan prefaced one response with the comment, "May I teach you something?" Thus, politely teaching and informing the interviewer seemed a better response than angrily "setting this guy straight." At another point in the interview, the interviewer asked if Dr. Jordan ever got tired of using his hands to sign. Dr. Jordan did not respond to the specific question, but instead humorously asked the interviewer, "Doesn't your mouth get tired of moving?"

Stigma management is important in social situations and even more important in job interviews or admission interviews. Explaining accommodations (how they work, their expense, and how they would allow the PWD to do the job), explaining the disability and its impact (or lack of impact) on the job, or explaining the gap in a resume due to a hospitalization all require skillful stigma management. Further, this type of stigma management has clear-cut effects for the PWD. Stigma is hurtful, stressful, and in the case of PWDs, it is very personally directed toward a single person. For someone who has been teased and harassed as a child, managing stigma as an adult can be overwhelming.

Filing formal complaints is a type of stigma management. A study that reviewed the complaints of discrimination by PWDs under the Americans with Disabilities Act (ADA) between 1992 and 1996 (McMahon, et al., 1995) found that the two disability categories with the highest numbers of complaints were mental illness and learning disabilities. Examining the records of the Equal Employment Opportunity Commission (EEOC), as McMahon and his colleagues did, supports the idea that there is more stigma directed toward cognitive and psychiatric disabilities. These researchers interpreted their findings: "Members of both groups have been erroneously perceived as having sub-average intelligence, and this and other respects are historically misunderstood by the general public....This makes the matter of disability harassment appear all the more cowardly and insidious" (p. 11).

Stigma by Association

Families with a member with a disability also experience stigma, only in this case it is termed, "stigma by association." Leah Hager Cohen, Ruth Sidransky, and Lou Ann Walker wrote books about their deaf parents and all spoke of the stigma of having relatives who are deaf and of the need to conceal their parents' deafness. Potential boyfriends/husbands did not want deaf in-laws or deaf children and thus, dating and social opportunities for these women, all of whom were hearing, were unnecessarily limited. These authors relate many instances of stigma by association. Families with members with mental illnesses feel stigma by association (Friesen, 1996) and many have responded to this by engaging in advocacy and educational efforts, such as the National Alliance for the Mentally Ill (NAMI). Reread the excerpt in Chapter 8 from the Westbrook and Legge Australian study. These family members thought the presence of a child with a disability in the family decreased the other children's chances of marriage.

Professionals who serve PWDs are often stigmatized by association. Professionals who have chosen to work with stigmatized individuals (PWDs) are thought to "lack initiative, training, and ambition" (Fink & Tasman, 1992, p. 204). Indeed, Fink and Tasman assert that many talented psychiatrists leave the profession because they are aware of the stigmatization, feeling undervalued. Due to the fact that psychiatrists treat patients with the most stigmatized disabilities (mental illness), these psychiatrists often feel themselves to be stigmatized. Also professionals who work with individuals with mental retardation are often thought to be less capable than professionals who work with higher functioning clients/students/patients.

THE DEGREE OF VISIBILITY OF THE DISABILITY

In this section, look for—
- ▶ *how there is no correlation between degree of visibility and degree of impairment*
- ▶ *how some episodic disabilities can be invisible during times of symptom remission*
- ▶ *how choosing the point of disclosure requires careful timing*
- ▶ *how, often, it is the PWD's family who wishes to keep the disability hidden*

Some disabilities are readily apparent to others; other disabilities are not apparent to others unless the PWD chooses to disclose, and other types of disabilities are hidden from the individual himself/herself. Disabilities, such as diabetes, may be hidden from the individual for a prolonged period of time.

As you will remember from Chapter 5, there is no correlation between degree of visibility and degree of impairment. However, many PWODs, whether consciously or subconsciously, do view the degree of visibility to be related to the degree of severity. In other words, these PWODs mistakenly believe that hidden disabilities are not as severe as visible disabilities. Indeed many individuals with hidden disabilities report, "You get tired of defending yourself all the time." Or, occasionally, individuals with hidden disabilities become angry and tell others, "It's none of your damned business." Often PWODs do not consider them to have a disability.

In addition, legally (under the ADA) the individual with a hidden disability is required to disclose the disability in order to receive accommodations. If he or she chooses not to disclose, often functioning is sacrificed. Visibility of assistive technology, such as insulin pumps or hearing aids, can render a disability visible (which heretofore was considered to be a hidden disability).

Disabilities with an episodic course are often visible only in times of symptom exacerbation or "flare-ups." Nonetheless, since most disabilities with an episodic course are unpredictable, it is difficult for the individual to "hide" the disability. For example, someone with a seizure disorder may have a difficult time explaining why he or she does not have a driver's license. A woman with rheumatoid arthritis, an episodic disability, described how she made daily decisions whether or not to disclose her disability. She said, "I finally broke down and asked my doctor about a handicap sticker [parking sticker]. [Was that a big step for you?]....yeah, well I still didn't want the handicap license plate. The sticker I can not use it or hide it or whatever" (Gordon, Feldman, & Crose, 1998, p. 8).

Both a parking sticker and a metal license plate are accommodations for the woman with rheumatoid arthritis. However, the parking sticker can be hidden when the woman is experiencing symptom remission.

For many individuals with hidden disabilities, the question is not *whether* to disclose the presence of the disability, but *when* to disclose the disability. This is referred to as "choosing the point of disclosure." Individuals with these types of disabilities can allow relevant characteristics to be displayed, while establishing the relationship, and when they feel the time is right, they can tell others that they have a disability. For instance, the individual can settle into a new job and demonstrate his or her capabilities and productivity before informing his or her supervisor and coworkers of the disability. In this case, the job capabilities and productivity are the relevant characteristics and the individual with a hidden disability has availed himself/herself of the option to be viewed as an ordinary employee (i.e., an employee without a disability). As we have learned, many PWODs regard a disability to be the defining characteristic of the PWD; however, the individual with a hidden disability can avoid much of this labeling and stereotyping. In social relationships, the individual with a hidden disability can establish friendships and other types of relationships without the automatic and erroneous assumptions about disabilities interfering.

The timing of the disclosure requires a careful balance: The individual must judge when he or she has established his or her capabilities but cannot take too long before disclosing because others often feel betrayed. For example, in the case of a dating relationship, the individual with the hidden disability can wait until the relationship has become very serious and then reveal his or her disability. However, the dating partner may be angry that he or she was not told at the very beginning.

Of course, some individuals with hidden disabilities choose not to disclose at all. Even in the case of an individual who has disclosed to his or her employer, the ADA requires that the employer maintain confidentiality. In these cases, the worker could have accommodations but his or her coworkers and clients would not know about the disability. The ADA provides for locked personnel file cabinets and other safeguards of the individual's privacy. Nonetheless, it is difficult to "pass" as a PWOD. Work absences for hospitalizations, the need to take medication on a strict schedule, or time off for support group meetings become difficult to explain. Further, as many people with hidden disabilities understand, the truth may be better than the negative implications that others often draw. In the case of the individual with a seizure disorder who does not have a driver's license, it may be wise to disclose the reason why he or she does not drive rather than have others "believe the worst."

Exhibit 9–1 is the chart on the cost–benefit ratio of disclosure (also found in Chapter 5). Perhaps the greatest "cost" of concealing a disability is the stress of hiding a characteristic that is central to one's identity, feeling that no one really "knows" him or her. The person may feel that he or she is always being a "phony" and being untrue to oneself. Reread Cynthia Rich's excerpt in which she refers to hiding a disability as "one of the most serious threats to selfhood."

Some individuals with hidden disabilities experience "heightened marginality" (Whitt, 1984). Speaking of the self-identity of children, Whitt explained, "Some studies...report that children with diseases which produce little significant disability (e.g., epilepsy) may have more psychosocial problems than their physically disabled [sic] peers. Barker, Wright, Meyerson, and Gonick's (1953) concept of 'marginality' acknowledged the heightened ambiguity experienced by children with minimal disabilities. These youngsters neither enjoy the benefit of being "normal" nor evoke the environmental support and allowances accorded more clearly handicapped [sic] children" (Whitt, 1984, p. 83).

A student in our department retired from the Air Force as a colonel. While in the Air Force, he was selected for the highly competitive test-pilot flight school. During the routine physical examination, it was discovered that he had diabetes. He had to withdraw from test-pilot school and, indeed, discontinue his life's work as a

Exhibit 9–1

Benefits of Disclosure

1. Accommodations are provided;
2. The truth is often better than negative assumptions.

Costs of Disclosure

1. No accommodations are given;
2. Negative characteristics are attributed to the individual with the disability;
3. Others with the same disability who have disclosed consider the person who "passes" as disloyal;
4. It is stressful to hide something that is part of one's self-identity;
5. The individual has lost an opportunity to advocate and educate others about the disability;
6. There might be more problems if the disability is discovered by others;
7. The individual sacrifices the group solidarity, support, and understanding of associating with other PWDs.

---

pilot. He jokingly referred to this career change as "flying a desk." Diabetes, a hidden disability, is often considered to be a relatively minor disability, one that does not impair an individual's functioning very much. However, for this colonel, it ended his flying career. While we cannot presume to understand the way in which the colonel responded to his disability, we can see that a hidden disability requires a different response and change in self-identity than a visible disability does. Of course, the type of onset, in the colonel's case, an insidious onset, also influences the individual's response.

Occasionally, it is not the PWD who wishes to hide or minimize the disability. Family members may encourage the individual with a hidden disability to keep the disability concealed. The family members understand the advantages of avoiding the "disabled role" for the PWD, and moreover, they may want to avoid the "stigma by association" for themselves. Weinberg & Sterritt (1991) explained the rationale:

> Many parents of children with physical disabilities would like to have their children develop a primary identification with the able-bodied world. Parents of children with disabilities know that society views people with disabilities as less acceptable, and that people with disabilities have difficulty in establishing satisfying social relationships and obtaining jobs....To improve their children's chances of succeeding, parents may encourage their children to appear, and to behave, as able-bodied as possible. To the extent that children can "pass" as able-bodied, these parents believe that the likelihood of their children's being accepted and succeeding is increased....(p. 68)

> Finally, if children with disabilities identify with and succeed in being a part of the able-bodied world, the parents' place in the able-bodied world is less disturbed. If, however, the parents have children who are unacceptable to able-bodied society, this reflects negatively on them, for they inevitably share their children's negative social identity....(p. 69)

Weinberg & Sterritt also explained the effect on these children:

In stressing the importance of "passing," as able-bodied, parents may also be communicating that being able-bodied is good and being disabled [*sic*] is bad....Children with disabilities are thus being told, "As you are, you are inferior, and to the extent that you can emulate able-bodied people, this is the extent to which you can overcome your inferiority." Yet achieving full able-bodied status is inherently impossible, so children with disabilities may be condemned to always feel inferior, always to work to cover up their deficiencies, and always be on guard lest their disabilities show. They can rarely be at ease with who they are (p. 69).

DEGREE OF DISFIGUREMENT OF THE DISABILITY

In this section, look for—

▶ *how disabilities can be disfiguring*
▶ *how symptoms of the disability can be disfiguring*
▶ *how treatments can be disfiguring*

Not all disabilities involve "disfigurement." Amputations, facial disfigurements, and burns are examples of disabilities that are considered to be disfiguring. Others, such as myasthenia gravis in which the individual's eyelids "droop," or rheumatoid arthritis in which the individual's joints are swollen and misshapen, are thought of as having disfiguring symptoms. Treatments can also be disfiguring. Medications often cause weight gain, radiation treatments cause the individual to lose his or her hair, and antipsychotic medications often have unpleasant and unattractive side effects. Disfiguring side effects of antipsychotic medications include: perioral tremor ("rabbit syndrome") in which the individual involuntarily moves his or her lips rapidly in movements that mimic a rabbit, and tardive dyskinesia, involuntary face, trunk, and limb movements, some of which are rocking, twisting, and jerking (Maxmen & Ward, 1995). Parenthetically, it is not difficult to understand why many individuals with psychiatric disabilities quit taking their medication.

BODY IMAGE

In this section, look for—

▶ *body image*
 1. *is (partly) the result of how we think others perceive us*
 2. *changes as the individual progresses through development stages*

Since the concept of disfigurement is closely related to an individual's image of his/her body, we will briefly discuss body image. An individual's body image is the mental picture of oneself, including the physical self, physical appearance, sexuality, health, and physical skills (Bramble & Cukr, 1998). Or, stated differently, body image is how the individual's body appears to himself/herself. The body is a reflection of oneself (Berkman, Weissman, & Frielich, 1978). Obviously, the use of multiple senses—visual, tactile, and kinesthetic—are involved in forming an individual's body image. Even more important in forming one's body image, however, is the individual's perception of how others view his or her body. Interacting with others in establishing body image is circular: How we think others perceive us influences our image of our physical self, and our image of our physical self influences how we perceive the world. Indeed, the "bad hair day" theory has been proven in research; individuals who think their hair is a mess, feel bad and perform poorly. Much of an individual's self-esteem is tied to his or her body image.

The development of body image changes as the individual progresses through physical and developmental stages of life (Lerner & Jovanovic, 1990; Pruzinsky, 1990). For instance, infants have no body image; children begin to develop a body image (and a sexual identity) (Weinberg, 1982), and "adolescence is a time of exquisite body image sensitivity" (Bramble & Cukr, 1998, p. 285). Indeed, during adolescence, the individual's body image is more influenced by others, especially peers, rather than his or her own judgment (Blumberg, Lewis, & Susman, 1984). Adults have usually come to terms with their body image and because of this, it is very difficult for adults to adjust their body image. Nonetheless, the aging process requires a shift in body image. Fortunately, the aging process is a gradual one, allowing the individual time to redefine his or her body image. The aging process is also a universal one, meaning that one's agemates also look bad and are experiencing sensory loss and loss of functional abilities.

In addition to the developmental stage of the individual, body image is influenced by the gender of the person. Girls and women are more critical of their appearance than are males; but they are more comfortable with body changes than men are (Pruzinsky & Cash, 1990). It is also safe to say that women are judged more on their appearance than are men (Asch & Fine, 1997).

DISFIGUREMENTS AS SOCIAL HANDICAPS

In this section, look for—

▶ *disfiguring disabilities*
   1. *age of onset (or stage of development) influences the individual's response)*
   2. *pace of onset (acute or gradual) influences the individual's response*

Since an individual's body image is a reflection of how the individual thinks that others are perceiving him or her, a disfiguring disability is truly a social handicap. Further, females and males respond differently to disfigurements because each gender thinks of body image in a somewhat different way. Finally, because an individual's body image evolves with each stage of development, the time of onset of a disfigurement is important (Rybarczyk, et al., 1995).

Disability scholars (Bernstein, 1989; Macgregor, Abel, Bryt, Laver, & Weissmann, 1953) have used the term "social death" to describe the effect of a major disfigurement and the term "closet people" to describe individuals with these types of disfigurements. "Closet people" withdraw from all social contact and stay at home; therefore they have experienced "social death"; these individuals feel they have no place in the world. Feminist disability scholars Adrienne Asch and Michelle Fine have asserted that women with disabilities, especially disfiguring disabilities, because they cannot attain the widely accepted standard of feminine beauty, often turn toward "male standards of achievement" (1997, p. 251), which probably means career advancement. Another feminist disability scholar, Rosemarie Garland Thomson (1997b) stated that political subordination is linked "to the cultural valuing and devaluing of bodies on the basis of their appearance" (p. 297). Thomson also asserts that many feel that virtue is linked to feminine beauty and that "beauty brings fulfillment" (p. 299). Further, Thomson stated that many believe that women with disfiguring disabilities must lead tortured, miserable lives (1997a).

Finally, the age of onset of the disfigurement is important. Those with congenital disabilities do not have to adjust their body image. "Children with congenital physical disabilities are only familiar with their already impaired bodies (Livneh & Antonak, 1997). Generally speaking, it is adolescents who have the most difficulty in responding to a disfiguring disability simply because adolescence is a time when individuals are very concerned about their appearance and the opinions/judgments of others. Indeed, it can take years for adolescents (and some adults) to adjust their body image after the onset of a disfiguring disability. Elderly individuals may not feel a disfiguring disability to be a great challenge simply because they have already come to terms with physical losses and diminished attractiveness.

The pace of onset of the disfiguring disability influences the individual's response. Disabilities, such as rheumatoid arthritis, which have a slow and gradual onset are considered to present fewer adjustment demands on the individual's body image. Robert Neumann described his teenage experience with rheumatoid arthritis. Note the use of the third person—Neumann writes of the person in the mirror as if the person were not himself:

> One day, almost by chance, I could avoid it no longer. I caught a good look at myself in a full-length mirror and was appalled at what I saw. I had remembered myself as having an able body. The person I saw looking back at me had a face swollen from high doses of cortisone, hands with unnaturally bent fingers, and legs that could barely support his weight" (1988, p. 157).

However, the majority of disfiguring disabilities have acute onset, many of them traumatic (Bernstein, 1976; 1989; 1990; Goldstein, 1986; Patterson, et al., 1993). For example, individuals who experience severe burns confront an unexpected, sudden change in body image (Weinberg & Miller, 1983). One little girl with facial burns remembered: "There were no mirrors in my house, so I wouldn't get scared" (Holaday & McPhearson, 1997, p. 354).

The Importance of Social Support

Anyone with any type of disability needs social support. However, individuals with disfiguring disabilities require even greater degrees of social support due to the fact that their disability elicits a great deal of rejection and avoidance from others (Bernstein, Breslau, & Graham, 1988; Bernstein, 1990; Love, et al., 1987). During World War II, a group of English Royal Air Force (RAF) pilots, who had acquired disfiguring disabilities (mostly burns), formed an organization. They all wore the same blazer and continued to meet 40 years after the end of the war. The importance of group solidarity, common understanding, and shared experiences filled a need for these men. (The blazer may have also served to inform others of the way in which they acquired their disfigurement: combat service in the RAF.)

Read the following excerpts. The first three are from individuals with severe burns. They all express the importance of social support.

When I got burned at age 18, I found out who my real friends were: They were the ones who came to see me and they still are my friends (Holaday & McPhearson, 1997, p. 349).

They (friends) made me use my burned hand to play games like ping-pong, so it wouldn't get stiff (ibid, p. 349).

Another severely burned interviewee (now a grandfather)...had been given the last rites and was expected to die. Against hospital rules, his wife brought their infant son into his room to say goodbye. It was at that moment the new father decided that he would fight to live despite his injuries because he wanted to watch his son grow up. "My family became my motivation to survive" (ibid, p. 348).

Read the lack of social support these individuals experienced:

Amy Hagadorn, a 9-year-old girl with cerebral palsy, limiting the use of her fingers on her right hand and resulting in a limp and impairment in speech, wrote a letter to Santa Claus sponsored by a local radio station: "Kids laugh at me because of the way I walk and run and talk. I want just one day where no one laughs at me or makes fun of me" (Holzbauer & Berven, 1996, p. 479).

A vignette by Henry Viscardi, whose legs were congenitally deformed, on his first day of grade school: "My sister Terry took me to school the first day. Clutching her hand, I hoisted myself up the steps to the schoolyard. It was crowded with children....I heard laughter. 'Hey, Louis, looka the ape man.' Three big boys came toward me....The crowd of jeering boys had grown. One of them...came over and shoved me. I shoved back against his knee. 'Oh, you wanta fight, kid?'....'I want to go home.' I hung on Terry's arm, tears rolling down my cheeks. 'Sissy, sissy' (ibid, p. 479).

Scapegoating of a family member with a disability can occur, sometimes with grisly consequences...a young child who had been severely burned became a 'whipping boy' to his poor, alcoholic, and dysfunctional family for many years. Nearly every evening his parents, two siblings, and two cousins would become drunk and make vicious fun of his disfigurement. One evening when the group had been more abusive than usual, he systematically lured each inebriated individual into a different room of the house, bludgeoning each of them to death (ibid, p. 349).

THE TREATMENT OF INDIVIDUALS WITH DISFIGURING DISABILITIES

In this section, look for—
 ▶ *treatment of disfiguring disabilities*
 1. is a battle against societal reactions
 2. usually does not concern itself with loss of function (mobility or sensory)
 3. takes years of rehabilitation

Treatment of individuals with disfiguring disabilities is different than other types of treatment or interventions. One disability scholar (Bernstein, 1989) described these different treatments and interventions as the result of three factors:

> First, treatment is a battle against societal values and community reactions. Second, it involves a problem of appearance and symbolism rather than a problem of mobility, pain, or sensory loss. And finally, there is an element of chronic grief over the situation. It is critical to be aware of time scale: for most of these individuals adjustment to a disfigurement takes years and rehabilitation takes years more—sometimes a lifetime (pp. 155–156).

In their interviews, Holaday and McPhearson (1997) found that "Burn survivors insisted that patients also be told about normal and predictable emotional distress following a severe burn so that they could be prepared for the possibility of depression, sleep disorders, nightmares, and physical reactions to reminders of the burn or treatments....'No one told me about the mood swings. I thought I was crazy. They should tell you these things. One of my day-care workers told me I was possessed because I had such terrible nightmares'" (p. 353).

Individuals respond to their disfiguring disabilities in several ways (Goldstein, 1986). Some individuals develop compassion for the strangers who stare; one person with severe facial scars stated, "I'd stare if I saw someone like me too!" (Holaday & McPhearson, 1997, p. 351). Some sequester themselves in their homes while others decide that cosmetic devices, designed to make them appear more "normal", are not worth the loss of function or the discomfort and inconvenience. Others do not incorporate the disfigurement into their identity, referring to their facial scarring as a "mask"; indeed, one woman insisted that she removed the mask when she was at home with her family (Morris, 1991). Wright (1960) included a short excerpt from Katherine Butler Hathaway:

> Over and over I forgot what I had seen in the mirror. It could not penetrate into the interior of my mind and become an integral part of me. I felt as if it had nothing to do with me; it was only a disguise. But it was not the kind of disguise which is put on voluntarily by the person who wears it, and which is intended to confuse other people as to one's identity. My disguise had been put on me without my consent or knowledge like the ones in fairy tales, and it was on me for life. It was there, it was there, it was real. Every one of those encounters was like a blow on the head. They left me dazed and dumb and senseless every time, until slowly and stubbornly my robust persistent illusion of well-being and of personal beauty spread all through me again....(p. 157)

Another way in which to respond is explained in the title of the video, *My Body Is Not Who I Am*. Obviously, for these individuals, their self-esteem and self-identity is not associated with their physical bodies.

Susan Wendell (1997) theorized that if PWODs were to understand the experience of PWDs, including individuals with disfiguring disabilities, PWODs would no longer be "oppressed" by their bodies. She summarized: "Our physical ideals change from time to time, but we always have ideals. These ideals are not just about appearance; they are also ideals of strength and energy and proper control of the body. We are perpetually bombarded with images of these ideals, demands for them....Idealizing the body prevents everyone, able-bodied and disabled, from identifying with and loving his/her real body" (p. 267).

Prognosis of the Disability

In the strictest sense, the definition of the word, "prognosis," is the prospect of a cure or recovery and, therefore, since disabilities are long-term, chronic conditions, the concept of a prognosis does not actually apply to most disabilities. As you remember, the idea of a prognosis is that of two outcomes: cure or death. The idea of prognosis is probably considered in those few disabilities which do have a terminal course, such as muscular dystrophy, AIDS, or cystic fibrosis. The key word in the last sentence is "course," because due to the advances in medical science, individuals with these disabilities often live years after the onset.

Nonetheless, there are a few disabilities that eventually result in the individual's death. Some scholars have termed this experience, "living with death," and, as would be expected, the tasks of the individual with this type of disability do not include long-term management of the disability, ensuring the highest quality of life, and emotionally preparing oneself and one's family for death (Allen & Sawyer, 1983). Certainly, the time of onset of these terminal disabilities has an impact on the individual's response. For example, muscular dystrophy (MD) is usually diagnosed by age 5 and the individual usually does not live beyond age 20 or 30. Therefore, the individual preparing for death is a child or a teenager. In contrast, amyotrophic lateral sclerosis is a disability with a terminal course, but it is a late onset disability and the individual is usually elderly. Individuals with MD and their families report that emotional and psychological issues are greater concerns than are physical symptoms. This seems reasonable because it is more difficult for a child or young adult to die than it is for an elderly person.

In addition to age of onset, the duration of the period between the diagnosis and the death of the individual influences response. It is safe to state that many individuals who experience a period of years between diagnosis and death often deny the reality of their impending death. This long interval also allows the individual to undertake the typical developmental tasks, such as school, work, marriage, and family. For others, the interval between diagnosis and death is relatively short and issues to be confronted are (1) pain, (2) fear of being separated from loved ones, (3) concern about being a burden on family, and (4) concern about family grieving after the death. Also, different types of disabilities require varied treatments during the final stages. Naturally, the living–dying interval is unique to each individual.

For many individuals with terminal disabilities, and their families, religious/spiritual/philosophic questions and answers are of great importance. However, many professionals are not trained or experienced in supporting the individual's spiritual search for meaning. This is probably due to the long-held view of the medical, psychological, and counseling professions that holds that the spiritual/religious/philosophical concerns of clients and patients are private, personal matters. Also, Freudian psychology has long been biased against religion, viewing it as an infantile escape from reality. Indeed, until the fourth edition of the *Diagnostic and Statistical Manual* published by the American Psychiatric Association (1994), religious beliefs of patients and clients were either pathologized or ignored (Smart & Smart, 1997). In spite of this, Taylor, Jones, and Burns (1998) stated, "Spirituality is clearly a core dimension and critical determinant of health-related quality of life" (p. 215).

Many professionals (and others) assume that a disability with a terminal course brings only pain, suffering, and despair. However, many individuals with these types of disability experience a high-quality life and report a feeling of mastery and satisfaction, which often includes ascribing religious meaning and purpose to both the disability and their impending death.

TREATMENT

> ### In this section, look for—
>
> ▶ *five general types of services*
> 1. *medical services*
> 2. *educational services*
> 3. *vocational services*
> 4. *residential services*
> 5. *mutual support groups*

The last factor that influences an individual's response to a disability concerns the type of treatment/services the individual receives. As we have discussed, in the past, disability was thought to be a personal or family concern, meaning that the family took care of all of the PWD's needs (Chubon, 1994). Moreover, it is safe to state that there are some people who continue to think that society should not concern itself with providing services to PWDs. Nonetheless, broadly speaking, these types of services can be conceptualized as falling within these categories: (1) medical services, (2) educational services, (3) vocational services, (4) residential services, and (5) mutual support groups. Obviously, due to the fact that each of these five broad types of services is provided by different types of individuals and in different settings, it is important that services be both comprehensive, continuous, and coordinated. As stated before, a perfect world is not a world without disabilities, but rather, a world in which (1) treatment and accommodations are provided to PWDs, and (2) there is full social, educational, vocational, and political integration of PWDs.

Medical treatment includes hospitals and regional rehabilitation centers where individuals, especially those with spinal cord injuries, learn the various skills and the use of assistive technology (Boswell, Dawson, & Heninger, 1998). Medical treatment also includes psychologists. Some PWDs, after the medical stabilization of their disability, will not utilize medical services more than anyone else. For other PWDs, there are symptom exacerbations, secondary disabilities, and complications which may require careful medical monitoring and treatment throughout the individual's life (Berkman, Weissman, & Frielich, 1978). Other PWDs take medication, thus requiring careful medical monitoring so as to maximize the therapeutic benefit while limiting side effects. As we have stated before, a PWD has two medical goals: (1) to manage and treat the disability, preventing complications, and (2) to maintain the highest quality of life possible. Rereading the section on the Medical Model of Disability in Chapter 2, we can see that the relationship between the medical profession and PWDs has been ambivalent. On the one hand, medical practitioners and scientists have greatly improved the lives of PWDs, including saving their lives. On the other hand, medical providers have often not viewed their patients as individuals with social, familial, and vocational roles.

The Difference Between Eligibility Programs and Entitlement Programs

Community educational services are a relatively new development. Indeed, the "birth" of special education is considered to have occurred during the decade of the 1960s. Of course, there were residential schools for children who were deaf and/or blind; but other than these there were no educational services available for children with disabilities. Education, for both children with and without disabilities, is an entitlement program, meaning that there are no eligibility requirements to be admitted to school. Continuity of services is often difficult to achieve when children with disabilities leave the public school due to (1) the shift from children's services to adult services, and (2) the shift from an entitlement program to eligibility programs. Naturally, in the past, individuals with severe disabilities lived their entire lives in institutions and, therefore, continuity of services was not an issue.

The Different Philosophical Orientation of Vocational Rehabilitation (VR) and Independent Living (IL)

Vocational rehabilitation (VR), a state and federal program, is both an adult program (minimum age for service is 16 years old) and an eligibility program. The eligibility criteria include: (1) the presence of a disability, (2) the disability is an impediment to employment, and (3) there must be a reasonable expectation that services will result in job placement. An individual applying for services must meet all three criteria. Because of this, many PWDs were refused services. These individuals had severe disabilities and therefore met the first two criteria but, due to the severity of their disability, were not able to meet the third criterion and consequently were refused services. The members of the Independent Living (IL) movement fought hard against, as they viewed it, considering an individual only in economic terms. Indeed, the state/federal VR system is a program that pays for itself and, moreover, makes a profit for the government. This is to say, when PWDs are placed in jobs, they pay taxes during their working lifetime and do not need public assistance (welfare), thus repaying many times what their VR services cost the government. Individuals in the IL movement have often viewed this as seeing the PWD only as an economic investment. Individuals in VR claim that working and economic empowerment mean more than money. Such factors as self-esteem, social contact, adult status, the chance to use creativity and to learn new things, and the opportunity to make a contribution and serve others are a few of the "rewards" of working. And, as we have seen, Louis Harris polls have shown that most PWDs express a desire to work.

There is a continuum of vocational placement from sheltered employment, supported employment using a job coach to what is termed "competitive" employment, meaning that the individual "competes" with PWODs for the same job (and is paid the same as PWODs). Sheltered employment, for example in workshops, is not used as much as it once was and has been the subject of a great deal of criticism. However, there are some PWDs for whom sheltered workshops is the best placement. This continuum of vocational placement is another new concept that has allowed PWDs to work in the community, but at the same time, receive appropriate support.

Residential services and living arrangements are far different than they were 40 years ago. Indeed, there are many professionals at the point of retirement, who remember when individuals with certain types of disabilities were automatically institutionalized for life. In contrast, most individuals entering professions serving

PWDs will not see people who have spent decades of their lives in institutions. Of course, for a few PWDs, institutionalization is necessary (Singer, 1996). However, for the majority of PWDs, there is a continuum of living arrangements, beginning at full community integration, to halfway houses, supported living arrangements, and group homes. The rationale of this continuum is to allow the individual as much community integration as possible while providing the support and care necessary. This is often referred to as "the most enabling environment" or "the least restrictive environment." A single individual during his or her lifetime, may move from one group home to a supported living arrangement in an apartment and so on. The importance of comprehensive treatment can be seen here. Some PWDs require good medical care and support and supervision in their living arrangement and their jobs. All service providers must work together to ensure that the individual has the highest quality of life possible.

The Advantages for Newcomers and "Veterans" of Mutual Support Groups

The last type of treatment to be discussed is not provided by professionals, but rather by mutual support groups. There are all types of mutual support groups, some for children, others for adults. Most mutual support groups are disability-specific, that is, individuals with cancer or individuals with mental retardation (Power & Rogers, 1979). Some groups are comprised of PWDs, others are comprised of family members of PWDs. Also, the level of organization and goal attainment varies; some groups have clear-cut goals while other groups are more informal and simply offer support. Once mutual support groups were viewed as a challenge to the medical profession. Today, however, physicians recognize the value of such groups and encourage their patients to participate. Some of the benefits of these types of groups include: the opportunity to learn about and associate with others who are living with the same type of disability (often those who have had the disability for a longer period of time are called "veterans"). Veterans can describe the likely course of the disability, help others to view their emotional responses as typical (this is referred to as "normalizing"), help others to establish realistic expectations, and assist others in accessing services and other resources in the community. Most medical professionals do not live 24 hours a day with a disability and it is natural that PWDs, and their families, would seek out others who are living the same experience. A sense of mastery and competence results for the newcomers. Also, the veterans often report that assisting others to deal with a disability helps them to find meaning in their own disability. Commonality and support are the hallmarks of mutual support groups. Read Joan Tollifson's feelings about associating with other PWDs:

> After a lifetime of isolating myself from other disabled [sic] people, it was an awakening to be surrounded by them. For the first time in my life, I felt like a real adult member of the human community. Finally, identifying myself as a disabled person was an enormous healing. It was about recognizing, allowing, and acknowledging something that I had been trying to deny, and finding that disability does not equal ugliness, incompetence, and misery" (Tollifson, 1997, p. 107).

Two Perspectives—The Service Provider and the Recipient of Services

Naturally, in order for a therapeutic alliance to be established, both professional and client/consumer should work toward an open and collaborative relationship. However, service providers and recipients of services often do not operate under the same set of assumptions and these conflicting assumptions work against establishing a collaborative relationship. We shall briefly discuss both the client/consumer's perspective and the perspective of professionals.

THE PERSPECTIVE OF THE CLIENT/CONSUMER

In this section, look for—
- ▶ *the concept of a "rescuer"*
- ▶ *why some PWDs have felt themselves to be "pawns" in agencies' struggles for survival*
- ▶ *the concept of iatrogenic treatment*
- ▶ *how professionals can contribute to prejudice and discrimination*

Disability is expensive. For example, Livneh and Antonak (1997) stated, "It is estimated that the cost of lifelong treatment for an individual with traumatic brain injury may exceed $4.5 million. The cost of traumatic brain injury to society each year was estimated recently...to approach a staggering $5 billion for medical intervention, rehabilitation, residential care, and lost earnings and may be several times that amount if consideration is given to the costs incurred by family, friends, and neighbors" (pp. 151–152). Considering the cost of a single disability, traumatic brain injury, it is not remarkable that both disability and rehabilitation are businesses (Albrecht, 1992). The nation spends billions of dollars annually responding to disability (Berkowitz, 1989). Higgins (1992) summarized the effects of this businesslike atmosphere:

> Disability is a business and many people would be unemployed. Disability is big business. Medical professionals, counselors, special educators, and other human service professionals earn their living by serving disabled [*sic*] people....Consequently, we should not be surprised when such organizations expand disability to encompass more conditions and more people or perpetuate people's status as disabled....Many organizational professionals "live off of" disability. Academics do, too (p. 220).

For the client/consumer, the experience of a disability is both personal and unique to himself/herself. It is easy to see how professionals and clients often work under different assumptions. The following is a brief list of some of the criticisms/concerns that PWDs have expressed about the services and treatments they have received.

The Perspective of the Recipient of Services

1. Many service providers have abused their power, often wanting to control the PWD, rather than allow him or her to make decisions and choices. Much of this, if not most, was the result of good intentions. Indeed, the term "rescuer" has been used to describe care providers who see professional services as "rescuing" and thereby controlling the individual. Billy Golfus (1994) was especially outspoken about this: "When you're disabled and these Do-Gooders pull their shit, there is allegedly nothing that you can do. I know. I've suffered years of the Do-Gooders' afflictions. Their game is about wanting to be in control of other people's lives" (cited in Charlton, 1998, p. 167).

2. Some PWDs have felt themselves to be "pawns" in agencies' or programs' struggle for survival. The disability rights movement uses the derisive term, "warm bodies" to describe the need for agencies to document the number of PWDs they serve. Therefore, at times, there was the temptation to pathologize PWDs or, at minimum to reinforce the disability, in order for the agency or program to remain operating.

3. Some PWDs (and a few care providers) have termed some of the treatments as iatrogenic. Iatrogenic means that the caregiver or the institution causes the patient harm. Certainly, PWDs who had been institutionalized for years were not allowed to develop skills and abilities to live in the community and, therefore their lack of skills were not due to the disability but rather due to the treatment (the institutionalization). This is also a criticism that has been leveled at agencies and programs for individuals with psychiatric disabilities (Deegan, 1990). Anthony (cited in Garske & Stewart, 1999) stated, "Recovery from mental illness involves much more than recovery from the illness itself. People with mental illness may have to recover from the stigma they have incorporated into their very being, from the iatrogenic effects of treatment settings" (p. 7).

4. Especially in medical settings, the care providers with whom PWDs have the most contact are the least trained and least paid. Until recently, there were no background checks for criminal records for these types of employees and moreover, employee turnover was high. Attendants, orderlies, and aides provide most of the "treatment" many PWDs receive (Adams & Gentry, 1999). Eisenberg summarized: "Individuals of low social value, such as people with disabilities, are served by providers of low competence and low professional prestige" (Wolfensberger & Tullman, 1991, p. 212).

5. Professionals have, at times, defined the problems and social agenda of PWDs, even to the point of representing PWDs (without their permission) to the world (Stubbins, 1988). Disability rights advocates have been calling for organization *of* PWDs, rather than organizations *for* PWDs.

6. Many PWDs feel that they have not been treated as complete individuals. Their experiences with prejudice, stigma, and discrimination have not been regarded as relevant to their treatment and rehabilitation (Stubbins, 1988). A disability scholar explained: "Concepts such as sick role, prejudice, normalization, the social order, the power elite, and how these concepts shed understanding on issues in disability are regarded as interesting, but deemed only marginal in clinical practice" (Stubbins, 1988, p. 23).

7. PWDs, especially those in the Deaf Culture, feel that professionals have, in the past, contributed to prejudice, discrimination, and their lives of limited choices and reduced opportunities. The most clear-cut example of this is that of hearing teachers for deaf children advocating oralism, rather than sign language. Teaching oralism, or the ability to speak (and read lips) was an attempt to make the children appear to be hearing children. The result of decades of this teaching method left many of the Deaf without a culture and unable to communicate. Other professionals have needlessly limited the range of choices available to PWDs (within their abilities).

8. Finally, some professional care providers view PWDs as objects of charity and, therefore, the services they provide to PWDs are "gifts" for which the PWDs should have no expectation, and they must be appropriately grateful. Further, these "gift" services should not be questioned or challenged.

WHAT DO PWDs WANT FROM PROFESSIONAL CARE PROVIDERS?

In this section, look for—

▶ *four resources that professionals can bring to the therapeutic alliance:*
1. *hope*
2. *ideas*
3. *understanding of the prejudice and discrimination PWDs face*
4. *willingness to stand by the PWD*

Joe Marrone (1997), a rehabilitation counselor, outlined four resources that professionals can bring to the therapeutic relationship: (1) hope, (2) ideas, (3) an understanding of the prejudice and discrimination that PWDs encounter, and (4) a willingness to stand by the person. Hope, according to Marrone, is not ill-informed optimism, that everything will be all right. Patricia Deegan, speaking of individuals with psychiatric disabilities, succinctly summarized hope. Deegan tells people with schizophrenia, "People *do* get better." Neither Marrone nor Deegan is saying that recovery is fast or easy; they are simply saying that there is hope and many people do get better. Ideas that professionals bring to the relationship include knowledge of the disability, of adaptative technology, and of the legal mandates against discrimination.

As would be expected, PWDs want easy access to services (often difficult in bureaucratic, eligibility programs); they want to be treated as people rather than as a disability, and they do not want to be blamed (implicitly or explicitly) for the disability. PWDs know that they have the right to be informed consumers, which includes: knowing the training, experience, credentials, and theoretical orientation of professionals. Even more important, PWDs understand that they have the right to full explanations of the treatment goals, which includes the right to question, challenge, or appeal any part of the treatment/service. Reading the list, these needs of PWDs seem both legitimate and straightforward, but, nonetheless, until recently PWDs were not accorded these rights.

The Perspective of Professionals

If disability and rehabilitation are businesses, they are also political programs. Berkowitz, the foremost authority on government disability programs, summarized his book in which he described all the government programs designed to respond to disability. Berkowitz stated

Disability does not represent an exception to the general pattern of anachronistic and uncoordinated programs that are resistant to change....Reform has therefore taken place within the existing contours of the program and involved incremental, rather than fundamental change....In disability, as in social welfare in general, the only avenue of fundamental reform is to add another program to existing programs and to cope with the resulting confusion....Because of these tendencies, our disability policy, viewed in its historical context, consists of layers of outdated programs (p. 227).

Professionals must provide services to PWDs under these types of institutional constraints. Professionals bring technical knowledge, years of experience and training, and, for most, a desire to do a good job. There are other difficulties with which professionals deal, including the complexity and uniqueness of each individual and of each disability. Treatment is individualized (rather than standardized) and such individualization requires a high level of skill. Further, while everyone would quickly agree that it is not possible to measure anything of human value in terms of dollars and cents, most professionals must work within financial constraints. Clients/consumers may think of professionals, such as rehabilitation counselors, as controlling a great deal of money and other resources. In contrast, the rehabilitation counselors probably view themselves as operating with a very limited budget and within strict guidelines.

Another difficulty faced by professionals who serve PWDs is the fact that these professionals are not in control of the outcome (Stav & Florian, 1986). Inherent in the relationship is the right of the PWD to make his or her own decision. Reread the essay by Dr. Krauthammer. Focus on the individual with a spinal cord injury who decided to lie in the bed for seven years, and if after the seven years, a cure for spinal cord injuries had not been developed, he planned to commit suicide. Since this man was a hospital-mate of Krauthammer's when Krauthammer first sustained his injury 22 years ago, it is interesting to imagine what happened to this man. Attempting to view this man from a professional caregiver's perspective, he would seem to be the type that does not "engage" the system, but allows himself to be "processed" through it. Physicians, psychologists, and rehabilitation counselors probably advised this man to capitalize on his remaining abilities and to make plans for the future. Did he change his mind and try to look forward to a future? Whether he did or not, this man must have been a very difficult patient for service providers.

Medical and rehabilitation providers work in a system which has, for centuries, been pathology oriented. The technical language of these professions is often pathological. In addition, professionals are, to some extent, a product of their training. Read the following excerpt, focusing on what (and whom) this woman with autism, considered to be most helpful:

> As I grew older, the people who were of the greatest assistance were always the more creative, unconventional types. Psychiatrists and psychologists were of little help. They were too busy trying to analyze me and discover my deep dark psychological problems. One psychiatrist thought if he could find my "psychic injury," I would be cured. The high school psychologist wanted to stamp out my fixations on things like doors instead of trying to understand them and use them to stimulate learning (cited in Mackelprang & Salsgiver, 1999, p. 155).

CONCLUSION

As these last two chapters have discussed, the many factors of a disability make each disability a unique experience. Even disabilities of the same type and severity will have different courses; the symptoms will present in different ways, may require somewhat different treatment, and will have varied prognoses. Carolyn Vash, the disability scholar, developed a model of the factors that influence an individual's response to a disability, dividing these factors into three broad categories. These three categories are: (1) factors in the individual, (2) factors in the environment, and (3) factors of the disability. As you will remember, factors in the individual include such aspects as the individual's coping abilities, level of education, and financial resources. The environment includes such aspects as family support, other social support, assistive technology available, services provided, and the amount of prejudice and discrimination in society. These last two chapters have focused on the 10 factors in the disability. We have only briefly discussed the three broad types of factor issues, but, nonetheless, it can be seen that each disability is a unique experience for the individual.

In-Class Activities

- View the 57-minute video *Breaking the Silence Barrier Inside the World of Cognitive Disabilities.* The producers describe this video: "This program reports on creative technologies that are being used to help people with autism, traumatic brain injuries, and learning and speech disabilities. Temple Grandin, an autistic woman with a PhD in animal science, explains her "squeeze machine" which uses deep pressure therapy to help ease the hyperacute sensory dysfunction that often accompanies autism. Renowned neurologist Oliver Sacks shares his views on how people with autism can find meaning in their own distinctive way. Also profiled is Bob Williams, who is the first person with a significant speech disability to hold a major federal office, and several people with learning disabilities and traumatic brain injuries who have improved their lives by using multimedia software programs."
- View the 29-minute video, *Pain Management.* The producers describe this video: "Pain, a frequent part of recovery from illness and injury, is actually controllable in the vast majority of cases. This program. . . illustrates approaches to pain control for patients healing after surgery, dealing with cancer, and coping with chronic back and nerve conditions." Available from Films for the Humanities and Sciences, PO Box 2053, Princeton, NJ 08543–2053, or at their Web site: www.films.com 800–257–5126.

Learning Activities

Read and discuss any of the following books:

- *Staring Back: The Disability Experience from the Inside Out* edited by Kenny Fries. (1997, Plume Books, New York.) This book is a compilation of writings, nonfiction, poetry, fiction, and drama, by PWDs. Many of these authors are well known including John Hockenberry, Adrienne Rich, and Mark O'Brien (who was the subject of the Academy Award winning documentary, *Breathing Lessons.*) The publisher's "blurb" states, "The passionate, evocative pieces included here help to dispel the myth that disabilities limit insight and productivity, and focus instead on understanding and redefining the experience of disability.
- *Violence and Abuse in the Lives of People with Disabilities: The End of Silent Acceptance?* By Dick Sobsey. (1994, Paul H. Brookes Publishing Company, Baltimore). This book clearly describes the violence, abuse, and neglect that PWDs experience, using both statistical information and case studies. Sobsey also offers some explanations as to why this abuse occurs and then outlines ways in which to (1) detect abuse, (2) combat abuse by altering specific social situations, and (3) help to heal the consequences of abuse.
- *Women with Disabilities: Essays in Psychology, Culture, and Politics* edited by Michelle Fine and Adrienne Asch. (1988, Temple University Press, Philadel-

phia). In their introduction, the editors pose these questions: "How do being female and having a disability interact? How do women with disabilities view their experience? What can we learn about disability from literature, folklore, social science, law, and public policy? How do race, social class, social circumstances, and sexual orientation influence the lives of women with disabilities?" (p.1). This book answers these questions.

- *The Deaf Way: Perspectives from the International Conference on Deaf Culture* edited by Carol J. Erting, Robert C. Johnson, Dorothy L. Smith, and Bruce D. Snider. (1989, Gallaudet University Press, Washington, DC). During the week of July 9–14, 1989, over 6,000 people with hearing disabilities from all over the world came to Washington, DC, and this book is the compilation of the presentations. We learn about the Deaf in Sweden, Japan, Italy, African nations, the United States, and many more countries. The foreword of the book states, "Most important of all, perhaps, was the sense of peopleness that was everywhere prevalent. This book will provide, in some measure, an enduring documentation of many of the formal presentations. But above and beyond these serious overtones on the reality and vitality of deaf people, on empowerment, advancement, pride, and self-identity, the week was a deaf Woodstock, an exhilarating and unbelievable extravaganza brimming with the wonder of self-fulfillment and realization" (p. 414).

References

Adams, C., & Gentry, C. (1999, December 31). Nurse shortage hurts families of the disabled. *Wall Street Journal,* p. A12.

Albrecht, G. L. (1992). *The disability experience: Rehabilitation in America.* Newbury Park, CA: Sage.

Allen, H. A., & Sawyer, H. W. (1983). Individuals with life-threatening disabilities: A rehabilitation counseling approach. *Journal of Applied Rehabilitation Counseling, 15,* 26–29, 37.

American Psychiatric Association. (1994). *Diagnostic and statistical manual of mental disorder* (4th ed.). Washington, DC: Author.

Asch, A., & Fine, M. (1997). Nurturance, sexuality, and women with disabilities: The example of women and literature. In L. J. Davis (Ed.). *The Disability Studies Reader* (pp. 242–259). New York: Routledge.

Barker, R. G., Wright, B. A., Meyerson, L., & Gonick, M. R. (1953). *Adjustment to physical handicap and illness: A survey of the social psychology of physique and disability* (rev. ed.). New York: Social Science Research Council.

Berkman, A., Weissman, R., & Frielich, M. (1978). Sexual adjustment of spinal cord injured veterans living in the community. *Archives of Physical Medicine and Rehabilitation, 59,* 22–23.

Berkowitz, E. D. (1989). *Disabled policy: America's programs for the handicapped.* Cambridge, England: University of Cambridge.

Bernstein, N. R. (1976). *Emotional care of the facially burned and disfigured.* Boston: Little Brown.

Bernstein, N. R. (1989). Psychological problems associated with facial disfigurement. In B. W. Heller, L. M. Flohr, & L. S. Zegans, (Eds.). *Psychosocial interventions with physically disabled persons* (pp. 147–161). New Brunswick, NJ: Rutgers University.

Bernstein, N. R. (1990). Objective bodily damage: Disfigurement and dignity. In T. F. Cash & T. Pruzinsky (Eds.). *Body Images: Development, deviance, and change* (pp. 131–148). New York: Guilford.

Bernstein, N. R., Breslau, J. J., & Graham, J. A. (Eds.) (1988). *Coping strategies for burn survivors and their families.* New York: Praeger.

Blumberg, B. D., Lewis, M. J., & Susman, E. J. (1984). Adolescence: A time of transition. In M. G. Eisenberg, L. C. Sutkin, & M. A. Jansen (Eds.). *Chronic illness and lifespan: Effects on self and family* (pp. 133–149). New York: Springer.

Bonica, J. J. (Ed.) (1990). *The management of pain.* Philadelphia: Lea & Febiger.

Boswell, B.B., Dawson, M., & Heninger, E. (1998). Quality of life as defined by adults with spinal cord injuries. *Journal of Rehabilitation, 64,* 27–32.

Bowman, J. M. (1994). Experiencing the chronic pain phenomenon: A study. *Rehabilitation Nursing, 19*(2), 91–95.

Bramble, K., & Cukr, P. (1998). Body image. In I. M. Lubkin & P. D. Larsen (Eds.). *Chronic illness: Impact and interventions* (pp. 283–298). Sudbury, MA: Jones & Bartlett.

Charlton, J. I. (1998). *Nothing about us without us: Disability oppression and empowerment.* Berkeley, CA: University of California.

Chubon, R. A. (1994). *Social and psychosocial foundations of rehabilitation.* Springfield, IL: Charles C Thomas.

Cook, D. W. (1991). Disability, psychopathology, and vocational adjustment. In M. G. Eisenberg & R. L. Glueckauf (Eds.). *Empirical approaches to psychosocial aspects of disability.* (pp. 85–105). New York: Springer.

Corbin, J., & Strauss, A. (1988). *Unending work, and care: Managing chronic illness at home.* San Francisco: Jossey-Bass.

Cott, C., & Wilkins, S. (1993). Aging, chronic illness and disability. In M. Nagler (Ed.). *Perspectives on disability* (2nd ed.) (pp. 363–377). Palo Alto, CA: Health Markets Research.

Crewe, N. M (1997). Life stories of people with long term spinal cord injury. *Rehabilitation Counseling Bulletin, 41,* 26–42.

Curtin, M., & Lubkin, I. (1998). What is chronicity? In I. M. Lubkin & P. D. Larsen (Eds.). *Chronic illness: Impact and interventions* (4th ed.) (p. 325). Sudbury, MA: Jones & Bartlett.

Deegan, P. (1990). Spirit breaking: When the helping professions hurt. *The Humanistic Psychologist, 18,* 301–313.

DeLoach, C., & Greer, B. G. (1981). *Adjustment to severe physical disability: A metamorphosis.* New York: McGraw-Hill.

Ducharme, S., Gill, K., Biener-Bergman, S., & Fertitta, L. (1993). Sexual functioning: Medical and psychological aspects. In J. DeLisa (Ed.). *Rehabilitation medicine: Principles and practices* (2nd ed.) (pp. 763–782). Philadelphia: Lippincott.

Dunn, D. S. (1996). Well-being following amputation: Salutary effects of positive meaning, optimism, and control. *Rehabilitation Psychology, 41,* 285–301.

Elliott, T. R., Shewchuk, R., Hagglun, K., Rybarczyk, B., & Harkings, S. (1996). Occupational burnout, tolerance for stress, and coping among nurses in rehabilitation units. *Rehabilitation Psychology, 41,* 267–284.

Fabian, E. S. (1991). Using quality of life indicators in rehabilitation program evaluation. *Rehabilitation Counseling Bulletin, 34,* 344–356.

Falvo, D. R. (1991). *Medical and psychosocial aspects of chronic illness and disability.* Gaithersburg, MD: Aspen.

Feldman, D. (1974). Chronic disabling illness: A holistic view. *Journal of Chronic Diseases, 27,* 287–291.

Fink, P. J., & Tasman, A. (Eds.) (1992). *Stigma and mental illness.* Washington, DC: American Psychiatric Association.

Friesen, B. J. (1996). Family support in child and adult mental health. In G. H. S. Singer, L. E. Powers, & A. L. Olson (Eds.). *Redefining family support: Innovations in public–private partnerships* (pp. 259–274). Baltimore: Brookes.

Gallagher, R. M. (2000) Treating depression in patients with comorbid chronic pain, Part 1. *Directions in Rehabilitation Counseling, 1,* 15–32.

Garske, G. G., & Stewart, J. R. (1999). Stigmatic and mythical thinking: Barriers to vocational rehabilitation services to persons with severe mental illness. *Journal of Rehabilitation, 65,* 4–8.

Goldstein, R. K. (1986). Adjustment of the burned patient. In D. W. Krueger (Ed.). *Emotional rehabilitation of physical trauma and disability.* (pp. 87–104). New York: Pergamon.

Gordon, P. A., Feldman, D., & Crose, R. (1998). The meaning of disability: How women with chronic illness view their experiences. *Journal of Rehabilitation, 64,* 5–11.

Gordon, P. A., Lewis, M.D., & Wong, D. (1994). Multiple sclerosis: Strategies for rehabilitation counselors. *Journal of Rehabilitation,* 34–38.

Gulick, E. E. (1994). Social support among persons with multiple sclerosis. *Research in Nursing and Health, 17*(3), 195–206.

Hadjistavropoulos, H. D., & Craig, K. D. (1994). Acute and chronic low back pain: Cognitive, affective, and behavioral dimensions. *Journal of Consulting and Clinical Psychology, 62,* 341–349.

Hardman, M. L., Drew, C. J., Egan, M. W., & Wolf, B. (1993). *Human exceptionality: Society, school, and family.* (4th ed.). Boston: Allyn & Bacon.

Higgins, P. C. (1980). *Outsiders in a hearing world: A sociology of deafness.* Newbury Park, CA: Sage.

Higgins, P. C. (1992). *Making disability: Exploring the social transformation of human variation.* Springfield, IL: Charles C Thomas.

Higgins, P. C., & Nash, J. E. (Eds.). (1987). *Understanding deafness socially.* Springfield, IL: Charles C Thomas.

Holaday, M., & McPhearson, R. W. (1997). Resilience and severe burns. *Journal of Counseling and Development, 75,* 346–356.

Holzbauer, J. J., & Berven, N. L. (1996). Disability harassment: A new term for a long-standing problem. *Journal of Counseling and Development, 74,* 478–483.

Huberty, D. J. (1980). Adapting to illness through family groups. In P. W. Power & A. E. Dell Orto (Eds.). *Role of the family in the rehabilitation of the physically disabled* (pp. 433–443). Austin, TX: ProEd.

Jubala, J.A. (1990). Spinal cord injuries. In M. Hersen & V. B. Van Hasselt, (Eds.) *Psychological aspects of developmental and physical disabilities* (pp. 229–245).

Kilpatrick, S. D., and McCullough, M. E. (1999). Religion and spirituality in rehabilitation psychology. *Rehabilitation Psychology, 44,* 388–402.

Knight, S. E. (1989). Sexual concerns of the physically disabled. In B. W. Heller, L. M. Flohr, & L. S. Zegans (Eds.). *Psychosocial interventions with physically disabled persons* (pp. 183–199). New Brunswick, NJ: Rutgers University.

Kohler, K., Schweikert-Stary, M. T., & Lubkin, I. (1998). Altered mobility. In I. M. Lubkin & P. D. Larsen (Eds.) *Chronic illness: Impact and interventions* (4th ed.) (pp. 122–148). Sudbury, MA: Jones and Bartlett.

Kosciulek, J. F., & Lustig, D. C. (1998). Predicting family adaptation from brain injury-related family stress. *Journal of Applied Rehabilitation, 29*(1), 8–12.

Kozloff, R. (1987). Networks of social supports and the outcome from severe head injury. *Journal of Head Trauma Rehabilitation, 2,* 14–23.

Latham, J., & Davis, B. D. (1994). The socioeconomic impact of chronic pain. *Disability and Rehabilitation, 16,* 33–44.

Lerner, R. M., & Jovanovic, J. (1990). The role of body image in psychosocial adjustment across the lifespan: A developmental contextual perspective. In T. F. Cash & T. Pruzinsky (Eds.). *Body images, development, deviance, and change* (pp. 110–127). New York: Guilford.

Linton, S.J. (1986). Chronic back pain: Integrating psychological and physical therapy—an overview. *Pain, 24,* 101–104.

Livneh, H., & Antonak, R. F. (1997). *Psychosocial adaptation to chronic illness and disability.* Gaithersburg, MD: Aspen Publishers, Inc.

Love, B., Bryne, C., Roberts, J., Browne, G., & Brown, B. (1987). Adult psychosocial adjustment following childhood injury: The effect of disfigurement. *Journal of Burn Care and Rehabilitation, 8,* 280–285.

Lubkin, I., & Jeffrey, J. (1998). Chronic pain. In I. M. Lubkin & P. D. Larsen (Eds.) *Chronic illness: Impact and interventions* (4th ed.) (pp. 149–178). Sudbury, MA: Jones and Bartlett.

Lubkin, I. M., & Larsen, P. D. (Eds.) (1998). *Chronic illness: Impact and interventions* (4th ed.). Sudbury, MA: Jones and Bartlett.

Macgregor, F. C., Abel, J. M., Bryt, A., Laver, E., & Weissmann, S. (1953). *Facial deformities and plastic surgery: a psychosocial study.* Springfield, IL: Charles C Thomas.

Mackelprang, R., & Salsgiver, R. (1999). Disability: A diversity model approach in human service practice. Pacific Grove, Ca: Brooks/Cole.

Marrone, J. (1997, May 21). Job placement for individuals with psychiatric disabilities. Presented at the Utah State Office of Rehabilitation. 75th Anniversary Conference, Provo, Utah.

Maslach, C., & Florian, V. (1988). Burnout, job setting, and self-evaluation among rehabilitation counselors. *Rehabilitation Psychology, 33,* 85–93.

Maxmen, J. S., & Ward, N. G. (1995). *Psychotropic drugs: Fast facts* (2nd ed.). New York: Norton.

McCarthy, H. (1995). Understanding and reversing rehabilitation counseling's neglect of spirituality. *Rehabilitation Education, 9,* 187–199.

McDaniel, J. W. (1976). *Physical disability antihuman behavior* (2nd ed.). New York: Pergamon.

McMahon, B. T., Shaw, L. R., & Jaet, D. N. (1995). An empirical analysis: Employment and disability from an ADA litigation perspective. *NARPPS Journal and News, 10*(1), 3–14.

McReynolds, C. J., Koch, L.C., & Rumrill, P. D., Jr. (1999). Psychosocial adjustment to multiple sclerosis: Implications for rehabilitation counselors. *Journal of Vocational Rehabilitation, 12,* 83–91.

Mechanic, D. (1978). *Medical sociology* (2nd ed.). New York: Free Press.

Mishel, M. (1993). Reconceptualization of the uncertainty in illness theory. *Image: The Journal of Nursing Scholarship, 22*(45), 256–262.

Morris, J. (1991). *Pride against prejudice: Transforming attitudes to disability.* Philadelphia: New Society.

Muller-Rohland, J. (1987). The medical aspects of disabling conditions: An overview. In B. Caplan (Ed.). *Rehabilitation Psychology Desk Reference* (pp. 473–499). Rockville, MD: Aspen Publishers, Inc.

Neumann, R. J. (1988). Personal statement: Experiencing sexuality as an adolescent with rheumatoid arthritis. In P. W. Power, A. E. Dell Orto, & M. B. Gibbons (Eds.). *Family interventions throughout chronic illness and disability* (pp. 156–163). New York: Springer.

Patterson, D. R., Everett, J. J., Bombardier, C. H., Questad, K.A., Lee, V. K., & Marvin, J.A. (1993). Psychological effects of severe burn injuries. *Psychological Bulletin, 113,* 362–368.

Peterson, C., Maier, S.F., & Seligman, M. E. P. (1993). *Learned helplessness: A theory for the age of personal control.* New York: Oxford University.

Power, P. W., & Rogers, S. (1979). Group counseling for multiple sclerosis patients: A preferred mode of treatment for unique adaptive problems. In R. G. Lasky & A.E. Dell Orto (Eds.). *Group counseling and physical disability* (pp. 115–127). North Scituate, MA: Duxbury.

Power, P. W., Dell Orto, A. E., & Gibbons, M. B. (1988). *Family interventions through chronic illness and disability.* New York: Springer.

Pruzinsky, T. (1990). Psychopathology of body experience: Expanded perspectives. In T. F. Cash & T. Pruzinsky (Eds.). *Body images: Development, deviance, and change* (pp. 170–189). New York: Guilford.

Pruzinsky, T., & Cash, T. F. (1990). Integrative themes in body-image development, deviance, and change. In T. F. Cash & T. Pruzinsky (Eds.). *Body images: Development, deviance, and change* (pp. 337–347). New York: Guilford.

Robinson, I. (1988). Managing symptoms in chronic disease: Some dimensions of patients' experience. *International Disability Studies, 10*(3), 112–119.

Rolland, J. S. (1988). A conceptual model of chronic and life threatening illness and its impact on family. In C.S. Chilman, E. W. Nunnally, & F. M. Cox (Eds.). *Chronic illness and disability: Families in trouble* (pp. 17–68). Newbury Park, CA: Sage.

Roessler, R., & Bolton, B. (1978). *Psychosocial adjustment to disability.* Baltimore: University Park Press.

Rousso, H. (1993). *Disabled, female and proud! Stories of ten women with disabilities* Westport, CT: Bergin & Garvey.

Rybarczyk, B., Nyenhuis, D. L., Nicholas, J.J., Cash, S. M., & Kaiser, J. (1995). Body image, perceived social stigma, and the prediction of psychosocial adjustment to leg amputation. *Rehabilitation Psychology, 40,* 95–110.

Sasao, T., & Sue, S. (1993). Toward a culturally anchored ecological framework of research in ethnic-cultural communities. *American Journal of Community Psychology, 21,* 705–772.

Scherer, M. J. (1993). *Living in the state of stuck: How technology impacts the lives of people with disabilities.* Cambridge, MA: Brookline.

Shinn, M., Rosario, M., Morch, H., & Chesnut, D. (1984). Coping with job stress and burnout in the human services. *Journal of Personality and Social Psychology, 46,* 864–876.

Shontz, F. C. (1971). Physical disability and personality. In W. S. Neff (Ed.). *Rehabilitation psychology.* Washington, DC: American Psychological Association.

Sinacore-Guinn, A. L. (1995). The diagnostic window: Culture and gender-sensitive diagnosis and training. *Counselor Education and Supervision, 35,* 18–32.

Singer, G. H. S. (1996). Introduction: Trends affecting home and community care for people with chronic conditions in the United States. In G. H. S. Singer, L. E. Powers, & A. L. Olsen (Eds.). *Redefining family support: Innovations in public–private partnerships* (pp. 3–38). Baltimore: Brookes.

Smart, D., & Smart, J. (1997). DSM-IV and culturally sensitive diagnosis: Some observations for counselors. *Journal of Counseling & Development, 75,* 392–398.

Spector, R. E. (1991). *Cultural diversity in health and illness* (3rd ed.). Norwalk, CT: Appleton & Lange.

Stav, A., & Florian, V. (1986). Burnout among social workers working with physically disabled persons and bereaved families. *Journal of Personality and Social Psychology, 46,* 864–876.

Strauss, A., & Glaser, B. (1975). *Chronic illness and the quality of life.* St. Louis, MO: Mosby.

Strauss, A. L., Corbin, J., Fagerhaugh, S., Glaser, B. G., Maines, D., Suczek, B., & Weiner, C. L. (1984). *Chronic illness and the quality of life* (2nd ed.). St. Louis, MO: Mosby.

Stubbins, J. (1988). The politics of disability. In A. E. Yuker (Ed.). *Attitudes toward persons with disabilities* (pp. 22–32). New York: Springer.

Taylor, E. J., Jones, P., & Burns, M. (1998). Quality of life. In I. M. Lubkin & P. D. Larsen (Eds.). *Chronic illness: Impact and interventions* (4th ed.) (pp. 207–226). Sudbury, MA: Jones & Bartlett.

Thomson, R. G. (1997a). Feminist theory, the body, and the disabled figure. In L. J. Davis (Ed.), *Disability studies reader* (pp. 279–292). New York: Routledge.

Thomson, R. G. (1997b). Integrating disability studies into the existing curriculum: The example of "Women and Literature" at Howard University. In L. J. Davis (Ed.). *The disability studies reader* (pp. 295–306). New York: Routledge.

Tollifson, J. (1997). Imperfection is a beautiful thing: On disability and meditation. In K. Fries (Ed.). *Staring back: The disability experience from the inside out* (pp. 105–112). New York: Plume.

Trieschmann, R. B. (1988). *Spinal cord injuries: Psychological, social, and vocational rehabilitation.* (2nd ed.). New York: Demos.

Vash, C. L. (1981). *The psychology of disability.* New York: Springer.

Weinberg, N. (1982). Growing up physically disabled: Factors in the evaluation of disability. *Rehabilitation Counseling Bulletin, 25,* 219–227.

Weinberg, N., & Miller, N. J. (1983). Burn care: A social work perspective. *Health and Social Work, 8,* 97–106.

Weinberg, N., & Sterritt, M. (1991). Disability and identity: A study of identity patterns in adolescents with hearing impairments. In M. G. Eisenberg & R. L. Glueckauf (Eds.). *Empirical approaches to psychosocial aspects of disability* (pp. 68–75). New York: Springer.

Weisgerber, R. S. (1991). *Quality of life for persons with disabilities.* Gaithersburg, MD: Aspen.

Wendell, S. (1997). Toward a feminist theory of disability. In L. J. Davis (Ed.). *The disability studies reader* (pp. 260–278). New York: Routledge.

White, N., & Lubkin, I. (1998). Illness trajectory. In I. M. Lubkin & P. D. Larsen (Eds.). *Chronic illness: Impact and interventions* (4th ed.) (pp. 53–76). Sudbury, MA: Jones & Bartlett.

Whiteneck, O. G. (1994). Measuring what matters: Key rehabilitation outcomes. *Archive of Physical Medicine and Rehabilitation, 75,* 1073–1076.

Whitt, J. K. (1984). Children's adaptation to chronic illness and handicapping conditions. In M.G. Eisenberg, L. C. Sutkin, & M. A. Jansen. *Chronic illness and disability through the life span: Effects on self and family* (pp. 69–102). New York: Springer.

Wolfensberger, W., & Tullman, S. (1991). A brief outline of the principle of normalization. In M. G. Eisenberg & R. L. Glueckauf (Eds.). *Empirical approaches to the psychosocial aspects of disability* (pp. 202–215). New York: Springfield.

Woog, P. (1992). *The chronic illness trajectory framework: The Corbin and Strauss nursing model.* New York: Springer.

Wright, B. (1960). *Physical disability: A psychological approach.* New York: Harper & Row.

Yalom, I. D. (1980). *Existential psychotherapy.* New York: Basic Books.

Zola, I. (1988). Policies and programs concerning aging and disability: Toward a unifying agenda. In S. Sullivan & M. Lewin (Eds.). *The economics and ethics of long-term care and disability* (pp. 90–130). American Enterprise Institute for Public Policy Research.

List of Sources

CHAPTER 1

Exhibit 1–13 *Source:* Reprinted with permission from Girls' weight, boys' height affects earning power, p. 4A, July 13, 1994, © 1994, *Standard-Examiner*.

Figure 1–1 *Source:* Reprinted from National Health Interview Survey, National Center for Health Statistics tabulations compiled by the Disability Statistics Rehabilitation Research and Training Center, University of California, San Francisco.

Table 1–1 *Source:* Reprinted from 1995 CPS data from unpublished tabulations provided by John M. McNeil, U.S. Bureau of the Census.

CHAPTER 2

Exhibit 2–1 *Source:* Reprinted with permission from Athletes Face Charges Over Handicapped Parking Scam, pg. 2, July 11, 1999, © 1999, *Herald Journal*, Associated Press.

CHAPTER 3

Exhibit 3–1 *Source:* Permission granted by Ann Landers and Creators Syndicate.

Exhibit 3–2 *Source:* Permission granted by Ann Landers and Creators Syndicate.

Exhibit 3–3 *Source:* From THE ORIGINS OF NAZI GENOCIDE: FROM EUTHANASIA TO THE FINAL SOLUTION by Henry Friedlander. Copyright © 1995 by the University of North Carolina Press. Used by permission of the publisher.

Exhibit 3–4 *Source:* Reprinted with permission from A Monumental Mistake, *Time*, Vol. 149, No. 17, © 1997, Time Life Syndication.

Exhibit 3–5 *Source:* Permission granted by Ann Landers and Creators Syndicate.

CHAPTER 4

Exhibit 4–1 *Source:* Permission granted by Ann Landers and Creators Syndicate.

CHAPTER 5

Excerpt *Source:* The excerpt on page 157 is from *Pride Against Prejudice* by Jenny Morris, published in Great Britain, 1991, by The Women's Press Ltd, 34 Great Sutton Street, London, EC1V 0LQ.

Excerpts *Source:* The first and second excerpts on page 165 are from *Pride Against Prejudice* by Jenny Morris, published in Great Britain, 1991, by The Women's Press Ltd, 34 Great Sutton Street, London, EC1V 0LQ.

Exhibit 5–1 *Source:* Permission granted by Ann Landers and Creators Syndicate.

Exhibit 5–3 *Source*: Reprinted with permission from Charles Krauthammer, Restoration, Reality, and Christopher Reeve, *Time*, Vol. 155, No. 6, p. 100, © 2000, Time Life Syndication.

CHAPTER 6

Excerpt *Source:* The excerpt on page 201 is from *Pride Against Prejudice* by Jenny Morris, published in Great Britain, 1991, by The Women's Press Ltd, 34 Great Sutton Street, London, EC1V 0LQ.

Exhibit 6–1 *Source:* Permission granted by Ann Landers and Creators Syndicate.

Exhibit 6–2 *Source:* Permission granted by Ann Landers and Creators Syndicate.

CHAPTER 7

Appendix 7–B *Source:* Courtesy of Donald C. Linkowski, PhD, CRC.

CHAPTER 8

Table 8–1 *Source:* C.S. Chilman, et al., *Chronic Illness and Disability*, p. 72, Copyright © 1998 by Sage Publications, Inc., Reprinted by permission of Sage Publications, Inc.

CHAPTER 9

Excerpt *Source:* The first excerpt on page 315 is from *Pride Against Prejudice* by Jenny Morris, published in Great Britain, 1991, by The Women's Press Ltd, 34 Great Sutton Street, London, EC1V 0LQ.

Excerpt *Source:* The second excerpt on page 315 is reprinted from N.M. Crewe, Life Stories of People with Long Term Spinal Cord Injury, *Rehabilitation Counseling Bulletin*, Vol. 41, p. 38. © 1997 ACA. Reprinted with permission. No further reproduction authorized without written permission of the American Counseling Association.

Excerpts *Source:* The third and fourth excepts on page 315 are reprinted with permission from B.B. Boswell, M. Dawson, and E. Heninger, Quality of Life as Defined by Adults with Spinal Cord Injuries, *Journal of Rehabilitation*, Vol. 64, p. 30, © 1998.

Index